Communications
in Computer and Information Science 196

David C. Wyld Michal Wozniak
Nabendu Chaki Natarajan Meghanathan
Dhinaharan Nagamalai (Eds.)

Advances in Network Security and Applications

4th International Conference, CNSA 2011
Chennai, India, July 15-17, 2011
Proceedings

Springer

Volume Editors

David C. Wyld
Southeastern Louisiana University, Hammond, LA 70402, USA
E-mail: david.wyld@selu.edu

Michal Wozniak
Wroclaw University of Technology, 50-370 Wroclaw, Poland
E-mail: michal.wozniak@pwr.wroc.pl

Nabendu Chaki
University of Calcutta, Calcutta, India
E-mail: nchaki@gmail.com

Natarajan Meghanathan
Jackson State University, Jackson, MS 39217-0280, USA
E-mail: nmeghanathan@jsums.edu

Dhinaharan Nagamalai
Wireilla Net Solutions PTY Ltd, Melbourne, VIC, Australia
E-mail: dhinthia@yahoo.com

ISSN 1865-0929
e-ISSN 1865-0937
ISBN 978-3-642-22539-0
ISBN 978-3-642-22540-6 (eBook)
DOI 10.1007/978-3-642-22540-6
Springer Heidelberg Dordrecht London New York

Library of Congress Control Number: 2011931555

CR Subject Classification (1998): C.2, K.6.5, D.4.6, E.3, H.3-4, D.2

Typesetting: Camera-ready by author, data conversion by Scientific Publishing Services, Chennai, India

Printed on acid-free paper

Springer is part of Springer Science+Business Media (www.springer.com)

Preface

The 4th International Conference on Network Security & Applications (CNSA 2011) was held in Chennai, India, during July 15–17, 2011.The conference focuses on all technical and practical aspects of security and its applications for wired and wireless networks. The goal of this conference is to bring together researchers and practitioners from both academia and industry to focus on understanding the present-day security threats and to propose and discuss counter-measures to defend against such attacks. In the past few years, the enthusiastic participation of a large number of delegates in different AIRCC–organized conferences, like the International Conference on Network Security and Applications (CNSA), International Conference on Networks and Communications (NECOM), International Conference on Web and Semantic Technology (WEST), International Conference on Wireless and Mobile Networks (WIMON), the First International Conference on Advances in Computing and Information Technology (ACITY), reflect the fact that the parent body of the Academy and Industry Research Collaboration Center (AIRCC) is successful in providing a platform toward promoting academic collaboration. We believe that this spirit of co-working was further strengthened during CNSA 2011.

The CNSA 2011, NECOM 2011, WEST 2011, WIMoN 2011 and AICTY 2011 committees invited original submissions from researchers, scientists, engineers, and students that illustrate research results, projects, survey works, and industrial experiences describing significant advances in the areas related to the relevant themes and tracks of the conferences.

Thanks to the authors whose effort as reflected in the form of a large number of submissions for CNSA 2011 on different aspects of network security including Web security, cryptography, performance evaluations of protocols and security application, etc. All the submissions underwent a scrupulous peer-review process by a panel of expert reviewers. Besides the members of the Technical Committee, external reviewers were invited on the basis of their specialization and expertise. The papers were reviewed based on their technical content, originality, and clarity. The entire process, which includes the submission, review, and acceptance processes, was done electronically. This hard work resulted in the selection of high-quality papers that expand the knowledge in the latest developments in networks security and applications.

There were a total of 1,285 submissions to the conference, and the Technical Program Committee selected 195 papers for presentation at the conference and subsequent publication in the proceedings. The book is organized as a collection of papers from the 4th International Conference on Network Security and Applications (CNSA 2011), the Third International Conference on Networks and Communications (NeCoM 2011), the Third International Conference on Web and Semantic Technology (WeST 2011), the Third International Conference on

Wireless and Mobile Networks (WiMoN 2011), and the First International Conference on Advances in Computing and Information Technology (ACITY 2011). This small introduction incomplete would be without expressing our gratitude, and thanks to the General and Program Chairs, members of the Technical Program Committees, and external reviewers for their excellent and diligent work. Thanks to Springer for the strong support. Finally, we thank all the authors who contributed to the success of the conference. We also sincerely wish that all attendees benefited academically from the conference and wish them every success in their research.

David C. Wyld

Michal Wozniak
Nabendu Chaki
Natarajan Meghanathan
Dhinaharan Nagamalai

Organization

General Chairs

David C. Wyld	Southeastern Louisiana University, USA
S. K. Ghosh	Indian Institute of Technology, Kharagpur, India
Michal Wozniak	Wroclaw University of Technology, Poland

Steering Committee

Krzysztof Walkowiak	Wroclaw University of Technology, Poland
Dhinaharan Nagamalai	Wireilla Net Solutions PTY LTD, Australia
Natarajan Meghanathan	Jackson State University, USA
Nabendu Chaki	University of Calcutta, India
Chih-Lin Hu	National Central University, Taiwan
Selma Boumerdassi	CNAM/CEDRIC, France
John Karamitsos	University of the Aegean, Samos, Greece
Abdul Kadhir Ozcan	The American University, Cyprus
Brajesh Kumar Kaushik	Indian Institute of Technology - Roorkee, India

Program Committee Members

A.P. Sathish Kumar	PSG Institute of Advanced Studies, India
Abdul Aziz	University of Central Punjab, Pakistan
Abdul Kadir Ozcan	The American University, Cyprus
Ahmed M. Khedr	Sharjah University, UAE
Alejandro Garces	Jaume I University,Spain
Andy Seddon	Asia Pacific Institute of Information Technology, Malaysia
Ashutosh Dubey	NRI Institute of Science and Technology, Bhopal, India
Ashutosh Gupta	MJP Rohilkhand University, Bareilly, India
Atilla Elci	Toros University, Turkey
Atilla Elci	Eastern Mediterranean University, Cyprus
B. Srinivasan	Monash University, Australia
Babak Khosravifar	Concordia University, Canada
Balaji Sriramulu	drsbalaji@gmail.com
Balakannan S.P.	Chonbuk National University, Jeonju, Korea
Balasubramanian Karuppiah	MGR University, India
Bhupendra Suman	IIT Roorkee, India
Bong-Han Kim	Cheongju University, South Korea

Boo-Hyung Lee	KongJu National University, South Korea
Carlos E. Otero	The University of Virginia's College at Wise, USA
Chandra Mohan	Bapatla Engineering College, India
Charalampos Z. Patrikakis	National Technical University of Athens, Greece
Chih-Lin Hu	National Central University, Taiwan
Chin-Chih Chang	Chung Hua University,Taiwan
Cho Han Jin	Far East University, South Korea
Cynthia Dhinakaran	Hannam University, South Korea
Danda B. Rawat	Old Dominion University, USA
David W. Deeds	Shingu College, South Korea
Debasis Giri	Haldia Institute of Technology, India
Dimitris Kotzinos	Technical Educational Institution of Serres, Greece
Dong Seong Kim	Duke University, USA
Durga Toshniwal	Indian Institute of Techniology, India
Emmanuel Bouix	iKlax Media, France
Farhat Anwar	International Islamic University, Malaysia
Firkhan Ali Bin Hamid Ali	Universiti Tun Hussein Onn Malaysia, Malaysia
Ford Lumban	Gaol University of Indonesia
Genge Bela	Joint Research Centre, European Commission, Italy
Girija Chetty	University of Canberra, Australia
Govardhan A.	JNTUH College of Engineering, India
H.V. Ramakrishnan	MGR University, India
Haller Piroska	Petru Maior University, Tirgu Mures, Romania
Henrique Joao Lopes Domingos	University of Lisbon, Portugal
Ho Dac Tu	Waseda University, Japan
Hoang Huu Hanh	Hue University, Vietnam
Hwangjun Song	Pohang University of Science and Technology, South Korea
Jacques Demerjian	Communication & Systems, Homeland Security, France
Jae Kwang Lee	Hannam University, South Korea
Jan Zizka	SoNet/DI, FBE, Mendel University in Brno, Czech Republic
Jayeeta Chanda	jayeeta.chanda@gmail.com
Jeong-Hyun	Park Electronics Telecommunication Research Institute, South Korea
Jeong-Hyun	Park Electronics Telecommunication Research Institute, South Korea
Jeyanthy N.	VIT University, India
Jivesh Govil	Cisco Systems Inc., USA
Johann Groschdl	University of Bristol, UK

Rajendra Akerkar	Technomathematics Research Foundation, India
Rajesh Kumar Krishnan	Bannari Amman Institute of Technology, India
Rajesh Kumar P.	The Best International, Australia
Rajeswari Balasubramaniam	Dr. MGR University, India
Rajkumar Kannan	Bishop Heber College, India
Rakhesh Singh Kshetrimayum	Indian Institute of Technology, Guwahati, India
Ramayah Thurasamy	Universiti Sains Malaysia, Malaysia
Ramin Karimi	Universiti Teknologi Malaysia
Razvan Deaconescu	University Politehnica of Bucharest, Romania
Reena Dadhich	Govt. Engineering College Ajmer, India
Rituparna Chaki	rituchaki@gmail.com
Roberts Masillamani	Hindustan University, India
S. Bhaskaran	SASTRA University, India
Sagarmay Deb	Central Queensland University, Australia
Sajid Hussain	Acadia University, Canada
Salah M. Saleh Al-Majeed	Esses University, UK
Saleena Ameen	B.S. Abdur Rahman University, India
Salman Abdul Moiz	Centre for Development of Advanced Computing, India
Sami Ouali	ENSI, Campus of Manouba, Manouba, Tunisia
Samodar Reddy	India School of Mines, India
Sanguthevar Rajasekaran	University of Connecticut, USA
Sanjay Singh	Manipal Institute of Technology, India
Sara Najafzadeh	Universiti Teknologi Malaysia
Sarada Prasad Dakua	IIT-Bombay, India
Sarmistha Neogy	Jadavpur University, India
Sattar B. Sadkhan	University of Babylon, Iraq
Seetha Maddala	CBIT, Hyderabad, India
Serban	Ovidius University of Constantza, Romania
Sergio Ilarri	University of Zaragoza, Spain
Serguei A. Mokhov	Concordia University, Canada
Seungmin Rho	Carnegie Mellon University, USA
Sevki Erdogan	University of Hawaii, USA
Shivan Haran	Arizona state University, USA
Shriram Vasudevan	VIT University, India
Shubhalaxmi Kher	Arkansas State University, USA
Solange Rito Lima	University of Minho, Portugal
Sriman Narayana Iyengar	VIT University, India
Subir Sarkar	Jadavpur University, India
Sudip Misra	Indian Institute of Technology, Kharagpur, India
Suhaidi B. Hassan	Office of the Assistant Vice Chancellor, Economics Building
Sundarapandian Vaidyanathan	Vel Tech Dr. RR & Dr. SR Technical University, India

SunYoung Han	Konkuk University, South Korea
Susana Sargento	University of Aveiro, Portugal
Swarup Mitra	Jadavpur University, Kolkata, India
Tsung Teng Chen	National Taipei University, Taiwan
Virgil Dobrota	Technical University of Cluj-Napoca, Romania
Vishal Sharma	Metanoia Inc., USA
Wei Jie	University of Manchester, UK
William R. Simpson	Institute for Defense Analyses, USA
Wojciech Mazurczyk	Warsaw University of Technology, Poland
Yannick Le Moullec	Aalborg University, Denmark
Yedehalli Kumara Swamy	Dayanand Sagar College of Engineering, India
Yeong Deok Kim Woosong	University, South Korea
Yuh-Shyan Chen	National Taipei University, Taiwan
Yung-Fa Huang	Chaoyang University of Technology, Taiwan

External Reviewers

Abhishek Samanta	Jadavpur University, Kolkata, India
Amit Choudhary	Maharaja Surajmal Institute, India
Anjan K.	MSRIT, India
Ankit	BITS, PILANI, India
Aravind P.A.	Amrita School of Engineering, India
Cauvery Giri	RVCE, India
Debdatta Kandar	Sikkim Manipal University, India
Doreswamyh Hosahalli	Mangalore University, India
Gopalakrishnan Kaliaperumal	Anna University, Chennai, India
Hameem Shanavas	Vivekananda Institute of Technology, India
Hari Chavan	National Institute of Technology, Jamshedpur, India
Kaushik Chakraborty	Jadavpur University, India
Lavanya	Blekinge Institute of Technology, Sweden
Mydhili Nair	M. S. Ramaiah Institute of Technology, India
Naga Prasad Bandaru	PVP Siddartha Institute of Technology, India
Nana Patil	NIT Surat, Gujrat
Osman B. Ghazali	Universiti Utara Malaysia, Malaysia
P. Sheik Abdul Khader	B.S.Abdur Rahman University, India
Padmalochan Bera	Indian Institute of Technology, Kharagpur, India
Pappa Rajan	Anna University, India
Pradeepini Gera	Jawaharlal Nehru Technological University, India
Rajashree Biradar	Ballari Institute of Technology and Management, India
Ramin Karimi	University Technology, Malaysia
Reshmi Maulik	University of Calcutta, India
Rituparna Chaki	West Bengal University of Technology, India

S.C. Sharma	IIT - Roorkee, India
Salini P.	Pondichery Engineering College, India
Selvakumar Ramachandran	Blekinge Institute of Technology, Sweden
Soumyabrata Saha	Guru Tegh Bahadur Institute of Technology, India
Srinivasulu Pamidi	V.R. Siddhartha Engineering College Vijayawada, India
Subhabrata Mukherjee	Jadavpur University, India
Sunil Singh	Bharati Vidyapeeth's College of Engineering, India
Suparna DasGupta	suparnadasguptait@gmail.com
Valli Kumari Vatsavayi	AU College of Engineering, India

Technically Sponsored by

Software Engineering & Security Community (SESC)
Networks & Communications Community (NCC)
Internet Computing Community (ICC)
Computer Science & Information Technology Community (CSITC)

Organized By

AIRCC

ACADEMY & INDUSTRY RESEARCH COLLABORATION CENTER (AIRCC)
www.airccse.org

Table of Contents

Network Security and Applications

Vulnerability Assessment Methods - A Review 1
Hiran V. Nath

Collaborative Polling Scheme to Detect and Isolate the Colluding Packet Droppers in Mobile Ad Hoc Networks 11
K. Gopalakrishnan and V. Rhymend Uthariaraj

Defense Strategy against Network Worms Causing ICMP Attacks and Its Forensic Analysis 23
K.S. Aathira and Thulasi N. Kutty

Analysis of Algebraic Attack on TRIVIUM and Minute Modification to TRIVIUM 35
Ashji S. Raj and Chungath Srinivasan

Design of Secure Chaotic Hash Function Based on Logistic and Tent Maps 43
P. Jhansi Rani, M. Sambasiva Rao, and S. Durga Bhavani

Detecting Anomalous Application Behaviors Using a System Call Clustering Method over Critical Resources 53
Grandhi Jyostna, Pareek Himanshu, and P.R.L. Eswari

Behavioral Malware Detection Expert System – Tarantula 65
Sandeep Romana, Swapnil Phadnis, Pareek Himanshu, and P.R.L. Eswari

Tool for Prevention and Detection of Phishing E-Mail Attacks 78
Shamal M. Firake, Pravin Soni, and B.B. Meshram

Improvement of QoS Performance in MANET by QoS-TORA: A TORA Based QoS Routing Algorithm 89
Govind Kumar Jha, Neeraj Kumar, Himanshu Sharma, and K.G. Sharma

Authentication Process in IEEE 802.11: Current Issues and Challenges 100
Dinesh Yadav and Anjali Sardana

Network Level Anomaly Detection System Using MST Based Genetic Clustering 113
P. Kola Sujatha, R. Arun, P.V. Shanthoosh, I. Ezra Prince Jebahar, and A. Kannan

A Hybrid Approach to Texture Classification 123
B. Vijayalakshmi and V. Subbiah Bharathi

Completeness of LAN Attack Detection Using Discrete Event Systems 131
F.A. Barbhuiya, N. Hubballi, S. Biswas, and S. Nandi

Designing Dependable Web Services Security Architecture Solutions 140
D. Shravani, P. Suresh Varma, B. Padmaja Rani, M. Upendra Kumar, and A.V. Krishna Prasad

Protocol for Simultaneous Ownership Transfer of Multiple RFID Tags with TTP 150
Wei Zhou and Selwyn Piramuthu

A Preventive Measure to Protect from Denial of Service Attack 157
Manas Ku. Dasmohapatra, Kamalika Datta, and Indranil Sengupta

Review of Some Checkpointing Algorithms for Distributed and Mobile Systems 167
Sunil Kumar Gupta and Parveen Kumar

Using Raga as a Cryptographic Tool 178
Sandip Dutta, Soubhik Chakraborty, and N.C. Mahanti

Combining Power of MATLAB with SystemVerilog for Image and Video Processing ASIC Verification 184
Dhaval Modi, Harsh Sitapara, Rahul Shah, Ekata Mehul, and Pinal Engineer

Memory Attack Detection of Cryptographic Algorithm 194
K. Rahimunnisa, Rincy Merrin Varkey, and S. Sureshkumar

Performance Comparison of Queueing Disciplines for Aeerg Protocol in Manet 204
S. Rajeswari and Y. Venkataramani

Design of a Cryptographic Tamper Detection Scheme for Network Security 214
B. Srinivasa Rao and S.D.V. Prasad

Energy Efficient and Congestion Control Multipath Routing in Wireless Sensor Networks 225
M. Nesa Sudha, Sapna E. John, and M.L. Valarmathi

Intrusion Prevention by Native Language Password Authentication Scheme 239
SreeLatha Malempati and Shashi Mogalla

An Improved Uncertainty Reduction Scheme Based on Bayesian Prediction in MANETs 249
B. Lydia Elizabeth, S. Sudha, A. John Prakash, and V. Rhymend Uthariaraj

Scalable Implementation of Active Detection Mechanism for LAN Based Attacks 258
G. Bansal, N. Kumar, F.A. Barbhuiya, S. Biswas, and S. Nandi

A Survey of Recent Intrusion Detection Systems for Wireless Sensor Network 268
Tapolina Bhattasali and Rituparna Chaki

Secure Network Steganographic Scheme Exploiting TCP Sequence Numbers 281
Vengala Satish Kumar, Tanima Dutta, Arijit Sur, and Sukumar Nandi

Intrusion Detection System Based on Real Time Rule Accession and Honeypot 292
Abhay Nath Singh, Shiv Kumar, and R.C. Joshi

Key Predistribution in 3-Dimensional Grid-Group Deployment Scheme 302
Samiran Bag

Novel Methods for Montgomery Modular Multiplication for Public Key Cryptosystems 320
V.R. Venkatasubramani, M. Surendar, and S. Rajaram

Protection against Denial of Service and Input Manipulation Vulnerabilities in Service Oriented Architecture 331
Alwyn Roshan Pais, D.J. Deepak, and B.R. Chandavarkar

Highly Resilient Key Predistribution Scheme Using Transversal Designs and Reed Muller Codes for Wireless Sensor Network 344
Samiran Bag, Amrita Saha, and Pinaki Sarkar

Improving Fairness in Network Traffic by Controlling Congestion and Unresponsive Flows 356
M. Azath, R.S.D. Wahida Banu, and A. Neela Madheswari

Authenticated Routing for Ad-Hoc On-Demand Distance Vector Routing Protocol 364
Preeti Sachan and Pabitra Mohan Khilar

Passblot: A Usable Way of Authentication Scheme to Generate One Time Passwords 374
Sainath Gupta, Pruthvi Sabbu, Siddhartha Varma, and Suryakanth V. Gangashetty

Safeguarding Web Services Using Self-adaptive Schema Hardening Algorithm..... 383
Vipul Patel, Radhesh Mohandas, and Alwyn Pais

Modeling and Performance Analysis of QAM System 393
T.P. Surekha, T. Ananthapadmanabha, C. Puttamadappa, and A.P. Kavya

An IDS Evaluation-Centric Taxonomy of Wireless Security Attacks..... 402
Khalid Nasr, Anas Abou-El Kalam, and Christian Fraboul

Rational Secret Sharing with Honest Players over an Asynchronous Channel 414
William K. Moses Jr. and C. Pandu Rangan

Agent Based Cross Layer Intrusion Detection System for MANET 427
V. Anjana Devi and R.S. Bhuvaneswaran

Evaluating Machine Learning Algorithms for Detecting DDoS Attacks..... 441
Manjula Suresh and R. Anitha

Insecure Query Processing in the Delay/Fault Tolerant Mobile Sensor Network (DFT-MSN) and Mobile Peer to Peer Network..... 453
Rahul Johari and Neelima Gupta

Financial Time Series Volatility Forecast Using Evolutionary Hybrid Artificial Neural Network 463
Anupam Tarsauliya, Rahul Kala, Ritu Tiwari, and Anupam Shukla

Data Security in Free Roaming Mobile Agents 472
G. Geetha and C. Jayakumar

End-to-End Security for At-Home Medical Monitoring 483
Mohanavalli Seetha Subramanian and Sheila Anand

Web Mining Research and Future Directions 489
G. Dileep Kumar and Manohar Gosul

Difference between Intrusion Detection System (IDS) and Intrusion Prevention System (IPS) 497
Asmaa Shaker Ashoor and Sharad Gore

Conditional Proxy Re-Encryption - A More Efficient Construction 502
S. Sree Vivek, S. Sharmila Deva Selvi, V. Radhakishan, and C. Pandu Rangan

Study of Malware Threats Faced by the Typical Email User 513
Anthony Ayodele, James Henrydoss, Walter Schrier, and T.E. Boult

Ad Hoc, Sensor and Ubiquitous Computing

Sequential Multi-Clustering Protocol Using a Node Deployment Protocol for Efficient Multiclustering in Wireless Sensor Networks 526
Pradipta Ghosh, Joydeep Banerjee, Swarup Kumar Mirta, Souvik Kumar Mitra, and Mrinal Kanti Naskar

Online Based Fuzzy Analyzer for Arrhythmia Detection 537
K.A. Sunitha, N. Senthil kumar, S.S. Dash, and K. Prema

A Novel Autonomic Design Pattern for Invocation OF Services 545
V.S. Prasad Vasireddy, Vishnuvardhan Mannava, and T. Ramesh

A Novel Way of Providing Dynamic Adaptability and Invocation of JADE Agent Services from P2P JXTA Using Aspect Oriented Programming 552
Vishnuvardhan Mannava, T. Ramesh, and V.S. Prasad Vasireddy

A Novel Way of Providing Dynamic Adaptability in P2P JXTA Multicast Sockets and P2P JXTA-WS Using Aspect Oriented Programming 564
Vishnuvardhan Mannava, T. Ramesh, and Bangaru Babu Kuravadi

Intelligent Energy Efficient Routing for Ad-Hoc Sensor Network by Designing QCS Protocol 577
Debaditya Ghosh, Pritam Majumder, and Ayan Kumar Das

Peer-to-Peer Networks And Trust Management

A New Approach for Securing Mobile Adhoc Network with an Improved Trust Calculation Method 587
Amit Chauhan and Nidhi Shah

A Routing Protocol for Facilitating Multimedia Transmission over 802.11e Based Mobile Ad Hoc Networks 598
Sujatha.P. Terdal, V.D. Mytri, A. Damodaram, and Uday S.B.

A Survey on Dataspace 608
Mrityunjay Singh and S.K. Jain

A Novel Social Network Model for Business Collaboration 622
Sreedhar Bhukya

A Novel Way of Providing Dynamic Adaptability in P2P JXTA Sockets Using Aspect Oriented Programming 631
Vishnuvardhan Mannava and T. Ramesh

A Novel Way of Providing Dynamic Adaptability in P2P JXTA Services Using Aspect Oriented Programming 640
Vishnuvardhan Mannava and T. Ramesh

Trust Management for Grid Environment Using Rule Based Fuzzy Logic 649
Mohd Noman Siddiqui, Vinit Saini, and Ravinder Ahuja

Author Index 659

Vulnerability Assessment Methods – A Review

Hiran V. Nath

TIFAC CORE in Cyber Security Centre,
Amrita School of Engineering Coimbatore, India
hiranvnath@gmail.com

Abstract. This paper reviews the major contributions in the field of Vulnerability Assessment from 1990 onwards. Even well administered networks are vulnerable to attack .Vulnerabilities are weaknesses in the requirements, design, and implementation, which attackers exploit to compromise the system. Researchers have proposed a variety of methods like graph-based algorithms to generate attack trees (or graphs), "black-box" and "whitebox" analysis, using Mobile Ambients, using Honepots, different Vulnerability tools and their Scoring System's, and so on. After surveying lot of research papers in the field, the amount of existing works for each method is identified and classified. Especially, the graph-based algorithms itself is a major area for researchers. The paper concludes with some inferences and results obtained in each method so can be used as a guideline for researchers.

Keywords: Vulnerability Assessment, graph-based algorithms, attack trees, Mobile Ambients, Honepots.

1 Introduction

With the advent of open systems, intranets, and the Internet, information systems and network security professionals are becoming increasingly aware of the need to assess and manage potential security risks on their networks and systems. Vulnerability assessment is the process of measuring and prioritizing these risks associated with network and host based systems and devices to allow rational planning of technologies and activities that manage business risk. Some tools allow customization of security policy, automated analysis of vulnerabilities, and creation of reports that effectively communicate security vulnerability discoveries and detailed corrective actions to all levels of an organization. Implementing network- and host-based scanning products together offers powerful security protection against the three types of risks: vendor, administrative, and user introduced [1].

Developing secure software systems is challenging because errors and misspecifications in requirements, design, and implementation can bring vulnerabilities to the system. Attackers most often exploit vulnerabilities to compromise the system. In security engineering, vulnerability is an error or weakness of the IT system or its environment that in conjunction with an internal or external threat can lead to a security failure [2].

D.C. Wyld et al. (Eds.): CNSA 2011, CCIS 196, pp. 1–10, 2011.

In recent years, software companies and government agencies have become particularly aware of security risks that vulnerabilities impose on the system security and have started analyzing and reporting detected vulnerabilities of products and services. For instance, the IBM Internet Security Systems X-Force [3] has detected and analyzed 6,437 new vulnerabilities in 2007, of which 1.9% is critical and 37% are high risk. 20% of the 5-top critical vulnerabilities were found to be unpatched. Of all the vulnerabilities disclosed in 2007, only 50% can be corrected through vendor patches, and 90% of vulnerabilities could be remotely exploited. These statistics show the critical urgency of the vulnerabilities affecting software services and products. Various web portals and on-line databases of vulnerabilities are also made available to security administrators. For example, the National Vulnerability Database [4] SANS top-20 annual security risks [5], and Common Weakness Enumeration (CWE) [6] provide updated lists of vulnerabilities and weaknesses. The Common Vulnerability Scoring System (CVSS) [7] also provides a method for evaluating the criticality of vulnerabilities.

Existing software engineering frameworks focus on various aspects for eliciting security requirements such as design of secure components [8], security issues in social dependencies among actors [9] and their trust relationships [10], attacker behavior [11, 12] and attacker goals [13], and events that can cause system failure [14]. However, they rarely use vulnerabilities to elicit security requirements. Liu et al. [9] propose a vulnerability analysis approach for eliciting security requirements. However, vulnerabilities in this framework are different from the ones defined in security engineering (i.e., weaknesses in the IT system). Liu et al. refer to vulnerabilities as the weak dependencies that may jeopardize the goals of depender actors. Only few security software engineering approaches consider analyzing vulnerabilities, as weaknesses in the systems, during the elicitation of security requirements. For instance, in [15], vulnerabilities are modeled as beliefs inside the boundary of attackers that may positively contribute to attacks. However, the resulting models do not specify which actions or assets introduce vulnerabilities into the system, and which actors are vulnerable. In addition, the impact of countermeasures on vulnerabilities and attacks is not captured. The CORAS framework [16, 17] provides a way for expressing how one vulnerability leads to another vulnerability and how a vulnerability (or combination of vulnerabilities) lead to a threat. However, similar to [18], CORAS does not investigate which design choice, requirement, or process has brought the vulnerabilities to the system [19].

Networks are inevitably vulnerable. The term "network vulnerabilities" refers to exploitable errors in configurations (e.g., ports and services enabled) and server software implemented to provide network services (e.g., Apache Chunked-Code software on web servers, operating environments Windows XP SP2, and Oracle and TNS Listener software for database servers). Although commercial vulnerability scanners (e.g., Nessus [20], ISS [21]) can detect software vulnerabilities within individual host configurations, networks that provide simultaneous services can still be attacked through sequences of exploitable vulnerabilities. Thus, perfectly secure isolated services by individual hosts do not guarantee secure combined services in a network configured from these hosts. Furthermore, removal of all software vulnerabilities may not be possible, especially for the software that provides necessary network services. The goal of network security is to maintain sufficient security while still allowing the network to provide its services. To do this, there is a need to analyze the network from existing vulnerabilities (e.g., Bugtraq [22], NVD [4]). Network vulnerability analysis generates chains of vulnerabilities that can be exploited by an attacker to compromise network security. The chains of possible exploits are then used to determine the work required to secure the network, typically by repairing the vulnerabilities and configuration errors. These exploit chains are organized as a directed graph (or a tree) whose nodes represent network states. Although various forms of attack graphs have been defined (e.g., access graph [23], multiple-prerequisite graph [24]), they share the same basic elements described above [25]. Authenticating the legitimacy of network devices and preserving the integrity of the network landscape is paramount because it is the key enabler for our critical operational capabilities. This involves accounting for every key networking device that enable the close integration of systems to detect illegitimate host or router connections made possible by insider threats [26]. Proper network accountability will eventually prevent the escalation of such attacks because clusters of compromised computer networks can be more responsively isolated and recovered [27].

Vulnerability analysis tools are usually categorized into Host scanning, Network scanning, Web application scanning, Database application scanning & Vulnerability and patch management. Vulnerability assessment tools, in general, work by attempting to automate the first three steps often employed by hackers like Performing footprint analysis, Enumerate targets, Test / obtain access through user privilege manipulation [28].

In the case of network-based tools, a network footprint analysis is performed by scanning for accessible hosts. The tools enumerate available network services (e.g., file transfer protocol, hypertext transfer protocol) on each host as accessible hosts are identified. Some advantages to vulnerability assessment tools are that they:

- More clearly define an asset,
- Discover technological and network vulnerabilities,
- Provide multi-perspective view points,
- Help properly scope the analysis,
- Reference public catalogs,
- Highlight design, implementation, and configuration vulnerabilities.

Almost all scanning tools perform tests based on their database of vulnerabilities. Just as anti-virus products must be constantly updated with new signatures, assessment tools must be continually updated with revisions to their vulnerability databases. In [29] they have described the value of honeynets for computer vulnerability assessment. Honeynet aids in collecting detailed information about attackers' behavior and help in analyzing their tools, techniques and motives.

This paper is organized as follows: Section 2 is various methods, where we describe in detail various methodologies developed for vulnerability assessments. Section 3 is conclusion where we provide some inferences and results obtained in each method so can be used as a guideline for researchers.

2 Various Methods

2.1 Attack Graphs

An attack graph is a succinct representation of all paths through a system that end in a state where an intruder has successfully achieved his goal. Usually Red Teams determine the vulnerability of networked systems by drawing gigantic attack graphs by hand. Researchers and commercial companies have recently developed differing approaches to generating attack graphs [30, 31, 32, 33, 34]). Attack graphs are constructed by starting an adversary at a given network location and, using information about the network topology and host vulnerabilities, examining how the attacker can progressively compromise vulnerable hosts that are reachable from already compromised hosts. Vulnerability scanners and analyses of filtering performed by firewalls and routers are used to obtain information about host vulnerabilities and to determine host-to-host reachability in a network. In addition, most of the existing implementations provide some type of attack graph display. However, the abstract nature of attack graphs has proven to be a serious practical weakness in creating an effective display.

Formal Analyses of Attack Graphs
Constructing attack graphs by hand is tedious, error-prone, and impractical for large systems. By viewing an attack as a violation of a safety property, researcher shows interest in using off-the-shelf model checking technology to produce attack graphs automatically: a successful path from the intruder's viewpoint is a counterexample produced by the model checker. Researchers were interested in presenting a minimization analysis technique that allows analysts to decide which minimal set of security measures would guarantee the safety of the system. They provided a formal characterization of this problem: they proved that it is polynomially equivalent to the minimum hitting set problem and presented a greedy algorithm with provable bounds. The conclusion was that by interpreting attack graphs as Markov Decision Processes we can use the value iteration algorithm to compute the probabilities of intruder success for each attack the graph [35].

2.2 Description Logics

In [36] uses description logics for network vulnerability analysis. The justification is as follows. While analyzing network vulnerabilities, considering the hosts in isolation is not sufficient and their relationships should be taken into account [37]. Also an attacker may exploit poorly configured network devices. The complexity of analyzing network vulnerabilities can be augmented as the number of hosts and services increase. As a result, an automated approach to vulnerability analysis is necessary. Here they propose a formal model for TCP/IP networks using Description Logics and as a case study use it to analyze the network vulnerability against man in the middle attacks.

Description logics are an extension of frame-based systems that can express definitions of classes and relations [38]. Class definitions can include disjunction and negation. Relations can be defined between classes. They can be constrained in cardinality and type. The cardinality constraint is used extensively in network vulnerability model. This hierarchy is used to associate instances to classes whose definitions are satisfied by the features of the instance [38]. Several reasons exist to use DL for network vulnerability analysis. The first one is that DL is decidable. The next reason is that DL has sound and complete reasoning mechanisms which guarantee the results accuracy and reliability. Finally, wide range of logics has being developed till now, from very simple to very expressive, so we can choose which logic satisfies our needs in a minimum computational complexity. In [36] they have used the proposed model to represent a sample network and analyze it against the man in the middle attack.

2.3 Agent Based Network Vulnerability Analysis Framework

In [39] an agent based network vulnerability analysis framework is proposed. This approach can be described in terms of three steps:

1. Vulnerability Metrics: In this step we identify the metrics to be used to analyze the network vulnerability;
2. System State Characterization: In this step we define the thresholds to be used to characterize the node/system state to be in one of three states: Normal State, Uncertain State, and Vulnerable State and
3. Vulnerability Index Evaluation: In this step we evaluate the vulnerability of the network or application with respect to the vulnerability metrics defined in the first step. The vulnerability index can also be used as an indicator to trigger proactive and survivable methodologies to aid fast recovery at the earliest possible stages.

2.4 Vulnerability in X86 Binary Using Symbolic Execution

In [40] proposes a new system, IntScope, which can automatically detect integer overflow vulnerabilities in x86 binaries before an attacker does, with the goal of finally eliminating the vulnerabilities. IntScope first translates the disassembled code into our own intermediate representation (IR), and then performs a path sensitive data flow analysis on the IR by leveraging symbolic execution and taint analysis to identify the vulnerable point of integer overflow. Compared with other approaches, IntScope does not run the binary directly, and is scalable to large software as it can just symbolically execute the interesting program paths. Experimental results show IntScope is quite encouraging: it has detected more than 20 zero-day integer overflows (e.g., CVE-2008-4201, FrSIRT/ADV-2008-2919) in widely-used software such as QEMU, Xen and Xine.

2.5 Model-Based Vulnerability Analysis

Most vulnerability arises from unexpected interaction between different system components such as server processes, file system permissions and content, and other operating system services. Existing vulnerability techniques (such as those used in COPS and SATAN) are based on enumerating the known causes of vulnerabilities in the system and capturing these causes in the form of rules, e.g., a world- or group- writable .login file is a well known vulnerability that enables one user to gain all access privileges of another user. Issues such as system complexity, race conditions, many possible interleaving, hidden assumptions etc. make it very hard even for experts to come up with all such rules. In [41] a new model-based approach is proposed, where the security-related behaviour of each system component is modelled in a high-level specification language such as CSP or CCS. These component models can then be composed to obtain all possible behaviours of the entire system. Finding system vulnerabilities can now be accomplished by analyzing these behaviours using automated verification techniques (model checking in particular) to identify scenarios where security-related properties(such as maintaining integrity of password files) are violated.

2.6 Vulnerability Assessment Using Honeynets

Honeypots are electronic bait, i.e. network resources (computers, routers, switches, etc.) deployed to be probed, attacked and compromised. Honeypots run special software which permanently collects data about the system and greatly aids in post-incident computer and network forensics. Several honeypots can be assembled into networks of honeypots called honeynets. Because of the wealth of data collected through them, honeynets are considered a useful tool to learn more about attack patterns and attacker behavior in real networks. Spitzner defines a honeypot to be "a resource who's value is in being probed, attacked or compromised." [42]. Honeypots are equipped with special software (usually a patched operating system) that make them indistinguishable from "normal" network nodes from the outside but they permanently collect detailed data about network connections, user activity etc. In contrast to similar data collected on "normal" machines, the wealth of this data can be used to better study attack patterns and attacker behavior and greatly aids in post-incident computer and network forensics. For example, the specialized tools used by an attacker can easily be intercepted on a honeypot and would be hard to obtain on a normal desktop computer since they are usually removed by the attacker after a break-in. In contrast to previous work in this area [43, 44] which collected data in an ad-hoc, post-incident manner, honeypots offer a more systematic approach for studying attack patterns and general vulnerability assessment. To investigate the usefulness of honeynet technology, they have deployed a honeynet at RWTH Aachen University within the Laboratory for Dependable Distributed Systems.

2.7 Combined "Blackbox" and "Whitebox" Analysis

The increased reliance on advanced networking technologies to integrate cutting-edge capabilities has posed tremendous challenges in assuring user legitimacy and preserving the integrity of our network landscape. Without proper network accountability and holistic vulnerability assessment, insider threats can exploit the security vulnerabilities that result from creating an integrated system-of-systems. To detect security illegitimacies, such as unauthorized connections, network security administrators need to have a comprehensive network map to identify potential entry points. In [27] they proposes a systematic way to combine "black-box" and "white-box" analysis for network exploration and vulnerability assessment. In the analytical model design, a modular approach is adopted to select tools and techniques from both analysis approaches. The "black-box" analysis was able to map active hosts and networking devices, but "white-box" analysis was able to detect those that are inactive or do not respond to pings. Moreover, "black-box" analysis provides a focal point for "white-box" analysis approach to derive in-depth information regarding unauthorized connections.

2.8 Featherweight Virtual Machine (FVM) Technology

Although there are many commercial vulnerability assessment tools in the market, none of them can formally guarantee that the assessment process never compromises the computer systems being tested. In [45] they propose a featherweight virtual machine (FVM) technology to address the safety issue associated with vulnerability testing. Compared with other virtual machine technologies, FVM is designed to facilitate sharing between virtual machines but still provides strong protection between them. The FVM technology allows a vulnerability assessment tool to test an exact replica of a production-mode network service, including both hardware and system software components, while guaranteeing that the production-mode network service is fully isolated from the testing process. In addition to safety, the vulnerability assessment support system described they can also automate the entire process of vulnerability testing and thus for the first time makes it feasible to run vulnerability testing autonomously and frequently.

2.9 Vulnerability Take-Grant Model (VTG)

In [46], they propose a new vulnerability analysis method based on the Take-Grant protection model. They extend the initial Take-Grant model to address the notion of vulnerabilities and introduce the vulnerabilities rewriting rules to specify how the protection state of the system can be changed by exploiting vulnerabilities. The analysis was based on a bounded polynomial algorithm, which generates the closure of the Take-Grant graph regarding vulnerabilities. The closure helps to verify whether any subject can obtain an access right over an object.

3 Conclusion

We came into a conclusion that, it is not sufficient just to use a single method for vulnerability analysis but to use a combination of multiple methods one after other in an automated sequential manner. The survey reveals that initially the only research which was going on was attack graph method, but by 2003 the research in other fields also emerged out. Even the research went deeper than just to analyse the attack graph manually they came up with automated attack graph generation methods and its tool kits. Many vulnerability analysis tools emerged out which were open source as well as commercial ones like CAULDRON Topographical Vulnerability Analysis.

Now the researchers have given equal importance to the role of insider threats in the area of vulnerability analysis. Since as an insider one could make a network vulnerable just by inserting a highly vulnerable host into that network. The overall vulnerability of the network is the vulnerability that is imparted by the most vulnerable machine in that network. Method proposed in [29] aid in collecting detailed information about attackers' behaviour and help in analyzing their tools, techniques and motives. From their implementation they were able to collect a wealth of data on attack patterns which currently prevail in the Internet. Method proposed in [41] has the potential to automatically seek out and identify known and as-yet-unknown vulnerabilities, where as the previous approaches mainly address only well-known vulnerabilities.

References

1. Network and Host-based Vulnerability Assessment - A guide for information systems and network security professionals, ISS, Atlanta
2. Anderson, R.: Security Engineering: a Guide to Building Dependable Distributed Systems. John Wiley and Sons, Chichester (2001)
3. IBM Global Technology Services, IBM Internet Security Systems X-Force 2007 Trend Statistics (2008)
4. Mell, P., Grance, T.: NVD National Vulnerability Database, `http://nvd.nist.gov`
5. SANS, `http://www.sans.org/`
6. Common Weakness Enumeration, `http://cwe.mitre.org/`
7. Common Vulnerability Scoring System, `http://www.first.org/cvss/`
8. Jurjens, J.: Secure Systems Development with UML. Springer, Heidelberg (2004)
9. Liu, L., Yu, E., Mylopoulos, J.: Security and Privacy Requirements Analysis within a Social Setting. In: Proceedings of the 11th IEEE International Conference on Requirements Engineering, pp. 151–161. IEEE Computer Society, Los Alamitos (2003)
10. Giorgini, P., Massacci, F., Mylopoulos, J., Zannone, N.: Requirements Engineering for Trust Management: Model Methodology and Reasoning. International Journal of Information Security 5(4), 257–274 (2006)
11. Sindre, G., Opdahl, A.: Eliciting security requirements with misuse cases. Requirements Engineering 10(1), 34–44 (2005)
12. Schneier, B.: Attack trees. Dr. Dobb's Journal 24(12), 21–29 (1999)
13. Lamsweerde, A.V.: Elaborating Security Requirements by Construction of Intentional Anti-Models. In: Proceedings of the 26th International Conference on Software Engineering, pp. 148–157. IEEE Computer Society, Los Alamitos (2004)
14. Asnar, Y., Moretti, R., Sebastianis, M., Zannone, N.: Risk as Dependability Metrics for the Evaluation of Business Solutions: A Model-driven Approach. In: Proceedings of the 2008 Third International Conference on Availability Reliability and Security, pp. 1240–1248. IEEE Computer Society, Los Alamitos (2008)
15. Matulevicius, R., Mayer, N., Mouratidis, H., Dubois, E., Heymans, P., Genon, N.: Adapting Secure Tropos for Security Risk Management in the Early Phases of Information Systems Development. In: Bellahsène, Z., Léonard, M. (eds.) CAiSE 2008. LNCS, vol. 5074, pp. 541–555. Springer, Heidelberg (2008)
16. Braber, F., Hogganvik, I., Lund, M.S., Stolen, K., Vraalsen, F.: Model-based security analysis in seven steps – a guided tour to the CORAS method. BT Technology Journal 25(1), 101–117 (2007)
17. Braber, F., Dimitrakos, T., Gran, B.A., Lund, M.S., Stolen, K., Aagedal, J.O.: The CORAS methodology: model-based risk assessment using UML and UP. In: UML and the Unified Process, pp. 332–357. IGI Publishing (2003)

18. Matulevicius, R., Mayer, N., Mouratidis, H., Dubois, E., Heymans, P., Genon, N.: Adapting Secure Tropos for Security Risk Management in the Early Phases of Information Systems Development. In: Bellahsène, Z., Léonard, M. (eds.) CAiSE 2008. LNCS, vol. 5074, pp. 541–555. Springer, Heidelberg (2008)
19. Elahi, G., Yu, E., Zannone, N.: A Vulnerability-Centric Requirements Engineering Framework: Analyzing Security Attacks Countermeasures and Requirements Based on Vulnerabilities. Requirements Eng. 15, 41–62 (2010)
20. Beale, J., Deraison, R., Meer, H., Temingh, R., Walt, C.: Nessus Network Auditing. Syngress Pub. (2004)
21. Klaus, C.: Internet Security System, http://www.iss.net
22. Chasin, S.: Bugtrag mailing list, http://www.securityfocus.com/archive/
23. Ammann, P., Pamula, J., Street, J., Ritchey, R.: A host-based approach to network attack chaining analysis. In: Proc. of the 21st Annual Computer Security Applications Conference, pp. 72–84 (2005)
24. Ingols, K., Lippmann, R., Piwowarski, K.: Practical Attack Graph Generation for Network Defense. In: Proc. of Comp. Sec. App. Conf., pp. 121–130 (2006)
25. Hewett, K.R., Kijsanayothin, P.: Host-Centric Model Checking for Network Vulnerability Analysis. In: IEEE Annual Computer Security Applications Conference (2008)
26. Brackney, R.C., Anderson, R.H.: Understanding the Insider Threat. In: Proceedings Corporation Conference, RAND National Security Research Division, Santa Monica, California (2004)
27. Meng, P.C.W.: Network Exploration and Vulnerability Assessment using a Combined Blackbox and Whitebox Analysis Approach. Naval Postgraduate School Monterey California (2010)
28. Skousen, R.A.: Information Assurance Tools Report - Vulnerability Analysis, 5th edn (2009)
29. Dornseif, M., Gärtner, F.C., Holz, T.: Vulnerability Assessment using Honepots. K.G. Saur Verlag, München (2004)
30. RedSeal Systems Inc., http://www.redseal.net/
31. Skybox Security Inc., http://www.skyboxsecurity.com
32. Ingols, K., Lippmann, R., Piwowarski, K.: Practical attack graph generation for network defense. In: Proceedings Computer Security Applications Conference, pp. 121–130 (2006)
33. Noel, S., Jajodia, S.: Understanding complex network attack graphs through clustered adjacency matrices. In: Proceedings Computer Security Applications Conference (ACSAC), pp. 160–169 (2005)
34. Ou, X., Govindavajhala, S., Appel, A.W.: Mulval: a logic- based network security analyzer. In: Proceedings of the 14th Usenix Security Symposium 2005, pp. 113–128 (2005)
35. Jha, S., Sheyner, O., Wing, J.: Two Formal Analyses of Attack Graphs. In: Proceedings of 15th IEEE Computer Security Foundations Workshop (2002)
36. Zakeri, R., Abolhassani, H., Shahriari, R.H., Jalili, R.: Using Description Logics for Network Vulnerability Analysis. In: Proceedings of the International Conference on Networking, International Conference on Systems and International Conference on Mobile Communications and Learning Technologies (2006)
37. Campbell, C.: A stateful framework for multi-stage network attack modeling. University of Tulsa (2003)
38. Baader, F., Calvanese, D., McGuinness, D., Nardi, D., Patel-Schneider, P.F.: The Description Logic Handbook: Theory, Implementation and Applications. Cambridge University Press, Cambridge (2003)

39. Qu, G., JayaPrakash, R., Hariri, S., Raghavendra, C.S.: A Framework for Network Vulnerability Analysis. Scientific Commons (2008)
40. Wang, T., Wei, T., Lin, Z., Zou, W.: IntScope: Automatically Detecting Integer Overflow Vulnerability in X86 Binary Using Symbolic Execution. LNCS, vol. 5927, pp. 336–345 (2009)
41. Ramakrishnan, C.R., Sekar, R.: Model-Based Vulnerability Analysis of Computer Systems. In: Proceedings of the Second International Workshop on Verification, Model Checking and Abstract Interpretation (1998)
42. The Honeynet Project, Know Your Enemy: Defining Virtual Honeynets, `http://www.honeynet.org/papers/virtual/`
43. Stoll, C.: Stalking the wily hacker. CACM 31(5), 484–497 (1988)
44. Cheswick, W.: An Evening with Berferd in which a cracker is Lured Endured and Studied. In: Proceedings of USENIX (1990)
45. Guo, F., Yu, Y., Chiueh, T.: Automated and Safe Vulnerability Assessment. In: Proceedings of the 21st Annual Computer Security Applications Conference on ACSAC 2005 (2005)
46. Shahriari, H.R., Sadoddin, R., Jalili, R., Zakeri, R., Omidian, A.R.: Network vulnerability analysis through vulnerability take-grant model (VTG). In: Qing, S., Mao, W., López, J., Wang, G. (eds.) ICICS 2005. LNCS, vol. 3783, pp. 256–268. Springer, Heidelberg (2005)

Collaborative Polling Scheme to Detect and Isolate the Colluding Packet Droppers in Mobile Ad Hoc Networks

K. Gopalakrishnan and V. Rhymend Uthariaraj

Ramanujan Computing Centre, College of Engineering Guindy,
Anna University, Chennai – 600025, Tamil Nadu, India
mrkrishauc@yahoo.in, rhymend@annauniv.edu

Abstract. In mobile ad hoc network, the cooperation between the nodes is essential to discover and maintain routes. The node cooperation is not always guaranteed because of the misbehaving nodes which exist due to its constraint resources such as battery, bandwidth and computational power. When the node colludes to misbehave, it further makes the routing process difficult due to frequent network partitioning and it results in degrading the overall network throughput. This paper addresses three different kinds of packet dropping misbehavior and proposes a collaborative polling scheme to detect and isolate the colluding packet droppers. The simulation result shows that packet drop ratio, malicious packet drop and false detection has been greatly reduced when compared to the existing system under both entity and group mobility scenario.

Keywords: Routing Security, Reputation System, Collaborative Polling, Colluding Packet Droppers, Ad Hoc Networks.

1 Introduction

Mobile Ad hoc Networks (MANETs) is a collection of mobile nodes that are dynamically and arbitrarily located in such a manner that communication between nodes does not rely on any fixed network infrastructure. The communication medium is broadcast and the nodes in a mobile ad hoc network are usually portable mobile devices with constrained resources such as battery power, computation and storage capacity. The absence of static infrastructure and centralized administration makes these networks to be self organized and relying on the cooperation of neighboring nodes in order to find the routes between the nodes for reliable communication. Due to the limited transmission power of mobile nodes the cooperation between the nodes is very essential for discovering routes and forwarding packets when the source and destination nodes are not within the direct communication range of each other. However, the cooperative behavior such as forwarding packets on behalf of other nodes cannot be taken for granted because a node might agree to forward packets during route discovery but would fail to do so [12] due to malicious/non malicious behavior.

D.C. Wyld et al. (Eds.): CNSA 2011, CCIS 196, pp. 11–22, 2011.

The non-malicious packet dropping exists due to network congestion, mobility and node malfunction. When the node colludes to mischief, it further increases the complexity in discovering routes and also results in frequent network partitioning and performance degradation. This paper addresses colluding packet dropping misbehavior and proposes a collaborative polling scheme to detect and isolate such kind of misbehaving nodes. The rest of the paper is organized as follows. In Section 2, the related works are described. The proposed work is described in Section 3. In Section 4 and 5, the simulation study and the results are discussed respectively. Finally Section 6, concludes the work and discusses about the future work.

2 Related Works

Marti et al. [4] proposed a scheme which contains two components namely watchdog and path rater in each and every node to detect and mitigate the routing misbehavior in ad hoc network. The watchdog is used to identify misbehaving nodes and path rater helps the routing protocol to avoid these nodes. Buchegger et al. [6] proposed a protocol called CONFIDANT (Cooperation Of Nodes: Fairness In Dynamic Ad-hoc NeTwork) to detect and isolate misbehaving nodes. Every node in this scheme has four components a monitor for observation, a trust manager to control trust, a reputation system for maintaining reputation records and a path manager to maintain routes according to reputation. These components interact with each other to provide and process protocol information. The reputation value of a node is calculated based on direct observation and trusted second-hand reputation messages. Michiardi et al. [7] proposed a mechanism called CORE (COllaborative REputation mechanism) to enforce node cooperation in MANETs. This scheme uses a collaborative monitoring technique and a reputation mechanism. The reputation is a measure of a node contribution to network operations. Bansal et al. [9] proposed a reputation mechanism termed as OCEAN (Observation-based Cooperation Enforcement in Ad hoc Networks) based on direct observation experienced by a node from its neighbors. All the traffic from a misbehaving node is rejected and it is considered to be useful again after some time out period.

Hu et al. [10] proposed a scheme called LARS - A Locally Aware Reputation System, in which the reputation of nodes is derived by using direct observation. When a selfish node is identified then its $k - hop$ neighbors become aware of the selfishness, where k is a parameter which is adaptive to the security requirement of the network. Gopalakrishnan et al. [12] proposed a Local Monitoring based Reputation System with Alert to Mitigate the Misbehaving Nodes in Mobile Ad Hoc Networks. This scheme is similar to watchdog mechanism and imposes strong malicious traffic rejection mechanism along with alerting the source of the packet about the misbehaving link. The proposed system differs from the related works by means of using a timeout approach for detecting the active neighbors before monitoring the transmissions which involves it and also the existing schemes did not consider the colluding packet dropping misbehavior.

3 Proposed Work

The proposed *Collaborative Polling Scheme (CPS)* consists of three main components: a monitor to detect the packet dropping misbehavior, reputation system to maintain the trust value for the neighborhood nodes and a path manager to maintain the routes without containing packet droppers in it. These components are added as an add-on into the existing routing functionality of *Dynamic Source Routing (DSR)* [2] protocol. This enables each node in the network to execute this add-on functionality along with the usual routing protocol operations. Whenever a node overhears a packet from the neighboring node for the first time then the neighboring node information is stored in the *Neighbor Connectivity List (NCL)* along with the timestamp at which the packet is overheard and its trust value is initialized into 0. The timestamp and the trust value are updated for the subsequent packet overhearing from the neighboring node.

The monitor component is responsible for tapping and registering the sent packets. It has an internal component called detectors which are used to identify the different kinds of packet dropping misbehavior. A positive event is registered for a successful forwarding of a packet by a node in the neighborhood otherwise a negative event is registered by the monitor. The second component is a Reputation System which is used to maintain the trust value for the nodes in the neighborhood with the help of an internal component called Trust Manger based on the events reported by the Monitor. If the Trust Manger receives a positive event from the Monitor then the trust value of the corresponding node is incremented by α or the trust value is decremented by β in the case of negative event being received. Once a nodes reputation value reaches the *Negative Threshold* limit then it will be added into the faulty list and any traffic to and from the misbehaving node will be rejected. As soon as a node is added into the faulty list, a second chance timer will be initiated for that node. The misbehaving node information is communicated to the path manger in order to prune the routes which have the misbehaving link in it and also an explicit route error packet will be sent to the source of the packet to inform about the misbehaving link.

Once the source or an intermediate node receives an explicit route error packet then it checks whether it is originated by the source of the misbehaving link or from the neighborhood of the misbehaving link. The route which contains the misbehaving link will be pruned if the packet is originated by the source of the misbehaving link else routes containing the destination of the misbehaving link will be pruned from both primary and secondary route cache. When the second chance timer of the misbehaving node reaches 100s then the node is removed from the faulty list and reintroduced into the network by considering it to be useful again after reducing its trust value by half. The reason for not resetting the trust value of the reintroduced node to 0 is that the node might still continue to misbehave. The Reputation System also maintains faulty table which contains a list of misbehaving nodes whose accused count is greater than $k + 1$, which is shared by rest of the nodes in the network during polling. The *RREQ* packet is not monitored because it can be dropped due to network operations [8]. A node rejects the control packets used in the polling scheme, a route discovery and maintenance packets, if its faulty table contains a node present in the source route of the received packet. A neighboring node is considered to be active if any kind of packet is overheard from it within last $3000ms$ at the time of checking. Once a neighboring node is found to be active for an ongoing transmission then its behavior will be monitored. The procedure for packet monitoring and trust evaluation of the proposed system is shown in Fig. 1.

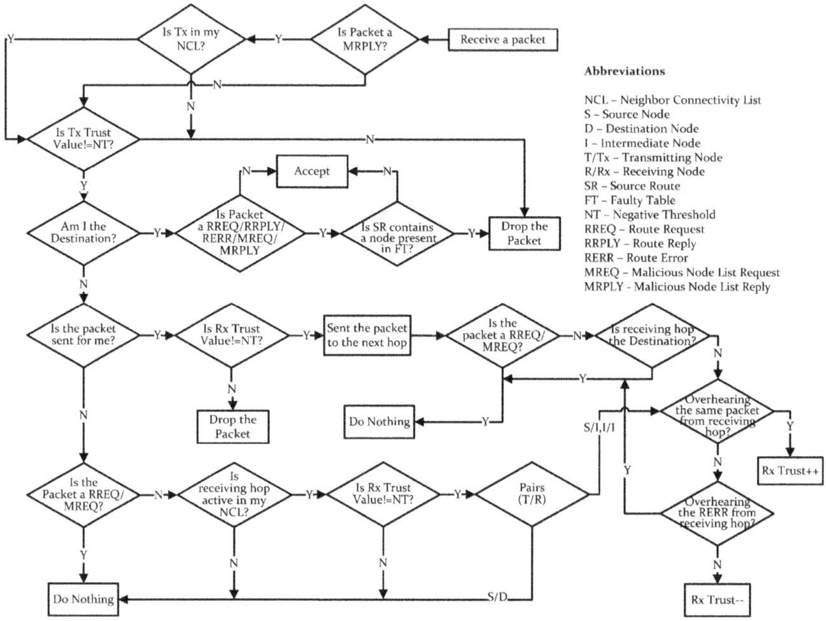

Fig. 1. Packet Monitoring and Trust Evaluation of CPS

3.1 Colluding Packet Dropping Misbehavior

As shown in Fig. 2, the solid circle represents a node and a solid line between them shows that the nodes are within the communication range of each other. Assume that the node N_1 communicates with the node N_{11} via the intermediate nodes $N_4 \rightarrow N_7 \rightarrow N_{10}$ and the nodes N_7 and N_{10} colludes to misbehave. If N_{10} drops the packet then the previous hop N_7 will not monitor and report to the source of the packet about this spiteful behavior because N_7 colludes to mischief with N_{10}.

In this scenario the neighboring nodes N_5, N_6, N_8 and N_9 are within the transmission range of N_{10} so they can identify this spiteful behavior and report to the source of the packet about this misbehaving link. Once the trust value of the misbehaving node N_{10} reaches the *Negative Threshold* limit in the neighboring nodes then the node N_{10} is added into their faulty list and they wait for the timeout period to overhear an explicit route error packet from the previous

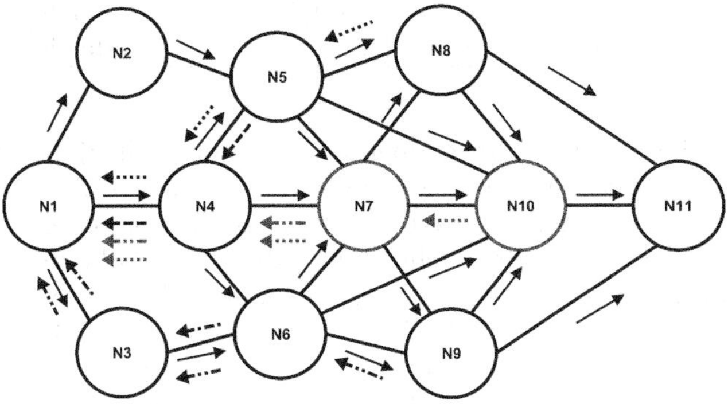

Fig. 2. Propagation of Malicious Node List Request and Reply

hop of the misbehaving node N_{10}. If they don't overhear an explicit route error packet from node N_7 within the timeout period then they decides that N_7 colludes to misbehave with N_{10}, adds N_7 into their faulty list and then send an explicit route error packet to the source of the packet to inform about this misbehaving link $N_7 \rightarrow N_{10}$. The source route of an explicit route error packet should not contain node N_7 in it because it colludes to misbehave with N_{10}. Once the source or the intermediate node receives an explicit route error packet then they will prune the routes from both the primary and secondary cache as described in section 3.

3.2 Polling Scheme

The polling scheme is used to identify the colluding/non colluding misbehaving nodes beyond the direct communication range of a node. It uses two additional control packets along with the *DSR* routing packets to carry out the polling operation. The first one is the *Malicious Node List Request (MREQ)* which is broadcasting in nature and the second one is the *Malicious Node List Reply (MRPLY)* which is unicast in nature. As shown in Fig.2., the solid arrow shows the propagation of malicious node list request and the dotted arrow shows the unicasting malicious node list reply. The proposed system also considers that the misbehaving node might also accuse the benevolent neighboring nodes as a misbehaving one during the polling process. The colluding misbehaving nodes are at least surrounded by double the amount of benevolent nodes to monitor and detect the misbehavior or at most it should satisfy the byzantine fault tolerance equation (1) then only the colluding misbehavior detection is possible.

$$n > 3t \tag{1}$$

where, n is the number of benevolent nodes which are within the communication range of colluding misbehaving nodes and t is the total number of nodes that colludes to mischief. Each node is allowed to poll the malicious node list from the rest of the nodes in the network by broadcasting the *MREQ* based on equation (2) and also it should satisfy the equation (3). It gives the time slot for each node to broadcast the *MREQ*. The *CycleNo* and *NodeId* starts with 0. Upon receiving the *MREQ*, the neighboring nodes will rebroadcast it and if it has a non empty faulty list then it sends a *MRPLY* to the requester by incorporating its faulty list into it.

$$PollingTime = PollingStartTime + ((No.of Nodes * PollingInterval * CycleNo) + (NodeId * PollingInterval)) \tag{2}$$

$$PollingTime \leq PollingEndTime \tag{3}$$

The malicious node list requester accepts an unique *MRPLY* from the rest of the nodes in the network and stores it into a mapping table called *Map Polled Misbehaving Node List* which consists of *Node Id* to hold the node address from which the *MRPLY* has been received and a *List* to hold its corresponding misbehaving node list. After receiving all malicious node list reply, it starts processing the *Map Polled Misbehaving Node List* mapping table and converts it into another mapping table called *Process Polled Misbehaving Node List* which consists of two fields to hold the *Misbehaving Node Id* and the *List* to hold the number of nodes which accused it. After completing the process, the mapping table is checked for any reverse accusations, if it exists then the node which is accused by maximum number of nodes and if the accused count is greater than or equal to $k+1$, it will be added into the faulty table. The rest of the entries in the *Process Polled Misbehaving Node List* mapping table which has the accused count greater than or equal to the threshold limit $k+1$ will be automatically added into the faulty table. The selection of k is critical for detecting the colluding misbehaving nodes as well as the independent misbehaving nodes present away from the direct communication range of the requester.

In order to thwart the Sybil attack [13], the malicious node list requester accepts *MRPLY* from and via the nodes present in its *NCL* as well as it would not update the *NCL* from the *MRPLY* because the nodes might spoof its identity in order to forge the *MRPLY*. The malicious node list requester flushes the mapping and faulty table immediately after broadcasting the *MREQ* during the next cycle in order to hold the new malicious node list and misbehaving nodes because the node which is identified as a misbehaving node during the last cycle at time t may not hold true after $t+1$ time due to reintroduction of misbehaving nodes as described in section 3.

4 Simulation Study

This paper assumes bidirectional communication symmetry on every link between nodes and the wireless interfaces support promiscuous listening mode for their operation. In promiscuous listening mode, if a node X is within the range of node Y then it can overhear communications to and from Y even if those communications does not directly involve node X. The proposed system was implemented in *ns-2.34* as an add on to the *DSR* protocol and used two different mobility models to mimic the real world movement of the mobile nodes. The first one is a *Random Way Point (RWP)* mobility model based on *Entity (E)* mobility model in which the mobile nodes movements are independent of each other. The other one is a *Reference Point Group Mobility (RPGM)* Model [1] based on *Group (G)* mobility model in which the mobile nodes move as a group. The *RWP* is based on *Carnegie Mellon University(CMU) Monarch v2* implementation and *RPGM* based on [5].

There exists multiple group of mobile nodes and each group work towards different goal but there exists communication between groups [3], [5] so the group mobility model utilizes both inter and intra group *Constant Bit Rate (CBR)* traffic patterns. Each node is assigned an initial value of *Energy (E)* by using an uniform distribution function in the interval $(E_i\text{–}3J, E_i + 3J)$ where the energy is expressed in *Joules (J)* and the initial energy $E_i = 500J$. The consequence of this choice is that every node will run out of energy at different times in the simulation. The simulation introduced three different kinds of packet droppers [11] to evaluate the *CPS* and the simulation parameters that were used in the simulation are shown in Table 1.

Table 1. Simulation Parameters

Parameter	Value
Simulation Area	900 m x 900 m
Simulation Time	900 s
Transmission Range	250 m
Number of Nodes	50
Number of Groups	5
Nodes Per Group	10
Node Mobility	10 m/s
Pause Time	30 s
Data Rate	8.0 kbps
Traffic Type	CBR (UDP)
Maximum Connections	15
Seed Value	1-20
Negative Threshold	-1
Positive Threshold	1
α	0.025
β	0.05
k	2
Polling Start Time	100 s
Polling Interval	5 s
Polling End Time	800 s

4.1 Performance Metrics

The performance of the proposed system has been measured by using the following parameters

1. Packet Loss Ratio (%) - The packet Loss Ratio is measured in terms of the ratio of data packets not delivered to the destinations to those generated by the *Constant Bit Rate (CBR)* sources
2. Normalized Routing Load (Packets) - The number of routing packets including polling control packets transmitted per data packet delivered at the destination. Each hop-wise transmission of a routing packet is counted as one transmission
3. Average End-End Delay (Seconds) - This includes all possible delays caused by buffering during route discovery latency, queuing at the interface queue, retransmission delays at the *MAC*, propagation and transfer times
4. Average Energy Dissipation (Joules) - The average amount of network energy dissipated over the simulation period
5. Malicious Drop (Packets) - The total number of data packets dropped by the different kind of packet droppers
6. False Detection (%) - The percentage of nodes detected falsely as a misbehaving node over the simulation period
7. Send Buffer Drop (Packets) - The number of data packets dropped in the send buffer of the packet originated node due to non availability/delay in finding the route to the destination

The measurements of the network performance were made using a script that parses and analyzes the trace file output generated from the simulation. The trace file provides information about a set of defined events that occurred in the simulation such as medium access control layer events, routing layer events and agent level events.

5 Results and Discussions

The simulation results of the proposed system were compared with *DSR* and the existing scheme *OCEAN*. This paper calculates a 95% confidence interval for the unknown mean and plots the confidence intervals on the graphs. The packet loss ratio of *CPS* has been decreased by 25-52% and 11-28% when compared to *DSR*, 14-16% and 7-15% when compared to *OCEAN* under both entity and group mobility scenario respectively as shown in a, b of Fig. 3. As shown in a, b of Fig. 4, the malicious drop of *CPS* has been decreased by 59-82% and 69-78% when compared to *DSR*, 17-34% and 45-65% when compared to *OCEAN* under both entity and group mobility scenario respectively. The false detection of *CPS* has been decreased from 29-39% and 37-54% when compared to *OCEAN* under entity and group mobility scenario respectively as shown in a, b of Fig. 5. As shown in a, b of Fig. 6, the normalized routing load of *CPS* has been minimum in the case of entity mobility model but where as in the case of group mobility model it gradually increased when compared to *OCEAN*.

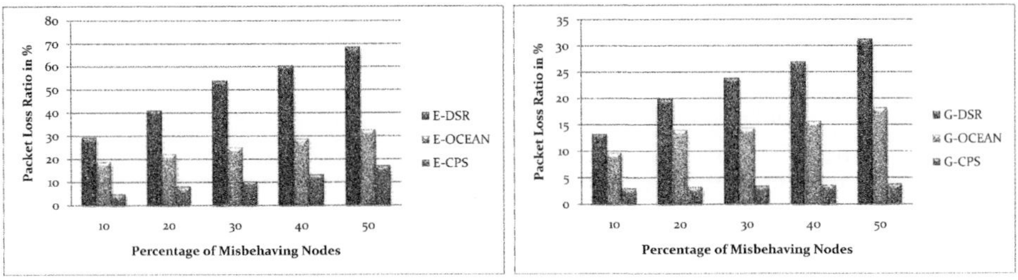

(a) Entity Mobility Scenario (b) Group Mobility Scenario

Fig. 3. Packet Loss Ratio in %

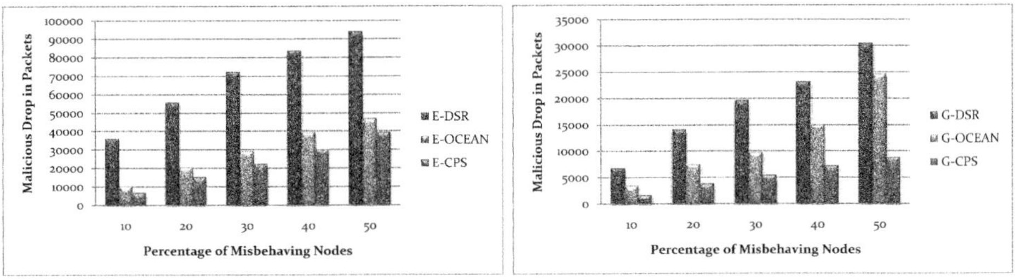

(a) Entity Mobility Scenario (b) Group Mobility Scenario

Fig. 4. Malicious Drop in Packets

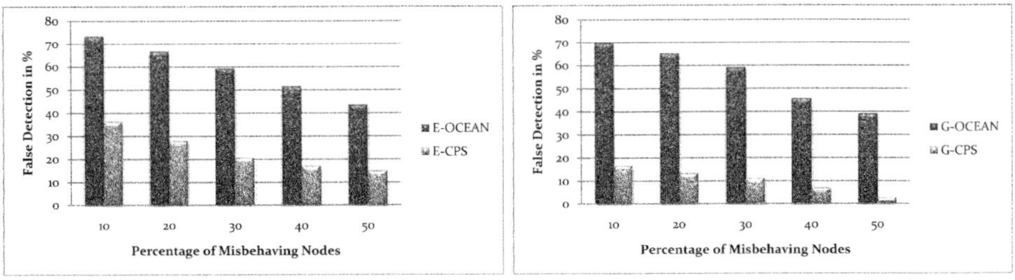

(a) Entity Mobility Scenario (b) Group Mobility Model

Fig. 5. False Detection in %

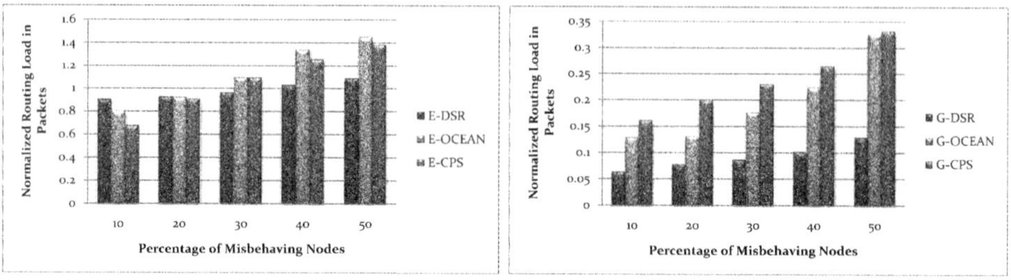

(a) Entity Mobility Model (b) Group Mobility Model

Fig. 6. Normalized Routing Load in Packets

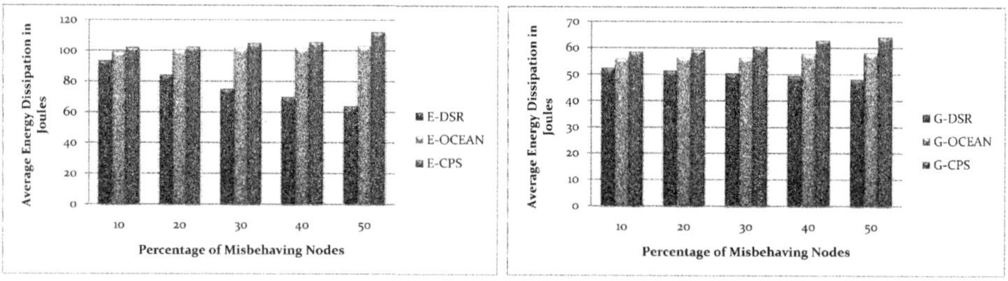

(a) Entity Mobility Model (b) Group Mobility Model

Fig. 7. Average Energy Dissipation in Joules

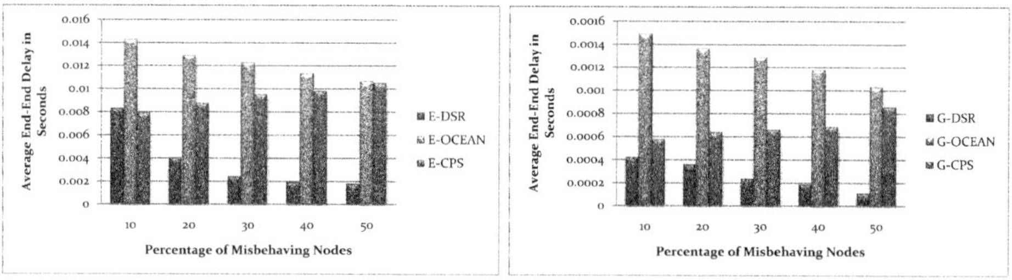

(a) Entity Mobility Model (b) Group Mobility Model

Fig. 8. Average End-End Delay in Seconds

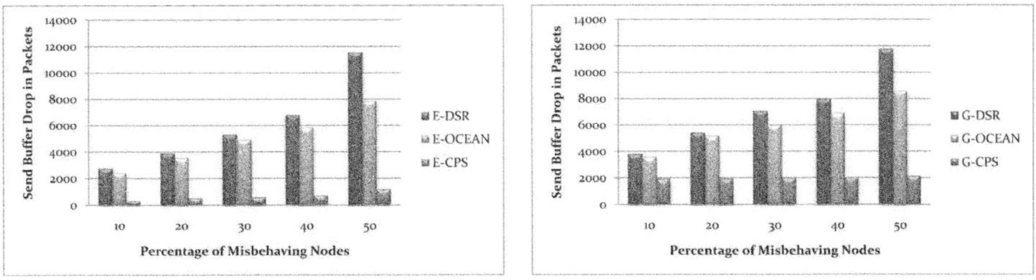

(a) Entity Mobility Model (b) Group Mobility Model

Fig. 9. Send Buffer Drop in Packets

Since the average energy dissipation is directly proportional to the overall network throughput and control packets spent, the average energy dissipation of *CPS* has been gradually increased when compared to *OCEAN* under both entity and group mobility scenario respectively as shown in a, b of Fig. 7. The average end-end delay of *CPS* has been reduced when compared to *OCEAN* under both entity and group mobility scenario respectively as shown in a, b of Fig. 8. This result shows that the proposed system finds trusted and shorter routes than the *OCEAN*. As shown in a, b of Fig. 9, the send buffer drop of *CPS* has been decreased by 87-90% and 50-83% when compared to *DSR*, 85-89% and 47-76% when compared to *OCEAN* under both entity and group mobility scenario. It shows that the proposed system has enough alternative routes to the destination even with the presence of colluding packet droppers when compared to OCEAN.

6 Conclusions and Future Work

The simulation result shows that the packet loss ratio, malicious drop, false detection and send buffer drop were greatly reduced. It shows the effectiveness of the proposed system in detecting the misbehaving nodes and finding out the alternative routes. The proposed system is immune to colluding packet dropping misbehavior because of the combination of timely generation of an explicit route error packet by the neighboring nodes and the polling process. This scheme is also immune to overhearing technique drawbacks mentioned in [4] due to neighborhood monitoring approach and the reintroduction of misbehaving nodes. In future work, more kind of misbehaving nodes will be considered and also find a way to decrease the control overhead occurred due to polling. This scheme is suitable for both entity and group mobility based applications.

Acknowledgment. The first author would like to acknowledge the support received from CSIR-HRDG (Council of Scientific and Industrial Research-Human Resource Development Group), India, through Senior Research Fellowship.

References

1. Hong, X., Gerla, M., Pei, G., Chiang, C.: A Group Mobility Model for Ad Hoc Wireless Networks. In: 2nd ACM International Workshop on Modeling and Simulation of Wireless and Mobile Systems, pp. 53–60. ACM, Seattle (1999)
2. Johnson, D.B., Maltz, D.A., Broch, J.: The Dynamic Source Routing Protocol for Mobile Ad Hoc Networks. Internet Draft, The Internet Engineering Task Force (1999)
3. Hong, X., Gerla, M., Pei, G., Chiang, C.: A Wireless Hierarchical Routing Protocol with Group Mobility. In: IEEE Wireless Communications and Networking Conference, pp. 1536–1540. IEEE, New Orleans (1999)
4. Marti, S., Giuli, T.J., Lai, K., Baker, M.: Mitigating Routing Misbehavior in Mobile Ad Hoc Networks. In: 6th International Conference on Mobile Computing and Networking, pp. 255–265. ACM, Boston (2000)
5. Camp, T., Boleng, J., Davies, V.: A Survey of Mobility Models for Ad Hoc Network Research. J. Wireless Communication and Mobile Computing 2, 483–502 (2002)
6. Buchegger, S., Le Boudec, J.Y.: Performance Analysis of the CONFIDANT Protocol (Cooperation Of Nodes: Fairness In Dynamic Ad-hoc NeTworks). In: IEEE/ACM Symposium on Mobile Ad Hoc Networking and Computing, pp. 226–236. ACM, Lausanne (2002)
7. Michiardi, P., Molva, R.: CORE: A COllaborative Reputation Mechanism to enforce node cooperation in Mobile Ad hoc Networks. In: 6th Joint Working Conference on Communications and Multimedia Security, vol. 228, pp. 107–121. Kluwer, Portoroz (2002)
8. Tseng, Y.C., Ni, S.Y., Chen, Y.S., Sheu, J.P.: The Broadcast Storm Problem in a Mobile Ad Hoc Network. J. Wireless Networks 8, 153–167 (2002)
9. Bansal, S., Baker, M.: Observation-based Cooperation Enforcement in Ad hoc Networks. Technical Report, Stanford University (2003)
10. Hu, J., Burmester, M.: LARS A Locally Aware Reputation System for Mobile Ad Hoc Networks. In: 44th Annual Southeast Regional Conference, pp. 119–123. ACM, Melbourne (2006)
11. Gopalakrishnan, K., Rhymend Uthariaraj, V.: Scenario based Evaluation of the Impact of Misbehaving Nodes in Mobile Ad Hoc Networks. In: 1st IEEE International Conference on Advanced Computing, pp. 45–50. IEEE Computer Society, Chennai (2009)
12. Gopalakrishnan, K., Rhymend Uthariaraj, V.: Local monitoring based reputation system with alert to mitigate the misbehaving nodes in mobile ad hoc networks. In: Das, V.V., Vijaykumar, R. (eds.) ICT 2010. CCIS, vol. 101, pp. 344–349. Springer, Heidelberg (2010)
13. Piro, C., Shields, C., Levine, B.N.: Detecting the Sybil Attack in Mobile Ad hoc Networks. In: Proceedings of Securecomm and Workshops, pp. 1–11. IEEE Digital Library, Baltimore (2006)

Defense Strategy against Network Worms Causing ICMP Attacks and Its Forensic Analysis

K.S. Aathira and Thulasi N. Kutty

TIFAC Core Cyber Security Department,
Amrita School of Engineering Coimbatore, India
{aathiramanikutty,thulasi.nk}@gmail.com

Abstract. The network forensic analysis process involves preparation, collection, preservation, examination, analysis, investigation and presentation phases. The proposed system addresses the major challenges in collection, examination and analysis processes. The model is for collecting network data, identifying suspicious packets, examining protocol features misused and validating the attack. This model has been built with specific reference to security attacks on ICMP protocol that enables forensic experts to analyze the marked suspicious network traffic, thus facilitating cost effective storage and faster analysis of high bandwidth traffic. The ICMP attacks initiated by worms can be detected using this system. The ability of worms to spread at rates that effectively preclude human-directed reaction has elevated them to a first-class security threat to distributed systems. Thus worm detection has become a vital part in the Intrusion Detection Systems. A reaction mechanism that seeks to automatically patch vulnerable software is also proposed. This system employs a collection of sensors that detect and capture potential worm infection vectors. The size of the log file generated by different sensors, used for detecting worm infection vectors can be efficiently reduced by the forensic architecture. It automatically tests the effects of these vectors on appropriately-instrumented sandboxed instances of the targeted application, trying to identify the exploited software weakness. Network forensics relates to the monitoring and analysis of computer network traffic for the purpose of information gathering, legal evidence or intrusion detection.

Keywords: Network forensics, pcap, ICMP, Intrusion Detection System, network worms, auto-patching, honeypots.

1 Introduction

Network forensics is a dedicated investigation technology that enables capture, recording and analysis of network packets and events for investigative purposes. It is an extension of the network security model which traditionally emphasizes prevention and detection of network attacks. When attacks are successful, forensic techniques enable investigators to catch the attackers. The ultimate goal is to provide sufficient evidence to allow the attacker to be prosecuted [8]. It refers to a dedicated investigation infrastructure that allows for the collection and analysis of network

D.C. Wyld et al. (Eds.): CNSA 2011, CCIS 196, pp. 23–34, 2011.

packets and events for investigative purposes. It is proposed to complement the mentioned network security model. Network forensics is of a great importance for today's organizations [10]. The proposed network forensic system for ICMP based network attacks can be extended to any of the network attacks. This model enables forensic experts to analyze the marked suspicious network traffic, thus facilitating cost effective storage and faster analysis of high bandwidth traffic. The significant features are identified which enable security attacks on ICMP protocol and mark suspicious packets. The header information of protocols in the TCP/IP suite encapsulated in the packet capture file is ported to a database. The protocol attributes of each packet are stored as a record. Rule sets for various ICMP attacks have been designed and are queried on the database to calculate various statistical parameters and thresholds. This information is used for validating the presence of attacks. The packet capture information in database records and related attack data is available for investigation process. This model gives the investigation phase a qualitative data.

The self-propagating code, also known as "network worms", has the ability to infect large numbers of hosts, exploiting vulnerabilities in the largely homogeneous deployed software base. Even when the worm carries no malicious payload, the direct cost of recovering from the side effects of an infection epidemic can be tremendous. Thus, countering worms has recently become the focus of increased research. However, these epidemics have also demonstrated the ability of worms to achieve extremely high infection rates [2]. This implies that a hypothetical reaction system must not, and in some cases cannot, depend on human intervention for containment. The dynamic nature of malware keeps most security experts constantly on the lookout for new types of malware and new vectors for attack. Due to the complex technical nature of malware, it is helpful to examine overall attack trends to better understand how attacks using malware are evolving. As mentioned previously, the use of malware is becoming more sophisticated and targeted. Attackers are using increasingly deceptive social engineering techniques to entice users to seemingly legitimate web pages that are actually infected and/or compromised with malware [1]. Malware is now spread around the world and rankings tend to show that a whole host of countries across the developed and the developing world are home to online criminals using malware. The ICMP attacks generated by worms are directed to network forensic architecture and size of various log files collected by different sensors are efficiently reduced. This minimizes storage requirement to a great extend. Although attacks originating from one country may have local targets, the predominant trend is attacks that originate internationally relative to their targets. In addition, geography may play a role depending on the end goal of the attacker. For example, broadband Internet speeds differ from country to country. If an attacker wishes to maximize network damage, he/she may use compromised computers located in countries where broadband is prevalent. If the goal is to degrade service or steal information over time, the attacker may use compromised computers from a variety of geographical locations. Geographical distribution allows for increased anonymity of attacks and impedes identification, investigation and prosecution of attackers. A reaction mechanism that tries to automatically patch vulnerable software, thus circumventing the need for human intervention in time critical infection containment is proposed. In our system, the issue of performance is of diminished importance since the primary use of the protection mechanisms is to identify the source of weakness in the application. The approach presented here employs a combination of techniques such as the use of honeypots, dynamic code analysis, auto-patching, sandboxing, and software updates. The ICMP attacks generated by worms are directed to network forensic architecture and size of various log files collected by different sensors are efficiently reduced. This minimizes storage requirement to a great extend. The ability to use these techniques is contingent upon a number of realistic assumptions. Dynamic analysis relies on the assumption that known classes of attacks can be tackled. Our architecture can be deployed on a per-network or per-organization basis, reflecting the trust relationships among entities. This can be further dissected to distributed sensors, anomaly detection, and the sandboxed environment. For example, an enterprise network may use a complete instantiation of our architecture while also providing remote-sensor functionality to other organizations.

2 Background

A key challenge in network forensics is to first ensure that the network is forensically ready. For a successful network investigation, the network itself must be equipped with an infrastructure to fully support this investigation. The infrastructure should ensure that the needed data exists for a full investigation. Designing a network forensic infrastructure is a challenging task because of the many possibilities in this design space.

2.1 ICMP Attacks

ICMP facilitates sending one-way informational message to a host and informs the source host about errors in datagram processing. These two operations are heavily exploited by the attackers to launch the following attacks:

2.1.1 ICMP Sweep

An ICMP sweep is not a direct attack on network, but is definite threat to security. By using a sweep, attackers can determine active hosts and perform more direct targeted attacks specific to those hosts. By sending a series of ICMP “echo request” packets to every IP on a network segment, an attacker will receive ICMP replies confirming that a host is alive. This process is fairly “noisy” as the attackers are broadcasting across a whole network range [9].

In any typical attack scenario, the attacker will first engage in some reconnaissance and scanning activities in order to

1. Better understand the environment of the target
2. Gather information about the target so as to plan the attack approach
3. Employ the right techniques & tools for the subsequent attack phases

One of the most common and most well understood techniques for discovering the range of hosts which are alive in the target’s environment is to perform an ICMP sweep of the entire target’s network range. An ICMP sweep involves essentially sending a series of ICMP request packets to the target network range and from the list of ICMP replies infer whether certain hosts are alive and connected to the target's network for further probing.

2.1.2 Inverse Mapping

Networks are protected by filtering devices such as firewalls and gateways that prevent internal hosts from being reached externally. Attacker uses inverse mapping to obtain a map of an internal network. ICMP reply messages are sent to internal routers about the hosts nearby by and getting the information about the network. This is accomplished without the filtering devices knowing.

An Inverse Mapping attack is illustrated below:

Step 1. Attacker sends an ICMP reply message to a range of IP addresses presumably behind a filtering device.

Step 2. Upon receiving the series of ICMP reply messages, since the filtering device does not keep state of the list of ICMP requests, it will allow these packets to their destination.

Step 3. If there is an internal router, the router will respond with a ICMP "Host Unreachable" for every host that it cannot reach, thus giving the attacker knowledge of all hosts which are present behind the filtering device [9].

2.1.3 Traceroute Network Mapping

Microsoft Windows and all Linux derivatives include a network tool known as traceroute that provides a mechanism for tracking the path of packets flowing between the host and a destination host. It achieves this by utilising the IP protocols TTL (time to live) field, where it attempts to elicit an ICMP "time exceeded" response from each gateway/router along the path to some host. By default the Linux version of the traceroute application uses UDP to perform its tracing, but it also provides an argument (-I) that allows the tool to use ICMP instead. What this command essentially does is, it will send out progressively a series of packets with an increasing TTL (Time to Live) value set. When an intermediate router receives a forwarding packet, it'll decrement the TTL value of the packet before forwarding it to the next router. At this time if the TTL value of the packet reaches zero, an ICMP "time exceeded" message will be send back to the originating host. By sending the packet with initial TTL value of 1 will allow the first router in the path of the packet to now send back an ICMP "time exceeded" message which will then allow the attacker to know the IP address of the first router. Subsequent packets are send by increasing the TTL value in the packet by 1 each time, thus the attacker will be able to know every hop between him and the target.Using this technique, the attacker could not only trace the path taken by a packet as it travels to the target but also gives him information on the topology of the target network [9].

2.1.4 OS Fingerprinting

Often an attacker will need to identify what system they are about to attack before they can exploit a vulnerability. In this technique, the attacker relies upon the operating system manufacturer to have built their communications system slightly differently from other operating systems, the steps to recreate this technique are: The attacker sends malformed ICMP packets to the destination. The destination host will respond with numerous answers to the given requests. Each operating system will send slightly different results back to the host. The installed operating system is determined by a process of elimination by evaluating the responses.

2.1.5 ICMP Smurf Attack

This attack exploits the weakness in the ICMP and IP protocols by forging the original source address of the packet with the address of the machine to be attack [11]. This "spoofing" hides the attacker, and begins a chain reaction of network disruption.

Step 1. Attacker finds some intermediary network that will respond to the network's broadcast address [9].

Step 2. Attacker spoofs the IP address of the victim host and sends a great number of ICMP echo request packets to the broadcast address of the above intermediary networks

Step 3. Now all the hosts on that network will respond to that ICMP echo request with a corresponding ICMP reply request back to the spoofed IP address (the victim).

Step 4. This will send a whole bunch of ICMP echo replies to the victim and its network thus causing network degradation or a total denial of service.

2.2 Scanning and Attack Patterns

The spread of the worm in its most basic sense depends most greatly on how it chooses its victims [5]. This not only affects the spread and pace of the worm network, but also its survivability and persistence as cleanup efforts begin. Classically, worms have used random walks of the Internet to find hosts and attack. However, new attack models have emerged that demonstrate increased aggressiveness.

2.2.1 Random Scanning

The simplest way for a worm to spread as far as it can is to use random network scanning. In this method, the worm node randomly generates a network to scan, typically a block of 65,000 hosts (a /16 network) or 256 hosts (a /24) in a target network block. This worm node then begins to search for potential victims in that network space and attacks vulnerable hosts. This random walk is the classic spread model for network-based worms.

However, there are some issues with this method, of course. The first is that the pool of addresses in use on the Internet tends to cluster to the middle, typically between 128/8 and 220/8. However, sizable and interesting networks reside outside of this, such as cable modem networks in 24/4 and 64/4, along with several large, well-known corporate networks in this range. To be effective, the worm should focus its efforts on hosts that are likely to be vulnerable to its exploits as well as being widely found. Secondly, it is easy to pick a network block that is sparsely populated. This then wastes the node's time by scanning a network section that will contain few, if any, hosts it can attack or compromise. The likelihood of this is dependent on the network space chosen. Several of the class A networks below 127/8 those are almost completely unused. Thirdly, it is important to have a good random number generator in use to achieve almost complete coverage of the chosen range. A weak random number generator will mean that some networks will be disproportionately scanned. Some networks may not be scanned at all when this occurs.

The advantages of this type of scanning are that, when properly executed, near total coverage of the Internet can be accomplished within a brief period of time. This can be of value for an attacker who wishes to gain access to the maximum number of hosts in a reasonable amount of time. Second, this type of worm is bound to be more persistent than a directed or island-based scanning worm. Not every network will be able to eradicate the worm infestation, and the worm will hop from one network to others randomly, constantly finding a host to infect.

This type of scanning has a few disadvantages. The first is that the worm network will not achieve deep penetration behind firewalls, unlike other methods. While the worm is likely to find a vulnerable host it can compromise within a potentially rich network, it is likely to hop out of the network again as it randomly generates a new network to scan. Also, this type of scanning pattern is very noisy and highly visible. As described above, the scanning of sparsely populated networks is likely, and a simple tracking of this will reveal the presence of a worm.

2.2.2 Random Scanning Using Lists

The next type of scanning mechanism is related to random scanning but selects from a reduced section. In this method, the worm carries a list of numbers used to assist in the generation of the networks to probe and attack [6]. This list is built from assigned and used address space from the Internet. By using this approach, the worm is able to focus on locations where hosts are likely to be present, improving the worm's efficiency.

Such lists are relatively easy to amass, and now that they have been used in several worms which have received considerable analysis, they can be recycled or updated as needed. Routing registries such as ARIN and regular nameservers can be exhaustively queried to find unused network segments. Furthermore, many routing databases are available that can provide this information.

The address generators that use these lists must be carefully designed. Otherwise, this can be used against the worm to predict where it will go next based on this hardcoded list. As such, sites that appear more frequently than others can set up detection or defense measures more rapidly and help stave off the worm's spread. But when a network range is scanned, the number of addresses attempted can grow to the tens of thousands, causing a significant delay in the worm's overall spread.

2.2.3 Island Hopping

The third type of network scanning that worms perform is typically called island hopping. This is so named because it treats network blocks as islands on which it focuses attention before hopping away to a new, random destination. This spread pattern has proven to be highly effective in the long term.

The advantages of this worm, for the attacker, are that it achieves a high degree of network penetration. All that it needs is one network host that can be infected by the worm, and then it can have trusted access to the network. Multihomed hosts are ideal for this kind of attack, because they can provide access to internal networks even if they are not directly forwarding network packets. This can include private address space that is not accessible from the global Internet, such as RFC 1918-compliant corporate or campus networks, typically behind strong filtering devices.

One major disadvantage for the attackers, and a boon to those who protect networks, is that the local bias of the worm means that it is typically easier to isolate and stop. These hosts typically show themselves on their local networks (assuming a /16 or larger network), meaning the network managers can take steps to isolate and remove the affected machines.

2.2.4 Directed Attacking

Another targeting and direction method that can be used by a worm is that of directing its attack at a particular network. In this scenario, a worm carries a target network it is to penetrate and focuses its efforts on that network. This type of worm attack would be used in information warfare.

This type of attack can be achieved in two major ways. In the first, the worm network is introduced and immediately begins its assault on the target network. In doing this, the worm can maximize its assault before the target network's defenses are raised. However, the relatively small number of sources can make it easy to filter based on the source location. In the second, the worm begins its attack only after some period of activity. This may include a widespread infection over the period of a few days, allowing it to exploit the trust of certain source networks now compromised. Alternatively, the worms may turn on the target network after a predefined number of iterations. In either scenario, the wide number of sources can overwhelm the target network and find a vulnerable host as a method of entry.

By choosing this method, an attacker can cause concentrated damage against the target network, including the release of sensitive documents and the disruption of network services. Such a worm would no doubt be useful in scenarios of corporate or military espionage, a campaign of terrorism against a corporation or a government, or the introduction of malicious software or information. While these attacks are possible with the other spread mechanisms described here, this gives an attacker a focused effort, which would be useful in overwhelming an enemy's defenses.

This method of choosing targets has several disadvantages. First, unless an introduction of the worm is done at widespread points, it would be easy to selectively filter the sources based on the attack type and location. Because of this, a worm that turns on a target after some period of random spreading would be preferred. This method introduces a second disadvantage, however. By spreading to other networks, researchers would be able to identify the worm and develop countermeasures, making them available to the target network.

2.2.5 Hit-List Scanning

When a node is attacked and compromised, the hit list splits in half and one-half remains with the parent node and the other half goes to the child node. This mechanism continues and the worm's efficiency improves with every permutation. This infection design is highly effective.

This mechanism has several drawbacks. First, the necessary scans are likely to be noticed. While widespread vulnerability scanning has become commonplace on the

Internet and is possibly accepted as background noise by some, widespread scanning for the same vulnerability still generates enough traffic in the monitoring community to raise some flags. Second, the network bandwidth consumed by a fast moving worm is likely to choke itself off of the network. As more worms become active, network connections fill, restricting the ability for the worm to move as efficiently. However, if the hit list were to be sorted hierarchically, so that larger bandwidth networks were hit first and the children nodes were within those networks, concerns about bandwidth could be minimized.

2.3 Introduction Mechanisms

Just as the way the worm network finds its next victim is important for its speed and its long-term survivability and penetration, the way in which the worm is introduced is another concern. A common scenario to imagine is a malicious attacker introducing a worm in a public computer lab one evening. By carefully considering the point and variety of introduction mechanisms, Internet worms can achieve different goals.

2.3.1 Single Point

The classic paradigm of the introduction of a worm is to use a single point of origin, such as a single Internet system. This host is set up to launch the worm and infect a number of child nodes, carrying the worm with it. These new nodes then begin the next round of target identification and compromise.

A well-connected and reasonably poorly monitored host is to be found out. To achieve the maximum introduction from a single point, this node will have to infect several new hosts, which are also capable of a wide area of infection. This will be crucial in establishing the initial presence of the worm when it is most vulnerable, existing on only a few nodes. An obvious weakness in this scenario is that the worm may be identified back to its source and ultimately its author. By combining a number of factors, including usage patterns of the source host or network, with the code base, investigators can sometimes establish the identity of the author of the malicious software.

One variation of this theme is to introduce the malicious software at a single point but use an accepted distribution mechanism to gain entry to the Internet. This includes a Trojan horse software package or a malicious file in a peer-to-peer network. While only a single point of entry for the software is used, it is then introduced to several computers which can then launch the worm onto multiple networks.

For the attacker, however, this is the easiest avenue of introducing a worm. It involves the fewest resources and, if the worm takes hold of the network early and establishes it quickly, gives the quickest path to a stable infection.

2.3.2 Multiple Point

The introduction of a worm at multiple points in the network overcomes several limitations of the single-point introduction method described. First, it has a higher chance of gaining a strong foothold within the network earlier than when compared to a single node starting out. This is due to the presence of multiple, redundant nodes. These can compensate for failure at any one node.

Second, this affords an added element of speed, which can be quite significant if the introduction is over a wide number of hosts [9]. By quickly ramping up the number of worm nodes, the worm network can be several generations ahead of a single-point worm introduction. Obviously, a nontrivial number of nodes are required to make this impact noticeable. Lastly, when executed properly, it can help to obscure the location of the worm's author. This is because of the diffusion of the worms' source, which is quickly obscured by the activity of the network. However, this can easily backfire and provide a method of network triangulation to the real source, unless the tracks are well obscured.

This path obviously creates a much larger amount of work for the malicious attacker. They must gain control of enough systems on the Internet to make this approach feasible and worthwhile, which takes time and effort. Given the relative speed of a typical worm, the time it would take a worm to reach the numbers of affected hosts can quickly reach that of an active attacker working manually.

2.2.3 Widespread Introduction with a Delayed Trigger

Another mechanism by which a worm can be introduced into the Internet is through the use of a delayed trigger in an existing software component. This can include the use of a compromised software repository to lead to a Trojan horse condition, where a piece of software carries malicious components with it.

The first and major advantage to this mechanism is the widespread nature of the initial round of infection. Presumably many hosts have downloaded the modified software, forming a wide base for the worm's launching point. Additionally, if these hosts are targeted as hosts with good connectivity, the initial rounds of infection by the worm can proceed more efficiently due to the increased visibility of the network.

3 Architecture

The architecture, shown in Figure 1,is a combined network worm vaccine architecture and the forensic analysis system of ICMP attacks , caused by the worms. The worm vaccine architecture makes use of five types of components: a set of worm-detection sensors, an anomaly-detection engine, a sandboxed environment running appropriately-instrumented versions of the applications used in the enterprise network, an analysis[4] and patch generation engine, and a software update component. The worm-detection sensors are responsible for detecting potential worm probes[3] and, more importantly, infection attempts. Several types of sensors may be employed concurrently: Host-based sensors are used for monitoring the behavior of deployed applications and servers. Special-purpose honeypots [7], which simulate the behavior of the target application and capture any communication in the network.

The potential infection vector (i.e., the byte stream which, when "fed" to the target application, will cause an instance of the worm to appear on the target system) is forwarded to a sandboxed environment, which runs appropriately-instrumented instances of the applications which are to be protected. Several patches can be tested (potentially even simultaneously, if enough resources are available), until satisfiable output, that the application is no longer vulnerable to the specific exploit. To ensure that the patched version will continue to function, regression testing can be used to

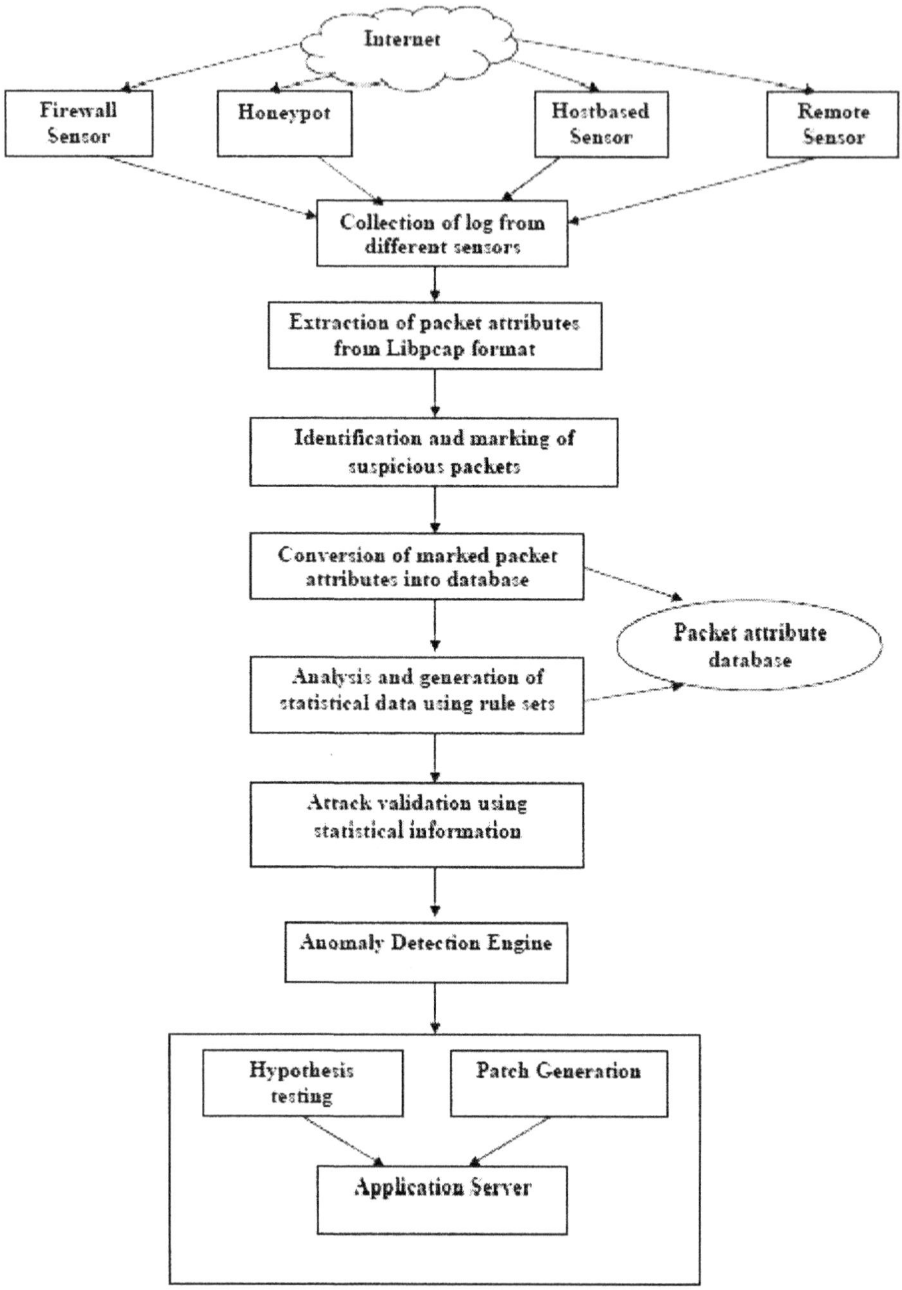

Fig. 1. A combined Architecture for Network Worm Vaccine and Forensic Analysis

determine what functionality (if any) has been lost. The test suite is generated by the administrator in advance, and should reflect a typical workload of the application, exercising all critical aspects [2].

Once a worm-resistant version of the application is developed, it must be instantiated on the server. Thus, the last component of our architecture is a server-based monitor. To achieve this, either a virtual-machine approach can be used or assume that the target application is somehow sandboxed and implement the monitor as a regular process residing outside that sandbox [1]. The monitor receives the new version of the application, terminates the running instance (first attempting a graceful termination), replaces the executable with the new one, and restarts the server.

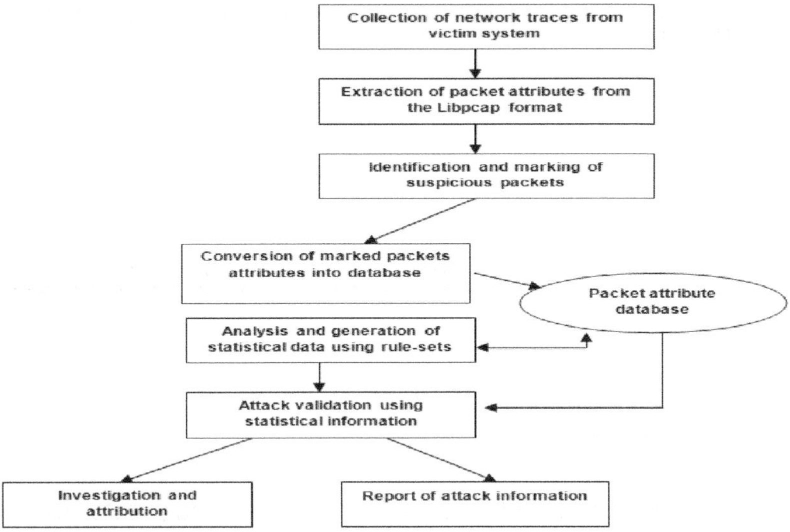

Fig. 2. Forensic System Architecture

The architecture for network forensic includes collection of network data, identification of suspicious packets, examining protocol features misused and validation of the attack. This model is built to address the major issue of the large amount of data to be examined for correlation of network features and attacks. This model is elaborated with reference to the network attacks on ICMP protocol [9]. After achieving significant reduction in the network data we validate the system by analyzing the statistics from the database of the protocol header parameters encapsulated in packet captures. The desired results are reported and used for investigation phase.

4 Conclusion

The major challenge in network forensics is handling the massive size of network packet capture. It is difficult to store, manage and analyze. This problem was addressed by reducing the packet capture file size by marking the attack packets using the packet header information only. For marking the attack packets, various attacks were correlated and its corresponding identified significant features. We focused on some specific attacks on ICMP protocol that are propagated by worms and have tested our approach onto a packet capture files from a victim system. The size of the log file generated by different sensors,used for detecting worm infection vectors can be efficiently reduced by the forensic architecture. An architecture for countering selfpropagating code (worms) through automatic softwarepatch generation is also proposed. In the architecture a set of sensors to detect potential infection vectors, and uses a cleanroom (sandboxed) environment running appropriately instrumented instances of the applications used in the enterprise network to test potential fixes are used. This system employs a collection of sensors that detect and capture potential worm infection vectors. Those which are identified as malicious are send to the Anomaly detection engine. Appropriate fix for vulnerable software (detected by the anomaly detection engine) is found out using sandboxed environment and server can be updated.

References

1. Sidiroglou, S., Locasto, M.E., Keromytis, A.D.: Self healing software services. In: Workshop on Architectural Support for Security and Anti-Virus, vol. 33(1) (2008)
2. Sidiroglou, S., Keromytis, A.D.: A NetworkWorm Vaccine Architecture. In: Proceedings of the Proceeding WETICE 2003 Proceedings of the Twelfth International Workshop on Enabling Technologies: Infrastructure for Collaborative Enterprises (2004)
3. Einwechter, N.: Identifying and Tracking Emerging and Subversive Worms Using Distributed Intrusion Detection Systems, SecurityFocus.com
4. Hong, S.-C., Zhao, L.-Q., Ju, H.-T., Hong, J.W.: Worm Traffic Monitoring and Infected Hosts Detection Algorithm for Local Network. In: Proceedings of 10th ACM Conference on Computer and Communications Security(CCS 2003), pp. 190–199 (2003)
5. Nazario, J.: Defense and Detection Strategies against Internet Worms. Artech House, Boston (2004) ISBN 1-58053-537-2
6. Zamboni, D., Riordan, J., Yates, M.: Boundary detection and containment of local worm infections. In: Proceedings of the 18th Annual FIRST Conference (2007)
7. Karthik, S., Samudrala, B., Yang, A.T.: Design of Network Security Projects Using Honeypots. Journal of Computing Sciences in Colleges 20(4)
8. Yasinsac, A., Manzano: Policies to Enhance Computer and Network Forensics. In: IEEE Workshop on Information Assurance and Security (2001)
9. Kaushik, A.K., Joshi, R.C.: Network Forensic System for ICMP Attacks. International Journal of Computer Applications 2(3), 975–8887 (2010)
10. Almulhem, A., Traore: Experience with Engineering a Network Forensics System. In: Proceedings of International Conference on Information Networking (2005)
11. Kumar, S.: Smurf-based Distributed Denial of Service(DDoS) Attack Amplification in Internet. In: Proceedings of International Conference on Internet Monitoring and Protection (2007)

Analysis of Algebraic Attack on TRIVIUM and Minute Modification to TRIVIUM

Ashji S. Raj[1] and Chungath Srinivasan[2]

[1] Amal Jyothi College of Engineering, Kanjirapally, Kottayam, India
ashjisraj@gmail.com
[2] TIFAC CORE in Cyber Security, Amrita Vishwa Vidyapeetham, Coimbatore, India
chungathsrinivasan@gmail.com

Abstract. In recent times, each user needs to secure the information from unwanted disclosure of secret. Encryption is the most wildly used technique to secure the information. LFSR based cipher systems called stream ciphers are commonly used for applications which requires high speed encryption and implementation. Even though these systems provide secrecy to information stream ciphers are highly vulnerable to attacks. The securities of these systems are calculated mostly in terms of correlation attacks and algebraic attacks. In these attacks the key is found by solving this multivariable system of equations. This paper presents a careful analysis on Stream Cipher TRIVIUM. The study has been performed on how the equations are generated and how much they are vulnerable to various attacks. Finally a minor variation has been made on TRIVIUM to prevent algebraic attack by guessing apposite nonlinear variables. Here propose a new design to the key generation of Trivium that has better correlation properties.

Keywords: Stream Ciphers, Correlation attack, Algebraic attack, multivariate nonlinear equations, TRIVIUM.

1 Introduction

TRIVIUM is a synchronous stream cipher designed to provide a flexible trade-off between speed and gate count or area in hardware. It is hardware oriented Stream Cipher; even though it works reasonably well in software implementations. TRIVIUM has been designed very simple and securely. It shows how simple a stream cipher can be designed without compromising its security. While simple designs are more likely to be vulnerable to attacks. Its design doesn't use more complex algorithm to introduce security.

Trivium is a synchronous stream cipher designed to generate up to 264 bits of key stream from an 80-bit secret key and an 80-bit initial value (IV). Design consists of two phases: first the internal state of the cipher is initialized using the key and the IV, and then the state is repeatedly updated and used to generate keystream bits [3]. This stream cipher consists of an NLFSR, which operates on a 288-bit state denoted by (s_1, . . , s_{288}) put together by a linear filter function. The linear filter function takes a linear combination of the state bits to produce the keystream. At each clock Trivium updates

D.C. Wyld et al. (Eds.): CNSA 2011, CCIS 196, pp. 35–42, 2011.

three bits of the state and outputs one bit of keystream. It has two other variants: BIVIUM-A and BIVIUM-B. It uses one register of 177 bits. The following section gives a concise description of the design of Trivium and its two variants, Bivium A and B. The security requirement that impose on Trivium is that any type of cryptographic attack should not be significantly easier to apply to Trivium than to any other imaginable stream cipher with the same external parameters.

In this paper, after giving a brief description of the design of TRIVIUM and its variants we show how to generate a system of equations over F_2 for Trivium and Bivium. Here it uses two methods: in the first method after each clock three new variables will be introduced in the cipher and in the second it uses only the 288 bits (or 177 bits for Bivium) of the internal state at the beginning. The last section describes how Groebner basis is applicable on these two methods.

2 TRIVIUM Specification

Trivium consists of a non-linear feedback shift register (NLFSR) coupled with a linear filter function. The NLFSR operates on a 288-bit state. Let $x_i^t \in F_2$ denote the value of the variable xi at clock time t. The 288 bit register is divided into three registers. The keystream is produced by taking a linear combination of the state using linear function. At each clock the cipher updates three bits of the state and outputs one bit of keystream, denoted by $z_i^{(t)}$. The cipher continues to run until the required numbers of keystream bits are produced. The full algorithm for the keystream generation is given in [8]. The ANF equations follow directly from this description where each clock introduces three new variables and four new equations (three from the NLFSR and one from the linear function). Trivium incorporates 80 bit Key and IV setup stage, where the cipher is clocked 4×288 times to initialize the state. Our analysis does not depend on the initialization process and will not be discussed further. Here it deals only from the keygeneration phase.

The register is divided in three registers of length 93, 84 and 111 bits:

$$s_1 \cdots s_{288} = s_1 \cdots s_{93} \mid s_{94} \cdots s_{177} \mid s_{178} \cdots s_{288} \tag{1}$$

A pictorial representation of the keystream generation process of TRIVIUM and BIVIUM can be found in Figure 5.1 and also the specification of which is given in Table 1 [3].

2.1 Variants of Trivium: BIVIUM A and B

BIVIUM-A and BIVIUM-B are two reduced variants of Trivium. This truncated version has only one register and a total state size of 177 bits. It is divided in two blocks of 93 and 84 bits. At each clock it updates two bits of the state and outputs one bit of keystream. Each clock of these ciphers introduces two new variables and three new equations. Size of each block is given in the following table Table 1.

Table 1. Bivium and Trivium Specification

Description	Specification A:B:C	Size
TRIVIUM	93:84:111	288
BIVIUM	93:84: --	177

The following figure (Fig. 1) shows the working of Bivium and Trivium class of stream cipher. Bivium contains only A and B divisions (only 177 registers) where as Trivium contains all the three (288 registers).

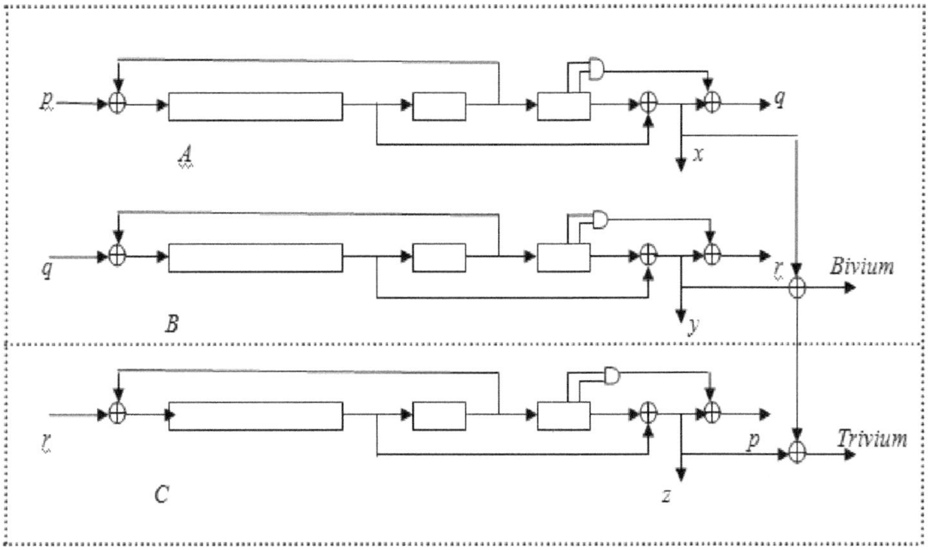

Fig. 1. Bivium and Trivium Class of Stream Ciphers

3 Algebraic Attack against Trivium

It is possible to attack Trivium and its variant Bivium in two ways. The first one is a state recovering attack: they try to guess the value of some state bit or the value of the product of some state bits. In suitable case, they reduce the system to a system of linear equations, which can be solved, using for example the Gaussian elimination. The other technique is a distinguishing attack: this technique allows to collect statistics on keystream and to build a distinguisher. Here more attention has been given to state recovery attack.

The obvious cryptanalytic approaches (to recover the state) involve creating a set of equations and then trying to solve them. Mainly two approaches are in use.

- Consider a single 288-bit state register at some point during the generation of keystream. Let these 288 bits be the unknown variables. Express known keystream bits as equations in these unknown variables, simplify and solve.
- Start with an initial set of 288 variables as above. But each time when clocked the register, add three new variables x, y and z (so the number of variables grows). Derive equations in terms of newly generated variables.

With the first approach, the number of variables is smaller but the individual equations become more complex. With the second approach, the number of variables is larger but the equations are simpler (sparse and of degree ≤ 2).

In the first approach, do not add any new variable to obtain a system which uses only 288 unknowns. At the clock i we get one equation, which expresses the bit z_i of the keystream as a non-linear function of the initial state variables $s_1, \ldots, s_{288}$. Obviously the degree of equations increases after 66 clocking. In fact, for example, in case of Trivium for the first 66 clocks the equations are linear, then for $67 \leq i \leq 148$ they have degree two and for $149 \leq i \leq 214$ the degree becomes three and so on.

In the second approach, it introduces three new variables to the next state, which can be expressed as non-linear combination of some of the bits from the initial state. This procedure is repeated as many number of keystream required. At each clocking of the generator, it adds three new variables and four equations. Among this four, three sparse degree-2 equations (no single equation consist of too many variables) for generator update and one linear for the new output keystream bit. After k clocks of the generator this gives 3k degree-2 equations and k linear equations in 288+3k unknowns. In which 66 linear equations are obtained without introducing any more unknowns, only by looking at the next 66 keystream bits. So totally 3k degree-2 equations and 66+k linear equations in 288+3k unknowns.

For the Trivium cipher a single register of 288 bits is used. Since the output function and all the three update functions are linear for Trivium, decomposition or linearization is performed very easily. It is enough to decompose 1st, 94th and 178th components given in the follows. The best linear approximations for these are achieved by eliminating the sparse degree-2 equations with probability 3/4 [4].

$$\begin{aligned} s_1 &= s_{243} + s_{288} + s_{286}.s_{287} + s_{69} \\ s_{94} &= s_{66} + s_{93} + s_{91}.s_{92} + s_{171} \\ s_{178} &= s_{162} + s_{177} + s_{176}.s_{175} + s_{264} \end{aligned} \tag{2}$$

The best linear approximations can be finding by decreasing the number of degree-2 equations in the sparse system. This can be achieved via guessing suitable variables. The approach that were used to guess the suitable variables consist of:

- Guessing variables occurring with the highest frequency
- Reduces the non-linearity of the system by guessing the variables occurring in the nonlinear equation.
- Select alternate variables – in Trivium all quadratic monomials are the products of two adjacent bits

It is clear from the Trivium analysis that, guessing suitable variables will results in the reduction of degree of equations. Different strategies were used to guess state bits. In fact, TRIVIUM contains nonlinear equations, products of some register values ie. $s_{91}\ s_{92}$, $s_{175}\ s_{176}$ and $s_{286}\ s_{287}$. This choice seems to work better if the attacker guesses alternate variables. Similarly, the attacker guesses consecutive variables between s_{91} and s_{287}, which come out more often than the other variables in term of degree greater than 1, in sparse system of equations. So these guessing make algebraic attack more feasible on Trivium and its variants.

By introducing a minor variation in the tapping positions in Trivium, tries to make guessing variable as rigid as possible. Hence the attacker is not able to reduce as many quadratic monomials as when it uses the original design. Alternate and consecutive guessing has less effect on the new system.

4 Proposal for the Selection of State Bits

In this section, propose a new method for keystream generation which is very similar to the original. The only difference is related to the selection of state bits to update the system; tapping positions are different from the original. Here rather taking consecutive bits we used Full Positive Difference Set (FPDS). It is already proven that FPDS are more resistant to correlation attacks [6]. As a result even if the attacker guesses suitable variables it will not end up with a desirable reduction in the degree-2 equations. Estimating values for FPDS variables are much trickier than estimating consecutive variables.

Like Trivium, this is also done by ensuring that any state bit is not used for at least 66 iterations after it has been modified. First 66 states of the three block of registers (A:B:C of fig.1) remain unused for next 66 iteration after it has been modified to provide parallelism. The key initialization and key generation process is given bellow.

Key Initialization Process
This process also uses key, K=80 and IV=80 bit length

$$s_1, s_2 \cdots s_{93} \leftarrow (K_1 \cdots K_{80}, 0, \cdots, 0)$$

$$s_{94}, s_{95} \cdots s_{177} \leftarrow (IV_1 \cdots IV_{80}, 0, \cdots, 0)$$

$$s_{178}, s_{179} \cdots s_{288} \leftarrow (0, \cdots, 0, 1, 1, 1)$$

for i=1 to 4. 288 do

$$t_1 = s_{66} + s_{91} + s_{70}.s_{84} + s_{169}$$

$$t_2 = s_{160} + s_{177} + s_{163}.s_{176} + s_{270}$$

$$t_3 = s_{243} + s_{281} + s_{257}.s_{277} + s_{79}$$

$$s_1, s_2 \cdots s_{93} \leftarrow (t_3, s_1, s_2 \cdots s_{92})$$

$$s_{94}, s_{95} \cdots s_{177} \leftarrow (t_1, s_{94}, s_{95} \cdots s_{176})$$

$$s_{178}, s_{179} \cdots s_{288} \leftarrow (t_2, s_{178}, s_{179} \cdots s_{287})$$

End for

Keygeneration Process

The proposed design contains a 288-bit internal state denoted by ($s_1 \ldots s_{288}$). The keystream generation consists of an iterative process which extracts the values of 15 specific state bits and uses them both to update 3 bits of the state and to compute 1 bit of keystream z_i.

$$t_1 = s_{66} + s_{91}$$
$$t_2 = s_{160} + s_{177}$$
$$t_3 = s_{243} + s_{281}$$
$$z_1 = t_1 + t_2 + t_3$$

$$t_1 = s_{66} + s_{91} + s_{70}.s_{84} + s_{169}$$
$$t_2 = s_{160} + s_{177} + s_{163}.s_{176} + s_{270}$$
$$t_3 = s_{243} + s_{281} + s_{257}.s_{277} + s_{79}$$

$$s_1, s_2 \cdots s_{93} \leftarrow (t_3, s_1, s_2 \cdots s_{92})$$
$$s_{94}, s_{95} \cdots s_{177} \leftarrow (t_1, s_{94}, s_{95} \cdots s_{176})$$
$$s_{178}, s_{179} \cdots s_{288} \leftarrow (t_2, s_{178}, s_{179} \cdots s_{287})$$

Once the design process has been finished, keystream will be generated. The randonmness of keystream is tested using NIST test suite. The NIST (National Institute of Standards and Technology) Test Suite is a statistical testing package consisting of 16 tests that were developed to test the randomness of (arbitrarily long) binary sequences produced by either hardware or software based cryptographic random or pseudorandom number generators. These tests focus on a variety of different types of non-randomness that could exist in a sequence. The results and observations are shown bellow.

5 Result and Observations

Trivium and the modified Trivium properties had been checked. The later system uses nonconsecutive variables to update the system. So it is infeasible to evaluate the unknown variables. And it also uses lesser variables than the original Trivium for the linear equations (66 equations). So it requires more number of equations than the original to find the 288 unknown values. This implies additional number of nonlinear equations has to be considered for the attack. Since the initial state bits are not continuous guessing one value from the other is not easy. The properties had been tested in NIST test suite. Original Trivium and the modified Trivium show approximately same characteristics. The results of NIST test is given in the table 2. For a cipher to be secure it has to satisfy all the 16 tests of NIST based on the p-values. Here modified Trivium also satisfies all the 16 tests.

Table 3 shows a comparative study of the original and modified Trivium. Analysis has been done on the basis of number of equations, NIST test and the guess and determines attack.

Table 2. Observations from the NIST Test

Statistical Tests	p-value	
	Modified Trivium	Trivium
Frequency	0.40990767	0.41168017
Block Frequency (m = 100000)	0.315025167	0.360247333
Cumulative Sum - Forward	0.3945735	0.458758833
Cumulative Sum - Backward	0.444528333	0.376714167
Runs	0.4150103	0.5832368
Long Runs of Ones (M = 10000)	0.383624	0.46369033
Rank	0.55134783	0.55454483
Spectral DFT	0.395437	0.652191
Non-periodic Templates (m = 9, B = 000000001)	0.555050167	0.562700833
Overlapping Template (m = 9)	0.582771	0.425887167
Universal (L = 9, Q = 5120)	0.399206	0.598426833
Approximate Entropy (m = 10)	0.39852783	0.45380233
Random Excursions (x = +1)	0.4842565	0.408874
Random Excursions Variant (x = -1)	0.632287	0.55614675
Linear Complexity (M = 500)	0.5694885	0.577206
Serial (m = 16)	0.505686667	0.359164333
	0.5224915	0.394415167
Lempel Ziv Complexity	0.48805367	0.605006

Performance analysis table gives a clear idea about the behavior of the modified Trivium. The next sessions gives conclusion to this work.

Table 3. Performance Analysis

Name	Modified Trivium	Trivium
Number of equations	More	Less
NIST test	Success	Success
Guess and Determine	Difficult	Medium

6 Conclusion

This paper demonstrates algebraic attack and algebraic equations on the stream cipher TRIVIUM. It is noted that even though the nonlinear structure is present TRIVIUM cipher is vulnerable to attack due to some structural limitations. The modified version of TRIVIUM is capable of resisting such sort of attack in an increased level. It also contains a new tapping strategy to prevent algebraic attack by guessing variables to decrease degree of equations.

In the future work, as a substitute to Groebner basis analysis of algebraic equations using fastest and efficient algorithms like F4/F5, XL, XSL are highly recommended. And other various techniques can be tried in order to solve the system, thus break the system. As an extension of linear cryptanalysis, in the use of multiple linear approximations different approximations for the same output bits can be found and combined to make better approximations.

References

1. Lee, D.H.: Algebraic Attacks on Stream Ciphers (Survey). Mathematics Information Center for Mathematical Sciences 8, 133–143 (2005)
2. Czapor, S.R., Geddes, K.O.: On Implementing Buchbergers Algorithm for Groebner Basis. In: ACM Symposium on Symbolic and Algebraic Computation, pp. 233–238 (2000)
3. Maximove, A., Briyukov, A.: Two Trivial attacks on Trivium. In: Proceedings of the 14th International Conference on Selected Areas in Cryptography, Ottawa, Canada, pp. 36–55 (2007)
4. Raddum, H.: Cryptanalytic Results on Trivium. LNCS, vol. 4876, pp. 36–55. Springer, Heidelberg (2007)
5. The home page for eSTREAM, the ECRYPT Stream Cipher Project, `http://www.ecrypt.eu.org/stream/`
6. Courtois, N., Meier, W.: Algebraic attacks on stream ciphers with linear feedback. In: Biham, E. (ed.) EUROCRYPT 2003. LNCS, vol. 2656, pp. 345–359. Springer, Heidelberg (2003)
7. Canniere, C.D., Preneel, B.: TRIVIUM Specifications. In: ECRYPT Stream Cipher Project Report (2005)

Design of Secure Chaotic Hash Function Based on Logistic and Tent Maps

P. Jhansi Rani, M. Sambasiva Rao, and S. Durga Bhavani

Department of Computer & Information Sciences,
University of Hyderabad, Hyderabad, India

Abstract. The main contribution of the paper is two-fold: Building step by step a chaotic hash function starting from a weak but basic algorithm and analyzing its strengths and weaknesses in order to make it stronger. We start with a basic chaotic hash function with a 128-bit message digest based on Baptista's encryption algorithm. In the next steps, a pseudo-random number generator using chaotic tent map is incorporated within the hash algorithm and perturbation and block chaining approaches are used to strengthen the hash function. In the literature on chaotic cryptography we have not seen preimage and second-preimage resistance analyis being done which we carry out and show that the proposed hash function is strong against both these attacks. Further, the standard collision analysis is performed in the space of 1-bit neighbourhood of a given message. The hash function is shown to exhibit diffusion effect with average hamming distance between message digests obtained as 63 bits which is close to the ideal of 50%. The collision performance compares favourably with that of chaotic hash functions proposed in the recent literature. It is to be emphasized that the existing chaotic hash functions in the literature use a multitude of chaotic maps whereas we show in this paper that using two chaotic maps judiciously achieves a secure hash function.

1 Introduction

A secure hash function is a function that takes a variable-length input string and converts it to a fixed-length (smaller) output string called hash value or message digest. $h : (0,1)^\star \rightarrow (0,1)^n$ is such that h satisfies the three security properties: **collision resistance**, **preimage** and **second preimage resistance** [1].

Recent investigations reveal that several well-known methods such as MD5, SHA1 and RIPEMD too are not immune to collisions [2,3]. Chaotic maps provide another potential avenue to look for secure encryptions [4,5,6]. The crucial property of sensitivity to initial conditions for a chaotic function proves to be very useful in this context [7]. A function f is said to be sensitive at a point x, if the trajectories of the dynamical system defined by f change drastically for points y that are initially very close to x. Hence sensitivity seems to be a tailor-made feature that satisfies the collision resistance requirement while constructing a hash function.

During the last three decades chaotic dynamics played a major role in the field of nonlinear sciences. The important characteristics like the randomness of

D.C. Wyld et al. (Eds.): CNSA 2011, CCIS 196, pp. 43–52, 2011.

dynamical behaviour, sensitivity to initial conditions and possession of positive Lyapunov exponents, that the chaotic maps possess make these prime candidates for many cryptographic applications.

2 Background

The seminal paper of Baptista [8] on chaotic cryptography inspires us to propose a one-way hash function based on chaotic maps. A thorough analysis of Baptista's scheme was carried out by Alvarez et al [9] and they show that Baptista's algorithm is vulnerable to all the four of cipher text only, known plain text, chosen plain text and chosen cipher text attacks. On the other hand, it was shown in the literature that Baptista's scheme has a lot of potential and could be modified to build a hash function. K.W.Wong modified Baptista's algorithm by adopting a dynamic look-up table to avoid collisions and preimage attack [11] and then came up with a hashing scheme in 2003 [12]. X.Yi [13] in 2005 proposed a hash function based on chaotic tent maps which is claimed to be better than Wong's scheme in its computational complexity. More recently H.Yang et al [14] have published another hash function based on a chaotic map network and Q.Yang et al [15] have published a hash function based on cell neural network.

These approaches use a multitude of chaotic maps [16,17,18,19] and we show in this paper that using two chaotic maps judiciously achieves a secure hash function. The novelty in this paper is that we propose the method in a systematic fashion. We consider a basic chaotic hash algorithm based on Baptista's encryption scheme and start strengthening it conducting analysis for security along the way. The hash function is proposed taking advantage of the strengths of Baptista's scheme and it is shown by computational analysis that the performance of the hash function is on par with recent chaotic hash function proposed in the literature without requiring a network of chaotic maps as in [14] thus improving the time complexity of the algorithm.

3 Basic Algorithm (Hash Function Based on Baptista's Scheme)

Baptista divides the input domain into ϵ-intervals I_a where I_a is associated with the character a. The encryption algorithm maps each character a of the message to the number of iterations n that the logistic map takes to reach I_a. We modify Baptista's encryption algorithm to build a hashing function which we call the basic algorithm in the paper. Experiments showed that the basic algorithm is not secure against collisions. Two variations of the basic algorithm are proposed to strengthen the security of the hash function.

The block diagram of the above algorithm is depicted in the Figure 1. Note that in the algorithm, hash value h_i that emerges for each block B_i is n_k where

$$f^{n_{k-1}}(\cdots f^{n_2}(f^{n_1}(f^{n_0}(x_0)))) \in I_{k-1}$$

n_{k-1} is the integer number of iterations that corresponds to the $(k-1)$-th byte. We show that this scheme is not secure from preimage resistance point of view.

Algorithm 1. Basic Algorithm

Divide the input bit sequence into 8 blocks, $B_0, B_1, \ldots, B_7$ each block having k bytes, $k \in N$.
Choose a secret value $0 < x_0 < 1$, $\lambda \in (3.8, 4.0)$ the control parameter of the logistic equation $f_\lambda(x) = \lambda x(1-x)$ and I_m intervals associated to character m. Let $x(0) = x_0$.
for $B_i = 0$ to 7 **do**
  for byte $m = 0$ to $k-1$ of the message of block B_i **do**
    Iterate the logistic map until $f^{n_m}(x(m)) \in I_m$.
    Re-Set $x(m+1) = f^{n_m}(x(m))$
  end for
  Define for the block B_i, $h_i = n$.
  Thus the block gets encrypted by 16 bits.
end for
The final hash value of the plain text P is obtained by concatenating h_i's

$$h(P) = (h_0 h_1 h_2 h_3 h_4 h_5 h_6 h_7)$$

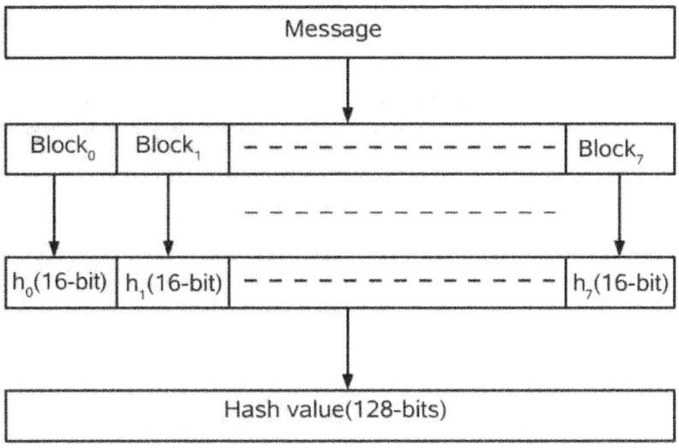

Fig. 1. Block diagram of hash function

3.1 Preimage and Second Preimage Resistance

Proposition: Given a hash value y for the proposed hash function in basic algorithm, one can produce an input (preimage) x such that $h(x) = y$.

Proof: Given $y = n$ say, find a character a such that $f^n(x_0) \in I_a$. So trivially a one character preimage exists for the given y. Assume that the minimum length of the message is greater than 1. First note that

$$f^{n_{k-1}}(\cdots f^{n_2}(f^{n_1}(f^{n_0}(x_0)))) = f^{n_0+n_1+\ldots n_{k-1}}(x_0).$$

Choose any sequence of integers that ends in n, such as $n_0 n_1 \ldots n_{k-1} n$. We can construct the preimage of y as follows: Find character p_0 where $f^{n_0}(x_0) \in I_{p_0}$. Now reset x_0 as $f^{n_0}(x_0)$. Then find p_1 such that $f^{n_0+n_1}(x_0) \in I_{p_1}$ and so on. Finally we get p_{k-1} such that

$$f^{n_0+n_1+\ldots n_{k-1}}(x_0) \in I_{n_{k-1}}.$$

Then the required preimage for $y = n$ is $p_0 p_1 \ldots p_{k-1}$.

Following the above scheme, second preimages can be found. Since a collision resistant hash function is second preimage resistant, the hash function will be automatically prone to collisions.[20]

This algorithm is quite weak and we strengthen it in a step by step fashion increasing the security of the algorithm along the way. In Scheme A proposed below, perturbation of initial value along with block-chaining method is adopted to strengthen the hash function. A pseudo-random number generator using chaotic tent map is incorporated within the hash algorithm to strengthen it further in Scheme B.

4 Stronger Algorithms for Chaotic Cryptographic Hash Functions

4.1 Scheme A

- *Perturb*$_{IC}$: In this section we rectify the vulnerability of the hash function using two schemes *Perturb*$_{IC}$ and *Vote*$_{PRNG}$. *Perturb*$_{IC}$ requires perturbing x_0 using character of the message at each step. This scheme is clearly depicted in Figure 2. In this case for a given n to find a one character preimage a such that $f^n(x_0 + 0.a) \in I_a$ is infeasible, as this equation may not be satisfied in most cases. Longer messages only lead to more infeasible requirements. The initial condition x_0 is perturbed when it gets reset for every byte in the inner loop of the Basic algorithm. This scheme is clearly depicted in Figure 2 with the following notation. Let $byte_i = a_i$ then $A_i = ASCII(a_i)$ and $I_i = I_{a_i}$.

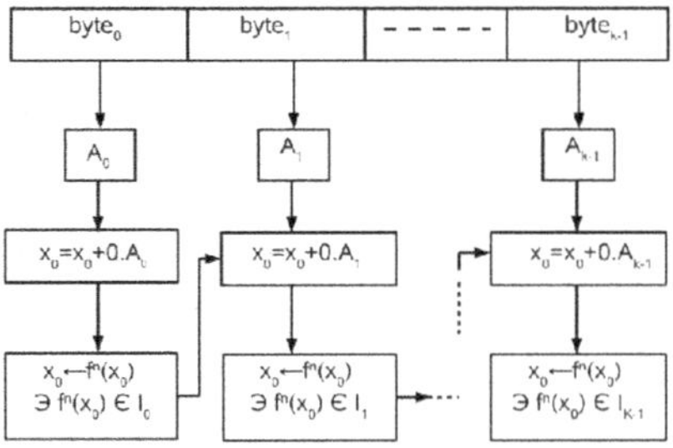

Fig. 2. Perturbing x_0 and evolving a compression function

4.2 Scheme B

- $Vote_{PRNG}$: It was also found in the experiments the small integers that get generated as hash values in the Basic algorithm 1 lead to collisions. We propose to take a vote by a pseudo-random number generator (PRNG) to decide if n that emerges at the end of the inner loop is to be chosen as h_n or iterate f further to pick the next possible n. Thus larger integers get produced for h_n. Fix an $\eta > 0$ check if the random number t generated using pseudo-random number generator (PRNG) is such that $t < \eta$. If yes, accept n else repeat the iteration step of the algorithm to find the next bigger n. Scheme B is depicted in the Figure 3.

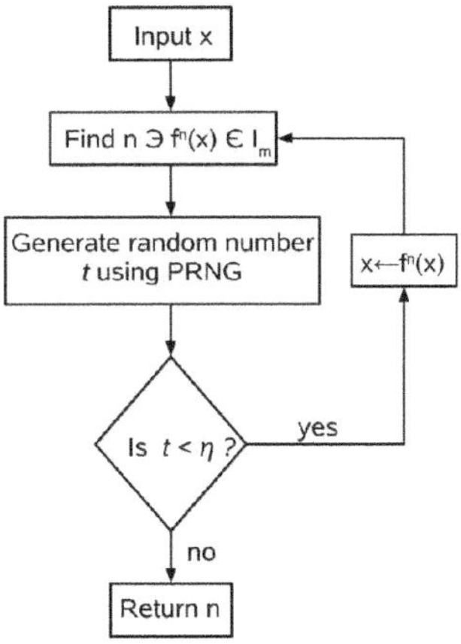

Fig. 3. Scheme to find large n

Plugging in Schemes A and B in the basic algorithm gives what we call the **strong algorithm** which uses PRNG provided in the ANSI 'C' library. We propose that the performance can be further improved by using a chaotic PRNG in the $Vote_{PRNG}$ scheme which is utilized in the final *strong chaotic hash function using* $PRNG_{Tent}$ proposed in the next section.

5 Strong Chaotic Hash Function Using $PRNG_{Tent}$

We strengthen the Scheme B further, by taking a PRNG based on the one-dimensional chaotic tent map $PRNG_{Tent}$.

Tent Map

$$f(x) = \begin{cases} 2x & \text{if } 0 \le x < \frac{1}{2} \\ -2x + 2 & \text{if } \frac{1}{2} < x \le 1 \end{cases}$$

The tent map is iterated and the PRNG algorithm outputs the iteration number at which the value falls within a prefixed ϵ-interval. Since the tent map is almost a linear map, the computations are inexpensive as compared to other non-linear chaotic maps. Good results are obtained when the PRNG is tested for randomness using NIST(National institute of standards and technology) test suite. The strong secure hash function that incorporates Schemes A and B is proposed below.

Algorithm 2. Strong Chaotic Algorithm using $PRNG_{Tent}$

Divide the input bit sequence into 8 blocks $B_0, B_1, \ldots, B_7$ and each block is an integer number of bytes
Choose a secret value x_0, λ the control parameter of the logistic equation and set a threshold $0 < \eta < 1$
for Block $B_i = 0$ to 7 **do**
  $x'(0) = x_0$.
  for Byte $m = 0$ to $k - 1$ of the message of a block B_i **do**
    $A(m) =$ ASCII value (m), $a(m) = 0.A(m)$
    Perturb x': $x'(m) = (a(m) + x'(m))$ mod 1
    $n = Vote_{PRNG}(x'(m)$
    $x'(m+1) \leftarrow f^{n_m}(x'(m))$
  end for
  Define for the block B_i, $h_i = n_{k-1}$. Thus a block gets encrypted by 16 bits.
end for
The final hash value of the plain text P is obtained by concatenating h_i's i.e

$$h(P) = (h_0 h_1 h_2 h_3 h_4 h_5 h_6 h_7)$$

6 Results and Analysis of Secure Hash Function

It is argued earlier that the proposed hash function satisfies preimage and second preimage resistance properties. In this section the function is empirically tested for collision resistance following similar work proposed in the literature.

6.1 Collision Resistance

A hash function is said to be resistant to collisions if it is computationally infeasible to find two inputs $x,\ x', x \neq x'$ that will get hashed to the same output i.e., $h(x) = h(x')$. Collision analysis can be done in two ways.

6.2 Looking for a Collision in the Whole Space i.e for a Large Number of Different Randomly Generated Messages

N input messages say $P_1, P_2, P_3, \cdots P_N$ of length 800 bits are chosen randomly to test for collisions. Hash values are computed for $P_i, i = 1, \ldots, 13000$ here and it is observed that no two hash values coincide and completely different hash values are obtained for all the 13,000 input messages. Hence the strong chaotic algorithm is found to have zero collisions in this experiment. Of course this experiment has to be done for $2^{128/2}$ messages to really show that the hash function is not prone to birthday attack. The hash values obtained for a sample of five input messages is shown in the Table 1.

Table 1. MD generated for the input messages $P_1, P_2, P_3, \cdots P_5$

Input	Message Digest
P1	84F30572BCB9F7F6D9FD5B5FDB1990AD
P2	DBEE2C5D040506F20A5F09D4760D15C5
P3	2EAE98A9266D3A9D8B9C25A303BF2F0F
P4	3E922FE86567624E687C543112B86754
P5	B5E870D72A544A01D0EB8A83D3C99CBC

6.3 Looking for Collision in 1-Bit Neighborhood of Message

If a plain text is changed randomly in one bit and this experiment is carried out for a large number of times, say N, the difference in the hash value then obtained could be quantified by looking at the minimum hamming distance and maximum hamming distance. The ideal diffusion effect should be that any minor change in the plain text leads to a 50% changing probability in the bit sequence of the Message digest.

In order to measure the collision resistance, four measures are proposed [14]. Let P be the input message and P' denotes the message in which ith bit is toggled. Then $d_H(h(P), h(P'))$ denotes the number of bits changed in output with a 1 bit change in the input. The minimum hamming distance,

$$d_{min} = \min_{1 \leq i \leq N} d_H(h(P), h(P'))$$

and maximum hamming distance ,

$$d_{max} = \max_{1 \leq i \leq N} d_H(h(P), h(P'))$$

are computed. Further, the average d_{avg} and the standard deviation d_{std} of the distribution of Hamming distances over N trials are computed to get a better idea of the distribution. We tabulate the performance of the hash function in terms of these four Hamming measures.

Data Set. Input message of size 720KB is taken for generating hash value say MD which is a 128 bit stream. A bit i is randomly chosen and toggled in the message. Let the hash value of the perturbed input be MD_i. The performance of the hash functions basic one and the strong ones are all evaluated in terms of the four Hamming measures defined above.

Results. The experiments are carried out for $N = 2000$ toggled messages for Basic Algorithm1 and Strong algorithm (which does not use $PRNG_Tent$ but the standard PRNG) . It can be clearly seen from Table 1 that the inclusion of $Perturb_{IC}$ and PRNG to choose bigger n makes a significant difference in the diffusion effect in the message digest. The messages obtained by changing one bit in the original message exhibit hash values that have, on average, nearly 47% of the bits different from the original Message Digest. Further note that in

Table 2. Hamming distance measures to evaluate collision resistance for basic and strong algorithms

N	256		512		1024		2000	
	basic	strong	basic	strong	basic	strong	basic	strong
d_{min}	16	46	16	44	16	44	16	44
d_{max}	42	70	44	77	46	77	49	77
d_{avg}	31.54	59.79	31.38	59.33	31.23	59.15	31.32	59.28
d_{std}	2.46	4.30	2.45	4.45	2.43	4.52	2.44	4.52

each experiment, the average number of bits changed in the MD gets doubled for the strong algorithm. All the values of $d_{min}, d_{max}, d_{avg}$ and d_{std} for the strong algorithm are much greater than that of the basic algorithm.

These results are improved considerably by using the chaotic tent map to generate pseudo-random numbers in the Scheme B of $Vote_{PRNG}$ for strong chaotic hash function. The Figure 4 shows that the proposed strong chaotic algorithm which uses $PRNG_{T}ent$ exhibits desirable security with the number of changed bits due to a 1-bit toggle in plain text being 63 which is very close to the ideal value of 50% probability. Inorder to compare the performance with that obtained by Yang, the same experiment is carried out for $N = 10,000$ number of toggled messages. In order to validate the proposed strong *chaotic* algorithm (Algorithm 2) and also compare with Yang's results which are noted in the last column of the table. These results are projected in Table 3. Further all the results achieved are comparable to those of the recent work of Yang et al as shown in the Table 3.

Table 3. Collision resistance analysis for strong chaotic algorithm using $PRNG_{T}ent$

N	256	512	1024	2048	4096	8192	10000
d_{min}	49	47	44	44	44	43	43
d_{max}	75	76	80	80	83	84	84
d_{avg}	63.05	63.03	63.10	63.03	63.21	63.06	63.03
d_{std}	4.92	4.92	4.93	4.92	4.94	4.93	4.92

The space in which the tests are conducted is large enough to indicate that the values obtained by d_{avg} etc lie close to the true values of the distribution.

It is important to note that the proposed strong chaotic algorithm makes use of only iteration of two maps, the logistic map and the chaotic tent map and acheives 63-bit diffusion where as the scheme proposed by Yang et al. which uses a 16 chaotic map network which is only improved by 1.03 bit confussion and significantly increases the chaotic complexity.

The Table 4 shows the comparision of existing algorithm in the literature.

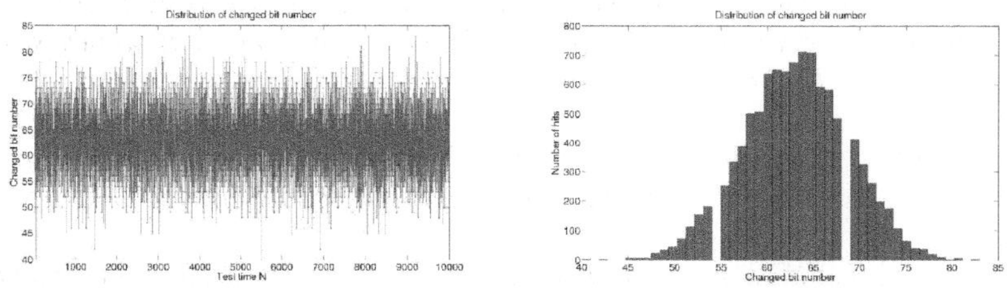

Fig. 4. Distribution of number of changed bits captured by the hamming distance of MD from MD_i for N=10,000 for strong chaotic algorithm

Table 4. Comparision with the existing algorithms in the literature

Scheme	d_{avg}	Number of functions used
Proposed	63.03	2
Yang [14]	64.06	16

7 Conclusions

A new one-way chaotic hash function is developed based on Baptista's encryption algorithm that gives an output of 128 bit message digest. The algorithm can be adapted to evolve 256 or 512 bit length message digest.

The secure hash functions that follow Merkel-Damgard construction schemes generally have a multitude of functions networked together to make the compression function secure. In general, there are no logical arguments provided for the proposed design. In this paper, starting with a nice encryption scheme that is proposed by Baptista which is used to design a hash function, it is argued logically why certain plug-ins are required and how these schemes help in making the function secure. It is not possible to prove collision resistance theoretically, hence following similar work in literature we present computational results to show that the proposed chaotic hash function exhibits 50% mixing of bits in the output of message digest on a one-bit change in the input message and hence is collision resistant. The function is further analyzed and shown to possess preimage and second preimage resistance.

It is shown that the performance of the hash function is comparable with some of the latest algorithms proposed in the literature.

References

1. Stinson, D.R.: Cryptography: Theory and Practice. CRC Press, Boca Raton (1995)
2. Wang, X., Yu, H.: How to break MD5 and other hash functions. In: Cramer, R. (ed.) EUROCRYPT 2005. LNCS, vol. 3494, pp. 19–35. Springer, Heidelberg (2005)

3. Wang, X., Yin, Y.L., Yu, H.: Finding collisions in the full SHA-1. In: Shoup, V. (ed.) CRYPTO 2005. LNCS, vol. 3621, pp. 17–36. Springer, Heidelberg (2005)
4. Jakimoski, G., Kocarev, L.: Chaos and cryptography: Block encryption ciphers based on chaotic maps. IEEE Trans. on Circuits and Systems I: Fundamental Theory and Applications 48(2), 163–169 (2001)
5. Jakimoski, G., Kocarev, L.: Analysis of some recently proposed chaos-based encryption algorithms. Phys. Lett. A 291, 381–384 (2001)
6. Kocarev, L.: Chaos-based cryptography: a brief overview. IEEE Circuits and Systems Magazine 1(3), 6–21 (2001)
7. Devaney, R.L.: An introduction to chaotic dynamical systems. Addison-Wesley, Reading (1989)
8. Baptista, M.S.: Chaos in cryptography. Phys. Lett. A 240, 50–54 (1998)
9. Alvarez, G., Montoya, F., Romera, M., Pastor, G.: Cryptanalysis of an ergodic chaotic cipher. Physics Letters A 311, 172–179 (2003)
10. Wong, W., Lee, L., Wong, K.: A modified chaotic cryptographic method. Comput. Phys. Commun. 138, 234–236 (2001)
11. Wong, K.W.: Modified Baptista type chaotic cryptosystem. Phys. Lett. A 298, 238–242 (2002)
12. Wong, K.: A combined chaotic cryptographic and hashing scheme. Phys. Lett. A 307, 292–298 (2003)
13. Yi, X.: Hash function based on chaotic tent maps. IEEE Transactions on Circuits and Systems-II: Express Briefs 52(6), 354–357 (2005)
14. Yang, H., Wong, K.W., Liao, X., Wang, Y., Yang, D.: One-way hash function construction based on chaotic map network. Chaos, Solitons & Fractals 41(5), 2566–2574 (2009)
15. Yang, Q., Gao, T., Fan, L., Gu, Q.: Analysis of one-way alterable length hash function based on cell neural network. Journal of Information Assurance and Security 5, 196–200 (2010)
16. Wang, Y., Liao, X., Xiao, D., Wong, K.: One-way hash function construction based on 2D coupled map lattices. Inform. Sci., 1391–1406 (2008)
17. Wong, K.W.: A fast chaotic cryptographic scheme with dynamic look-up table. Phys. Lett. A 298, 238–242 (2002)
18. Xiao, D., Liao, X., Deng, S.: One-way hash function construction based on the chaotic map with changeable-parameter. Chaos, Solitons & Fractals 24, 65–71 (2005)
19. Zhang, J., Wang, X., Zhang, W.: Chaotic keyed hash function based on feedforward-feedback nonlinear digital filter. Phys. Lett. A, 439–448 (2007)
20. Delfs, H., Knebl, H.: Introdution of Cryptography. Springer, Heidelberg (2002)
21. Wang, S., Hu, G.: Hash function based on chaotic map lattices. CHAOS 17, 0231191–0231198 (2007)

Detecting Anomalous Application Behaviors Using a System Call Clustering Method over Critical Resources

Grandhi Jyostna, Pareek Himanshu, and P.R.L. Eswari

Centre for Development of Advanced Computing,
Hyderabad, India
{gjyostna,himanshup,prleswari}@cdac.in
http://www.cdachyd.in

Abstract. Malware attacks which focus on exploiting an application to launch the payload have become major security threat. We present the methodology and algorithm which is able to detect anomaly in application behavior and prevent such type of attacks. Our approach is to represent the normal behavior of an application, detect deviations from this normal behavior and prevent them. We represent normal behavior using system calls made over critical resources by clustering of these system calls and then monitor the behavior of applications for any deviations from the normal behavior, by means of an enforcement algorithm. Any mismatch from the normal behavior indicates an anomaly. We provide a description of our approach. We have implemented and tested the proposed approach and the results are encouraging. As compared to previous research in this direction, we implement on Windows OS instead of Linux OS and use minifilter and registry callback techniques instead of raw system call interception which is prohibited in latest operating system versions.

Keywords: Behavior Analysis, Anomaly Detection, Behavior Model.

1 Introduction

In this paper we describe a method for capturing the normal behavior of a software application based on system calls. Our aim is to first model the normal behavior of an application, and later be able to detect the deviations from the normal behavior as malicious behavior. Our approach is as follows: When an application executes, it makes resource requests to the Operating System. The kind of request made (read, write, modify, delete, etc) is very important based on the resource for which the request is made. Therefore, during modeling of the normal behavior of an application, we monitor all the system calls made over the resources. We categorize our approach as a resource specific approach based on system calls. The rest of the paper is organized as follows. In section 2, we discuss the problem statement. Section 3 describes the related work in application based anomaly detection. In section 4 system call based anomaly detection is discussed.

D.C. Wyld et al. (Eds.): CNSA 2011, CCIS 196, pp. 53–64, 2011.

In section 5 we describe the approach for the resource specific model generation and enforcement. The advantages and limitations of our approach are discussed in section 6. In Section 7 we present the implementation details. In section 8 the experimental results are given.

2 Background

There are two types of detection systems, signature based detection and anomaly based detection[1]. Signature based detection systems look for well-defined patterns of known attacks or vulnerabilities. The limitation of signature based detection is that it cannot detect previously unseen attacks[1]. As a result, the computer systems protected solely by signature based detection systems face the risk of being compromised without detecting the attacks. Moreover, signature based detection requires explicit representation of attacks and hence the nature of the attacks should be well understood. This implies that human experts must work on the analysis and representation of attacks, which is usually time consuming and error prone. These limitations are overcome by anomaly detection systems. In anomaly detection, it is assumed that the nature of the intrusion is unknown, but that the intrusion will result in behavior different from that normally seen in the system. Our proposal is based on anomaly detection.

3 Related Work

The use of system call sequences to model program behaviors was first suggested by Forrest et al.[2], [3], [4]. Forrest et al demonstrated that effective intrusion detection techniques can be developed by learning normal program behaviors, and detecting deviations from this normal behavior. In contrast with users, programs tend to have more narrowly defined behaviors. This enables more accurate learning of normal behaviors, and thus improves the accuracy of intrusion detection. Forrest et al's approach characterizes normal program behaviors in terms of sequences of system calls made by them. Anomalous program behavior produces system call sequences that have not been observed under normal operation. Another approach by Mazeroff[5] describes the use of probabilistic models modeling the sequence of system calls made during the execution of a software application. Sequences of predetermined system calls are intercepted using which a probabilistic suffix tree (PST) that represents the probability of each system call given a finite-length sequence of previously observed system calls is constructed. The model can subsequently be used for real-time data monitoring by means of a matching algorithm. An alternative approach is to use finite-state automata (FSA), as demonstrated by R. Sekar [6], [7], [8], [9], [10]. Unlike the algorithm proposed by Forrest which limits both the length and number of sequences, an FSA can capture an infinite number of sequences of arbitrary length using finite storage.

4 Basic Approach

The basic approach can be summarized as building a normal behavior model and identifying anomalous behavior as any deviation from this normal model. A model is defined as the representation of the normal behavior of an application. The formal definition of a model is given in section 4.2. As said earlier, the basis of this model is system calls made to the operating system. The system calls that are captured are classified as file system based and registry based system calls. Registry based system calls allow us to read, write, create, delete, rename or enumerate various registry keys and values. Some examples are RegCreateKey, RegSetValue, RegQueryValue etc. As a part of building the model, we first record the system calls made by an application over various resources. We capture the system call number and the argument which specifies the resource. We also capture some additional information (value) for registry based system calls. This process is known as profiling. After creating several such normal behavior profiles for an application, the next step is to build the model. The model generation algorithm takes as input all these normal profiles and builds a single model file. After the model is built, the application can be monitored for anomalies by identifying deviations from the model. We describe our approach in three stages, profiling an application, model generation and model enforcement.

4.1 Profiling an Application

The profiling module logs the resource, system call, value and a category. The resources are broadly divided into categories like current directory, windows directory etc. The category field tells which category the logged resource belongs to. The purpose of this category field is for facilitating an efficient implementation of the model. This log is generated every time a process is created for the application which is being monitored. We monitor critical system calls (such as CreateFile, ReadFile, WriteFile, RegCreateKey etc) and critical resources (such as \Device\HarddiskVolume1\Windows etc.). The profile is written in binary format. Several normal profiles are generated for the given application. This system call information is used as a learning database for the model generation.

4.2 Model Generation

After the normal profiles are generated a model is built from these profiles. We follow a resource specific clustering approach for the model generation. The process for model generation is explained in detail. We divide the profiles into clusters, where every cluster is identified by a resource and value. A model is a set of clusters

$$M \equiv \{C_1, C_2, C_3, .., C_N\} \tag{1}$$

where N denotes the total number of clusters. And a cluster can be defined as three tuple:

$$C \equiv \{R_i, V_i, S\} \tag{2}$$

where R_i is the name of the resource, V_i is the value and S is the set of system calls made over that resource. These Clusters are generated in the first step of profiling the application. The Resource R_i is chosen if one of the following is true:

1. It is an executable resource.
2. $$R_i \in D \tag{3}$$

   Where D is the set of directories to be profiled.

Let S denote the universal set of system calls which are being monitored.

$$S \equiv \{s_1, s_2, ..s_m\} \tag{4}$$

where m represents the total number of system calls being monitored. Also there exists an integer such that

$$1 \leq x \leq m \tag{5}$$

For system calls s_1 to s_x, the value is NULL. For system calls s_{x+1} to s_m, the value is not NULL. The model can be defined as a set of clusters, where every cluster represents the resource-value pair and the system calls for that resource. For example, we have profiled the following sequence of system calls as the normal behavior of an application (Table 1).

Table 1. Sequence of system calls as the normal behaviour of an application

System call	Value	Resource
Open	0	A
Read	1	A
Open	0	B
Write	0	B
Close	0	A
Close	0	B
Open	0	C
Write	0	C
Close	0	C
Open	0	B
Write	0	B
Close	0	B

Every line in the sequence in figure 1 represents the system call, value and resource respectively. This sequence has four system calls (open, read, write and close). Let us consider that the open, write and close system calls have no value associated with them. Hence the value for these system calls is always zero. The read system call on the other hand has some value associated with it (1 in this example). On clustering these system calls based on the resource and value, the sequence can be represented as four clusters ({A, 0}, {A, 1}, {B, 0} and {C, 0}). Here A, B and C are the three resources and the numbers represent the value.

The four clusters that will be generated for the sequence in Table 1 are (Figure 1): < A, 0, {1,4}>, <A, 1, {2}>, <B, 0, {1,3,4}>, <C, 0, {1,3,4}>. Several profiles can be generated for an application, which are all used to build one model.

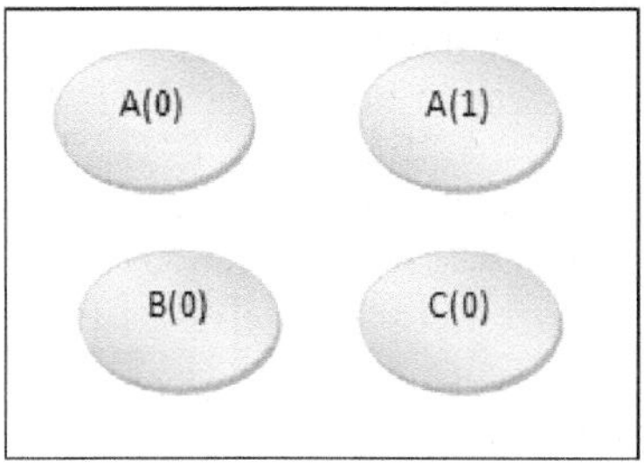

Fig. 1. Model consisting of four clusters

4.3 Model Enforcement

Model enforcement is run time verification of the application behavior with the generated model. When a request is made to the operating system, the resource, value and system call are matched with the model to see if it is present in the model. If the system call is not present for the resource, value pair, then it can be said that the application is deviating from its normal behavior. The procedure for anomaly detection can be better explained with the help of the following examples. Consider the normal model in Figure 1. The sequence of system calls to be verified is shown in Table 2. Every system call in this sequence (Table 2) has to be matched with the clusters <A, 0, {1,4}> ,<A, 1, {2}> and <B,0,{1,3,4}> from the model (figure 2). Enforcement for the sequence in Table 2 is shown in the table 3. Since all the system calls made during enforcement (Table 2) are matched with the model, the behavior is considered to be normal.

Now we verify another system call sequence (shown in table 4) against the same normal model in Figure 1.

Table 2. Example of system calls to be verified during enforcement

System call	Value	Resource
Open	0	A
Open	0	B
Read	1	A
Write	0	B
Close	0	A
Close	0	B

Table 3. Model Enforcement for the system calls

Sequence to be verified			Cluster	Match \ Mismatch
Resource	**Value**	**System call**		
A	0	1	<A,0,{1,4}>	Match
B	0	1	<B,0{1,3,4}>	Match
A	1	2	<A,1{2}>	Match
B	0	3	<B,0{1,3,4}>	Match
A	0	4	<A,0{1,4}>	Match
B	0	4	<B,0{1,3,4}>	Match

Table 4. Example of system calls to be verified during enforcement

System call	Value	Resource
Open	0	A
Open	0	B
Read	1	A
Write	0	B
Close	0	A
Close	0	B

Every system call in this sequence (Table 4) has to be matched with the clusters <A,0,{1,4}>, <A,7,{2}>, <B,0,{1,3,4}> from the model (Figure 1). Enforcement for the sequence in Table 4 is shown in table 5.

Table 5. Model Enforcement for the system calls

Sequence to be verified			Cluster	Match \ Mismatch
Resource	**Value**	**System call**		
A	0	1	<A,0,{1,4}>	Match
B	0	1	<B,0{1,3,4}>	Match
A	7	2		**Mismatch**
B	0	3	<B,0{1,3,4}>	Match
A	0	4	<A,0{1,4}>	Match
B	0	4	<B,0{1,3,4}>	Match

Since the value 7 for the read operation (system call 2) is not present in the model for resource A, there is a mismatch. Hence a deviation from the normal behavior has been detected. We will consider another sequence now. Every system call in the sequence shown in Table 6 has to be matched with the clusters <A,0,{1, 4}> and <D,0 {1, 4}> from the model (Figure 1).

Enforcement for the sequence in Table 6 is shown in the Table 7.

Since the resource D is not present in the model, there is a mismatch. Hence a deviation from the normal behavior has been detected. The steps for verification can be summarized as follows (Figure 2):

Table 6. Example of system calls to be verified during enforcement

System call	Value	Resource
Open	0	A
Open	0	D
Close	0	D
Close	0	A

Table 7. Model Enforcement for the system calls

Sequence to be verified			**Cluster**	**Match \ Mismatch**
Resource	**Value**	**System call**		
A	0	1	<A,0,{1,4}>	Match
D	0	1		**Mismatch**
D	0	4		**Mismatch**
A	0	4	<A,0{1,4}>	Match

1. For every system call to be identified
   (a) Check if the resource and value to be verified are in the model. If either the resource or the corresponding value is not in the model, it is a mismatch.
   (b) If the resource and value are in the model, then check if that system call to be verified is in the cluster of that particular resource. If the system call is not present, then it is a mismatch.

5 Advantages and Limitations

The resource based approach has the advantage of monitoring operations on critical resources. The efficiency of our approach depends on choosing these critical resources. Another advantage in our approach is that we do not consider sequences of system calls. Considering a sequence of system calls generates a number of false positives because the system call sequence is not fixed and varies to a very large extent. The size of the model using our approach is much smaller when compared to other techniques especially models that are built on sequence of system calls. The limitation of the model is that it does not capture inter-resource dependency. Future work in this area is capturing Inter-resource dependency by considering the snap sequence of the system calls.

6 Implementation

The algorithm is implemented in three different modules (Profiling, Model generation and Model enforcement). The first step is profiling of an application.

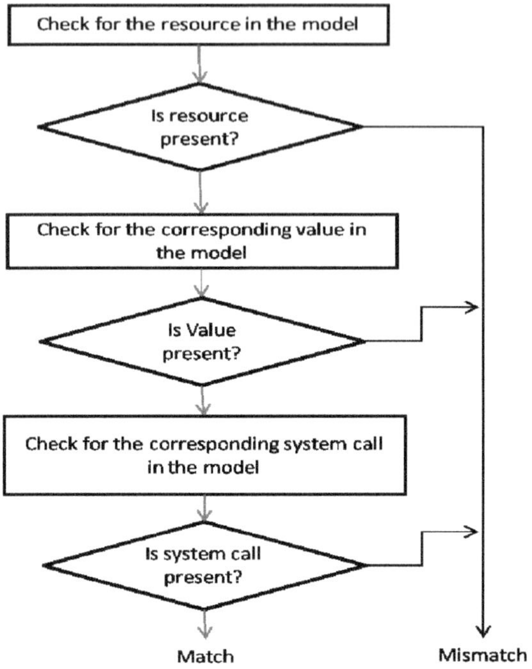

Fig. 2. Flow chart for model enforcement

Previous work in this area use system call interception approach to intercept the system call and its argument. Our profiling module is built using a mini filter driver for the Windows operating system family. This is a similar approach as taken in capture[11]. The mini filter driver records the system call activity of an application. The model generation code generates a model from these profiles.

The steps for model generation are summarized in Figure 3.

Before model enforcement, we check for the existence of some critical behavior signatures in the model. These are the signatures for some suspicious behaviors such as disabling regedit, disabling task manager etc [12]. The result of this check is added in the header of the model. (1 = verified successfully, 2 = verified but not successful, 3 = not yet verified). The model generation program also adds a header in the model which tells the name of the application and the status of verification of behavior signatures with this model. The data structure used to store the model is shown in figure 4. After generating the model, we do the model enforcement which is summarized in Figure 5.

The model enforcement is a matching algorithm which searches for the system call, argument and value in the model. If a match is not found, the applications behavior is regarded as anomalous.

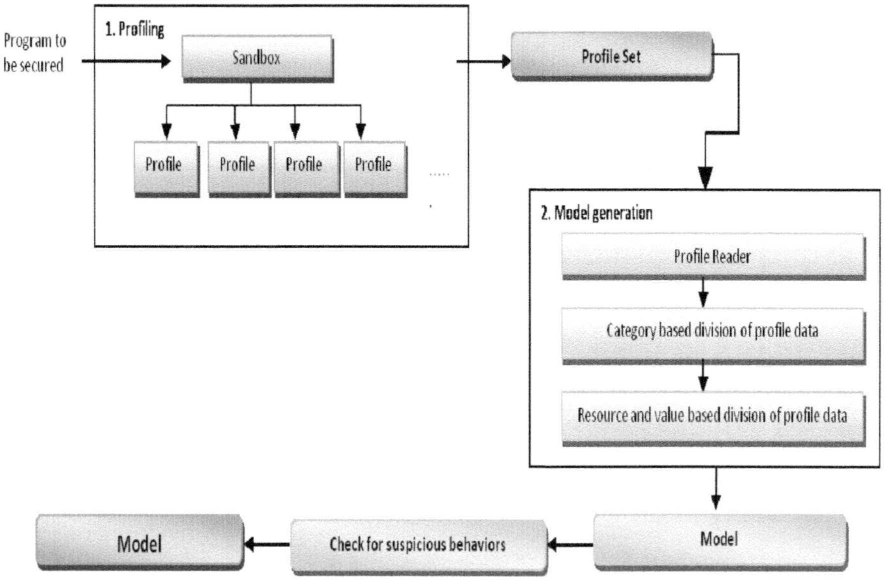

Fig. 3. Steps for model generation

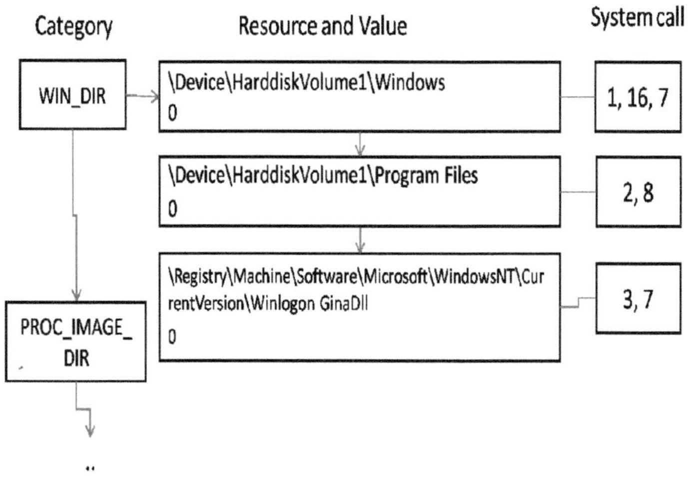

Fig. 4. Data structure representation of the model

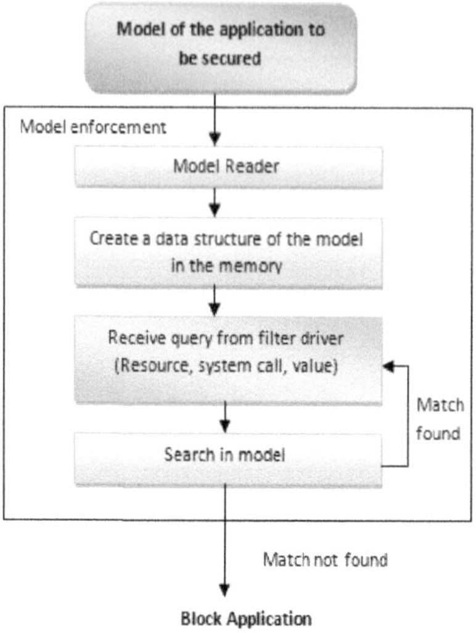

Fig. 5. Steps for model enforcement

7 Experimental Results

In this section we report the results of testing our model with various applications in a live environment. Our approach detects and stop the attacks before the system is compromised. First we generated an application behavior model for Microsoft Word 2003, 2007, Excel 2003, Excel 2007, Powerpoint 2003, Powerpoint 2007, Adobe Reader 9.3. When we want the model for various versions of the application, our approach allows to have a single model file for them. The model includes the behaviors of these applications in terms of the system calls made over the resources. Our solution could detect and prevent attacks. With our approach false positive rate is also very low discussed later in the section.

1. **Attack Prevention.** We tested the solution with various malicious document collected from different sources like offensivecomputing.net and our own honeypot setup. We tested with 80 malicious documents of pdf, doc, xls and ppt. Solution was able to detect all the malicious documents and prevent attacks. We also tested the solution with a keylogger program installed and solution denied the code injection in the benign process by keylogger. Till now, solution's detection rate is 100%.
2. **Performance.** We tested the performance of the solution with various applications like Microsoft Word, Excel, Adobe Reader etc. We made use of xperf[14] tool to calculate the overhead introduced by our solution. These benchmarks are calculated on a x86 PC installed with Windows Vista SP2, Intel Core 2 Duo 2.20 GHz and 2 GB of RAM.
3. **False Positives.** We collected more than 6000 documents of various formats like doc, pdf, xls and ppt from our highly secured network. These documents

Table 8. Performance: Overhead due to our Solution

Application	%CPU usage by process		Overhead
	Without Solution	With Solution	
Acrord32.exe	0.044	0.053	20.45%
Excel.exe	0.025	0.03	20%
Firefox.exe	0.08	0.09	12.50%
Powerpoint.exe	0.06	0.075	25%
Winword.exe	0.123	0.145	17.80%

were first scanned for any known malware signatures. We tested our solution against these documents. Every event generated was logged and classified as whether normal or deviation. We then analyzed all deviations manually and with automated malware analysis tools. After we made sure that none of the deviations was malicious we could calculate false positive rate. Out of total 1939800 events generated only 5302 events were classified as false positives. According to these experiments false positive rate was calculated to only 0.2%.

8 Conclusion

The goal of this paper is to describe a method for obtaining system calls made by an application and building the model based on these system calls. We have presented a method for capturing and representing the normal behavior of an application. We have also described the method to detect abnormal behavior during run time. Effectiveness of the proposed approach in detecting malicious behavior depends on the extent to which the normal behavior of the application has been captured. The proposed approach can be used to capture the normal behavior and detect abnormal behavior of any application executing on any operating system. However, similar to the behavior analysis tool for applications and documents[11], this is the first implementation (in our knowledge) of application behavior modeling approach using mini filter driver. This approach makes the system call monitoring deployable for 64 bit systems too without any need to turn off the kernel patch protection[15]. Moreover, updating the behavior model may be required in case of application plug-ins and as vendor releases more patches and features to the application and cluster based approach makes it easier to update the application behavior model.

References

1. Idike, N., Mathur, A.P.: A Survey of Malware Detection Techniques. Technical Report, Purdue University (2007)
2. Warrender, C., Forrest, S., Pearlmutter, B.: Detecting Intrusion Using System Calls: Alternative Data Models. In: IEEE Computer Society Symposium on Research in Security and Privacy (1998)

3. Forrest, S., Hofmeyr, S.A., Somayaji, A., Longstaff, T.A.: A Sense of Self for UNIX Processes. In: IEEE Symposium on Security and Privacy (1996)
4. Hofmeyr, S.A., Forrest, S., Somayaji, A.: Intrusion Detection using Sequences of System Calls. Journal of Computer Security (1998)
5. Mazeroff, G., Cerqueira, V.D., Gregor, J., Thomason, M.G.: Probabilistic Trees and Automata for Application Behavior Modeling. In: ACM Southeast Regional Conference Proceedings (2003)
6. Parampalli, C., Sekar, R., Johnson, R.: A Practical Mimicry Attack Against Powerful System-Call Monitors. In: ACM Symposium on Information, Computer and Information Security (2008)
7. Sekar, R., Cai, Y., Segal, M.: A Specification-Based Approach for Building Survivable Systems. In: Proceedings of the NISSC (1998)
8. Sekar, R.: On Preventing Intrusions by Process Behavior Monitoring. In: USENIX Intrusion Detection Workshop (1999)
9. Sekar, R., Venkatakrishnan, V.N., Basu, S., Bhatkar, S., Daniel, DuVarney, C.: Model-Carrying Code: A Practical Approach for Safe Execution of Untrusted Applications. In: ACM Symposium on Operating system principles (2003)
10. Sekar, R., Bendre, M., Dhurjati, D., Bollineni, P.: A Fast Automaton-Based Method for Detecting Anomalous Program Behaviors. IEEE Symposium on Security and Privacy (2001)
11. Seifert, C., Steenson, R., Welch, I., Komisarczuk, P., Endicott-Popovsky, B.: Capture A behavioral analysis tool for applications and documents. In: Digital Forensics Research Conference (2007)
12. Rieck, K., Holz, T., Willems, C., Dussel, P., Laskov, P.: Learning and Classification of Malware Behavior. In: Conference on Detection of Intrusions and Malware and Vulnerability Assessment (2008)
13. Wagner, D., Soto, P.: Mimicry Attacks on Host Based Intrusion Detection Systems. In: ACM Conference on Computer and Communication Security (2002)
14. Xperf: `http://msdn.microsoft.com/en-us/performance/cc825801.aspx`
15. Solomon, R.: Windows Internals: Kernel Patch Protection. Microsoft Press, Redmond (2008)

Behavioral Malware Detection Expert System – Tarantula

Sandeep Romana, Swapnil Phadnis, Himanshu Pareek, and P.R.L. Eswari

Centre for Development of Advanced Computing,
Hyderabad, India
{sandeepr,swapnilp,himanshup,prleswari}@cdac.in
http://www.cdachyd.in

Abstract. The number of new malware samples and their complexity is increasing rapidly because of which protecting the system with signature based detection has become increasingly challenging task. In this work we present a novel behaviour-based malware detection expert system named tarantula which makes use of suspicious behaviour rules to detect malicious activity on the system. In our research, we observed that malware targets critical system resources such as system files and registry of operating system in order to execute; shield itself and propagate to other hosts. We identified the critical system resources such as system files and registry in Microsoft Windows and evolved suspicious behaviour rules at a granular level. These behavioural rules are enforced using monitoring and enforcement layer. Through extensive experimentation and testing, we conclude that tool has high detection rate and very less overhead and false positives. The implementation details of prototype (Tarantula) developed for Microsoft Windows XP and Vista operating systems are also provided.

Keywords: Malware detection, Expert system, Mini-filter driver, Malicious behaviour.

1 Introduction

Antivirus software relies on signature and behaviour based techniques to protect the systems from malware. Present antivirus software (using anomaly, specification and signature based detection techniques [1]) combined with firewall and continuous patching up of the operating system provides a fair degree of defence against malware threats. But there are enormous news reports stating the incidences in which malwares have bypassed installed antivirus software.

In this research paper, we present the novel behaviour-based technique to restrict the malware execution. We identified the critical system resources such as files and registry in Windows and evolved the suspicious behaviour rules at a granular level. These suspicious behaviour rules represent various operations over critical system resources. These rules are enforced at the end system using monitoring and enforcement layer to detect and stop malware execution. In order

D.C. Wyld et al. (Eds.): CNSA 2011, CCIS 196, pp. 65–77, 2011.

to evolve these rules we have identified the typical operating system resources and operations carried out on them by genuine applications during their execution. We have also explored the behaviour of malware [2], [3], [4] such as trojans, rootkits, worms, viruses, spyware etc. over these system resources.

Typical operations carried out by malware in Windows operating system include disabling automatic updates, driver installation, accessing SAM file, modifying master boot record, running a packed executable, service installation [5], format operation, and privilege escalation attack. To hide its presence on the system, malware usually disables task manager, registry editor, modifies logon, explorer registry keys, changes host configuration file, runs hidden processes. Operations made on registry keys and files while performing the above mentioned activities are identified to represent the suspicious behaviour rules.

In this research paper we describe how the operating system resources are modified to carry out malicious operations. With this as the background, we arrive at suspicious behaviour rules and also evolve the mechanism used to enforce these rules for restraining malware execution. The prototype has the capability to detect and restrain zero-day malware on Windows OS. The developed prototype (Tarantula) can be categorised as an expert system according to taxonomy presented by G. Jacob [6]. The implementation details of tarantula are presented in the following sections. Few of the malware studied are presented in section 2. Our approach in evolving the suspicious behaviour rules as well as enforcing them at runtime is presented in section 3. We evaluate our prototype in section 4 whereas conclusions are given in section 5.

2 Background

Windows registry is a repository of configuration information for installed software and hardware. Malware targets the registry to change the configuration of Windows operating system and application software. Malware also targets important files stored in %Windir%, %System%, %SystemRoot% and %programfiles% directories. Malwares use packers to compress and encrypt binaries to make reverse engineering difficult and put some extra hurdles in the process of making antivirus signatures. We studied behaviour of around 2000 malwares and details of few malware samples are listed below:

Recent wide spread threat Stuxnet [25] which was discovered in July 2010 tried to copy following files into %WinDir%\inf and %System%\drivers directory

%System%\drivers\mrxcls.sys
%System%\drivers\mrxnet.sys
%Windir%\inf\oem6C.PNF
%Windir%\inf\oem7A.PNF
%Windir%\inf\mdmcpq3.PNF
%Windir%\inf\mdmeric3.PNF

and created following new registry keys

HKEY_LOCAL_MACHINE\SYSTEM\CurrentControlSet\Services\MRxCls\ "ImagePath" = "%System%\drivers\mrxcls.sys"
HKEY_LOCAL_MACHINE\SYSTEM\CurrentControlSet\Services\MRxNet\ "ImagePath" = "%System%\drivers\mrxnet.sys"

The Code Red worm [7] which was released in July 2001 accesses and modifies various registry keys [8] as described below.
For disabling the System File Cache

HKLM\SOFTWARE\Microsoft\WindowsNT\CurrentVersion\Winlogon\Sfc disable = -99

Sets the following registry entries

HKLM\SYSTEM\CurrentControlSet\Services\W3SVC\Parameters\Virtual Roots\/C = C:\,,217
HKLM\SYSTEM\CurrentControlSet\Services\W3SVC\Parameters\Virtual Roots\/D = D:\,,217

Changes the following registry keys

HKLM\SYSTEM\CurrentControlSet\Services\W3SVC\Parameters\Virtual Roots\/Scripts
HKLM\SYSTEM\CurrentControlSet\Services\W3SVC\Parameters\Virtual Roots\/MSADC

Conficker [9], [10] modifies various registry keys and files. The worm removes the following registry key to prevent Windows Defender [11] from running on system start-up:

HKLM\Software\Microsoft\Windows\CurrentVersion\Run\ Windows Defender

Following registry key is removed to suppress Windows Security Centre (utility for managing Windows Firewall, Automatic Updates and Internet Options) notifications:

HKLM\Software\Microsoft\Windows\CurrentVersion\explorer\ ShellServiceObjects\fFD6905CE-952F-41F1-9A6F-135D9C6622CCg

Conficker.C [10] deletes the following key to disable booting Windows in safe mode:

HKLM\SYSTEM\CurrentControlSet\Control\SafeBoot

Sasser worm [12] sets the following logon registry entry allowing virus executable to run each time a user logs on:

HKLM\Software\Microsoft\Windows\CurrentVersion\Run\avserve = avserve.exe

Netsky worm [13] also created the following logon registry entry:

```
HKLM\Software\Microsoft\Windows\CurrentVersion\Run\service=
"C:\\WINDOWS\\services.exe -serv
```

Rustock rootkit [14] copies *.sys file into %SystemRoot%\driver\ and *.dll into %SystemRoot% folder and modified \HKEY_LOCAL_MACHINE\SOFTWARE \Microsoft\Windows NT\CurrentVersion\Winlogon\Notify registry key.
Troj/FakeAV-QN Trojan [15] creates logon registry keys and modifies - %SystemDirectory%\driver\etc\hosts file.

3 Implementation

In this section, the derived behaviour rules are described and then we explain the monitoring and enforcement layer. Finally we discuss working of decision making engine.

3.1 Behaviour Rules

Behaviour rules were derived using the knowledge gained from the malware study. Also a severity level has been allotted to the behaviour rule according to the suspiciousness associated with the behaviour. These rules were formulated as three tuple as: BR = <R, O, S>. Where BR is the behaviour rule, R is the resource; O is the operation over the resource and S is the severity associated with the behaviour rule. Table 1 gives the brief discussion of the formulated behaviour rules:

Table 1. Behaviour Rules

Behaviour	Severity	Description	Behaviour Rule
Create Logon entry	3	Malware modifies logon registry keys and files so that they can be run automatically every time the user logs onto the system.	BR1 = < Logon registry keys *, RegSetValue, 3 > and BR2 = < Logon files*, CreateFile/WriteFile/DeleteFile, 3 >
Create Explorer entry	3	Malicious software modifies explorer registry keys so that they can execute the code specified in the registry, each time windows explorer is run.	BR = < Explorer registry keys*, RegCreateKey/ RegSetValue, 3 >

*Refer to Appendix for details.

Table 1. *(continued)*

Create Win logon Entry	3	Malicious software modifies winlogon registry keys and files so that they can be run automatically and modifies the winlogon sequence	BR1 = < Winlogon registry keys*, RegCreateKey/RegSetValue, 3 > and BR2 = < Winlogon files*, CreateFile/WriteFile/ DeleteFile, 3>
Disable Registry editing tool	5	Usually malware disables the registry editor so that the administrator should not be able to revert back the changes done by the malicious software.	BR = < disable registry keys*, RegSetValue, 5>
Disable Task Manager	5	Malware disables the task manager to restrain the administrator from killing the malicious processes	BR = < Disable task manager registry key* RegSetValue, 5 >
Installation of Drivers	3	Kernel rootkits installs drivers	BR = < Services registry key*, RegSetValue, 3 >
Disable Auto update	5	Malware disable windows automatic updating so that latest patches should not be installed automatically.	BR = < Disable Auto Update registry keys*, RegSetValue, 5 >
Modifying hosts file	5	Malware change the hosts configuration file to divert the traffic to some particular domain from where the malicious program is controlled	BR = < %SystemDirectory%\drivers\etc\hosts file, WriteFile, 5 >
Disable processing of GDI metafiles	3	Modifying this prevents some documents from printing.	BR= < Disable GDI Meta Files registry key*, RegSetValue, 3 >
Disable command prompt	5	Malware disables command prompt so that administrator can't run certain commands	BR = < Disable CMD registry keys*, RegSetValue, 5 >
Disable specified windows applications	5	Can be used to disable any windows applications (e.g. Antivirus)	BR1 = < Disallow run registry key*, RegSetValue, 5 > and BR2 = < Registry.pol/gpt.ini files, WriteFile, 5>
DLL injection	3	Some keyloggers and user mode rootkits use this technique to execute their code through genuine processes	BR = < AppInit Dlls registry key*, RegSetValue, 3 >

Table 1. (*continued*)

Add service to svchost	5	A malware can run its service under svchost which makes it difficult to detect	BR = < Services registry keys*, RegSetValue, 5 > When there is RegSetValue at ImagePath key with value svchost.exe and RegSetValue at ServiceDll key with name of dynamic link library.
Disable user account control	5	So that executable can be run without giving Run As Administrator pop up.	BR = < EnableLUA registry key*, RegSetValue, 5 >
Disable LMHOST lookup	3	Prevent system from referring to LMHOSTS file for name resolution	BR = < EnableLMHOSTS registry key*, RegSetValue, 3 >
Modifying netbios settings	3	Malware may use netbios for name resolution of malicious server. To achieve this it may need to enable netbios	BR = < Netbiosoptions registry key*, RegSetValue, 3 >
Addition of WINS server	3	Malware may add or modify entry for resolving name to point to malicious IP	BR = < NameServerList registry key*, RegSetValue, 3 >
Addition of DNS server	3	Malicious domain can be added to DNS list	P = < NameServer registry key*, RegSetValue, 3 >
Layered Service Provider installation	3	Can be used by malware to intercept TCP/IP packet and redirect to malicious server	BR = < Catalog entries registry key*, RegSetValue, 3 >
Booting time execution	3	To load malicious executable in memory at boot time and run it	BR = < Boot execute registry key*, RegSetValue, 3 >
Disable show hidden files	3	To disallow user to delete malicious hidden files stored on the disk	BR = < Show all registry key*, RegSetValue, 3 >
Writing to executable	3	Viruses attach themselves to existing executables	BR = < file with exe extension, WriteFile, 3 >
An executable writes itself	3	Polymorphic viruses exhibit this kind of behaviour to defeat signature based malware detection	BR = < Process's own executable, WriteFile, 3 >

Table 1. (*continued*)

Writing to system directory	3	Malware can copy its files to system directory to given a feel as if the malware files are genuine	BR = < %SystemRoot%, WriteFile, 3 >
Changing the access rights	3	Can change access rights of malicious files/directories for making them difficult to remove	BR = < Device object, IRP_MJ_SET_INFORMATION, 3 >
Delete disk partition	5	Causes formatting of hard-disk and loss of data.	BR = < Device object, IOCTL_DISK_DELETE_DRIVE_LAYOUT, 5 >

3.2 Monitoring and Enforcement Layer

In order to monitor the applications running on the system for the identified suspicious behaviours and enforce the derived behaviour rules we used minifilter drivers [16], [17] for file activity monitoring [18] and registry callback [19] for monitoring registry on Windows platform. Choosing minifilter driver for implementation and interception gives us flexibility over other techniques [17]. The activity monitor minifilter driver intercepts CreateProcess, ReadFile, WriteFile, DeleteFile and DeviceIoControl file system calls and NtCreateKey, NtDeleteKey, NtDeleteValueKey, NtSetInformationKey, NtSetValueKey and NtRenameKey registry calls. The position of activity monitor driver in the file system stack is given below in Fig. 1.

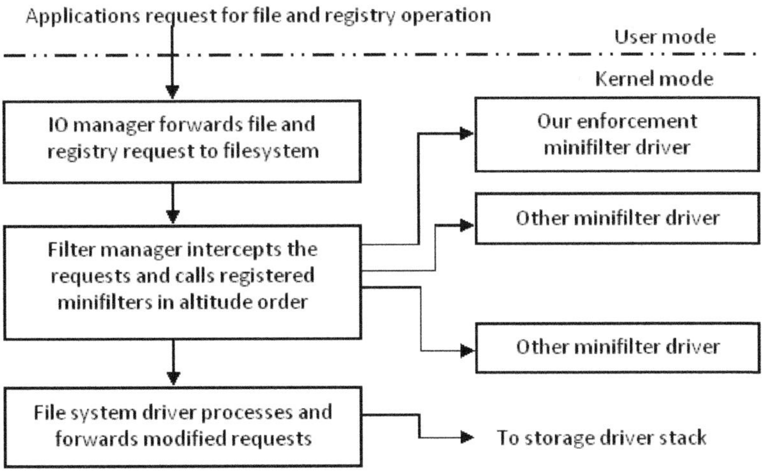

Fig. 1. Position of activity monitor minifilter driver on file system stack

Every file and registry access is compared with the derived behaviour rules. When any of the process does the activity defined in the behaviour rules the total severity of the process is increased with the severity value associated with that behaviour rule. Hence the total number of suspicious behaviours exhibited by a process adds to the total severity of the particular process. If any of the behaviour defined through the above mentioned security policies is found, the user is notified about the possible malicious activity and prompted to allow or block the operation.

3.3 Packed Executable Detection

Apart from the behaviour database we also do static analysis of Portable Executable's section headers to arrive at a conclusion whether it is packed or not. We first make two lists. One list contains the known normal section names while the other contains known packed section names. The algorithm gives the packed score (PS) as output where

$$0 \leq PS \leq 3 \tag{1}$$

The algorithm devised is as follows:

Step 1. If any of the section names of the executable files in the list of known packed section names then PS = 3
Step 2. If no section of the executable file is set with IMAGE_SCN_CNT_CODE then PS = 3
Step 3. If at least one section of the executable file is set with IMAGE_SCN_MEM_EXECUTE and IMAGE_SCN_MEM_WRITE then
  a. If all of the section names are present in the list of normal section names then PS = 2
  b. If any unknown section names appears in the executable file header then PS = 3
Step 4. In any other case PS = 0

3.4 Decision Making Engine

The total severity of process is calculated by

$$T_p = \sum_{i=0}^{n} S_i + PS(1) \tag{2}$$

Where, T_p is the total severity of the process p, S_i is the severity of the corresponding behaviour, n is the total number of behaviours exhibited by a process p and PS is the packed score. If we denote threshold value by W, then if

$$T_p \geq W \tag{3}$$

user is notified about malicious activity attempted by a process p. The threshold value is the integer decided based upon the knowledge we gained by studying various malwares and PS is calculated by the algorithm derived in section 3.3. The complete flow of enforcement of behaviour rules is presented in Fig. 2.

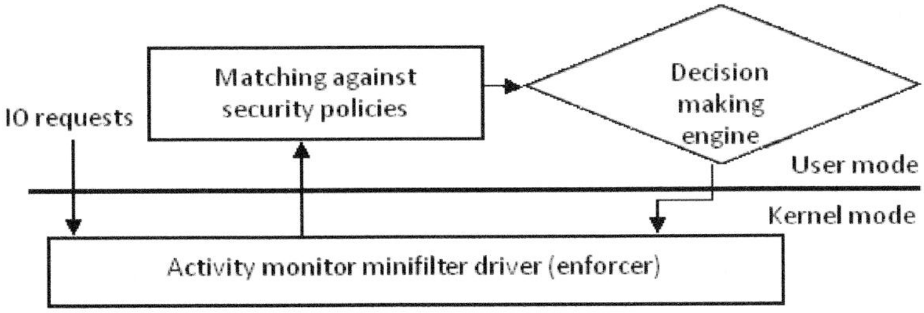

Fig. 2. Enforcement using monitoring and enforcement layer

4 Evaluation

In this section we first evaluate the performance of tarantula. Then, analyze overhead caused by tarantula. Finally we compare tarantula with other expert systems.

4.1 Performance

We used xperf [24] and PCMark05 [23] to evaluate the performance of tarantula. The benchmarks were calculated on a x86 based PC installed with Microsoft Windows Vista Business, Service Pack 2, build 6002 with Intel(R) Core(TM)2 Duo CPU E4500 @ 2.20GHz, 2200 Mhz, 2 Core(s), 2 Logical Processor(s) and 2 GB of RAM. Using xperf we calculated the idle %CPU usage time in normal conditions and with tarantula running on the system and calculated the overhead by subtracting these. Table 2 shows the results of CPU benchmarks with PCMark05 and Table 3 shows the %CPU usage by process with xperf.

Table 2. Benchmark with PCMark05

Benchmark	Normal	With Tarantula	Overhead (%)
File Compression (B/s)	5.40	6.43	19.07
File Encryption (B/s)	30.16	26.97	10.17
File Decryption (B/s)	60.40	60.59	0.32
HDD - Virus Scan (B/s)	47.56	49.69	4.3

Table 3. %CPU usage by process with xperf

Benchmark	Normal	With Tarantula	Overhead (%)
% CPU usage by idle process (B/s)	99.49	99.24	0.25

4.2 Overhead Analysis

Tarantula intercepts eleven system calls in order to monitor all the running processes on the operating system. Overhead calculated using xperf and PCMark05 reveals that tarantula is very much suitable to be installed on a Windows operating system with an average overhead of less than 20 percent.

5 Advantages and Limitations

Our approach does not rely on frequent update of threat database as in case of antivirus software's. Moreover suspicious behaviours are independent of any specific process or program which makes the technique generic and is applicable to any process running on the specific operating system. For enforcing the behaviour rules, built in mechanisms like minifilter driver technology and registry callbacks provided by Windows operating system are used, which makes the implementation reliable and efficient. The prototype developed is also portable on other versions of windows which support the above mentioned technologies.

Currently, our prototype tarantula enforces behaviour rules for file and registry access. More malicious behaviours can be explored to arrive at exhaustive set of behaviour rules. The approach presented in this paper can be extended to detect the malicious network behaviours.

6 Conclusions and Future Work

Formulating behaviour rules derived from knowledge of various kinds of malware and enforcing them at run time, is a promising technique for restraining the malware. However, MAPMon[20] and Argus[21] do the malware detection based on run time behaviour of the program by making use of various API hooking techniques whereas approach presented in this paper is the first implementation (in our knowledge) of malware detection based on runtime behaviour using minifilter driver. This approach makes the behaviour monitoring deployable for 64 bit systems without any need to turn off the kernel patch protection [22]. Moreover, updating the behaviour rule database may be required in case we identify more critical suspicious behaviours.

References

1. Idike, N., Mathur, A.P.: A Survey of Malware Detection Techniques. Technical Report, Purdue University (2007)
2. Skoudis, E., Zelster, L.: Malware Fighting malicious code. Prentice Hall, Englewood Cliffs (2003)
3. Szor, P.: Art of Virus Research and Defense. Addison-Wesley, Reading (2005)

4. Bayer, U., Habibi, I., Balzarotti, D., Krida, E., Kruegel, C.: A view on current malware behaviors. In: Proc of LEET (2009)
5. Bleeping Computer Advanced Spyware Removal Tutorial, http://www.bleepingcomputer.com/tutorials/tutorial83.html
6. Behavioral detection of Malware: from a survey towards established taxonomy (Febraury 2008)
7. Code Red Worm Exploiting Buffer Overflo In IIS Indexing Service DLL, http://www.cert.org/advisories/CA-2001-19.html
8. Sophos, Security Analysis for Viruses and Spyware, W32/CodeRed-II, http://www.sophos.com/security/analyses/viruses-and-spyware/w32coderedii.html
9. Technical Cyber Security Alert TA09-088A, Conficker Worm Targets Microsoft Windows Systems (April 09, 2009), http://www.us-cert.gov/cas/techalerts/TA09-088A.html
10. Fitzgibbon, N., Wood, M.: Conficker.C: A Technical Analysis (April 1, 2009), http://www.sophos.com/sophos/docs/eng/marketing_material/conficker-analysis.pdf
11. Windows Defender homepage, http://www.microsoft.com/windows/products/winfamily/defender/default.mspx
12. Sophos, Security Analysis for Viruses and Spyware, W32/Sasser-A, http://www.sophos.com/security/analyses/viruses-and-spyware/w32sassera.html
13. Sophos, Security Analysis for Viruses and Spyware, W32/Netsky-A, http://www.sophos.com/security/analyses/viruses-and-spyware/w32netskya.html
14. Sophos, Security Analysis for Viruses and Spyware, Troj/Rustock-C, http://www.sophos.com/security/analyses/viruses-and-spyware/trojrustockc.html
15. Sophos, Security Analysis for Viruses and Spyware, Troj/FakeAV-QN, http://www.sophos.com/security/analyses/viruses-and-spyware/trojfakeavqn.html
16. Windows Driver Kit Documentation, http://msdn.microsoft.com/en-us/library/default.aspx
17. Seifert, C., Steensona, R., Welcha, I., Komisarczuka, P., Endicott-Popovsky, B.: Capture - A behavioural analysis tool for applications and documents
18. Nagar, R.: Windows NT File System Internals. O'Reilly, Sebastopol (1997)
19. Honeycutt, J.: The Windows XP Registry Guide. Microsoft Press, Redmond (2002)
20. Dai, S.-Y., Kuo, S.-Y.: MAPMon: A Host-Based Malware Detection Tool. In: Dependable Computing, PRDC 2007 (2007)
21. Hu, Y., Chen, L., Xu, M., Zheng, N., Guo, Y.: Unknown Malicious Executables Detection Based on Run-Time Behavior. In: Fuzzy Systems and Knowledge Discovery, FSKD 2008 (2008)
22. Kernel Patch Protection, http://www.microsoft.com/whdc/driver/kernel/64bitpatching.mspx
23. FutureMark PCMark05, http://www.futuremark.com/products/pcmark05/
24. Xperf, http://msdn.microsoft.com/en-us/performance/cc825801.aspx
25. W32.Stuxnet, http://www.symantec.com/security_response/writeup.jsp?docid=2010-071400-3123-99

Appendix

Logon registry keys
HKLM\Software\Policies\Microsoft\Windows\System\Scripts\Startup
HKCU\Software\Policies\Microsoft\Windows\System\Scripts\Logon
HKCU\Software\Microsoft\Windows\CurrentVersion\Policies\System
HKLM or HKCU \SOFTWARE\Microsoft\Windows\CurrentVersion\Run
HKLM\SOFTWARE\Microsoft\Windows\CurrentVersion\RunOnceEx
HKLM or HKCU \SOFTWARE\Microsoft\Windows\CurrentVersion\RunOnce
HKCU\Software\Microsoft\WindowsNT\CurrentVersion\Windows
HKCU\Software\Microsoft\WindowsNT\CurrentVersion\Windows\Run
HKLM or HKCU\SOFTWARE\Microsoft\Windows\CurrentVersion\Policies\Explorer\Run
HKCU\Software\Policies\Microsoft\Windows\System\Scripts\Logoff
HKLM\Software\Policies\Microsoft\Windows\System\Scripts\Shutdown
Logon files
C:\ProgramData\Microsoft\Windows\Start Menu\Programs\Startup
C:\Users\xxx\AppData\Roaming\Microsoft\Windows\StartMenu\Programs\Startup
Explorer registry keys
HKLM\SOFTWARE\Classes\Protocols\Filter, HKLM\SOFTWARE\Classes\Protocols\Handler
HKCU\SOFTWARE\Microsoft\Internet Explorer\Desktop\Components
HKLM\SOFTWARE\Microsoft\Active Setup\Installed Components
HKLM\SOFTWARE\Microsoft\Windows\CurrentVersion\Explorer\SharedTaskScheduler
HKLM or HKCU\SOFTWARE\Microsoft\Windows\CurrentVersion\ShellServiceObjectDelayLoad
HKLM\Software\Microsoft\Windows\CurrentVersion\Explorer\ShellExecuteHooks
HKCU or HKLM\Software\Classes*\ShellEx\ContextMenuHandlers
HKCU or HKLM\Software\Classes\AllFileSystemObjects\ShellEx\ContextMenuHandlers
HKCU or HKLM \Software\Classes\Directory\ShellEx\ContextMenuHandlers
HKCU or HKLM \Software\Classes\Directory\Shellex\DragDropHandlers
HKCU or HKLM\Software\Classes\Directory\Shellex\PropertySheetHandlers
HKCU or HKLM \Software\Classes\Directory\Shellex\CopyHookHandlers
HKCU or HKLM\Software\Classes\Folder\Shellex\ColumnHandlers
HKCU or HKLM \Software\Classes\Folder\ShellEx\ContextMenuHandlers
HKCU or HKLM \Software\Classes\Directory\Background\ShellEx\ContextMenuHandlers
HKCU or HKLM \Software\Microsoft\Windows\CurrentVersion\Explorer\ShellIconOverlayIdentifiers
HKCU or HKLM \Software\Microsoft\Ctf\LangBarAddin,
HKCU or HKLM \Software\Microsoft\Windows\CurrentVersion\Shell Extensions\Approved
Winlogon registry keys
HKLM\SOFTWARE\Microsoft\WindowsNT\CurrentVersion\Winlogon key System, UIHost, GinaDLL, Taskman, Userinit, Shell, SaveDumpStart
HKCU\SOFTWARE\Microsoft\WindowsNT\CurrentVersion\Winlogon key Shell
HKLM\SOFTWARE\Microsoft\WindowsNT\CurrentVersion\Winlogon\Notify
HKCU\Control Panel\Desktop key Scrnsave.exe
HKLM\System\CurrentControlSet\Control\BootVerificationProgram key ImagePath
Winlogon files
%SystemRoot%\Win.ini, %SystemRoot%\System.ini, %SystemRoot%\Wininit.ini
Disable registry editing keys
HKU or HKLM \SID\Software\Microsoft\Windows\CurrentVersion\Policies\System keyDisableRegistryTools
Disable task manager keys
HKU or HKLM \SID\Software\Microsoft\Windows\CurrentVersion\Policies\System key DisableTaskMgr
Services Registry key
HKLM\SYSTEM\CurrentControlSet\Services\xxx
Disable GDI metafiles registry key
HKLM\SOFTWARE\Microsoft\Windows NT\CurrentVersion\GRE_Initialize key DisableMetaFiles
Disable CMD registry key
HKCU\Software\Microsoft\Windows\CurrentVersion\GroupPolicyObjects\xxx\Software\Policies\Microsoft\Windows\System key DisableCMD
HKCU\Software\Policies\Microsoft\Windows\System key DisableCMD
Disallow Run registry key
HKCU\Software\Microsoft\Windows\CurrentVersion\GroupPolicyObjects\xxx\Software\Microsoft\Windows\CurrentVersion\Policies\Explorer key DisallowRun
AppInit Dlls registry key
HKLM\SOFTWARE\Microsoft\WindowsNT\Current Version\Windows key AppInit_DLLs
EnableLUA registry key
HKLM\Software\Microsoft\Windows\CurrentVersion\Policies\System key EnableLUA
Disable LMHOSTS

HKEY_LOCAL_MACHINE\SYSTEM\CurrentControlSet\Services\netbt\Parameters\ key EnableLMHOSTS

Netbiosoptions registry key

HKLM\SYSTEM\CurrentControlSet\Services\netbt\Parameters\Interfaces key Netbiosoptions

NameServerList registry key

HKLM\SYSTEM\CurrentControlSet\Services\netbt\Parameters\Interfaces key NameServerList

NameServer registry key

HKLM\SYSTEM\CurrentControlSet\Services\Tcpip\Parameters\Interfaces key NameServer

Catalog entries registry key

HKLM\System\CurrentControlSet\Services\WinSock2\Parameters\ Protocol_Catalog9\ Catalog_Entries

Boot execute registry key

HKLM\System\CurrentControlSet\Control\Session Manager key BootExecute

Show all registries key

HKLM\SOFTWARE\Microsoft\Windows\CurrentVersion\Explorer\Advanced\ Folder\Hidden\SHOWALL key Type and CheckedValue

Set disk layout and geometry control codes

IOCTL_DISK_CREATE_DISK, IOCTL_DISK_FORMAT_TRACKS, IOCTL_DISK_FORMAT_TRACKS_EX, IOCTL_DISK_GROW_PARTITION, IOCTL_DISK_INTERNAL_CLEAR_VERIFY, IOCTL_DISK_INTERNAL_SET_VERIFY, IOCTL_DISK_REASSIGN_BLOCKS, IOCTL_DISK_SET_CACHE_INFORMATION, IOCTL_DISK_SET_DRIVE_LAYOUT, IOCTL_DISK_SET_DRIVE_LAYOUT_EX, IOCTL_DISK_SET_PARTITION_INFO, IOCTL_DISK_SET_PARTITION_INFO_EX, IOCTL_DISK_UPDATE_DRIVE_SIZE, IOCTL_DISK_VERIFY

Tool for Prevention and Detection of Phishing E-Mail Attacks

Shamal M. Firake, Pravin Soni, and B.B. Meshram

Computer technology Department
V.J.T.I., Matunga, Mumbai
shamal@inbox.com, pravindsoni@gmail.com, bbmeshram@vjti.org.in

Abstract. In today's world, the major security threat is due to Phishing attacks. Phishing attack makes web users believe that they are communicating with a trusted entity for the purpose of stealing account information, login credentials, and identity information in general. This attack method most commonly initiated by sending out e-mails with links to spoofed website that harvest the information. We propose a methodology to detect and prevent the phishing attacks on e-mail. In its more general form it is an end user application that uses hyperlink feature set to detect phishing attacks and digital signature to prevent the attack. Thus our application will act as an interface between a user and its e-mail service provider to provide secure communication. We believe that this will be a better and more cost effective way to prevent people from losing their private information due to phishing.

Keywords: E-mail, Phishing Attack, HyperLink Detection, Digital Signature.

1 Introduction

Computer and technology dictionary Webopedia.com defines phishing as: "The act of sending an e-mail to a user falsely claiming to be an established legitimate enterprise in an attempt to scam the user into surrendering private information that will be used for identity theft."

Phishing has actually been around for over 15 years, starting with America Online (AOL) back in 1995.There were programs (like AOHell) that automated the process of phishing for accounts and credit card information [2]. The frequently used attack method is to send e-mails to potential victims, which seemed to be sent by banks, online organizations, or ISPs. In these e-mails, they will makeup some causes, e.g. the password of your credit card had been mis-entered for many times, or they are providing upgrading services, to allure you visit their Web site to conform or modify your account number and password through the hyperlink provided in the e-mail. You will then be linked to a counterfeited Web site after clicking those links. You will then enter your personal data in these websites assuming , you are communicating to a legitimate site.

The phishing problem is a hard problem for a number of reasons [3]. Most difficulties stem from the fact that it is very easy for an attacker to send mass emails or to do email forging to spoof e-mail addresses. Previous work indicates that the

D.C. Wyld et al. (Eds.): CNSA 2011, CCIS 196, pp. 78–88, 2011.

ability to create exactly similar looking copies of legitimate e-mails, as well as users' unfamiliarity with browser security indicators, leads to a significant percentage of users being unable to recognize a phishing attack. Unfortunately, the ease with which copies can be made in the digital world also makes it difficult for computers to recognize phishing attacks. As the phishing websites and phishing emails are often nearly identical to legitimate websites and emails, current filters have limited success in detecting these attacks, leaving users vulnerable to a growing threat.

According to the statistics provided by the Anti-Phishing Working Group (APWG) [1], in March 2010, email reports received by APWG from consumers were 30,577.The number of unique phishing sites detected ,in March 2010 were 29879.Payment Services returned to being the most targeted industry sector after Financial Services held top position during H2 2009. However, the category of ,Other' rose from 13 percent to nearly 18 percent from Q4 2009 to Q1 2010, an increase of nearly 38 percent. Amongst the affected industry sector Payment services hold 37% and Financial services 35.9%[20].

In this paper we propose a method to detect and prevent phishing attacks on e-mails. We will see the basic architecture and workflow of an application. Architecture includes main two featured modules as Detection module and Prevention module. Detection module uses the hyperlink feature set, blacklist and whitelist of URLs to detect phishing attacks. Prevention module uses Digital signature to send the official e-mails which include confidential data. The rest of the paper is organised as follows. Section II discuss the literature survey of approaches used to detect or prevent phishing attacks. Section III gives basic architecture of our model. It also includes the workflow of overall application as well as workflow of Detection module and Prevention module is explained. IV concludes the paper.

2 Literature Survey

Phishing being a form of online crime that lures people into giving up personal or corporate information, is a growing security threat that already costs victims billions of dollars every year [8]. The different techniques studied for analysis purpose are presented in tabular form in Table 1.

Table 1. Survey analysis of different Phishing Mail detection techniques

Sr No	Author Name	Tool	Description
1	I. Fette, N. Sadeh, and A. Tomasic [3].	PILFER	The tool can be deployed in a standalone configuration without a spam filter to catch a large percentage of phishing emails. PILFER Phishing email filter combines a set of features aimed at catching deception along with advanced machine learning techniques.

Table 1. (*Continued*)

2	Engin Kirda and Christopher Kruegel [6].	AntiPhish	AntiPhish is an anti phishing solution to guard users against a spoofed web site based phishing attack. The tool keeps track of the sensitive information of a user and generates warnings whenever sensitive information is typed on a form generated by a website that is considered as not trusted .
3	Juan Chen and Chuanziong Guo [4].	----------	They have proposed an algorithm named **LinkGuard** which analyses the generic characteristics of the hyperlinks in the phishing emails to deduce whether a site is spoofed or not.
4	Kapil Oberoi and Anil K. Sarje [16].	An Anti-Phishing Application for the End User	They have developed an end user application that makes use of user provided data to check the authenticity of the destination URL and hence is able to give a more accurate prediction about the validity of the destination website.
5	Kristofer Beck, Justin Zhan [9].	Thin Client	A thin client is created to allow a secure connection between a client and the institution. We believe that this is a better way to prevent people from losing their private information due to phishing.
6	B. Adida, S. Hohenberger, and R. L. Rivest [13].	Trusted Email Approach	Trusted Email Approach proposed the solution to authenticate certain email messages for the purpose of distinguishing legitimate business emails from spam and phishing attempts.

Table 1. (*Continued*)

7	Wilfried N. Gansterer, David Polz [15]	-----------	They had done e-mail classification for phishing defense based on different features of an-email. The approach introduces new sixteen features. These newly introduced features belong to three different groups: • The first group contains six "off-line" features. • The second group contains eight "online" features. • The third group is a control group of presumably class independent features containing two features: Subject length (SubjectLen) counts the number of characters in the subject field, and Sender length (SenderLen) counts the number of characters in the sender field of a message.
8	M. Chandrashekaran, K. Narayana, S. Upadhyaya [7].	Structural properties	They analysed the structural properties of e-mail to separate phishing mails from legitimate e-mails.
9	Shamal Firake, Pravin Soni,B.B.Meshram	**Our approach**	The approach that we present here is unique in a way that we are providing detection as well as prevention of phishing e-mails which is not done before , again it will be beneficial to general user as well as a corporate user also. Phishing Email detection is based on Phishing URL characteristics as well as general E-mail characteristics.

3 Proposed Model to Detect and Prevent Phishing Attacks

Now a days phishing e-mail attacks are very easy for fradulents to carry out. As mass e-mails are sent , the number of affected victims are also large. To fight against such attacks, we proposed an anti-phishing tool to detect and prevent e-mail phishing attacks.

Problem Statement : **Detection and Prevention of Phishing Attacks on Email.**

3.1 Modules of the Application

The tool mainly implements following modules

1. User Interface Module
User friendly graphical interface will be developed by using java technology for ease of use. It facilitates the use of tool for naive users also.

2. Database Maintenance Module
Data storage module storing, managing and if needed update the URL and IP address information of trusted and non-trusted websites.

3. Business Logic Module
This module implements the core functionality of the application. It uses data provided by user emails and database. It contains sub modules as

Detection Module	Prevention Module
Communication Module	Messenger Module

Fig.1 Shows the basic architecture of the tool whereas fig. 2 shows the overall workflow.

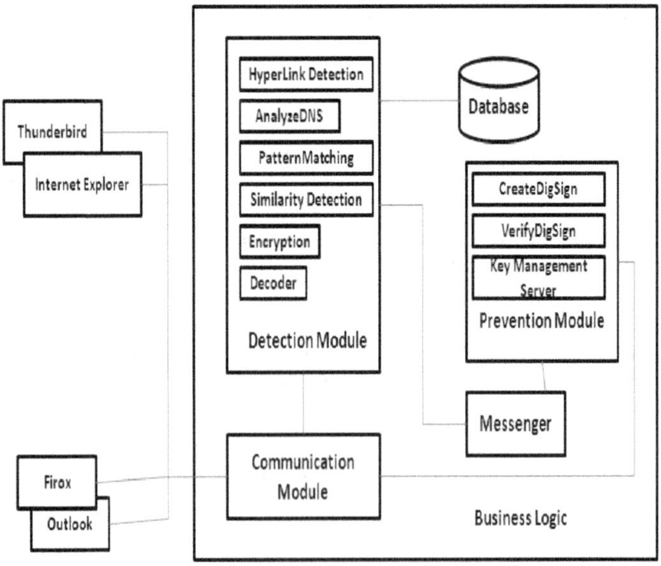

Fig. 1. Architecture of tool to detect and prevent phishing attacks

3.2 Business Logic Module

As said above Business logic module is the heart of application. It communicates to the outside world using Communication module. Each of the module is explained below :

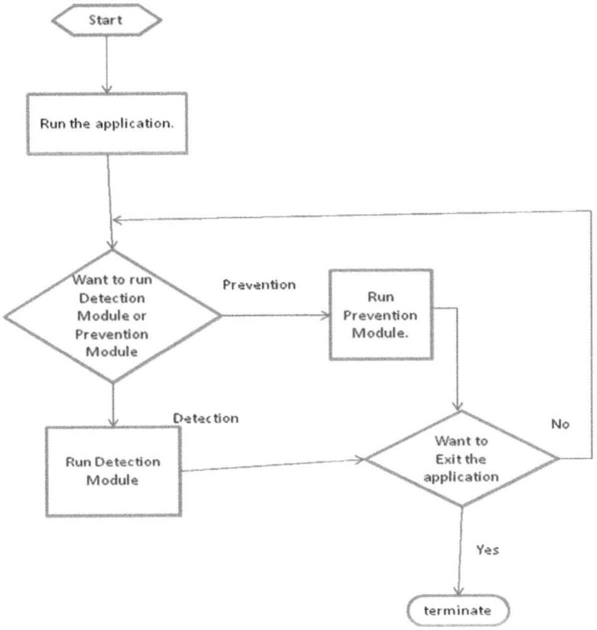

Fig. 2. Workflow of the Tool

3.2.1 Detection Module

Detection Module reads the mails from inbox of mail client of user. It scans all messages and detects for any phishing attack , by using generic characteristics of Hyperlinks. Fig. 3 shows the workflow of the Detection Module. The Detection Module includes following sub-modules,

a. **Hyperlink Detection Module**

Hyperlink Detection Module fetches the DNS names of actual link and visual links of hyperlinks. If both the links are not empty and are different then it warns user about the phishing attack, fig. 4 shows workflow of HyperLink Detection Module. It checks whether the actual DNS name is directly used as dotted decimal then returns possible phishing attack. Many times to confuse the user the actual links and visual links are encoded by using Hexadecimal code or ASCII code. To handle such situations module calls the respective DECODER modules and then compare the decoded links. Module also checks the JavaScript attack if any present in an email. It just checks for the keyword "Java Script" in the email text and if it present, module warns user as possible phishing Attack. This module implements DetectHyperLink Algorithm.

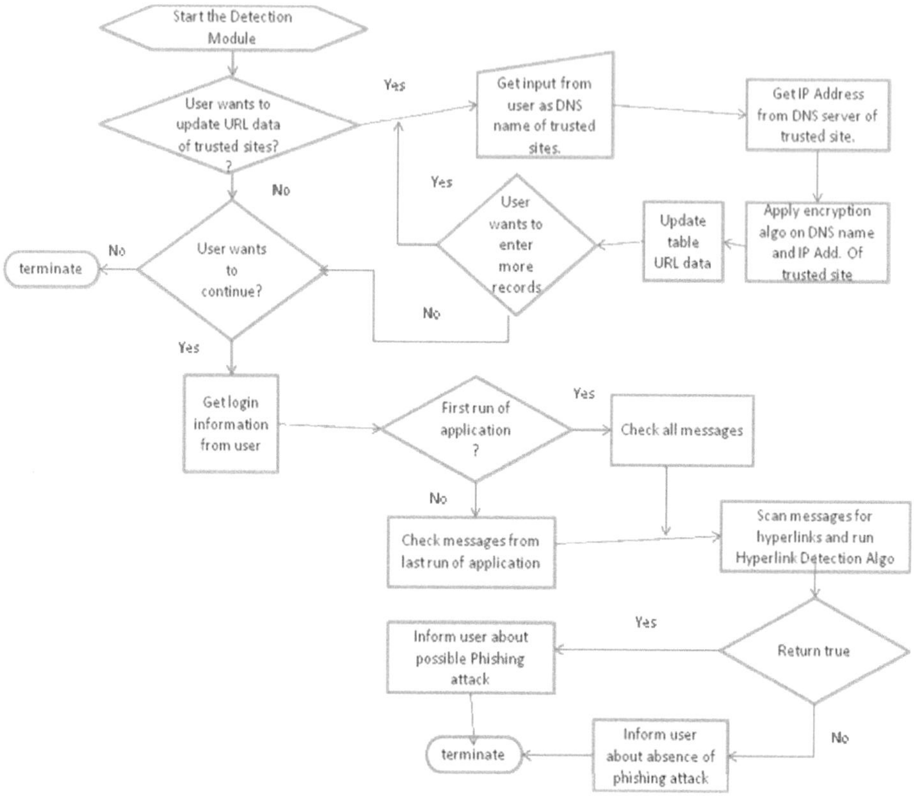

Fig. 3. Workflow of Detection Module

b. AnalyzeDNS Names Module

AnalyzeDNS Names module is used if visual link is null in the hyperlink. The module then check the DNS of hyperlink in Blacklist and whitelist respectively. If It doesn't find there also, then it calls the pattern matching module. This module is implemented using AnalyzeDNS algorithm.

c. PatternMatching Module

It implements the PatternMatching algorithm. Pattern matching module first extracts the DNS name from sender's email address.If this senders DNS name and actual link DNS name are different then it is possibly a phishing attack.If both are same then module checks the previously accessed links database maintained as SEED_SET .SEED_SET is a list of possible phishing links previously accessed or identified. Module then checks the DNS name of actual link against each item in the SEED_SET. If match is found module returns as POSSIBLE PHISHING attack .To compare it calls the Similarity algorithm module.

d. Similarity Detection Module

This module checks how much similar is the actual link DNS name with an item in the SEED_SET. If similarity is beyond a threshold value then it returns true otherwise false. This module uses Similarity algorithm.

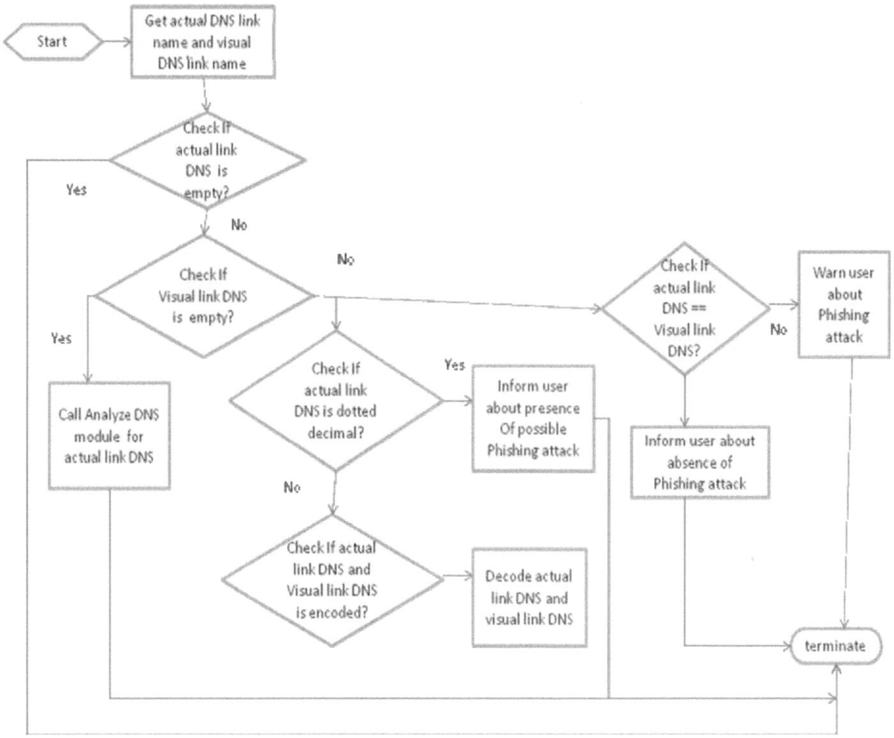

Fig. 4. Workflow of the HyperLink Detection Module

e. DECODER Module

This module consist of two parts as

- **Hexadecimal Decoder**

Many times the hyperlinks are mentioned in Hexadecimal format so that normal user may get confused. To understand the actual DNS name of encoded hyperlink , it must be first decoded. Hexadecimal Decoder algorithm decodes the given Hexadecimal given format into normal text.

- **ASCI I Decoder**

Likewise , the hyperlinks are mentioned in Hexadecimal format also so that normal user may get confused. To understand the actual DNS name of encoded hyperlink , it must be first decoded. The algorithm decodes the given ASCII given format into normal text.

3.2.2 Prevention Module

Prevention Module helps user to prevent from phishing attacks. It allows user to create Digital Signatures to send the official messages .The receiver will verify the Digital Signature at other end and authenticates the sender of the message. A message signature is essentially a sophisticated one-way hash value that uses aspects of the sender's private key, message length, date and time. In general the module does the following things

- Create a personal public/private key pair

Upload their public key to respected key management servers so that other people who may receive emails from the user can verify the messages integrity.

- Enable, the automatic signing and verification of emails

Create the digitally signed e-mails.Verify all signatures on received emails and be careful of unsigned or invalid signed messages – ideally verifying the true source of the email

3.2.3 Communication Module

Communicate with all of the monitored processes, collect data related to user input from other processes (e.g. IE, outlook, firefox, etc.), and send these data to the Business Logic module, it can also send commands (such as block the phishing sites) from the Business Logic executive to other modules.

3.2.4 Messenger

Messenger receives a warning messages from Business Logic module and shows the related information to alert the users . Messenger also send the reactions of the user back to the Business Logic module. One can save the alert messages received and sent.

4 Conclusion

The spectre of online identity threat was never so real as it is today primarily due to rapid growth of the Internet and increase in online trading activities which offer a cost effective method to service providers, such as banks, retailers etc., to reach out to their customers via this medium. This has also provided the phishing community an excellent tool to try and fool the netizans into divulging sensitive information about their banking accounts, credit cards details, etc. Recent years have witnessed a host of phishing scams with each doing the other in terms of reach to the users and the level of sophistication.

Though the best measure available against such scams is user awareness , it is highly impossible also. So many tools have been developed to fight against the e-mail phishing attacks. To contribute in this regard we, have also taken a step ahead. This paper gives the literature survey of the approaches till now used by different people to detect and prevent e-mail phishing attacks. We have also proposed our own approach to fight against the e-mail phishing attacks. The modules include the detail specification of their functionality. Thus , we assure that this solution will help to the normal end user as well as the corporate people from loosing their private credentials and to send the highly confidential data.

References

1. The Anti-phishing working group, http://www.antiphishing.org/
2. Williams, A.: Phishing Exposed. Syngress Publishing Inc., (2005)
3. Fette, I., Sadeh, N., Tomasic, A.: Learning to detect phishing emails. Technical Report CMU-ISRI-06-112, Institute for Software Research, Carnegie Mellon University (June 2006), http://reports-archive.admcs.cmu.edu/anon/isri2006/abstracts/06-112.html
4. Chen, J., Guo, C.: Online Detection and Prevention of Phishing Attacks. In: IEEE Communications and Networking, ChinaCom 2006, pp. 1–7 (October 2006)
5. Ollmann, G.: The Phishing Guide. NGS Software Insight Security Research (2005), http://www.ngssoftware.com/papers/NISRWPhishing.pdf
6. Kirda, E., Kruegel, C.: Protecting Users Against Phishing Attacks. In: 29th Annual International Conference on Computer Software and Applications (COMPSAC 2005), Edinburgh, Scotland, July 26-28, vol. 1, pp. 517–524 (2005)
7. Chandrashekaran, M., Narayana, K., Upadhyaya, S.: Phishing Email Detection Based on Structural Properties. In: Symposium on Information Assurance: Intrusion Detection and Prevention, New York (2006)
8. Suriya, R., Saravanan, K., Thangavelu, A.: An Integrated Approach to Detect Phishing Mail Attacks A Case Study. In: SIN 2009, North Cyprus, Turkey, October 6-10, vol. 3. ACM, New York (2009) 978-1-60558-412-6/09/10
9. Beck, K., Zhan, J.: Phishing in Finance. IEEE, Los Alamitos (2010) 978-1-4244-6949-9/10/$26.00
10. Huang, H., Zhong, S., Tan, J.: Browser-side Countermeasures for Deceptive Phishing Attack. In: Fifth International Conference on Information Assurance and Security (2009)
11. Irani, D., Webb, S., Giffin, J., Pu, C.: Evolutionary Study of Phishing. IEEE, Los Alamitos (2008) 978-1-4244-2969-1/08/ c_
12. Crain, J., Opyrchal, L., Prakash, A.: Fighting Phishing with Trusted Email. In: International Conference on Availability, Reliability and Security (2010)
13. Adida, B., Hohenberger, S., Rivest, R.L.: Fighting phishing attacks: a lightweight trust architecture for detecting spoofed emails, draft (February 2005)
14. Kumaraguru, P., Rhee, Y., Acquisti, A., Cranor, L.F., Hong, J., Nunge, E.: Protecting people from phishing: the design and evaluation of an embedded training email system. In: CHI 2007: Proceedings of the SIGCHI Conference on Human Factors in Computing Systems, pp. 905–914. ACM, New York (2007)
15. Gansterer, W.N., Pölz, D.: E-Mail Classification for Phishing Defense
16. Oberoi, K., Sarje, A.K.: An Anti-Phishing Application for the End User. In: 3rd Hackers Workshop on Computer and Internet Security. Prabhu Goel Research Centre for Computer & Internet Security Department of Computer Science and Engineering Indian Institute of Technology Kanpur (March 17-19, 2009)
17. Yu, W.D., Nargundkar, S., Tiruthani, N.: PhishCatch – A Phishing Detection Tool. In: 33rd Annual IEEE International Computer Software and Applications Conference (2009)

18. Beck, K., Zhan, J.: Phishing in Finance. IEEE, Los Alamitos (2010) 978-1-4244-6949-9/10/
19. Phishing Activity Trends Report (2009), http://www.antiphishing.org/reports/apwg_report_pdf
20. Phishing Activity Trends Report, 1st Half (2010), http://www.antiphishing.org/reports/apwg_report_h1_2010.pdf

Improvement of QoS performance in MANET by QoS-TORA: A TORA Based QoS Routing Algorithm

Govind Kumar Jha, Neeraj Kumar, Himanshu Sharma, and K.G. Sharma

Assistant Professor, GLA University Mathura
gvnd.jha@gmail.com, javaneeraj@gmail.com,
himanshusharma19@gmail.com,
hollyhoc@gmail.com

Abstract. Due to the growth of multimedia applications, Quality-of-Service (QoS) is becoming one of the most desirable features of mobile ad hoc networks (MANETs). However, mobility of nodes, limited bandwidth and highly dynamic nature of network topologies make it difficult to provide QoS support in MANETs. In this paper we propose a QoS routing protocol based on TORA (QoS-TORA). This protocol provides not only multiple routes between a given source and destination but also, it selects the optimized route according to applications of QoS requirements. Experimental result shows that QoS-TORA provides better performance than TORA in terms of packet delivery fraction and end to end delay. Experiments are done on NS-2 simulator.

Keywords: Quality of Service, QoS Routing, TORA, QoS-TORA, Ad hoc Network.

1 Introduction

A mobile ad hoc network (MANET) is a collection of mobile nodes that form a wireless network without the use of a fixed infrastructure and there is no any centralized administration.

The most desirable feature for MANETs is Quality-of-Service (QoS) due to the growing need of multimedia like applications. Lack of available bandwidth, QoS assurance is a challenging task, so it is necessary to manage the proper bandwidth to accommodate these applications. Several approaches have been proposed to provide QoS assurance in wired networks [2] . However, due to the different characteristics of the wireless medium, wire-based QoS models are not appropriate for mobile adhoc networks.

In recent years, many routing protocols have been developed for MANETs. Temporally-Ordered Routing Algorithm (TORA) is a source initialized on-demand or proactive routing protocol for MANET.

TORA attracted great attention because of its simplicity, low computational complexity and low processing overhead [3]. It is an on demand routing protocol, so that a route is only discovered when required by a source node. This eliminates periodic routing updates and only necessary information is propagated to minimize control overhead. That's TORA is an eminent one. It is one of a family of protocols

D.C. Wyld et al. (Eds.): CNSA 2011, CCIS 196, pp. 89–99, 2011.

which termed as 'link reversal' algorithm. According to routing height mechanism, TORA can build a directed acyclic graph (DAG) from source to destination. TORA is highly adaptive, efficient and scalable and due to these features this is best-suited for use in large dense, mobile networks.

In this paper we proposed QoS-TORA routing protocol. Although TORA can create and maintain multiple paths from source to destination, A QoS extension for TORA can be used in a QoS routing protocol based on TORA with IEMP support to select the best suited paths among the multiple existing path that satisfy the QoS requirements. This extension in the form QoS-TORA includes the bandwidth or delay requirement of an application as parameter. The number of time slots is considered as the bandwidth requirement of the applications.

A QoS extension is added to the TORA routing table and the control packets, and routes are required which have sufficient bandwidth for multimedia application. A local repair mechanism may help to provide a better packet delivery ratio.

The only QoS metric considered here is bandwidth for a QoS flow, because finding a route for QoS flow is subject to multiple metrics is inherently difficult and in many cases it is considered to be an NP-complete problem [8].

Organization of Paper

Section 2 describes related work in this field. The proposed protocol is presented in Section 3 and its simulation environment is discuss in section 4 performance is evaluated and compared with that of TORA in Section 5 and Section 6 discuss about conclusions and future enhancements about this literature.

2 Related Work

2.1 TORA Protocol

The mechanism of TORA is similar to water-supplying system. Communication links between routers can be treated as pipelines, and routers can be treated as pipeline junctions, while data packets should be treated as water stream. In the network, every router maintains a "Routing Height" metric for each destination respectively. When two adjacent routers communicate with each other, the one with lower routing height will be treated as downstream router. TORA defines that data packets can only be routed from upstream router to downstream router; just like water can only flows from high to low. With the direction of routing height, data packets can flow from source to destination without any loop. TORA operates by creating a Directed Acyclic Graph (DAG) that is rooted at the destination. The DAG is extremely useful in our scheme since it provides multiple routes from the source to the destination. We use this routing structure to direct the flow through routes that are able to provide the resources for the flow according to the QoS requirements of the flow.

The Temporally Ordered Routing algorithm presented by Park and Corson belongs to the family of link reversal routing algorithms [9]. TORA also maintains a DAG by means of an ordered quintuple with the following information:

- T- Time of a link failure
- O - Originator id
- R- Reflection bit that indicates 0=original level & 1=reflected level
- d -integer to order the nodes that is relative to the reference level
- i- the nodes id

The triplet (T,O,R) is called the reference level.Each node maintains a neighbors routing table containing the height of the neighbor nodes. Initially the height of all the nodes is NULL. (This is not zero "0" but NULL "-") so their quintuple is (-,-,-,-,i). The height of a destination neighbor is (0,0,0,0,dest).

When a node has detected a partition it sets its height and the heights of all its neighbors for the destination in its table to NULL and it issues a CLR (Clear) packet. The CLR packet consists of the reflected reference level (T,O,1) and the destination id. If a node receives a CLR packet and the reference level matches its own reference level it sets all heights of the neighbors and its own for the destination to NULL and broadcasts the CLR packet. If the reference level doesn't match its own it just sets the heights of the neighbors its table matching the reflected reference level to NULL and updates their link status.

There Are Two Special Routing Heights That Are Defined as Follows

1. (0,0,0,0,i)- Zero routing height which is only associated with destination nodes.
2. (-,-,-,-,i) - Null routing height which is equivalent to infinite routing height.

If the local repair request is succeed unreachable destinations and their known sequence number, and invalidates all the active routing entries in its routing table that use the downstream node of the broken link as the next hop.

3 Proposed QoS-TORA

3.1 Modification in TORA

In TORA, router always selects the downstream with minimum hop count to destination as their next hop. The δ value in routing height reflects the hop count to the destination, although it is not equal to the real value. Minimum δ value means minimum hop count. In QoS-TORA we modify the route selection strategy when a router has more than one down streams, Route selection factor α expresses the combination delay performance that includes total transmission delay determined by route hop count and media access delay determined by MAC packet queue length if the data packet routed from the downstream router j. The longer delay will lead to smaller route selection factor. In next step, we normalize the route selection factor (α) into route selection probability (Pi) according to the formula.

$$\alpha_i = 1/[(\beta_i + 1)T_m + (\delta_i + 1)T_t$$

Tt=Length of routed data packet /Data rate of transmitter
βi= Packet queue length
Tm= Average media access time

Route selection probability:

$$P_i = (\alpha_i)^2 / \sum_{i=1}^{n} (\alpha_i)^2$$

We take the square in order to be greedier with respect to the better paths. Finally, we will generate a random number which is uniformly distributed from 0.0 to 1.0 and use it to select a downstream. It is obvious that QoS-TORA is based on probabilistic routing algorithm which leads to network load spreading with consequent automatic load balancing. Probability routing algorithm is very popular for MANETs' resource management especially in multi-path routing protocols. Some new routing protocols [6][7] have made use of this from the previous introduction, we can imagine when a path is clearly worse than the others, its selection probability will be smaller and intentionally avoided in route selection. So its congestion will be relieved. Better path will undertake more network traffic. When the downstream paths have similar performance, the network traffic will be spread in the multiple paths, which will decrease the delay and reduce the energy consumption of the backbone routers and make energy consumption more fairly. By continuously adapting the data traffic, the routers will spread the data load evenly over the network. This is quite important in MANETs, because the bandwidth of the wireless channel is very limited.

3.2 QoS Routing in TORA

QoS routing protocols search for routes with sufficient resources for the QoS requirements. These protocols work with the resource management mechanisms to establish the paths through the network that meet end-to-end QoS requirements, such as delay or jitter bounds, bandwidth required [3]. CEDAR[5] is an example of a routing protocol where the QoS provision mechanism is intrinsically tied to the routing protocol. However, QoS routing is difficult in MANETs. The over head is too high for the bandwidth limited MANETs because there need to be mechanisms for a mobile node to store and update link information. Also due to the dynamic nature of MANETs, obtaining precise link information is very difficult. Moreover, the traditional meaning that the required QoS should be maintained once a feasible path is established is no longer true. The reserved resource may not be guaranteed because of the mobility caused path breakage . While QoS-TORA is trying to find a better route for the qos flow following the admission control failure at an intermediate node, that packets are transmitted as best effort(BE) packets from the source to the destination. It should also be noted that there is no any interruption in the transmission of a flow that has not been able to find a route in which resources have been reserved all the way from the source to the destination. Because of the nature of the Directed Acyclic Graph (DAG), QoS-TORA tries to get a route which satisfies QoS requirements locally. When this fails, the search for a route which satisfies the QoS requirement becomes globally.

In the worst case, we would have searched the entire DAG for a QoS route. The state introduced in the nodes due to this search is soft. So, there is no overhead in maintaining the state. This search, which goes on in the background does not affect the delivery of the packets of the flow. Also, the scope of search for the routes is the DAG. QoS-TORA only chooses an appropriate route from the set of routes given by

TORA. It does not trigger any route-querying mechanism to find routes which will satisfy the QoS requirements. The philosophy of OoS-TORA is that it tries to find a better route for a flow while the transmission of the flow continues without interruption governed by the service requirements of end user applications. In [1], the authors of TORA claim: "This distance information can be used, if desired, to favor routing over links with shorter distances; although under heavy traffic conditions we would not advocate routing all packets over a single path due to the congestion enhancing the effect of single path routing. It is clearly shows that the authors of TORA do not recommend to use any single or shortest path routing in any case. But the authors do not provide further solution for making use of these multiple paths. The TORA always chooses the downstream with minimum hop count when routing data packets. The traffic load from Source node to Destination node will always be routed in the path shown by dotted line. This route selection strategy may lead to congestion and energy over-consumption of intermediary nodes (Node 2 and Node 5 in Fig.1) on the path. So the selection of routing path with minimum routing height is not always the best choice.

The basic idea of QoS-TORA is to present a new routing path selection strategy which takes into account of not only hop count but also the packet queue length in MAC layer. In this way QoS-TORA can sufficiently make use of the multiple Paths and selecting those paths that provide the QoS assurance. In Fig.1, each node with multiple down streams (such as Node 2 and Node 3) can select the appropriate one according to their own status. The modifications based on TORA are on the aspects by modifying the selection strategy in classical TORA protocol.

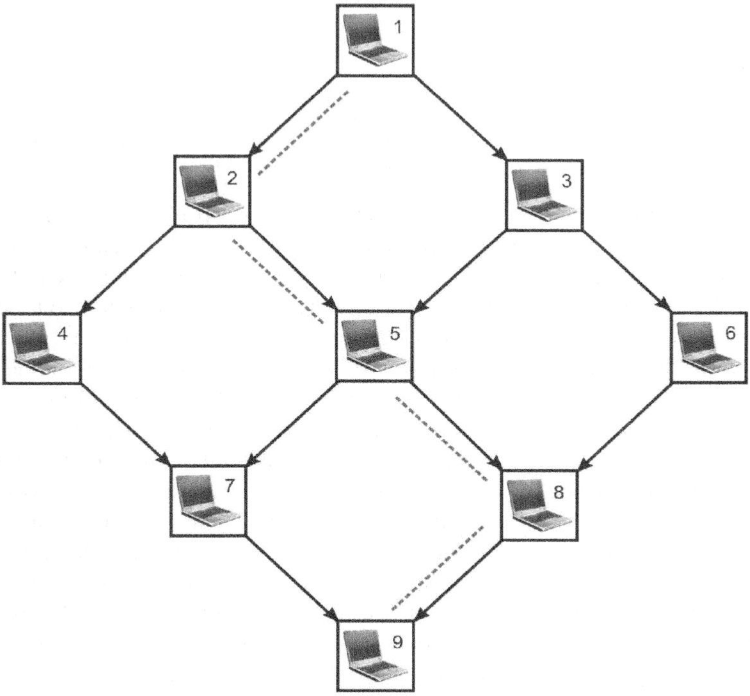

Fig. 1. Routing mechanism of QoS-TORA

A QoS extension for IMEP routing packets [6] is used in QoS-TORA, it is added to QRY and UPD packets to discover and create routes. This QoS extension includes the application bandwidth requirements, and a "session ID" issued to identify each QoS flow that is established. The session ID and required QoS parameters are recorded in the routing tables to identify different QoS flows. QoS-TORA modifies the route discovery and maintenance mechanisms of TORA to provide QoS assurance.

Step1:
Tora provides multiple path from source to destination. But our aim is to choose that path that satisfies the required qos flow. In TORA there may exist a DAG (Directed Acyclic Graph) that is responsible for providing multiple paths.

But all these paths do not take guarantee to satisfy our required QoS flow. When the search for a route that satisfies the QoS requirements is failed, it becomes a global issue. In our worst-case scenario, we have to search among all paths that are associated with DAG.

It is very difficult to find that particular path, which always takes guarantee of QoS flow. This is not possible at all, because of dynamic changing topologies at any unpredictable time. Our QoS-TORA provides an appropriate route among the multiple routes given by TORA.

Step 2:
As mentioned above, QoS TORA tries to select that path which provides the QoS flow and during establishment of this path if any node fails to satisfy the required QoS flow, it send NCM (Negative Control Message) to its previous node.

Step 3:
If any node get to know that it's next hope does not satisfy the requirement of our QoS flow, then that node Re-Routes the QoS flow through any other downstream neighbor provided by TORA.

Step 4:
If reachable path to a node has sufficient bandwidth to satisfy the QoS requirements then QoS TORA selects that path.

Step 5:
If a node realizes that it does not satisfies QoS requirements because it is overloaded by all the downstream neighbors that was provided by TORA then it sends an NCM to its previous node, indicating that none of its down streams neighbors satisfy QoS requirements .

Step 6:
As a result of this approach, our QoS -TORA tries with other down streams neighbors for the possibility of a path that provides QoS assurance.

Step 7:
Finally, QoS-TORA tries to find a better route for the QoS requirements at intermediate nodes, which does not have appropriate path for QoS flow.

Algorithm 1. Proposed QoS-TORA Algorithm

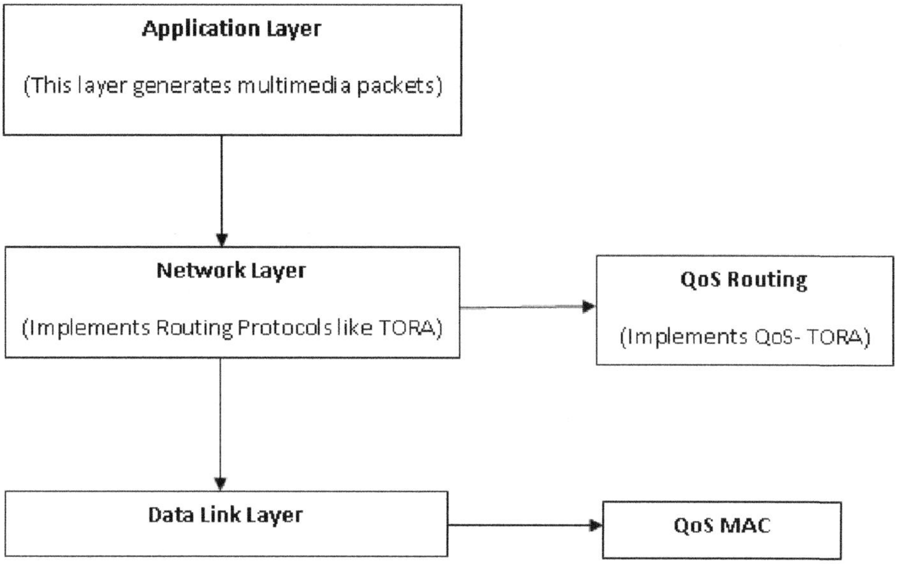

Fig. 2. Layres Perspective of QoS Model

4 The Simulation Environment

Our conclusions are based on the results of extensive network simulation of the proposed protocol. Network Simulator NS-2 [10] was used for the simulation.

A. Traffic and Mobility Model

In our simulations, 50 nodes move in a 1200m × 300m rectangular area according to the random waypoint mobility model. In this model, each node is randomly distributed in the area.

The nodes move towards a random destination and pause for a certain time after reaching this destination before moving again. When a node reaches the boundary, it reflects back with the same angle of incidence [8]. The nodes move at a speed uniformly distributed between 0m/s and a maximum of 10m/s. The simulation time is

Table 1. Network parameter in NS-2

Channel	Wireless Channel
Propagation model	Random waypoint mobility model
Network Interface	Wireless PHY
MAC Layer	IEEE 802.11
Data Link Layer	LL
Antenna	Omni Antenna

Table 2. Simulation Parameters

Number of Nodes	50
Maximum Delay	0.1s
Minimum Bandwidth	2 Mbps
Topology	1200m x 300m
Pause Time	300s
Traffic	CBR
Packet Size	512 bytes
Data Rate	8,20 packets/s
Simulation Time	600s

600s, ten different simulations were executed with different pause times, where a higher pause time reflects lower mobility. 0s indicates a high mobility scenario, while a pause time of 300s is considered a very stable network.

We use Constant-Bit-Rate (CBR) data in the traffic model. Sources generate 512 byte packets at rates of either 8 packets/s or 20 packets/s. The link bandwidth is assumed as 2Mbps, and a resource scheduling and reservation protocol is assumed to be used to schedule and reserve the required resources at each mobile node along the route.

In our our simulations environment number of nodes, mobility and topology may be changed from scenario to scenario.

B. Parameters Monitored

We evaluated the performance of QoS-TORA by measuring two parameters: data packet delivery ratio, and end-to-end data packet delay [8] but we will also discuss one more metric normalized routing overhead ratio.

• **Data packet delivery ratio:** This is the ratio of the number of packets sent by the sources into the network to the number of packets successfully received by the destinations. This measures the reliable data delivery nature of the protocol.

• **Normalized routing overhead ratio:** the ratio of the total number of routing packets transmitted to the number of data packets delivered. For packets sent over multiple hops, each transmission of a packet over a hop counts as one transmission. Protocols that generate large amounts of routing overhead increase the probability of packet collision and data packet delays in network interface queues.

• **End-to-end delay:** This gives the time delay that a data packet has encountered from the time it was sent by a source to the time it was received at the destination.

And this is equal to the delay in transmitting data packets through wireless links plus the delay in the network interface queues due to network congestion.

5 Performance Evaluation

The performance of QoS-TORA was evaluated by comparing it with TORA [4]. We considered various numbers of sessions with different packet rates and mobility models.

5.1 Effects of Traffic Loads

Figs. 3 and 4 show the performance of QoS-TORA and TORA with different numbers of CBR sources and packet rates, and a pause time of 400s. At a packet rate of 8 packets/s, when the number of sessions increases, the packet delivery ratios of both QoS-TORA and TORA decrease. When the traffic is light (number of sessions less than 10), sufficient bandwidth can be guaranteed to provide a high packet delivery ratio, small normalized routing overhead and low end-to-end delay. QoS-TORA has a comparable packet delivery ratio to that with TORA, but it needs more routing overhead and has more delay . The reason is that TORA has the advantage of using routing information in the intermediate nodes.. On the other hand, a UPD packet can only be generated by a destination node in QoS-TORA, which results in more routing overhead and more time to find a route. As a consequence, TORA has slightly better performance than QoS-TORA under light traffic - this is also observed at 20 packets/s.

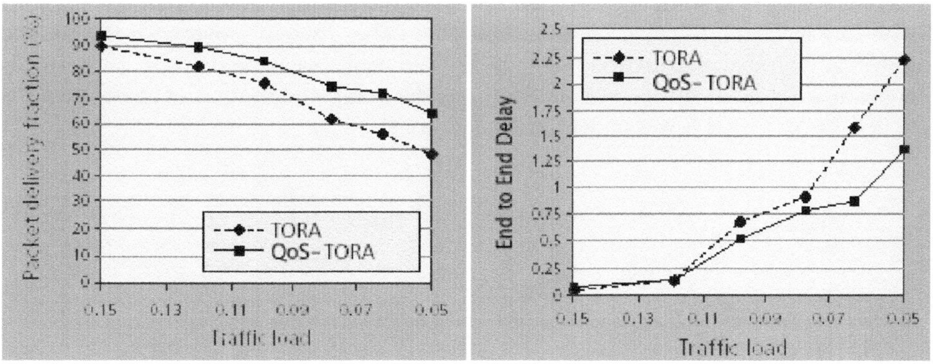

Fig. 3.

When the number of sessions increases to 20, QoS-TORA provides better performance than TORA, and this becomes more pronounced as the traffic load increases. At 8 packets/s, the packet delivery ratio of TORA is lower than QoS-TORA by 2% to 5% . At 20 packets/s, the packet delivery ratio of QoS-TORA outperforms TORA by 8 % to 12%. Under these conditions, QoS-TORA uses less routing overhead than TORA at the cost of slightly more end-to-end delay because some QoS routes are not the shortest. Heavy network traffic causes congestion and buffers to fill quickly, so packets take longer to be sent, and packets are lost if a buffer is full. The routes created by QOS-TORA guarantee the bandwidth requirements of each session, while TORA only finds the shortest path and is not concerned with available of bandwidth. Thus with QoS-TORA the traffic load is more balanced, and the probability of packet loss is also reduced. Furthermore, in congested conditions, routes become invalid more easily with TORA, resulting in a significant increase in routing overhead and some delays in finding new routes or repairing routes.

5.2 Effect of Node Mobility

Different mobility models were simulated by using different pause times. It was observed that mobility has a great impact on the performance of both QoS-TORA and TORA. In [6] similar observations for TORA were discussed. Figs. 3 and 4 show the performance of QoS-TORA and TORA with 20 CBR sessions and different packet rates. QoS-TORA has a lower packet delivery ratio than TORA at 0s pause time (high mobility), and the routing overhead is less than with TORA. At 300s pause time (low mobility), QoS-TORA has higher packet delivery ratio than TORA, and requires some less routing overhead than TORA. Similar results were also observed with a 20 packets/s data rate. This is because TORA creates a route for each destination, and so benefits from route information stored in the nodes. QoS-TORA creates a route for each session even if they are for the same source and destination nodes, and a route reply can only be generated by the destination node. Thus, a QoS route is harder to find than a best effort route at high mobility, and the difference in routing overhead and delay between TORA and QoS-TORA is larger with high mobility (short pause time), than with low mobility (long pause time). Furthermore, with low mobility, routes do not break as often after route discovery, so the network traffic is more balanced with QoS-TORA. Data packets can be delivered faster if the nodes usually have sufficient bandwidth, as the delay and routing overhead required to deliver packets is lower under these conditions.

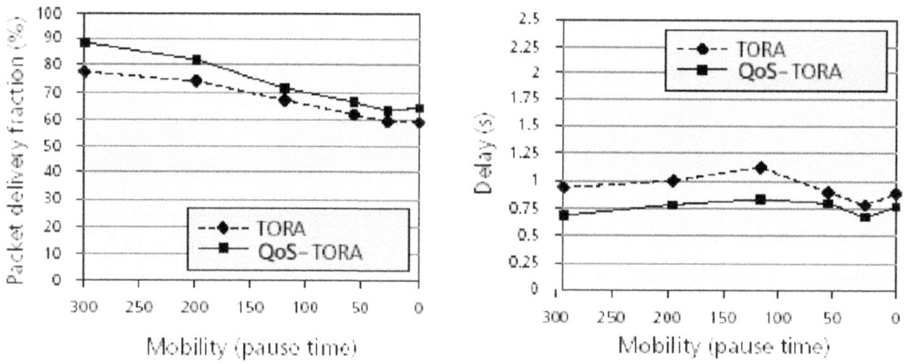

Fig. 4.

6 Conclusion

In this paper, QoS-TORA was proposed to provide QoS assurance in ad hoc networks, and the difference between QoS-TORA and TORA was examined. Results were presented under a number of conditions to show the effectiveness of our approach. It is clear that QoS-TORA can provide a better performance comparable to TORA. Mobility affects the performance of both protocols, but it has little bit more impact on QoS-TORA than on TORA. In simulation experiment we have shown that QoS-TORA has some clear advantages over TORA. First of all, QoS-TORA gives a much smaller packet delay than TORA in most scenarios. The construction of multiple paths during route setup, and the continuous information update of neighbor's MAC layer information ensure that QoS-TORA can always select the best downstream path which has a small hop count and a short MAC layer congestion delay. Secondly, QoS-TORA has much better packet delivery ratio performance than TORA. Probabilistic routing algorithm leads to data load spreading with consequent automatic load balancing and reducing load of backbone router. Multi-path routing contributes less congestion possibility so fewer packets will be destroyed in MAC layer. In the case of TORA, it is easy to cause some important node in best routing path to fail too early. An interesting issue for our future research is taking some more selection parameters such as energy status or geographical information of mobile nodes taken into account. We also plan to do further work with QoS-TORA in congestion control because congestion in a wireless network at a node is related to congestion in its one-hop neighborhood and it can be avoided by a QoS flows.

References

1. Chlamtac, I., Conti, M., Liu, J.J.N.: Mobile ad hoc networking: Imperatives and challenges. Ad Hoc Networks 1(1), 13–64 (2003)
2. Braden, R., Clark, D., Shenker, S.: Integrated services in the Internet
3. Wu, K., Harms, J.: QoS Support in Mobile Ad Hoc Networks. Crossing Boundaries- the GSA Journal of University of Alberta 1(1), 92–106 (2001)
4. Park, V., Corson, S.: Temporally Ordered Routing Algorithm (TORA) version 1 functional specification, draft-ietf-manet-tora-spec-04:txt (July 2001)
5. Sinha, P., Sivakumar, R., Bhargavan, V.: CEDAR: a Core- Extraction Distributed Ad hoc Routing Algorithm. In: IEEE INFOCOM, New York, NY (1999)
6. Baras, J.S., Mehta, H.: A probabilistic emergent routing algorithm for mobile ad hoc networks. In: WiOpt 2003: Modeling and Optimization in Mobile, Ad Hoc and Wireless Networks (Febaury 2003)
7. Hussien, O.H., Saadawi, T.N., Lee, M.J.: Probability Routing Algorithm for Mobile Ad Hoc Networks Resources Management. IEEE Journal on Selected Areas in Communications 23(12) (December 2005)
8. Wang, Z., Crowcroft, J.: Quality-of-service routing for supporting multimedia applications. IEEE J. Select. Areas Commun. 14(7), 1228–1234 (1996)
9. Park, V., Corson, S.: Temporally Ordered Routing Algorithm (TORA) Version 1 Functional Specification, draft-ietf-manet-tora-spec-00.txt, work in progress (November 1997)
10. UCB LBNL VINT Group, Network Simulator (Version 2)
11. `http://mash.cs.berkeley.edu/ns`

Authentication Process in IEEE 802.11: Current Issues and Challenges

Dinesh Yadav and Anjali Sardana

Department of Electronics and Computer Engineering,
Indian Institute of Technology Roorkee,
Roorkee, India
{dyiitpec,anjlsfec}@ iitr.ernet.in

Abstract. Authentication is a challenging area in wireless networks. The authentication process of IEEE 802.11i is using the standards of IEEE 802.1X for authentication; and for key management and distribution 4-way handshake protocol is used. In this paper, we exhaustively review the authentication technique in IEEE 802.11i. The work presents a security analysis of authentication technique which shows its strengths against various threats and some flaws which are responsible for security breaches. The paper compares and contrasts the techniques and points out current issues and challenges.

Keywords: Wireless LAN, IEEE 802.11i, 4-way handshake, network security.

1 Introduction

Wireless Local Area Networks have flexibility in deployment and use along with high transmission rate in comparison to cellular systems. However, security is a major concern because the signals of wireless networks are open for public access within a certain range. Initially IEEE 802.11 [1], also known as WLAN, was providing the security and authentication using Wired Equivalent Privacy (WEP) protocol. But major design flaws have been indicated in [2-7]. Therefore, a Temporal Key Integrity Protocol (TKIP) was introduced by Wi-Fi Alliance to provide better security through Message Integrity Code (MICHAEL), Sequence counter (TSC) and a key mixing function. Instead of using open system authentication or shared key authentication mechanism, a new mechanism called IEEE 802.1X/Extensible Authentication Protocol (EAP) was developed for authentication. Recently, another standard, the IEEE 802.11i [8], was proposed for providing data confidentiality, integrity and replay protection. In it, for authentication purpose combination of IEEE 802.1X authentication method and key management procedure 4-way handshake protocol were used. However, for using IEEE 802.11i security mechanism a hardware upgrade is needed to the WEP or TKIP users.

In this paper, we analyze the authentication process in IEEE 802.11i. In section 2, we present the general authentication process of IEEE 802.11i. In section 3, various attacks and their solutions related to IEEE 802.11i's authentication process have been discussed. And finally, the problems which still remain unsolved are presented in the final section of conclusion and future work directions.

D.C. Wyld et al. (Eds.): CNSA 2011, CCIS 196, pp. 100–112, 2011.

2 IEEE 802.11i Authentication

Open system authentication and shared key authentication schemes are two authentication schemes defined by IEEE 802.11. But both the mechanisms have been compromised completely. Then, IEEE 802.11i standard was introduced which has WEP, TKIP and Counter with CBC-MAC Mode Protocol (CCMP) encryption algorithms. WEP and TKIP are not long term solutions as they have the flaws of the RC4 encryption algorithm and are vulnerable to many attacks defined in [2, 5]. Thus, CCMP remains the only practical solution for data confidentiality and integrity. For the authentication purpose IEEE 802.11i [8, 9] defines the operations of the Robust Security Networks (RSN) and a 4-way handshake protocol.

2.1 Robust Security Network Association (RSNA)

In RSNA, first information about network security and capability are exchanged between the station and access points. Then mutual authentication is performed using IEEE 802.1X standard for port based network access control and Extensible authentication protocol (EAP). As shown in the Fig. 1, both supplicant and authenticator contain a port access entity (PAE) that manages the authentication mechanism in IEEE 802.1X [8]. Before the authentication, only IEEE 802.1X messages are transferred using the uncontrolled port.

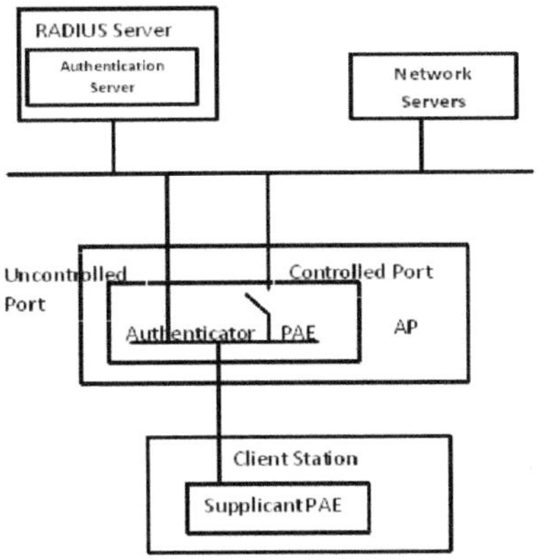

Fig. 1. IEEE 802.1X framework

Authentication process of IEEE 802.11i has three components supplicant, authenticator and authenticator server, i.e., the remote authentication dial in user service (RADIUS). Authentication process starts as shown in the Fig. 2. Initially, either AP broadcasts its security capabilities in a specific channel through the beacon frame periodically or responds to a supplicant's probe request through a probe response frame. After network discovery an open system authentication process is used for backward compatibility. After this step, the access point and the supplicant are authenticated and associated, but IEEE 802.1X port remains blocked.

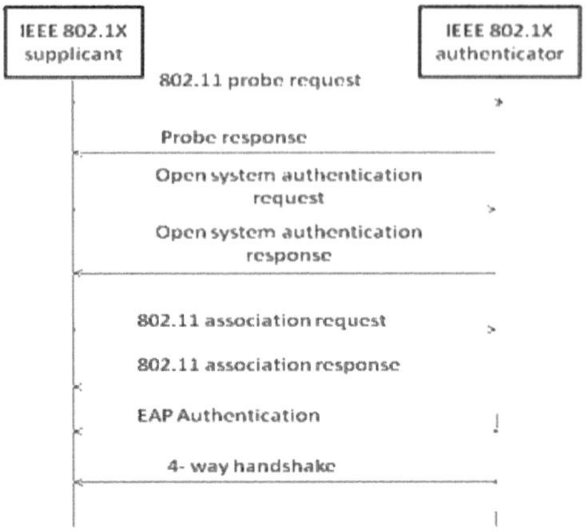

Fig. 2. Robust security network association

Now the supplicant and the authentication server mutually authenticate them using the authenticator (AP) as a relay and one of the authentication protocol of IEEE 802.1X (e.g. EAP-TLS). Now the supplicant and the authentication server generate master session key (MSK) which is further used in generating Pairwise Master Key (PMK). This step can also be skipped if the static Pre Shared Key (PSK) is used, or when a cached PMK is used during Re-association. Regardless of whether the PMK is derived from IEEE 802.1X protocol or based on a static PSK, a 4-way handshake protocol must be executed for generating fresh Pairwise Transient Key (PTK) for each new session.

2.2 4-Way Handshake Protocol

After generating the PMK, the 4-way handshake protocol is executed as shown in the Fig. 3. In the form of first message the access point sends the random number ANonce and MAC address of itself. In response, the supplicant generates another random number, SNonce, and sends it to the AP with the MAC address and message integrity code (MIC) using PTK. The PTK is generated with the help of PMK, MAC addresses of AP and the supplicant, and ANonce and SNonce.

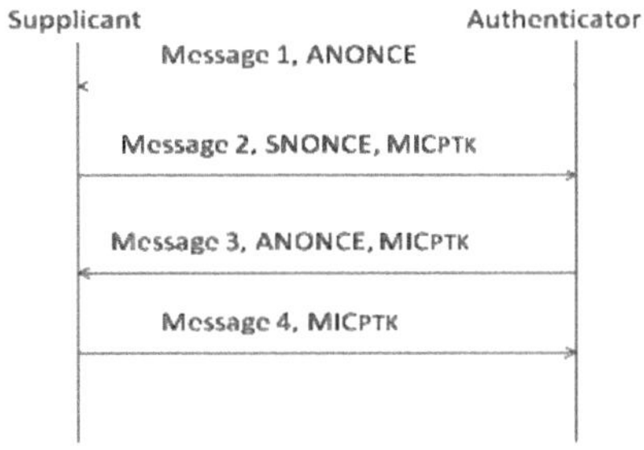

Fig. 3. 4-way handshake protocol

Now a third message is sent by the AP after generating PTK and verifying MIC. Now supplicant verifies MIC of message 3 and sends a MIC and install PTK at supplicant. After receiving message 4, AP also installs PTK. PTK is divided into three parts: Key Confirmation Key (KCK), Key Encryption Key (KEK) and Temporal Key (TK). KCK is used to authenticate message 2, 3 and 4; KEK is used to protect group key distribution and TK is used to provide confidentiality during subsequent data transmissions.

The PTK can be renewed either periodically or on the request from the supplicant to the authenticator by executing another 4-way handshake with the same PMK. Authenticator and supplicant silently discard the received message having erroneous MIC. When the supplicant does not receive message 1 within the expected time interval after a successful IEEE 802.1X authentication, it will dissociate, de-authenticate and try another authenticator. On the other hand, the authenticator will timeout and retry the message if it does not receive the expected reply within the configured time interval.

2.3 Security Analysis

Complete analysis of authentication has been done considering possible threats. Since the management frames are not protected in a WLAN, an adversary is capable of interfering with initially step of AP discovery and IEEE 802.11 association and authentication. Spoofed security capabilities and topological views of the network can be sent to a supplicant on behalf of an authenticator by an adversary. Once this occurs, the supplicant will be forced to use inappropriate security parameters to communicate with the legitimate authenticator, or associate with a malicious AP. if no further protections are used, an adversary can forge association requests to the authenticator with weak security capabilities, which might cause problems. Fortunately, these threats are eliminated in IEEE 802.1X authentication if a strong mutual authentication is implemented. The main purpose of authentication is to prevent an intruder from modifying, and forging authentication packets.

If PSK is used instead of PMK, then the AP and the supplicant can authenticate each other by verifying shared key (PSK or cached PMK) and active and passive eavesdropping and message interception can be eradicated. Session hijacking can be possible even if a strong authentication mechanism is implemented. However, it does not pose any threat more than eavesdropping, because the adversary can disconnect a station by forging de-authentication or disassociation messages and hijack the session with AP on behalf of the legitimate station. In this case, the adversary can only accept packet which are encrypted using PTK, so he can't know what is inside the packet.

Man in the middle attack can be launched, if mutual authentication mechanism is not appropriately implemented. This vulnerability is a weakness of the specific mutual authentication protocol instead of 802.11i and so the mutual authentication should be implemented carefully. The adversary can forward credentials between the AP and the station; but since the authentication packets cannot be used further like in replay attack, so an adversary can't cause more damage than eavesdropping, he can only relay the packets.

From the above discussion, the complete RSNA process seems to be secure for authentication process. Since the adversary could interfere with IEEE 802.11

authentication and association step, it might be able to fool the authenticator and the supplicant, and prevent completion of the RSNA. In addition, some implementations might also allow a reflection attack in the 4-way handshake protocol. Although the link between the authenticator and the authentication server is assumed to be secure, dictionary attacks will still be a threat for the shared secret in RADIUS. When a 256-bit PSK is used instead of PMK, this PSK could be derived from a passphrase, which makes the PSK vulnerable to dictionary attacks [10]. For eliminating this vulnerability, a good passphrase or a 256-bit random value should be chosen carefully.

3 Attacks and Countermeasures on Authentication Process in IEEE 802.11i

3.1 DoS Attacks

An adversary can launch DoS attacks because of much vulnerability in the authentication process and frame structure. Management frames and control frames are not secure in a WLAN, so an adversary can easily forge these frames and launch a DoS attack. The most efficient management frame attack is to forge and repeatedly send Deauthentication or Disassociation frames. The major problem with control frames lies in the virtual carrier-sense mechanism like RTS frame [11, 12]. Even in the presence of IEEE 802.11i security mechanism, this problem persists. Central Manager can be a solution for handling these frames and can identify the forged frames by their abnormal behavior [13]. However, extra functionality requirement in the authentication server and needs of keeping the state of all the supplicants makes it infeasible because of increase in the workload of server. Alternatively, if the Deauthentication and Disassociation frames are forged, then 4-Way Handshake can be restarted. This method could limit the impact of forged Disassociation and Deauthentication to the 802.11 MAC. However, periodically forcing a 4-Way Handshake could be an effective DoS attack. On the basis of above discussion, authenticating management frames seems to be a better approach. But the management and control frames appear frequently and authenticating them will add too much overhead and will make the system inefficient. Therefore, it might be a better approach to handle forged control frames by checking the validity of the virtual carrier-sense according to the knowledge of the specific frames. In [14], a new framework is proposed for management and control frames. It employs 16 bits, spared by replacing CRC32 in the FCS Field with CRC16, for authentication of these frames. But the replacement degrades the error detection capability but not very significantly. It also requires certain amendments in the 802.11 Control and Management Frames FCS field.

Now, several DoS attacks, that could exploit the unprotected EAP messages in 802.1X authentication, are described. Specifically, forging of EAPOL-Start messages can prevent the 802.1X authentication from succeeding, forge EAPOL-Success message can maliciously bring up the 802.1X data port in the supplicant without authentication, and forge EAPOL-Failure message and EAPOL-Logoff message can disconnect the supplicant. For eliminating this vulnerability, ignoring these messages is a good solution. This will not affect the functionality and logic of the protocol. The outcome of the subsequent 4-Way Handshake could take the role of EAPOL-Success and EAPOL-Failure to indicate the authentication result; EAPOL-Logoff could be replaced by Deauthentication to disconnect a client; and EAPOL-Start is not necessary for the protocol.

By flooding of forged Association Request frames on AP can also create a DoS attack. From this, the EAP Identifier space will be exhausted instantly, which is only 8 bits long (0-255). This flaw can be removed by careful considerations during implementation. When the EAP identifier space has been exhausted, then the AP can adopt a separate counter for EAP identifier for each association. Using this technique AP will not deny any association request and can serve all the requests.

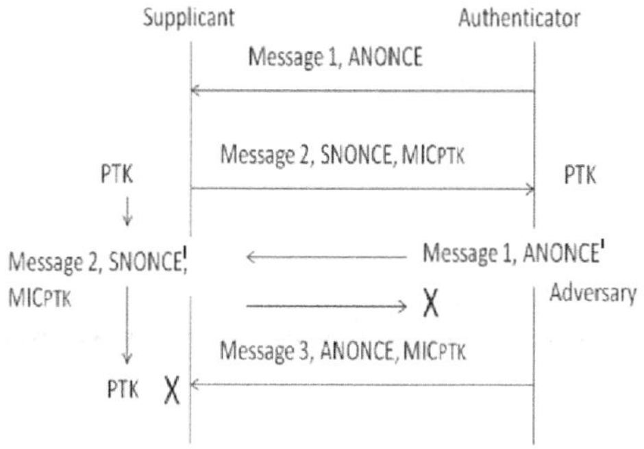

Fig. 4. DoS attack on 4-way handshake protocol

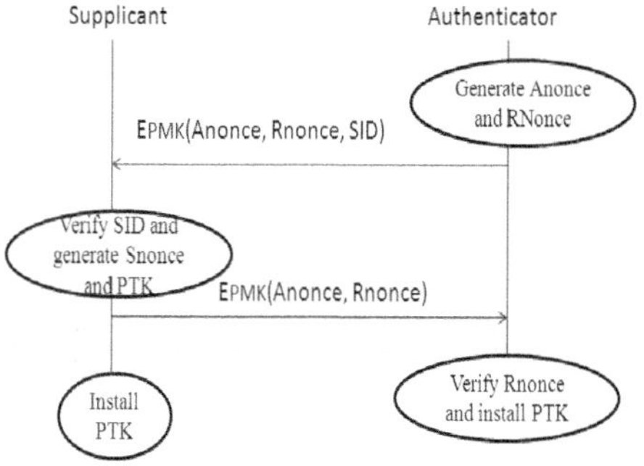

Fig. 5. 2-way handshake protocol

In 4-way handshake protocol, message1 is totally unprotected; therefore DoS attacks can be performed. For this purpose an adversary sends a fake message1 with a different ANonce' to the supplicant, before the message3 is sent by authenticator as shown in the Fig. 4. The supplicant treat it as a retransmission from authenticator and generate a new PTK' using ANonce' and then sends message2' to authenticator. This message2' is discarded and PTK synchronization is disrupted. Now supplicant has PTK' and authenticator is having PTK, so message3 sent by authenticator is invalidated by PTK' at supplicant and silently dropped and 4-way handshake protocol fails this way.

There are several approaches to address these vulnerabilities. In first approach, a queue with random-drop policy can be implemented by the supplicant [15]. This technique does not eliminate the vulnerability; it only helps to mitigate this flaw. In second approach, authentication of message1 can be used, because authentication has been already finished between authenticator and supplicant and they have shared some secret [15]. However, some modifications to the message format are required for applying this; besides this a monotonically increasing sequence number must be included to prevent replay attack. In third approach, same nonce can be used in the supplicant side for all received message1s until a 4-way handshake completes successfully. In this method, supplicant stores only one nonce, and calculates a PTK based on this stored nonce and the nonce received in the message1 from authenticator, and then verifies the MIC. In this approach minor modifications are needed in the algorithm on the supplicant side; the supplicant only needs to store one nonce, this eliminates the possibility of memory exhaustion. However, the supplicant will consume more computation power because it needs to calculate the same PTK twice for the received message1 and message3, given that the received nonces and derived PTKs are not stored. The supplicant needs to decide on the tradeoff between the memory and the CPU consumption. As a combined solution, the supplicant can re-use the same nonce for all message1s to eliminate this vulnerability, and store one entry of the derived PTK to improve the performance [15].

For handling this vulnerability, a 2-way handshake protocol is also proposed in [16]. As shown in the Fig. 5, the authenticator sends a message encrypted by PMK having ANonce, a big random number, RNonce, and other elements as in message1 of the 4-way handshake. After receiving this message, the supplicant generates PTK using ANonce and sends SNonce and RNonce. Then, the authenticator verifies the RNonce and installs PTK.

This method looks perfect but PMK is used for symmetric encryption of first message, which is a big flaw. In [17], it is shown that some tools like aircrack [18] can crack the PMK using dictionary attack, therefore it is not secure to encrypt by PMK. The authors then propose a multikey encryption scheme, which is more secure but requires more computational power.

3.2 Reflection Attack

This attack is possible when the authenticator and the supplicant are implemented on the same device. Then, an adversary can take advantage of symmetric cryptographic mechanism of 4-way handshake and shared PMK. When such a device (victim) is playing the role of authenticator, the adversary will start another 4-way handshake with the same parameters but with the victim device acting as the supplicant. Once the victim computes messages as a supplicant, the adversary could use these messages as valid response to the previous 4-way handshake initialized by the victim.

This scenario is mainly seen in ad-hoc networks, where each device has to serve the both roles to distribute their own GTKs. Some might argue that this is not a real threat because the adversary could not decrypt the following data packets without the appropriate key materials. However, it is still valuable to point out the problem because the attack violates mutual authentication and the attacker can save the encrypted data for further analysis.

For eliminating this vulnerability, the role of devices must be limited to only one either authenticator or supplicant. Another solution of this problem is use of different PMKs for different roles.

3.3 Rollback Attack

This attack is only feasible when the network supports the Pre-RSNA algorithms. IEEE 802.11i strictly prohibits the use of Pre-RSNA, but for migration support it also defines transient security network (TSN) which enables the use of both Pre-RSNA and RSNA. In this attack, the adversary either perform a man in the middle attack or forges the beginning management frames in a timely way, i.e., Beacon or Probe Response frame to the supplicant and Association Request frame to the authenticator.

In this attack, the attacker is impersonating as the authenticator, forge the Beacon or Probe Response frames to the supplicant, and indicate that only WEP (Pre-RSNA) is supported. Alternatively, the adversary can impersonate the supplicant, forging the Association Request frame in a similar way. Therefore, the supplicant and the authenticator will establish a Pre-RSNA connection, even though both of them could support RSNA algorithms. Since in the Pre-RSNA, there is no provision of cipher suite verification, the authenticator and the supplicant will not detect the forgery and confirm the cipher-suites and the adversary can also disclose the default keys by exploiting the weakness of WEP, which completely make the network insecure.

The solution of this problem is that both the authenticator and the supplicant could allow only RSNA connections. However, TSN will be a better choice for providing service to more number of supplicants using appropriate policies on the choice of the security level. Specifically, the supplicant should decide whether it wants a more confidential connection (using RSNA), or it wants more availability of Internet access (using Pre-RSNA). In any event, the supplicant should have a chance to deny the Pre-RSNA algorithms, prior to initiating a connection, either manually or through some form of policy configuration. Pre-RSNA can be used only for insensitive data.

This policy will provide a good level of security, although it might cause some inconvenience. But, it is absolutely unreliable to allow the devices to choose a security level transparently, because the supplicant and authenticator have no knowledge of the authenticity in the initial steps of network discovery and association.

3.4 Robust Security Network Information Element Poisoning

This is a type of DoS attack on IEEE 802.11i. Authentication and pairwise key cipher suite selectors, a single group key cipher suite selector, an RSN Capabilities field, the PMKID (Pairwise Master Key Identifier) count, and the PMKID list are the main components of Robust Security Network Information Element (RSN IE). The supplicant should put its chosen RSN IE inside the (Re)association request and the authenticator must put the supported RSN IEs inside the Beacon and Probe Response. The security suites, which are already negotiated, are used to perform the authentication and key management protocol between the authenticator and supplicant, and encrypted data communications has been done using negotiated cipher suites. The same RSN IE in Message2 of the 4-Way Handshake as in (Re)association Request must be included by supplicant to validate the authenticity of the RSN IEs. The authenticator is also required to include the same RSN IE in message3 of the 4-Way Handshake as in the Beacon or Probe Response. After receiving a message2, the bit wise comparison RSN IE will be done by the authenticator with the message it receives in the (Re)association request from the supplicant. The supplicant will also bit-wise compare the RSN IE in message3 with the one it receives in Beacon or Probe response. If the RSN IEs are not same, then de-authentication will be done between the supplicant and a security error should be logged. This process prevents an adversary to take advantage from the supplicant and the authenticator when they are using a using a weaker security scheme. However, it will make the system vulnerable to DoS attacks.

The authenticator verifies the MIC before the RSN IE In message2 of the 4-Way Handshake, which is correct; but in message3, the supplicant checks the RSN IE before the MIC verification, and aborts the connection if the RSN IE is unmatched. From the above discussion, we can easily understand that RSN IE in message3 can easily be modified to cause the handshake to fail [19]. As shown in fig. 6, even if the check order is correct, there is another fundamental attack that will cause the RSN IE confirmation process to fail. Several bits can easily be modified in the beacon frames of a legitimate authenticator frame that are "insignificant", where "insignificant" means that, the validity of the frame and the selection of the cipher suites will be unaffected even if these bits are modified. Reserved bits and the replay counter bits in the RSN Capabilities field are such insignificant bits. Only the insignificant bits are changed, so the authenticator and the supplicant are still able to continue the authentication and key management. However, the 4-Way Handshake will always fail because the RSN IE confirmation will not succeed.

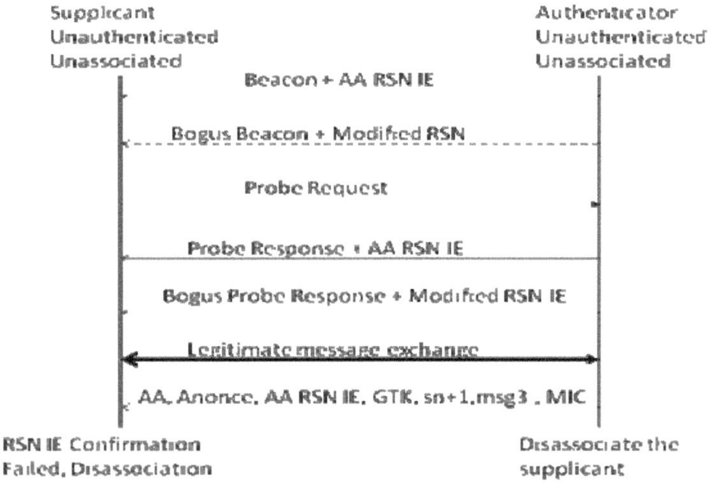

Fig. 6. RSN IE Poisoning

Based on above analysis, a DoS attack can always be launched by RSN IE poisoning. Since, the authenticator and the supplicant are not aware of this RSN IE poisoning, they will communicate regularly and will exchange an adequate amount of data, until the 4-Way Handshake fails. It means an attacker can interfere between the communication of authenticator and supplicant with a little amount of work.

This vulnerability is harmful because the management and control frames like Beacon, Probe Response, and (Re) association Request are not having any protection mechanism and message exchanges between the RSN IE negotiation and confirmation are consuming more resources and provide more time for an attacker [19]. The bit-wise comparison in the 4-way handshake is also unnecessarily strict to confirm RSN IE which makes this weakness exploitable.

This attack can be mitigated by simply ignoring the differences of the insignificant bits in the RSN IEs. In case of no change in authentication and key management suite by adversary, the RSN IE could be accepted and the correct authentication will be executed. And the supplicant and the authenticator can use the authenticated RSN IE in the 4-Way handshake for the subsequent data encryptions. However, if the authentication and key management suite selector is modified by the adversary, this can easily be detected at the beginning of the association. As a result of this, association will fail and the supplicant will retry quickly without continuing message exchanges. In the worst scenario, this modification will be detected and prevented in the 4-Way handshake.

4 Comparison among Various Solutions

Comparison of solutions of the vulnerabilities and attacks is shown in Table 1. From the table, it can easily be inferred that solutions which are suggested against DoS attacks are not sufficient. For example random drop queues are only effective when network has slow speed, not in the case of fast WLANs which are used in current scenario. Nonce reuse can cause the CPU exhaustion because of recomputation of PTK. If we use separate EAP counter in case of DoS attack generated by flooding of forged association requests, memory requirement will be very high. Therefore, we can see that almost every solution has some overheads in terms of either memory or

Table 1. Security Issues and their proposed solution in authentication process of IEEE 802.11i

S. No.	Solution	Issue addressed	Advantages	Disadvantages
1.	Use random drop queues	DoS attack due to unprotected message 1 of 4-way handshake protocol	More messages are needed to block 4-way handshake.	Increasing queue size is quite expensive and performance reductive and vulnerable in high speed networks.
2.	Nonce Reuse		Eliminate memory DoS attacks.	It can cause CPU exhaustion because of recomputation of PTK and MIC verification.
3.	Message 1 Authentication using sequence number		It will prevent the attacker from forging the message.	Vulnerable to replay attacks in case of PSK and cached PMK.
4.	2-way handshake instead of 4-way handshake and encrypt the 1st message by PMK		It costs less communication and computation time and more reliable key management.	Cached PMK and PSK is vulnerable to dictionary attack, so still not secure.

Table 1. (*Continued*)

5.	Authenticate the management and control frames using 16-bit pseudo random number in the spare bits of CRC16 which is used instead of CRC32		No need of up-gradation of hardware. It can employ for authentication of both management and control frames.	It requires certain amendments in the 802.11 Control and Management Frames FCS field and error checking capability will also be degraded.
6.	Limit a role of device either authenticator or supplicant	Reflection attack if a device is implemented to play the role of both the supplicant and authenticator.	Provide security against reflection attack.	This solution is not feasible in ad-hoc networks.
7.	Require separate roles to have different PMKs.		It can also work in ad-hoc network against reflection attack.	More PMK are needed and computation will be increased.
8.	Limit Pre-RSNA connection to only insensitive data.	Roll back attack due to Pre-RSNA algorithm support	Support migration in Pre-RSNA and RSNA networks.	Always depend on policy maker of network.
9.	Ignore the IE differences of insignificant bits of RSN IEs.	RSN IE Poisoning due to insecure management frames.	Remove the DoS attack due to RSN IE poisoning.	It requires minor modification to the algorithm.
10.	Use Multi key encryption scheme.	Vulnerable PMK towards dictionary attack.	It makes the PMK guessing almost impossible.	It does not secure message1 of the 4-way handshake protocol, so still vulnerable to DoS attacks.
11.	Use separate EAP counter for each association.	DoS attack by flooding forged association requests.	Removal of forged association requests	Memory required is high.

computational power. Most of the policy makers can also be the cause of attacks in the network, like in case of roll back attack, role of policy maker is vital and if they are having wrong information about Pre-RSNA support of the network, then the network will be flawed. In case of reflection attack, policy maker will decide that a device should not act as both authenticator and supplicant. Against the dictionary attacks, multi key encryption scheme is flawless, still it does not provide the security against the DoS attacks which are generated due to unprotected message1. From this comparison we can easily see that none of the solution provides the complete set of security against the various DoS attacks.

5 Conclusion and Future Work

Various solutions are proposed for many problems, but some issues still remain unsolved. Network and frequency jamming are still exist which can be the cause of DoS attacks. Due to backward compatibility, open system authentication is also present due to which various attacks like man in the middle attack and message forgery etc. are also possible. For removing the DoS attacks in 4-way handshake protocol, a 2-way handshake protocol has been proposed, but it is solely dependent on secrecy of PMK. However, PMK can be cracked using tools like aircrack which are based on dictionary attack. Therefore, key distribution also suffers from the DoS attacks. We conclude on the note that authentication mechanism is still vulnerable to DoS attacks. Future work can be directed to propose an efficient technique for authentication which can give security against all of these attacks.

References

1. Hiertz, G., Denteneer, D., Stibor, L., Zang, Y., Costa, X.P., Walke, B.: The IEEE 802.11 universe. IEEE Communications Magazine 48, 62–70 (2010)
2. Fluhrer, S., Mantin, I., Shamir, A.: Weaknesses in the key scheduling algorithm of RC4. In: Vaudenay, S., Youssef, A.M. (eds.) SAC 2001. LNCS, vol. 2259, pp. 1–24. Springer, Heidelberg (2001)
3. Arbaugh, W.A., Shankar, N., Wan, Y.C.J., Zhang, K.: Your 802.11 wireless network has no clothes. IEEE Wireless Communications 9, 44–51 (2002)
4. Cam-Winget, N., Housley, R., Wagner, D., Walker, J.: Security flaws in 802.11 data link protocols. Communications of the ACM 46, 35–39 (2003)
5. Walker, J.: Unsafe at any key size: An analysis of the WEP encapsulation. IEEE document 802, 362 (2000)
6. Manley, M.E., McEntee, C.A., Molet, A.M., Park, J.S.: Wireless security policy development for sensitive organizations. IEEE Information assurance and security 25, 150–157 (2005)
7. Bittau, A., Handley, M., Lackey, J.: The final nail in WEP's coffin. Proceedings of the 2006 IEEE Symposium on Security and Privacy, 515–525 (2006)
8. Chen, J.C., Jiang, M.C., Liu, Y.W.: Wireless LAN security & IEEE 802.11i. IEEE Wireless Communications 12, 27–36 (2005)
9. Edney, J., Arbaugh, W.A.: Real 802.11 security: Wi-Fi protected access and 802.11i. Addison Wesley Publishing Company, Reading (2004)
10. Moskowitz, R.: Weakness in passphrase choice in WPA interface (2003), `http://www.wifinetnews.com/archive/002452.html`
11. Bellardo, J., Savage, S.: 802.11 Denial-of-Service attacks: real vulnerabilities and practical solutions. In: Proceedings of the USENIX Security Symposium, pp. 15–28 (2003)
12. Chen, D., Deng, J., Varshney, P.K.: Protecting wireless networks against a Denial of Service attack based on virtual jamming. In: Poster Session of MobiCom 2003, San Diego, CA (2003)

13. Ding, P., Holliday, J., Celik, A.: Improving the security of Wireless LANs by managing 802.1X Disassociation. In: Proceedings of the IEEE Consumer Communications and Networking Conference, Las Vegas, NV (2004)
14. Khan, M.A., Hasan, A.: Pseudo Random Number Based authentication to counter denial of service attacks on 802.11. In: The proceedings of 5th IFIP International Conference on Wireless and Optical Communications Networks (WOCN 2008), Surabaya, pp. 1–5 (2008)
15. He, C., Mitchell, C.: Analysis of the 802.11i 4-way Handshake. In: Proceedings of the ACM Workshop on Wireless Security (WiSe 2004), Philadelphia, PA, USA, pp. 43–50 (2004)
16. Liu1, J., Ye, X., Zhang, J., Li, J.: Security Verification of 802.11i 4-way Handshake Protocol. In: ICC proceedings, pp. 1642–1647 (2008)
17. Hung, C.C., Wu, E.H., Wu, C.L., Gau, R.L., Chen, Y.C.: A Multi-Key Encryption Scheme for the Next Generation Wireless Network. Journal of Computers 18(4) (2008)
18. Aircrack-ng tool, http://www.aircrack-ng.org/
19. Changhua, H., Mitchell, J.C.: Security Analysis and Improvements for IEEE 802.11i. In: 12th Annual Network and Distributed System Security Symposium, California, pp. 90–110 (2005)

Network Level Anomaly Detection System Using MST Based Genetic Clustering

P. Kola Sujatha, R. Arun, P.V. Shanthoosh, I. Ezra Prince Jebahar, and A. Kannan

Anna Unniversity, Chennai, India
{pkolasujatha,kannan}@annauniv.edu

Abstract. With the ubiquitousness and far reaching effects of Internet, the role played by Internet security systems becomes very critical. There arises an imminent need for an in force Intrusion Detection Systems (IDS). In this paper, we propose a blend of an anomaly detection system and misuse detection system. A two-phase Intrusion Detection System (IDS) involves Misuse Detection System using supervised learning techniques and Anomaly Detection System using unsupervised learning techniques. Anomalies are outliers, corresponding to attacks characterized by isolated, sparse clusters. MST based Clustering identifies the outliers by exploiting the isolation property. But in this process, some group of normal packets may be broken into sparse clusters. Our Genetic Algorithm based Optimization combines the sparse normal clusters with sufficiently close normal clusters. The resulting clusters can directly correspond to normal or anomalous types. Experimental results performed using KDD Cup 1999 dataset proved that the proposed method provides significantly high detection rates compared to other techniques.

Keywords: IDS, Anomaly Detection, Misuse Detection, Supervised Learning, MST based Genetic Clustering.

1 Introduction

With the Internet playing a vital role in incessant communication, its effectiveness can diminish owing to effects –Intrusions. Intrusion is an activity that adversely affects the targeted system. An intrusion may compromise the integrity, confidentiality and availability of resources of the attacked system. With ever increasing network connectivity, there is an increasing threat of intrusions to systems. A network based intrusion detection system (NIDS) maintains a log of packet traffic to the system for intrusion detection. With the knowledge of signatures of known attacks, supervised learning techniques can be used to train the NIDS and detect these known attacks. However the knowledge about attack type of the logged packet data may not always be available. Attack signatures unknown to the Misuse Detection System, known as novel attacks cannot be detected correctly by the IDS. In such cases Anomaly Detection can be employed.

Anomaly Detection is based on unsupervised learning techniques, which can be used to detect novel or previously unknown attacks. This paper describes an Anomaly Detection System that employs clustering to partition the logged packet data. A

D.C. Wyld et al. (Eds.): CNSA 2011, CCIS 196, pp. 113–122, 2011.

cluster is a grouping of tuples or patterns in the data set such that intra-cluster similarity is high whereas inter-cluster similarity is low. An out-lier in the clustering result corresponds to an anomalous attack packet. Outliers are characterized by their sparseness and isolation from the rest of the clusters.

Many graph based clustering algorithms can cluster the data based on connectivity, viewing the tuples as vertices of a complete graph. Minimum Spanning Tree (MST) based clustering constructs a minimum spanning tree from the graph of data points. Other approaches to clustering exist such as k-means and k-medoids which result in a cluster arrangement with 'k' clusters based on a proximity measure from a cluster centre or a centroid. Such techniques cannot detect outliers. In fact, presence of outliers affects ideal clustering results. MST based techniques can easily identify outliers based on graph connectivity, by removing inconsistent edges.

Due to some constraints on the clustering algorithm, some normal data points end up being grouped as anomalies due to their sparseness. But unlike anomalies, they are not isolated from other clusters. This is resolved by our Genetic Clustering algorithm.

In clustering the number of clusters cannot be determined accurately. Many approaches have been proposed for estimating the number of clusters. The selection of the number of clusters affects the final clustering results. Similarly, the number of outliers and their groupings cannot be estimated before the application of the clustering algorithm. If the number of outliers expected is less than the actual number, the algorithm ends up missing some outliers. On the other hand, an overestimation results in normal points being grouped as outliers.

The proposed work first constructs a Minimum Spanning Tree from the tuples in the given data set. Assuming an upper bound on the number of outliers, the inconsistent edges are removed such that then sub graphs, on either side of the edge removed, remain connected. Then a Fitness function for Genetic Algorithm is defined that results in sparse normal clusters being combined to nearby normal clusters.

2 Related Works

KDD CUP 1999 Dataset [12] was to learn a predictive model (i.e. a classifier) capable of distinguishing between legitimate and illegitimate connections in a computer network. The competition task was to build a network intrusion detector, a predictive model capable of distinguishing between "bad" connections, called intrusions or attacks, and "good" normal connections. This database contains a standard set of data to be audited, which includes a wide variety of intrusions simulated in a military network environment.

KDD CUP '99 provided a training set with packet data along with the labels of attack types to train the IDS. It provided a training set that contained along with the known attack packets, a few attacks of unknown type. The test set provided only the packet information without providing the class of the attack. Misuse Detection Systems have been developed based on supervised learning techniques like Bayesian Classification, Neural Networks, Decision Trees and Rule Based Learning. Such systems typically need a substantially large training set with a dedicated time for training. After training, the system can be used on a test set.

Table 1. Basic features in KDD CUP 1999 Dataset from TCP/IP

feature name	*description*	*type*
duration	length (number of seconds) of the connection	continuous
protocol_type	type of the protocol, e.g. tcp, udp, etc.	discrete
service	network service on the destination, e.g., http, telnet, etc.	discrete
src_bytes	number of data bytes from source to destination	continuous
dst_bytes	number of data bytes from destination to source	continuous
flag	normal or error status of the connection	discrete
land	1 if connection is from/to the same host/port; 0 otherwise	discrete
wrong_fragment	number of ``wrong'' fragments	continuous
urgent	number of urgent packets	continuous

MINDS IDS was the first system to use deviation from normality as a case of a novel attack. Anomaly Detection Systems predominantly use clustering techniques. Many minimum spanning tree based clustering algorithms have been proposed. Many inconsistency measures have been defined for removing edges. [1] provides a strategy for reducing the time required for constructing a MST. It proposes to use a spanning tree, rather than a Minimum Spanning Tree and performs clustering on the data recursively. This paper follows the assumption that larger clusters correspond to normal data packets in an IDS during the application of the clustering algorithm.

Genetic Algorithms can be used as a search technique that searches among a set of solutions-called species, the ones that are the fittest. A fitness function gives the fitness of a species. The algorithm must also create newer search spaces from the existing population by means of reproduction. Reproduction is achieved by selecting two parents randomly from the current population of species and performing the genetic operations of crossover and mutation.

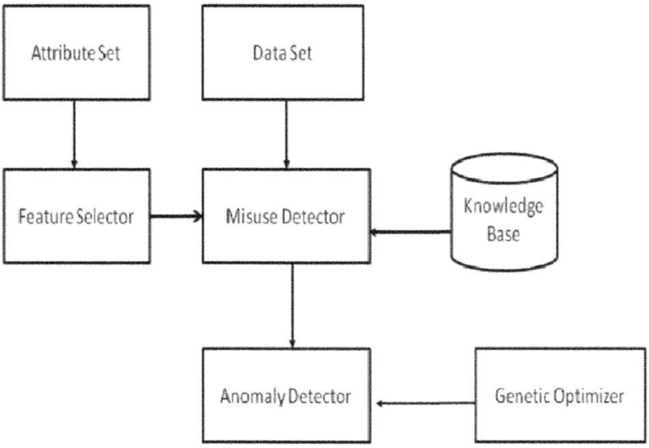

Fig. 1. System Architecture

The Schema Theorem proves that the number of species having fitness higher than average fitness of the current population increases geometrically with every population. Typically the genetic algorithm's fitness function closely follows the expected features of some clustering methods. We have combined Genetic Algorithms with traditional clustering techniques leading to hybrid method.

3 Minimum Spanning Tree Based Clustering

3.1 Outliers

Minimum spanning tree (MST) based clustering method is a graph based clustering technique [8]. Each point in the dataset is considered as a vertex in an undirected graph G. It can be assumed that the graph is complete, that is, every vertex has an edge to every other vertex. Traditional MST Based algorithms start by finding a minimum spanning tree of the graph G. For a graph with 'n' vertices, an MST has 'n'-1 edges.

Clusters from a MST have been formed by removing inconsistent edges. The removal of a single edge from a MST results in partitioning of the graph into a sub graph with two components. If 'k' inconsistent edges from a MST and the subsequent sub-graph are removed, we will be left with ('k'+1) components. Each component is considered as a cluster. Inconsistency of an edge is based on multiple factors. The most straight forward one is to use the largest edge in the sub graph as the most inconsistent.

The utility of MST lies in the fact that it can easily detect outliers. Outliers can be a sparse sub-cluster with one or more vertices. Our aim is to detect these outliers which correspond to anomalies in the data set. MST can be constructed by Prim's algorithm, Kruskal's algorithm or Reverse Delete Algorithm.

Other partition clustering algorithms like k-means and k-medoids include an out-lier to one of its nearest neighbor cluster center. As a result, clusters over-fit to include an out-lier to a cluster. For example, the k-means algorithm aims to minimize the intra cluster distance from a cluster center and is forced to assign outliers to some clusters. This assignment may shift the natural configuration of clusters in the actual data. As a result some natural clusters may be distorted or broken up and the cluster centers may be displaced. Further it is not possible to detect outliers easily.

It can be seen that if the partitioning caused by removing an inconsistent edge based on edge length results in a component with a few vertices, then the group of vertices correspond to outliers. By fixing a lower bound for the number of vertices in a valid cluster, we can easily determine the outliers. A new component is an outlier if the number of vertices is below the lower bound set.

In this approach, care must be taken to choose a correct value of number of clusters 'k', which is roughly determines the number of anomalous clusters. If k is too large, valid clusters will be broken and normal data points will be misrepresented as outliers. If 'k' is too small, some outliers will be left undetected. So choosing the correct value of 'k' is crucial to the detection of all outliers.

3.2 Sparse Normal Clusters

As seen before in order to identify the outliers we need to choose an appropriate value for ‘k’, the number of clusters. Usually before the algorithm finds all anomalous clusters, breaks sparse clusters from normal clusters. Now our task is to group the normal sub-clusters, lest they might be identified as outliers if they are sparse. A primary characteristic of normal data points as opposed to outliers is that normal clusters are relatively more crowded with many data points and are distributed close to other normal clusters. Thus a sparse cluster exhibiting this character can be a normal data point cluster and hence must not be misconstrued as an anomaly. We must devise a strategy to combine such sparse clusters to form larger clusters so that we can tell them apart from isolated sparse clusters.

To achieve this end, our initial clusters from the clustering algorithm have been combined to minimize intra cluster distance and maximize distance of separation of a cluster center to some near cluster centers. Our problem is to search for cluster centers with the above property and retain them in the final configuration. In such a configuration, the sparse clusters will correspond to anomalies and other clusters to normal packets. This search procedure is modeled as a —Genetic Algorithm Search .

4 Genetic Clustering

4.1 Coding

The clusters from the MST Based clustering can be used as the parameters to be coded. In a species of the population, a bit with value 1 indicates that the corresponding cluster is intact and the cluster center is preserved. A bit with value 0 indicates that the corresponding cluster is rejected. Before calculating the fitness function, every point in the rejected cluster is associated with a selected cluster in the species (with bit set 1) whose center is the nearest neighbor of that point.

4.2 Fitness Function

The aim of the Genetic Algorithm search is to find the clustering configuration such that all sparse clusters correspond to anomalous packets, while no normal packet is in a sparse cluster. This can be achieved by combining many sparse sub-clusters of normal cluster into larger clusters.

We aim to retain clusters with low intra cluster distance and high inter cluster distance to a set of near cluster centers. Average distance of all points in a cluster to its cluster center, known as the average cluster separation is an indication of the intra cluster distance. The distance of the *kn* nearest cluster centers from the current cluster center is an indication of the inter cluster distance of the current cluster. The value has to be maximized for a given configuration.

Fitness function maps the intra cluster and inter cluster distances of all selected clusters in the species to a real value in the range (0.0 - 1.0). So distance measures are normalized. The higher the value returned by the function, higher is the fitness of the configuration. But the intra cluster distance is minimized whereas the inter cluster distance is maximized. The fitness function maps lower intra cluster distances to better fitness by determining the difference between the current intra cluster distance and the highest intra cluster distance found in a generation. This when added to the intra cluster measure found out, can provide an appropriate value for fitness. Fitness of a species monotonically increases with the value returned by the fitness function.

$$\boldsymbol{\Phi(i) = \mu(i) + \beta(i, kn)}$$

$$\boldsymbol{\mu(i) = d_{max} - \delta(i)}$$

Φ - *Fitness Function*

μ - *Intra Distance Measure*

β - *Inter Distance Measure*

d_{max} - *Maximum Distance*

δ - *Average Cluster Separation*

where *i* is the bit set to 1 in the population corresponding to the ith cluster center and *kn* is the number of nearest cluster centers to consider for inter cluster distance.

d_{max} is the maximum average cluster separation of the species generated by GA so far.

4.3 Overall System

This section describes how the Genetic Clustering based MST Clustering Anomaly Detection System fits into the entire IDS. A misuse detection phase usually precedes the anomaly detection phase. During misuse detection a confidence value is attributed to the classification result. For trained attack classes the value will be sufficiently high. However for untrained types of packets both normal packets and novel attacks, the confidence will be low. During a session such low confidence packets are gathered and anomaly detection is applied only to such packets.

While anomaly detection can point out deviation from normality, the notion of normality is not well defined. Normality is usually assumed to correspond to the characteristics of the most prevalent behavior observed.. However if anomalous packets dominate the dataset during a session, this assumption will fail. This could be overcome if a known large normal set is combined with the data for which anomaly detection has to be applied, such that the normal data dominates the data set. In this way the normality assumption will hold and Anomaly Detection System will not be misled by the prevalence of abnormal behavior.

Table 2. Performance Measure before Optimization

Number Of Samples	True Positive	False Positive	Most Frequent Attack
5000	89.4	0.4	Smurf
5000	88.8	0.3	Guess_passwd
6000	88	0.45	Portsweep
5500	80.3	0.48	Satan
5500	82.8	0.5	Teardrop
6000	88	0.6	Loadmodule
5500	82.56	0.7	Pod
6000	82	0.69	Back
5500	89.5	0.6	Spy
5000	87.34	0.73	N-map

5 Experimental Results

The KDD CUP '99 dataset, used for the measurement of system performance over various test samples, was divided into 10 batches and the experiment was carried out for each batch of test set separately. The result is represented in Fig – 2 and 3 and the data is tabulated in Table – 2 and 3 for anomaly detection system before and after genetic optimization respectively. The figure shows False Positive Rate on y – axis and True Positive Rate on x – axis. False Positive Rate and True Positive Rate are independent of each other in the graph. The values are plotted for each test set. True Positive Rate is the proportion of attack packets identified correctly by the IDS to the total attack packets. False Positive Rate is the proportion of attack packets not identified by the IDS to the total attack packets.

During anomaly detection, we collect all suspected tuples and merge them with a known data set having a high prevalence of normal packets. This is done at the end of each session. Using the merged data, we apply the clustering algorithm and genetic

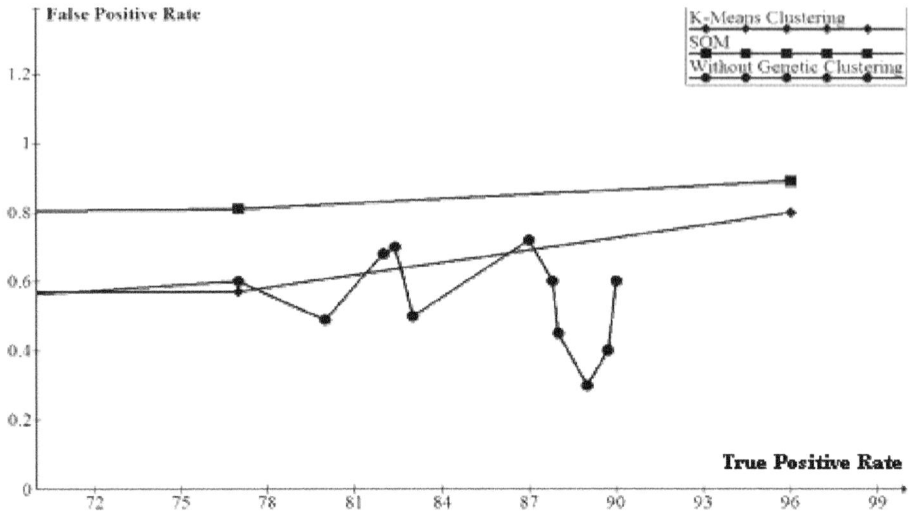

Fig 2. Performance Graph - Before Optimization

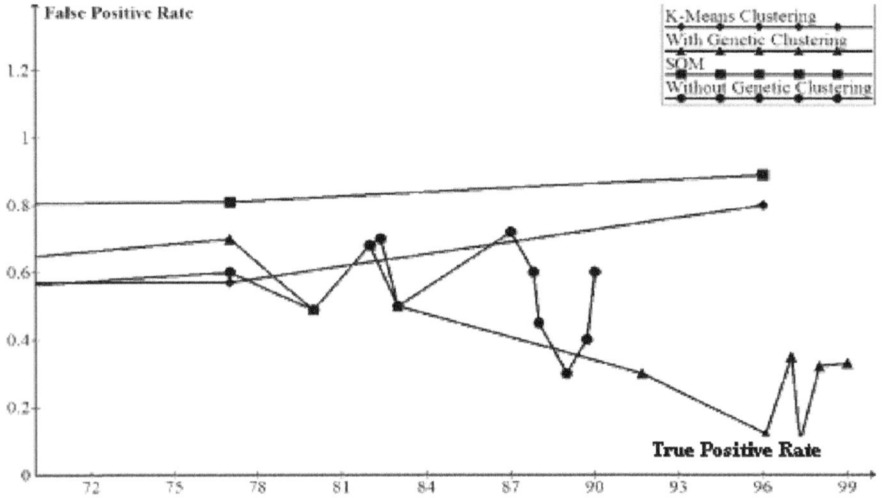

Fig. 3. Performance Graph - After Optimization

optimization. If a suspected tuple is clustered as an anomaly, then the system assumes that it corresponds to a novel attack. Otherwise the tuple corresponds to a normal packet.

For each sample the False Positive Rate and True Positive Rate are calculated as shown in the fig-3. The overall system can attain a Maximum True positive rate of 99.2% and Minimum false positive rate of 0.098 % for some test samples.

Table 3. Performance Measure after Optimization

Number of Samples	True Positive	False Positive	Most Frequent Attack
5000	97.2	0.098	Smurf
5000	98.2	0.105	Guess_passwd
6000	98.3	0.13	Portsweep
5500	96.1	0.12	Satan
5500	91.8	0.3	Teardrop
6000	97.0	0.34	Loadmodule
5500	98.4	0.33	Pod
6000	98.1	0.4	Back
5500	97.3	0.5	Spy
5000	99.2	0.32	N-map

Inferring the results in Table - 3, application of MST Based Clustering and Genetic Optimization increases the True Positive Rate significantly and reduces the False Positive Rate to some extent.

The false positive rate in the anomaly detection system is quite high, because some normal clusters in the additional data merged could be clustered as an anomaly, but we consider only the suspected packet's grouping for the final decision. The reduction in false positive rate of the IDS is mainly due to the sequencing of classification and clustering operations of the IDS.

6 Conclusion and Future Work

With the advent of improved attacks that compromise the overall security of the system, an IDS that is adaptable is necessary. We have designed such IDS that combine Clustering for Anomaly Detection and Supervised Learning for Misuse Detection. The storage of packet pattern in a knowledge base helps in determination of new attacks.

Minimum Spanning Tree (MST) is used for optimizing the clusters and the searching technique has been enhanced with the usage of Genetic Algorithm. This algorithm improves combination of existing clusters resulting in better attack pattern detection. A feature selector that we have used selects a number of features used during intrusion detection activity that is optimized by using GA-algorithm.

Our system can be deployed in a distributed environment using mobile agents so as to improve the scalability and reliability of the system. Such a system can be extended to detect distributed attacks.Instead of constructing an MST, clustering can be done by identifying the articulation points (nodes in the graph which upon removal disconnects the graph) and removing them from the graph depending upon number of clusters required.

References

1. Wang, X., Wang, X., Wilkes, D.M.: A Divide-and-Conquer Approach for Minimum Spanning Tree-Based Clustering. IEEE Transactions on Knowledge And Data Engineering 21(7), 945–958 (2009)
2. Lin, J., Ye, D., Chen, C., Gao, M.: Minimum spanning tree based spatial outlier mining and its applications. In: Wang, G., Li, T., Grzymala-Busse, J.W., Miao, D., Skowron, A., Yao, Y. (eds.) RSKT 2008. LNCS (LNAI), vol. 5009, pp. 508–515. Springer, Heidelberg (2008)
3. Jiang, M.F., Tseng, S.S., Su, C.M.: Two-Phase Clustering Process for Outliers Detection. Pattern Recognition Letters 22, 691–700 (2001)
4. Fries, T.P.: A Fuzzy-Genetic Approach to Network Intrusion Detection. Network and Computer Applications 30(1), 81–98 (2007)
5. Yu, Z., Tsai, J.J.P., Fellow, Weigert, T.: An Automatically Tuning Intrusion Detection System. IEEE Transactions on Systems, Man, And Cybernetics-Part B: Cybernetics 37(2) (April 2008)
6. Li, Y., Fang, B.-X., Chen, Y., Guo, L.: A Lightweight Intrusion Detection Model Based on Feature Selection and Maximum Entropy Model. IEEE, Los Alamitos (2004)
7. Xie, Z., Yu, L., Yang, J.: A Clustering Algorithm Based on Improved Minimum Spanning Tree. In: Fourth International Conference on Fuzzy Systems and Knowledge Discovery (FSKD 2007) (2007)
8. Jain, A.K., Dubes, R.C.: Algorithms for Clustering Data. Prentice-Hall, Englewood Cliffs (1988)
9. Goldberg, D.: Genetic Algorithms - An Introduction (1984)
10. Li, Y., Fang, B.-X., Chen, Y., Guo, L.: A Lightweight Intrusion Detection Model Based on Feature Selection and Maximum Entropy Model. IEEE, Los Alamitos (2004)
11. Han, J., Kamber, M.: Data Mining Concepts and Techniques, 2nd edn. Elsevier, Amsterdam (2006)
12. KDD cup (1999), dataset, `http://www.sigkdd.org`

A Hybrid Approach to Texture Classification

B. Vijayalakshmi[1] and V. Subbiah Bharathi[2]

[1]Assistant Professor, Dept. of MCA, Velammal College of Management and Computer Studies
vlakshmi752002@yahoo.co.in
[2] Dean (Academic), DMI College of Engineering

Abstract. The rapid expansion of the internet and the wide use of digital data have increased the need for both efficient image database creation and retrieval procedure. In this paper, texture classification based on the combination of texture features is proposed. Since most significant information of a texture often appears in the high frequency channels, the features are extracted by the computation of LBP and Texture Spectrum histogram. Euclidean distance is used for similarity measurement. The experimental result shows that 97.99% classification accuracy is obtained by the proposed method.

Keywords: Texture features, Local Binary Pattern, Texture Spectrum, Similarity measure, Texture Classification.

1 Introduction

Content based image retrieval uses only characteristics of image content without any additional caption or text information. Feature extraction is the basis for Content based image retrieval. Features may be text based features [such as keyword, annotation] or visual features [color, texture and shape]. Within visual feature scope, features can be classified as general features and domain specific features. The former include color, texture and shape, while latter is application dependent.

Texture contains important information about the structural arrangement of surfaces and their relationship to the surrounding environment. A variety of techniques ranging from statistical methods to multi resolution filtering have been developed for texture analysis. In texture analysis, the most important task is to extract texture features, which specifies textural characteristics of the original image. Tuceryan and Jain [22] divided texture analysis methods into statistical, geometrical, model based and signal processing. Recent study of human vision system indicates that spatial/frequency representation which preserves both global and local information is adequate for quasi periodic signal. This observation has motivated researchers to develop multi resolution texture models.

In the early 70's Haralick et al [5] proposed coocurrence matrix representation of texture feature. This approach explored gray level spatial dependent of texture. Tamura et al [2] explored texture representation from different angle and proposed a computational approximation on six visual properties like coarseness, contrast, directionality, linelikeness, regularity and roughness. The QBIC system and MARs system further improved Tamura's texture representation. In the early 90's, the

D.C. Wyld et al. (Eds.): CNSA 2011, CCIS 196, pp. 123–130, 2011.

wavelet transform was introduced for texture representation. Smith and Chang [28, 29] used the statistics such as mean and variance features are extracted from wavelet subbands as texture representation. Gross et al [4] used Wavelet Transform together with KL expansion and kohenon maps to perform texture analysis. Thyagarajan et al [30] and Kundu et al combined wavelet transform with coocurrence matrix to take the advantages of statistics based and transform based texture analysis. Ma and Manjunath [8] evaluated texture image annotation by using various wavelet texture representation including orthogonal and bi-orthogonal wavelet transform, tree structured wavelet transform and Gabor wavelet transform. They found that Gabor transform was best among others in the study of human vision.

The texture spectrum was initially used as a texture filtering approach (He and Wang, 1991). The key concept of this method is the computation of the relative intensity relations between the pixels in a small neighborhood and not on their absolute intensity values. The importance of the texture spectrum method is determined by the extraction of local texture information for each pixel and of the characterization of textural aspect of a digital image in the form of a spectrum. Also, Ojala *et al.* [21] proposed the uniformed local binary patterns (LBP) approach to extracting rotation and histogram equalization invariant features, which was extended by Huang, Li and Wang by computing the derivative-based local binary patterns and applied it to the application of face alignment. The approach of the conventional LBP is simple and efficient. It considers the uniform patterns in the images which will be local features of an image.

Most of the textural classification applies contextual (spatial) information. Spatial classification can be categorized into three groups 1) statistical approaches such as co-occurrence probabilities, 2) structural approach in which texture is viewed as many primitive elements such as Texel, Texton or texture unit and 3) model based approach such as Gaussian Markhov random fields and Gibbs random fields in which texture image is modeled as a probability model or linear combination of a set of basic function and coefficients of these models are the textural features.

In this paper, statistical methods are used for texture feature extraction and representation. The objective of this paper is to retrieve images accurately with the combined texture features. Local Binary pattern and Texture spectrum features are combined and provides better texture classification. The classes of texture features are investigated in classification experiments with arbitrary texture images taken from Brodatz album [12]. The classification accuracy rates are compared with that of Local Binary Pattern and Texture Spectrum methods and the results are found to be improved significantly.

This paper is organized as follows: Second section explains the model behind our work and the method of detecting the presence of texture features. In the third section, with the proposed set of textured images are represented by the global descriptor, namely Texture Spectrum and Local Binary Pattern and the experimentation with a set of standard Brodatz Textural Album. In fourth section, texture classification scheme has been explained and the classification results are presented. Finally, the conclusion about our approach and its application for unsupervised texture classification has been highlighted along with further scope of this work.

2 Methodology

2.1 Local Binary Pattern

Local Binary Pattern operator is a simple yet very efficient texture operator which labels the pixels of an image by thresholding the neighborhood of each pixel with the value of the center pixel and considers the result as a binary number. The original LBP method is a complementary measure for local image contrast. LBP extracts texture feature in spatial domain. The LBP value is determined as:

$$LBP = \sum_{i=1}^{8} E_i . 2^{i-1} \tag{1}$$

where

$$E_i = \begin{cases} 1 \text{ if } V_i \geq V_0 \\ 0 \text{ if } V_i < V_0 \end{cases} \tag{2}$$

2.2 Texture Spectrum

In a square raster digital image, each pixel is surrounded by 8 neighboring pixels. The local texture information for a pixel can be extracted from a neighborhood of 3×3 pixels, which represents the smallest complete unit. We define the corresponding texture unit by a set containing 8 elements such as: $TU = \{E_1, E_2, \ldots\ldots E_8\}$ where $E(i = 1,2,\ldots\ldots,8)$ is determined by the formula:

$$E_i = \begin{cases} 0 \text{ if } V_i < V_0 \\ 1 \text{ if } V_i = V_0 \\ 2 \text{ if } V_i > V_0 \end{cases} \tag{3}$$

for $i = 1,2,\ldots, 8$ and the element E, occupies the same position as the pixel i. As each element of TU has one of three possible values, the combination of all eight elements results in $3^8 = 6561$ possible texture units in total. The texture unit number is calculated by the following formula:

$$N_{TU} = \sum_{i=1}^{8} E_i . 3^{i-1} \tag{4}$$

Thus the statistics on frequency of occurrence of all the texture units over a large region of an image should reveal texture information. The computation of N_{TU} can be shown in Fig. 1.

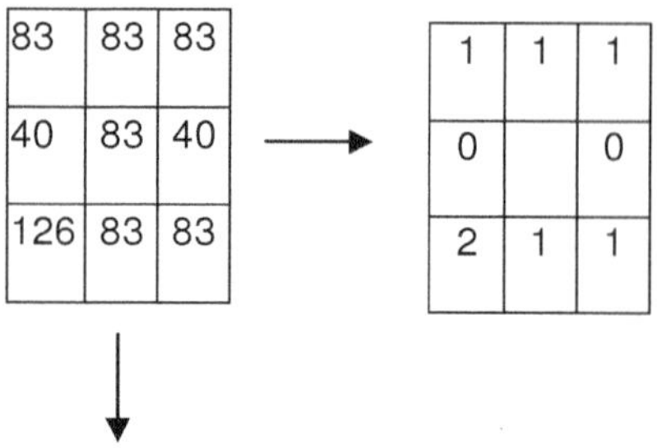

$$V = [83,83,83,83,40,83,83,126,40] \rightarrow TU = [1,1,1,0,1,1,1,2,0]$$

$$N_{TU} = 1795 .$$

Fig. 1. Transformation of neighborhood pixels to a Texture Unit with the Texture Unit number

2.3 Framework of Proposed Method

The algorithm involved in the proposed approach is as follows:-

1. Each 512×512 of Brodatz texture images are normalized to 64×64 of 64 sub images.
2. Local Binary pattern is applied to each sub images and the resultant images will be used for extracting features by texture spectrum.
3. Randomly selected 10 sub images are considered as training set and remaining sub images are testing set.
4. Compute the feature vectors for training set of images by applying Texture spectrum approach to calculate the Texture Unit (TU) number and then compute histogram and calculate mean of a feature vector.
5. Repeat step4 for compute feature vector for testing set of images.
6. Euclidean distance is used to determine the similarity measure between the trained and tested image set.

$$D_k(Q_i, D_i) = \sqrt{\sum_{i=1}^{n} (Q_i - D_i)^2} \tag{5}$$

Where Q_i represents the Query Image, D_i represents the Database Image, n is the number of feature vectors and $D_k(Q_i, D_i)$ is the distance vector between the query image and database image.

7. Images are classified based on the Minimum Distance Decision rule such as:

$$I_{sim} = \min \sum_{k=1}^{N} D_k \tag{6}$$

where I_{sim} is the similar image which belongs to the texture class and N is the number of texture classes.

3 Result and Discussion

In order to evaluate the texture features using Local Binary Pattern and Texture Spectrum in texture characterization and classification, several experimental studies carried out on 12 texture classes of brodatz texture images of 512×512 pixels which are depicted in Fig. 2. These texture images can be normalized to 64×64 pixels with 768 samples of sub images. Classification experiments were performed by using texture features extracted using local binary pattern and texture spectrum separately. Then classification performance was analyzed by extracting texture spectrum on LBP images. A quantitative study was performed using classification over 12 texture images based on the proposed method. The Euclidean Distance can be used to measure the similar images by determining the distance between training and testing set. The minimum distance decision rule is used for the texture classification. The classification accuracy of texture features of the various methods are shown in the Table1 and its performance is depicted as graph in Fig.3. The experimental result shows that the proposed approach has better classification performance than Local Binary pattern and Texture spectrum.

Table 1. Classification Accuracy (%) of the Texture Features

Classes	LBP	TS	Proposed method
Water	100	68.52	94.44
Raffia	98.15	92.59	98.15
Bark	92.59	98.15	100
D6	96.29	98.15	87.03
Weave	90.74	100	100
Leather	100	100	100
Handpaper	100	100	98.15
Sand	96.29	100	100
Oriental	100	100	98.15
Pressed cork	79.63	100	100
D52	68.52	100	100
D53	100	100	100
Average Precision	93.52	96.45	**97.99**

Fig. 2. Brodatz Images for Texture Classification

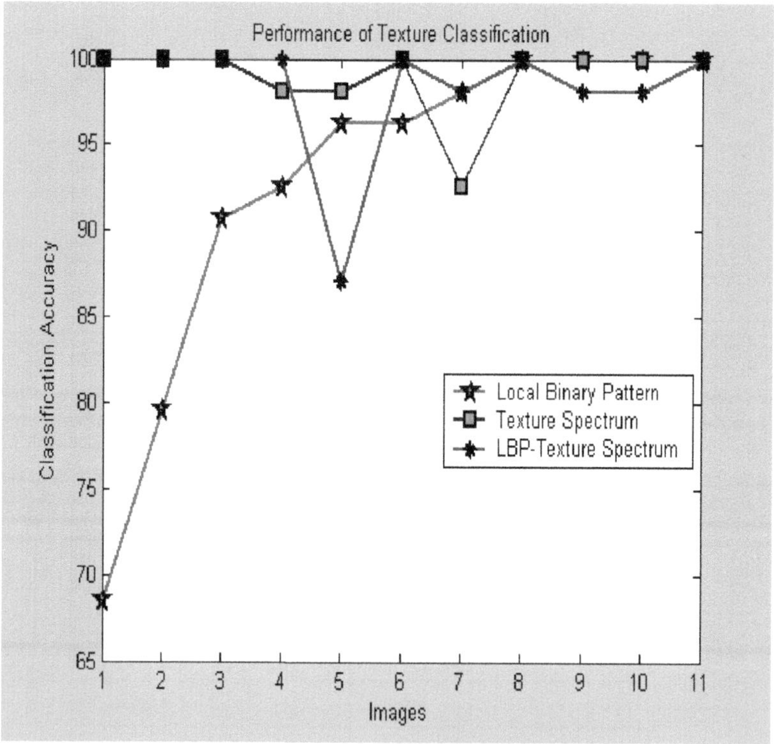

Fig. 3. Graph representing the performance analysis of Texture Feature

4 Conclusion

Texture analysis has been performed with the Local Binary Pattern images, Texture Spectrum and proposed method. The evaluation shows that Local Binary pattern is able to extract spatial texture features and it has promising discriminating performance for different textures. The combined approach performs better classification than the individual features and achieves 97.99% classification accuracy. In the future work, various other features can be combined with the proposed method and applied for various applications such as medical image retrieval.

References

1. Long, F., Zhang, H., Feng, D.D.: Fundamentals of Content Based Image Retrieval
2. Tamura, H., Mori, S., Yamawaki, T.: Textures Corresponding to Visual Perception. IEEE Trans. syst. Man Cybern, SMC 8(6), 460–473 (1978)
3. Rui, Y., Huang, T.S., Chang, S.-F.: Image Retrieval: Current Techniques, Promising Directions, and Open Issues. Journal of Visual Communication and Image Representation 10(1), 39–62 (1999)
4. Cross, G.R., Jain, A.K.: Markov random field texture models. IEEE Trans. Pattern Anal. Machine Intell. PAMI 5(1), 25–39 (1983)
5. Haralick, R.M., Shanmuga, K., Dinstein, I.: Textural Features for Image Classification. IEEE Transactions on Systems, Man and Cybernetics SMC 3, 610–621 (1973)
6. Chen, C.C.: Markov Random Fields in Image Analysis, Ph.D. Thesis, Computer Science Department, Michigan State University, East Lansing, MI (1988)
7. Rignot, E., Kwok, R.: Extraction of Textural Features in SAR Images: Statistical Model and Sensitivity. In: Proceedings of International Geoscience and Remote Sensing Symposium, Washington, DC, pp. 1979–1982 (1990)
8. Manjunath, B.S., Ma, W.Y.: Texture Features for Browsing and Retrieval of Image Data. IEEE Transactions on Pattern Analysis and Machine 18(8), 837–842 (1996)
9. Li, S.Z., Huang, X., Wang, Y.: Shape localization based on statistical method using extended local binary pattern. In: IEEE Proc. Conf. Image and Graphics, pp. 184–187 (2004)
10. Pass, G., Zabih, R.: Computer Science Department. Cornell University. Ithaca, Histogram Refinement for Content-Based Image Retrieval
11. Arivazhagan, S., Ganesan, L.: Texture classification using wavelet transform. Pattern Recognition Letters 24, 1513–1521 (2003)
12. Brodatz, P.: Textures: A Photographic Album for Artists and Designers. Dover, New York (1966)
13. Chang, T., Jay Kuo, C.C.: Texture analysis and classification with tree-structured wavelet transform. IEEE Trans. Image Process 2(4), 429–441 (1993)
14. Chellappa, R., Chatterjee, S.: Classification of texture using Gaussian Markov Random Fields. IEEE Trans. Acoustic Speech Signal Process, ASSP 33(4), 959–963 (1985)
15. He, D.C., Wang, L.: Texture unit, Texture spectrum and Texture Analysis. IEEE transactions on Geoscience and Remote Sensing 28(4) (July 1990)
16. He, D.C., Wang, L.: Texture classification using texture spectrum, vol. 23(8) (1990)
17. Jain, A.K.: Fundamentals of Digital image Processing. Prentice Hall, Englewood Cliffs (1989)

18. Hung, C.-C., Pham, M., Arasteh, S.: Image Texture Classification Using Texture Spectrum and Local Binary Pattern. IEEE transactions on pattern recognition, 2739–2742 (2006)
19. Zhitao, X., Minx, Y., Chengming, G.: Using Spectrum to Extract Texture Feature. IEEE transactions on image processing, 657–659 (2002)
20. Hiremath, P.S., Shivashankar, S.: Texture Classification using Wavelet Packet Decomposition. GVIP Journal 6(2) (September 2006)
21. Ojala, T., Pietikäinen, M., Mäenpää, T.: Multiresolution gray-scale and rotation invariant texture classification with Local Binary Patterns. IEEE Transactions on Pattern Analysis and Machine Intelligence 24(7), 971–987 (2002)
22. Tuceryan, M., Jain, A.K.: Texture Analysis handbook of Pattern Recognition and Computer Vision (1994)
23. Jian, M., Guo, H., Liu, L.: Texture Image Classification Using Visual Perceptual Texture Features and Gabor Wavelet Features. Journal of Computers 4(8) (August 2009)
24. Borchani, M., Stamon, G.: Texture features for Image Classification and Retrieval. In: SPIE, vol. 3229, p. 401(1997) (March 2005)
25. Karkanis, S., Galousi, K., Maroulis, D.: Classification of Endoscopic Images Based on Texture Spectrum
26. Wiselin Jiji, G., Ganesan, L.: Unsupervised Segmentation using Fuzzy Logic based Texture Spectrum for MRI Brain Images. World Academy of Science, Engineering and Technology 5 (2005)
27. Ojala, T., Pietikäinen, M.: Unsupervised Texture Segmentation Using Feature Distributions. Pattern Recognition 32, 477–486, 1495-1501 (1999), `http://www.cssip.elec.uq.edu.au/guy/meastex/meastex.html`
28. Smith, J.R., Chang, S.-F.: Visually searching the web for content, IEEE Multimedia Magazine 4(3), 12–20 (1997) (Columbia U. CU/CTR Technical Report 459-96-25)
29. Smith, J.R., Chang, S.F.: Transform features for texture classification and discrimination in large image databases. In: Proc. IEEE Int. Conf. on Image Proc. (1994)
30. Thyagarajan, K.S., Nguyen, T., Persons, C.: A maximum likelihood approach to texture classification using wavelet transform. In: Proc. IEEE Int. Conf. on Image Proc. (1994)

Completeness of LAN Attack Detection Using Discrete Event Systems

F.A. Barbhuiya, N. Hubballi, S. Biswas, and S. Nandi*

Department of Computer Science and Engineering
Indian Institute of Technology
Guwahati, India - 781039
{ferdous,neminath,santosh_biswas,sukumar}@iitg.ernet.in
http://www.iitg.ernet.in

Abstract. Address Resolution Protocol (ARP) based attacks are caused by compromised hosts in the LAN and mainly involve spoofing with falsified IP-MAC pairs. Since ARP is a stateless protocol such attacks are possible. The existing signature or anomaly intrusion detection systems are unable to detect these type of attacks. On one hand there are no signatures available for these attacks and on the other hand no significant statistical behavior change can be observed. Several schemes have been proposed in the literature to circumvent these attacks, however, these techniques either make IP-MAC pairing static, modify the existing ARP, violate network layering architecture, patch operating systems etc. In [1] Neminath et al. proposed a Discrete Event System (DES) based approach for detecting ARP attacks, which solved most of these issues. The approach is formal and can be applied to many attack cases whose nature is similar to that of ARP, e.g., ICMP informational message based attack. However, the work [1] did not show its completeness i.e., all possible scenarios of ARP spoofing can be detected by the scheme. In this paper we show which scenarios of spoofing are detected by the scheme and which are missed. Also the repercussions of the missed classes are analyzed.

Keywords: Network Security, Local Area Network (LAN) Attack, Address Resolution Protocol (ARP), Discrete Event systems, Failure Detection.

1 Introduction

A LAN is a high-speed communication system designed to link computers and other data processing devices together within a small geographic area, such as department or a building. Security threat to any computer, based on LAN specific attacks is from a compromised or malicious host in the LAN. The basic step involved in most of these attacks comprises cache poisoning with falsified IP-MAC pairs, which may then lead to other attacks namely, MiTM, denial of service etc. [2].

* The work reported in this paper is a part of the project "Design, Development and Verification of Network Specific IDS using Failure Detection and Diagnosis of DES", Sponsored by Department of Information Technology, New Delhi, INDIA.

D.C. Wyld et al. (Eds.): CNSA 2011, CCIS 196, pp. 131–139, 2011.

Computers in the internet are identified by their IP addresses. IP addresses are used by the network layer for identifying the machine uniquely. At the data link layer, computers use another address known as MAC address or hardware address. It is to be noted that IP addresses can be dynamic and change over a time but the MAC address of a computer is constant unless the Network Interface Card (NIC) is replaced. To deliver a packet to correct machine, IP address has to be mapped to some MAC address. This dynamic binding (since IP is dynamic) between the IP and MAC address is done by Address Resolution Protocol (ARP). ARP is responsible for finding the MAC address given the IP address. Data link layer uses the MAC address of the destination machine for sending the packets. If the host sending the packets does not know the MAC address of the destination host, it sends a broadcast request to know "What is the MAC address corresponding to the IP address". The host which has the IP address in the broadcast message sends a unicast reply message to the sender, mentioning its MAC address. In order to reduce the number of broadcast requests each machine maintains a table termed as ARP cache, which holds the mapping between the IP and MAC. Entries in the ARP cache can be either static or dynamic. In the dynamic cache the entries are erased as they get older than a predefined duration. The problem with ARP is that, it is a stateless protocol. Any host after receiving any ARP response message will update its cache without verifying wether it has earlier sent a request corresponding to the response. This enables the malicious hosts to craft custom ARP packets and forge the IP-MAC pair.

There are some solutions proposed in the literature to detect, mitigate and prevent ARP related attacks. These solutions and their merits/demerits are briefly discussed below.

- Static IP-MAC pairing [3]: In this scheme each host is manually assigned a MAC address and these static IP-MAC pairing are maintained in ARP caches of all hosts. This is the most foolproof way to prevent ARP attacks. However, this scheme is not acceptable in a dynamic environment.
- Enabling port security features in switch [4]: Security features are available in high end switches which tie a physical port to a MAC address. A change in transmitter's MAC address can result in port shutdown or ignoring the change. The scheme works fine only if the first packet received by the switch has correct IP-MAC pairing. Further, any genuine change in IP-MAC pair will be discarded (e.g., gratuitous request).
- Software security [5,6]: The basic notion of security features in switches (involving observation of changes in IP-MAC pairs) can been implemented in software solutions also. These software solutions are cheaper than switches with port security. However, they also suffer from the same drawbacks as that of port security in switches.
- Cryptographic techniques [7,8,9]: Cryptographic techniques can be used to authenticate ARP requests and responses. Cryptographic techniques increase computation overhead and violate the standard ARP.

In [1], a Discrete Event System (DES) based network IDS for detecting ARP related attacks has been proposed. A DES is characterized by a discrete state space and some event driven dynamics. DES have widely been used for failure detection and diagnosis of large systems like chemical reaction chambers, nuclear reactors etc. [10]. The basic idea is to develop a DES model for the system under normal condition and also under each of the failure conditions. Following that, a state estimator called diagnoser (or detector, if only detection of failure is required) is designed which observes sequences of events generated by the system to decide whether the states through which the system traverses correspond to the normal or faulty DES model. The DES based IDS could alleviate all the drawbacks of the existing schemes mentioned above. As reported in [1] the scheme has the following salient features

1. Follows standard ARP and do not violate the principles of network layering structure.
2. Generates minimal extra traffic in the network, as probes are sent only for unverified IP-MAC pairs
3. It involves installation of the DES detector (based network IDS) in just one host in the network.
4. Detects a large set of LAN attacks namely, malformed packets, response spoofing, request spoofing, man-in-the-middle and denial of service.
5. The only hardware requirement of the IDS is a switch with port mirroring facility.
6. This DES based approach is formal and can be applied to many cases whose nature is similar to that of ARP, e.g., ICMP informational message based attack.

The paper [1] did not show its completeness. In other words, working of the algorithms and the DES detector were shown by examples and no formal/semiformal proofs were given to illustrate its completeness in all possible scenarios of ARP spoofing attacks. In this paper we show which scenarios of spoofing are detected by the scheme and which are missed. Also the repercussions of the missed classes are analyzed.

The rest of the paper is organized as follows. Section 2 deals with proofs to analyze the completeness of the scheme [1]. Also the consequences of the spoofing cases which cannot be detected by the scheme are analyzed in this section. The paper is concluded in Section 3.

2 Completeness of the IDS for ARP Attacks

In this section we prove the completeness of the working of the DES detector based IDS [1] using different scenarios of ARP spoofing attacks. For the sake of brevity we do not discuss the details of the work presented in [1]. For details and reference to some figures used in explanation in this section we will refer to [1]. In this paper, hosts are identified by alphabets, a for example, and IP (MAC) address of the host is represented by IP(a) (MAC(a)). Before the proof, ceratin definitions are given.

Definition 1 ARP spoofing attack. *In ARP spoofing attack a malicious host m sends an ARP request/response packet to another host p in the LAN with falsified IP-MAC pair. In the response/request packet being sent, IP address of host v IP(v) is associated with MAC address of host k MAC(k), where $v \neq k$ and $v, k \neq p$. In other words, an ARP request or response packet is created and sent by m which has source IP-MAC pair as IP(v)-MAC(k). When response/request packet with IP(v)-MAC(k) is sent to p,* *it updates its cache with IP(v)-MAC(k) and all packets p wants to send v will reach k. The attack is said to be created with falsified IP-MAC pair "IP(v)-MAC(k)" against victim v by m.*

Definition 2 Victim Machine: *A machine in the LAN whose network traffic can be redirected to some other machine is called the victim machine. In Definition 1, host v is the victim machine as traffic being sent by p to v is redirected to k.*

An interesting case occurs if ARP attack is created with IP(v)-MAC(k), where v is the malicious host (i.e., $v = m$). In this case, malicious host m sends an ARP request/response packet with IP(m)-MAC(k) ($m \neq k$) to another host p. So all packets p wants to send m will reach k. So in this case attacker becomes the victim.

We assume the following in our arguments.

- The set of IP addresses in the LAN corresponding to which the hosts are up is I.
- The set of IP addresses in the LAN corresponding to which the hosts are down is I'.

We will study completeness of the IDS in two scenarios of the LAN. In the first case let all the machines in the LAN are up and running. In the second case, there may be some machines which are down. In this case will also see the situation when such machines are powered up after an attack is launched against them.

Theorem 1. *The DES detector based IDS detects all ARP spoofing attacks except the case where attacker becomes the victim, when all IP address in I are used.*

Proof. We prove the theorem by enumerating all possible combinations of IP-MAC pairs generated by malicious host. Let there be a single malicious host m in the LAN having IP-MAC pair IP(m)-MAC(m); latter we will show that the theorem holds for multiple malicious hosts also. It is assumed that Authenticated and Spoofed tables are empty.

There are 5 cases for IP-MAC combinations that can be generated by m–(A) IP(m)-MAC(m), (B) IP(v)-MAC(v) ($IP(v) \in I \neq IP(m)$), (C) IP(v)-MAC(m) ($IP(v) \in I \neq IP(m)$), (D) IP(m)-MAC(v) ($v \neq m$), (E) IP(v)-MAC(k) ($IP(v) \in I, v \neq k$ and $v, k \neq m$).

Now these cases are analyzed one by one. (A), (B) do not correspond to spoofed cases. The rest are analyzed as follows. The analysis is shown when the malicious host uses a request packet for sending the falsified IP-MAC pair. Same argument will hold when the malicious host uses a response packet for sending the falsified IP-MAC pair.

1. **Case 1–IP(v)-MAC(m) ($IP(v) \in I \neq IP(m)$):** If ARP request packet with IP(v)-MAC(m) is sent by m to any host, then IDS receives the packet due to port mirroring and REQUEST-HANDLER() generates a RQP event. As Authenticated and Spoofed tables are empty, probe request is sent by IDS for verification and $PRQP$ event is generated. As the probe request is broadcast it is received by all hosts. So this probe request is also received by the malicious host m and may respond in the ways enumerated below. However, in all cases the genuine host v will reply to the probe using an ARP response packet having source IP-MAC pair as IP(v)-MAC(v); for this the RESPONSE-HANDLER() generates a $PRSP$ event, whose MAC address is not same as that of MAC address of the request being verified.

Variations of Responses of m

(a) m may not give any reply. So there will be only one reply having IP(v)-MAC(v) (from genuine host v). So, in all, the following sequence of events is received by the detector –RQP,$PRQP$,$PRSP$; the MAC address of $PRSP$ (MAC address of IP-MAC pair sent with probe response, MAC(v)) is not same as that of MAC address of the request packet being verified (having MAC address MAC(m)). From Figure 7 (a) (of [1]) it may be noted that this sequence of RQP,$PRQP$,$PRSP$ corresponds to transitions $\tau_1', \tau_2', \tau_5'$ in the system and $a7, a8, a11$ in the detector (Figure 8 of [1]). $a7, a8, a11$ leads to state $z12$ in the detector that has only one system state $s6'$ which corresponds to request spoofing condition. *So IP(v)-MAC(m) is correctly identified to be spoofed.* Also, the reply from v with IP(v)-MAC(v) leads to tracking the attacker (MAC(m)). To avoid self identification, attacker m has to give a single reply to all queries asking for MAC of v with spoofed IP-MAC pair IP(v)-MAC(m); this mimics as if IP(v)-MAC(m) was normal. The IDS has no clue whether IP(v)-MAC(v) or IP(v)-MAC(m) is genuine; only possibility of spoofing is detected. In other words, to avoid being detected, if the attacker sends a spoofed packet IP(v)-MAC(m) say, then for all ARP requests for MAC of $IP(v)$ it would send a reply with the same spoofed MAC address (i.e., MAC(m)) that it has used in spoofing. This behavior of attacker is assumed for all queries for MAC address it has spoofed.

With this assumption, the case of one reply having IP(v)-MAC(m) from m is analyzed as follows.

(b) One reply having IP(v)-MAC(m) from m. It may be noted that the sequence in which host v and host m respond to the probe request is not fixed. Let v respond before m. The two response packets (one from v and the other from m) are processed by RESPONSE-HANDLER() as two $PRSP$ events. So, in all, the following sequence of events is received by the detector–RQP,$PRQP$,$PRSP$,$PRSP$; the MAC address of first $PRSP$ is different from the of MAC address of the request being verified and the MAC address of second $PRSP$ is same. From Figure Figure 7 (a) (of [1]) it may be noted that this sequence of RQP,$PRQP$,$PRSP$, $PRSP$ corresponds to transitions $\tau_1', \tau_2', \tau_5', \tau_6'$ in the system and $a7, a8, a11$ in the detector (Figure 8 of [1]). $a7, a8, a11$ leads to state $z12$ in the detector that has only one system state $s6'$ which corresponds to request spoofing condition. *So IP(v)-MAC(m) is correctly identified to be spoofed.*

Now, let m respond before v. In this situation, sequence of events received is by the detector is–RQP,$PRQP$,$PRSP$,$PRSP$, where the MAC address of first $PRSP$ is same as the MAC address of the request being verified and the MAC address of second $PRSP$ is different. From Figure Figure 7 (a) (of [1]) it may be noted that RQP,$PRQP$,$PRSP$, $PRSP$ corresponds to transitions $\tau_1', \tau_2', \tau_3', \tau_4'$ and $a7, a8, a9, a10$ in the detector (Figure 8 of [1]). $a7, a8, a9, a10$ leads to state $z11$ in the detector that has only one system state $s5'$ which corresponds to request spoofing condition. *So IP(v)-MAC(m) is correctly identified to be spoofed.*

It may be noted that spoofing is identified by transition which corresponds to $PRSP$ whose MAC address is different than the MAC address of the request being verified; τ_5' if first $PRSP$ has the different MAC address and τ_4' if second $PRSP$ has the different MAC address.

2. **Case 2–IP(m)-MAC(v) ($v \neq m$):** REQUEST-HANDLER() generates a RQP event on receipt of the request packet sent by m having IP(m)-MAC(v). Following that probe request is sent by IDS for verification of MAC address (MAC(v)) associated with IP address (IP(m)) of the request packet and $PRQP$ event is generated. This probe request sent to query MAC address of IP(m). Even of the request is received by all hosts, as all hosts except m are genuine, only m would respond. According to the assumption in Case-1, m will respond to the probe as IP(m)-MAC(v); the case is analyzed as follows.

   (a) One reply with IP(m)-MAC(v). REQUEST-HANDLER() generates event $PRSP$. So, in all, the following sequence of events is received by the detector –RQP,$PRQP$,$PRSP$; the MAC address of $PRSP$ is same as that of MAC address of the request being verified. From Figure Figure 6 (of [1]) it may be noted that RQP,$PRQP$,$PRSP$ corresponds to transitions $\tau_4, \tau_5, \tau_6, \tau_{10}$ in the system and $a7, a8, a9, a12$ in the detector (Figure 8 of [1]). In the detector $a7, a8, a9, a12$ leads to leads to state $z13$ that has only one system state $s1$ which corresponds to normal condition. *So IP(m)-MAC(v) is incorrectly identified to be genuine.* It may be noted that if response to the probe has same MAC address as that of the request being verified, it is determined to be genuine. In other words, if no response to the probe has different MAC address compared to the request being verified, it is determined to be genuine.

3. **Case 3–IP(v)-MAC(k)** ($IP(v), IP(k) \in$ ***I***, $v \neq k$ **and** $v, k \neq m$): REQUEST-HANDLER() generates a RQP event on receipt of the request packet sent by m having IP(v)-MAC(k). Following that probe request is sent by IDS for verification and $PRQP$ event is generated. As the probe request is broadcast it is received by all hosts. As v is genuine it will respond by a ARP response packet having IP(v)-MAC(v), whose MAC is different than the one in the request packet being verified. The attacker will respond to this probe as IP(v)-MAC(k). Attack is detected by the detector because there is at least one repone to the $PRQP$ whose MAC is different from the request packet being verified. *So IP(v)-MAC(k) is correctly identified to be spoofed.*

From the enumeration above, only Case 2 Subcase(a) is the condition when spoofing is detected as genuine; i.e., spoofing attack cannot be detected. Case 2 corresponds to IP(m)-MAC(v) ($v \neq m$). Let m send a request with IP(m)-MAC(v) ($v \neq m$) to host p, which updates its cache accordingly. So all traffic p wants to send m will reach v; so Case 2 corresponds to condition where m is also the victim (in addition to being a malicious host).

From the theorem the following corollary follows.

Corollary 1. *If all responses to the probe sent by IDS for verifying any request/response packet has same MAC address as that of the packet being verified, the detector determines normal condition.*

If at least one response to the probe sent by IDS for verifying any request/response packet has different MAC address compared to the packet being verified, then detector determines spoofed condition.

Proof. Follows from construction of detector and illustrated in Theorem 1.

In the next theorem we will show that Theorem 1 also holds when there is more than one malicious host. Before that Theorem 1 is restated as follows:

Let IP(v)-MAC(k) ($IP(v) \in I \neq IP(k)$) be sent in a spoofed request/response by malicious host m. Spoofing can be detected if $v \neq m$.

The elaborate proof given above for Theorem 1 can be summarized as follows.

As shown in Corollary 1, spoofing is detected if at least one response to the probe sent by IDS for verification has different MAC address compared to the packet being verified. If IP(v)-MAC(k) is sent (by m), then IDS sends a probe (by broadcast) to query the MAC address associated with IP(v). If $v \neq m$, then v is genuine and as $IP(v) \in I$ (i.e., v is up) it will reply with IP(v)-MAC(v); as the reply has different MAC address compared to the packet being verified, spoofing can be detected.

Hoverer, if $v = m$, then v is itself the attacker. The IDS probe request is sent to query MAC address of IP($v = m$) and no genuine host would reply. The malicious host m will reply with spoofed ARP reply whose MAC address is deliberately kept same as the one in the packet being verified. So IP(v)-MAC(k) is falsely determined to be genuine. It may be noted that IP($v = m$)-MAC(k) is the case where attacker is the victim.

Theorem 2. *Let the set of malicious hosts in a LAN be M. Let IP(v)-MAC(k) ($IP(v) \in I \neq IP(k)$) be sent in a spoofed request/response by malicious host $m \in M$. Spoofing can be detected if $v \notin M$.*

Proof. As shown in Corollary 1, spoofing is detected if at least one response to the probe sent by IDS for verification has different MAC address compared to the packet being verified. If IP(v)-MAC(k) is sent (by m), then IDS sends a probe to query MAC address associated with IP(v). As $v \notin M$, $IP(v) \in I$ (i.e., v is up) and malicious hosts cannot stop v from responding, it will reply with IP(v)-MAC(v). Along with the reply from v, other malicious hosts can also reply to the probe request, however, cannot stop detection of spoofing because reply sent by v has different (correct) MAC address compared to the packet being verified (which has spoofed MAC address).

Next we will study completeness of the IDS in the second scenario where some IPs in LAN may not be used, i.e., some of the machines are down. In this case we will also see the situation when such machines are powered up.

Theorem 3. *The DES detector based IDS detects all ARP spoofing attacks except the cases (i) where attacker becomes the victim (i.e., IP(m)-MAC(v), $v \neq m$), and (ii) the IP address used in the spoofing packet corresponds to a machine which is down (i.e., IP(v)-MAC(k), $IP(v) \in I' \neq IP(k)$)*

Proof. We prove the theorem by enumerating all possible combinations of IP-MAC pairs generated by the malicious host. Let there be a single malicious host m in the LAN having IP-MAC pair IP(m)-MAC(m)[1]. It is assumed that Authenticated and Spoofed tables are empty.

There are 8 cases for IP-MAC combinations that can be generated by m– (A) IP(m)-MAC(m), (B) IP(v)-MAC(v) ($IP(v) \in I \neq IP(m)$), (C) IP(v)-MAC(v) ($IP(v) \in I' \neq IP(m)$), (D) IP(v)-MAC(m) ($IP(v) \in I \neq IP(m)$), (E) IP(v)-MAC(m) ($IP(v) \in I' \neq IP(m)$), (F) IP(m)-MAC(v) ($v \neq m$), (G) IP(v)-MAC(k) ($IP(v) \in I$, $v \neq k$ and $v, k \neq m$), (H) IP(v)-MAC(k) ($IP(v) \in I'$, $v \neq k$ and $v, k \neq m$).

Case (A), (B), (C) do not correspond to spoofed cases. Case (D),(G) involve IP address $IP(v) \in I$; so this can be handled similarly as in Theorem 1. Also, Case (F) can be handled similarly as in Theorem 1 because it involves IP address $m \in I$ (attacker is the victim).

The rest of the cases ((E),(H)) are analyzed as follows. As in Theorem 1 the analysis is shown when the malicious host uses a request packet for sending the falsified IP-MAC pair. Same argument will hold when the malicious host uses a response packet for sending the falsified IP-MAC pair.

1. **Case 1–IP(v)-MAC(m) ($IP(v) \in I' \neq IP(m)$):** REQUEST-HANDLER() generates a RQP event on receiving the packet with IP(v)-MAC(m). A probe request is sent by IDS for verification and $PRQP$ event is generated. As machine with IP(v) is not up, there would not be any reply from v with IP(v)-MAC(v) (that has different MAC address than the packet being verified). Also, the malicious host m will send a reply with same MAC address. So, there is a condition when only one response to the probe request is received that has same MAC address as that of the packet being verified. By Corollary 1, *IP(v)-MAC(m) is incorrectly identified to be genuine*.
2. **Case 2–IP(v)-MAC(k) ($IP(v) \in I'$, $v \neq k$ and $v, k \neq m$).** This situation is similar to Case-1 (of Theorem 3)above. *IP(v)-MAC(k) is incorrectly identified to be genuine*.

In Theorem 3 we have seen two conditions when a spoofed packet is determined to be genuine. IP address in such spoofed packets correspond to system(s) which are down. Now we will see the condition when such a system system comes up.

Let a spoofed packet having IP(v)-MAC(k) ($IP(v) \in I' \neq IP(k)$) be detected as genuine; so IP(v)-MAC(k) is entered in Authenticated Table. After, v comes up, it sends a gratuitous request with IP(v)-MAC(v); REQUEST-HANDLER() generates a RQP event. Following that a probe request is sent to verify to the gratuitous request thereby generating event $PRQP$. Host v responds to the probe request with IP(v)-MAC(v). Now malicious host will respond to the probe by IP(v)-MAC(k) ($k \neq v$), which has different MAC address corresponding to the gratuitous request being verified. So, gratuitous request is incorrectly determined to be spoofed and the falsified IP-MAC pair IP(v)-MAC(k) ($v \neq k$) remains to be kept in the Authenticated table.

[1] As in Theorem 1 the current proof also holds for multiple malicious hosts.

The following points can be deduced from Theorem 1 and Theorem 3 regarding the consequences of the cases when a spoofed request/reply is determined to be genuine (i.e., false negative cases).

- Theorem 1: Spoofed IP-MAC pairs for the case "when attacker itself is the victim", is missed to be detected. This does not lead to a serious consequence because no genuine host can be victimized (by diverting its traffic to some other host). So other attacks like man-in-the-middle, denial of service etc. which require diverting traffic sent to genuine hosts (to malicious hosts) cannot be launched.
- Theorem 3: Spoofed IP-MAC pairs for cases "(i) when attacker itself is the victim" and "(ii)IP address used in a spoofed packet corresponds to a machine which is down" are missed to be detected. Further, even after the machine comes up, spoofing cannot be detected. Case (ii) may lead to serious consequence as traffic intended to a genuine host would be diverted to malicious host.

3 Conclusion

In this paper we have discussed completeness of the IDS for LAN attack detection [1]. It was shown formally (by exhaustive enumeration) that if all systems in an LAN are up then associating a false MAC address with a genuine IP can be detected. In other words, if all systems in an LAN are up then intention of diverting traffic for a genuine machine can be detected (i.e., effort to make a genuine host victim can be detected). However, if IP address of a host is associated with a false MAC address when it is down, then the host can be made victim (even after it comes up).

References

1. Hubballi, N., Biswas, S., Roopa, S., Ratti, R., Nandi, S.: LAN attack detection using discrete event systems. ISA Transactions 50(1), 119–130 (2011)
2. Held, G.: Ethernet Networks: Design, Implementation, Operation, Management, 1st edn. John Wiley & Sons, Ltd., Chichester (2003)
3. Kozierok, C.M.: TCP/IP Guide. No Starch (2005)
4. Switches, C.C.: `http://www.cisco.com/en/us/products/hw/switches/ps708/`
5. colasoft capsa: `http://www.colasoft.com`
6. arpwatch: `http://www.arpalert.org`
7. Gouda, M.G., Huang, C.: A secure address resolution protocol. Computer Networks 41(1), 57–71 (2003)
8. Lootah, W., Enck, W., McDaniel, P.: Tarp: Ticket-based address resolution protocol, pp. 106–116. IEEE Computer Society, Los Alamitos (2005)
9. Abad, C.L., Bonilla, R.I.: An analysis on the schemes for detecting and preventing arp cache poisoning attacks. In: ICDCSW 2007: Proceedings of the 27th International Conference on Distributed Computing Systems Workshops, pp. 60–67. IEEE Computer Society, Los Alamitos (2007)
10. Cassandras, C.G., Lafortune, S.: Introduction to discrete event systems, 1st edn. Kluwer Academic Publishers, Dordrecht (1999)

Designing Dependable Web Services Security Architecture Solutions

D. Shravani[1], P. Suresh Varma[2], B. Padmaja Rani[3], M. Upendra Kumar[4], and A.V. Krishna Prasad[5]

[1] Research Scholar Computer Science Rayalaseema University Kurnool A.P. India
sravani.mummadi@yahoo.co.in
[2] Principal and Professor Computer Science Adikavi Nannaya University A.P. India
vermaps@yahoo.com
[3] Associate Professor CSE JNTU CEH Hyderabad A.P. India
padmaja_jntuh@yahoo.co.in
[4] Research Scholar CSE JNTU Hyderabad A.P. India
uppi_shravani@rediffmail.com
[5] Research Scholar Computer Science S.V. University Tirupathi A.P. India
kpvambati@gmail.com

Abstract. Web Services Security Architectures have three layers, as provided by NIST standard: Web Service Layer, Web Services Framework Layer (.NET or J2EE), and Web Server Layer. In services oriented web services architecture, business processes are executed as a composition of services, which can suffer from vulnerabilities pertaining to secure data access and protecting code of Web Services. The goal of the Web services security architecture is to summary out the details of message-level security from the mainstream business logic, with a focus on Web Service contract design and versioning for SOA. Service oriented web services architectures impose additional analysis complexity as they provide much flexibility and frequent changes with in orchestrated processes and services. In this paper, we discuss about developing dependable solutions for Web Services Security Architectures in terms of Privacy and Trust negotiation. All this research is motivated by Secure Service Oriented Analysis and Design research domain. We initially validate this by a BPEL Editor using GWT for RBAC and Privacy. Finally a real world case study is implemented using J2EE, for validating our approach. Secure Stock Exchange System using Web Services is to automate the stock exchange works, and can help user make the decisions when it comes to investment.

Keywords: Web Services, Security Architectures, Agile Modeling, BPEL RBAC, Service Oriented Analysis and Design, Privacy for Business Processes.

1 Introduction to Web Services Security Architectures

Introduction. Service Orientation Engineering (SOE) (or Web Services) and Agile modeling software development presents promising solutions for contemporary software development projects to deal effectively with challenges in increasingly

D.C. Wyld et al. (Eds.): CNSA 2011, CCIS 196, pp. 140–149, 2011.

turbulent business environments typified by unpredictable markets, changing customer requirements, pressures of even shorter time to deliver, and rapidly advancing information technologies. Model-based agile security engineering is a promising approach that can help to fill the gap between vulnerabilities on the one hand and concrete protection mechanism on the other. Using security patterns to develop secure systems is a major research area.

Web Services Security Architectures. Web Services has emerged as a dominant paradigm for constructing and composing distributed business collaborations over the web. [1] Security is one of the major concerns when developing mission critical business applications and this concern motivated the Web Services Security specifications. This paper surveys current Security Mechanisms for Web Services and Security in a Web Services World Proposed Architecture and Roadmap, which includes secure communication protocol, authentication, Signature, Encryption, Authorization, and Transport Security etc. It provides Strong ways to protect information for Browser/Server applications. Some interesting web services securing mechanisms are XKMS, SAML, XACML and WS-Security. These mechanisms can be used to provide a wide variety of web services security models and encryption technologies. The goal of the Web services security architecture is to summary out the details of message-level security from the mainstream business logic [2]. Web Services Privacy for Business Processes is important because Web Services are increasingly being adopted for business and government applications as a viable means to access web-based applications. [3]

Secure Service Oriented Analysis and Design. The first step is to analyze the application and determine the services that describe the applications. [4] The logic encapsulated by each service, the reuse of the logic encapsulated by the service, and the interfaces to the service has to be identified. From a security policy of view, in defining the services we have to consider the security policies. What is the security level of the service? What are the policies enforced on the service? Who can have access to the service? When we decompose the service into smaller services to see how we can ensure that security is not violated. The next step is for the relationship between the services, including the composition of services, to be identified. In a top-down strategy, one has to identify all the services and the relationships before conducting the detailed design and development of the services. For large application design, this may not be feasible. In the case of bottom-up design, one has to identify services and start developing them. In agile design, both strategies are integrated. From a security policy point of view, there may be policies that define the relationship between the services. Furthermore, such an approach sets the stage for orchestration-based service-oriented architectures. Orchestration essentially implements workflow logic that enables different applications to interoperate with each other. Also, we have stated orchestrations themselves may be implemented as services. Therefore, the orchestration service may be invoked or different applications also implemented as services to interoperate with each other. Business services also promote reuse. From a security point of view we have yet to determine who can involve the business logic and orchestration services. A lot of work has gone into security for workflow systems including the BFA model. Therefore, we needed to examine the principles in this work for business logic and orchestration services. When a service is reused, what happens if there are confecting policies on reuse? Also, we have to make sure that there is no security violation through reuse.

Secure Service modeling. The main question is, how do you define a service? [4] At the highest level, an entire application such as order management can be one service. However, this is not desirable. At the other extreme, a business process can be broken into several steps, and each step can be a service. Te challenge is to group steps that carry out some specific task into a service. However, when security is given consideration, then not only do we have to group steps that carry out some specific task into a service, we also have to group steps that can be meaningfully executed. If security is based on multilevel security, then we may want to assign a security level for each service. In this way, the service can be executed by someone cleared at an appropriate level. Therefore, the challenge is to group steps in a way that is meaningful not only from a task point of view but also from a security point of view. Next, we must examine the service candidates and determine the relationships between them. One service may call other services. Two services may be composed to create a composite service. This would mean identifying the boundaries and the interface, and make the composition and separations as clear as possible. Dependencies may result in complex service designs. Te service operations could be simple operations such as performing calculations or complex operations such as invoking multiple services. Here again, security may impact the relationships between the services. If two services have some relationships between them, then both services should be accessible to a group of users or users cleared at a particular level. For example, if service A and service B are tightly integrated, it may not make sense for a service C to have access to A and not to B. If A is about making a hotel reservation and B is about making a rental car reservation, then an airline reservation service C should be able to invoke both services A and B. Once the candidate services and the service operations are indentified, the next step is to refine the candidates and state the design of the services and the service operations. Therefore, from a security point of view, we have to refine the services and service operations that are not only meaningful but also secure. Mapping of the candidate service to the actual service has to be carried out according to the policies.

Secure Services. Web Services and service-oriented architectures are at the heart of the next-generation web.[4] They are expected to make use of Semantic Web technologies to generate machine understandable web pages. Major initiatives like global information grid and network centric enterprise services are based o n web services and Service oriented architectures. A unified approach with a security model is required for securing Services Oriented Analysis and Design Life cycle.

Dependable Systems. Dependability includes trust, privacy and integrity.[4] Multilevel security is a part of dependability. Trust management and negotiation techniques should take the advantage of semantic web technologies. Standards such as P3P and appropriate technologies that enforce various privacy policies needs to be researched.

Secure SOAD approach using Secure UML for Services. Secure UML for services essentially developed secure UML for service-oriented analysis and modeling.[4] Several approaches to applying UML and other object-oriented analysis and design approaches to secure applications have been proposed. We need to extend these approaches to secure SOAD. We also need to examine the security impact on service-oriented discovery and analysis modeling, service-oriented business integration modeling, service-oriented logical design modeling, service-oriented conceptual architecture modeling, and service-oriented logical architecture modeling. [5]

2 Designing Solutions for Dependability

Secure Software Architectures. Software Engineering covers the definition of processes, techniques and models suitable for its environment to guarantee quality of results.[6] An important design artifact in any software development project is the Software Architecture. Software Architecture's important part is the set of architectural design rules. A primary goal of the architecture is to capture the architecture design decisions. An important part of these design decisions consists of architectural design rules. In an MDA (Model-Driven Architecture) context, the design of the system architecture is captured in the models of the system. MDA is known to be layered approach for modeling the architectural design rules and uses design patterns to improve the quality of software system. And to include the security to the software system, security patterns are introduced that offer security at the architectural level. More over, agile software development methods are used to build secure systems. There are different methods defined in agile development as extreme programming (XP), scrum, feature driven development (FDD), test driven development (TDD), etc.[7] Agile processing includes the phases like agile analysis, agile design and agile testing.[8] These phases are defined in layers of MDA to provide security at the modeling level which ensures that "security at the system architecture stage will improve the requirements for that system". [9] Dependable Solutions for Security Requirements involves Privacy, Trust negotiation, RBAC, Identity management etc.

Layered Services Design. Consider using a layered approach to designing service applications and avoid tight coupling across layers.[10] Separate the business rules and data access functions into distinct components where appropriate. Use abstraction to provide an interface into the business layer. This abstraction can be implemented by using public object interface definitions, abstract base classes, or messaging.

3 Business Process Execution Language RBAC and Privacy

BPEL RBAC. Security for Workflow and Business Processing, focuses on an important component that makes it possible to build and manage complex applications.[11] In a Web-based environment, business processes or workflows can be built by combining Web services through the use of a process specification language. Such languages basically allow one to specify which tasks have to be executed and the order in which those tasks to be executed. One such language is WS-BPEL, which provides syntax for specifying business processes based on Web Services. A problem of particular relevance for security is the development of access control techniques supporting the specification and enforcements stating which users can execute which tasks within a workflow, while also enforcing constrains such as separation of duty on the execution of those tasks.

BPEL Editor using Google Web Toolkit (GWT). GWT is an open source set of tools that allows web developers to create and maintain complex JavaScript front-end applications in Java. When the application is deployed, the GWT cross-compiler translates the Java application to JavaScript, CSS and HTML. GWT does not revolve only around user interface programming; it is a general set of tools for building any sort of high-performance client-side JavaScript functionality. BPEL is an orchestration language built on the foundation of the XML and Web services which use a XML based language that supports the Web Services technology Stack. If any application wants to work on multiple Web Services, for example if there is an application which involves three business processes using three Web Services of hotel reservations, cab reservations Airline reservations, then BPEL is the solution.[12]

Business Process Execution Language (BPEL) is a XML-based language used to define Enterprise business processes within Web services. The key objective of BPEL is standardize format of business process flow definition so companies can work together seamlessly using Web service. Processes written in BPEL can orchestrate interactions between Web Services using XML documents in a standardized manner. BPEL is used to model the Behavior of both executable and abstract processes. Executable processes model actual behavior in business transactions. Abstract

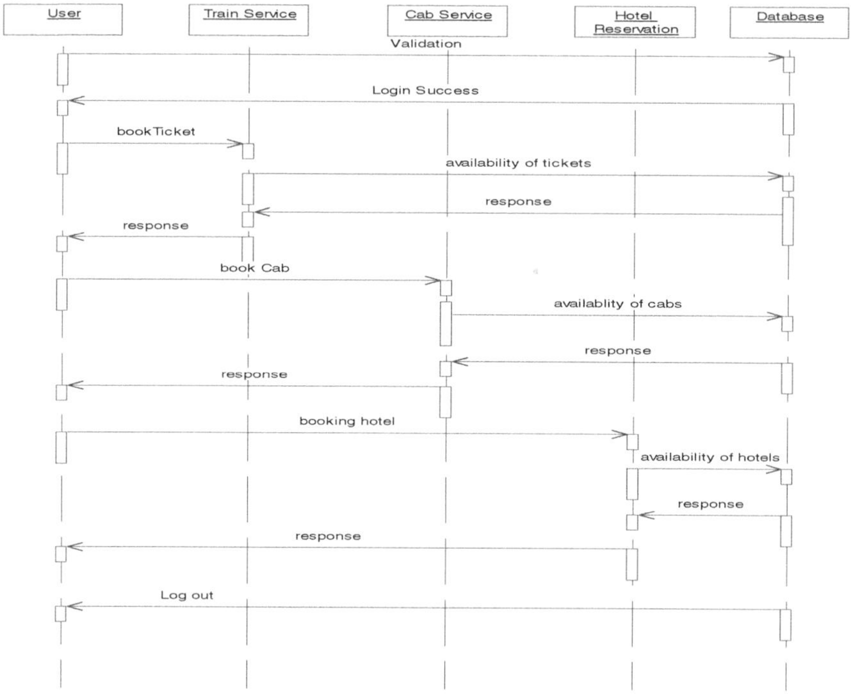

Fig. 1. Sequence diagram of the BPEL Editor application

Fig. 2. Class diagram of the BPEL Editor application

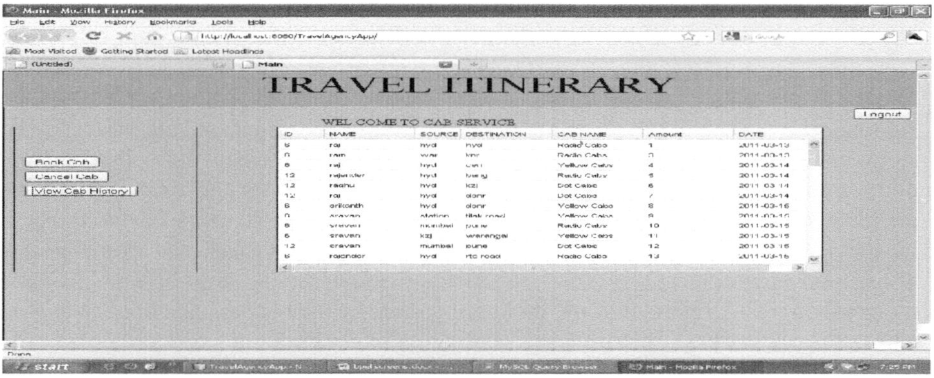

Fig. 3. Execution screen shot of the BPEL Editor application

processes interact without revealing their internal behavior. In the existing system, in order to access two or more interdependent web-services simultaneously, the client has to use one web-service, close the connection and then use the second service. In the proposed system we will create front end using GWT. For orchestration of several web services at a time we use BPEL. This would overcome the above drawbacks and also reduces overall cost and maintenance. First we will create an application with GWT as front end. The customer should register himself in order to proceed to access service. The user needs to input all the required particular details during the registration process. The web service will perform validation checks on customer input and length constraints. Upon successful login, the customer will be registered officially to the web service and he can login using his username and password. Second we will develop graphical user interface, connecting the several web services using BPEL and making the connection with the database for accessing the web services. Third we will show how the user can access service. Like retrieving information of availability of tickets and can book a ticket and if another services user needs may go for it and all the details will be stored in the database. Refer to the

Figure 1, Figure 2, Figure 3 below, which consists of sequence diagram, class diagram and execution screen shot respectively of this BPEL editor application.

4 Implementations and Validations

Secure Stock Market using Web Services

Secure Stock Exchange Web Services design in J2EE is all about Secure Stock Exchange System using Web Services containing the following: :Stock Markets & Investments, Stock Options, Related Information. A stock exchange is simply a market that is designed for the sale and purchase of securities of corporations and municipalities. This means that a stock exchange sells and buys stocks, shares, and other such securities. In addition, the stock exchange sometimes buys and sells certificates representing commodities of trade. Secure Stock Exchange system is simply a system that is designed for the sale and purchase of securities of corporations and municipalities. A stock exchange sells and buys stocks, shares, and other such securities. In addition, the stock exchange sometimes buys and sells certificates representing commodities of trade. At first, stock exchanges were completely open. Anyone who wished to buy or sell could do so at a stock exchange. However, to make stock exchange more effective, membership became limited to those in clubs and other associations. Today, professionals who have a seat at the exchange are the people who trade at the exchange if a broker approaches a post and sees that the price of the stock is what they are authorized to pay, the broker can complete the transaction themselves. As soon as a transaction occurs, the broker makes a memorandum and reports it to the brokerage office by telephone instantly. The buying and selling of stocks at the exchange is done on an area which is called the floor. All over the floor are positions which are called posts. Each post has the names of the stocks traded at that specific post. If a broker wants to buy shares of a specific company they will go to the section of the post that has that stock. If the broker sees at the price of the stock is not quite what the broker is authorized to pay, a professional called the specialist may receive an order. The specialist will often act as a go-between between the seller and buyer. What the specialist does is to enter the information from the broker into a book. If the stock reaches the required price, the specialist will sell or buy the stock according to the orders given to them by the broker. The transaction is then reported to the investor. If a broker approaches a post and sees that the price of the stock is what they are authorized to pay, the broker can complete the transaction themselves. As soon as a transaction occurs, the broker makes a memorandum and reports it to the brokerage office by telephone instantly. At the post, an exchange employee jots down on a special card the details of the transaction including the stock symbol, the number of shares, and the price of the stocks. The employee then puts the card into an optical reader. The reader puts this information into a computer and transmits the information of the buy or sell of the stock to the market. This means that information about the transaction is added to the stock market and the transaction is counted on the many stock market tickers and information display devices that investors rely on all over the world. Today, markets are instantly linked by the Internet, allowing for faster exchange.

The following are the modules implemented in this Secure Stock Exchange System using Web services: Securities: The securities view provides a list of all available securities. From here you can open charts and news headers specific to each security, and drag a security to populate other views. Watch List: The watchlist view allows you to keep track of the price trend of the securities. The watchlist wizard allows you to define the name of the watchlist and the columns to display. To add the securities to a watchlist drag a security from the securities view and drop it to the watchlist. The security will be added at the end of list. Charts: Chart views provide a graphical representation of the historical prices for a given security. The view's pull-down menu to add indicators and drawing objects to the chart that helps you to perform the technical analysis of the price trends. Indicators can be added over existing indicators, on a new tab in the same row with other indicators or alone in a row. Patterns: From the Watchlist or Securities views you can search each security for a pattern in the price history. The patterns search view provides a list of all performed search results. Accounts: The accounts view provides a list of trading accounts and keep track of your owned assets. All accounts are transaction-based. Portfolio: The portfolio view provides a list of all open positions for the available trading accounts. Trading: The trading feature allows you to submit orders to a broker using: Account, Security, Provider, Order. And keep track of the submitted orders and their status using the orders view.

For details of these implementations, please refer to the website http://sites.google.com/ site/upendramgitcse

5 Recent Related Research work

The References section from [13-33] provides recent related research work on Designing dependable Web Services Security Architecture Solutions.

6 Conclusions

In this paper we discussed about designing dependable web services security architecture solutions using layered agile modeling with appropriate case studies of BPEL RBAC and Privacy and another secure application. Future work includes developing privacy and RBAC for Business Processes for Business Intelligence applications which provide insights of Web Science and Web Engineering applications and Cloud computing virtualizations. Also securing Web services contract design, its vulnerability detection, prediction of effects of these detected vulnerabilities, for the business process under consideration needs to be examined. These security patterns needs to be formalized and model checked, verified for security, tool supported, detected threats needs to be stopped or mitigated, and run-time monitoring is required.

References

1. Mokbel, M.S., Jiajin, L.: Integrated Security Architecture for Web Services and this Challenging. Journal of Theoretical and Applied Information Technology JATIT, 518–525 (2005 – 2008)

2. li, M., Cheng-yan, J.: A research on Web Security Service Architecture. Journal of Chongqing Electric Power College China (2009)
3. Godbole, N.: Information Systems: Security Management, Metrics, Frameworks and Best Practices. Wiley India Publishers, Chichester (2009)
4. Thuraisingham, B.: Secure Semantic Service Oriented Systems. Auerbach Publications (2011)
5. Tiller, J.S.: Adaptive Security management Architecture. Auerbach Publications (2011)
6. Hans, K.: Cutting edge practices for Secure Software Engineering. International Journal of Computer Science and Security IJCSS 4(4), 403–408 (2010)
7. Kuhn, M.R., Schatten, E.: Towards an Architectural Framework for Agile Software Development. In: IEEE 17 International Conference and Workshop on Engineering of Computer Based Systems (ECBS), pp. 276–280 (2010)
8. Fernandez, E.B., Yoshika, N., Washizaki, H., Jurjens, J., VanHilst, M., Pernul, G.: Using Security Patterns to Develop Secure Systems, pp. 16–31. IGI Global (2011), doi:10.4018/978-1-61520-837-1.ch002
9. Spanoudakis, G., Zisman, A.: Discovering Services during Service-Based System Design Using UML. IEEE Transactions on Software Engineering 36(3), 371–389 (2010)
10. Hill, D.: Microsoft Application Architecture Guide, Patterns and Practices, 2nd edn. Microsoft Press, Redmond (2009)
11. Bertino, E., Martino, L.D., Paci, F., Squicciarini, A.C.: Security for Web Services and Service Oriented Architectures. Springer Publisher book, Heidelberg (2010)
12. Xian, L.L.: Research of B2B e-Business Application and development technology based on SOA. In: Song, W.W., et al. (eds.) Information Systems Development. Springer Science + Business Media, LLC 2011, pp. 367–375 (2011)
13. Gutierrez, C., Fernandez-Medina, E., Piattini, M.: Web Services Security Development and Architecture: Theoretical and Practical Issues. Information Science Reference publishers (2010)
14. Yang, S.J.H., Lan, B.C.W., Hsieh, J.S.F., Chung, J.-Y.: Trustworthy Web Services: An experience-based model for trustworthiness evaluation. International Journal of Information Security and Privacy 1(1), 1–17 (2007)
15. Goschka, K.M., Froihofer, L., Dustdar, S.: What SOA can do for Software Dependability pp. 1-6
16. Xu, T., Yi, C.: SOAP-Based Security interaction of Web Service in Heterogeneous Platforms. Journal of Information Security, 1–7 (2011)
17. Lodi, G., Querzoni, L., Beraldi, R., Baldoni, R.: Combining Service-Oriented and Event-driven architectures for Designing Dependable systems, pp. 1 – 13
18. Hohn, S., Lowis, L., Jurjens, J., Accorsi, R.: Identification of Vulnerabilities in Web Services using Model-based Security, pp. 1 – 32. IGI Global (2010)
19. Rodigues, D., Estrella, J.C., Branco, K.R.L.J.C.: Analysis of Security and Performance aspects in Service Oriented architectures. International Journal of Security and its application 5(1), 13–30 (2011)
20. Al-Jaroodi, J., Al-dhaheri, A.: Security issues of Service-oriented middleware. International Journal of Computer Science and Network Security 2(1), 153–160 (2011)
21. Basin, D., Burri, S.J., Karjoth, G.: Separation of duties as a service. In: Proceedings of the 6 th ACM Symposium on Information, Computer and Communications Security, pp. 1–7. ACM, China (2011)
22. Mohammad, A., Kannan, G., Kannan, R., Khdour, T., Bani-ahmad, S., Alarabeyyat, A.: Toward Access Control Model for Web Services applications. International Journal of Research and Reviews in Computer Science (IJRRCS) 2(2), 253–264 (2011)

23. Accorsi, R., Wonnemann, C.: Indico. Information flow analysis of Business Processes for confidentiality requirements pp. 1-16
24. Coppolino, L., Romano, L., Vianello, V.: Security Engineering of SOA applications via Reliability patterns. Journal of Software Engineering and applications, 1–8 (January 2011)
25. Barletta, M., Calvi, A., Ranise, S., Vigano, L., Zanetti, L.: Workflow and access control reloaded. A declarative specification framework for the automated analysis of web services. Scalable Computing 12(1), 1–20 (2011)
26. Tartanoglu, F., Issarny, V., Romanovsky, A., Levy, N.: Dependability in the Web Services Architecture. In: de Lemos, R., Gacek, C., Romanovsky, A. (eds.) Architecting Dependable Systems. LNCS, vol. 2677, pp. 90–109. Springer, Heidelberg (2003)
27. Nakamura, Y., Tatsubori, M., Imamura, T., Ono, K.: Model-Driven Security Based on a Web Services Security Architecture. In: Proceedings of the 2005 IEEE International Conference on Services Computing, (SCC 2005) (2005)
28. Singh, M.P., Huhns, M.N.: Service Oriented Computing, Semantics, Processes, Agents. John Wiley & Sons, Ltd., Chichester (2005)
29. Stojanovic, Z., Dahanayake, A.: Service-Oriented Software System Engineering: Challenges and Practices. Idea Group Publishing, USA (2005)
30. Nitto, E.D., Sassen, A.-M., Traverso, P., Zwegers, A.: Service-Oriented Computing from an EU perspective. The MIT Press, Cambridge (2009)
31. Hafner, M., Breau, R.: Security for SOA. Springer, Heidelberg (2009)
32. Gritzalis, D., Lopez, J. (eds.): SEC 2009. IFIP Advances in Information and Communication Technology, vol. 297. Springer, Heidelberg (2009)
33. Tatnall, A.: Web Technologies Concepts, Methodologies, Tools and Applications I Premier Reference Source (2010)

Protocol for Simultaneous Ownership Transfer of Multiple RFID Tags with TTP

Wei Zhou[1,2] and Selwyn Piramuthu[2,3]

[1] Information & Operations Management, ESCP Europe, Paris, France
[2] RFID European Lab, Paris, France
[3] Information Systems and Operations Management, University of Florida Gainesville, Florida 32611-7169, USA
wzhou@escpeurope.eu, selwyn@ufl.edu

Abstract. Ownership transfer of items that are RFID-tagged require more than physical means to accomplish the process. Their inherent ability to communicate with entities that are not necessarily in their close proximity necessitates supplementary ownership transfer measures that complement the transfer of the physical item. Over the past few years, several ownership transfer protocols have been developed with the explicit purpose of transferring ownership of a tag from one owner to another. While it generally suffices to transfer ownership of tags one by one, sometimes it is necessary to simultaneously transfer ownership of multiple tags from one owner to another. This is especially true when multiple items are required to belong together during and outside of the ownership transfer process. Extant literature on RFID ownership transfer protocol, however, does not consider this scenario. We propose a protocol that attempts to address this gap in the literature.

Keywords: RFID, ownership transfer, multiple tags.

1 Introduction

Over the past five years, several ownership transfer protocols for RFID tags have been proposed and studied (e.g., [1], [2], [3], [6], [8], [9]). A majority of these have been found to have vulnerabilities that can readily be taken advantage of by a resourceful active adversary (e.g., [6]). A majority of these ownership transfer protocols deal with the common single tag - single owner scenario. A few (e.g., [5]) consider variations of this scenario such as the single tag - multiple owners, multiple tag - single owner, and inclusion/exclusion scenarios where tags move in and out of the system.

Another stream of research related to RFID authentication protocols include published literature that followed as a direct result of the 'yoking proof' ([4]) protocol, 'grouping proof' ([7]) protocol and their variants. Essentially, these protocols purport to simultaneously authenticate the presence of multiple tags in the field of the reader. Such a scenario may include, for instance in the example presented in [4], the necessity of simultaneous presence of a given pharmaceutical

D.C. Wyld et al. (Eds.): CNSA 2011, CCIS 196, pp. 150–156, 2011.

item along with its instructions. Although the intention is to authenticate the presence of multiple tags simultaneously, these protocols and a majority of their variants accomplish this in a sequential manner whereby the authentication of the first tag is immediately followed by the authentication of the next tag, and so on. Since these authentications are done sequentially as a compact batch, the process is almost similar to comparable simultaneous authentication of these tags.

To our knowledge, extant published literature does not include the scenario where tags that need to be simultaneously present together change ownership together from the same previous owner to the same new owner. Given the need for 'yoking proof' protocol and its variants and the need for ownership transfer protocols, it is not hard to envision the need for protocols that incorporate the dynamic present in both these scenarios. We purport to fill this gap in extant literature by proposing a protocol for verifying the simultaneous presence of multiple tags in the field of the reader while ownership transfer involving these tags takes place.

We consider the scenario where two tags that need to be simultaneously present in the field of the reader change ownership in the presence of a trusted third party (TTP). We do not consider the case where a TTP is absent. Without the presence of a TTP, it is extremely difficult to transfer ownership of items between two entities even if these two entities share a common secret that is not known to any other entity. In this case, the protocol becomes an ownership *sharing* one and not an ownership *transfer* protocol since the previous owner may continue to maintain RF access to the tag. Since this paper is not about ownership sharing, we do not consider the case where a TTP is absent. The proposed protocol is an extension of the single owner - single tag ownership protocol presented in ([6]) with appropriate and necessary modifications to incorporate verification of the simultaneous presence of multiple tags.

This paper is organized as follows: The next section provides a sketch of the proposed protocol for two tags transferring ownership between two owners in the presence of a TTP. Section 3 provides a brief security analysis of the proposed protocol. Section 4 concludes the paper with a brief discussion.

2 Simultaneous Ownership Transfer Protocol with TTP

Notation

The following notations are used in this paper:

- N_J: random l-bit nonce generated by entity J
- R_i, T_i reader/owner i, Tag i
- s_i: shared keys between/among entities (including tags)
- H: one-way hash function $\quad \{0,1\}^* \rightarrow \{0,1\}^l$
- f'_k, f_k: keyed (with key k) encryption function
- t_i: shared secret between tag$_i$ and TTP
- r_i: shared secret between reader R_i and TTP

The Proposed Protocol

The proposed protocol for simultaneous ownership transfer of two items that belong together is given in Figure 1. This protocol comprises five 'loops' between pairs of entities with the first three initiated by the trusted third party (TTP) and the other two initiated by the new owner (R_2). Figure 1 illustrates transfer of ownership of entities with tags T_i and T_j that belong together from previous owner (R_1) to the new owner (R_2). The process begins when the previous and new owner decide to transfer ownership and inform the TTP of the same. This step is not explicitly or implicitly modeled in the protocol. Although this protocol models transfer of ownership of two related items, this can readily be extended to any number of related items that need to be in close proximity of one another.

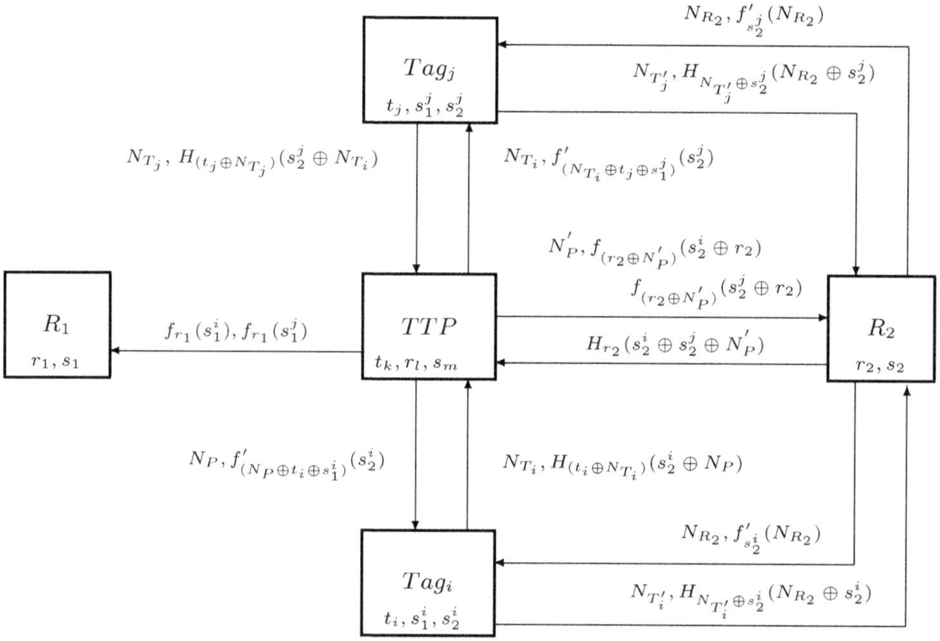

Fig. 1. Multi-Tag Simultaneous Ownership Transfer Protocol with TTP

The first 'loop' is between the TTP and one of the two tags (here, T_i). This step ($N_P, f'_{(N_P \oplus t_i \oplus s_1^i)}(s_2^i)$ from the TTP to tag T_i and $N_{T_i}, H_{(t_i \oplus N_{T_i})}(s_2^i \oplus N_P)$ from tag T_i to the TTP) essentially accomplishes generation of new shared key for the first Tag T_i (i.e., s_2^i) and secure transfer of this key to T_i. If the return message is blocked from getting back to the TTP for whatever reason, the TTP waits for a pre-determined amount of time and re-transmits the first message with a new nonce (N_P). Once the first loop is completed, the TTP uses the nonce (i.e., N_{T_i}) generated by the first tag (or, any tag, if there are several tags) to communicate with the second (or, next, if there are several tags) tag. The message used in the second loop follows a similar pattern as that in the first loop and the newly generated shared key (i.e., s_2^j) is securely sent to the second tag (T_j). The TTP again waits for reply from the second tag. If this reply is not received within a pre-determined amount of time, it repeats the entire process from the beginning by repeating the first loop. When there are more than two tags that belong together and need to verified of their simultaneous presence in the field of the reader, the second loop is modified appropriately - with the nonce generated by the previous tag in the sequence, the tag's shared key with the TTP, its current key, and its next key that is generated by the TTP - and repeated for each of these tags. The TTP verifies the acknowledgement from the tags for their authenticity.

The third loop is between the TTP and the new owner and is initiated by the TTP. This loop involves the transfer of the tags' secret keys (here, s_2^i, s_2^j) to the new owner. The new owner acknowledges receipt of these keys with $H_{r_2}(s_2^i \oplus s_2^j \oplus N_P^{'})$, where r_2 is the shared key between the TTP and this owner and $N_P^{'}$ is the nonce generated and sent by the TTP. When there are more than two tags, the messages are modified appropriately to incorporate the same. I.e., when c is the last tag in the sequence, the TTP modifies and includes the following for every tag that needs to be verified: $f_{(r_2 \oplus N_P^{'})}(s_2^c \oplus r_2)$ for the last tag in the sequence, with the appropriate s_2^* for each of the other tags in the sequence. Similarly, the new owner sends $H_{r_2}(s_2^i \oplus s_2^j \oplus \cdots \oplus s_2^c \oplus N_P^{'})$ to the TTP where c is the last tag in the sequence. Like in the first two loops, the TTP waits for acknowledgement from the reader. However, if the acknowledgement fails to materialize, the TTP repeats only this loop (unlike the case of the second loop or the last loop between TTP and the last tag in the sequence when there are more than two tags) with a freshly generated nonce ($N_P^{'}$).

Upon successful completion of this third loop in the protocol, the new owner is made aware of the tags' keys. The new owner completes the next two loops - i.e., the new owner authenticates the two tags using the next two loops - before acknowledging receipt of message to the TTP. I.e., the fourth and fifth loops are nested within the third loop. These next two loops (i.e., loops four and five) are initiated by the new owner (with $N_{R_2}, f_{s_2}^{\prime}(N_{R_2})$) and are similar in structure with the use of the same freshly generated nonce (N_{R_2}), except for the encryption keys used. The new owner waits for response from all the tags in the set that are verified for their simultaneous presence. If it does not hear back from even one of the tags, it re-transmits its message to *all* the tags with a different nonce (i.e., N_{R_2}). The response from the tags are verified for their authenticity. Once the tags' authenticity are verified, the new owner acknowledges the same to the TTP.

When the TTP gets the acknowledgement from the new owner, it sends the last message in the protocol (i.e., the message from TTP to the previous owner) informing the previous owner (i.e., R_1) with a message that is encrypted with the shared key (i.e., r_1) between the TTP and the previous owner that the previous keys (i.e., s_1^i, s_1^j) are no longer valid. The previous owner ceases to have access to these tags while the new owner begins to have access to these tags.

The protocol seems rather busy with several messages. However, it is a one-pass protocol between every pair of entities and we believe it is reasonable given what it accomplishes. We kept the following in mind while developing this protocol: (1) generate fresh nonce every time a new loop is run to ensure freshness of the message and to avoid repeating previously sent message, (2) reduce use of one-way hash functions since these are (computational) resource intensive, while using one-way hash function when necessary (3) the originating message in each loop is *synchronous* in a sense since it expects the recipient to acknowledge with a response, which when not received would trigger repeating the loop with a freshly generated nonce, (4) previous owner should not have access to the new tag secrets while the new owner does, (5) messages sent to the tags after the 'first' tag depend on and are derived from message sent to or generated by the 'previous' tag to ensure dependency among the authenticated set of tags and to prevent insertion of a fake tag by an adversary, and (6) not sending any identification information in cleartext. By following the above, the resulting protocol is free of obvious vulnerabilities that have been identified in the literature on cryptanalysis of existing RFID protocols. This, however, obviously does not provide any guarantees of the security of the proposed protocol. The security of this protocol can only be ascertained through detailed analysis and even then the nature of RFID protocols preclude any claims to its complete security against attacks from a resourceful adversary.

3 Security Analysis

We provide a brief security analysis of the proposed protocol. We do not attempt to provide a detailed analysis here since the proposed protocol is structurally similar to the one tag - one owner ownership transfer protocol presented in ([6]). Although the number of messages and the exact terms are slightly different and so are the number and type of entities participating in the proposed protocol, the essential structure of the message is similar from a security analysis perspective. Therefore, we omit the details in this paper and refer the interested reader to ([6]) for detailed security analysis using GNY and Strand logic. We now consider some of the common vulnerabilities that are generally present in such protocols and provide brief discussions on each.

1. Authenticity, secrecy, data integrity
   The messages that are seemingly vulnerable use one-way hash functions to ensure that they are not easily tampered with and other messages between any pairs of entities (tag, reader, TTP) are also encrypted and no clearly identifiable information is sent in cleartext.
2. DoS/Synchronization problem
   A means to denial of service (DoS) attack through blocking of messages or de-synchronization of secret keys is prevented through requirement of acknowledgement in all five loops in the protocol. I.e., the sender waits for the recipient to acknowledge its message before proceeding further. This mechanism facilitates alleviating issues including those associated with adversaries blocking messages between any two entities.

3. Relay attack
   Relay attack and its variants (e.g., Mafia attack, Terrorist attack) cannot be prevented using the proposed protocol since it is not protected against such attacks. A majority of existing RFID protocols are not immune to relay attacks. Although several means to address relay attacks exist, none of them *completely* prevent such attacks since these protocols use the round-trip time taken by messages between any two entities and measuring these necessitates access to extremely sensitive devices since these distances are generally small (e.g., a few centimeters to a few meters at the most) and it is extremely difficult to identify latency.
4. Prevention of Replay attack
   The proposed protocol addresses this issue through two means: (1) freshly generated nonce in every loop, and (2) no two messages between different pairs of entities are the same. While the former prevents an adversary from simply capturing and replaying the captured message to the same entity at a later point in time, the latter prevents copying message from an entity and replaying it with or without appropriate modifications to another entity.
5. Forward Security
   Knowing the current key, an adversary will not be able to decipher past messages between the entity of interest and any other entity. This is due to the one-way hash functions used to encrypt messages in every loop in the protocol.

4 Discussion

We developed a protocol that simultaneously accomplishes two tasks: verifying the simultaneous presence of multiple tags in the field of the reader and ownership transfer of multiple tags between two owners (represented by readers, here) in the presence of a trusted third party. Extant protocols accomplish either of these tasks separately but not both in one protocol. Incorporating both these tasks in one protocol accomplishes these with less overhead when a scenario dictates seamlessly accomplishing both these tasks. Clearly, given the existence of protocols for these individual tasks, there is no need to justify the rationale for the existence of each such protocol at this point in time. However, for the proposed protocol, it is necessary to justify the rationale for its need and its marginal benefits or advantages beyond what already exists in published literature.

Incidentally, the justification for the need for such a protocol is rather straightforward. It is not hard to imagine a scenario where two items need to be together (e.g., pharmaceutical item and its accompanying information materials; an electronic item and its necessary accessories such as a power cord) through a large part of their presence in a supply chain where they change ownership as a pair (or, as a group of items when there are > 2 items). There is, therefore, a need for such a protocol and we attempted to develop a protocol for such a scenario. We also presented a very brief security analysis of the proposed protocol.

While the proposed protocol only considered two tags, extensions to multiple tags is easily accomplished by appropriately modifying and repeating the messages between tag and TTP, tag and new owner, and TTP and new owner. The proposed protocol is certainly not immune to relay attacks like other extant ownership transfer protocols as well as 'yoking proof' protocol and its variants. We considered the scenario where a TTP is present. As was observed earlier (e.g., [6]), it is rather challenging to develop ownership transfer protocols without the presence of a trusted third party. The best one can do in such a situation (i.e., without a TTP) is a ownership *sharing* (as opposed to *transfer*) protocol where every previous owner continues to maintain RF access to the tag. Depending on the context of interest, this may not even be an issue. However, identifying a protocol as an ownership *transfer* protocol necessitates that it indeed strictly *transfers* ownership between entities and not a looser version where ownership is *shared* among current and all previous owners.

Given the track record of protocols developed for RFID authentication, such protocols are secure only until a vulnerability is identified regardless of any proof claiming otherwise. As have been illustrated in numerous other cases where protocols had been proven to be secure against attacks, only to be shown to be vulnerable to some attack by a resourceful adversary using an identified loophole. Regardless, we believe there is a need for protocols that seamlessly verify the simultaneous presence of multiple tags while accomplishing ownership transfer.

References

1. Chen, H.-B., Lee, W.-B., Zhao, Y.-H., Chen, Y.-L.: Enhancement of the RFID Security Method with Ownership Transfer. In: Proceedings of the ICUIMC, pp. 251–254 (2009)
2. Dimitriou, T.: RFIDDOT: RFID Delegation and Ownership Transfer Made Simple. In: Proceedings of the 4th International Conference on Security and Privacy for Communication Networks, (SecureComm) (2008)
3. Jäppinen, P., Hämäläinen, H.: Enhanced RFID Security Method with Ownership Transfer. In: Proceedings of the International Conference on Computational Intelligence and Security, pp. 382–385 (2008)
4. Juels, A.: Yoking Proofs for RFID Tags. In: Proceedings of the First International Workshop on Pervasive Computing and Communication Security. IEEE Press, Los Alamitos (2004)
5. Kapoor, G., Piramuthu, S.: Vulnerabilities in Some Recently Proposed RFID Ownership Transfer Protocols. IEEE Communications Letters 14(3), 260–262 (2010)
6. Kapoor, G., Piramuthu, S.: Single RFID Tag Ownership Transfer Protocols. IEEE Transactions on Systems, Man, and Cybernetics - Part C (2010)
7. Saito, J., Sakurai, K.: Grouping Proof for RFID Tags. In: Proceedings of the 19th International Conference on Advanced Information Networking and Applications (AINA 2005), pp. 621–624 (2005)
8. Song, B.: RFID Tag Ownership Transfer. In: Proceedings of RFIDSec 2008 (2008)
9. Yoon, E.-J., Yoo, K.-Y.: Two Security Problems of RFID Security Method with Ownership Transfer. In: Proceedings of the IFIP International Conference on Network and Parallel Computing, pp. 68–73 (2008)

A Preventive Measure to Protect from Denial of Service Attack

Manas Ku. Dasmohapatra[1], Kamalika Datta[1], and Indranil Sengupta[3]

[1] School of Computer Engineering, KIIT University,
Bhubaneswar- 756024, Orissa, India
[2] Dept. of Comp Sc. and Engg.
Indian Institute of Technology
Kharagpur- 721302
{manasd9,kdatta.iitkgp}@gmail.com
isg@iitkgp.ac.in

Abstract. As the number of users in the internet is increasing rapidly, various attacks are becoming an important issue which needs to be analyzed at the earliest. There exist various attacks like, ARP poisoning, IP spoofing, Denial of Service (DOS) etc. Now-a-days one of the major threats on the internet is Denial of Service (DOS) attack. As this attack slows down a particular system, the resources of that system becomes unavailable to others. DOS attack is mounted by consuming the resources of the victim system. By doing this, it can no longer provide the normal service to others. As the universe of DOS attack is large, there exists various different kind of DOS attacks like Distributive DOS attack, Low rate DOS attack etc. In this paper we have proposed a simple hashing based authentication technique which can protect computers from different DOS attacks. The main contribution of this paper is that, here prior to making a connection between source and destination, an authentication must take place at network layer. So before sending a packet to upper layer protocol such as TCP or UDP, this technique will ensure the authentication of the source in network layer. Here a Hash based DOS Attack Analyzer (HDAA) is used whose main job is to capture the packets in the network layer and perform an authentication. For the proposed method it is necessary for both source and destination to agree upon a set of rules and to pass the authentication process. If authentication passes, then it will deliver the data packet to upper layer protocol. If authentication does not pass then it will drop that packet and block that source address from entering the network. A thorough analysis have been made and compared with some existing techniques. The main advantage of this method lies in the application of simple hashing method in network layer which restricts the packet from entering our system initially. The computation overhead is also very less as this scheme can be implemented in network layer with respect to other techniques.

Keywords: DOS Attacks, Analyzer, Authentication, Network Security, Hash Function, Database.

D.C. Wyld et al. (Eds.): CNSA 2011, CCIS 196, pp. 157–166, 2011.

1 Introduction

With increasing dependency of computer users on internet, it has become extremely important to protect our computers from different network based attacks [3]. In general there exists various network attacks like IP spoofing, ARP poisoning, DOS attack, etc. Apart from some common attacks, each day new advanced attacks are been launched by attackers, essentially the hackers. To understand the importance and impact of these attacks, it is very much essential to analyze them a priori. Among various attacks, DOS attack is one of the common attacks, which is undoubtedly a very crucial attack in the internet. A DOS attack can be defined as an attack that prevent a legitimate user to get the normal service from the network. A DOS attack can be launched through various ways. There exists various forms by which DOS attacks can be launched. The attacker can consume resources of the victim machine such as bandwidth and processor time, so that it is unable to provide service to other computers. Also it can manipulate the routing information and state information for launching DOS attack [3].

So this paper puts an effort in analyzing the system first and then provides a mechanism which can detect as well as protect the system from DOS attacks. Rest of the paper is organized as follows, section 2 discusses different DOS attacks, section 3 gives a brief concepts of the protocol field and encapsulated data. Section 4 gives a detailed literature survey, section 5 provides the overall description of the proposed scheme and section 6 provides some information regarding the analysis of the scheme, followed by conclusion in the last section.

This paper gives a defense mechanism that is based on authentication principle. It will be able to detect the forge packet and also protect our communication network from various DOS attacks. Our main objective is to check the authentication of source before the data delivers to next higher level protocol from network layer at the destination side.

2 DOS Attack

There exists various different methods through which DOS attacks [4] can be mounted, such as ICMP flood attack, UDP flood attack, TCP/SYN attack, Smurf attack, low rate DOS attack, malformed packet attack and ping attack. Each of these attacks are explained in the following subsections.

2.1 ICMP Flood Attack

In ICMP protocol, ECHO REQUEST and ECHO REPLY messages are designed for diagnostic purposes. Sometimes one host checks whether the remote host is alive or not by sending ICMP ECHO REQUEST packets. Instead of sending a reply message, attacker sends large number of ICMP ECHO REPLY message to that requested sender. As a result it will increase the congestion of the network and the victim will remain busy by checking all forge packets.

2.2 UDP Flood Attack

This attack is designed by sending forge UDP packets to some random ports on the victim system. When victim system receives forge UDP packets, then only it realizes that there is no application waiting on the port. If large numbers of UDP packets are delivered to the ports of victim system then the system goes down.

2.3 Teardrop Attack

The main idea of this attack is that here attacker sends oversized payload to the victim system. This will crash different operating systems because it not supported by their TCP/IP fragmentation and re-assembly of packet.

2.4 Smurf Attack

In this attack, the attacker targets the victim source address. By using this source address the attacker broadcast ICMP ECHO REQUEST messages to the network. So all the machines connected to the network must send ICMP ECHO REPLY message to that victim. Therefore lot of unnecessary packets reach the victim address. It will unnecessarily consume resources.

2.5 Malformed Packet Attack

In malformed packet attack the attacker sends wrong IP packet to the victim. The packets contain the same source and destination addresses. So the victim system gets confused.

2.6 Distributed DOS Attack

A distributed DOS attack [2] occurs when multiple computers target the bandwidth or resources of one or more computers in the network.

2.7 TCP/SYN Attack

TCP is a transport layer protocol. Here each party must initialize communication and get approval from other party before any data are transferred.

In case of TCP/SYN attack, the client sends request (SYN) to the server. Then the server sends the "SYN+ACK" segment to the client and waits for final "ACK". In the mean time the client does not send the final "ACK" segment to the server. So connection remain half open. These half open connections saturate the number of available connections which the server is trying to make, keeping it from responding to legitimate requests until after the attack ends.

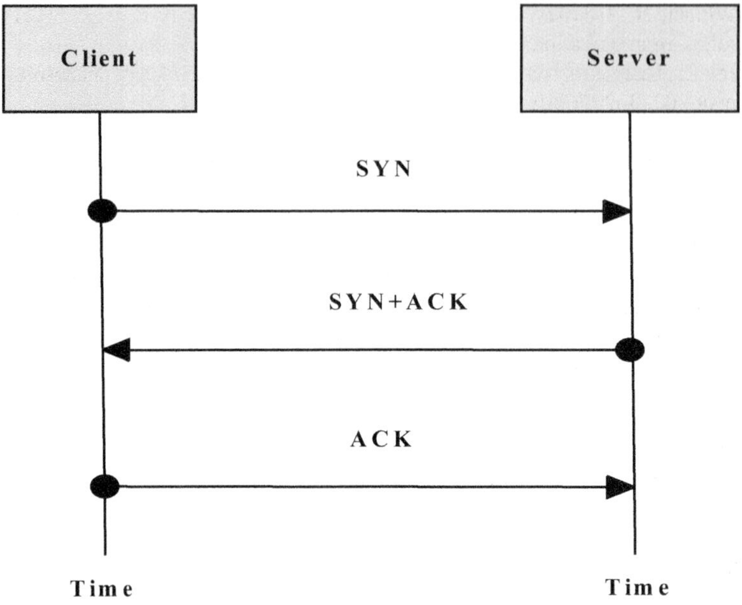

Fig. 1. Connection establishment in TCP

2.8 Low Rate DOS Attack

Low Rate DOS attack [5] is an attack, where attacker periodically sends large number of packet to the buffer which is shared by both attacker and sender. The main aim of the attacker is to keeping the buffer full for a sufficiently long time. So it forces the sender's TCP connection to timeout and increase the retransmission timeout interval, and decrease the congestion window by one packet. If such packet losses occur continuously, then the throughput of the TCP flow will decrease drastically.

2.9 Ping Attack

Ping attack is a very simple kind of DOS attack which can be mounted by sending a large number of ping packets to a target system using the "ping" command. These unnecessary packets cause flooding in the network and slows down the target system.

3 Protocol Field and Encapsulated Data

In network layer the IP datagram has a "protocol" field. The value of the protocol field defines to which protocol the data are to be transferred. According to this value, the data will get delivered to some higher level protocol such as TCP, UDP, ICMP, etc. Figure 2 shows the encapsulation of the data [3].

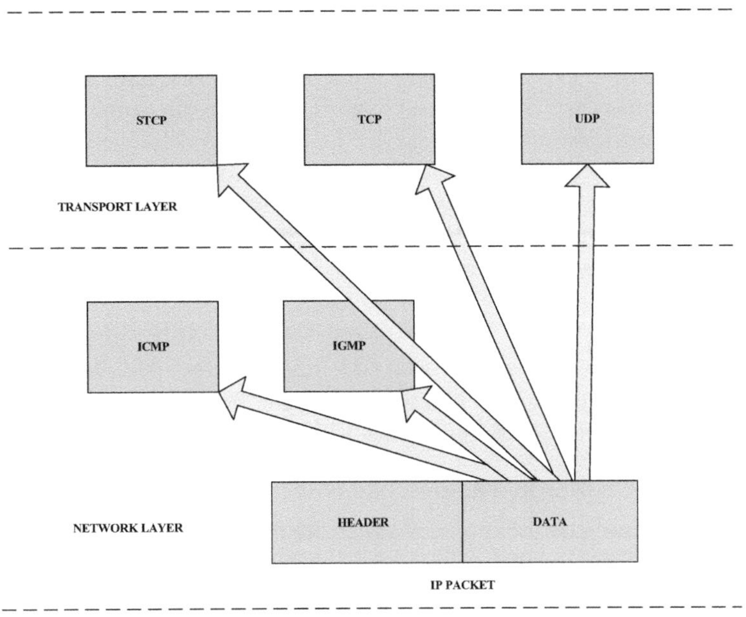

Fig. 2. Encapsulation of data

If value written in the protocol field is 1 then the data belongs to ICMP protocol. If the value of the protocol is 2, 6, 17, then data belongs to IGMP, TCP and UDP protocols respectively. Usually all the DOS attacks have been launched on transport layer or application layer protocols. So we can avoid it if we are able to detect the forge packets as early as possible.

4 Review of Existing Works

There exists a number of techniques that are developed to protect our network from different DOS attacks. Some are discussed below.

In [6] Haidari et al proposed an approach to detect the legitimate traffic and attack traffic with the help of entropy based scheme. First by doing some calculation they set a threshold value of entropy. According to the threshold value they send the legitimate packet into the first queue and others into second queue. The firewall will process the packet from the first queue first. If the first queue is found empty then the firewall will process the second queue. This scheme suffers from false positive decisions. If one legitimate packet measures as attack packet then it will send it to the second queue where it may have to wait for long time for execution.

In [1] Hyusand Choi et al proposed a scheme that is based on graphical signature. They take four different parameters such as: source address, destination address, destination port, and packet length for making graphical signature.

They consider some common DOS attacks and make graphical patterns for these attacks with the help of the four parameters and store it in a database. For detecting attacks, they capture a packet from the network and analyze the same through some analyzer. They form a graphical pattern from that packet and match it to some signature stored in database. This mechanism can only detect limited number of DOS attacks because they have also limited number of attack signatures present in the database. It will not be able to detect the attacker if the attacker attacks the network traffic in a different way.

In [5] Efstathopoulos proposed an approach which will protect our communication network from low rate TCP targeted DOS attack. According to this mechanism it will be more effective if we can randomly change the value of the minimum retransmission timeout (RTO), instead of using fixed value for the minimum RTO. So that it will difficult for the attacker to synchronize with RTO expiration interval. But randomizing the fixed minimum RTO will reduce the TCP connection performance in the absence of an attack.

In [7] Seonho Choi proposed a technique which uses one-way key chain and prediction hashing to protect the network against DoS attacks. Here the idea of prediction hashing is used where each block of packet carries authentication information which will be used to authenticate the next block packet. Here the sender is able to get a series of hash values by applying the same hash function again and again. These hash values will be assigned to the block of packets one by one in the backward order of their generation time. This is a very good technique which provides strong resistance against DOS attacks and it consumes less resources in comparison to other authentication methods.

5 Proposed Method

To secure our communication network from DOS attacks we propose a hash based authentication mechanism. It will work for a small organization. This scheme will work on Network layer. Many of the DOS attacks have been targeting to higher level protocols, such as ICMP, TCP and UDP. The attacker sends a lot of ICMP, TCP or UDP forge packets to the victim machine which consumes its resources. As a result of which the victim will not be able to do normal execution. So if we can perform the authentication of source before the data is delivered to higher level protocol from network layer at the destination side, then it will decrease the rate of DOS attack. After checking process, if that source is authenticated then only the packet will be send to upper level protocol and allocate resource for it. If it will not pass the authentication, then packet will not be sent to upper level protocol. It will drop that packet and also block that source.

5.1 System Design

In order to prevent the DOS attack we have designed a system of Hash based DOS Attack Analyzer (HDAA). For this scheme both sender and receiver of the organization have to agree upon a secret key. That means both the source and

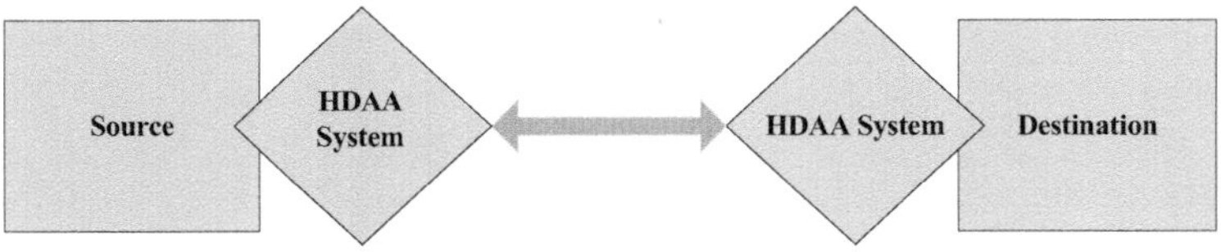

Fig. 3. Overview of HDAA system

destination has to use a common key for authentication purpose. The analyzer will provide these secret keys and store them in the database. We also use a hash key generator that will generate a random key. This random key is a public key. Any standard hash function can be used for this purpose. The hash function is also public. For example, we can use a function

$$H(x) = x^7 + x^5 + x^3 + 1 \tag{1}$$

The main objective is to check the authentication of source before the data is delivered to higher level protocol from network layer at the destination side. The HDAA consists of five modules: packet capturing tool, analyzer, database, hash function calculator and hash key generator. The packet capturing tool captures all packets from the network layer. Then the analyzer collects these packets and analyzes these packets thoroughly.

For every new session it will check against the rules of authentication. It checks the source address of the new arrival packets with its database entry. The database entry of the analyzer has four parameters, where it stores the address of the authenticated source, address of the attack source, hash key and result of the hash function. For every new session the analyzer will have to perform certain steps. Algorithm 1 shows the outline of the process. At first the analyzer checks whether the new IP address is present in the authenticated source or not; if present, it allows the packet to move forward. If it is not present in the authenticated source, it checks whether it is present in the attack list in the database. If that is also not present, then the hashing mechanism is performed for authentication purpose.

Algorithm 1
Steps performed by analyzer to check for new IP packet

```
begin
    if(IP packet present in authenticated address of database)
        Allow packet to get passed to higher level protocol;
    else if(IP packet present in attack list IP of the database)
        Drop the packet without checking further;
    else
        Apply hashing mechanism for authentication purpose;
end
```

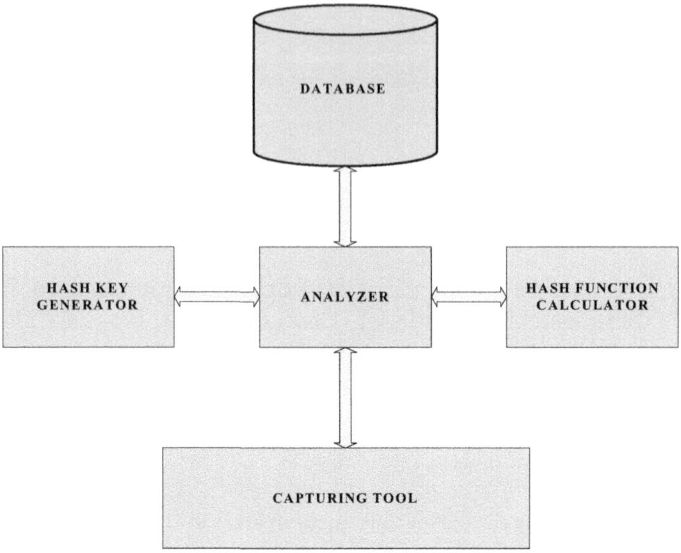

Fig. 4. System design of HDAA

We will explain the hashing mechanism with the help of an example. Suppose the secret key S which is shared between the source and the destination is 3. For the authentication purpose, first hash key generator of the HDAA System at the destination side generates a random key. Suppose the value of the random key X is 2.

After that it will send that random key to the analyzer which is the main part of the system. The analyzer adds both the keys (secret key and public key) and calculates the result with the help of the hash function calculator H.

$$C = S + X \tag{2}$$

where C is key which is used for calculations of the hash function If the hash function is $H(x) = x^7 + x^5 + x^3 + 1$, the resultant hash value will be 81376. The analyzer stores the result in the database of the HDAA system. It will then send the public key ($X = 2$) to the source and set the maximum waiting time for getting response from the source. Let the maximum waiting time is 1 second. If the analyzer does not receives the expected value within 1 second, then it will not appept the packet which is coming from that source.

Now we will discuss what will happen at the source end. When the source receives a hash key ($X = 2$) from destination, immediately it will send it to the analyzer part of the HDAA system. Already analyzer has its own secret key. It will add the secret key with the public key. Then the analyzer sends this key to the hash function calculator, where it can calculate the result with that hash function which is public to all. Obviously it will get the same result (81376) and return it to the analyzer, which in turn sends it to the destination.

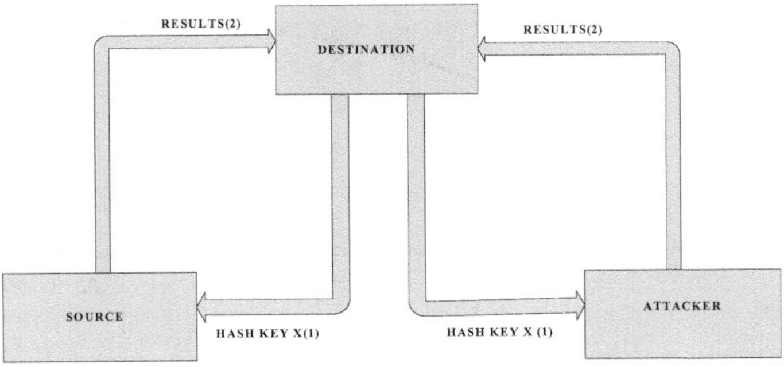

Fig. 5. HDAA Authentication

But in case of attacker, it does not have the secret key. So it is able to calculate the result of the hash function by using the public key ($X = 2$). It will send the result (169) to the destination.

After getting result from source, the analyzer of the destination will match this result with its result which is stored in the database. If both results are equal then it will deliver that data packet to upper level protocol and stores the source address to the "AUTHENTICATE ADDRESS" part of his database. If the results does not match then it will drop that packet and store the source address to the "ATTACK ADDRESS" part of database. For making it more secure we propose to change the secret key periodically, say, once in every ten days, so that it is difficult for attacker to gain access to the shared secret keys.

6 Analysis

There are many defense mechanisms present in communication networks for different types of DOS attacks. But none of them are fully able to give protection against various DOS attack. Each method has some flaws or the other. Different solutions exists for different DOS attacks, which also increases the CPU overhead for implementation.

The proposed defense mechanism (HDAA) will provide a strong defense against DOS attacks. Before a packet is delivered to upper level protocol and consume resources, HDAA will check it thoroughly. As a result congestion of the network automatically decreases.

Second disadvantage is that when analyzer does authentication for new source address, then it has to wait for some time for getting response from the source, which in turn increases the congestion as other new packets have to wait for authentication. One more problem can occur if the hash result sent by the source reaches the destination after exceeding the time limit. If this happens then sometime the authentic source will not be able to get access.

This proposed method proves to be a very simple solution to prevent DOS attacks. However, several improvements can be incorporated to enhance the performance.

7 Conclusion

A simple hash based preventive measure is proposed, which can protect our network from different DOS attacks. The work proposed in this paper can be implemented as an extension to the TCP/IP protocol stack. The software can be installed on individual machines which are connected to internet. The main advantage of this method is that it uses very simple mechanism and is computationally efficient. As the checking is performed in network layer, this is more advantageous as compared to other schemes. The technique provide significantly better resistance against many DOS attacks. The limitations discussed in the analysis section can be incorporated in future work to improve the proposed scheme.

References

1. Choi, H., Lee, H., kim, H.: Fast detection and visualization of network attacks on parallel coordinates. Science Direct 28, 276–288 (2009)
2. Douligeris, C., Mitrokosa, A.: DDoS attacks and defense mechanisms: classification and state-of-the-art, vol. 44, pp. 643–666 (2004)
3. Forouzan, B.A., Fegan, S.C.: Data Communication and Networking. Tata Mgraw Hill (2007)
4. Priselac, D., Marijic, D., MikucM: Analysis of DoS attack method on IMS system. In: Proceedings of 33rd Intl. convention on MIPRO, Opatija, Croatia, pp. 524–527 (2010)
5. Efstathopoulos, P.: Practical study of a defence against Low-rate TCP-targeted DoS attack. In: Proceedings of Intl. conf. on Internet Techonology and Secured Transactions, London, pp. 1–6 (2009)
6. AI-Haidari, F., Sqalli, M., Hamoodi, J.: An Entropy-based Countermeasure against Intelligent DoS Attack Targeting Firewalls. In: Proceedings of IEEE International Symp. on Policies for Distributed and Network, London, pp. 41–44 (2009)
7. Choi, S.: DoS Resistance Multicast Authentication Protocol with Prediction Hashing and One-Way Key Chain. In: Proceedings of Seventh IEEE Intl. Symp. on Multimedia, London, pp. 524–527 (2005)
8. Liu, Z., Guan, L.: Attack simulation and signature extraction of low-rate DoS. In: Proceedings of Third Intl. Symp. on Intelligent Information Technology and security Informatics, China, pp. 544–548 (2010)

Review of Some Checkpointing Algorithms for Distributed and Mobile Systems

Sunil Kumar Gupta[1] and Parveen Kumar[2]

[1] Beant College of Engineering and Technology, Gurdaspur-143521, India
skgbcet1965@rediffmail.com
[2] Meerut Institute of Engineering & Technology, Meerut (INDIA)-250005
pk223475@yahoo.com

Abstract. A distributed system is a collection of independent entities that cooperate to solve a problem that cannot be individually solved. A mobile computing system is a distributed system where some of processes are running on mobile hosts (MHs). Checkpoint is defined as a designated place in a program at which normal processing is interrupted specifically to preserve the status information necessary to allow resumption of processing at a later time. Checkpointing is the process of saving the status information. Over the past two decades, intensive research work has been carried out on providing efficient checkpointing protocols in traditional distributed computing. The existence of mobile nodes in a distributed system introduces new issues that need proper handling while designing a checkpointing algorithm for such systems. These issues are mobility, disconnections, finite power source, vulnerable to physical damage, lack of stable storage etc. Recently, more attention has been paid to providing checkpointing protocols for mobile systems. This paper surveys the algorithms which have been reported in the literature for checkpointing in distributed systems as well as Mobile Distributed systems.

Keywords: Fault tolerance, checkpointing, message logging, independent checkpointing, consistent global state, domino effect, coordinated checkpointing and mobile systems.

1 Introduction

A distributed system can be characterized as a collection of mostly autonomous processors communicating over a communication network. In mobile distributed computing system, some processes are running on mobile hosts (MHs). An MH is a computer that may retain its connectivity with the rest of the distributed system through a wireless network while on move or it may disconnect. It requires integration of portable computers within existing data network. An MH can connect to the network from different locations at different times. The infrastructure machines that communicate directly with the MHs are called Mobile Support Stations (MSSs). A cell is a logical or geographical coverage area under an MSS. All MHs that have identified themselves with a particular MSS, are considered to be local to the MSS. An MH can directly communicate with an MSS (and vice-versa) only if the MH is

D.C. Wyld et al. (Eds.): CNSA 2011, CCIS 196, pp. 167–177, 2011.

physically located within the cell serviced by the MSS. At any given instant of time, an MH may logically belong to only one cell; its current cell defines the MH's location [1].

There are two software based fault tolerance approaches for error recovery: (i) Forward Error Recovery, (ii) Backward Error Recovery.

In forward error recovery techniques, the nature of errors and damage caused by faults must be completely and accurately assessed and so it becomes possible to remove those errors in the process state and enable the process to move forward. In distributed system, accurate assessment of all the faults may not be possible. In backward error recovery techniques, the nature of faults need not be predicted and in case of error, the process state is restored to previous error-free state. It is independent of the nature of faults. Thus, backward error recovery is more general recovery mechanism [45].

There are three steps involved in backward error recovery. These are:

- Check pointing the error-free state periodically
- Restoration in case of failure
- Restart from the restored state

The global state (GS) of a distributed system is a collection of the local states of the processes and the channels. Local checkpoint is the saved state of a process at a processor at a given instance. Global checkpoint is a collection of local checkpoints, one from each process. A global state is said to be "consistent" if it contains no orphan message; i.e., a message whose receive event is recorded, but its send event is lost. A transit message is a message whose send event has been recorded by the sending process but whose receive event has not been recorded by the receiving process. To recover from a failure, the system restarts its execution from a previous consistent global state saved on the stable storage during fault-free execution. This saves all the computation done up to the last check pointed state and only the computation done thereafter needs to be redone. Processes in a distributed system communicate by sending and receiving messages.

Checkpointing can be uncoordinated, coordinated, communication induced based or message logging based. In uncoordinated or independent checkpointing, processes do not coordinate their checkpointing activity and each process records its local checkpoint independently [46]. It allows each process the maximum autonomy in deciding when to take checkpoint, i.e., each process may take a checkpoint when it is most convenient. It eliminates coordination overhead all together and forms a consistent global state on recovery after a fault. After a failure, a consistent global checkpoint is established by tracking the dependencies. It may require cascaded rollbacks that may lead to the initial state due to domino-effect. It requires multiple checkpoints to be saved for each process.

Coordinated checkpointing requires processes to orchestrate their checkpoints in order to form a consistent global state. Coordinated checkpointing simplifies recovery and is not susceptible to the domino effect, since every process always restarts from its most recent checkpoint. Also, coordinated checkpointing requires each process to maintain only one permanent checkpoint on stable storage, reducing storage overhead and eliminating the need for garbage collection. Its main disadvantage, however, is the large latency involved in committing output, since a global checkpoint is needed before messages can be sent to out side world [7, 37, 46].

Communication-induced checkpointing avoids the domino-effect without requiring all checkpoints to be coordinated [46]. In these protocols, processes take two kinds of checkpoints, local and forced. Local checkpoints can be taken independently, while forced checkpoints are taken to guarantee the eventual progress of the recovery line and to minimize useless checkpoints. As opposed to coordinated checkpointing, these protocols do no exchange any special coordination messages to determine when forced checkpoints should be taken.

Message logging and checkpointing can be used to provide fault tolerance in distributed systems in which all inter-process communication is through messages. Each message received by a process is saved in message log on stable storage. No coordination is required between the checkpointing of different processes or between message logging and checkpointing. The execution of each process is assumed to be deterministic between received messages, and all processes are assumed to execute on fail stop processes. When a process crashes, a new process is created in its place. The new process is given the appropriate recorded local state, and then the logged messages are replayed in the order the process originally received them. All message logging protocols require that once a crashed process recovers, its state needs to be consistent with the states of the other processes [46].

2 Checkpointing Protocols for Distributed Systems

In Chandy-Lamport [7] algorithm, each processor has a distinct set of neighbor processors. To communicate to a non-neighbor, a processor must send a message to the neighbor, which forwards the message onward. A master processor starts the algorithm by broadcasting a marker message to all its neighbors, and then committing its checkpoint. All other processors begin the algorithm upon receipt of the marker message. They too broadcast a marker Message to all their neighbors, and then commit a checkpoint. For each neighbor, a processor logs messages received from that neighbor from the time the processor starts checkpointing until the time a marker message is received from the neighbor. When markers have been received from all neighbors, no more messages have to be logged. This algorithm ensures that checkpoints compose a consistent cut. Moreover, all messages that cross the cut are logged by the receiving processor. Upon failure, all processors rollback to their checkpoints and replay messages from their logs.

Kim-Park [15] proposed a protocol for checkpointing recovery which exploits the dependency relationship between processes to achieve time-efficiency in checkpointing and rollback coordination. Unlike other synchronized protocols, in which the checkpointing coordinator collects the status information of the processes that it depends on and delivers its decision, the process in their protocol takes a checkpoint when it knows that all processes on which it computationally depends took their checkpoints. In this way, the coordinator of the checkpointing does not always have to deliver its decision after it collects the status of the processes it depends on; hence one phase of the coordination is practically removed. The checkpointing coordination time and the possibility of total abort of the checkpointing are substantially reduced. Reduction of the coordination roll back time is also achieved by sending the restart messages from the coordinator directly to the roll back processes, and concurrent activities of the checkpointing and roll back are effectively handled exploiting the process dependency relationship.

Koo- Toueg's [37] proposed a minimum process blocking checkpointing algorithm for distributed systems. The algorithm consists of two phases. During the first phase, the checkpoint initiator identifies all process with which it has communicated since the last checkpoint and sends them a request. Upon receiving the request, each process in turn identifies all processes it has communicated with since the last checkpoint and sends them a request, and so on, until no more processes can be identified. During the second phase, all processes identified in the first phase take a checkpoint. The result is a consistent checkpoint that involves only the participating processes. In this protocol, after a process takes a checkpoint, it can not send any message until the second phase terminates successfully, although receiving messages after the checkpoint is permissible.

Xu and Netzer [34] introduced the notion of ZigZag paths, a generalization of Lamport's happened-before relation and shown that notation of ZigZag path captures exactly the conditions for a set of checkpoints to belong to the same consistent global snapshot. They shown that a set of checkpoints can belong to the same consistent global snapshot iff no zigzag path exists from a checkpoint to any other.

Kumar et al. [24] proposed an all process non-intrusive checkpointing protocol for distributed systems, where just one bit is piggybacked onto normal messages. This is done by incurring extra overhead of vector transfer during checkpointing.

3 Checkpointing Protocols for Mobile Distributed Systems

The research on the problem of devising efficient checkpointing algorithms for distributed mobile systems was started by Acharya-Badrinath [1]. In their algorithm, hosts can take local checkpoints independently. This can be done because the checkpointing protocol ensures that every local checkpoint can become a part of global checkpoint. Moreover, the set of checkpoints with which a given local checkpoint has to be combined to form a global checkpoint is stored with the local checkpoint and in one round of messages an initiator can complete the formation of a global checkpoint.

Prakash-Singhal [35] has stated that a checkpointing algorithm for mobile distributed systems should have following characteristics: (i) It should be minimum process (ii) it should be non-intrusive (iii) it should not awake the MHs in "doze mode operations". They proposed a synchronous snapshot collection algorithm for mobile systems that neither forces every node to take a local snapshot, nor blocks the underlying computation during snapshot collection. Cao-Singhal [12] has shown that the algorithm [35] may lead to inconsistencies.

In [41], Kumar et al proposed a coordinated checkpointing scheme, in which, in the first phase, all concerned MHs will take soft checkpoint only. Soft checkpoint is similar to mutable checkpoint, which is stored on the memory of MH only. In this case, if some process fails to take checkpoint in the first phase, then MHs need to abort their soft checkpoints only. The effort of taking a soft checkpoint is negligibly small as compared to the tentative one. In this way, this scheme significantly reduce the loss of checkpointing effort when any process fails to take its checkpoint in coordination with others.

Gupta et al [44] proposed a minimum process coordinated checkpointing protocol. They used a concept of delaying some messages at the receiver end. By using this technique, only selective processes are blocked for a short duration and processes are allowed to do their normal computations and send messages in the blocking period. Every MSS maintains the dependency set for each process, on which it directly depends. The initiator process (say P_{in}) sends the checkpoint request to P_i only if P_{in} is directly dependent upon P_i. Similarly, P_i sends the checkpoint request to any process P_j only if P_i is directly dependent upon P_j.

Cao and Singhal [12] presented a minimum process checkpointing algorithm in which, the dependency information is recorded by a Boolean vector. This algorithm is a two phase protocol and saves two kinds of checkpoints on the stable storage. In the first phase, the initiator sends a request to all processes to send their dependency vectors. On receiving the request, each process sends its dependency vector. Having received all the dependency vectors, the initiator constructs an NxN dependency matrix with one row per process, represented by the dependency vector of the process. Based on the dependency matrix, the initiator can locally calculate all the processes on which the initiator transitively depends. After the initiator finds all the process that need to take checkpoints, it adds them to the set S_{forced} and ask them to take checkpoints. Any process receiving a checkpoint request takes the checkpoint and sends a reply. The process has to be blocked after receiving the dependency vectors request and resumes its computation after receiving a checkpoint request.

Cao-Singhal [11], proposed a minimum process coordinated checkpointing algorithm for mobile distributed systems. They introduced the concept of "mutable checkpoint", which is neither a tentative checkpoint nor a permanent checkpoint. It is saved on MH. The basic idea of the algorithm is as follows. In the first phase the initiator process, say , P_{in}, sends the checkpoint request to P_j iff P_{in} is directly dependent upon P_j. On getting the checkpointing request, P_j takes the following actions: (i) P_j takes its tentative checkpoint (ii) it finds the processes which are in its dependency vector but not in the minimum set received from the P_{in}. P_j sends the checkpointing request to such processes. Suppose P_i sends m to P_j after taking its tentative checkpoint. When P_j receives m and finds that it has not taken its tentative checkpoint for the current initiation, it can not conclude whether it will be included in the minimum set in the current initiation. In this case, if P_j takes its tentative checkpoint after receiving m, m will become orphan. Therefore, P_j, takes its mutable checkpoint before processing m. if P_j gets the checkpointing request, it converts its mutable checkpoint into tentative checkpoint; otherwise, at the time of commit, P_j discards its mutable checkpoint.

Weigang et al [42] presented a coordinated non-blocking algorithm for distributed mobile systems. They proposed to reduce the MHs' coordination message overhead by introducing an idea called proxy coordinator. The proxy coordinator is a process which is running on the MSS. When a process initiates the checkpointing operation, it takes its tentative checkpoint and sends the checkpointing request to all the dependent processes through its MSS. On receiving the checkpointing request by the initiator MSS, a process called proxy coordinator is started on this MSS. This proxy coordinator further coordinates the checkpointing process on behalf of the initiator process. They assumed that a process will not receive a checkpoint request associated with another initiator before the current executing one is completed. They shown that Cao-Singhal algorithm [11] may lead to inconsistencies during concurrent initiations.

Wang and Fuchs [43] proposed a coordinated checkpointing scheme in which they incorporated the technique of lazy checkpoint coordination into an uncoordinated checkpointing protocol for bounding rollback propagation. Recovery line progression is made by performing communication induced checkpoint coordination only when predetermined consistency criterion is violated. The notation of lazyness provides a trade off between extra checkpoints during normal execution and average rollback distance for recovery.

Awasthi-Kumar [2] proposed a minimum process coordinated checkpointing protocol for mobile distributed systems, where the number of useless checkpoints and the blocking of processes are reduced using the probabilistic approach and by computing the tentative minimum set in the beginning. This algorithm is the first one to combine blocking and non-blocking scheme in one algorithm.

Higaki-Takizawa [14] proposed a hybrid checkpointing protocol for mobile computing system. It is a hybrid of independent and coordinated checkpointing. The mobile Hosts take the checkpoint independently whereas the fixed stations take the coordinated checkpoint. The messages sent and received by MHs are stored in corresponding MSS. The algorithm has two defects. First, using independent checkpointing protocol may cause the domino effect. Second, coordinated and independent checkpointing protocols perform independently in mobile support stations and mobile hosts, and do not negotiate with each other. Therefore, it is difficult to obtain consistent global checkpoints.

4 Communication Induced Based Checkpointing Protocols for Distributed Systems and Mobile Computing Environment

Mannivannan and Singhal proposed a quasi synchronous checkpointing algorithm [31]. This algorithm is simple and has a merit of asynchronous checkpointing, low overhead, and a merit of synchronous checkpointing, low recovery time. In this algorithm, each process takes checkpoint independently, called basic checkpoints. Checkpoints triggered by message reception are called forced checkpoints. The checkpoint index is increased by one after taking a basic or forced checkpoint. When process P_i receives a message m, with piggybacked information $index_j$ from process P_j, and P_i's $index_i$ is smaller than $Index_j$, a forced checkpoint is taken to advance the recovery line. Although the algorithm has a low checkpoint overhead, it has to maintain multiple checkpoints.

In [8], Each process P_i maintains a logical clock lc_i that functions as P_i's checkpoint timestamp. The timestamp is an integer variable with initial value 0 and is incremented according to the following function:

1. lc_i increases by 1 whenever P_i takes a local checkpoint.
2. P_i piggybacks on every message m it sends a copy of the current value of lc_i. They denote the piggybacked value as m.lc.
3. Whenever P_i receives a message m, it compares lc_i with m.lc. If m.lc > lc_i, then P_i sets lc_i to the value of m.lc and takes a forced checkpoint before it can process the message.

The set of checkpoints having the same timestamps in different processes is a consistent state. There is always a recovery line corresponding to the lowest timestamp in the system, and the domino effect cannot happen.

5 Message Logging Based Checkpointing Protocols for Distributed Systems and Mobile Computing Environment

In [38] the authors proposed a checkpointing protocol CCUML-Coordinated Checkpointing with Unacknowledged Message Logging. A checkpoint initiator initiates taking of checkpoints at the end of each checkpoint interval. Processes take local checkpoints only after being notified by the initiator. However, there is no central initiator, but each process takes turn to act as the initiator at each checkpoint initiation. The guaranty that no message will be lost in case of failure, has been brought about by maintaining a log of unacknowledged messages along with the latest checkpoint in a process. The checkpointing algorithm proposed constructs consistent checkpointing in a distributed manner. The checkpointing protocol described eliminates the occurrences of both missing and orphan messages. Also, each and every checkpoint taken by a process contributes to a consistent global snapshot and hence only the last global snapshot has to be retained.

Elnozahy and Zwaenepoel [10] proposed a message logging protocol which uses coordinated checkpointing wth message logging. The combination of message logging and coordinated checkpointing offers several advantages, including improved failure free performance, bounded recovery time, simplified garbage collection and reduced complexity.

Johnson and Zwaenepoel [21] proposed sender based message logging for deterministic systems, where each message is logged in volatile memory on the machine from which the message is sent. The massage log is then asynchronously written to stable storage, without delaying the computation, as part of the sender's periodic checkpoint. Johnson and Zwaenepoel [20] used optimistic message logging and checkpointing to determine the maximum recoverable state, where every received message is logged.

David R. Jefferson [19] introduced the concept of anti-message. Anti-message is exactly like an original message in format and content except in one field, its sign. Two messages that are identical except for opposite signs are called anti-messages of one another. All messages sent explicitly by user programs have a positive (+) sign; and their anti-messages have a negative sign (-). Whenever a message and its anti-message occur in the same queue, they immediately annihilate one another. Thus the result of enqueueing a message may be to shorten the queue by one message rather than lengthen it by one.

6 Time Based Checkpointing Protocols

These protocols use time to avoid having to exchange messages during the checkpointing operation. These protocols make the coordination by having checkpoint timers at the different processes and these timers are approximately synchronized. In these protocols two techniques are used for synchronizing timers. When the process starts, the protocol sets the timer in all processes with a fixed value, the checkpoint period. Since processes do not begin at the same time, timers will expire at different times. The protocol [33] has a resynchronization mechanism that adjusts timers during the process execution. Each process piggybacks in its message, the time interval until the next checkpoint. When a process receives a message, it compares its local interval with the one just received. If the received interval is smaller, the process resets its timer with the received value. The protocol maintains a checkpoint number counter, CN, at each process to guarantee that the independently saved checkpoint verify the consistency property. The value of CN is incremented whenever the process creates a new checkpoint and is piggybacked in every message. The consistency property is ensured if no process receives a message with CN_m larger than the current local CN. The process creates a new checkpoint before delivering the message to the process if CN_m is larger than local CN. The recoverability property is guaranteed by logging at the sender all messages that might become in-transit. The sender processes also logs the send and receive counters. Duplicate messages are detected as they are during the normal operations.

7 Conclusion

A survey of the literate on checkpointing algorithms for mobile distributed systems shows that a large number of papers have been published. We have reviewed and compared different approaches to checkpointing in mobile distributed systems with respect to a set of properties including the assumption of piecewise determinism, performance overhead, storage overhead, ease of output commit, ease of garbage collection, ease of recovery, useless checkpointing, low energy consumptions.

References

[1] Acharya, A., Badrinath, B.R.: Checkpointing Distributed Applications on Mobile Computers. In: Proceedings of the 3rd International Conference on Parallel and Distributed Information Systems, pp. 73–80 (September 1994)

[2] Awasthi, L.K., Kumar, P.: A synchronous checkpointing protocol for mobile distributed systems: probabilistic approach. International Journal of Information and Computer Security 1(3), 298–314 (2007)

[3] Gupta, B., Rahimi, S., Liu, Z.: A new High Performance Checkpointing Approach for Mobile computing Systems. IJCSNS International Journal of Computer Science and Network Security 6(5B), 95–104 (2006)

[4] Lin, C.M., Dow, C.-R.: Efficient Checkpoint-based Failure Recovery Techniques in Mobile Computing Systems. Journal of Information Science And Engineering 17, 549–573 (2001)

[5] Subba Rao, C.D.V., Naidu, M.M.: A New, Efficient Coordinated Checkpointing Protocol Combined with Selective Sender-Based Message Logging. In: International Conference on Computer Systems and Applications, March 31-April 4, pp. 444–447. IEEE, Los Alamitos (2008)

[6] Men, C., Xu, Z.: Performance Analysis of Rollback Recovery Schemes for the Mobile Computing Environment. In: International Symposium on Parallel and Distributed Processing with Applications, ISPA 2008, December 10-12, pp. 371–378 (2008)
[7] Mani, C.K., Lamport, L.: Distributed Snapshots: Determining Global States of distributed systems. ACM transactions on computer systems 3(1), 63–75 (1985)
[8] Briatico, D., Ciuffoletti, A., Simoncini, L.: A distributed domino-effect free recovery algorithm. In: Proceedings of the IEEE International Symposium on Reliability, Distributed Software, and Databases, December, pp. 207–215 (1984)
[9] Elnozahy, E.N., Johnson, D.B., Zwaenepoel, W.: The performance of consistent checkpointing. In: Proceedings of 11th Symposium on Reliable Distributed Systems, pp. 39–47 (1992)
[10] Elnozahy, E.N., Zwaenepoel, W.: On the use and implementation of message logging. In: Digest of Papers: 24th Annual International Symposium on Fault Tolerant Computing, pp. 298–307. IEEE computer society, Los Alamitos (June 1994)
[11] Cao, G., Singhal, M.: Mutable Checkpoints: A New Checkpointing Approach for Mobile Computing Systems. IEEE Transactions On Parallel And Distributed Systems 12(2), 157–172 (2001)
[12] Cao, G., Singhal, M.: On the impossibility of Min-Process Non-Blocking Checkpointing and an efficient Checkpointing Algorithm for mobile computing system. In: Proceedings of International Conference on Parallel Processing, August 10-14, pp. 37–44 (1998)
[13] Li, G., Shu, L.: A low Latency Checkpointing Scheme for mobile computing system. In: Proceedings of the 29th Annual International Computer Software and Application Conference (COMPSAC 2005), pp. 491–496 (2005)
[14] Higaki, H., Takizawa, M.: Checkpoint- Recovery Protocol for Reliable Mobile Systems. In: Proceedings of the 17th Symposium on Reliable Distributed Systems, pp. 93–99 (October 1998)
[15] Helary, J.-M.: Observing global states of asynchronous distributed applications. In: Bermond, J.-C., Raynal, M. (eds.) WDAG 1989. LNCS, vol. 392, pp. 124–134. Springer, Heidelberg (1989)
[16] Kim, J.L., Park, T.: An efficient Protocol for checkpointing Recovery in Distributed Systems. IEEE Trans. Parallel and Distributed Systems, 955–960 (August 1993)
[17] Qiangfeng, J., Mannivannan, D.: An optimistic checkpointing and selective message logging approach for consistent global checkpoint collection in distributed systems. In: IEEE International on Parallel and Distributed Processing Symposium, IPDPS 2007, March 26-30, pp. 1–10 (2007)
[18] Juang, Venkatesan, S.: Crash recovery with little overhead. In: Proceedings of the 11th International Conference on Distributed Computer Systems, pp. 454–461 (1991)
[19] Jefferson, D.R.: Virtual Time. ACM Transactions on Programming Languages and Systems 7(3), 404–425 (1985)
[20] Johnson, D.B., Zwaenepoel, W.: Sender-based message logging. In: Proceedingss of 17th international Symposium on Fault-Tolerant Computing, pp. 14–19 (1987)
[21] Johnson, D.B., Zwaenepoel, W.: Recovery in Distributed Systems using optimistic message logging and checkpointing. Journal of Algorithms 11(2), 462–491 (1990)
[22] Plank, J.S.: Effect of checkpointing on MIMD architecture, Ph.D. thesis, department of computer science, Princeton University (1993)
[23] Kumar, P.: A low cost hybrid coordinated checkpointing protocol for mobile distributed systems. Journal of Mobile Information System 4, 13–32 (2008)
[24] Kumar, L., Mishra, M., Joshi, R.C.: Checkpointing in distributed computing systems. In: Concurrency in Dependable Computing, pp. 273–292 (2002)

[25] Lai, T.H., Yang, T.H.: On distributed snapshots. Information Processing Letters 25, 153–158 (1987)

[26] Li, H.F., Radhakrishnan, T., Venkatesh, K.: Global state detection in non-FIFO networks. In: Proceedings of the 7th International Conference on Distributed Computing Systems, pp. 364–370 (1987)

[27] Alvisi, L., Hoppe, B., Marzullo, K.: Nonblocking and orphan free message logging protocols. In: The Proceedings of 23rd Fault Tolerant Compting Symposium, pp. 145–154 (June 1993)

[28] Chandy, M., Lamport, L.: Distributed snapshots: Determining global states of distributed systems. ACM Transactions on Computer Systems 3(1), 63–75 (1985)

[29] Manabe, Y.: A distributed consistent global checkpoint algorithm for distributed mobile systems. In: 8th International Conference on Parallel and Distributed Systems (ICPADS 2001), Korea, June 26-29 (2001)

[30] Mandal, P.S., Mukhopadhyaya, K.: Checkpointing using Mobile Agents in Distributed Systems. In: Proceedings of the International Conference on Computing: Theory and Applications, (ICCTA 2007) (2007)

[31] Manivannan, D., Singhal, M.: A low overhead recovery technique using quasi synchronous checkpointing. In: Proceedings of the 16th International Conference on Distributed Computing Systems, pp. 100–107 (1996)

[32] Mattern, F.: Efficient algorithms for distributed snapshots and global virtual time approximation. Journal of Parallel and Distributed Computing 18, 423–434 (1993)

[33] Neves, N., Fuchs, W.K.: Adaptive Recovery for Mobile Environments. In: Proceedings of the IEEE High-Assurance Systems Engineering Workshop (October 1996)

[34] Netzer, R.H.B., Xu, J.: Necessary and sufficient conditions for consistent global snapshots. IEEE Transactions on Parallel and Distributed Systems 6(2), 165–169 (1995)

[35] Prakash, R., Singhal, M.: Low-Cost Checkpointing and Failure Recovery in Mobile Computing Systems. IEEE Transaction on Parallel and Distributed Systems 7(10), 1035–1048 (1996)

[36] Kumar, P., Lumar, L., Chauhan, R.K.: A Non-Intrusive minimum process synchronous checkpointing protocol for mobile distributed systems. In: Proceedings of IEEE ICPWC-2005 (2005)

[37] Koo, R., Toueg, S.: Checkpointing and rollback recovery for distributed systems. IEEE transactions on software engineering SE-13(1), 23–31 (1987)

[38] Neogy, S., Sinha, A., Das, P.K.: CCUML: a check pointing protocol for distributed system processes. In: TENCON 2004, Thailand, vol. B(2), pp. 553–556 (November 2004)

[39] Basu, S., Palchaudhuri, S., Podder, S., Chakrabarty, M.: A Checkpointing and Recovery Algorithm Based on Location Distance, Handoff and Stationary Checkpoints for Mobile Computing Systems, In: International Conference on Advances in Recent Technologies in Communication and Computing 2009, October 27-28, pp. 58-62 (2009)

[40] Silva, L.M., Silva, J.G.: Global checkpointing for distributed programs. In: Proc. 11th symp. Reliable Distributed Systems, pp. 155–162 (October 1992)

[41] Kumar, P., Garg, R.: Soft Checkpointing Based Hybrid Synchronous Checkpointing Protocol for Mobile Distributed Systems. International Journal of Distributed Systems and Technologies 2(1), 1–13 (2011)

[42] Ni, W., Vrbsky, S.V., Ray, S.: Low Cost Coordinated Nonblocking checkpointing in Mobile Computing Systems. In: Proceedings of the 8th IEEE International Symposium on Computers and Communication (ISCC 2003), pp. 62–69 (2003)

[43] Wang, Y.M., Fuchs, W.K.: Lazy checkpoint coordination for bounding rollback propagation. In: Proceedings of IEEE Symposium on Reliable Distributed Systems, pp. 78–85 (1993)
[44] Gupta, S.K., Chauhan, R.K., Kumar, P.: A Minimum-process Coordinated Checkpointing Protocol for Mobile Computing Systems. International Journal of Foundations of Computer Science 19(4), 1015–1038 (2008)
[45] Singhal, M., Shivaratri, N.: Advanced Concepts in Operating Systems. McGraw Hill, New York (1994)
[46] Elnozahy, E.N., Alvisi, L., Wang, Y.M., Johnson, D.B.: A Survey of Rollback-Recovery Protocols in Message-Passing Systems. ACM Computing Surveys 34(3), 375–408 (2002)

Using Raga as a Cryptographic Tool

Sandip Dutta[1,*], Soubhik Chakraborty[2], and N.C. Mahanti[2]

[1] Dept. of Information Technology, Birla Institute of Technology, Mesra,
Ranchi - 835215, India
sandipdutta@bitmesra.ac.in
[2] Dept. of Applied Mathematics, Birla Institute of Technology, Mesra,
Ranchi - 835215, India
soubhikc@yahoo.co.in,
ncmahanti@rediffmail.com
http://www.bitmesra.ac.in

Abstract. Music can be used as a special language of codes and ciphers. Music cipher is one possible way to communicate among many others. Musical notes with letters are equated in such a way as to make a work or phrase. Broadcast messages encrypted by the sender in the musical notes and decrypted by the receiver can help to protect the message from the intruder. The paper proposes raga as a cryptographic tool. Apart from the novelty, we discover some potential benefits.

Keywords: Encryption, Decryption, Musical Notes, Raga, Malkauns.

1 Introduction

Cryptography is not only meant to encrypt the message but also necessary to hide the information which is being sent. So Steganography and Cryptography together are used to encrypt the required data using a key. Encrypting algorithms can be classified into three broad categories. They are Symmetric, Asymmetric and Digest algorithms. In Symmetric algorithm encryption and decryption are done with the same key. Asymmetric algorithms are those which use public key for encryption and private key for decryption purpose. A message digest algorithms uses hashing algorithm to generate a key and encryption and decryption is done with the same key. This algorithm can be termed better of the symmetric, asymmetric and digest algorithms because it does not depend on the key. If the attacker can able to get the key while transferring and attacker knows the algorithm, the message can be easily decrypted. Another advantage of our algorithm is that the message is transferred as a musical note and it is very difficult for intruder to know the message.

2 Previous Work

Data hiding in music [1] and in speech signals [2]-[3] were conducted with the help of watermarking system. Deterioration of the sound quality is relatively small because

* Corresponding author.

D.C. Wyld et al. (Eds.): CNSA 2011, CCIS 196, pp. 178–183, 2011.

the human auditory system is less sensitivity to modulation masking and modulation detection. Previously most of the research is done on watermarking in music for copyright protection. We propose a new algorithm where the message is encrypted in the form of musical notes.

3 Attack

One of the most destructive and the most effective attack can be brought about by using a technique called packet sniffing. This is a process in which attacker machines on a network sniff the packets (capture the packet or the data streams) over a network resulting in data theft, illegitimate e-commerce and so on. The process of packet sniffing starts with intrusion into a network. The packet sniffer monitors the entire packet stream that is transferred to and from the target machine.

There might be a case of using honey pots. The concept is to provide a network to users which are manipulated to transfer all of the traffic through a machine (computer) that the attacker can use at ease. Thus, it becomes very easy for the attacker to misuse people's information. The packet sniffer and man in the middle attack is most applicable in network. In our algorithm it is very difficult to predict the hidden information because encrypted information is sent by the sender to receiver in term of musical nodes.

4 Description

A raga, which is the nucleus of Indian classical music, may be defined as a melodic structure comprising of fixed notes and a set of rules (specific note combinations and how they are to be rendered, allowable note sequences in ascent and descent, which notes to stress on and how etc.) characterising a certain mood conveyed by performance [4]. Here we have taken raga Malkauns to illustrate our technique. This is a pentatonic raga that consists of the five notes Sa, komal Ga (g), Sudh Ma (M), komal Dha (d) and komal Ni (n). The terms Sudh and komal means natural and flat respectively. In an earlier work [5], the raga sequence of 262 notes taken from a standard text [6] were put into three groups namely G1, G2, and G3. The group G1 comprised the first 87 notes, group G2 the next 87, and the group G3 the next last 88 notes. We analysed the group wise as well as the overall distribution of the notes. Chi-Square tests verified our null hypothesis that the overall relative note frequency is maintained in the three component groups. Hence the unconditional probability of a note can be taken to be not changing significantly from one instance to another. This, together with the overall independence of the notes, verified by a run test, confirmed a multinomial model. We next considered the conditional probabilities which are crucial since overall independence does not imply overall mutual independence, not even independence in pairs. Assuming a first order Markov chain, table 1 gives the transition probability matrix of the notes of the raga *Malkauns*. To find P (x/y) which is the probability for the next note to be **x** given that the present note is **y,** the number of times y is followed by x is divided by the total number of times y occurs in the entire sequence. If y is the last note in the sequence, there is no information of the next transition. Hence, in that special case, we simply subtract one from the denominator.

Let p(i,j) be the probability in the i-th row and j-th column of the transition probability matrix of raga Malkauns. A Malkauns note sequence is simulated by the algorithm MALKAUNS [5]. The choice of first order in Markov chain for generating the transition probability matrix has been justified in a related work through an ARIMA model of lag unity [7].

4.1 Algorithm MALKAUNS

Step 1: The note at the instance 1 is taken to be the tonic Sa or simply S.

Step 2: The next note is simulated by using the transition probabilities at S (table io5). The idea is to generate a uniform variate X in the range [0, 1] and the note at instance 2 is obtained as S, g, m, d, or n depending upon whether X falls in the range [0, p(1,1)], [p(1,1), p(1,1)+p(1,2)], [p(1,1)+p(1,2), p(1,1)+p(1,2)+p(1,3)], [p(1,1)+p(1,2)+p(1,3), p(1,1)+p(1,2)+p(1,3)+p(1,4)] or [p11+p12+p13+p14, 1]. The logic is that since X is a U [0, 1] variate, so P (a<X<b) = b-a.

Step 3: The next note is similarly simulated using the corresponding transition probability row of the previous note and the cumulative probabilities to form intervals. This process is repeated. For an extensive literature on algorithmic composition, refer to [8].

4.2 Raga as a Cryptographic Tool

In the present work, we prepare an array of independent U[0, 1] variates (four digits taken after the decimal point). The length of the array is kept as the maximum of the ASCII values of the possible distinct characters that can come in the message. Corresponding to each character, its ASCII value gives the index of the array. The corresponding array entry is then taken which is a U[0, 1] variate and the algorithm_MALKAUNS is followed to give the musical note. The next character in the message will give similarly the next U[0, 1] variate and hence we get another note by following the same procedure. If the characters are random, overall at least, we can assume we are getting a simulated Malkauns note sequence which, except for the first note which we fixed as Sa, also contains the hidden message! In other words, the simulated Malkauns note sequence is the encrypted message in terms of musical notes except the first. This simulated sequence is send to the receiver and the receiver will then decrypt the message reversing the process to get back the original message. Of course, this sequence may not be a correct Malkauns sequence, nor can we make changes to make it correct (as otherwise the message will change), but the target of hiding a message using raga notes is definitely accomplished. That said, we do however emphasize that Malkauns is one of the easiest and yet one of the serious ragas where you are more likely to be correct in terms of the raga note sequence unless you create something totally absurd. Hence, a simulated Malkauns sequence is more likely to be close to what could be an accepted Malkauns sequence as compared to a simulated sequence in any other raga being close to being an accepted sequence in the concerned raga. So we preferred to experiment with Malkauns than with other ragas.

Table 1. Transition Probability Matrix

	S	g	M	d	n
S	6/55	4/55	9/55	17/55	19/55
g	11/43	1/43	26/43	1/43	4/43
M	0/62	37/62	7/62	14/62	4/62
d	4/49	1/49	19/49	0/49	25/49
n	34/52	0/52	1/52	17/52	0/52

Table 2. Sequence Matrix

	S	g	M	d	n
S	(0.0000-0.1091)	(0.1092-0.1818)	(0.1819-0.3455)	(0.3456-0.6545)	(0.6546-1.000)
g	(0.000-0.2558)	(0.2559-0.2791)	(0.2792-0.8837)	(0.8838-0.9070)	(0.9071-1.000)
M	(0.000-0.000)	(0.000-0.5968)	(0.5969-0.7097)	(0.7098-0.9355)	(0.9356-1.000)
d	(0.000-0.0816)	(0.0817-0.1020)	(0.1021-0.4898)	(0.4898-0.4898)	(0.4899-1.000)
n	(0.000-0.6538)	(0.6538-0.6538)	(0.6539-0.6731)	(0.6732-1.000)	(1.000-1.000)

4.3 Algorithm for Encryption and Decryption

English alphabets (small and big) with the special characters can be accommodated in an array of size 150 (150 being the maximum ASCII value). Each array element is a four digited uniform U[0, 1] number and is unique in the array, generated with the formula a + (b-a).*rand(150,1), where a = 0.0001 and b = 1 using MATLAB. (1)

The ASCII value of each letter of the message is matched with the index of the array. For example if we want to send a message "Wish you a happy and prosperous New Year 2011". The corresponding ASCII values of the message are 87, 105, 115, 104, 32, 121, 111, 117, 32, 97, 32, 104, 97, 112, 112, 121, 32, 97, 110, 100, 32, 112, 114, 111, 115, 112, 101, 114, 111, 117, 115, 32, 78, 101, 119, 32, 89, 101, 97, 114, 32, 50, 48, 49, 49 and the corresponding unique random sequence turns out to be 0.8055, 0.6978, 0.2111, 0.3091, 0.6038, 0.5004, 0.0233, 0.5494, 0.6038, 0.2543, 0.6038, 0.3091, 0.2543, 0.1608, 0.1608, 0.5004, 0.6038, 0.2543, 0.1668, 0.6577, 0.6038, 0.1608, 0.9536, 0.0233, 0.2111, 0.1608, 0.7783, 0.9536, 0.0233, 0.5494, 0.2111, 0.6038, 0.3405, 0.7783, 0.4607, 0.6038, 0.3131, 0.7783, 0.2543, 0.9536, 0.6038, 0.8524, 0.2508, 0.2860, 0.2860. The above random sequence is again matched with the sequence matrix of table - 2 starting with S. The value is searched in the specific row of S and when it falls within a certain range, for example here the range for n, then the difference of the random number and the upper limit of the range is calculated (for n/S, we get 1 – 0.8055 = 0.1945). Again the next value is similarly searched from corresponding row of n. Like that the note sequence is generated along with the corresponding differences, which are as follows n/S, d/n, M/d, g/M, M/g, g/M, S/g, d/S, n/d, S/n, d/S, M/d, g/M, S/g, g/S, M/g, M/M, g/M, S/g, n/S, S/n, g/S, n/g, S/n, M/S, g/M, M/g, n/M, S/n, d/S, M/d, M/M, g/M, M/g, g/M, M/g, g/M, n/g, S/n, n/S, S/n, M/S & g/M and the corresponding differences are 0.1945, 0.3022, 0.2787, 0.2877, 0.2799, 0.0964, 0.2325, 0.1051, 0.3962, 0.3995, 0.0507, 0.1807, 0.3425, 0.095, 0.021, 0.3833, 0.1059, 0.3425, 0.089, 0.3423, 0.05, 0.021, 0.0464, 0.6305, 0.1344, 0.1183, 0.1054, 0.0464, 0.6305, 0.1051, 0.2787, 0.1059, 0.2563, 0.1054, 0.1361, 02799, 0.2837, 0.1054, 0.3425, 0.0464, 0.05, 0.1476, 0.403, 0.0595 & 0.3108. The above musical note sequence and the differences are sent to receiver. The sender previously sends to the receiver the value of a, b and the database of 262 notes or reference no from where the 262 notes can be generated. The values of a and b are unique for different users used for authentication purpose. The receiver generates the sequence matrix of Table -2 as the sender using the database of 262 notes supplied by the sender to the receiver and the unique random sequence using (1). The receiver then matches the corresponding note from sequence matrix of table-2 and subtracts the differences from the upper limit of corresponding ranges to get back the original random sequence. From the position of random sequence the corresponding ASCII value is generated and from the ASCII value the receiver gets back the original message.

5 Main Features of the Proposed Algorithm

a. It is very difficult for the intruder to know the message, which is encrypted as musical notes.

b. Values of a and b, while calculating random sequence in equation (1), can be changed for different persons to make it unique.

c. The proposed algorithm is tested for raga Malkauns but this can be used with any other raga.

d. In this algorithm, key such as public key or private key are not used, so the user does not require to search a public database for public key for encryption or remember a private key for decryption.

e. Authentication is done with the value of a and b described in equation (1).

6 Conclusion

The encryption and decryption based on musical notes have many advantages over the current encryption, decryption algorithm because the technique does not depend on the symmetric and asymmetric key. Users do not have to remember the key and it is safe from the attacker. The proposed method is tested with raga Malkauns but this algorithm can be easily modified for different ragas.

References

1. Nishimura: Audio watermarking based on sinusoidal amplitude modulation. In: Proceedings of ICASSP 2006, vol. IV, pp. 797–800. IEEE, Los Alamitos (2006)
2. Nishimura: Audio watermarking based on sub-band amplitude modulation. In: Proceedings of the 2006, Symposium on Cryptography and Information Security, vol. 3F4-2, IEICE (2006)
3. Nishimura, A.: Data hiding for speech sounds using sub-band amplitude modulation robust against reverberations and background noise. In: Proceedings of IIH-MSP, pp. 7–10. IEEE, Los Alamitos (2006)
4. Chakraborty, S., et al.: Analyzing the melodic structure of a North Indian raga: A Statistical approach. Electronic Musicological Review, Vol. XII (2009a)
5. Chakraborty, S., Kumari, M., Solanki, S.S., Chatterjee, S.: On What Probability can and cannot do: A case study in Raga Malkauns. Journal of Acoustical Society of India 36(4), 176–180 (2009b)
6. Dutta, D.: Sangeet Tattwa, Vol. 1, Brati Prakashani, 5th ed, (2006) (in Bengali)
7. Chakraborty, S., Shukla, R.: Raga Malkauns Revisited with Special Emphasis on Modeling, Ninad. Journal of ITC Sangeet Research Academy 23 (December 2009)
8. Nierhaus, G.: Algorithmic Composition: Paradigms of Automated Music Generation, 1st edn. Springer Publishing Company, Inc, Heidelberg (2008)

Combining Power of MATLAB with SystemVerilog for Image and Video Processing ASIC Verification

Dhaval Modi[1], Harsh Sitapara[2], Rahul Shah[3], Ekata Mehul[4], and Pinal Engineer[5]

The Fourth International Conference on Network Security & Applications (CNSA-2011)
[1] P.G. Student, L.D. College of Engineering, Ahmedabad, Gujarat, India
[2] P.G. Student, M.S. University, Baroda, Gujarat, India
[3,4] ASIC Division, E-INFOCHIPS Pvt. Ltd., Ahmedabad, Gujarat, India
[5] S.V.N.I.T., Surat, Gujarat, India
dhavalmodi045@yahoo.com, harsh.sitapara@einfochips.com, rahulv.shah@einfochips.com, ekata.mehul@einfochips.com, pje@eced.svnit.ac.in

Abstract. The ultimate Aim of ASIC verification is to obtain the highest possible level of confidence in the correctness of a design, attempt to find design errors and show that the design implements the specification. Complexity of ASIC is growing exponentially and the market is pressuring design cycle times to decrease. Traditional methods of verification have proven to be insufficient for Digital Image processing applications. We develop a new verification method based on SystemVerilog verification with MATLAB to accelerate verification. The co-simulation is accomplished using MATLAB and SystemVerilog coupled through the DPI. Here is used the Image Resize design verification as case study by using co-simulation method between SystemVerilog and MATLAB. Golden reference will be made using MATLAB In-built functions, while rest of the Verification Environment are in SystemVerilog. The goal is to find more bugs from the Design as compared to traditional method of Verification, reduce time to verify video processing ASIC, reduce debugging time, and reduce coding length.

Keywords: Code base, API, DPI, Design cycle time.

1 Introduction

Today the Integrated Circuits (IC) design industry is associated with very complex designs, reusable intellectual property (IP), and System-on-Chip (SoC) designs. Leading chip development teams report that functional verification has become the biggest bottleneck, consuming approximately 70% of chip development time and efforts. for Digital Image processing, RTL test-benches have become too complex to manage and slow to execute. New method has to be discovered to reduce verification cycle. Image processing designs begin with algorithmic modelling in the MATLAB environment. We believe that verification could be significantly improved and accelerated by reusing these golden references models in MATLAB.

D.C. Wyld et al. (Eds.): CNSA 2011, CCIS 196, pp. 184–193, 2011.

1.1 Verification Architecture Using Co-simulation Interface

The MATLAB environment is a high-level technical computing language for algorithm development, data visualization, data analysis and numerical computing which also include Simulink for multi-domain simulation and model-based design.

SystemVerilog has become a concrete RTL level verification language used by many industries. One of the good capabilities of SystemVerilog is to develop hierarchical modular verification environment random stimuli.

Here golden reference is in MATLAB and design Under Test is in HDL. Scoreboard compares the output of golden reference and DUT. We require an efficient transition between algorithmic level and RTL level design. Thus, we need a co-simulation between the MATLAB environment and SystemVerilog.

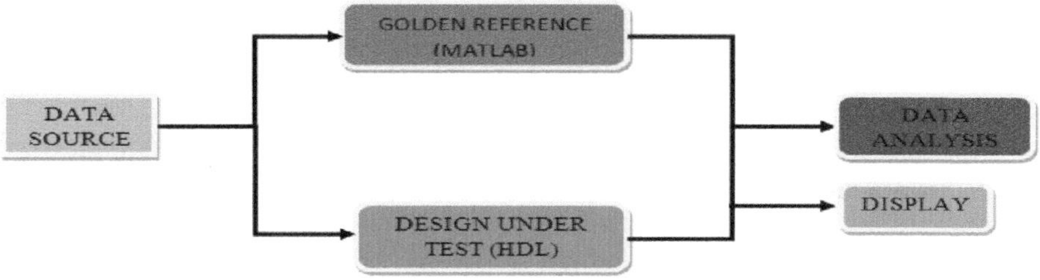

Fig. 1. Concept for Verification Environment

2 Co-simulation between SystemVerilog and MATLAB

SystemVerilog language doesn't provide any facility to directly call the MATLAB. The SystemVerilog Direct Programming Interface (DPI) is basically an interface between SystemVerilog and a foreign programming language. It allows the designer to easily call C functions from SystemVerilog and SystemVerilog function from C. We use the C program to call MATLAB Engine library.

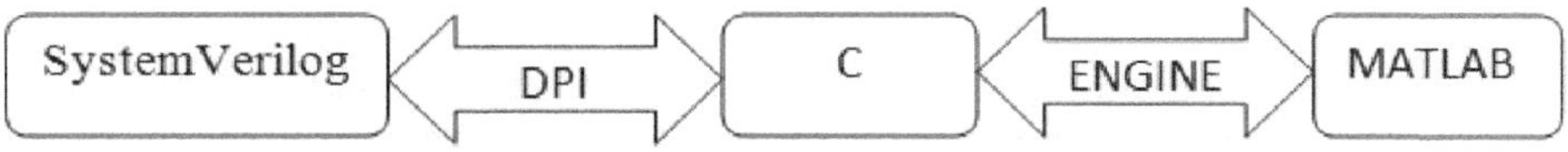

Fig. 2. Interface between SystemVerilog and MATLAB

With the link between SystemVerilog and MATLAB, it opens up a wide range of additional capability to SystemVerilog, like stimulus generation and data visualization. The first advantage of our technique is to use the right tool for the right task.

2.1 Co-simulation between MATLAB and C

2.1.1 The MATLAB Engine Library

To enable C to call MATLAB, we use 'engine' library available within MATLAB which contains library of routines that allow us to call MATLAB from our own program. They are standalone C/C++ programs that communicate with a separate MATLAB process via pipes. MATLAB provides a library of functions that allows us to start and end the MATLAB process, send data to and from MATLAB, and send commands to be processed in MATLAB.

The MATLAB language works with only a single object type: MATLAB arrays which are manipulated in C using the 'mx' prefixed application programming interface (API) routines included in the MATLAB engine. This API consists of over 60 routines to create access, manipulate, and destroy mxArrays. The engine library part of the MATLAB API contains routines for controlling the computation engine. The function begin with the three-letter prefix "eng". MATLAB libraries are not thread-safe.

2.1.2 How to Communicate with MATLAB

In this paragraph we show detail about how to write our application with use of MATLAB engine library. Write your application in C/C++ using any of the engine routines to perform computations in MATLAB. Use the mex script to compile and link engine programs. mex has a set of switches you can use to modify the compile and link stages. MATLAB supplies a mex options file to facilitate building MEX applications. This file contains compiler-specific flags that correspond to the general compile, prelink, and link steps required on your system. If you want to customize the build process, you can modify this file. The MATLAB Engine Library is an external library; so the Linker path has to be modified.

2.1.3 Compiling and Linking MATLAB Engine Programs

Step1.Write your application in C/C++ or FORTRAN using any of the engine routines to perform computations in MATLAB.

Step2. Build the Application. Use the mex script to compile and link engine programs.

Step3.Use of MEX Options File:- MATLAB supplies an options file to facilitate building MEX applications. This file contains compiler-specific flags that correspond to the general compile, prelink, and link steps required on your system. If you want to customize the build process, you can modify this file.

Step4.Building an Engine Application on LINUX Systems.

Build the executable file using the ANSI compiler for engine stand alone programs and the options file engopts.sh:

```
optsfile = [matlabroot '/bin/engopts.sh'];
mex('-f', optsfile, 'engdemo.c');
```

Verify that the build worked by looking in your current working folder for the file engdemo: dir engdemo

To run the demo in MATLAB, make sure your current working folder is set to the one in which you built the executable file, and then type: !engdemo

We can change compiler using mex -setup. We can choose GCC or LCC compiler for our application. MATLAB provides inbuilt compiler LCC for C/C++ programs.

2.2 Co-simulation between SystemVerilog and C

2.2.1 Introduction about Direct Programming Interface

It consists of two separate layers: the SystemVerilog layer and a foreign language layer. Both sides of DPI are fully isolated and allows a heterogeneous system to be built in which components can be written in a language other than SystemVerilog.

Methods implemented in C called import methods. Imported tasks or functions can have zero or more formal input, output, and inout arguments. Imported tasks always return an int result as part of the DPI-C disable protocol and, thus, are declared in foreign code as int functions. The syntax import method:

import {"DPI-C"}[context|pure][c_identifier =] [function task] function_identifier |task _ identifier] ([port_list]);

Methods implemented in SystemVerilog which can be called from C, such methods are referred to as exported methods. Syntax of export method is same as import method. The syntax import method:

export {"DPI-C"}[context|pure][c_identifier =] [function task][function_identifier |task _identifier] ([port_list]);

2.3 Co-simulation between SystemVerilog and MATLAB

2.3.1 Combining Power of SystemVerilog and MATLAB Using DPI

Here is combined the SystemVerilog DPI and MATLAB API. Here is used a wrapper of C around MATLAB Engine and use of DPI to communicate with SystemVerilog as shown in the figure 3.

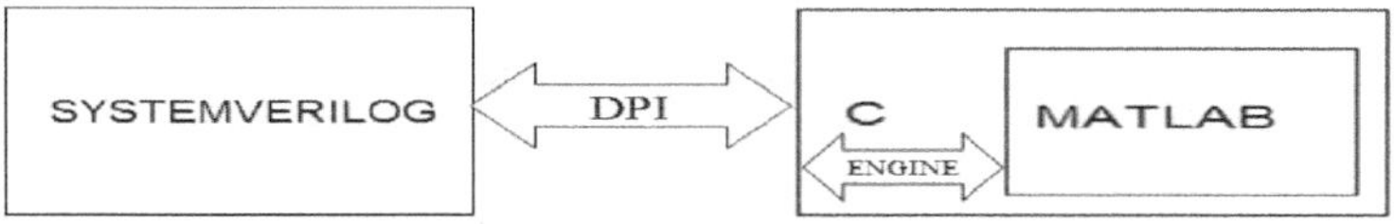

Fig. 3. Co-Simulation between SystemVerilog and MATLAB

Here is made a code which is named "engdemo.c" from SystemVerilog using import DPI method. First SV code is executing and with import DPI engdemo.c is executing. Output is combination of both MATLAB and SystemVerilog. To compile and simulate the above program we use following command.

Irun dpic.sv try1.c -I/opt/matlab2008/extern/include -L/opt/matlab2008/bin/glnx86 -leng

When the SystemVerilog compiler while encountering the C code, it calls GCC compiler to compile the C code in background. The final control however remains within the SV compiler.

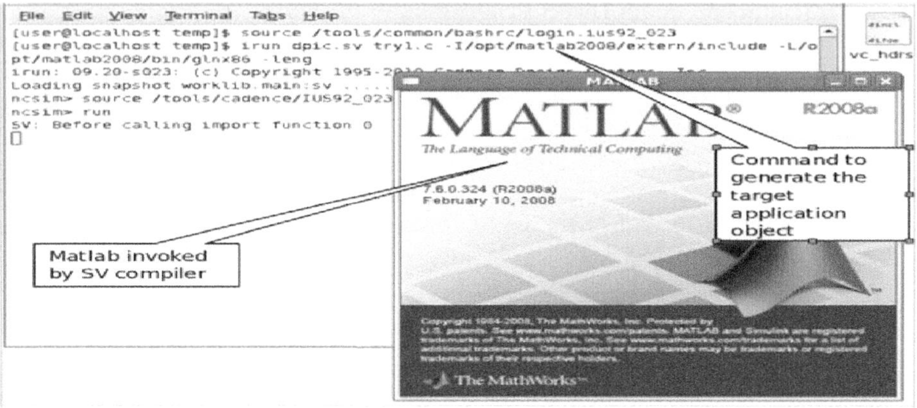

Fig. 4. MATLAB start

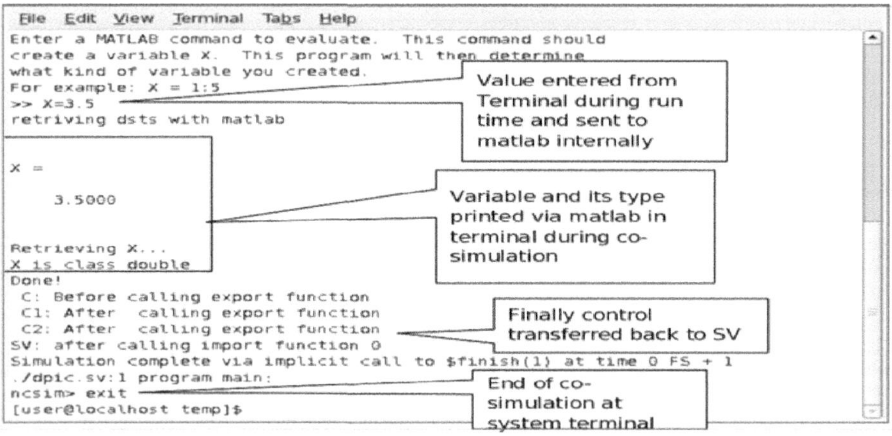

Fig. 5. Control back to SystemVerilog

2.4 Flow Chart of Co-simulation

The items existing in the SystemVerilog environment are in the left column. The middle two columns show tasks existing in the two interface C-layers. The far right column shows tasks existing in the MATLAB workspace.

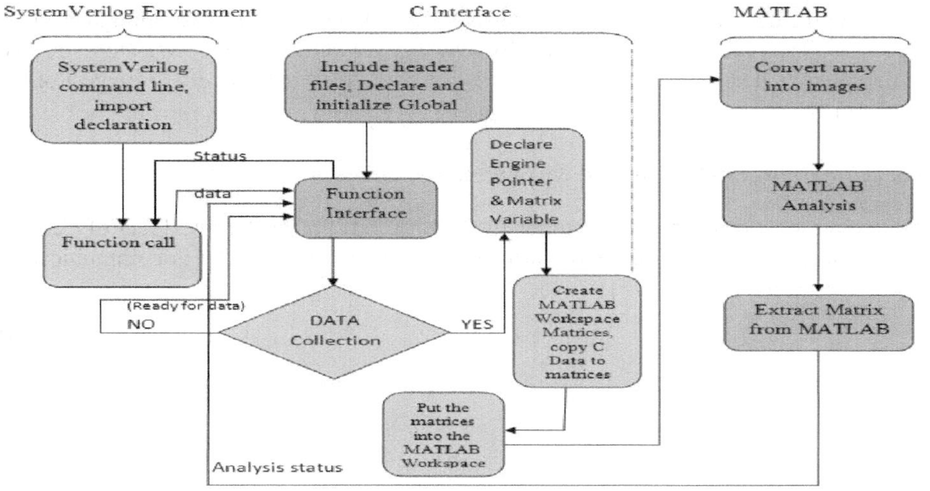

Fig. 6. Flow chart of Co-Simulation

3 Image Resizing as a Case Study

Supported features of Image Resizing Design are: Supports an image with a maximum size of 2K X 2K; Shrinks the image to any integral factor of the original image; Enlarges the image to any integral multiple of the original image; Maximum shrink ratio supported is 1/8; The maximum enlargement supported by the DUT is 8 times the maximum image size; The minimum image size that the DUT can support is 2 X 2; Indicates DONE and BUSY status depending upon the state of DUT.

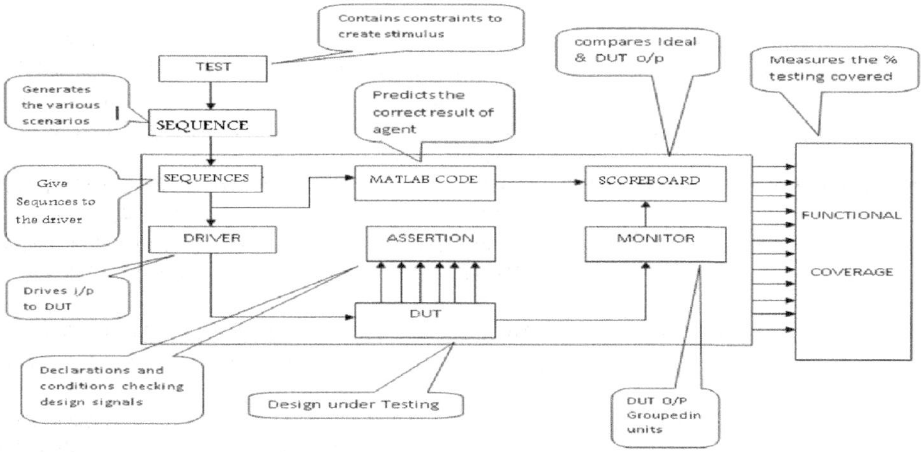

Fig. 7. Image Resizing Verification Environment

4 Verification Environment Architecture

As we know, Image processing Application is easily made in MATLAB. Due to visualization capability of MATLAB, it is very easily checked by human beings. So I can make Scoreboard is in MATLAB. The output of Scoreboard and DUT in checker is compared & with the help of co-simulation, the output of MATLAB is transferred in SystemVerilog. So checker is also in SystemVerilog. Rest of the blocks is in SystemVerilog. The other standard verification components were coded as per the routein fashion as done in any OVM based verification environment.

5 Integrating MATLAB with Open Verification Methodology

Establish of link between MATLAB and SystemVerilog is completed using SystemVerilog Direct Programming interface. Open Verification Methodology provides SystemVerilog along with its library of classes. To integrate MATLAB with Open Verification Methodology based environment, link between MATLAB and SystemVerilog is very useful. Here I represent the steps to integrate the MATLAB with Open Verification Methodology. I use Image resizing mean Enlargement or shrinking as a case study.

MATLAB has a in-built function for Image Resizing "imresize (image, ratio);". Enlargement or shrinking of image is possible by factor of ratio. Use of this function is possible in our verification environment of Open verification Methodology. This way our golden reference model is in the MATLAB. Now generating image is generated from SystemVerilog and Random transaction is generated from Open Verification Methodology. This transaction and Image array is given to the design and MATLAB. Steps to integrate MATLAB with OVM:

1. Write Image resizing logic with the help of MATLAB in-built functions.
2. Using import method call c function from OVM class ovm_matlab_test which is extend from ovm_component.
3. In import function pass transaction parameter which are used in MATLAB.
4. Declare MATLAB workspace matrixes in C using mxArray.
5. Allocate size to the variable as a matrix using mxCreateNumericMatrix.
6. Open MATLAB engine.
7. Put c variable into MATLAB workspace using engPutVariable.
8. Compile MATLAB .m file using engEvalstring.
9. Get MATLAB variable outputImageData1D into C variable using engGetVariable.
10. Copy the data of outputImageData1D into SV variable.
11. Close the engine.
12. Control back to SystemVerilog.
13. Enlarge or shrink Image is available in SystemVerilog.

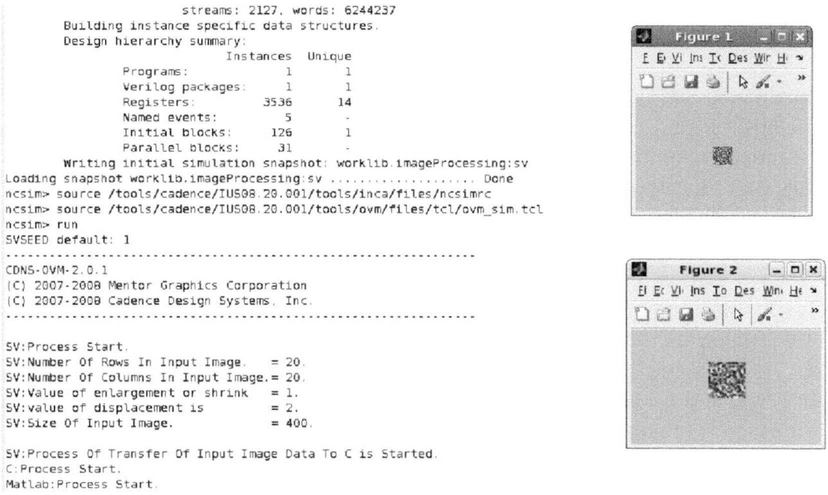

Fig. 8. Original and resized Image shown by MATLAB

Fig. 9. Compiling OVM package and MATLAB process start

6 Advantages Compare to Traditional Method of Verification

Here Golden reference is in MATLAB for Image Resizing ASIC. So we can reduce code length for the same Golden reference for Image Resizing logic if we can code in MATLAB. Another advantage is reduction in debugging time. We can use the MATLAB inbuilt function in our Verification architecture. So we have advantages of both SystemVerilog and MATLAB. This way we can reduce ASIC design Cycle for Image processing ASIC.

7 Conclusions

A sophisticated methodology is needed to build leading-edge test benches, ensure interoperability, and promote verification randomization and reuse. In this project a verification environment based on co-simulation interface between SystemVerilog and the MATLAB environment has been presented. The co-development and endorsement by Mentor and Cadence give the OVM credibility and viability and The OVM is clearly the only interoperable, open, and proven verification methodology. The Open Verification Methodology and libraries used to generate the advance stimulus for designing large test bench and verification IP in the form of transaction. The DPI C-layer can be used to interface to a wide variety of C base libraries and also the MATLAB Engine Library. The simulation stimulus could be generated from SystemVerilog; this would allow more robust image. Use of the MATLAB graphics capabilities could be more fully utilized.A more complete testbench can be build up in a shorter period of time than with traditional methods.

8 Future Work

The co-simulation between SystemVerilog and MATLAB has been used in the digital image processing application project. Instead of creating time consuming stimuli in SystemVerilog, data generated from MATLAB environment is used to drive the testbench. Further using the MATLAB, a golden reference model is created. This Golden reference model is used in SystemVerilog environment to compare behavior of the Design under verification. Use of the SystemVerilog and MATLAB could be extended in a variety of directions for various applications with this kind of hybrid simulation platform at hand along with the provision of the co-simulation provided here.

References

1. Compiling and Linking MATLAB Engine Programs, which is, `http://www.mathworks.com/help/techdoc/matlab_external/f39903.html`
2. MATLAB Application Program Interface Guide (December 1996)
3. Calling existing C code from MATLAB which is, `http://www.mathworks.com/support/compilers/interface_r13.html#Call_MATLAB_from_C`
4. SystemVerilog Language Reference Manual by Accellera's Extension to Verilog (2002, 2003)
5. Irun-user guide from cadence, product version 9.2, (July 2010)
6. Bailey, B.: CoVerification: From Tool to Methodology. white paper (June 2002), `http://www.mentor.com`
7. Boland, J.-F.: Using Matlab And Simulin In A Systemc Verification Environment. McGill University, QC, Canada
8. Stickley, J., Stone, W.: Accelerated Verification of a MATLAB-Driven Digital FIR Filter RTL Design Using Veloce and TBX. Mentor Graphics Corporation

9. Zuloaga, A., Martín, J.L., Bidarte, U., Ezquerra, J.A.: VHDL test bench for digital image processing systems using a new image format. Department of Electronics and Telecommunications, University of the Basque Country
10. Bergeron, J.: Writing Test benches using SystemVerilog. Springer, Heidelberg (2006)
11. Lam, W.K.: Hardware Design Verification. Pearson Education, Inc., London (2005)
12. Boland, J.F.: Cosimulation of Matlab with system C. Mcgill University, Canada (2004)
13. Spear, C.: SystemVerilog for Verification: A Guide to Learning the Testbench Language Features. Springer, Heidelberg (2006) ISBN:0387270361
14. Mintz, M., Ekendahl, R.: Hardware Verification with System Verilog. Springer, Heidelberg (2007) ISBN: 978-0-387-71738-8
15. Bergeron, J.: Writing Testbenches using SystemVerilog (2006) ISBN: 978-0-387-29221-2
16. The Art of Verification with SystemVerilog Assertions, (2006) ISBN-13: 978-0-9711994-1-5

Memory Attack Detection of Cryptographic Algorithm

K. Rahimunnisa[1], Rincy Merrin Varkey[2], and S. Sureshkumar[3]

[1,2] Department of ECE,
Karunya University, Coimbatore, India
{krahimunnisa,rincyvarkey09}@gmail.com
[3] Department of EEE,
Karunya University, Coimbatore, India
ssk@karunya.edu

Abstract. Embedded systems are becoming increasingly complex, networked, and functionally extensible through software, exposing them to a large number of security problems that have plagued general-purpose systems and thereby a need for an efficient monitoring method arises. Various security attacks exist and a major concern is memory attack. Any change in the memory content of the processor will change the flow of execution. In order to ensure secure execution and detect intrusion of an embedded processor, effective intrusion monitoring technique is proposed in this paper. The technique uses run-time verification of the program at instruction level. The instruction integrity is verified using hash function. Due to limited memory and processing capabilities of embedded systems this technique functions within the constraints, by focusing on effective detection and low overhead.

Keywords: Monitoring System, Intrusion, Blowfish Algorithm, Run-Time Verification, Security.

1 Introduction

With increasing trend in embedded system application in various areas like medical, military, education, security and communication purposes. And due to this embedded system will have a peak impact in technologies and applications of the future. The rising need of embedded system in safety critical applications like RFID, ATM, Smart Card and Mobile e-commerce. These devices are connected to various networks where sensitive data are exchanged between them. As being connected to a network there is an increasing probability that the devices will be subjected to attacks. The characteristic limitations of embedded system like limited protection capability: as it does not have a anti-virus protection tool nor a firewall and limited power as the devices are run on battery.

Security can be explained in terms of authorized communication channel between two entities which is been monitored by a third entity to obtain the information transferred or can be modified. Similarly in embedded system the data in the memory can be modified so as to change the behavior of the program[11]. The potential attacks in embedded system are :

D.C. Wyld et al. (Eds.): CNSA 2011, CCIS 196, pp. 194–203, 2011.

- Energy drainage (exhaustion attack like DoS or buffer overflow).
- Physical intrusion (tampering of device).
- Network intrusion (malware attack).
- Reprogramming of system for other users (stealing information).

These attacks are done in the memory of the device by changing the binary content stored in memory. The various attacks on memory include bit flips and buffer overflow attacks.

Our proposed technique focuses on two important criteria:

- Effective detection: This is an important criterion as it is necessary to detect attacks as quickly as possible.
- Low overhead: The security system implemented on it should consider these limitations in terms of using less computationally complex protocols for security due to the limited power and memory capabilities.

The remaining part of the paper is as follows: section 2 briefly discusses on related works, section 3 gives an overview of the monitoring system and section 4 explains the experimental results and section 5 gives the conclusion and future work.

2 Related Works

Over the years various methods have been found to ensure the security of the system in various aspects like physical, thermal or verifying the integrity of the program. Ravi et al. in [1] describes various techniques that can be implemented for physical security. For security of the system during run-time various approach using static analysis dynamic analysis. The paper [2] describes the use of control flow graph to verify the execution of the program at run time. This method is practical and compatible with existing software. Control flow graph can also be used with machine codes. It provides a useful foundation for security protocol. But the use of control flow graph method is vulnerable to attack when the same block structure as the original code will go undetected for a while during run-time. In paper [3] the permissible behavior of the application is captured at different level of granularity namely inter procedural, intra procedural and instruction stream integrity. This approach however detects deviation after a few instruction cycles unlike in paper [9]. Another approach is the SAFES method in [4] is a reconfigurable architecture. A SAFES reconfigurable architecture is proposed based on the following i) reconfigurable security primitive, ii) reconfigurable hardware monitor and iii) hierarchy of security controllers. This approach enables in dynamically configuring the monitoring of the system thereby making it flexible for detecting various attacks. Another approach for embedded security is SAFE-OPS [5]. It uses a combination of compiler and architecture technique. The authors R.G. Ragel and S. Parameswaran in [6] discuss about IMPRES technique which is related to fault detection in bit flips .The method described by the authors is verifying the application memory by method of checksum however it can handle code injection as well as bit flips but only deals with a basic block in a program and does not verify the integrity of the each instruction.

The authors in [7] Kurthartha Patel and Shri Paremeshwaran describes the method of using program map and trace file technique to verify the system during run-time to address code injection attacks.This method however is unable to detect data corruption. An approach to defending against buffer overflow attacks is described by Shao et al. in [8].

Our work is related to [9] where hashing of each instruction is stored in the memory which is compared with real time values obtained. In [9] the author does mention intrusion detection in single or few instructions. In [10] the author proposes a run-time monitoring technique using address pattern. Our work however focuses on improving the detection within a single instruction cycle and increasing the efficiency with the use of 128-bit hashing function.

3 Proposed Architecture

Our approach provides an efficient method to ensure the security of the system and to enable faster detection of attacks. It consists mainly of application file, memory, processor, MD5 module and monitoring logic as shown in Fig. 1. The application file consists of the binary file of the executable application used in the system. This is stored in the memory. When each instruction is been simultaneously accessed from the memory, its corresponding hash value which is stored in the monitoring logic. The application is loaded into memory where it is stored as binary file. When the processor fetches the instruction and executes it, the encrypted value of the instruction is generated using MD5 algorithm. This is done for verifying the instruction integrity.

3.1 Data Processing System

Fig 1 gives the block diagram of the proposed architecture. The application file comprises of binary representation of the program executed and is stored in memory. The control flow graph is obtained at off-line process by the programmer. The graph represents the control flow of the sequence between blocks and instructions. The application file is stored in a memory, from which each instruction is fetched. This instruction is accessed by the processor. The hash value is also generated simultaneously which is given to monitoring logic.

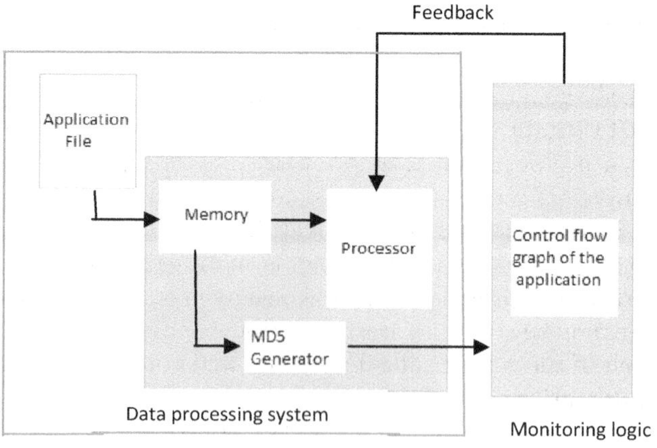

Fig. 1. Block Diagram of the Proposed Architecture

3.2 Monitoring Logic

The monitoring logic compares the run-time information obtained from the processor with the control flow graph. The ability to detect attacks clearly depends on the choice of information that is passed between the processor and the monitoring system. When monitoring within a basic block, the logic simply follows the sequence of patterns that is stored in the control flow graph. As the verification of instruction progresses the states are compared with the values stored in the monitoring system.

If there is any deviation in the program execution then an attack is detected. On the detection of an attack an interrupt is sent through the feedback to initiate shutdown. After which the system can recover by suitable recovery systems.

3.3 Message Digest (MD5) Algorithm

Though there are other hashing algorithms like SHA1, SHA2, SHA512, etc. MD5 is used as it has lesser computational rounds (i.e. 4) when compared to SHA (i.e. 80). This reduces the memory requirement for computation, enabling the available memory for utilization for the processor. MD5 is a message digest algorithm developed by Ron Rivest at MIT. This has been the most widely used secure hash algorithm particularly in Internet-standard message authentication. The processing involves the following steps [11].

Step 1. Append Padding Bits
The message is "padded" (extended) so that its length (in bits) is congruent to 448, modulo 512. That is, the message is extended so that it is just 64 bit of less being a multiple of 512 bits long.

Step 2. Append Length
A 64-bit representation of b (the length of the message before the padding bits were added) is appended to the result of the previous step

Step 3. Initialize MD Buffer
A four-word buffer (A, B, C, D) is used to compute the message digest. Here each of A, B, C, D is a 32-bit register. These registers are initialized to the following values in hexadecimal

Word A: 01 23 45 67
Word B: 89 AB CD EF
Word C: FE DC BA 98
Word D: 76 54 32 10

Step 4. Process Message in 16-Word Blocks

It defines four auxiliary functions, each take three 32-bit words as input and produces one 32-bit word as output. The functions used are as follows:

F(X, Y,Z) = (X^Y) +(not(X)^ Z)
G(X,Y,Z) = (X^Z) + (Y^ not(Z))
H(X,Y,Z) = X xor Y xor Z
I(X,Y,Z) = Y xor (X + not(Z))

On using the compressed hash values [9] it will reduce the memory space required for the storage but the reliability decreases as there is a probability for two instructions to have the same hash value. So in this paper we use MD5 to generate 128 bit hash value for each instruction. The hash value of a simple word "seek" is generated as shown in Fig 2 and is verified.

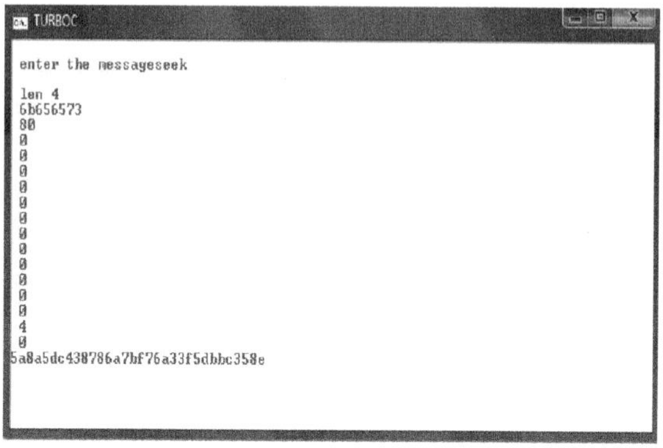

Fig. 2. The hash value of word "seek"

4 Experimental Results

A blowfish encryption is used as the application program. The flow chart of the program is as shown in Fig 3. This encryption algorithm is a symmetric block cipher algorithm with 16 rounds. A symmetric algorithm means the same key is used for both encryption and decryption. It can be effectively used for encryption and safeguarding of data. It takes a variable-length key, from 32 bits to 448 bits, making it ideal for securing data. This program is coded and compiled in TurboC.

Blowfish Algorithm is a **Feistel Network**, iterating a simple encryption function 16 times. The block size is 64 bits, and the key can be any length up to 448 bits. It is suitable for applications where the key does not change often, like a communications link or an automatic file encryptor. It is significantly faster than most encryption algorithms when implemented on 32-bit microprocessors with large data caches.

The algorithm keeps two subkey arrays: the 18-entry P-array and four 256-entry S-boxes. The S-boxes accept 8-bit input and produce 32-bit output. One entry of the P-array is used every round, and after the final round, each half of the data block is XORed w ith one of the two remaining unused P-entries. In each round the data xL and xR are xored with the element pf P-array and the function f(x) respectively. The function f(x) is as given in Fig 4. Here the 32-bit data is divided to four quarters and applied as inputs to the s-box and the results are Xored and added to get the final 32-bit output of function f(x) [12].

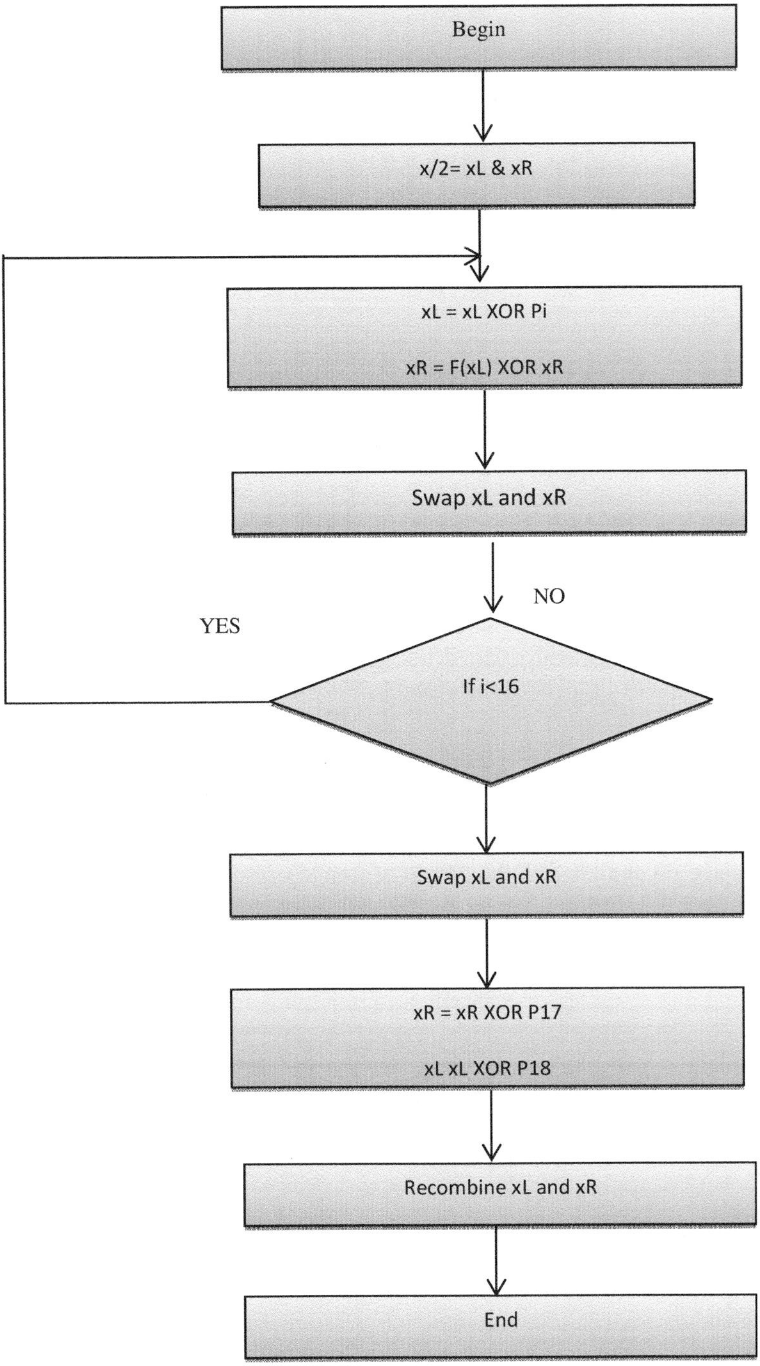

Fig. 3. The flow chart for the Blowfish algorithm program

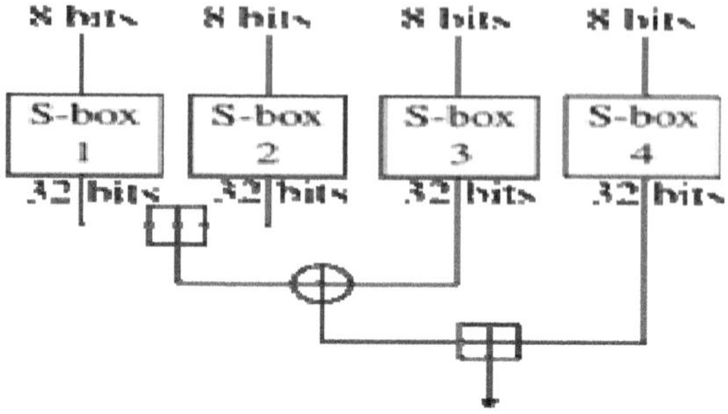

Fig. 4. The function f(x)

An important part of the algorithm is the subkey generation . The generation of subkeys are done using the P array and S array. The subkeys are calculated using the Blowfish algorithm[13]:

1. Initialize first the P-array and then the four S-boxes, in order, with a fixed string. This string consists of the hexadecimal digits of pi (less the initial 3): P1 = 0x243f6a88, P2 = 0x85a308d3, P3 = 0x13198a2e, P4 = 0x03707344, etc.
2. XOR P1 with the first 32 bits of the key, XOR P2 with the second 32-bits of the key, and so on for all bits of the key (possibly up to P14). Repeatedly cycle through the key bits until the entire P-array has been XORed with key bits.
3. Encrypt the all-zero string with the Blowfish algorithm, using the subkeys described in steps (1) and (2).
4. Replace P1 and P2 with the output of step (3).
5. Encrypt the output of step (3) using the Blowfish algorithm with the modified subkeys.
6. Replace P3 and P4 with the output of step (5).
7. Continue the process, replacing all entries of the P array, and then all four S-boxes in order, with the output of the continuously changing Blowfish algorithm.

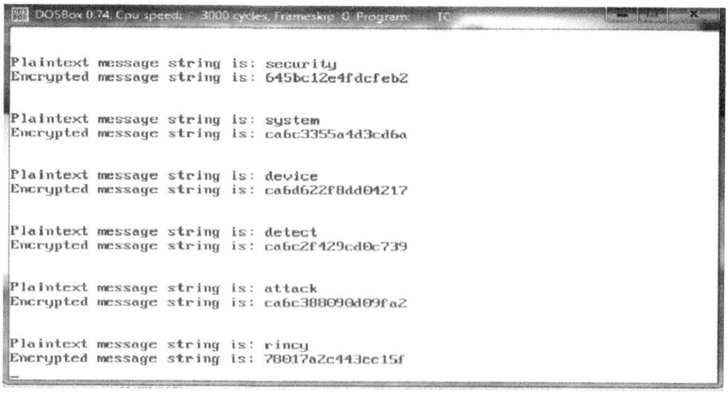

Fig. 5. Output of the blowfish encryption program

The output of the application program is as shown in Fig. 5. The programmer generates the encrypted value of each instruction of the program which is stored in the memory of the monitoring logic. The encryption program reads each instruction from the program file stored in the memory of the processor. These values are verified with the values stored by the programmer during offline process. Fig 6 shows the hash value generated for each instruction of the application program.

Fig. 6. The hash value of each instruction

The pre-calculated hash value is stored the monitoring logic which is used to verify the integrity of the instruction during run-time.

Fig. 7. The output when the program behaves normally

The Fig. 7 shows a scenario when the program behaves as per its permissible behavior. If an error occurs it stops the execution indicating an attack. Here the content in the binary file is changed at a particular memory location. During verification of the affected memory location, a mismatch is found for which the execution stops abruptly as shown in Fig 8. Any deviations in execution of the application program will initiate a feedback which halts the execution of the system.

Fig. 8. The output when the program is under attack

5 Conclusion

An efficient intrusion detection system which can be used to monitor software attack like code injection or bit flip attack for any specific applications is explained . The system is efficient as it performs verification at lowest level of granularity and it's economical as the attack is been detected within one instruction cycle. Here the checksum of each instruction is generated during run-time using MD5 hash function which is then verified with the offline stored values. Once the checksum is matched the particular instruction is indicated as secure and the next instruction is verified. If a mismatch occurs the execution is halted and the particular instruction is indicated as not secure.We have presented an efficient security protocol which will enable faster detection. Here the security is ensured at the finest level. We are presently working on improving the monitoring technique in terms of speed and efficiency of detection.

Acknowledgments

The authors would like to thank Karunya University for the facilities provided for research.

References

1. Ravi, S., Raghunathan, A., Chakradhar, S.: Tamper Resistance Mechanisms for Secure, Embedded Systems. In: Proc. 17th Int'l Conf Very Large Scale Integration Design, VLSI Design 2004 (2004)
2. Abadi, M., Budiu, M., Erlingsson, U., Ligatti, J.: Control-Flow Integrity Principles, Implementations, and Applications. In: Proc. ACM Conf. Computer and Comm. Security (CCS), pp. 340–353 (November 2005)
3. Arora, D., Ravi, S., Raghunathan, A., Jha, N.K.: Hardware Asisted run-Time Monitoring for Secure program execution on embedded processors. IEEE Transaction Very Large Scale Integration Systems (VLSI) 14(12), 1295–1307 (2006)
4. Gogniat, G., Wolf, T., Burleson, W., Diguet, J.-P., Bossuet, L., Vaslin, R.: Reconfigurable Hardware for High-Security/High-Performance Embedded Systems: The SAFES

Perspective. IEEE Trans. Very Large Scale Integration (VLSI) Systems 16(2), 144–155 (2008)

5. Zambreno, J., Choudhary, A., Simha, R., Narahari, B., Memon, N.: SAFEOPS: An Approach to Embedded Software Security. ACM Trans. Embedded Computing Systems 4(1), 189–210 (2005)
6. Ragel, R.G., Parameswaran, S.: IMPRES: Integrated Monitoring for Processor Reliability and Security. In: Proc. 43rd Ann. Conf. Design Automation(DAC), pp. 502–505 (July 2006)
7. Patel, K., Paremeshwaran, S., Shee, S.L.: Ensuring Secure program execution in multiprocessor embedded systems. In: Proceedings of the 5th IEEE/ACM International Conference on Hardware/Software Co-Design and System Synthesis, pp. 57–62 (2007)
8. Shao, Z., Zhuge, Q., He, Y., Sha, E.H.-M.: Defending Embedded Systems Against Buffer Overflow via Hardware/Software. In: Proc. 19th Annual Computer Security Applications Conf (ACSAC), pp. 352–363 (December 2003)
9. Mao, S., Wolf, T.: Hardware Support for Secure Processing in Embedded Systems. IEEE Transactions on Computers 59(6) (June 2010)
10. Rahimunnisa, K., Suresh Kumar, S., Kavya, T.S., Anoop Suraj, A.: Intrusion Detection Using Address Monitoring. International Journal of Recent Trends in Engineering 3(2) (May 2010)
11. Stallings, W.: Cryptography and Network Security, 2nd edn. PHI Publishers (2007)
12. `http://en.wikipedia.org/wiki/Blowfish_cipher`
13. `http://www.schneier.com/paper-blowfish-fse.html`

Performance Comparison of Queueing Disciplines for AEERG Protocol in Manet

S. Rajeswari[1] and Y. Venkataramani[2]

[1]Associate professor, Dept. of Electronics and Communication Engineering, Saranathan college of Engineering
rajee_ravi@sify.com
[2] Principal, Saranathan college of Engineering
diracads@saranathan.ac.in

Abstract. Queuing disciplines have been a subject of intensive discussion and research in the network field for scheduling packets from different traffic flows for processing at a specific node. When that particular node is selected for the transmission of all traffic flows since it has been chosen as an emerging node for the shortest path in the adaptive energy efficient algorithm, queue scheduling disciplines have been used to improve the quality of service. In this paper, we evaluate the performance of three queuing disciplines (FIFO, PQ and RED) which is implemented in the AEERG protocol. We carry out simulation using NS-2 and compare their relative performance based on queuing delay, packet drop rate and end-to-end delay with drop-tail policies and RED.

Keywords: Ad hoc Networks, Queuing schedule, Drop-Tail, Priority, RED.

I Introduction

Ad Hoc network is a wireless, mobile, multi-hop self-organizing network, no infrastructure. The node's mobile features of Ad Hoc network make the network topology change frequently. They are connected through wireless channel, there is no specific routing facilities, each node in the network also acts as a router, forwarding data packets for other nodes, there is also no naming service, directory services and other functions, these features make the traditional wired networks QoS policies no longer apply to mobile Ad Hoc Networks[1]. The current routing protocols of Ad Hoc networks proposed by IETF are all suitable to a certain network environment, to our knowledge, there is no a protocol itself has QoS mechanism [2]. In a mobile environment, the changing of queue is quite different from those in static conditions.

The cheapest and most common approach is scheduling mechanisms and packet discarding policies. A queue scheduling discipline manages the allocation of network resources among different traffic flows by selecting the next packet to be processed. Also when packets arrive faster than they can be processed, arriving packets are dropped and thus control the congestion in the network. Furthermore, it can reduce the impact of ill-behaved flows on other flows especially when having a mixture of real-time and non-real-time traffic. The queueing disciplines considered in this paper

D.C. Wyld et al. (Eds.): CNSA 2011, CCIS 196, pp. 204–213, 2011.

are: First-In-First-Out (FIFO), Priority Queueing (PQ). We also scrutinize the effect of two dropping policies, drop-tail and random-early drop (RED) [7], on their performance.

The remainder of the paper is organized as follows. In the next section, we review related work and briefly discuss the operational aspects of the selected queue scheduling disciplines with some comments on their performance in section 3. We describe the simulation model and traffic scenarios with the simulation results in Section 4. Finally, we conclude our paper and summarize results in Section 5.

2 Related Work

Shensheng Tang and Wei Li [3] discussed about an analytical traffic (Markov) model and three queue management schemes are developed for a heterogeneous multihop mobile ad hoc network (MANET). Babak Abbasov[5] proposed a new active queue management algorithm based on RED, called AHRED has been designed and compared with different AQM schemes. Peter Marbach proposed a distributed scheduling and active queue management mechanism for wireless ad hoc networks which is based on a random access scheduler. P. G. Kulkarni et al. presented a proactive prediction based queue management scheme called PAQMAN [7] that captures variations in the underlying traffic accurately and regulates the queue size around the desirable operating point. PAQMAN harnesses the predictability in the underlying traffic by applying the Recursive Least Squares (RLS) algorithm to estimate the average queue length for the next prediction interval given the average queue length information of the past intervals. Jamal N. AI-Karaki et al. propose a QoS routing protocol, called Quality Virtual Routing (QVR), for heterogeneous [8] MANETs. QVR operates on a fixed virtual rectilinear architecture (called virtual grid architecture) that is built on top of the physical topology which consists of a few, but possibly more powerful, mobile nodes known as ClusterHeads (CHs) that are elected periodically and discover multiple QoS routes on the virtual grid using an extended version of the Open Shortest Path First (OSPF) routing protocol and an extended version of WFQ scheduling policy that takes into account the wireless channel state. Liu Ping et al. proposed a mathematical model to calculate the queue delay [10] for MANET, which has a better effect on improving the multimedia stream with delay sensitive. Jianyong Chen et al. a new self-tuning RED [2] is proposed to improve the performance of TCP-RED network.

Hesham N. Elmahdy et al. studied the effect of the packet size and the effect of random early detection (RED) parameters [1] on the Two Rate Three Color Marker (trTCM) and Single Rate Three Color Marker (srTCM). P. Kulkarni et al. presents a predictive queue management strategy named PAQMAN that proactively manages the queue, is simple to implement and requires negligible computational overhead (and hence uses the limited resources efficiently). Xinyu JIN et al. implemented a novel minimum energy routing scheme based on the mobile node's energy consumption [9] and the hierarchical node's congestion levels, which is named RED based Minimum Energy Routing (REDMER) scheme. S.Radha Rammohan et al. proposed an effective architecture system [11] to provide a good Quality of Service in Mobile Ad hoc Network.

3 Proposed Queue Implementation in AEERG Protocol

In this protocol, the nodes can be in active mode with probability 1-p or sleep mode with probability p which is fixed at the initial stage. We set a counter B to adapt the number of neighbors to which a packet is forwarded. B represents the current number of neighbors at each node which are kept in active state [12]. The value of B is adaptively adjusted based on the packet delivery ratio. This results in less energy consumption and more reliability in the communication networks. When the same node is selected for the forwarding of packets from different flows, congestion will occur. To ease the congestion and to increase the throughput, different scheduling mechanisms are implemented and the results are discussed.

First-In-First-Out **(FIFO)** queuing is the most popular queue scheduling discipline that has been extensively examined in the literature. It also serves as a baseline for comparing the performance of other queue scheduling disciplines. In FIFO queuing, all packets placed into a single queue and then served in the same order on which they arrived. Hence, it is also known as first come-first-serve (FCFS) queuing. Although it is simple and has predictable behavior and extremely low computational load on the system, it has some severe limitations for wireless network traffic. It is incapable of providing differentiated service and can not isolate the effect of ill-behaved flow on other flows. A bursty flow can consume the entire buffer space and causes all other flows to be denied service until after the burst is serviced. This can result in increased delay, jitter and loss for the other well-behaved flows traversing the queue. To reduce the impact of ill-behaved sources, other queue disciplines have been proposed to isolate traffic flows into separate queues. These queues can be serviced according to some scheduling scheme. Among these are priority queuing, fair queuing, and weighted fair queuing, weighted round robin or class-based queuing, and deficit weighted round robin.

Priority Queuing **(PQ)** is a simple approach to provide differentiated services to different packet flows. Packets of different flows are assigned a priority level according to their QoS requirements. When packets arrive at the output link, they are first classified into different classes enqueued separately based on their priorities. Then, queues are served in order. The highest priority queue is served first before serving lower priority queues. Packets in the same priority class are serviced in a FIFO manner. As soon as high-priority packets are served, packets from the lower priority class are served. But if a higher-priority packet arrives while serving a lower-priority packet, the server waits until complete the service of the current packet then goes back to serve the higher priority queue (non-preemptive PQ). The limitation of PQ is that lower-priority packets may receive little attention when a higher-priority class has a continuous stream of packets. This problem is known as starvation problem [1]. Also it lacks fairness. The closed form analytical solution of a two-class priority queue is given in [8].

Random early detection (RED): It is also known as random early discard or random early drop and it is also an active queue management algorithm. It is also a congestion avoidance algorithm. This algorithm plays an important role in avoiding full queues, reducing the packet delay and loss. It monitors the average queue size and dropped packets based on statistical probabilities. The RED is also known as a threshold based queuing discipline. It statistically drops packets from flows before it reaches its threshold value. So it is considered a good queue for situations where the complexity of per-session state tracking needed by fairness queuing is not affordable. Assume that each node has a single buffer. Let λn be the packet arrival rate to the buffer at node n; let D_n be the expected delay of a packet at node n, and let P_n be the probability that a packet is dropped at node n due to a buffer overflow. For $\lambda = N$,

$$X(\lambda) = \sum_{1}^{N} \lambda n \tag{1}$$

Let $X(\lambda)$ be the network throughput under the network arrival rate λ. We list the schedulers with the following property.

Property: For a single-cell wireless network consisting of nodes n = 1, ..., N, we say that a scheduler implements a distributed buffer with service rate μ if the following is true.

(a) The expected delay D_n is identical at all nodes, i.e. we have $D_n = D$, for values n = 1, ...,N.

(b) The packet-drop probability P_n is identical at all nodes, i.e.

we have $P_n = P$, for values n = 1, ...,N.

(c) The throughput $X(\lambda)$ is a non-decreasing function in λ with

$\lim_{\lambda \to \infty} X(\lambda) = \mu$.

The above property states that a fair scheduler should serve packets as if the network traffic shares a common buffer that is served at rate μ, i.e. all packets entering the network should experience the same expected delay and the same probability of being dropped.

For every packet arrival, the RED gateway calculates the weighted moving average queue size (avg). It then compares the results with minimum (min_{th}) and a following schema [5,6].

- When $avg < min_{th}$ the packet is dropped with probability one.
- When $min_{th} \leq avg < max_{th}$ the packet is dropped with some probability.
- When $max_{th} \leq avg$ the packet is not dropped.

The value of the average queue size (avg) is computed as follows:

After each idle period the average queue size (avg) is additively decreased by a constant $\alpha > 0$ and after each busy period the average queue size (avg) is additively increased by a constant $\beta > 0$. Note that this rule follows the intuition that average queue size (avg) should be increased when the channel is busy, and be decreased when the channel is idle.

It is well known that by employing FIFO, throughput is not as good as priority Queue which is lesser than RED.

4 Performance Evaluation

For queuing disciplines specification, we set the maximum queue size to be 500 packets. There are three types of classes in all queues (except FIFO) whose queue buffer size increases from highest priority to lowest one. Finally when RED is enabled, we used minimum and maximum threshold as 100 and 200 respectively while keeping the mark probability denominator (the fraction of packets dropped when the average queue size is at maximum threshold) as 10. We set exponential weight factor (used to calculate average queue size based on the previous average and current queue size) to be 9.

4.1 Simulation Parameters

NS2 is used to simulate the proposed algorithm. In our simulation, the channel capacity of mobile hosts is set to the same value: 2 Mbps. For the MAC layer protocol the distributed coordination function (DCF) of IEEE 802.11 (for wireless LANs) is used. It has the functionality to notify the network layer about link breakage.

In the simulation, mobile nodes move in a 600 meter x 400 meter region for 50 seconds simulation time. The number of mobile nodes is varied from 10-60. We assume each node moves independently with the same average speed. All nodes have the same transmission range of 250 meters. In our simulation, the speed is set as 20m/s. The simulated traffic is Constant Bit Rate (CBR). The pause time of the mobile node is kept as 20-120 sec.

4.2 Performance Metrics

The simulated values of Throughput, Queuing delay and Packet delivery ratio with the increasing number of nodes and for varying Simulation Pause Time are plotted as shown in the figures below.

4.2.1 Throughput

The successful number of packets received by the destination is termed by Throughput and it is measured by bytes/sec. For varying number of nodes, Throughput is measured for different queuing and the figure is plotted as in Fig.1.

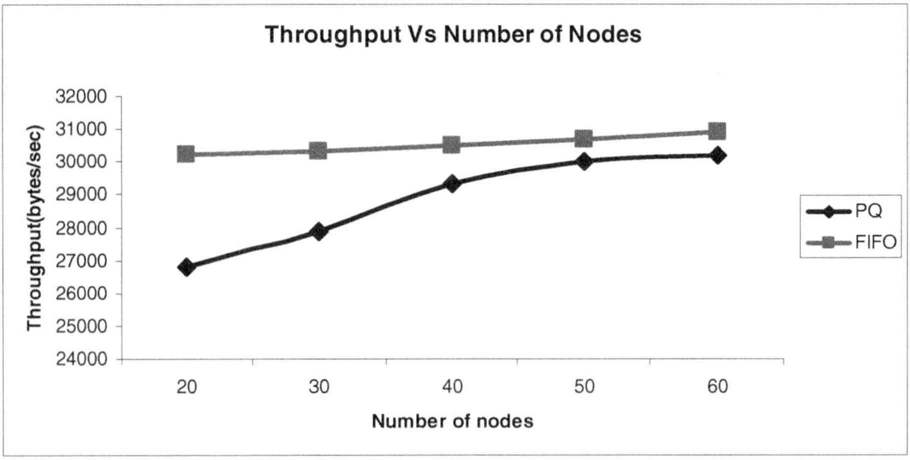

Fig. 1. Throughput Vs Number of Nodes with Drop-Tail policy

Fig.1 gives the Throughput of two queue scheduling mechanisms when the number of nodes is increased. When the number of nodes is increased, number of flows will increase leads to many number of packets. From the figure, we can see that if we employ FIFO, more number of packets will drop due to fixed buffer size. So, the throughput will be increased by RED policy both in the Priority Queue and FIFO scheduling mechanism which is shown in the fig.2

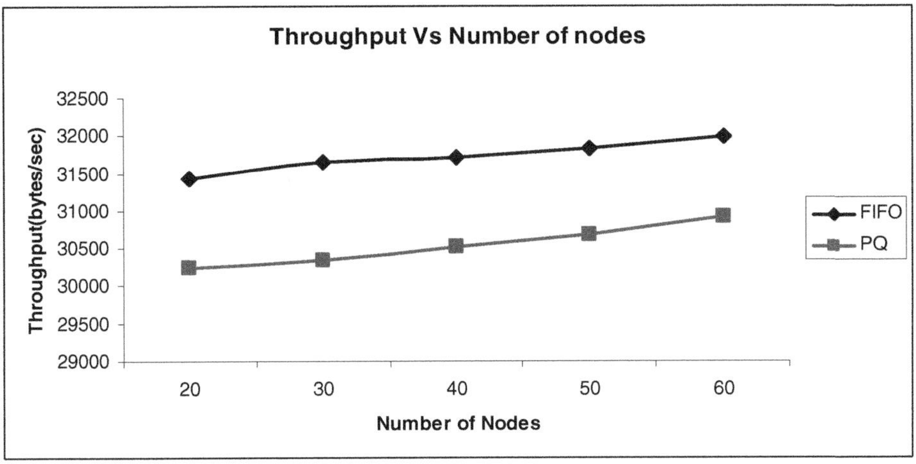

Fig. 2. Throughput Vs Number of Nodes with RED policy

4.2.2 Packet Delivery Ratio

Packet delivery ratio is calculated by dividing the number of packets received by the destination through the number of packets originated by the application layer of the

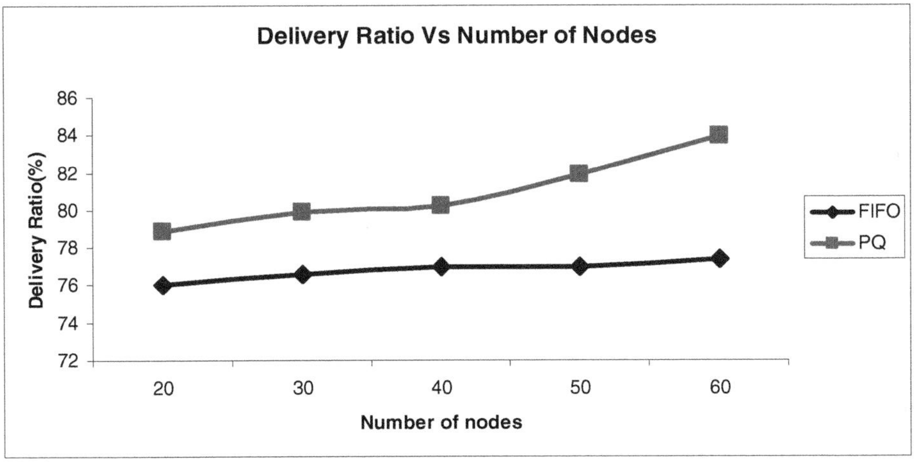

Fig. 3. Packet Delivery Ratio Vs Number of Nodes with Drop-Tail policy

source. It specifies the packet loss rate, which limits the maximum throughput of the network. The better the delivery ratio, the more complete and correct is the routing protocol. For different queuing disciplines, Packet Delivery Ratio is computed with increasing number of nodes and the graph is plotted in figure.3 and various Simulation Pause Time and the graph is plotted in figure.4 with drop tail policy.

Fig.3 gives the Packet Delivery Ratio of different queue scheduling mechanisms when the number of nodes is increased. This figure helps us to study about the efficiency of the queue scheduling mechanisms. This result is obtained for non-real

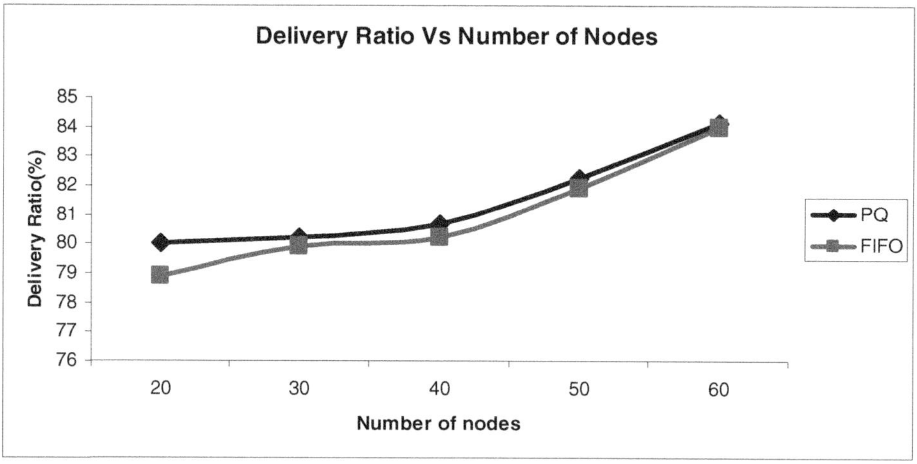

Fig. 4. Packet Delivery Ratio Vs Number of Nodes with RED policy

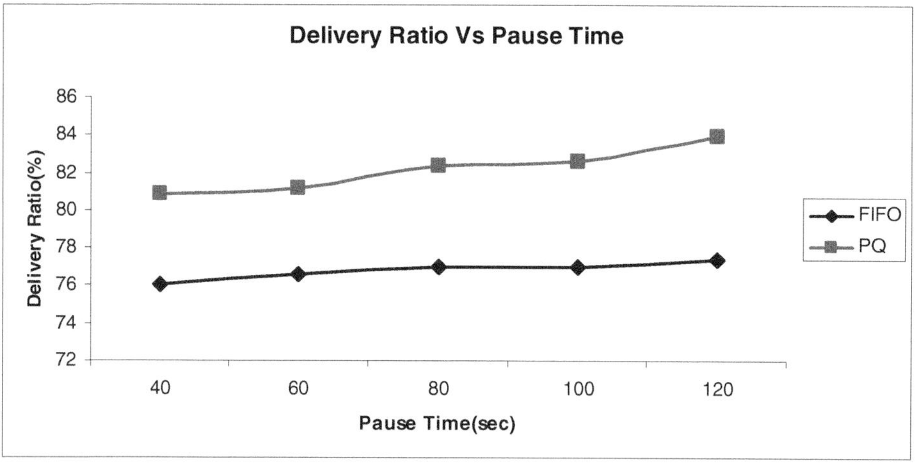

Fig. 5. Packet Delivery Ratio Vs Simulation Pause Time with Drop-Tail policy

time communications. When the number of nodes is increased, number of flows will increase leads to generation of many number of packets. From the figure.4, we can see that if we employ Drop-Tail, more number of packets will drop due to fixed buffer size. So, the Delivery Ratio will be increased by RED policy in both the queue scheduling mechanism.

Fig.5 gives the Packet Delivery Ratio of different queue scheduling mechanisms when the pause time is increased. This figure helps us to study about the adaptive queue buffer size change mechanisms. When the Simulation Pause Time is increased, number of free space in the buffer is adaptively changed for RED.

4.2.3 Queuing Delay

Figure 6 and 7 shows the average queuing delay of the two queue disciplines (with drop-tail policy) versus increasing number of nodes and with simulation pause time. We can see that FIFO has the worst behavior (more than 2.5 msec) as compared to other disciplines.

To study the load effect on the queuing-delay performance, we run the simulator under different loads and plot the queuing delay variation versus load for different traffic scenarios which may be used for multimedia communication. We may change the traffic from UDP to FTP and the results will be obtained as it is planned in extension of this work.

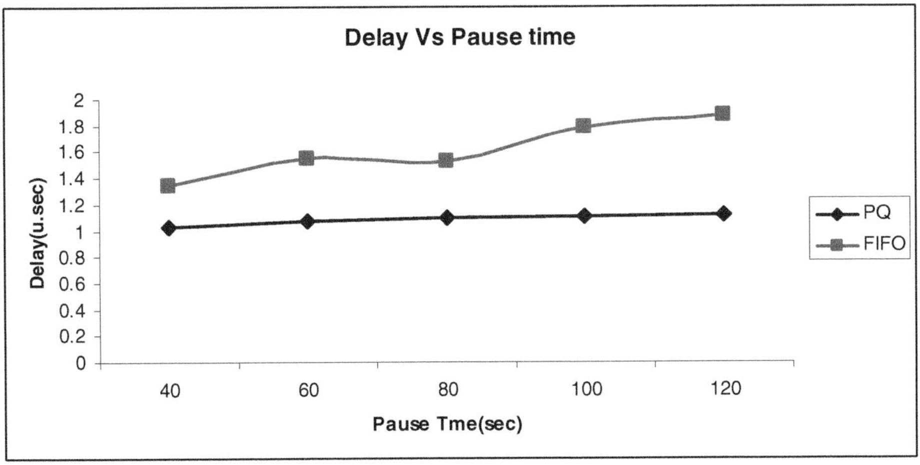

Fig. 6. Queuing Delay Vs Simulation Pause Time with Drop-Tail policy

Figure 6 and 7 show the Queuing delay versus pause time drop-tail and RED policies respectively. At some points, delay rate is higher in case of Drop-Tail which sounds logical as RED relies merely on probabilistic packet drop to avoid congestion and starvation problem.

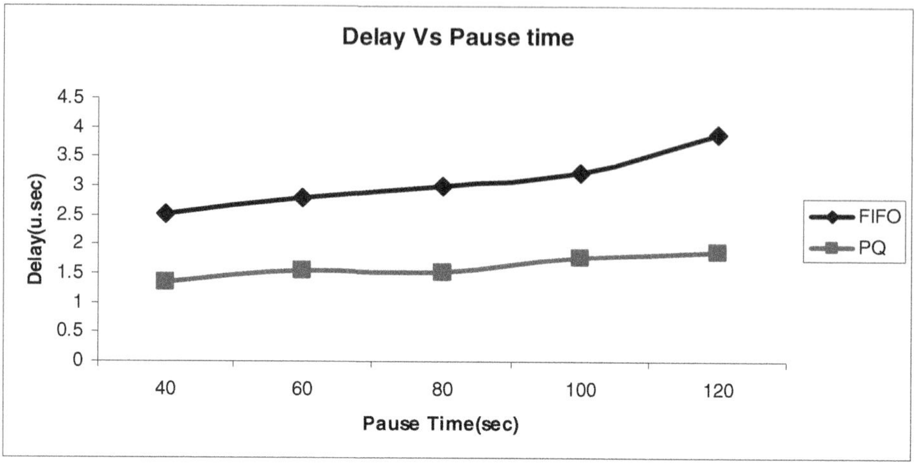

Fig. 7. Queuing Delay Vs Simulation Pause Time with RED policy

5 Conclusion

In this study we presented a simulation-based performance evaluation and comparison of two queuing scheduling disciplines for different number of nodes and pause time for the impact of using random-early drop as compared to drop-tail policy and priority. The simulation results show RED that outperforms other disciplines in terms of average queuing delay and packet delivery ratio although PQ and FIFO are also very close to it for the considered node scenarios. We also noticed that using RED has greatly improved all the performance measures especially with FIFO. The reason is that RED monitors the average queue size and randomly drops packets when congestion is detected. Further work is still required to change the type of traffic to examine these queuing disciplines and to study the impact of different traffic scenarios and the use of traffic shapers at the edges of the network.

References

1. Elmahdy, H.N., Taha, M.H.N.: The Impact of Packet Size and Packet Dropping Probability on Bit Loss of VoIP Networks. ICGST-CNIR Journal 8(2), 25–29 (2009)
2. Chen, J., Hu, C., Ji, Z.: Self-Tuning Random Early Detection Algorithm to Improve Performance of Network Transmission. Mathematical Problems in Engineering journal,17 pages Article ID 872347 (2011), doi:10.1155/2011/872347
3. Tang, S., Li, W.: QoS Provisioning and Queue Management in Mobile Ad hoc Networks. In: Wireless Communications and Networking Conference, pp. 400–405 (April 2006)
4. Wei, S., Bai, G., Shen, H.: An Adaptive Queue Management Mechanism for Video Streaming over Mobile Ad Hoc Networks. In: WiCOM 2009 Proceedings of the 5th International Conference on Wireless communications, networking and mobile computing (October 2009)

5. Abbasov, B.: AHRED: A Robust AQM algorithm for wireless Adhoc Networks. In: International Conference on Application of Information and Communication Technologies, pp. 1–4 (October 2009)
6. Marbach, P.: Distributed Scheduling and Active Queue Management in Wireless Networks. In: INFOCOM, pp. 2321–2325 (2007)
7. Kulkarni, P.G., McClean, S.I., Parr, G.P., Black, M.M.: Proactive Predictive Queue Management for improved QoS in IP Networks. In: Proceedings of the International Conference on Networking, International Conference on Systems and International Conference on Mobile Communications and Learning Technologies (April 2006)
8. Al-Karaki, J.N., Kamal, A.E.: Supporting Quality of Service In Mobile Ad hoc Networks. In: ACS/IEEE 2005 International Conference on Computer Systems and Applications, (AICCSA 2005) (2005)
9. Ping, L., Peiyan, Y.: An Approach to Calculate Queue Delay in Mobile AdHoc Networks. In: International Conference of Information Science and Management Engineering (August 2010)
10. Cai, W., Jin, X., Zhang, Y., Chen, K., Wang, R.: ACO Based QoS Routing Algorithm for Wireless Sensor Networks. In: Ma, J., Jin, H., Yang, L.T., Tsai, J.J.-P. (eds.) UIC 2006. LNCS, vol. 4159, pp. 419–428. Springer, Heidelberg (2006)
11. Radha Rammohan, S., Rengarajan, K.: Study of Possible Packets Travelling Algorithm for Effective Mobile Ad hoc Networks. International Journal of Soft Computing 4, 162–167 (2009)
12. Rajeswari, S., Venkataramani, Y.: An Adaptive Energy Efficient and Reliable Gossip Routing Protocol For Mobile Adhoc Networks. IJCTE 2(5) (October 2010)

Design of a Cryptographic Tamper Detection Scheme for Network Security

B. Srinivasa Rao and S.D.V. Prasad

Department of Computer Science and Engineering, Malla Reddy Engineering College, Maisammaguda, Dulapally, Hyderabad-500014
bmsssaditya_1997@yahoo.co.in

Abstract. In the present research work an attempt has been made to design and implement a tamper detection scheme that provides an additional procedure which detects tampering, given two signatures, whether one of them was generated by the forger. In this system, emails and files are signed digitally. The scheme automatically computes a hash based on the exact content of the email message, and then encrypts the value with the sender's private key. The recipient of the email will use their tamper evidence software to compute the same calculation. The matching of the calculation with the hash value is a proof that the message has not been altered. It ensures the data integrity, confidentiality and authentication.

Keywords: Network security, Tampering, Hash Function, Encryption and Decryption.

1 Introduction

Tampering is basically related to the data security which aims at ensuring that data is safe from corruption and that access to that is suitably controlled. Thus data security helps to improve privacy of the data like passwords, user info, etc. To avoid tampering of the data various encryption techniques are used like SHA1, MD5 etc., so that private data can't be reverse engineered to get the actual data. It is important for the Internet users to understand that the regular emails and file transfers offers no privacy and can actually be read by many people other than to whom it is sent to. The Internet Service Provider (ISP) probably keeps a copy on its computer and copies of documents sent from a networked computer are probably kept behind and all of the internet computers the email goes through on its way to the recipient can keep a copy. The administrators of all these computers can read the documents if they choose to and they can send it to anyone they might want to. Anyone that can intercept the document can alter the file content and anyone can send document that looks as if original sender sent it. Key exposure is a well-known threat for any cryptographic tool. For signatures, exposure of secret key compromises the corresponding public key. After the exposure is detected, the compromised keys can be revoked [1-6]. This detection of the exposure has previously been dealt with outside the scope of cryptography. Recently, Gene Itkis et al proposed a cryptographic scheme for tamper

D.C. Wyld et al. (Eds.): CNSA 2011, CCIS 196, pp. 214–224, 2011.

detection [7]. Considerable amount of research is being done in this direction. Many real-world applications wish to collect tamper evident logs for forensic purposes [8]. Matt Franklin presents a survey of key evolving cryptosystems in the public key setting, focusing on two main approaches: 'forward security' and 'intrusion resilience'. The essential feature of this design strategy is that the secret key changes over time, while the corresponding public key remains unchanged. Key evolving cryptosystems can limit the damage caused by an attacker who occasionally learns your secret key [9]. In our present work we propose a cryptographic solution to the above posed problem in the frame work of Itkis.

2 Tamper Detection Scheme

In the present research work an attempt has been made to design and implement a tamper detection scheme and its variants. The scheme automatically computes a hash based on the exact content of the email message, and then encrypts the value with the sender's private key. The recipient of the email will use their tamper evidence software to compute thesamecalculationasshowninFig.1. In Fig.1, at the Sender end the message M is subjected to a hash function H to compute a hash value H (M) which is encrypted by an encryption algorithm E using private key $PR_{a.}$ The cipher text E (PRa, H (M)) is appended to the plaintext message M and sent to the Receiver. At the receiving end, the same computation is performed on M using decryption algorithm and public key $PU_{a.}$ The computed value is compared with H (M) received by the Receiver. The matching of the calculation with the hash value is a proof that the message has not been altered.

3 Design of the Tamper Detection Scheme

The entire procedure consists of processes at Sender end and Receiver end. At Sender side the text is first encrypted. Hash code is created for the original text by using hash table techniques and DSA algorithm. The encrypted data and hash code are merged and sent through a data communication channel. At the Receiver side the received text is decrypted .A hash code is created for the received text and then compared with the hash code received. If both the hash codes do not match then the received text is tampered, thus providing evidence. The scheme consists of the following modules.

3.1 Encryption

Encryption is the conversion of data into a form, called a cipher text that cannot be easily understood by unauthorized people. Suppose Alice wants to send a message M to Bob. Alice creates the cipher text C by exponentiation C = I mod N, Where E and N are Bob's public key. Alice sends C to Bob. The input is plain text file and the data is encrypted and output will be the encrypted file. The purpose of Encryption is to encrypt the message digest or intelligent plain text file.

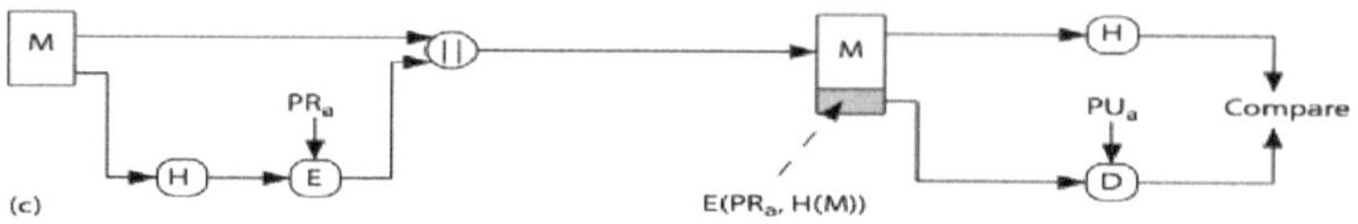

Fig. 1. Authentication with Public Key Encryption using a Hash function

3.2 Hash Function

A hash value is generated by a function H of the form H =H (M) Where M is a variable length message and H (M) is the fixed length hash value. The hash value is appended to the message at the source at a time when the message is assumed or known to be correct. The receiver authenticates the message by recomputing the hash value. Because the hash functions are typically quite complex, it is useful to examine next some very simple hash functions to get a feel for the issues involved. We then look at several approaches to hash function design. The purpose of a hash function is to produce a "fingerprint "of a file, message, or other block of data. To be useful for message authentication, a hash function H must have the following properties can be applied to a block of data of any size produces a fixed length out put H (X) is relatively easy to compute for any given x , making both hardware and software implementation practical. For any given code h, it is computationally infeasible to find x such that H(X) =h. This is some times referred to in the literature as the one way property for any given block x , it is computationally infeasible to find y!=x with H(y)= H(x).this is some times referred to s weak collision resistance. It is computationally infeasible to find any pare (x, y) such that H(x) = H(y). This is sometimes referred to as strong collision resistance.

3.3 RSA Algorithm

Ronald Rivest, Adi Shamir and Leonard Adleman developed the RSA system in 1977. RSA is a public-key cryptosystem. The algorithm is as follows:

Take two large prime numbers, P and Q.

Compute their product,

$$N = P*Q.$$

Compute the function if N as

$$F (N) = (P-1) (Q-1).$$

Choose a number, E less than N and relatively prime to F (N). This means that E and F (N) have no common factors other than 1.

Find another number D such that

$$D*E \bmod F (N) = 1.$$

The values E and D are called the public and private exponents respectively. The public key is the pair (N, E) and the private key is (N, D). Decryption by someone who doesn't know E would involve finding the Dth root of the encrypted message (mod N) which is accepted as a computationally intractable problem even with fairly small numbers it would take powerful computers hundreds of years to do this. It is also important to determine E given the public key. To find E, you Need to know D and M. As N = P*Q and F (N) = (P-1) (Q-1), to find M you would have to break N up into its prime factors. Again, this is a computationally intractable problem. Provided large prime numbers are used for P and Q. They should be on the order of 10^{75} to 10^{100}. Then, even if we take powerful computers it takes hundreds of years to determine the secret key from the public key.

3.4 Merging

Merging is a technique that brings together several existing process models and creates a new process model. Merge the encrypted message and the Hash value and send the message to the receiver by E-mail. Both the files i.e.; encrypted text and hash file are combined and merge.mer file will be generated. The merge.mer file is transferred to the receiver.

3.5 Decryption

Decryption is the process of converting encrypted data back into its original form the cipher text is converted back to the normal text. To decrypt the cipher text C, Bob also exponentiates: $M = C^D \bmod N$. The relationship between E and D ensures that Bob correctly recovers M. Since only Bob knows D, only Bob can decrypt the message.

3.6 Demerging

In the process of demerging the data will be separated. The encrypted text and the SHA code are separated in the demerging process. The file merge.mer which is received from the sender is demerged in the receiver side. The received file merge.mer is separated to encrypted text and the hash code. The data is divided into encrypted text and hash code.

3.7 Tamper Detection

The input recovered hash code and created hash code are compared for the tamper detection. We compare the hash code which is sent from the sender and the hash code which is generated after the process of decryption. Comparing these two hash codes, we can display the message which describes intelligent message is tampered or not. The received file is authenticated if the two hash codes are same and no tampering is done. The file is not authenticated if manipulations are done in the hash code and send to the receiver. Minute manipulations can be detected in the tamper detection.

4 System Design

In logical database design we approach database development from two perspectives. First, we transform the conceptual data model into a standard notation called relations, based on relational database theory. During bottom-up analysis we verify exactly what data are to be maintained in the database and the nature of those data as needed for each transaction, report, and so forth. The final step in logical database design is to transform the combined and reconciled for well-structured data specification. Fig.2 and Fig.3 show the sequence diagram both in sender and receiver perspective.

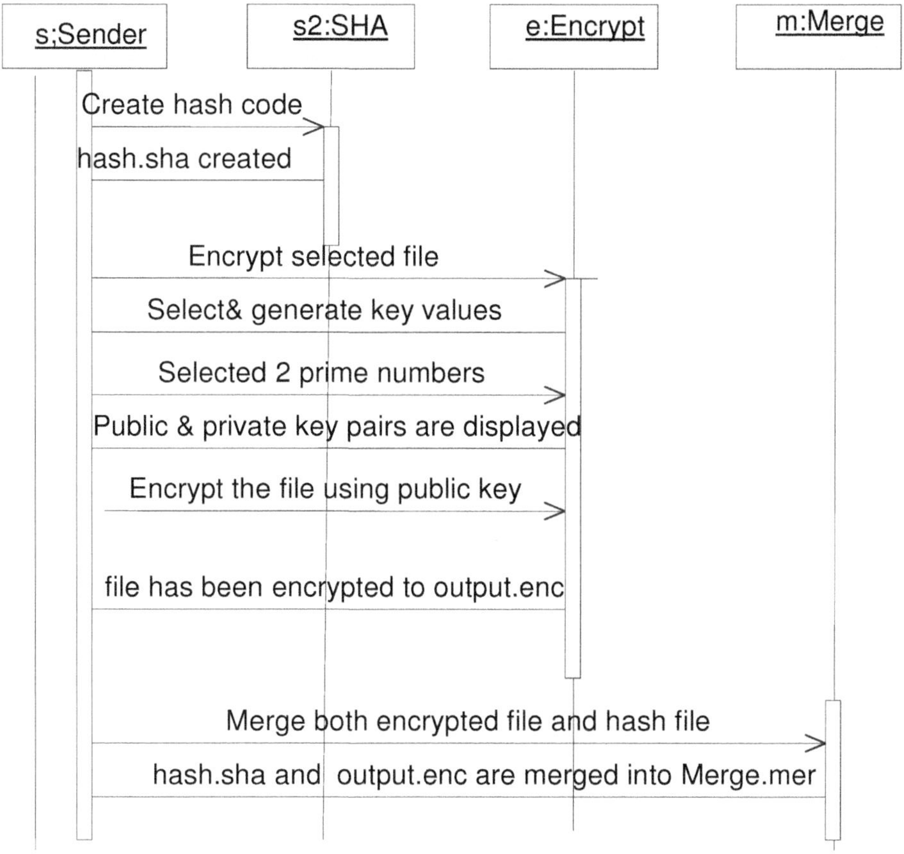

Fig. 2. Sequence diagram from sender' view

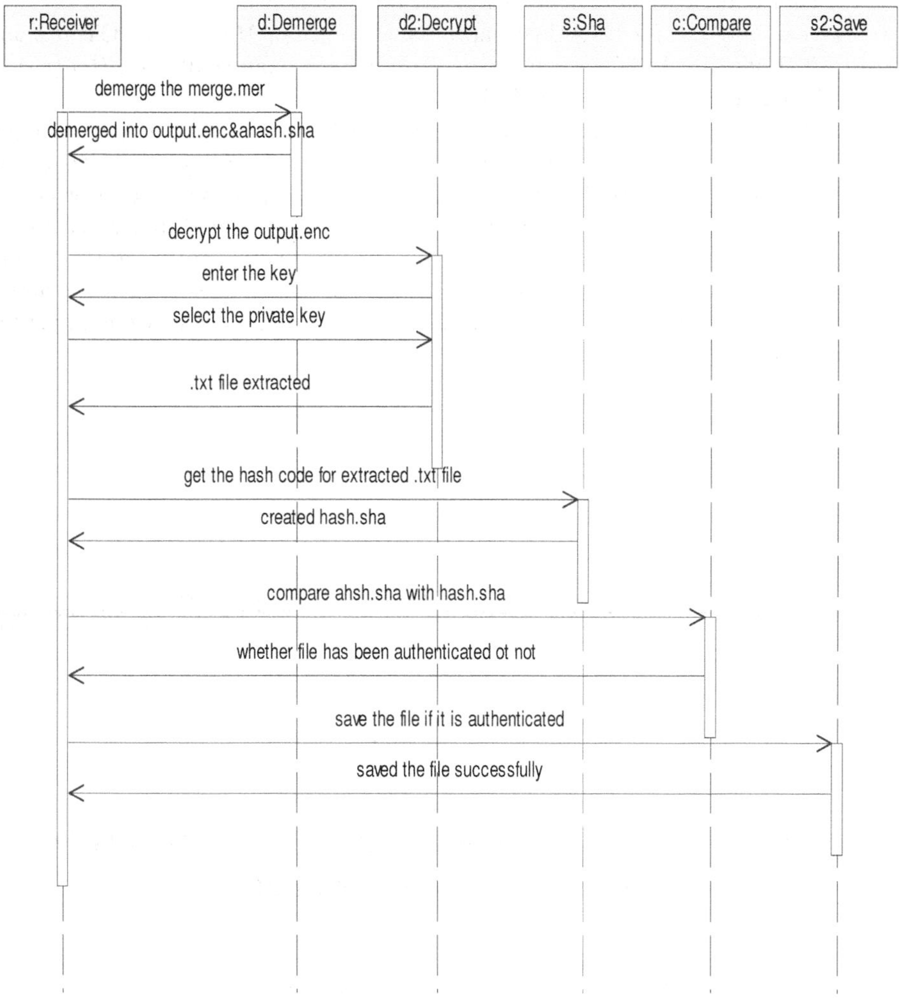

Fig. 3. Sequence diagram from Receiver' view

5 System Requirements

5.1 Hardware Requirements

Intel Processor (Giga hertz)
RAM 128 MHz
Network Connection Card

5.2 Software Requirements

Operating System: Windows
Java 2 Runtime Environment

Java Standard Development Kit 1.4.0
Java Servlet Development Kit 2.0 or higher versions.

6 System Testing

Testing is done to ensure reliability of the software, to recover form errors and from errors and unknown bugs that are present. During testing, the program to be tested is executed with a set of test cases and the output of the program for the test cases is evaluated to determine if the program delivers the performance as expected. There are chances for various errors to occur during any phase of the software development cycle. Verifications are done at the output of each phase. Each modules and sub modules are checked for errors at the output of each phase.

6.1 Testing Strategies

Test cases are devised with the purpose of finding errors. A test case is a set of data that the system will process as normal input. For this system, the test data is devised to check if the adjustments are done correctly. The other test cases devised is to check the situation in which no data is available for adjustment for a specific condition. System testing is designated to uncover weakness that was not detected in the earlier tests. The total system is tested for recovery and fallback after various major failures to ensure that no data are lost. An acceptance test is done to ensure the user about the validity and reliability of the system. The philosophy behind the testing is to find error in project. There are many test cases designed with this mind .the flow of testing is as fallows: Code testing, Unit testing and System testing.

6.2 Code Testing

Specification testing is done to check if the program does what it should do and how it should behave under various condition or combination and submitted for processing in the system and it is checked if any overlaps occur during the processing. This strategy examines the logic of the program. Here only syntax of the code is tested. In the testing syntax errors are corrected .To ensure that the code is perfect we performed unit testing and system testing.

6.3 Unit Testing

The first level of testing is called unit testing. Here different modules are tested against the specification produced during the design of the modules. Unit testing was done to test the working of the individual modules with test oracles. Unit testing comprises the set of tests preformed by an individual programmer prior to integration of the units into a large system. A program unit is usually small enough that the programmer who developed it can test it in great detail. Unit testing focuses first on the modules to locate errors. There errors are verified and corrected so that unit perfectly fits to the project.

6.4 System Testing

The next level of testing was system testing and acceptance testing. This testing was done to check if the system has met its requirements and to find the external behavior of the system. System testing involves two kinds of activities: Integration testing and Acceptance testing.

Integration Testing

The next level of testing is called the integration testing. In this many tested modules are combined into subsystems, which were then tested. Test case data was prepared to check the control flow of all the modules and to exhaust all the possible inputs to the program. Situation like treating the modules when there is no data entered in the file was also tested. This testing strategy dictates the order in which modules must be available, and exerts strong influence on the order in which the modules must be written, debugged and unit tested. In the testing all the modules / units on which unit testing is performed are integrated together and tested altogether.

Acceptance Testing

This testing is performed finally by user to demonstrate that the implemented system satisfies its requirements. The users give various inputs to get required outputs.

Specification Testing

Specification testing is done to check if the program does what it should do and how it should behave under various condition or combination and submitted for processing in the system and it is checked if any overlaps occur during the processing.

Performance Time Testing

Performance time testing is done to determine how long it takes to accept and respond, the total time for processing when it has to handle quite a large number of records. It is essential to check the exception speed of the system that runs well with only a handful of test transactions might be slow when fully loaded. So testing is done by providing large number of data for processing.

7 Implementation

The implementation of the Tamper Detection Scheme is as shown in screen shots 1 to 14. Screen shots 1 to 7 depict the various actions that take place at the sender side. At sender' side the following actions take place: creation of hash code, encrypting the selected file, generation of public and private keys, encrypting the file using public key, and merging of encrypted and hash file. The merged file is sent to the receiver. At the receiver's end reverse process takes place. The merged file is demerged into encrypted file and hash file. The encrypted file is decrypted using private key. The hash code is computed to the decrypted file. The computed hash code is compared with hash code received from the sender. During the comparison if both hash codes are same it is supposed that no tampering has occurred. Otherwise it can be understood that tampering has occurred.

7.1 Senders' Side

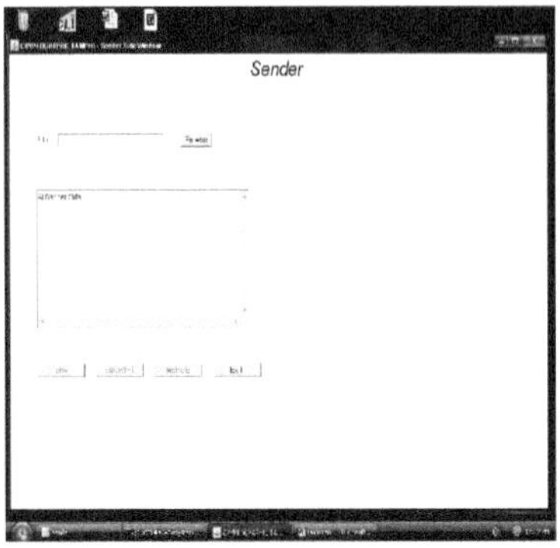

Fig. 4. Screen Shot -1

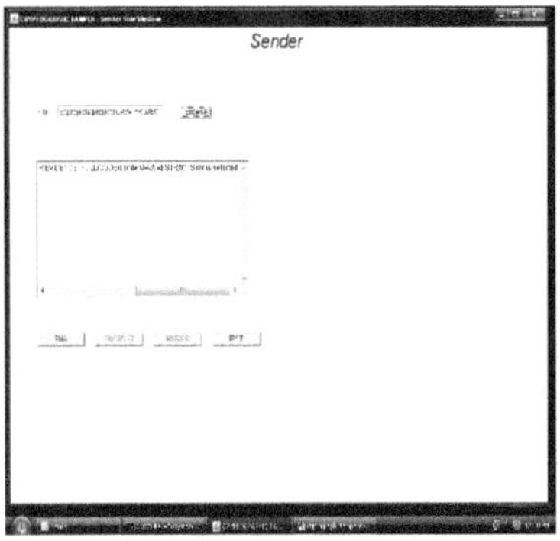

Fig. 5. Screen Shot -2

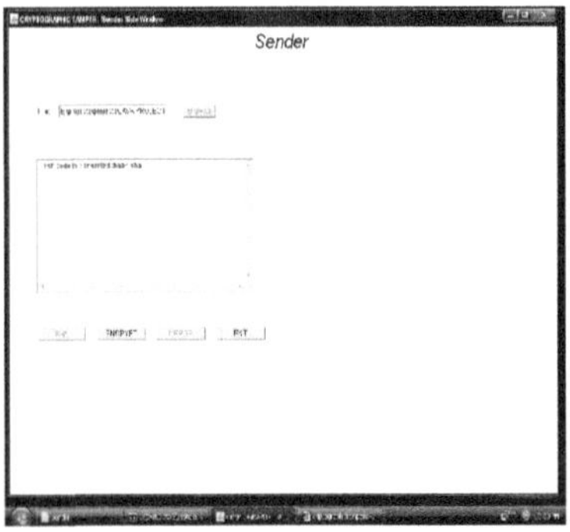

Fig. 6. Screen Shot -3

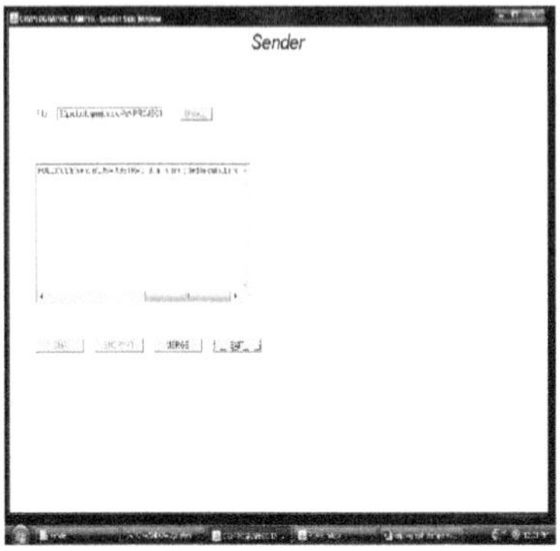

Fig. 7. Screen Shot -4

Fig. 8. Screen Shot -5

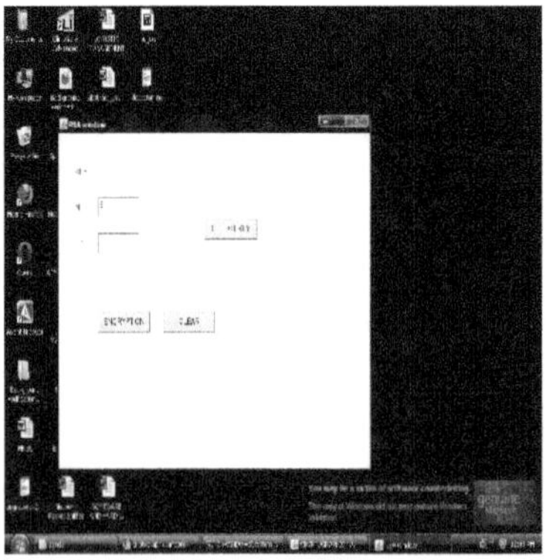

Fig. 9. Screen Shot -6

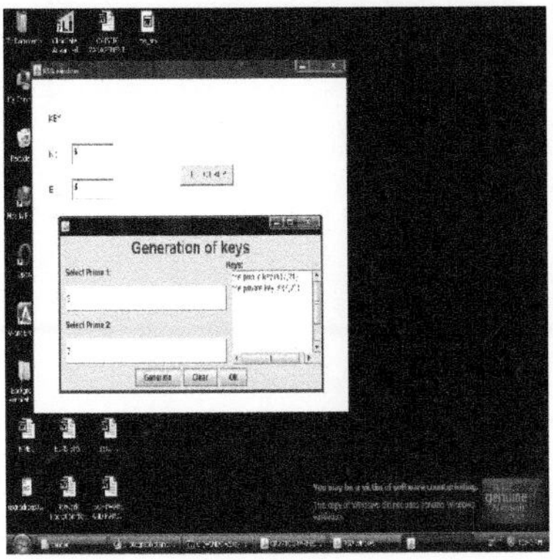

Fig. 10. Screen Shot -7

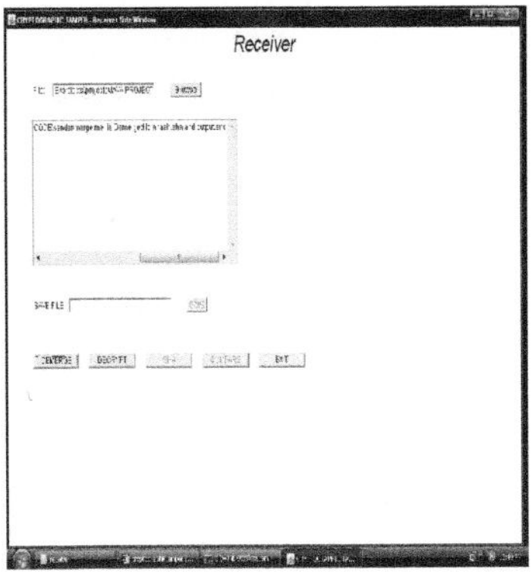

Fig. 13. Screen Shot -10

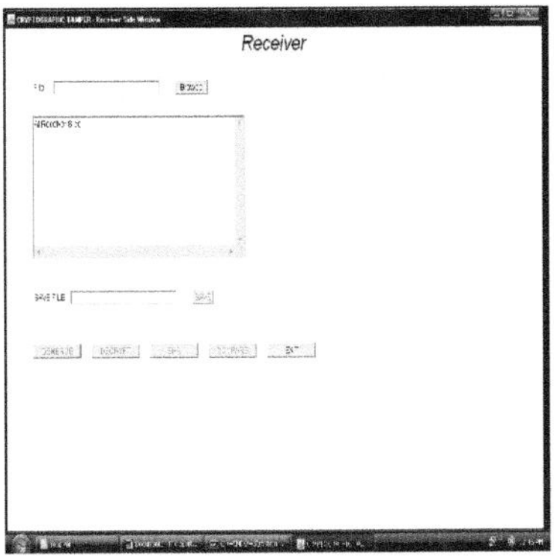

Fig. 11. Screen Shot -8

Fig. 14. Screen Shot -11

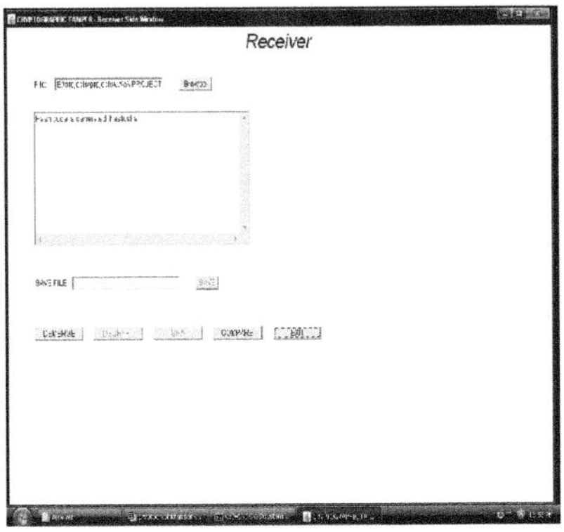

Fig. 12. Screen Shot -9

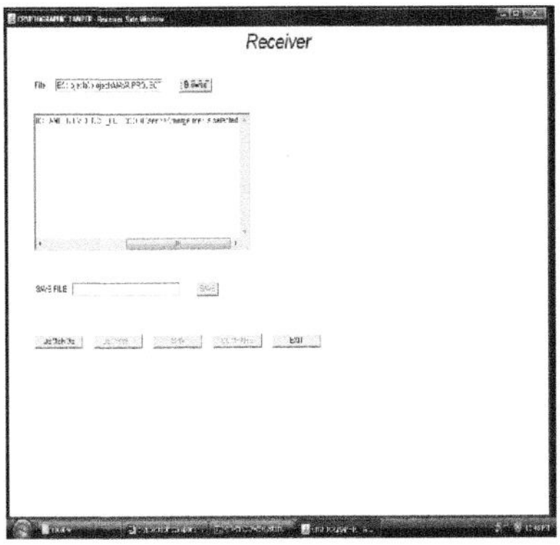

Fig. 15. Screen Shot -12

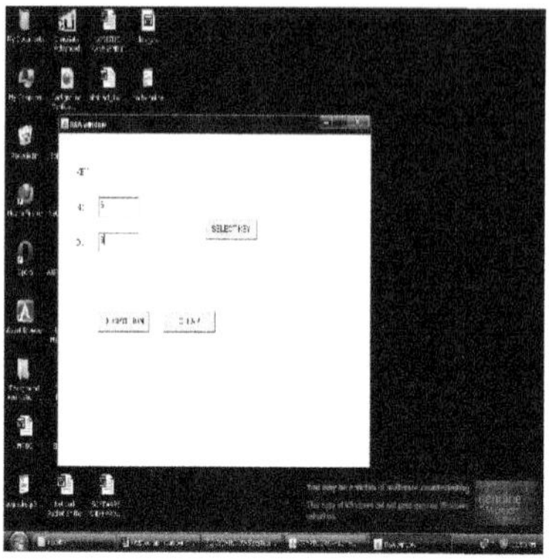

Fig. 16. Screen Shot -13

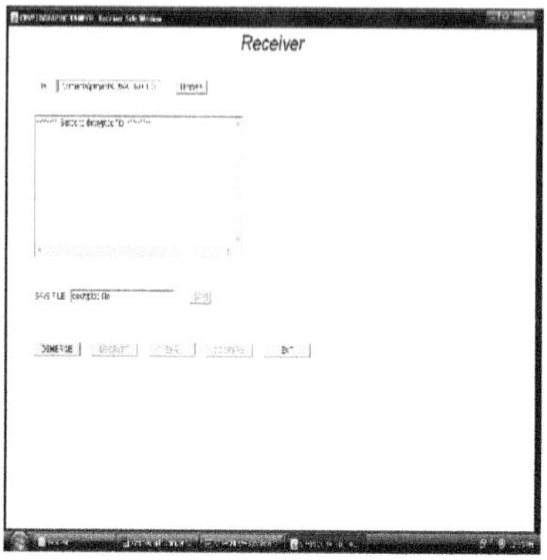

Fig. 17. Screen Shot -14

8 Conclusion

The challenge of cryptography is developing a system in which it is impossible to determine the key. This is accomplished the use of a one-way function. With a one-way function, it is relatively easy to compute a result given some input values. To encrypt data, enter the data "plain text" and an encryption to the encryption portion of the algorithm. To decrypt the "cipher text" a proper decryption key is used at the decryption portion of the algorithm. The work done herewith has given a lot of insight into the working of the Networking-programming environment. The program written for encryption and decryption using IDEA Algorithm is tested on several textual files and results are observed. The results are in the form of screen shots for effective presentation. The program could achieve a better secure transferring of files between the server and various clients. The program written could be extended to higher order to achieve a better secure transferring of files between server and the various clients. In future different types of hash functions may be used for improvement of the present scheme.

References

1. Gasser, M.: Building a Secure Computer System. Van Nostrand Reinhold, New York (1988)
2. Gollmann, D.: Computer Security. Wiley, New York (1999)
3. Cheswick, w., Bellovin: Internet Security. Repelling the Wily Hacker,
4. Felten, E.: Understanding Trusted Computing: Will Its Benefits Outweighs Its Drawbacks? IEEE Security and Privacy (May 2003)
5. Rosette, J.L.: Improving Tamper-Evident Packaging: Problems, Tests and Solutions (1992)
6. Waksman, A., Sethumadhavan, S.: Tamper Evident Microprocessors (2010)
7. Itkis, G.: Cryptographic tamper evidence. In: Proceedings of the 10th ACM Conference on Computer and Communications Security, Washington D.C., USA, October 27-30 (2003)
8. Crosby, S.A., Wallach, D.S.: SSYM 2009 Proceedings of the 18th conference on USENIX Security Symposium. USENIX Association, Berkeley (2009)
9. Franklin, M.: International Journal of Security and Networks 1 (½), 46–53 (2006)

Energy Efficient and Congestion Control Multipath Routing in Wireless Sensor Networks

M. Nesa Sudha[1], Sapna E. John[1], and M.L. Valarmathi[2]

[1] Department of ECE , Karunya University, Coimbatore, India
[2] Department of CSE, Govt.College of Technology, Coimbatore, India
nesasudha@yahoo.com, saapaul@gmail.com,
ml_valarmathi@rediffmail.com

Abstract. An important factor concerning routing protocol in wireless sensor networks is energy consumption. Single path routing protocols are not optimal in maximizing network lifetime. An energy efficient cost function used in multipath routing protocol that maximizes network lifetime using minimum energy path is proposed. Multipath routing protocol splits the load among multiple paths instead of routing all traffic along a single path. Here the paths with minimum energy are discovered and out of the discovered paths, required paths are selected. The protocol uses a least cost path in terms of cost function that calculates node's transmission energy, residual energy, and buffer space and signal strength threshold. The cost function is used to find the next preferred hop through the path construction phase. A primary path and alternate path is discovered using cost function and data is transmitted. If a node in selected path has high utilized buffer ratio and the residual energy of nodes in selected paths are different, there is a chance of congestion in the paths. Consequently the network can avoid congestion by assigning traffic to different paths. When congestion is occurred, it can help to detect congestion by using the values of transmitting capacity and alleviate congestion by reassigning traffic. The results of simulations validate that the proposed energy efficient and congestion control mechanism can avoid and alleviate congestion, and has reasonable effects of low energy consumption and high throughput.

Keywords: wireless sensor networks, multipath routing, cost function, path selection, congestion control.

1 Introduction

The present advances in micro electro-mechanical systems, low power and highly integrated digital electronics, small scale energy supplies, tiny microprocessors, and low power radio technologies have created low power, low cost and multifunctional wireless sensor devices [1]. Due to low-cost of these nodes, the deployment can be in order of magnitude of thousands to million nodes. The nodes can be deployed 1either in random fashion or a pre-engineered way. The sensor nodes perform desired measurements, process the measured data and transmit it to a base station, commonly referred to as the sink node, over a wireless channel. The base station collects data from all the nodes, and analyzes this data to draw conclusions about the activity in the area of interest [2].

D.C. Wyld et al. (Eds.): CNSA 2011, CCIS 196, pp. 225–238, 2011.

The main areas of applications of sensor networks vary from military [3], civil [4], health care and environmental [3] to commercial. So energy-efficient protocol designs with specific consideration of the unique features of sensor networks are necessary [5]. Sensor's energy resources must be utilized efficiently and maximizing the network lifetime are the main design consideration for most proposed protocols and algorithms for sensor networks. Key issues like stringent energy constraint and vulnerability of sensors to dynamic environmental conditions, still remain to be addressed. They create a demand for energy-efficient and robust protocol designs with specific consideration of the unique features of sensor networks, such as data-centric naming and addressing convention, high network density and power limitation. Recently, various routing protocols have been proposed for WSNs [6]. Most of them use a single path to transmit data.

A Wireless Sensor Network (WSN) contain hundreds or thousands of sensor nodes. These sensors have the ability to communicate either among each other or directly to an external base-station (BS). A greater number of sensors allows for sensing over larger geographical regions with greater accuracy. Basically, each sensor node comprises sensing, processing, transmission, mobilizer, position finding system, and power units The fig 1 shows the communication architecture of a WSN [7] .Sensor nodes are usually scattered in a sensor field, which is an area where the sensor nodes are deployed. Sensor nodes coordinate among themselves to produce high-quality information about the physical environment. A base-station may be a fixed node or a mobile node capable of connecting the sensor network to an existing communications infrastructure or to the Internet where a user can have access to the reported data.

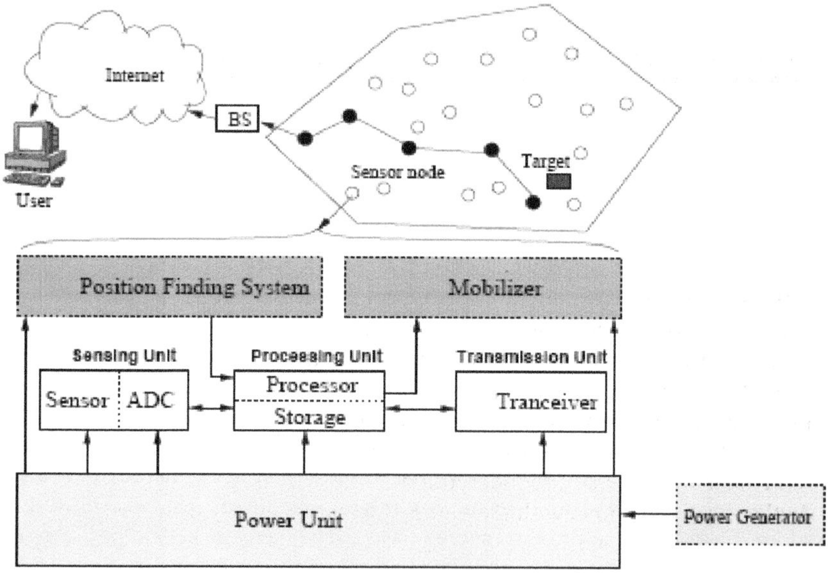

Fig. 1. Schematic diagram of sensor node components

Energy is conserved in Wireless Sensor Networks(WSN) by using a cost function which helps in discovering energy efficient route for transmitting data in multipath routing protocol.Here multiple paths are established between the source and the destination. Multipath routing is used for two reasons [8]. The first is load balancing. Load or traffic between the source and destination is split across multiple paths. The second use of multipath routing is to increase the reliability of data delivery and fault tolerance. In these approaches multiple copies of the data are sent along different paths allowing for resilience to failure of a certain number of paths.

Section 2 deals with related work. Section 3 explains the proposed energy efficient path discovery and section 4 explains about congestion avoidance and control mechanism using cost function .The performance analysis and simulation results are presented in section 5. Section 6 gives the conclusion.

2 Related Works

In this section some proposals related to routing and multipath protocol is discussed and presented. A survey of routing techniques in wireless sensor networks is presented [9]. The common objective is to extend the lifetime of the sensor network, without compromising data delivery.

In energy efficient and quality of service aware multi-path routing protocol which is designed specifically for wireless sensor networks provides service differentiation by giving real-time traffic absolute preferential treatment over the non-real-time traffic. The protocol uses the multi-path paradigm together with a Forward Error Correction (FEC) [10] technique to recover from node failures without invoking network-wide flooding for path-discovery.

The number and the quality of the paths selected dictate the performance of a multipath routing scheme. An energy efficient adaptive multipath routing technique which utilizes multiple paths between source and the sink, adaptive because they have low routing overhead is proposed [11]. This protocol is intended to provide a reliable transmission environment with low energy consumption, by efficiently utilizing the energy availability and the received signal strength of the nodes to identify multiple routes to the destination.

Congestion in wireless sensor networks not only causes packet loss, but also leads to excessive energy consumption [12]. Therefore congestion in WSNs needs to be controlled in order to prolong system lifetime. In addition, this is also necessary to improve fairness and provide better quality of service (QoS), which is required by multimedia applications in wireless multimedia sensor networks. In this paper, a novel upstream congestion control protocol for WSNs, called Priority based Congestion Control Protocol (PCCP) [13] is proposed. Unlike existing work, PCCP innovatively measures congestion degree as the ratio of packet inter-arrival time along over packet service time. Based on the introduced congestion degree and node priority index, PCCP utilizes a cross-layer optimization and imposes a hop-by-hop approach to control congestion.

For solving the issue of congestion in WSN, proposed a congestion avoidance control mechanism for multiple paths routing protocol (MR-CACM) [14], which integrates fairness, status of congestion and level of energy. Consequently the network can avoid congestion by assigning traffic to different paths. When congestion is occurred, it can help to detect congestion by using the values of transmitting capacity and alleviate congestion by reassigning traffic. The results of simulations validate MR-CACM can avoid and alleviate congestion, and has reasonable effects of reliability, low energy consumption and high throughout.

3 Energy Efficient Path Selection-Proposed Method

One of existing algorithm [9] proposed to route data through a path whose nodes have the largest residual energy. The path is changed whenever a better path is discovered. The primary path will be used until its energy falls below the energy of the backup path at which the backup path is used. The path with the largest residual energy when used to route data in a network may be very energy expensive too. So, there is a tradeoff between minimizing the total power consumed and the residual energy of the network. Taking these limitations we are using a new cost function for this protocol.

In proposed method, nodes used in the network are homogeneous and stationary. All the 50 nodes have the same transmission range, and enough battery power to carry their sensing, computing, and communication activities. The network is fully connected and dense. All nodes are willing to participate in communication process by forwarding data. Each sensor node is capable of computing its transmission energy, hop count, residual energy, free buffer space and received signal strength.

3.1 Path Discovery Phase

A cost function is used by the node to select the next hop during the path discovery phase. The cost function proposed in this paper has transmission energy, residual energy, buffer space and received signal strength as parameters. The protocol uses the formula for next hop function.

$$NEXTHOP = TE_{\min} + RE_{\max} + FB_{\max} + SST_{\min} \tag{1}$$

If i and j are two nodes in the network, TE is the transmission energy of node 'i' for transmitting a bit to node 'j'.

$$TE = 1 + \beta d_{ij}^{\ 2} \tag{2}$$

where d_{ij} is the Euclidean distance between the two nodes 'i' and 'j' and the value of β=2. RE is the residual energy (remaining energy) of node 'j'.

$$RE = E_{initial} - E_{transmitted} \tag{3}$$

$$RE = E_{initial} - \delta_{ij}\left(1 + \beta d_{ij}^{\ 2}\right) \tag{4}$$

where δ_{ij} is the amount of data. FB is free buffer space and SST is signal strength threshold that indicate the minimum distance in order to receive all the data's transmitted to that node.

The scenario of multipath discovery phase is shown in fig.2.The sink node [13] starts the multiple paths discovery phase to create a set of neighbours that is able to forward data towards the sink from the source node. The constructed multi-paths are node-disjoint paths (i.e. have no common nodes except the source and the destination). In the initialization phase each sensor node broadcast a HELLO message to its neighbouring nodes. Each sensor node maintains and updates its neighbouring table during this phase. The neighbouring table contains information about the list of neighbouring nodes of the sensor node.

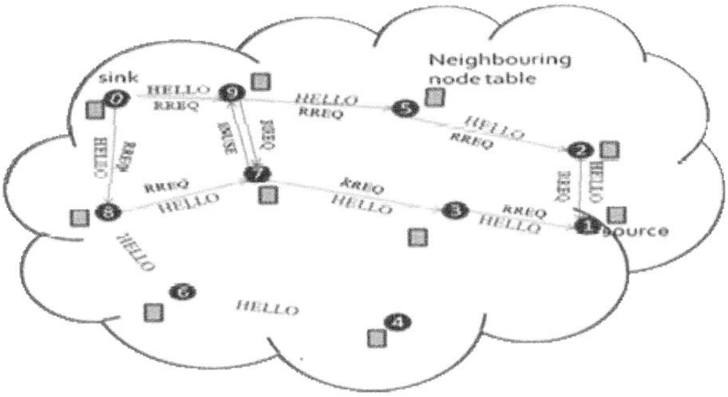

Fig. 2. Scenario for multipath discovery

Fig .3. illustrates the structure of the HELLO message. The source ID contains the node's identity of the message originator. The HC- hop count [13] gives the hop distance of the message that has been passed from its originator using algorithm given below.

Fig. 3. HELLO message frame format structure

Algorithm 1

```
      Hop count
      Begin
  Initialize the sink node with Hop Count (HC) value 1.
  Get the HC value for all the nodes.
  Increment the count by i + 1 of all nodes in the
  network .
  Select node with the lowest hop count value
  Else go for node with least residual energy.
          End
```

The TE-transmission energy, RE-residual energy, FB-free buffer and SST-signal strength threshold are calculated using (2) and (3). After initialization phase, each sensor node has enough information to compute the cost function for its neighbouring nodes. Then, the sink node locally computes its preferred next hop node using (1) the cost function, and sends out a RREQ (route request) message to its most preferred next hop.

Fig.4 shows the structure of the RREQ message.D-ID gives the destination node identity. RC-route cost [14] is calculated by $\frac{\text{transmitted energy} - \text{residual energy}}{\text{number of nodes}}$, Through the link cost function, the preferred next hop node of the sink computes locally its most preferred next hop in the direction of the source node, and sends out a route request message to its next hop, the operation continues until source node For finding the second alternate path, the sink node sends an alternate path route request message to its next most preferred neighbour.Each parameters one byte each.

S-ID	D-ID	HC	TE	RE	FB	SST	RC

Fig. 4. RREQ message frame format structure

To avoid having paths with shared node, each node must accept only one route request message. Nodes that receive more than one route request message will accept only the first route request message and reject the remaining messages. If a node is already in the primary path it sends an already in use message indicating it is in usage (Fig. 2).The requesting node will go for the next preferred node and the procedure continues till it reach the source node.

4 Congestion Control Mechanism

Reasons for congestion in multipath can be due to the buffer utilized ratio in nodes, the energy remain of nodes in the selected paths are different, the degree of disturbed state in the selected paths is different and the nodes in the paths can be used by other sources.

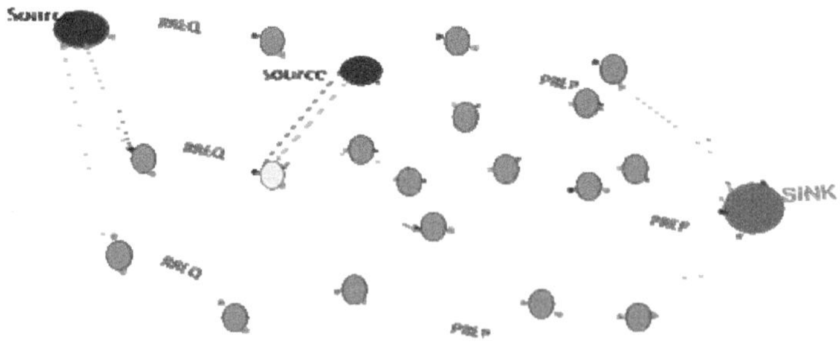

Fig. 5. Scenario for multipath congestion control

The scenario of multipath congestion is shown in fig. 5.. The source nodes starts the multiple paths discovery phase to create a set of neighbours that is able to forward data towards the sink from the source node. The multipath are not node-disjoint paths. If an intermediate node in a set of node-disjoint paths fails, only the path containing that node is affected, and data can be transmitted through alternate path.

4.1 Traffic Assignment

The buffer utilized ratio in node i is denoted as BUi, which means the ratio of the data buffered to buffer size. The parameter directly implies the busy degree of node i. The value is greater, the congestion more easily happen in the paths which node i participates in. The load factor of node i is denoted as $LF_i = \frac{r_i}{C_i}$ where ri is the sum of all incoming packets. Ci is the sum of all the outgoing packets.

- When $BUi < 1$, if $LFi \geq 1$ [9], the value of BUi may become more and more large, implies the incoming packets is more than the outgoing packets, and data are piling up in buffer, so congestion is emerging or aggravated.
- If $LFi < 1$, the value of BUi may become more and more small, implying the inflow is less than the outflow, and the network is in proper state.
- When $BUi = 1$, it implies buffer is used up, and node i can't receive data any more. And $LFi = 0$, congestion is emergence. But when node i is leisure, $BUi = 0$, the sum of all inflow is zero, and $LFi = 0$ too.

Utilized frequency of node, denoted as UFi, means the number of paths using node i. For some paths of one source may comprise node i at the same time, the frequency isn't equal to the number of sources used.

Before sending data, the source must select several paths having good performance The source sends RREQ information as in fig.6 used in the proposed method.

S-ID	D-ID	HC	RE	FB

Fig. 6. RREQ message format structure

The nodes receiving the RREQ information send PREP (path response) to source. Eventually, several paths are constructed between source and destination.The format for PREP is shown in fig.7.

BL	PF	EP	PU

Fig. 7. PREP message format structure

BL is used to store the utilized ratio of buffer, *PF* is used to store the load factor, *EP* is used to store the residuary energy. *PU* is used to store the utilized frequency of the path.Each time when a node receives a PREP the node updates corresponding values in PREP as [15].

The traffic assign mechanism can be described as in the given algorithm.

Algorithm 2

Traffic Assign

Begin:

Get *BOp*, *LFp*, *EP* of every path;

Computes Cp which is the cost function , and sorts *Cp* by descending order, $C_P = \frac{E_P(1-BU_P)F(LF_P)}{UF_P}$

Selects *N* paths having maximum *CF* from *m*, and assign traffic as $\frac{CF_P}{\sum_{1\le P\le N} CF_P} S$ for *p* path.

If $\left(\frac{CF_P}{\sum_{1\le P\le N} CF_P} S \bullet\right) >= E_P$; set $S = S - \frac{E_P}{\lambda}, E_P = 0$

Else set $E_P = E_P - \left(\frac{CF_P}{\sum_{1\le P\le N} CF_P} S \bullet\right)$; $S = S - \left(\frac{CF_P}{\sum_{1\le P\le N} CF_P} S\right)$

End

By algorithm, traffic is assigned fairly to the paths, which have enough energy, excellent receiving capability and forwarding capability. So congestion can be avoided considerably. The algorithm 2 is formulated whenever a congestion is detected.

4.2 Congestion Detection and Mitigation

The congestion mechanism integrates the utilized ratio of buffer and level of channel load to measure congestion, and automatically adjusts traffic. *NCi* is communication capability factor of node [15].

$$NCi = (1- BUi)F(LFi), NCCi \in [0,1]. \quad (5)$$

It implies the receiving and forwarding capability of node. From *BOi* and formula (4), and using the format in fig.7 conclusions can be made.The PREP message is sent by each node to the source node for detecting congestion.

BL	PF	EP	NC

Fig. 8. PREP message format structure for congestion detection

- When BOi =1 or $LFi \geq 1$, $NCCi$ = 0. This implies node is in a state of congestion and begins to throw away coming data.
- When BOi <1 or LFi <1, $NCCi$ > 0. This implies node is in a proper state.

When forwarding data, each node in path computes *NCCi* and sends it to upstream by PREP. If *NCCi* equals 0 , the node stops receiving data. Upstream nodes (not source) get PREP, do:

- If *NCCi*, in PREP, is 0, it implies the downstream nodes are in congestion. The node stops to forward data to downstream nodes and forwards PREP to upstream.
- If $NCCi$ > 0 , it implies the downstream nodes are in order. The node goes on forwarding data to downstream, and forwards PREP to upstream. If the *NCi* of the node is less than the *NCi* in PREP, the node updates the *NCi* in PREP by itself.

Finally, source readjusts the traffic on all paths based on received *NCi* from all paths. If *NCCi*=0 in any one path, the source calls algorithm 2.

5 Performance Analysis

The energy efficient routing is simulated using Network Simulator (NS2) which is a discrete event driven simulator developed at UC Berkeley. The goal of NS2 is to support networking research and education. It is suitable for designing new protocols, comparing different protocols and traffic evaluations.

The simulations results are compared with

1. Existing method which uses the residual energy as the only parameter for determining the next hop node. Here the paths are node disjoint paths with a single source and sink.
2. Proposed path discovery method which uses transmission energy, residul energy, hop count, buffer size and signal strength threshold as the parameters for determing the next hop node. Here also the paths are node disjoint paths with a single source and sink.
3. Congestion control mechanism which has two source and together of five paths. The paths are not node disjoint paths. A node in a source can be part of another source also. Every time the source is updated of the utilization of a node by another source so that it can take an alternate path.

The performance metrices compared are average energy consumption, average packet delivery ratio, average delay, average throughput and the packet drop.

5.1 Performance Metrics and Simulation Results

5.1.1 Comparison of Average Energy Consumption

Energy is an important parameter in WSN. Since the life time of the WSN depends on energy resources and their consumption by sensors the energy consideration has a great influence on route design. The average energy consumption is shown in fig.9. The initial energy assigned to every node was 100 joules .Using the congestion mechanism about 22% of energy is consumed. The proposed mechanism has consumed 30% of the network energy and the existing method has consumed 38% of energy. It measures the average residual energy conserved by the nodes in multipath after transmitting assigned data packets from the source to the sink. Eventhough the number of paths is increased the energy consumed is less because the mechanism detects the congestion and reduces traffic through that path which helps in conserving 78% of the network energy.

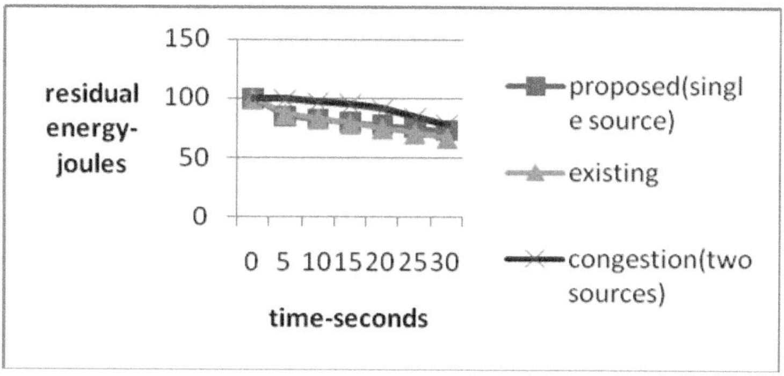

Fig. 9. Comparison of average energy consumption

5.1.2 Comparison of Average Packet Delivery Ratio

This metric represents the ratio of time at which the number of data packets that are sent by the source and the number of data packets that are received by the sink.

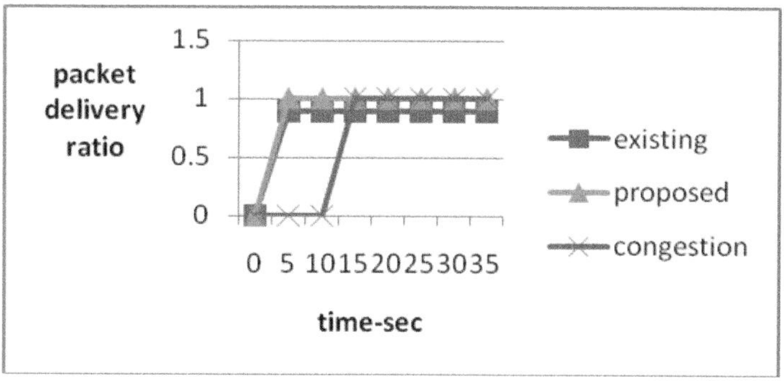

Fig. 10. Comparison of average packet delivery ratio

$$\text{Packet delivery ratio} = \frac{\text{successfully delivered data}}{\text{required data}}$$

In the ideal case the ratio should be equal to 1. Fig.10 shows that the proposed protocol and the congestion control mechanism has ratio equal to 1 and for existing it is less than 1.If the ratio falls below the ideal ratio, then it could be an indication of some faults in the protocol design. If the ratio is higher than the ideal ratio, then it is an indication that the sink receives a data packet more than once and reception of duplicate packets consumes the network's valuable resources.

5.1.3 Comparison of Average Throughput

Throughput or network throughput is the average rate of successful message delivery over a communication channel. This data may be delivered over a physical or logical link, or pass through a certain network node. The throughput is usually measured in bits per second (bit/s or bps), and sometimes in data packets per second or data packets per time slot. The system throughput or aggregate throughput is the sum of the data rates that are delivered to all terminals in a network. Fig.11 shows that the performance of congestion conrol mechanism is much higher than the proposed and existing methods. The higher the throughput , the network has good performance.

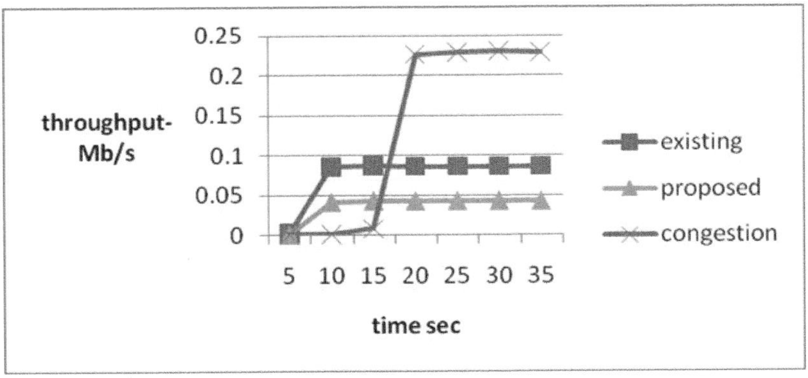

Fig. 11. Comparison of average throughput

5.1.4 Average Delay

It is defined as the average time between the moment a data packet is sent by a data source and the moment the sink receives the data packet.Fig.12 shows the end-to-end average delay performance of the three mechanisms. Both route availability delay and propagation delay of data packets contribute to the data latency. Delay grows slowly with the increase of node population. The results show energy efficient multipath routing protocol's ability to sustain application performance even for large node densities. Here in congestion control mechanism as the number of paths and sources are more as the time increases delay is more.

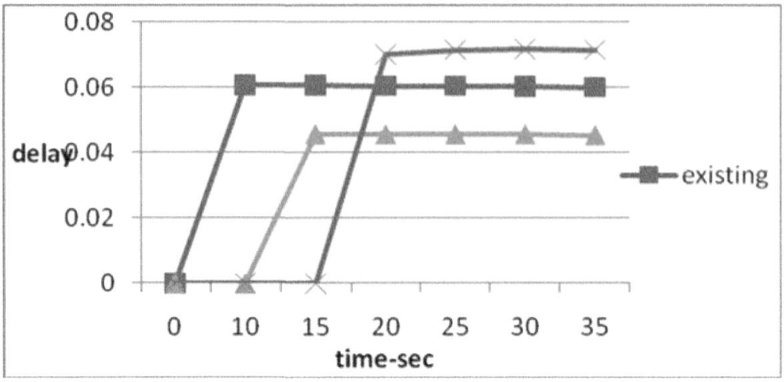

Fig. 12. Comparison of average delay

5.1.5 Packet Drop

Packet loss occurs when one or more packets of data travelling across a computer network fail to reach their destination. Packet loss is distinguished as one of the three main error types encountered in digital communications; the other two being bit error and spurious packets caused due to noise.

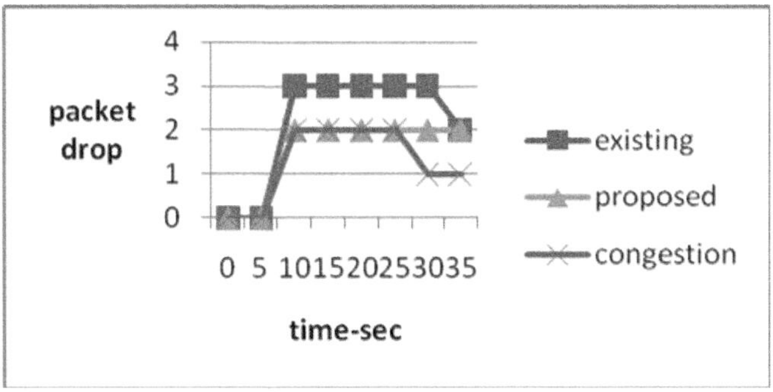

Fig. 13. Comparison of Packet Drop

The fraction of lost packets increases as the traffic intensity increases. Therefore, performance at a node is often measured not only in terms of delay, but also in terms of the probability of packet loss. Lost packet may be retransmitted on an end-to-end basis in order to ensure that all data are eventually transferred from source to destination. Although TCP can recover from packet loss, retransmitting missing packets causes the throughput of the connection to decrease. This retransmission causes the overall throughput of the connection to drop. Here in fig.13 the existing method has more packet drop due to congestion and less number of paths. In congestion control mechanism the packet loss is less and the retransmissions are also less.

6 Conclusion

Energy conservations are of priority concern in sensor networks. Balancing the load by using multipath routing has impact on system lifetime. The energy efficient routing protocol is capable to search multiple paths and aims to allocate the traffic rate to each path optimally. Simulation results show that the proposed cost function protocol has energy conservation and less delay, than the existing protocol. The limitation in the proposed scheme is the throughput but the bandwidth requirement is minimum. When several paths transmit data simultaneously, even if node disjoint multipath are used, there is still a potential for collisions that result in high packet loss rate and bad data transmission performance. As enhancement, how to avoid congestion in multipath due to heavy traffic is focused. For solving the issue of congestion in WSN (wireless sensor network), proposed a congestion avoidance control mechanism for multiple paths routing protocol which integrates fairness, status of congestion and level of energy. Consequently the network can avoid congestion by assigning traffic to different paths. The results of simulations validate the method can avoid and alleviate congestion, and has reasonable effects of reliability, low energy consumption and high throughout. But, in fact, along with the decreasing of energy and increasing of source, congestion may emerge in some areas. WSN needs congestion detection and mitigation mechanism. When congestion is occurred, it can help to detect congestion by using the values of transmitting capacity and alleviate congestion by reassigning traffic.

References

1. Bokareva, T., Hu, W., Kanhere, S., Ristic, B., Gordon, N., Bessell, T., Rutten, M., Jha, S.: Wireless Sensor Networks For Battlefield Surveillance. In: Proceedings Of The Land Warfare Conference, Lwc Brisbane, Australia, October 24–27 (2006)
2. Xu, N., Rangwala, S., Chintalapudi, K., Ganesan, D., Broad, A., Govindan, R., Estrin, D.: A Wireless Sensor Network For Structural Monitoring. In: The Proceedings Of The 2nd International Conference On Embedded Networked Sensor Systems, Baltimore, Md, Usa, November 03–05, pp. 13–24 (2004)
3. Mainwaring, J., Polastre, R., Szewczyk, D., Culler, J.A.: Wireless Sensor Networks For Habitat Monitoring. In: The Proceedings Of The 1st Acm International Workshop On Wireless Sensor Networks And Applications, Acmwsna, Atlanta, Georgia, USA, September 28–28, pp. 88–97 (2002)
4. Yahya, B., Ben-Othman, J.: Towards A Classification Of Energy Aware Mac Protocols For Wireless Sensor Networks. Journal Of Wireless Communications And Mobile Computing 9(12), 1572–1607 (2009)
5. Lou, W., Liu, W., Zhang, Y.: Performance Optimization Using Multipath Routing In Mobile Ad Hoc And Wireless Sensor Networks. In: Combinatorial Optimization In Communication Networks Book. Kluwer, Dordrecht (2005) ISBN: 978-0-387-29025-6
6. Al-Karaki, J.N., Kamal, A.E.: Routing Techniques in Wireless Sensor Networks: A Survey, Dept. of Electrical and Computer Engineering, Iowa State University, Ames, Iowa 50011

7. Ganesan, D., Govindan, R., Shenker, S., Estrin, D.: Highly Resilient, Energy-Efficient Multipath Routing In Wireless Sensor Networks. ACM Sigmobile Mobile Computing And Communications Review 5(4), 11–25 (2001)
8. Lu, Y.M., Wong, V.W.S.: An Energy Efficient Multipath Routing Protocol For Wireless Sensor Networks. International Journal Of Communication System 20(7), 747–766 (2007)
9. Ben-Othman_, J., Yahya, B.: Energy efficient and QoS based routing protocol for wireless sensor networks, Department of Computer Science. PRiSM Laboratory, University of Versailles Saint Quentin, 45 Avenue des Etats-Unis
10. Vidhyapriya, R., Vanathi, P.T.: Energy Efficient Adaptive Multipath Routing for Wireless Sensor Networks. IAENG International Journal of Computer Science, IJCS 34(1) _34_1_8
11. Intanagonwiwat, C., Govindan, R., Estrin, D., Heidemann, J., Silva, F.: Directed Diffusion For Wireless Sensor Networking. ACM/IEEE Transactions On Networking (TON) 11(1), 2–16 (2002)
12. Rossi, M., Zorzi, M.: Probabilistic Algorithms for Costbased Integrated MAC and Routing in Wireless Sensor Networks. Dept. of Engineering, University of Ferrara via Saragat 1, 44100 Ferrara, Italy
13. Dulman, S., Nieberg, T., Wu, J., Paul: Havinga,Trade-Off Between Traffic Overhead And Reliability In Multipath Routing For Wireless Sensor Networks. In: The Proceedings Of IEEE Wireless Communication And Networking Conference (2003)

Intrusion Prevention by Native Language Password Authentication Scheme

Sreelatha Malempati[1] and Shashi Mogalla[2]

[1] Dept. of Computer Science & Engineering
R.V.R. & J.C. College of Engineering
Chowdavaram, Guntur, A.P.
lathamoturi@rediffmail.com

[2] Dept. of Computer Science & System Engineering
Andhra University College of Engineering
Visakhapatnam, A.P.
smogalla@yahoo.com

Abstract. In a multi-user system, user name and password serves to authenticate the user. Generally users select alphanumerical passwords or textual passwords in English. It is easy for the intruder to crack these passwords by eaves dropping, password stealing, dictionary attack and shoulder surfing. To overcome these vulnerabilities, graphical password schemes have been introduced. An intruder can easily break the simple graphical password authentication schemes by shoulder surfing and hidden cameras. In this paper a new shape based textual authentication scheme for native language passwords is proposed. User selects a character from his native language and the shape of this character becomes password criteria. The proposed authentication scheme is resistant to attacks like password stealing, eves dropping, shoulder surfing and hidden cameras because every time user enters a new password.

Keywords: Shape based authentication, Textual Password, Native language character, Intrusion prevention.

1 Introduction

The main objective of the intruder is to gain access to a system with the knowledge of some user's password and login to a system like a legitimate user. The first step of defense against intruders is the password system. In all multi-user systems, user provides login ID and password which serves to authenticate the user. Generally users select a password that is too short or too easy to guess. The password length and the guessable passwords are two main problems in password protection. When users select a password that is guessable such as their first name, birthday, mobile number, child's name, favorite actor and so forth, the password cracking is straight forward. If the password length is too short, it is easy for intruder to find the password. If users select long passwords, it would be difficult for most of the users to remember their passwords. Users select English for their textual passwords and it makes password

D.C. Wyld et al. (Eds.): CNSA 2011, CCIS 196, pp. 239–248, 2011.

guessing, eaves dropping, dictionary attacks and shoulder surfing easy. To overcome these vulnerabilities graphical password schemes have been introduced.

The graphical password schemes use images or shapes for authenticating the user. Users remember the images or shapes better than textual password. But for graphical schemes, shoulder surfing and hidden cameras are the main problems. As an alternative to textual passwords, biometrics, such as finger prints, iris scan or facial recognition have been introduced but not yet widely adopted. The major drawback of this approach is that such systems can be expensive and the identification process can be slow. This approach requires a special sensor for the biometric. In this paper, a new shape based textual authentication scheme for native language passwords is proposed. Users can remember their native language passwords better than any other language. User selects a character from his native language and submits the shape of that character in a grid during password creation. Later based on this information, the user is authenticated.

This paper is organized as follows: Related work is discussed in section 2. In section 3, the new shape based textual authentication scheme is introduced. Security analysis is done in section 4. conclusion and future work are proposed in section 5.

2 Related Work

Graphical password schemes have been proposed as a possible alternative to text-based schemes, motivated partially by the fact that humans can remember pictures better than text. There exist various approaches that focus on graphical authentication schemes. Blonder [1] designed a graphical password scheme in which a password is created by having the user click on several locations on an image. During authentication, the user must click on the approximate areas of the locations. Dhamija and perrig [2] proposed a graphical authentication scheme in which the user selects a certain number of images from a set of random pictures. Later user has to identify the pre-selected images for authentication. Jansen [4,5] proposed a graphical password scheme for mobile devices. During password creation, a user selects a theme consisting of photos in thumbnail size and set a sequence of pictures as a password. During authentication, user must recognize the images in the correct order. Each thumb nail image is assigned a numerical value, thus the sequence of the chosen images will create a numerical password. As the no. of images is limited to 30, the password space of this scheme is not large. Weinshall and Kirkpatrick [10] proposed several authentication schemes such as picture recognition, object recognition and pseudo word recognition and conducted user studies on these. The results declared that pictures are most effective than the other two proposed schemes. Goldberg [3] designed a technique known as "passdoodle". This is a graphical password authentication scheme using handwritten design or text usually drawn with a stylus onto a touch sensitive screen. Jermyn et al [6] proposed a technique called " Draw A Secret"(DAS) where a user draws the password on a 2D grid. The coordinates of this drawing on the grid are stored in order. During authentication user must redraw the picture. The user is authenticated if the drawing touches the grid in the same order. All these graphical authentication schemes are vulnerable to shoulder surfing.

To overcome the shoulder-surfing problem, many techniques were proposed. Zhao and Li [12] proposed a shoulder-surfing resistant scheme “S3PAS”. The main idea of the scheme is as follows. In the login stage, they must find their original text passwords in the login image and click inside the invisible triangle region. The system integrates both graphical and textual password scheme and has high level security. Man, et al, [8] proposed another shoulder-surfing resistant technique. In this scheme, a user chooses many images as the pass-objects. The pass-objects have variants and each of them is assigned to a unique code. In the authentication stage, the user must type the unique codes of the pass-objects variants in the scenes provided by the system. Although the scheme shows perfect results in resisting hidden camera, it requires the user to remember code with the pass-object variants. Luca, et al. [7] proposed a stroke based shape password for ATMs. They argued that using shapes will allow more complex and more secure authentication with a lower cognition load. More graphical password schemes have been summarized in a recent survey paper [9]. Zheng et al [13] designed a hybrid password scheme based on shape and text. The basic concept is mapping shape to text with strokes of the shape and a grid with text. The user has to select a shape which can be a number, character (in English), geometric shape or a random shape. But selecting simple and common shapes makes the process easy for the intruder. Though the random and arbitrary shapes are strong, it is difficult for the user to remember them. Naturally, users remember their native language passwords better than any other language. This paper focuses on authentication based on native language passwords..

3 The Authentication Scheme

The new shape based textual authentication scheme consists of three steps:

- password creation
- password entry
- password verification

3.1 Password Creation

User selects a character from his native language character set. Each character may contain one or more strokes. A stroke is an ordered list of cells. A password is represented by a sequence of strokes. The length of a stroke is the number of cells it contains. The length of the password is the sum of the lengths of its strokes. An interface consisting of a grid of size 5x 5 will be displayed on the screen. User has to select an ordered list of grid cells to represent the shape of the character selected for password.

Consider the following character

This character consists of two strokes, each consisting of a set of ordered grid cells.

The first stroke of the character starts from the grid cell (2,4) and ends with (4,2). The second stroke starts with (1, 2) and ends with (1, 4).

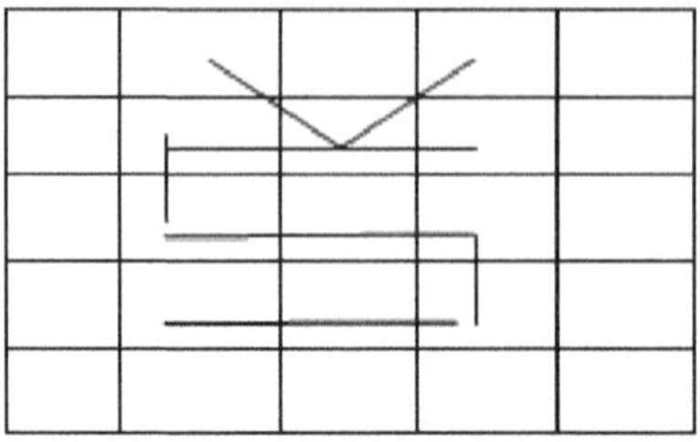

Fig. 1. Password character

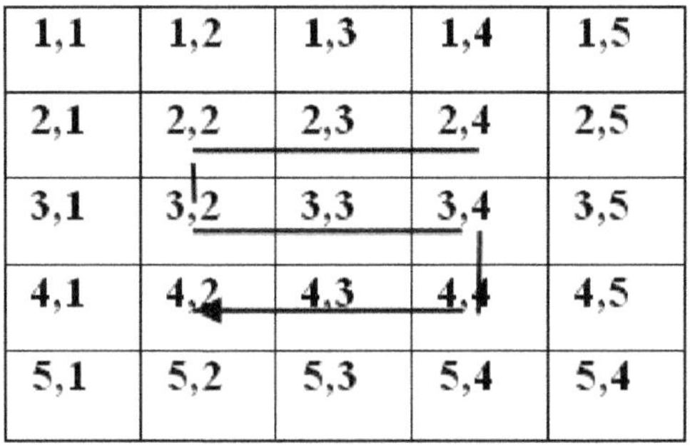

Fig. 2. The first stroke of the character

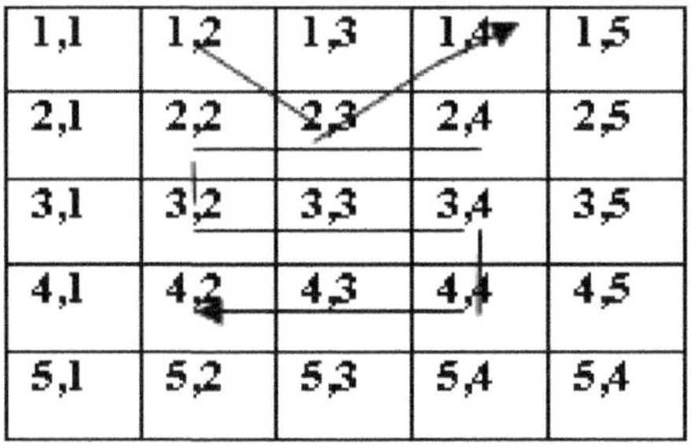

Fig. 3. The two components of the character

Totally the shape of the character can be represented by the grid cells { (2,4), (2,3),(2,2),(3,2),(3,3),(3,4),(4,4),(4,3),(4,2),(1,2),(2,3),(1,4) } .User has to select the grid cells in this order at the time of password creation.

3.2 Password Entry

At the time of login, user has to enter his login ID and password. An interface consisting of grid of size 5x5 will be displayed. The grid contains a symbol in each cell. Based on the symbol in the grid cells and shape of the character selected by him, user has to enter his password.

1	1	0	0	1
0	1	1	0	0
1	1	0	1	0
1	0	1	0	1
0	1	0	1	1

Login ID: ______________
Password: ______________

Fig. 4. Login interface grid with symbols

For this interface, suppose the user enters the password: **011101010110.**

3.3 Password Verification

After password entry, the authentication scheme will verify the password. It will compare the symbols of the interface in the positions of the grid cells selected by the user at the time of password creation with the symbols of the password entered by the user at the time of login. If the password entered is not correct, the system will generate another login interface grid with different symbols. At each login step, the symbols vary, but the shape of the character and the order of the grid cells that represent the shape of the character do not vary and the password entered by the user varies. So, the text-based brute force attack will not work.

For the above interface, the password will be verified in this manner:

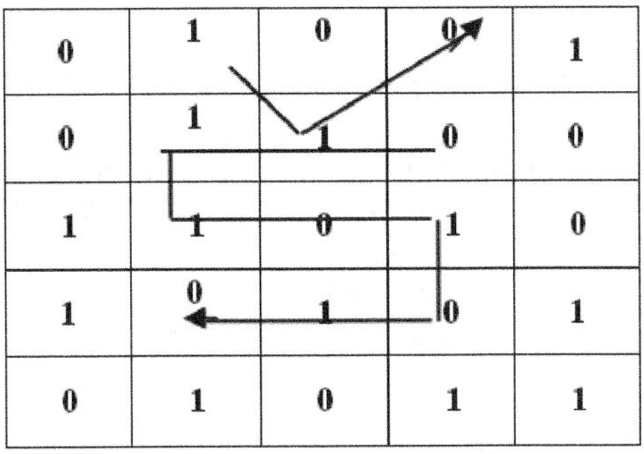

Fig. 5. Grid with shape of the character

The shape of the character is represented by the cells:

{(2,4), (2,3),(2,2),(3,2),(3,3),(3,4),(4,4),(4,3),(4,2),(1,2),(2,3),(1,4)}

For this interface, by considering the symbols of the cells in the above order, actual password is 011101010110 and the password entered by the user is 011101010110. In this example, the user is authenticated.

4 Security Analysis

4.1 Size of the Grid

If the grid size is small, it is easy to enter the password and at the same time it is easy for the intruder to crack the password. With a grid of small size it may not be possible to represent all the characters of the native language properly. If the grid size is large, then it is difficult for the intruder to break the password. Each character can be represented in many ways and user has to remember the representation.

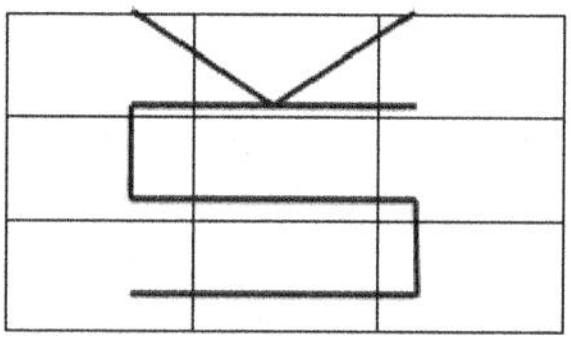

Fig. 6. 3x3 grid

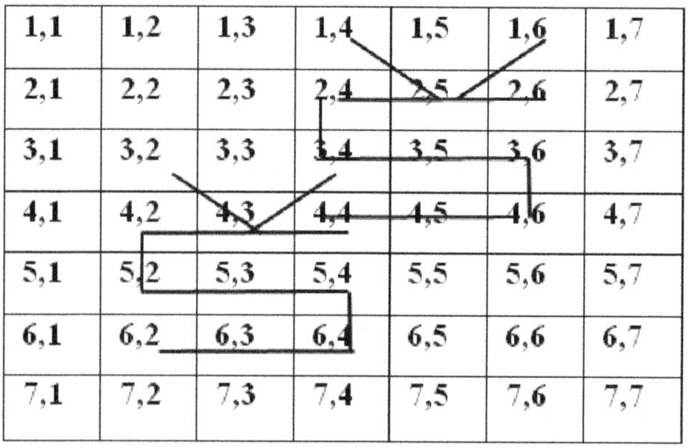

Fig. 7. 7x7 grid

4.2 Complexity

In this paper, Telugu language is selected as the native language of the user. Telugu is one of the official languages of India. There are 18 vowels and 36 consonants in the language. A syllabic unit could be a vowel, a consonant or their combination. In a combination, the vowel part is indicated using a diacritic sign known as maatra. The shape of a maatra is often completely different from the corresponding vowel. The shape of the consonant also changes when it combines with a vowel or with another consonant. Each character is represented by one or more strokes with some strokes extending above or below the main part of the character. There may be overlapping of these strokes in many of the characters. This overlapping of strokes leads to repetition of grid cells in the password creation.

The grid consists of 3 types of cells-internal cells, boundary cells and corner cells. An internal cell of the grid consists of 8 neighbors, a boundary cell consists of 5 neighbors and a corner cell consists of 3 neighbors. The actual complexity depends on the type of cells selected by the user for his password. For simplicity, we are considering that all selected cells are internal cells.

Case 1: The character contains a single stroke:

Suppose the shape of the character selected for password contains n cells.

(a) Without repetition of grid cells:
Theoretically, the password space is 25*24*23*...(25-(n-1)) .
But, practically it is less than that value. Every cell in the stroke (except the first cell) is a neighbor of the previous cell. After selection of the first cell with 25 possibilities, the no. of possibilities of selection of the second cell is 8 and third cell is (8-1). The total password space is 25 * 8 * 7 ^ (n-2).

(b) With repetition of grid cells, theoretically the no. of possibilities is 25 ^ n. Practically the password space is 25 * 8 ^ (n-1).

Case 2: The character contains two or more strokes

(a) Without repetition of grid cells:
If there are two strokes with n and m symbols then the password space is 25 * 8 * 7 ^ (n-2) of the first stroke and (25-n) * 8* 7 ^ (m-2) for the second component for internal cells.

(b) With repetition of grid cells
With repetition, the password space is 25 * 8 ^ (n-1) of the first stroke and 25 * 8 ^ (m-1) of the second stroke. With more no. of components, it will be more difficult to crack the password.

4.3 Eaves Dropping/Shoulder Surfing

These attacks do not work with the proposed shape based textual authentication scheme even though intruder has a copy of the password entered by the authenticated user. Every time the symbols of the login interface grid changes and the password varies. Suppose that the intruder has obtained the interface grid and the password entered during login step. Now , the intruder has to guess the shape of the password based on strokes. A single password represents many stroke variants. The total password space depends on number of 1's and 0's in interface grid and the password entered. Suppose, the interface grid consists of m number of 1's and n number of 0's and the password consists of p number of 1's and q number of 0's. The password space is (m ^ p) * (n ^ q).

4.4 Random Input

The possible symbols for the password are {0,1}. By giving random input, the possibility of guessing the correct password of length k is (1/2) ^ k = 1 / (2 ^ k).

4.5 Hidden Camera

Suppose the intruder has a copy of the login interface grid and the password entered by the authenticated user captured by hidden cameras. For the login interface grid in fig:4, the password entered by the user is 011101010110. When the intruder tries to find the character of the password, he may find many characters of the language.

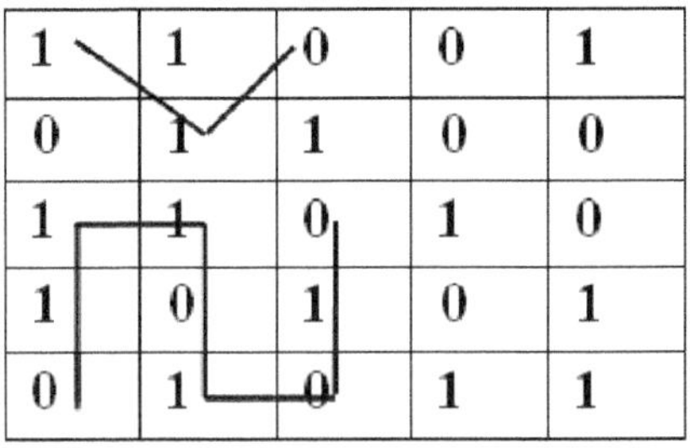

Fig. 8. The letter "sa"

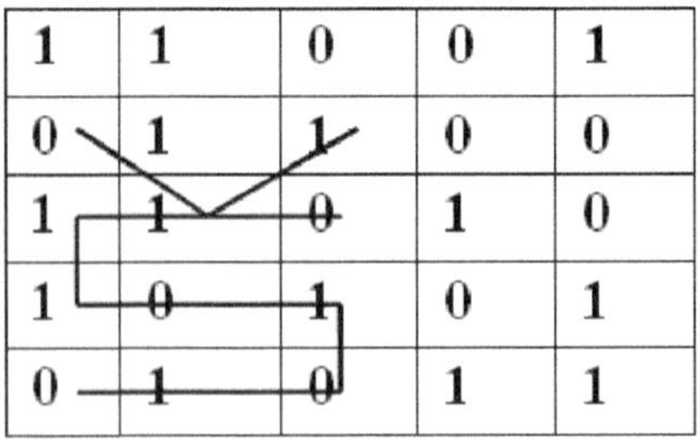

Fig. 9. The letter "ka"

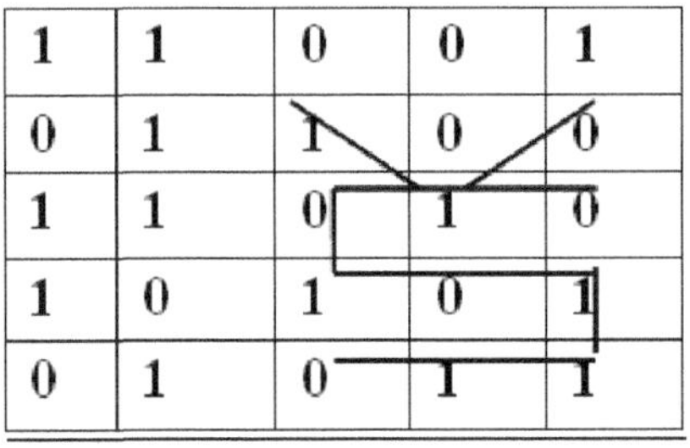

Fig. 10. The letter "ka"

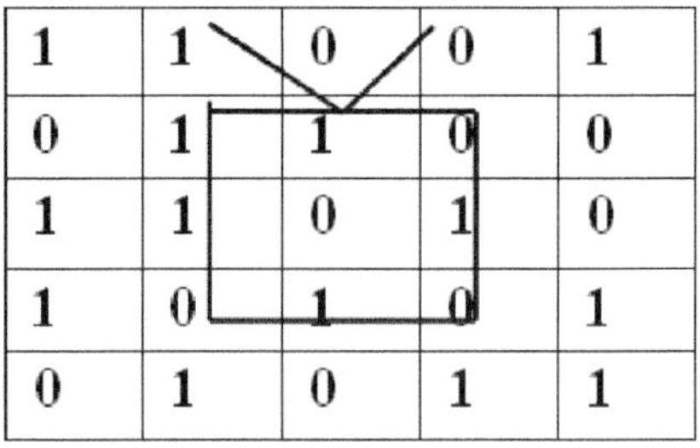

Fig. 11. The letter "ra"

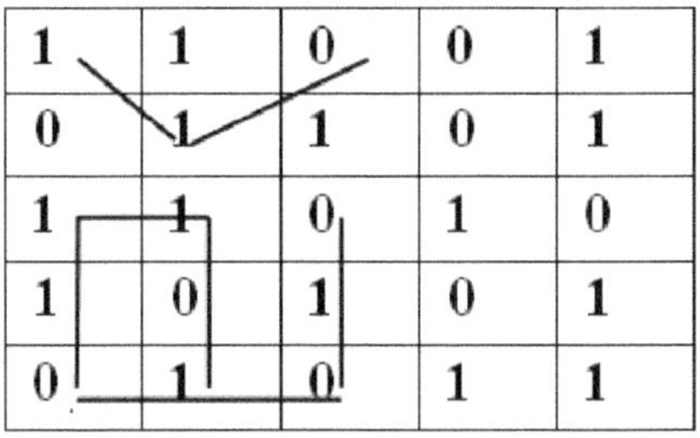

Fig. 12. The letter "pa"

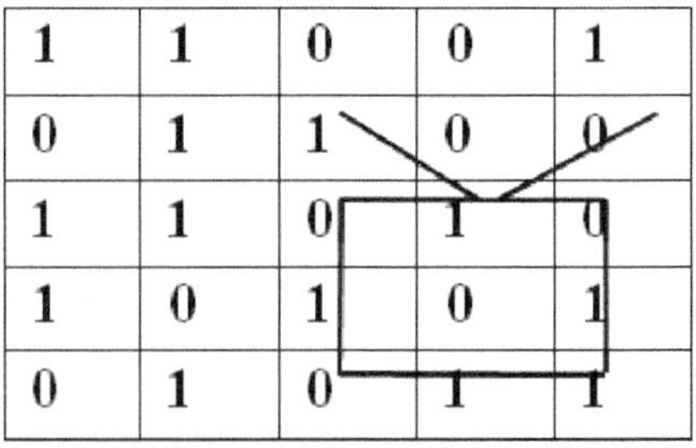

Fig. 13. The letter "ra"

With the same password, the login interface grid may represent number characters of the language. Even though generally the strokes of the language go from left to right and top to bottom, it may depend upon the writing style of the user. The user takes freedom in writing characters of the language. For example, in fig 9 , the letter "ka" contains two strokes –one goes in the correct order but the second component {110} goes from right to left i.e. {(2,3),(3,2),(2,1)}. It can be accepted considering the writing style of the user.

5 Conclusion and Future Work

In this paper a new authentication scheme based on native language passwords is proposed. In this paper, Telugu language is selected as the native language of the user. Telugu is one of the official languages of India. The proposed scheme is resistant to eves dropping, brute force attack, shoulder surfing and hidden camera. Users can remember their native language passwords better than any other language. The intruder should have the knowledge of native language of the user to guess the password to break the system. During registration, user selects sequence of cells on the grid based on the shape of the character selected by him for password. For log-in, user has to enter the symbols in the grid in the same sequence selected by him during registration. The process of creating the password and entering the password are time taking and vulnerable activities. To reduce these problems, a more advanced scheme is to be designed, which is the future work for this paper.

References

[1] Blonder, G.E.: Graphical Passwords, in Lucent Technologies, Inc., Murray Hill, NJ, U. S. Patent, Ed.United States (1996)

[2] Dhamija, R., Perrig, A.: Deja Vu: A User Study using Images For Authentication. In: 9th USENIX Security Symposium (2000)

[3] Goldberg, J., Hagman, J., Sazawal, V.: Doodling Our Way To Better Authentication. In: CHI 2002 extended abstracts on Human Factors in Computer Systems (2002)

[4] Jansen, W.: Authenticating Mobile Device User through Image Selection. Data Security (2004)

[5] Jansen, W.: Authenticating Users on Handheld Devices. In: Proceedings of Canadian Information Technology Security Symposium (2003)

[6] Jermyn, I., Mayer, A., Monrose, F., Reiter, M., Rubin: The design and analysis of graphical passwords. In: Proceedings of USENIX Security Symposium (August 1999)

[7] Luca, A.D., Weiss, R., Hussmann, H.: PassShape:stroke based shape passwords. In: Proceedings of the conference of the computer-human interaction special interest group (CHISIG) of Australia on Computer-human interaction: design: activities, artifacts and environments, Adelaide, Australia, November 28-30, pp. 239–240 (2007)

[8] Man, S., Hong, D., Mathews, M.: A shouldersurfing resistant graphical password scheme. In: Proceedings of International conference on security and management, LasVergas, NV (2003)

[9] Suo, X., Zhu, Y., Owen, G.S.: Graphical passwords: A survey. In: 21st Annual Computer Security Applications Conference (ASCSAC 2005), Tucson (2005)

[10] Weinshall, D., Kirkpatrick, S.: Passwords You'll Never Forget, but Can't Recall. In: Proceedings of Conference on Hman Factors in Computing Systems (CHI). ACM, Vienna (2004)
[11] Stallings, W.: Cryptography and Network Security, 4th edn. Pearson Education Inc., London
[12] Zhao, H., Li, X.: S3PAS: A Scalable Shoulder-Surfing Resistant Textual-Graphical Password Authentication Scheme. In: 21st International Conference on Advanced Information Networking and Applications Workshops (AINAW 2007), Canada, vol. 2, pp. 467–472 (2007)
[13] Zheng, Z., Liu, X., Yin, L., Liu, Z.: A Hybrid password authentication scheme based on shape and text. Journal of Computers 5(5) (May 2010)

An Improved Uncertainty Reduction Scheme Based on Bayesian Prediction in MANETs

B. Lydia Elizabeth[1], S. Sudha[2], A. John Prakash[1], and V. Rhymend Uthariaraj[1]

[1] Anna University, Chennai, India
{lydiajohn,johnprakash,rhymend}@annauniv.edu
[2] Madras Institute of Technology, Chennai, India
sudha.ssr.23@gmail.com

Abstract. Formulating and evaluating trust is important for ensuring security and collaboration among the nodes in MANETs. The dynamic nature of mobile ad hoc networks may contribute to uncertainty in trust opinions. Uncertainty in trust opinions reflects the sufficiency of trust information obtained by a trustor node so that it can accurately compute the trust values of its neighboring nodes. Uncertainty can therefore be reduced by the collection and dissemination of more trust information proactively, exploiting mobility. But the infinite collection and dissemination process leads to communication and cost overhead. And when the trust convergence time increases due to the network size, the possibility of stale opinions also arises. To overcome these overhead, we propose to include the probabilistic Bayesian prediction of trust values, along with gathering of trust information at periodic intervals, before needed, thereby reducing frequent information collection and dissemination. This reduces the communication and cost overhead considerably. The prediction process also prevents aging of opinions when done at desired time intervals. Simulation results are presented to support the performance of the Mobility and Prediction Assisted Uncertainty Reduction Scheme (MPAURS).

Keywords: Trust, Uncertainty, Probabilistic Prediction, Bayesian, MANETs.

1 Introduction

A mobile ad hoc network (MANET) is a network of wireless mobile nodes which does not need the support of an existing network infrastructure. Because of the limited transmission range of nodes in mobile ad hoc networks, they seek the support of the neighboring nodes to forward packets to the respective far off destinations. Thus collaboration between the nodes of a MANET is vital to perform the desired network operations. Certain malicious nodes either do not extend their cooperation and support to achieve the aimed functionalities of the network or pretend to be cooperative.

Trust is a belief level that a node called trustor, can have on another node called trustee, in the network for a particular task, based on functioning of the trustee. Trust management is required in MANETs when the nodes, with and without knowledge about the neighboring and remote nodes, need to form a network where an adequate trust relationships need to exists among themselves. The dynamic nature of mobile ad

D.C. Wyld et al. (Eds.): CNSA 2011, CCIS 196, pp. 249–257, 2011.

hoc networks may contribute to uncertainty in trust opinions. Feng Li et al. (2010) defined uncertainty in [6] as a degree to which a node cannot accurately predict the behavior of the neighboring nodes. The uncertainty level also reflects the adequacy and accuracy of knowledge about other nodes in the network.

We propose to use probabilistic prediction techniques along with the proactive trust information collection and dissemination process to reduce uncertainty. This leads to a considerable reduction in cost and communication overhead that is involved with infinite collection and dissemination process. The problem of opinion aging can also be reduced when predictions are done at regular and desired intervals until the next collection and dissemination process.

2 Related Work

Feng Li et al. (2010) defined a certainty oriented reputation system where the uncertainty component was included into the opinion set of a node to reflect its confidence in the sufficiency of its past experience with the other nodes and also studied how the collection of trust information affects uncertainty in trust opinions. In [6] mobility assisted schemes were proposed for the reduction of uncertainty by enabling collection and dissemination of more trust information, proactively and reactively. Three proactive schemes namely the Town Hall Scheme, Travelling Preacher Scheme and the Hierarchical Scheme were proposed. [6] also analyses the three schemes based on their delay, cost, and uncertainty reduction. The results show that the Hierarchical Scheme is appropriate when short convergence time at a controllable cost is required. The collection and dissemination process takes place infinitely and when the network size is large, the communication and cost overhead would increase.

[1, 7] review the literature on trust and reputation management based on trust semantics and implementation overhead. Probabilistic prediction techniques are considered to be better with respect to the meaningfulness of the computed trust values. These techniques incur low implementation overhead. There are number of parameter estimation and prediction techniques namely the Maximum Likelihood Estimation (MLE), Bayesian prediction, Maximum A Posteriori estimation (MAP) etc. In MLE prior knowledge about the parameters is not used and with small samples, MLE may not be very precise and may even be biased. The idea behind MAP is to make predictions based on most probable hypothesis unlike Bayesian approach where predictions are made considering all the hypotheses weighted by their probabilities. [3, 4, 5, 8] suggest Bayesian approaches as one of the appropriate probabilistic tool for evaluating the future behavior and the trust worthiness of the nodes based on the past interactions with them. The prior probability in Bayesian approach allows incorporating a prior knowledge about a particular hypothesis providing a solid decision framework. It also allows the aggregation of information from multiple sources.

3 Mobility and Prediction Assisted Uncertainty Reduction Scheme (MPAURS)

3.1 Reputation Model

We've chosen the reputation model developed by Feng Li and Jie Wu in [6]. The idea of uncertainty is the main focus of their model as a basic element to support evidence. Therefore a node uses a triplet $b, d, u \in \{0, 1\}^3$ to represent a node's opinion (belief, disbelief and uncertainty respectively) toward a trustee/neighbor, such that $b + d + u = 1$. The reputation value of a node is represented using Beta distributions, *Beta* (α, β), where the uncertainty, u is obtained from the normalized variance of the beta distribution.

3.2 Algorithm

Assuming the behavior of the nodes to be consistent, MPAURS is proposed where Hierarchical Uncertainty Reduction Scheme in [6] is assisted with probabilistic predictions. We use Bayesian prediction where the reputation of a node Ø is treated as random and the analysis is conditioned on the observed data. We first describe how the observed data modify the subjective views about the reputation of a node through the posterior distribution and then how the posterior is used to build a predictive distribution for future values of reputation.

1) The grid-based network of size $2^g \times 2^g$ is divided regions $R_1, R_2, R3 \ldots R_r$ based on application requirements.
2) The nodes in the each region interact with each other for a certain period of time H_t *(Halt Time)*. During H_t the nodes observe the behavior of their neighboring nodes using watchdog mechanism.
3) After the observations the following process takes place:
   a. Nodes compute the opinion triplet *(b, d, u)* based on the observations collected and update recommendations from other nodes using subjective logic operators defined in [6].
   b. Opinions are updated using the Bayesian Inference (*Section 3.3*).
4) Choosing of intra and inter region trust information collectors based on computed trust values.
5) Movement of the above chosen representatives to their target places for the collection of trust information
6) Dissemination of collected trust information to the nodes in the home grid/region.
7) Until the next collection and dissemination, the trust value is obtained using probabilistic prediction.
   a) The nodes $n_1, n_2, n_3 \ldots n_m$ in the network predict the trust values of their neighboring and remote nodes, using *Equation 3*, based on the posterior probabilistic values obtained from Bayesian Inference in *step 3b*.

b) Prediction Errors are computed for measuring the accuracy and precision of the predicted value as given in *Section 3.5*.

8) Then continue *step 5* to *7*.

The Frequency of dissemination can be set based on the application requirements and uncertainty reduction requirements.

3.3 Bayesian Inference

Bayesian approach provides a conceptually simple process for updating uncertainty in the light of evidence. The posterior distribution for the reputation of a node is obtained by combining the prior reputation value and the likelihood behavior of the node. Bayes Theorem is used for this purpose.

Let $\emptyset$ represent the reputation value of node and prior observations about $\emptyset$ are represented by $p(\emptyset)$ called the prior probability. Let $\boldsymbol{x} = \{x1,...,xn\}$ be a set of observations obtained from watchdog. $p(x \mid \emptyset)$ represents the likelihood that the trust value is equal to x when $\emptyset$ is the prior trust value. The updated or conditional posterior probability (obtained via Bayes Theorem) is given by,

$$p(\emptyset|x) = \frac{p(x|\emptyset)\cdot p(\emptyset)}{p(x)} \tag{1}$$

where $\emptyset \in \{b, d, u\}$ of the respective node and $p(x)$ is the normalization constant (i.e. the evidence) where $x \in \text{observed}\,\{b, d, u\}$ about a node. The normalization constant is formulated as:

$$p(x) = p(\emptyset) \cdot p(x|\emptyset) + p(\neg\emptyset) \cdot p(x|\neg\emptyset) \tag{2}$$

The posterior distribution computed using *Equation* (1) becomes the prior distribution for the next opinion computation that is based on the new observations.

3.4 Bayesian Prediction

In [2] Al-Hussaini presents references on the use of Bayesian approach in predicting observables and in various areas of applied statistics. The objective of Bayesian Prediction is to provide an estimate of the posterior predictive density function of the future reputation of a node. *Fig 2* explains the Bayesian Prediction from posterior probability that is obtained from Bayesian Inference.

The Predictive distribution is given by:

$$p(\widehat{\boldsymbol{x}} \mid x_1 \dots x_n) = \int_0^1 p(\widehat{\boldsymbol{x}}|\emptyset) \cdot p(\emptyset|x)\, d\emptyset \tag{3}$$

where $p\ (\emptyset|x)$is the posterior distribution of the reputation value $\emptyset$ and $p\ (\widehat{\boldsymbol{x}}|\emptyset)$ is the likelihood of future instance of reputation $\widehat{\boldsymbol{x}}$ given a prior reputation value of $\emptyset$. Thus *Equation (3)* gives the probable future behavior of a node.

3.5 Evaluation of Bayesian Prediction

To obtain a comprehensive trust prediction, assessment of trust prediction accuracy is required. There exist a number of evaluation measures to determine the accuracy and reliability of the prediction. We intend to use Mean Squared Prediction Error and Absolute Prediction Error to assess the Bayesian prediction of trust values.

The Mean Squared Prediction Error (MSPE) is considered the most important criterion used to evaluate the performance of a predictor. The mean square error is also useful to relay the concepts of bias, precision, and accuracy in statistical estimation and prediction. The *MSPE* calculated from the one-step-ahead forecasts is given by,

$$MSPE = \left[\frac{1}{n}\right] SSE \tag{4}$$

where n indicates the total number of predictions and *SSE* , Sum of Squared Errors is given by,

$$SSE = \sum_{t=1}^{n} (\emptyset_t - \widehat{\emptyset}_t)^2 \tag{5}$$

where $\widehat{\emptyset}_t$ is the predicted reputation value and $\emptyset_t$ is the actual reputation value.

We also use Absolute Prediction Error *(APE)* as another measure of accuracy of prediction. The *APE* value is computed as the absolute difference between the actual and predicted reputation value. An APE of *0* indicates an accurate prediction of reputation values.

$$APE = |\, \emptyset - \widehat{\emptyset} | \tag{6}$$

where $\widehat{\emptyset}$ is the predicted reputation value and $\emptyset$ is the actual value.

4 Simulation and Analysis

The performance of the trust information collection and dissemination process is evaluated based on trust convergence time, communication and cost overhead.

4.1 Simulation Parameters

Several parameters influence the trust convergence time and cost of the Mobility and Prediction Assisted Uncertainty Reduction Scheme. Table 1 presents the various network parameters used for analyzing the performance of the MPAURS.

Table 1. Simulation Parameters

Parameters	Values
Simulation Area	1000 × 1000
Network Size, $(2^g \times 2^g)$	$2^3 \times 2^3$
Number of Regions, (4re)	4
Number of nodes per (1 × 1) grid	5
Mobile Node Speed, (ϑ)	0.5 m/s
Halt Time, (H_t)	9 s
Routing Protocol	AODV
Traffic Rate	CBR (Constant Bit Rate)
Cost of a Message Exchange, c_{me}	1.0
Cost of Moving per unit Distance, c_{md}	1.0

4.2 Analysis

4.2.1 Trust Convergence Time

The trust convergence time is the time involved in obtaining a new trust value of a node. The convergence time of Hierarchical Scheme and MPAURS would be the same. Fig 1 presents the frequency of obtaining a new trust value of the neighboring/remote nodes.

Time (s)	0	35	70	105	140
Hierarchical	Start	1st D	2nd D	3rd D	4th D
Modified	Start	1st D	Pred	2nd D	Pred

Fig. 1. Frequency of obtaining the new trust value: D - Dissemination; Pred - Bayesian Prediction

From Simulation it is observed that in Hierarchical Scheme the 2nd dissemination occurs at about 70th second. While in MPAURS at 70th second Bayesian prediction of trust value is made to obtain the new trust value about the other nodes. Based on the requirement of uncertainty in trust opinions, the collection and dissemination interval can be decreased / increased. This might lead to an increase/decrease in communication and moving cost respectively.

4.2.2 Communication Cost

The Communication Cost is associated with the number of message exchanges that are involved between the nodes during the process of collection and dissemination. [6] states that the Communication Cost (CC) of the Hierarchical Scheme is

$$CC = 4^{re} \times \left(\left(\frac{n\cdot(n-1)+4^{g-re}\cdot(4^{g-re}-1)}{2} + 4^{re}\right)\cdot(P_t)\cdot c_{me}\right) \tag{7}$$

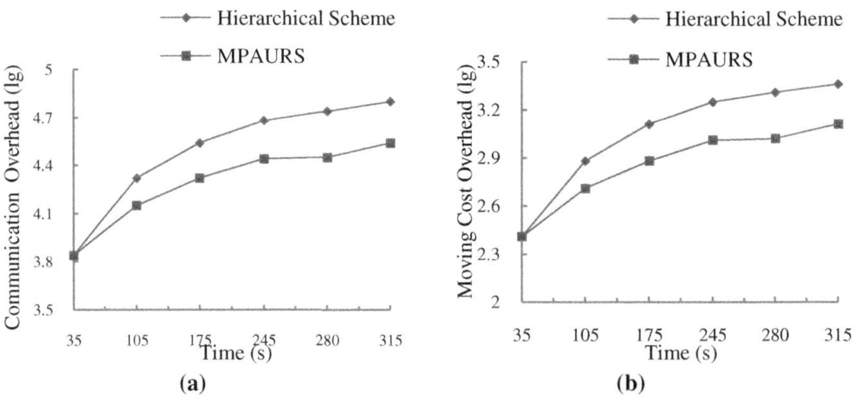

Fig. 1. **(a)** Communication Overhead and **(b)** Moving Cost Overhead at Different Instances of Time

The communication cost of the Hierarchical Scheme for the above simulated network scenario at 70th second, would be 4.15 (lg). In MPAURS the dissemination happens at every 70 seconds after the first dissemination of trust information. Thus the communication cost at 70th second would be nearly halved. *Fig 1a* presents the analysis of the communication cost at different time instances.

4.2.3 Moving Cost Overhead

Moving Cost *(MC)* is the cost associated with the movement of the trusted representatives and the ambassadors to and fro their target regions for uncertainty reduction process. *MC* is given by [6]:

$$MC = 4^{re} \times (8^{g-re} + 2^{g-4}) \times c_{md} \tag{8}$$

In MPAURS the cost associated with the moving of trusted representatives considerably reduces. *Fig 1b* presents the moving cost of both the schemes at different time instances.

4.2.4 Impact of Region Size on Cost

A network size of $2^5 \times 2^5$ is used for *Fig 2a and 2b* and the number of regions is varied from 4^0 to 4^4 to present the effect of region size on the communication cost and moving cost overhead at 70th second.

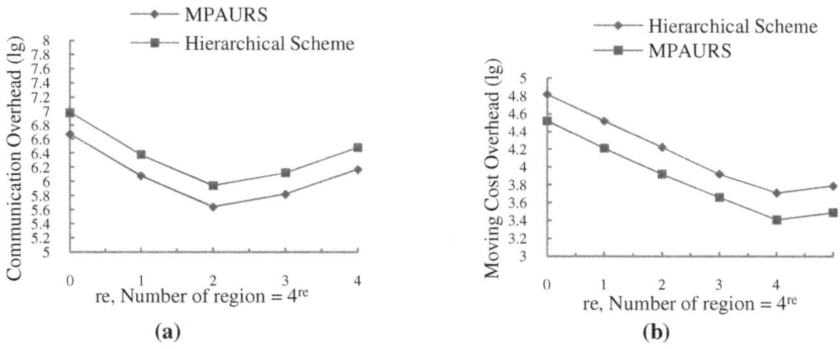

Fig. 2. With varying number of regions: a) Communication Overhead and b) Moving Cost Overhead

4.2.5 Accuracy of Bayesian Prediction of Trust Values

We use Absolute Error between the predicted reputation value and actual reputation value to measure the prediction accuracy. *Fig 3* plots the prediction error between the real reputation and Bayesian predicted reputation. Most of the prediction errors are less than 0.01, which demonstrates that the Bayesian prediction can capture the real reputation effectively.

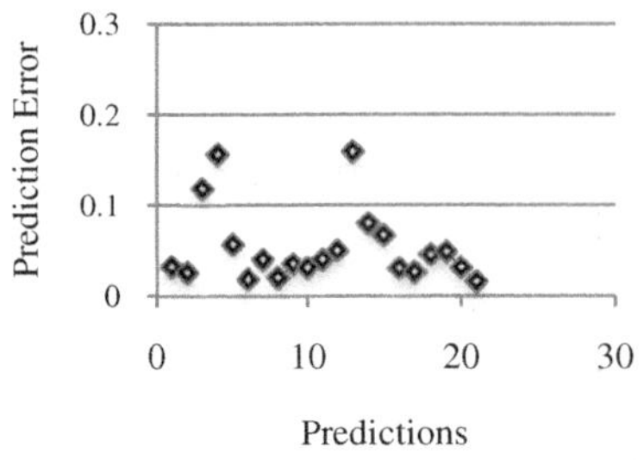

Fig. 3. Prediction errors of Bayesian Prediction

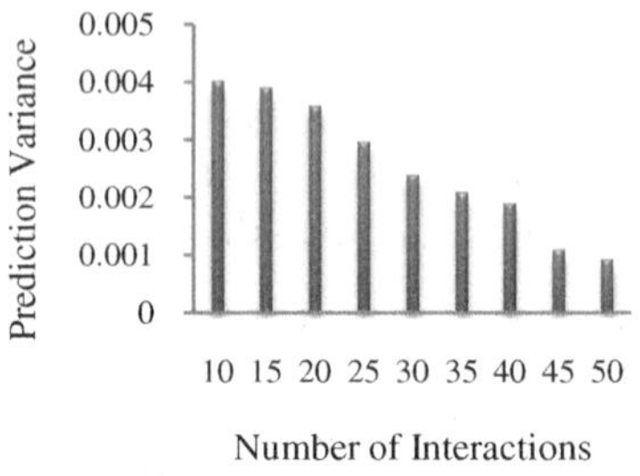

Fig. 4. Prediction Variance with Varying Number of Interactions

Fig 4 presents the prediction variance *(MSPE)* with varying number of interactions. It shows that the prediction variance gradually decreases with the increase in Halt time (H_t) that is as more trust information is accumulated the variance between the actual trust value and predicted trust value reduces.

5 Conclusion

To reduce the communication and cost overhead involved in the frequent collection and dissemination process in the Hierarchical Uncertainty Reduction Scheme, we propose to include the Bayesian prediction technique to predict the future reputation value of the neighboring nodes, thereby reducing the frequency of trust information collection and dissemination. This also enables to prevent aging of opinions when the convergence time increases with the network size. Simulation results support the performance of the Hierarchical Scheme Assisted with Bayesian Prediction and the accuracy of Bayesian predicted trust values. In future we will the study the impact of dynamic network conditions on the uncertainty of trust information collected.

References

1. Aberer. K. and Despotovic. Z.: Possibilities for managing trust in P2P networks, EPFL Technical Report, IC/2004/84, Lausanne (2004)
2. AL-Hussaini: Predicting observables from a general class of distributions. Journal of Statistical Planning and Inference (1999)
3. Buchegger, S., Le Boudec, J.Y.: The effect of rumor spreading in reputation systems for mobile ad-hoc networks. In: Proc. of WiOpt 2003: Modeling and Optimization in Mobile, Ad Hoc and Wireless Networks (2003)
4. Hang, C.-W., Singh, M.P.: Trustworthy Service Selection and Composition. ACM Transactions on Autonomous and Adaptive Systems, TAAS (July 2010)
5. Ermon, S., Schenato, L., Zampieri, S.: Trust Estimation in autonomic networks: a statistical mechanics approach. In: Proc. of the 48th IEEE Conference on Decision and Control, Shanghai (2009)

6. Li, F., Wu, J.: Uncertainty Modeling and Reduction in MANETs. IEEE Transactions on Mobile Computing 9(7) (July 2010)
7. Sun, Y.L., Yu, W., Han, Z., Liu, K.J.R.: Information Theoretic Framework of Trust Modelling and Evaluation for Ad-hoc Networks. IEEE Journal on Selected Areas in Communications (2006)
8. Zouridaki, C., Mark, B.L., Hejmo, M., Thomas, R.K.: A Quantitative Trust Establishment Framework for Reliable Data Packet Delivery in MANETs. In: The 3rd ACM Workshop on Security of Ad-hoc and Sensor Networks (2005)
9. Despotovic, Z., Aberer, K.: P2P reputation management: Probabilistic estimation vs. Social networks. The International Journal of Computer and Telecommunications Networking - Management in peer-to-peer systems 50(4) (March 2006)

Scalable Implementation of Active Detection Mechanism for LAN Based Attacks

G. Bansal, N. Kumar, F.A. Barbhuiya, S. Biswas, and S. Nandi*

Department of Computer Science and Engineering
Indian Institute of Technology
Guwahati, India - 781039
{gunjan,niteesh,ferdous,santosh_biswas,sukumar}@iitg.ernet.in
http://www.iitg.ernet.in

Abstract. The function of Address Resolution Protocol (ARP) is critical in local area networking as well as for routing Internet traffic across gateways. *ARP*, being a Stateless protocol, is prone to various attacks such as ARP spoofing, ARP flooding and ARP poisoning. This work discusses about an efficient scalable implementation of an Intrusion Detection System (IDS) with active detection, to detect ARP spoofing, flooding and related attacks like Man-in-the-Middle(MiTM) and Denial-of-Service(DoS) etc.

1 Introduction

The basic step involved in most of LAN based attacks is to compromise ARP cache, by poisoning it with falsified IP-MAC pairs. Some of the tools to perform such attacks are Ettercap, Cain and Abel, Dsniff, Parasite, ArpPoison, and ARP-SK. These tools easily enable eavesdropping, denial-of-service, data manipulation and communication hijacking. By maintaining the Static ARP Entries [1], ARP attacks can be countered. However, in a dynamic environment this is not a practical solution. ARP attacks can be handled by enabling port security, a feature available in managed switches, which ensures that a change in the transmitters MAC address is countered with port shutdown or ignoring the change. However, if the first sent packet itself is spoofed, then the whole system fails. A few Software based solutions are available namely, ARPWATCH [2], ARPDEFENDER [3], COLASOFT-CAPSA [4]. They work Like "Port Security", by observing the change in IP-MAC pairs. These solutions have slower response time compared to switches and suffer from the drawbacks as that of port security in switches. The main problem signature based IDSs like Snort [5] is that they tend to generate a high number of false alarms. Furthermore, ability of IDS to detect all forms of ARP related attacks is limited [6]. Hsiao et al. [7], have proposed an anomaly IDS to detect ARP attacks based on SNMP statistics. Reported results show that false negative rates are as high as 40%.

A few cryptography based techniques have been proposed to prevent ARP attacks namely S-ARP [8], TARP [9]. Addition of cryptographic features in ARP may lead to performance penalty [6]. Also, upgradation of network stacks is not feasible.

* The work reported in this paper is a part of the project "Design, Development and Verification of Network Specific IDS using Failure Detection and Diagnosis of DES", Sponsored by Department of Information Technology, New Delhi, India.

D.C. Wyld et al. (Eds.): CNSA 2011, CCIS 196, pp. 258–267, 2011.

An Active techniques for detecting ARP spoofing is proposed by Ramachandran et al. in [10], where detection of any change in IP-MAC pairs is verified by sending a probe with TCP SYN packet. This scheme violates the network layering architecture.

Neminath et. al. [11] proposed an active detection mechanism in which each pair of IP-MAC is validated by sending verification probes upon receiving ARP requests or replies. On receiving the probe response, the system matches it with the ARP request or reply received earlier and tries to conclude if there is any attack. This is a comprehensive approach to detect most of the ARP related attacks, but suffer from scalability issues and fail to detect a case of *DoS* attack. Apart from this capturing ARP traffic in high speed network is difficult. Fabian describes General Problems in packet capturing in [12]. Although many hardware based solutions are available in commercial domain but they are not cost effective.

In this work, we propose a scalable IDS for ARP attacks using optimal data structure and algorithms which make it suitable for high speed networks. Also the scheme is augmented to detect possible *DoS* attacks.

2 Proposed Scheme

The scalability issues makes it mandatory to have data structures that support faster data manipulation. We propose to handle ARP traffic to and/or from IP's within the network and IP external to the network separately, as spoofing for a IP outside the network can be easily detected by comparing corresponding MAC with gateway MAC. This classification helps to reduce processing overload and memory requirements.

Also information, now stored in objects, for which the space complexity can be scaled down to $O(2^m)$, m being number of bits in Host Identifier (*HOSTID*) of a IP address inside *LAN* (See Section 2.2), is marked obsolete and memory is reused. Sliding window mechanism, explained in subsequent subsection, reduce time taken to invalidate/delete information.

2.1 Sliding Window for Data Deletion/Invalidation

Window refers to a data structure that stores the data accumulated in unit time. If threshold time, till which the data is valid, is τ units, then each object (except for Unsolicited Response) is composed of $\tau + 1$ such windows. We discard/invalidate the contents of an entire window after $\tau + 1$ unit time (from when it was created) instead of removing individual entries. Although it seems that we keep invalid information for an extra time unit, but calculating exact value of τ is difficult and only an approximate value is used. We also want to make sure that information is not discarded before it is still valid in our program. This technique helps us to save memory, as time-stamps are not required for data invalidation and can be removed from most of the objects (Section 2.2). The data structures are designed to minimize amount of time spent in deletion/invalidation of contents of a window.

Henceforth in the discussion, we will use the following abbreviations.

- *IPS* - Source IP Address
- *IPD* - Destination IP Address

- *MACS* - Source MAC Address
- *MACD* - Destination MAC Address
- *GWIP*, *GWMAC* - Gateway IP and MAC address respectively (Assuming they are known to us)
- *IPIDS*, *MACIDS* - IDS IP and MAC address respectively
- $index_i$ - Integer value of *HOSTID*
- *IPEXT* - IP Address for hosts which are not in the same subnet i.e., external to the LAN
- *AMOUNT_ELEMS* - $65536(2^{16})/256(2^8)$ for networks with 16 and 8 bit *HOSTID* respectively

The information of any packet having either $IPS \in IPEXT$ or $IPD \in IPEXT$ is not stored. The data structures used, described below, can perform well only up to 16 bit *HOSTID*.

2.2 Objects Used in the Implementation

1. *Response Object :-* This object (*RST*) substitute the response table. Source IP(RSP_{IPS}), Source MAC (RSP_{MACS}), Destination IP (RSP_{IPD}) and Destination MAC (RSP_{MACD}) in *RSP* are stored in *RST*. The time when *RSP* arrived (RSP_τ) is also recorded. The data is arranged according to following scheme, with $index_i$ being *HOSTID* of RSP_{IPS} :-
   - RST_{IP_BITS}: Array (of bits), with each index signifying a unique IP address(common among all arrays in RST). Bit at $RST_{IP\_BITS}[i]$ is set if a RSP arrived, for which $index_i$ is equal to i.
   - RST_{HEADS}: Array (of pointers) with $RST_{HEADS}[index_i]$ pointing to start of a list, in which a node is composed of RSP_{MACS}, RSP_{MACD}, RSP_{IPD} and RSP_τ. The common thing among all nodes of a list is IPS
   - RST_{FLAGS}: Array (of bits), with $RST_{FLAGS}[i]$ set if more than one MAC address is associated with IP address corresponding to i
   - RST_{TAILS}: Array (of pointers) with $RST_{TAILS}[index_i]$ pointing to the rear of the list
   - RST_{VALID_HEADS}: Array (of pointers) for storing $RST_{HEADS}[i]$ such that $RST_{HEADS}[i]$ points to a list which is yet to be deleted and $i < RST_{COUNT}$
   - RST_{COUNT}: Counter for keeping track on number of entries in RST_{VALID_HEADS}

   Each array is composed of AMOUNT_ELEM elements. RST_{IP_BITS} and RST_{COUNT} are initialized to 0.The space complexity of *RST* is $O(n)$ were n is number of *RSP* stored in *RST*.

   (a) *Insertion* of data in a window, explained in Algorithm 1, has time complexity of $O(1)$.
   (b) *Deletion* of data within a window, given in Algorithm 2, has time complexity $O(n)$ were n is the number of packets in the window. Although information in RST_{VALID_HEADS}, RST_{HEADS}, RST_{TAILS} is invalid after delete operation, it is no longer used which is evident in insert and search mechanisms (Algorithm 1 and Algorithm 3).

Algorithm 1. Insertion of data in RST

```
if ( RST_{IP_BITS}[index_i] set) then
   if (RST_{TAILS}[index_i] → MACS ≠ RSP_{MACS}) then
      RST_{FLAGS}[index_i]=1
   end if
   Create node containing RSP_{MACS}, RSP_{MACD}, RSP_{IPD} and RSP_τ
   Join new node to list and update RST_{TAILS}[index_i]
else
   SET RST_{IP_BITS}[index_i]
   RESET RST_{FLAGS}[index_i]
   Create node containing RSP_{MACS}, RSP_{MACD}, RSP_{IPD} and RSP_τ
   Point RST_{HEADS}[index_i] and RST_{TAILS}[index_i] to this new node
   RST_{VALID_HEADS}[RST_{COUNT}]=RST_{HEADS}[index_i]
   RST_{COUNT}++
end if
```

Algorithm 2. Deletion data in RST

```
Reset RST_{IP_BITS}
for all i such that 0 ≤ i < RST_{COUNT} do
   Delete list pointed by RST_{VALID_HEADS}[i]
end for
RST_{COUNT}=0
```

Algorithm 3. Search Operations in RST

```
for all window do
   if (RST_{IP_BITS}[j]) == 1 for j = HOSTID of IP then
      if (RST_{FLAGS}[j] == 1) then
         Return MAC mismatch
      else if (RST_{TAILS}[j] → MACS ≠ MAC to be searched) then
         Return MAC mismatch
      end if
   end if
end for
Return IP address not found
```

(c) *Search* operation, shown in Algorithm 3, has time complexity of $O(k)$ were k is number of windows. $k \ll n$, n being the number of RSP stored.

2. *Verification Object :- IPS* and *MACS* of the request/response packets (*RP*) are stored in this object (*VRFT*). The organization of data in each window is given below, with $index_i$ calculated using *HOSTID* of *IPS* in RP (denoted as RP_{IPS}).

   - $VRFT_{IP\_BITS}$:-Array (of bits), with each index signifying a unique IP address (common among all arrays in $VRFT$). Bit at $VRFT_{IP\_BITS}[i]$ is set if a RP arrived, for which $index_i$ is equal to i.
   - $VRFT_{MACSS}$: Array (of MAC addresses), in which $VRFT_{MACSS}[index_i]$ being MACS of RP (denoted as RP_{MACS})

Each array contain AMOUNT_ELEM elements. $VRFT_{IP\_BITS}$ is initialized to 0. At any instance only one of the windows will have $VRFT_{IP\_BITS}[i]$ set ($\forall i : 0 \leq i \leq AMOUNT\_ELEM$). The space complexity of *VRFT* is $O(2^m)$, m being the number of bits in $HOSTID$.

(a) For *insertion* of data, set $VRFT_{IP\_BITS}[index_i]$ and store RP_{MACS} at $VRFT_{MACSS}[index_i]$. The time complexity of insert operation is $O(1)$.
(b) *Invalidation* of data in a window, is done by resetting $VRFT_{IP\_BITS}$, time complexity being $O(1)$.
(c) *Search* for an IP ($IP_{SearchVRFT}$) will return true if $VRFT_{IP\_BITS}[index_i]$ ($index_i$ calculated using $IP_{SearchVRFT}$) is set in any of the valid windows. The corresponding MAC can be accessed at $VRFT_{MACSS}[index_i]$. Search operation has time complexity of $O(k)$, k being number of windows.

3. *Authenticated binding object :-* The genuine IP-MAC bindings, are stored in this object (*AUTHT*). The implementation of *AUTHT* is similar to *VRFT* with $AUTHT_{IP\_BITS}$, $AUTHT_{MACSS}$ taking place of $VRFT_{IP\_BITS}$, $VRFT_{MACSS}$ respectively. $index_i$ calculated using *HOSTID* of IP address in an authenticated binding. Also F_{AUTHT}(IP) = MAC : IP-MAC is an authenticated binding pair in any of the windows.
4. *Log Object :-* Any detected spoofing attempt is stored in this object (*LOGT*). The logs for forensic purposes are made separately. This object holds *IPS, MACS, IPD* of spoofed *RP*'s. This information is stored using hash technique. In each window a hash table is maintained, with RP_{MACS} being the key. The value of each key, is combination of two sets (no duplicate entries), one storing *HOSTID* of RP_{IPS} and other storing *HOSTID* of RP_{IPD}. As we need to have search facility in these sets, we again hash corresponding *HOSTID*. For a spoofed gratuitous ARP packet, only Source IP and Source MAC is stored. If $RP_{IPS} \in$ *IPEXT*, GWIP are stored as Source IP corresponding to RP_{MACS} without storing RP_{IPD}.
   (a) *Insertion* of [*IPS, MACS, IPD*] involves two steps: If MACS is already present in *LOGT*, then *IPS & IPD* are added. Otherwise, a new entry for *MACS* is created and *IPS, IPD* are stored. Insertion as done in MAP & SET Classes in C++, has time complexity is $O(log(n))$, where n is number of elements to be inserted [13].
   (b) *Deletion* is done by clearing the hash table (including containers of *IPS & IPD*). Time complexity is $O(n)$, n being number of entries in MAP.
   (c) *Searching for data :-* After locating the presence of *MACS* in LOGT, *IPS* and *IPD* are searched in corresponding value. Time complexity is $O(log(n))$, n being number of entries in MAP.
5. *Unsolicited response Object :-* This object (*URSPT*) is used for storing the number of unsolicited response packets received by a host. Array $URSPT_{Ts}$ and $URSPT_{Counters}$ indexed with *HOSTID* of *IPD*, which stores time of arrival of packet and count of such packets that arrived within threshold time respectively. The space complexity of *URSPT* is $O(2^m)$, m being the number of bits in $HOSTID$. The information at an index is updated when required and no specific procedure is followed for deletion/invalidation of complete information apart from validation checks (on $URSPT_{Ts}[index_i]$).

Algorithm 4. ARP Request Handler

```
if (RQP is UNICAST) then
    Enter RQP in Log-File
    Continue to next packet
end if
if (RQP_IPS == IPIDS && RQP_MACS == MACIDS) then
    Continue to next packet
end if
if (RQP_IPS ∈ IPEXT) then
    Flood Detected, Enter in Log-File
    Continue to next packet
end if
if (RQP_IPS == RQP_IPD) then
    Gratuitous Packet
    VERIFY-IP-MAC(RQP_IPS,RQP_MACS)
    Continue to next packet
end if
if (RQP_IPS ∈ AUTHT ) then
    if (RQP_MACS == F_AUTHT(RQP_IPS)) then
        Genuine Packet
        Continue to next packet
    else
        Spoof Detected, Enter in LOGT and Log-File
        Continue to next packet
    end if
else
    VERIFY-IP-MAC(RQP_IPS,RQP_MACS)
    Continue to next packet
end if
```

3 Implementation

For achieving the goal of active detection, following modules are invoked as threads based on events like *RP* arrival, Spoof Detection etc.

3.1 Main Thread

Main thread capture *ARP* packets, logs anomalous packets or packets having changes in the immutable fields (considered as malformed [11]) and distribute non malformed *RQP's* and *RSP's* to Request handler and Response handler respectively.

3.2 ARP Request Handler

Input :- *RQP*, RQP_τ-time at which *RQP* arrived, *VRFT, AUTHT, LOGT*
Output :- Updated *LOGT*

RQP with $RQP_{IPS} \in$ *IPEXT*, are not expected inside network, hence they are reported as flooding attempt. There is no need to process these packets any further. Also

RQP are not stored in any table or object. This helps us in saving memory with minimal increase in false positives (See subsequent subsection). Algorithm 4 explains working of Request handler.

3.3 ARP Response Handler

Input :- RSP, RSP_τ, *AUTHT, LOGT, RST*
Output :- Updated *RST* and *LOGT*

RSP's are processed by this module (Algorithm 5). A *RSP* with $RSP_{IPS} \in$ *IPEXT* is expected to have RSP_{MACS} as *GWMAC*, otherwise it can be marked as spoofed. *GWIP* (in place of source IP), RSP_{MACS} and NULL is stored in LOGT. This is because MiTM can happen only when a spoofed packet with GWIP as RSP_{IPD} and a spoofed source MAC with some RSP_{IPS} is sent (Flipped pair). Also *RSP's* with $RSP_{IPD} \in$ *IPEXT*, are marked as flooding attempt.

As a possible solution to undetected case of a *DoS* attack in [11], assuming that a machine is not expected to receive more than threshold number of packets within DoS threshold time, we propose to continue without checking whether an *ARP* request for RSP_{IPS} was made in the network by some host (This check was done in algorithm given in [11]) and call unsolicited response handler for each response packet for which $RSP_{MACS} \notin$ *AUTHT*. This may give us some false positives (only for DoS attacks). The false positives will generally be only for machines which provide service in the network such as a proxy server, and to a much extent can be dealt with a white-list. This saves memory (*RQT* is not stored) and processing overhead.

3.4 VERIFY_IP_MAC, Spoof Detector and Unsolicited Response Handler

The algorithm of these modules are left unaltered ([11]). Using the data structure and the above mentioned classification of IPs,these modules preform upto expectations. After sending a request probe *VERIFY_IP_MAC* invokes *Spoof Detector* which waits for some β waiting time. β incorporates waiting time before a packet is processed and estimated round trip time. β depends on network speed as well as available processing power. This value must be lower then time τ after which data is invalidated. Choice τ and β depend on several factors and it is fare enough to let administrator choose these values. To reduce inter-thread communication modules VERIFY_IP_MAC and Unsolicited Response Handler can be included in response and request handler.

3.5 MiTM Detector

Input :- LOGT, IP-MAC pair passed from Spoof Detector
Output :- Updated *LOGT*
Neminath et al.[11] used a time interval δ, within which if spoofing is detected, there is a chance of MiTM. We discard δ as we invalidate all the data in *LOGT* after τ seconds. The choice of τ is made taking this into account. This may result in few false positives but saves us from storing more information in *LOGT* which may increase the Space/Time complexity.

Algorithm 5. ARP Response Handler

```
if (RSP_IPS ∈ IPEXT) then
   if (RSP_MACS ≠ GWMAC) then
      Spoof Detected, Enter in LOGT and Log-File
   end if
   if (RSP_IPD ∈ IPEXT) then
      Flood Detected, Enter in Log-File
      Continue to next packet
   else
      UNSOLICITED RESPONSE HANDLER(RSP_IPD)
      Continue to next packet
   end if
end if
if (RSP_IPD ∈ IPEXT) then
   Flood Detected, Enter in Log-File
   Continue to next packet
end if
INSERT IN RESPONSE OBJECT(RSP)
if (RSP_IPS == RSP_IPD) then
   Gratuitous Packet
   VERIFY_IP_MAC(RSP_IPS,RSP_MACS)
   Continue to next packet
end if
if (RSP_IPD == IPIDS) then
   if (RSP_MACD == MACIDS) then
      Continue to next packet
   else
      Spoof Detected, Enter in LOGT and Log-File
      Continue to next packet
   end if
end if
if ( RQP_IPS ∈ AUTHT ) then
   if (RSP_MACS == F_AUTHT( RSP_IPS )) then
      Genuine
      Continue to next packet
   else
      Spoof Detected, Enter in LOGT and Log-File
   end if
   VERIFY_IP_MAC(RSP_IPS,RSP_MACS)
   UNSOLICITED RESPONSE HANDLER(RSP_IPD)
end if
```

4 Implementation and Comparison

To verify resource utilization of the proposed scheme, it was implemented and tested on a self developed testbed. The IDS was running in a system with Intel Core2-Duo 2.0 GHz processer, 4GB RAM and Ubuntu 9.10) OS. The band with of the LAN was 1 Gbps.

In the testbed, we injected different amount of attack packets (up to 400000) and measured CPU utilization of the processer running the IDS, memory utilization of the system running the IDS and bandwidth utilization in the LAN. Figure 1 illustrates memory utilization in MB, CPU utilization in percentage and bandwidth in Mbps, respectively for different amount of attack packets injected per second.

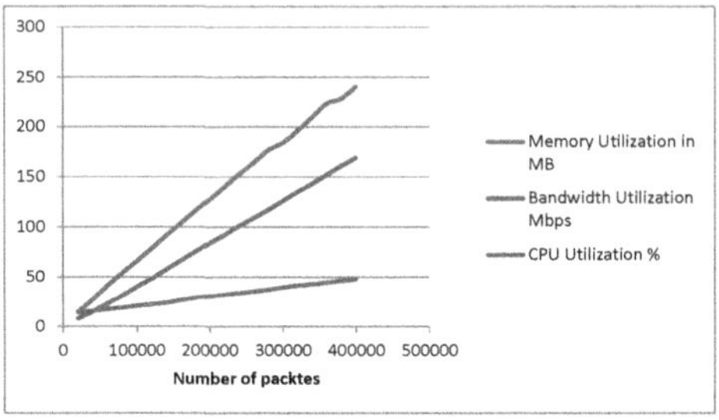

Fig. 1. Memory, CPU and Bandwidth utilization of IDS

It may be noted that in the worst case of our experiment, where 400000 attack packets were injected per second, CPU utilization is around 50% (including consumption by OS), memory utilization is about 250 MB and bandwidth utilization is around 170Mbps. Considering the ARP cache timeout in modern OS varies from 15 sec to a few minutes, the number of ARP packets in a LAN with about 100 hosts should not exceed a few hundred. Hence we can conclude that under extremely high number of attack packets also the IDS works without any problem in terms of resources.

5 Conclusion

In this paper we discussed a scalable implementation of active detection mechanism LAN based attacks. Classification of IP as internal and external IPs has helped in reducing the cardinality of the set of IPs for further analysis. The use of proposed data structure has reduced space and time complexities for most of data manipulation. Also algorithm has been augmented further to detect even those possible *DoS* attack that were missed by Neminath et al[11]. The performance can be further enhanced by using multiprocessor systems with better network interface cards.

References

1. Kozierok, C.M.: TCP/IP Guide, 1st edn (October 2005)
2. ARPWATCH
3. Arpdefender
4. Colasoft-capsa
5. Snort

6. Abad, C.L., Bonilla, R.I.: An Analysis on the Schemes for Detecting and Preventing ARP Cache Poisoning Attacks. In: ICDCSW 2007: Proceedings of the 27th International Conference on Distributed Computing Systems Workshops, p. 60 (2007)
7. Hsiao, H.W., Lin, C.S., Chang, S.Y.: Constructing an ARP attack detection system with SNMP traffic data mining. In: ICEC 2009: Proceedings of the 11th International Conference on Electronic Commerce, pp. 341–345 (2009)
8. Gouda, M.G., Huang, C.-T.: A Secure Address Resolution Protocol. Computer Networks 41(1), 57–71 (2003)
9. Lootah, W., Enck, W., McDaniel, P.: TARP: Ticket-based Address Resolution Protocol, pp. 106–116 (2005)
10. Ramachandran, V., Nandi, S.: Detecting ARP Spoofing: An Active Technique. In: Jajodia, S., Mazumdar, C. (eds.) ICISS 2005. LNCS, vol. 3803, pp. 239–250. Springer, Heidelberg (2005)
11. Hubballi, N., Roopa, S., Ratti, R., Barbhuiya, F., Biswas, S., Sur, A., Nandi, S., Ramachandran, V.: An Active Intrusion Detection System for LAN Specific Attacks. In: Kim, T.-h., Adeli, H. (eds.) AST/UCMA/ISA/ACN 2010. LNCS, vol. 6059, pp. 129–142. Springer, Heidelberg (2010)
12. Schneider, F., Wallerich, J.: Performance evaluation of packet capturing systems for high-speed networks. In: CoNEXT 2005: Proceedings of the 2005 ACM conference on Emerging network experiment and technology, pp. 284–285 (2005)
13. Devadithya, T., Chiu, K., Lu, W.: C++ reflection for high performance problem solving environments. In: SpringSim 2007: Proceedings of the 2007 spring simulation multiconference, pp. 435–440 (2007)

A Survey of Recent Intrusion Detection Systems for Wireless Sensor Network

Tapolina Bhattasali[1] and Rituparna Chaki[2]

[1] Techno India College of Technology, Kolkata, India
tapolinab@gmail.com
[2] West Bengal University of Technology, Kolkata, India
rituchaki@gmail.com

Abstract. Security of Wireless sensor network (WSN) becomes a very important issue with the rapid development of WSN that is vulnerable to a wide range of attacks due to deployment in the hostile environment and having limited resources. Intrusion detection system is one of the major and efficient defensive methods against attacks in WSN. A particularly devastating attack is the sleep deprivation attack, where a malicious node forces legitimate nodes to waste their energy by resisting the sensor nodes from going into low power sleep mode. The goal of this attack is to maximize the power consumption of the target node, thereby decreasing its battery life. Existing works on sleep deprivation attack have mainly focused on mitigation using MAC based protocols, such as S-MAC, T-MAC, B-MAC, etc. In this article, a brief review of some of the recent intrusion detection systems in wireless sensor network environment is presented. Finally, we propose a framework of cluster based layered countermeasure that can efficiently mitigate sleep deprivation attack in WSN. Simulation results on MATLAB exhibit the effectiveness of the proposed model in detecting sleep-deprivation attacks.

Keywords: WSN, Sleep Deprivation Attack, Cluster, IDS, Insomnia.

1 Introduction

Wireless sensor network (WSN) refers to a system that consists of number of low-cost, resource limited sensor nodes to sense important data related to environment and to transmit it to sink node that provides gateway functionality to another network, or an access point for human interface. WSN is a rapidly growing area as new technologies are emerging, new applications are being developed, such as traffic, environment monitoring, healthcare, military applications, home automation. WSN is vulnerable to various attacks such as jamming, battery drainage, routing cycle, sybil, cloning. Due to limitation of computation, memory and power resource of sensor nodes, complex security mechanism can not be implemented in WSN. Therefore energy-efficient security implementation is an important requirement for WSN.

A sleep deprivation attack (battery drainage) is a particularly severe attack in WSN because recharging or replacing node batteries in WSN may be impossible. In this type of attack, intruder forces the sensor nodes to remain awake; so that they waste their energy.

D.C. Wyld et al. (Eds.): CNSA 2011, CCIS 196, pp. 268–280, 2011.

This attack imposes such a large amount of energy consumption upon the limited power sensor nodes that they stop working and give rise to denial of service through denial of sleep.

In this paper a survey of on-going research activity is presented. This is followed by a comparative analysis of the recent ID schemes. This paper concludes with a glimpse of the proposed model for detecting sleep deprivation attack.

2 Related Works

Intrusion detection for WSN is an emerging field of research. This section presents a category-wise report of on-going research activities.

Distributed Approach

- In [1], a semantic based intrusion detection framework is proposed for WSN by using multi-agent and semantic based techniques, where security ontology is constructed according to the features of WSN to represent the formal semantics for intrusion detection. This distributed technique is based on cooperative mechanism. In this mechanism, each selected rule of security ontology is mapped to sensing data collected from common sensor nodes to detect anomaly.
- In [2], an energy efficient learning solution for IDS in WSN has been proposed. This schema is based on the concept of stochastic learning automata on packet sampling mechanism. Simple Learning Automata based ID (S-LAID) functions in a distributed manner with each node functioning independently without any knowledge about the adjacent nodes.

Hierarchical Approach

- In [3], a location-aware, trust-based detection and isolation mechanism of compromised nodes in wireless sensor network is proposed. In this technique, probabilistic model is used to define trust and reputation.
- In [4], a method using isolation table is proposed to isolate malicious nodes by avoiding consumption of unnecessary energy by IDS (ITIDS).This hierarchical structure of IDS based on cluster network can detect serious attacks such as hello flooding, denial of service (DoS), denial of sleep, sinkhole and wormhole attack. In this mechanism, malicious nodes can be detected by considering remaining energy and trust values of sensor nodes.
- In [5], a lightweight ranger based IDS (RIDS) has been proposed. It combines the ranger method to reduce energy consumption and the isolation tables to avoid detecting anomaly repeatedly. This lightweight IDS model relates ontology concept mechanism about anomaly detection. In this technique, rough set theory (RST) is used for preprocessing of packets and anomaly models will be trained by support vector machine (SVM).
- In [6], a hierarchical overlay design (HOD) based intrusion detection system is proposed, using policy based detection mechanism. This model follows core defense strategy where cluster-head is the centre point to defend intruder and concentrates on saving the power of sensor nodes by distributing the responsibility of intrusion detection to three layer nodes.

- In [7], a Hybrid Intrusion Detection System (HIDS) has been proposed in heterogeneous cluster based WSN (CWSN).The attacks such as spoofed, altered, or replayed routing information, sinkhole, sybil, wormholes, acknowledgment spoofing, select forward, hello floods can be detected using this model.
- In [8], a hierarchical model (three layer architecture) is proposed based on weighted trust evaluation (WTE) to detect malicious nodes by monitoring its reported data.
- In [9], a dynamic model of intrusion detection (DIDS) has been proposed for WSN. This is a hierarchical model of IDS based on clustered network to battle the low energy. It can use distributed defense which has the advantage of detecting multiple intruders, albeit, with an increased rate of energy consumption with increase in cluster size.

3 Comparative Analysis of Recent ID Schemes

Table 1. Strength, Weakness and Future Scope of Existing IDS

Existing IDS	Strength	Weakness	Future Scope
Semantic IDS[1]	1) Agent node stores the whole ontology in its memory. 2) Energy efficient	1) Mapping of security ontology with sensor data is vague. 2) Decision making function is not clearly specified.	Algorithms can be improved by using more complex semantics of security ontology.
Simple Learning Automata based IDS [2]	1) Distributed nature avoids all other nodes being sacrificed when a single node is affected. 2) Energy efficient 3) Self-learning nature optimizes packet sampling efficiency.	Computational complexity increases because of using dynamic topology by distributed self-learning automation technique.	S-LAID solution can be tested in different application domains of sensor network.
Location Aware Trust based IDS [3]	1) Reputation-based monitoring facilitates detection and isolation of malicious nodes efficiently. 2) Location awareness enhances integrity.	Use of encryption algorithm consumes more energy.	Location verification protocol can be extended.
Isolation Table based IDS [4]	Primary experiment proves that ITIDS can prevent attacks effectively in terms of live nodes and transmission accuracy.	When the remaining nodes decrease, the intruders can penetrate WSN more easily.	Anomaly detection technique can be extended for improvement.

Table 1. (*Continued*)

Ranger based IDS [5]	1) Intruder can not attack WSN through isolated anomalous nodes. 2) Lightweight model works in energy-efficient manner.	It mainly focuses on Sybil attack.	It can be implemented through standard protocols (e.g. Zigbee) for performance evaluation.
Hierarchical Overlay Design based IDS [6]	1) Reliability, efficiency and effectiveness are high for a large geographical area. 2) Distributed four level hierarchy results in highly energy saving structure. 3) ID becomes very fast and effective.	1) IDS needs to wait for intruders to reach the core area whereas nodes can be captured at any area without any notice. 2) Total cost of network set up is increased for using policy based mechanism.	Election procedure can be implemented; IDS scalability and definition of detection policy need to be determined, more specifically.
Hybrid IDS [7]	1) Its detection rate and accuracy are high for using hybrid approach. Decision making model is very simple and fast. 2) Cluster head is used to reduce energy consumption, amount of data in the entire network and to increase network lifetime.	Rules in the anomaly detection model are defined manually, so performance can not be verified through simulation.	Feature selection in anomaly detection can be done by data mining; Rule based approach can be extended to provide anomaly detection model with better performance and flexibility.
Weighted Trust Evaluation based IDS [8]	1) It detects misbehaved nodes accurately with very short delay. 2) Light-weight algorithm incurs little overhead.	It gives rise to high misdetection rate.	More detailed analysis regarding the performance will be studied in the ongoing research.
Dynamic Model of IDS [9]	1) It has remarkable improvement in security, stability and robustness as compared to static IDS. Distributed nature of this model increases security and network's lifetime. 2) Upgradation of defense structure increases flexibility.	1) It needs more time to detect all intrusions. 2) Distributed detection consumes more energy.	It can be tested with real life applications to ensure perfectness of the model.

Table 2. Analysis of Some of the Recent IDS for WSN

Intrusion Detection System	**Featurewise differences**		
	Node Density	**Detection Rate**	**Energy consumption**
S-LAIDS [2]	Node density medium.	Penalty threshold of 0.2 detects 63 to 71% malicious packets, that of 0.8 is able to detect 25 to 33% malicious packets.	Both the reward and the penalty functions are calculated on basis of the residual energy. Removal of malicious node requires less energy.
Location aware trust based IDS [3]	Number of sensor nodes within 5 to 100 are deployed randomly in 50 m^2 area.	Probability of compromised node detection is certain when the number of neighb oring nodes is 15 or less. As the number of neighboring nodes increases, the probability of blacklisting decreases.	No evaluation regarding energy consumption is found.
ITIDS[4]	200 sensor nodes are deployed uniformly within 10000 square meters area.	95% detection accuracy is achieved when number of monitor nodes equals to 100.	Energy consumption is less for WSN having 50 nodes compared to 100 or 200 nodes.
HIDS [7]	Node density is not specified.	99.81% detection rate, 0.57% phantom intrusion rate and 99.75% accuracy are achieved. Individual detection rate is very low when the training sample is not substantial.	Its energy consumption is very low.
WTE based IDS [8]	Number of nodes are within a range from 9 to 900. It has high scalability.	Detection is terminated after more than 25% of all nodes are detected as malicious nodes. Weight penalties values in the range of 0.04 -0.1 can improve detection rate with low misdetection rate.	No evaluation regarding energy consumption is found.

Table 2. (*Continued*)

DIDS [9]	70 nodes within transmission range of 4 to 15 m, having cluster size equals to 10 for the overall area of 80m *100m.	When number of nodes equals to 20, all types of defenses can detect intrusion, but when number of nodes is greater than or equal to 40, only distributed defense can detect intrusion. DIDS detection rate is higher within smaller range (90% with a range of at least 15m).	If consumed energy in any node is greater than or equal to 30% before activation of IDS, it can not be selected. Distributed defense results in high energy consumption. The lowest energy in DIDS is about 57%, which is 17% higher than that in SIDS. DIDS can prolong the lifetime of network by 8% on average.

4 Proposed Model

Our objective is to detect the sleep deprivation attack in sensor network. In this section, a lightweight model, **INSOMNIA MITIGATING INTRUSION DETECTION SYSTEM (IMIDS)** is proposed for heterogeneous wireless sensor network (HWSNET) to detect insomnia of stationary sensor nodes. It uses cluster based mechanism in an energy efficient manner to build a five layer hierarchical network to enhance network scalability, flexibility and lifetime. The low energy constraints of WSN necessitate the use of a hierarchical model for IDS. We divide sensor network into clusters which are again partitioned into sectors. It will minimize the energy consumption by avoiding all the nodes needing to send data to a distant sink node. It uses anomaly detection technique in such a way so that phantom intrusion detection can be avoided logically.

4.1 Assumptions

- A sensor can be in any one of the following states:

NEW→MEMBER→ SUSPECTED→MALICIOUS→ISOLATED
↓ ↕ ↓
GENUINE → DEAD

- Each sensor node has a unique id in the network.
- Each member node has authentic wake-up token.
- A protocol is used to assign a secure wakeup and sleep schedule for the sensor nodes.
- Sink node is honest gateway to another network.
- The threshold values are pre-calculated and set for the entire network.
- If any of cluster coordinator, forwarding sector head, sector monitor or sector coordinator is found to be compromised, reconfiguration procedure takes place dynamically.

- Sensor nodes excluding leaf nodes and forwarding sector heads in the system participate in intrusion detection process.
- Generally, sector coordinator is responsible for anomaly detection and sector monitor is responsible for detection of intrusion.
- Initially, probability of sleeping schedule and wake-up schedule are same (p=0.5) for any normal node.
- Initially, trust value of each node is represented by a nibble $t_3\, t_2\, t_1\, t_0$ containing all 1's, belief is set to 1.
- SM may be more than one within a sector.
- SN selects CC and CC selects SC, SM, FSH.
- Anomaly can be detected on the basis of energy consumption rate, allotted wakeup schedule, authentic wakeup token, number of packets received within a time interval. Reputation of sensor node needs to be considered during intrusion detection.

4.2 Data Definition

- *Definition 1: Leaf Node* LN– A node N is defined to be a *Leaf Node* if $Child_N\{\ \} = \{\emptyset\}$ AND $Parent_N\ \{\ \} \neq \{\emptyset\}$. Its detection power(DP) $\leftarrow$0.

- *Definition 2: Setor Coordinator SC* – A node N is defined to be a *Sector Coordinator* if Rem_eng_N = MAX_ENG {FN[ ]}, where FN[] $\rightarrow$ follower nodes.

- *Definition 3: Setor Monitor SM* - A node N is defined to be a *Sector Monitor* if DP_N =MAX_DETECT {N [ ]}, where N$\notin$ {CC_k, SN} AND $DP_N\rightarrow$ power required by a node for intrusion detection.

- *Definition 4: Forwarding Sector Head FSH* - A node N is defined to be a *Forwarding Sector Head, where* $hop\_distance_N$ *{}* = *min{hop_* $distance_N$ *from* CC_k},where N $\notin CC_k$. Its detection power (DP) $\leftarrow$0.

- *Definition 5: Cluster Coordinator CC* - A node N is defined to be a Cluster Coordinator, if Rem_eng_N = MAX_ENG{N[ ]}AND $CAPACITY_N$=MAX($CAPACITY_N$),where N$\notin$SN AND $CAPACITY_N$ = ($DEGREE_N$/ $INITIAL\_ENG_N$)*Rem_Eng_N, $DEGREE_N\rightarrow$number of nodes within its radio range.

- *Definition 6: Sink Node SN* - A node N is defined to be a *Sink Node* if $Child_N\ \{\ \} \neq \{\emptyset\}$ AND $Parent_N\ \{\ \} = \{\emptyset\}$.

4.3 System Model

Figure 1 describes the main building block of the system model. Here SN–> SINK NODE; CC–>CLUSTER COORDINATOR; SM–>SECTOR MONITOR; FSH–>FORWARDING SECTOR HEAD; SC–>SECTOR COORDINATOR; LN–> LEAF NODE;

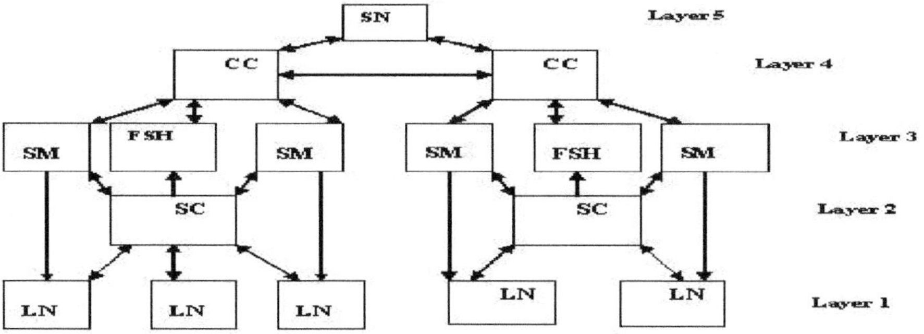

Fig. 1. Layered Model

4.3.1 Description of Each Layer

The five layers of sensor network are described below-

- **Layer 1:** In this lowest layer leaf nodes sense environmental data and send it to its immediate next higher layer i.e. layer 2. Layer 1 has no anomaly detection capacity.
- **Layer 2:** This layer includes sector coordinator (SC) of each sector that collects data from layer 1 and checks for anomaly. Sector coordinator maintains membership list [] of all leaf nodes within a sector, normal profile [] (tuple space that consists of sensor node's attribute) and knowledge base [] (system parameters, application requirements). Suspected nodes are penalized and legitimate nodes are rewarded by SC. Reputation list [] is updated. Suspected node details are inserted in suspected list [] before forwarding to SM and valid packets are forwarded to FSH of layer 3.
- **Layer 3:** This layer includes sector monitor(SM) and forwarding sector head (FSH). Sector monitor maintains suspected list [], normal profile [], knowledge base [], reputation list []. SM can detect intruders, compromised nodes and isolate them by inserting the details into quarantine list [] and forwards the information to cluster coordinator (CC).FSH (nearest neighbor of cluster coordinator) acts as router that inserts valid packet details to forwarding table [] and forwards valid packet of legitimate nodes to CC of layer 4.
- **Layer 4:** This layer constitutes the cluster coordinator (CC) which controls SM and FSH of each Sector within a cluster. It inserts valid packets details to valid list [] and forwards data to the sink node. Cluster coordinators (CC) can cooperate with each other to form global IDS.CC contains backup copy of its own cluster.
- **Layer 5:** The topmost layer is the sink node that collects data from lower layer and it acts as a gateway between sensor network and other networks or acts as access point. SN contains backup copies of all clusters.

4.3.2 IMIDS: Insomnia Mitigating Intrusion Detection System

The entire heterogeneous sensor field is divided into overlapping or disjoint clusters like C_k, for $k \in \{1,..,r\}$, r being the number of clusters in the sensor network. Each cluster consists of its member nodes including a cluster coordinator (CC). Let mem_1, mem_2, ...,mem_n be the members of a cluster C_k, which are unaware of their locations and n is the number of members within a cluster excluding CC. Clusters are partitioned into non-overlapping sectors like S_j, for $j \in \{1,\ldots,m\}$,where m is the number of sectors within a cluster, where r<<m. We assume three types of sensor nodes in this five layered model: (i) leader nodes or LDN (in layer 3 and 4) (ii) follower nodes or FN (in layer 1 and 2) and (iii) sink node or SN (in layer 5). Leader nodes can be equipped with EXIDS (extended IDS), but only the node designated as sector monitor can activate it. Cluster coordinator (CC) and sink nodes (SN) are also using EXIDS for detecting intrusion during its requirement. SIDS (simple IDS) can be loaded in all follower nodes, but can be activated only at sector coordinator of layer 2 for detecting anomaly. Sector coordinator collects sensing data within allotted TDMA time slot of each leaf node in a sector. Sector coordinator (SC) monitors the sensor nodes for detecting anomaly by SIDS. Suspected nodes are penalized and legitimate nodes are rewarded. Forwarding sector head (FSH) forwards valid packets to CC. Sector monitor (SM) decides whether a suspected node is malicious or not. EXIDS has the responsibility to declare the suspected node as malicious and to drop fake or corrupted packets. To avoid phantom intrusion detection logically, suspected nodes get chance to increase their reputation by SM, if it is not decided as malicious. Intruder/Malicious nodes are isolated in quarantine list; so that no intrusion occurs through these nodes.

If HWSNET is considered as a graph G (V, E), any edge E between two nodes n_i and n_j is valid if and only if distance between two nodes $D_{i,j} <= R_{tr}$ (transmission range).Detection power of LN and FSH are 0%, SC,CC,SN are 50% and SM is

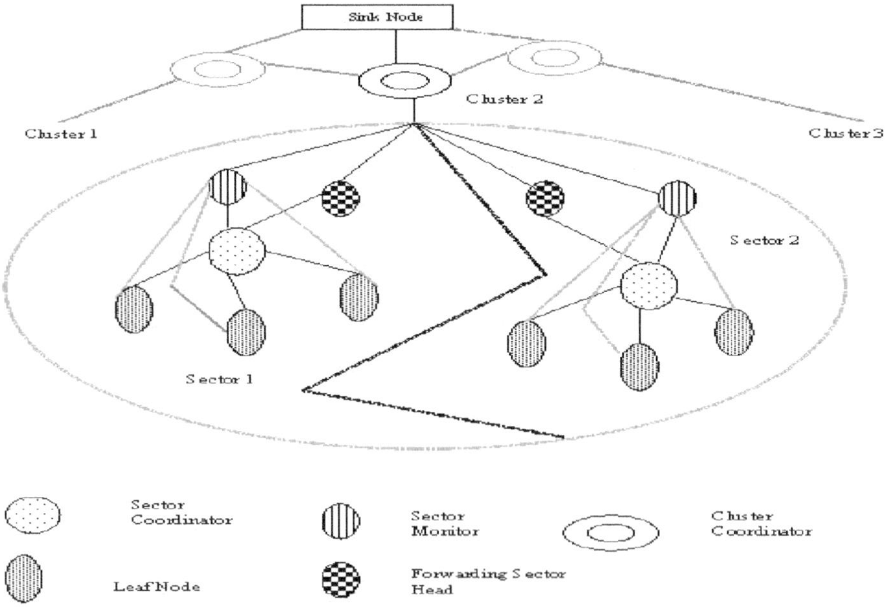

Fig. 2. Cluster Based Heterogeneous Sensor Network

80%.When detection power reaches to minimum threshold, detection capacity is automatically disabled. Reconfiguration procedure takes place dynamically if any node found to be suspected i.e. energy consumption rate greater than normal consumption rate. Each of leader and follower nodes must be included within a cluster. If any node is under more than one CC then RSSI value need to be checked. If there is a tie, it is broken randomly. Anomaly is detected by SC. But there is a possibility of false positive or false negative. If any genuine node is suspected by SC (false positive), SM can detect it and takes final decision. If any compromised node is treated as genuine and forwarded to FSH (false negative), CC can detect it.

4.3.3 Procedural Steps of IMIDS

- **Initialization Phase:**

Sensor nodes are deployed in the sensor field during this phase. A unique identification number consisting of the geographical position vectors is assigned to each new node. The sink node searches for its neighbors to acquire energy details of all nodes after broadcasting advertised message.

- **Cluster Coordinator Selection and Cluster Formation Phase:**

Cluster coordinator is selected among all leader nodes and its coverage area is considered as cluster. The Cluster-head details are broadcasted to all its neighbors. The neighbor nodes collect advertised messages during a given time interval and send a join message to nearest cluster coordinator for all nodes within the range of any specific cluster coordinator. Intersection of two cluster domains may or may not be NULL.

- **Sector Coordinator Selection and Sector Formation Phase:**

Sector coordinator is selected among all follower nodes and its detailed information along with node-id is broadcasted to all of its neighbors. Its coverage area is considered as sector. Intersection of domains of two sectors must be NULL. Sector monitors and forwarding sector heads are selected for each sector.

- **IDS Activation Phase:**

Activate IDS preinstalled in cluster coordinators, sector monitors and sector coordinators.

- **Reconfiguration Phase:**

When cluster coordinator or sector coordinator's behavior deviates from normal, reconfiguration procedure takes place.

- **Data Transfer and Intrusion Detection Phase:**

After sector coordinator selection is done each follower node (leaf node) sends data to the sector coordinator that transfers genuine packet to its cluster coordinator through forwarding sector head. Cluster coordinator collects valid data from all sectors within its coverage area and then forwards aggregated packets to sink node.

4.3.4 Selection Procedure

(i) Sink node broadcasts its node-id and query message to acquire current residual energy of each sensor node within its coverage area.

(ii) According to response from sensor nodes, sink node categorized sensor nodes into leader nodes having high energy and follower nodes having comparatively low energy.
(iii) Leader node having minimum distance from sink node, maximum residual energy among all other leader nodes and high reputation, is selected as cluster coordinator.
(iv) Remaining leader nodes within a cluster having high detection power is selected as sector monitor, whereas leader nodes having minimum distance from cluster coordinator is selected as forwarding sector head.
(v) Follower nodes having maximum energy among all follower nodes are selected as sector coordinator, other follower nodes are considered as leaf nodes.

5 Performance Analysis

In this section, we validate our analysis using simulation in MATLAB. Performance has been studied by simulating sensor nodes in the existing ITIDS and proposed IMIDS. In figure 3, the result of the simulation shows that number of alive nodes with respect to increasing time in second is more in IMIDS. Therefore it can be said that HWSNET lifetime is better by using IMIDS than ITIDS. Because IMIDS uses dynamic configuration and cluster is further partitioned into sectors. In figure 4, the result shows that accuracy is comparatively high in IMIDS because here sector monitors which have high detection power are used to detect intrusion; whereas in ITIDS low energy member nodes are considered as monitor nodes. In figure 5, energy consumption is compared with respect to the density of sensor nodes with clusterization and sectorization and without clusterization or sectorization. The result of simulation shows energy consumption is comparatively less when sensor field is partitioned into clusters and sectors. After analyzing performance, it can be said that proposed IMIDS can prolong network lifetime, detect intrusion accurately and consumes less energy to mitigate sleep deprivation attack.

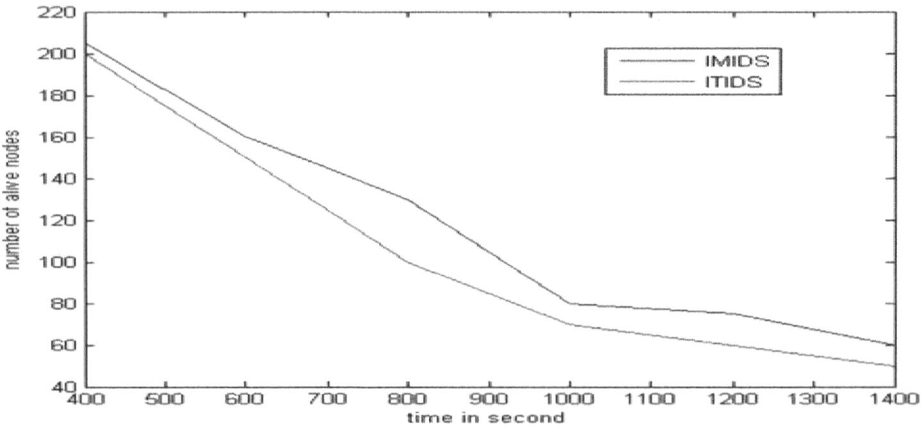

Fig. 3. Comparison of the number of alive nodes between ITIDS and IMIDS

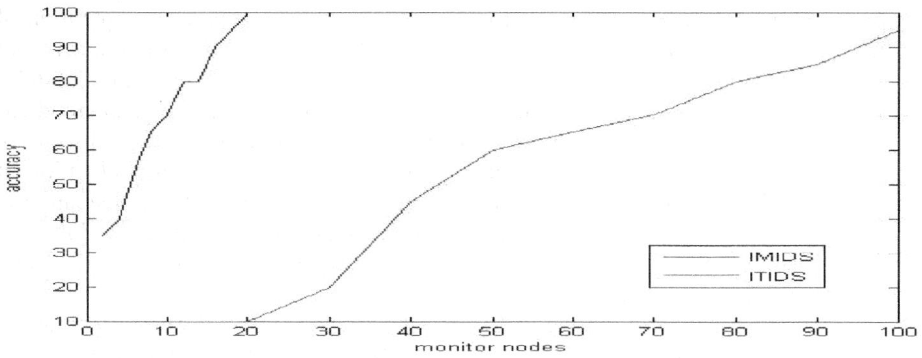

Fig. 4. Comparison of the accuracy between ITIDS and IMIDS

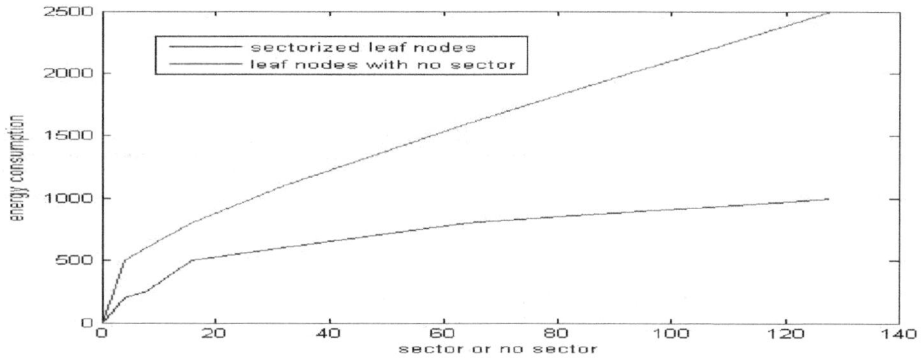

Fig. 5. Energy consumption with sectorization and without sectorization in IMIDS

6 Conclusion

In this paper, we present a review of recent works on different approaches of IDS for WSN. It has been observed that these intrusion detection systems are not adequate for protecting WSN from intruders efficiently. The need of the day is an IDS for detecting intrusions accurately in an energy-efficient manner. Among the different types of prevalent attacks, sleep deprivation attack at link layer has been found to be the most devastating one for sensor nodes, exhausting the battery life very quickly. This paper comes up with the idea of a novel IDS that can mitigate sleep deprivation attack without using MAC based protocols like S-MAC, T-MAC, B-MAC, G-MAC. The outline of layer based approach using cluster technique to design a lightweight IDS capable of detecting insomnia of sensor nodes with less energy consumption has been documented here. The aim of this proposed model is to extend the lifetime of the WSN, even in the face of sleep deprivation attack. Generally, intruder attacks lower layer leaf nodes in HWSNET. In this model, intrusion detection is mainly focused on layer 1 that has no intrusion detection capacity of its own. Simulation proves the effectiveness of proposed model. At present work is on for more detailed analysis of IMIDS in a simulated environment.

References

1. Mao, Y.: A Semantic-based Intrusion Detection Framework for Wireless Sensor Network. In: 6th International Conference on Networked Computing (INC), Gyeongju, Korea, South (2010)
2. Misra, S., Venkata Krishna, P., Abraham, K.I.: Energy Efficient Learning Solution for Intrusion Detection in Wireless Sensor Networks. In: Proceedings of the 2nd international conference on Communication systems and Networks COMSNETS 2010 (2010)
3. Crosby, G.V., Hester, L., Pissinou, N.: Location-aware, Trust-based Detection and Isolation of Compromised Nodes in Wireless Sensor Networks. International Journal of Network Security 12(2), 107–117 (2011)
4. Chen, R.-C., Hsieh, C.-F., Huang, Y.-F.: An Isolation Intrusion Detection System for Hierarchical Wireless Sensor Network. Journal of Networks 5(3) (March 2010)
5. Chen, R.-C., Huang, Y.-F., Hsieh, C.-F.: Ranger Intrusion Detection System for Wireless Sensor Networks with Sybil Attack Based on Ontology. New Aspects of Applied Informatics, Biomedical Electronics and Informatics and Communications (2010)
6. Mamun, M.S.I., Sultanul Kabir, A.F.M.: Hierarchical Design Based Intrusion Detection System For Wireless Ad Hoc Sensor Network. International Journal of Network Security & Its Applications (IJNSA) 2(3) (July 2010)
7. Yan, K.Q., Wang, S.C., Liu, C.W.: A Hybrid Intrusion Detection System of Cluster-based Wireless Sensor Networks. In: Proceedings of the International MultiConference of Engineers and Computer Scientists, IMECS 2009, Hong Kong, March 18 - 20, vol. I (2009)
8. Atakli, I.M., Hu, H., Chen, Y., Ku, W.-S., Su, Z.: Malicious Node Detection in Wireless Sensor Networks using Weighted Trust Evaluation. In: The Symposium on Simulation of Systems Security (SSSS 2008), Ottawa, Canada, April 14 –17 (2008)
9. Huo, G., Wang, X.: DIDS: A Dynamic Model of Intrusion Detection System in Wireless Sensor Networks. In: IEEE, International Conference on Information and Automation, Zhangjiajie, China, June 20 –23 (2008)
10. Techateerawat, P., Jennings, A.: Energy Efficiency of Intrusion Detection Systems in Wireless Sensor Networks. In: IEEE WIC 2006 (2006)

Secure Network Steganographic Scheme Exploiting TCP Sequence Numbers

Vengala Satish Kumar, Tanima Dutta, Arijit Sur, and Sukumar Nandi

Department of Computer Science and Engineering
Indian Institute of Technology, Guwahati
Guwahati-781039, India
{vengala,d.tanima,arijit,sukumar}@iitg.ac.in

Abstract. Network steganography is a relatively new area of research. Various network steganographic schemes that modifies the header of protocols like TCP and IP are present in literature. An observation suggests that packet length based schemes are suitable for transferring secret information across the network. This paper attempts to propose a novel steganographic scheme which uses the length of the TCP segments to transfer secret information. This scheme embeds the secret information in the TCP sequence number by adjusting the payload of TCP segments. Experiments and results show that this scheme is better than other existing schemes based on adjusting the length of packets.

Keywords: Network steganography, covert channels, information hiding.

1 Introduction

Protection of information that is sent over network can be done by using the principles of cryptography. It is thought that the use of encryption is sufficient for secure communication in network. However, it is possible for an attacker to find the existence of encrypted channel between two remote entities and decrypt the captured traffic. Steganography in network layers eliminates this problem by concealing the existence of the messages.

Network Steganography is synonym to covert channels which is introduced by Lampson [2]. Various covert channels are present in literature which uses the header fields of protocols like TCP [27], [8] and IP [12], [1] for data hiding. Detection schemes [28] are also introduced for those schemes. Network Steganography is divided into three broad categories.

1. Methods modifying network packet's header or payload.
2. Methods modifying the structure of packet streams.
3. Hybrid Schemes.

The classification of Network Steganography shown in following figure 1.

In methods that modify network packet's header, the data hiding is carried out by modifying the protocol-specific fields. For example TCP, IP or UDP headers are modified to inject secret messages as discussed in literatures [1] and [12].All the

D.C. Wyld et al. (Eds.): CNSA 2011, CCIS 196, pp. 281–291, 2011.

steganographic techniques under this method have high steganographic capacity but they are highly detectable using some existing steganalytic techniques as mentioned in [19]. Some of the application layer based steganographic techniques modify payloads of the packets. The detection of these techniques are difficult and the amount of hidden data that can be sent through them are relatively less. There is another method which involves hiding the data in both header and payload of the network packet as stated in [3] and HICCUPS [20](Hidden Communication System for Corrupted Networks). This method offers high steganographic capacity but the implementation is more diffcult than any of the other methods. It needs reprogramming of Network Interface Cards. Drawbacks include increased frame error rate. Data Hiding can also be done through modifying the packet streams of the network as described in [11]. Some of the examples in this method are those which affect the sequence order of the packets [21], those which modify the inter packet delay [22] and those that introduce intentional losses by skipping sequence numbers [23] at the sender. The main problem with these schemes includes synchronization between sender and receiver. Other drawback is that delays may affect transmission quality. In hybrid scheme, the packet header and their time dependencies are modified. Lost Audio Packets Steganography [24] and Retransmission Steganography [15] is one of the examples which fall under this scheme. Compared to the other methods, this method has higher steganographic capacities. Another advantage of this method is that it is hard to detect. A detailed survey of network steganography is given in [13].

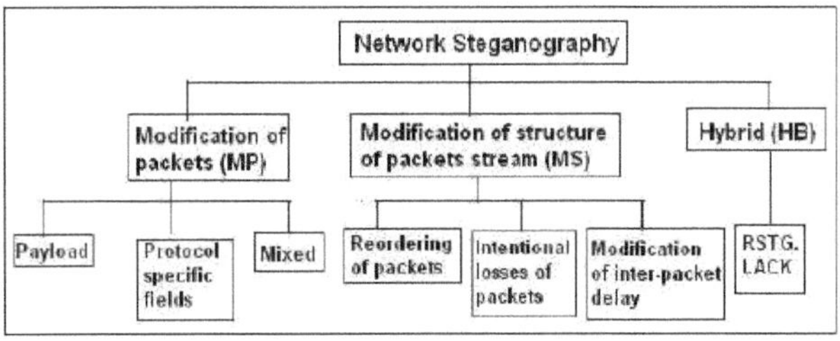

Fig. 1. Classification of Network Steganography

Rest of the report is organized as follows. Section 2 outlines the literature survey. Section 3 describes the proposed work. Results of experiments are presented in Section 4. Description of future plan of our work along with conclusion is presented in Section 5.

2 Literature Survey

We analyze the various existing steganographic schemes present in the literature. Network Protocol stack have various layers that contains various header fields for proper communication. These fields can be used as covert storage channels for covert communication. The OSI model is the standard network model against which nearly all current network models are compared. The OSI model includes TCP,IP, and ICMP protocols which are implemented at different layers.

2.1 Covert Channels

A covert channel is a vessel in which information can pass, but this vessel is not ordinarily used for information exchange. Covert channels are first introduced by Lampson [2]. Definition of covert channel is Any communication channel that can be exploited by a process to transfer information in a manner that violates the system's security policy [25]. In theory, almost any process or bit of data can be a covert channel. In practice, it is usually quite difficult to elicit meaningful data from most covert channels in a timely fashion. Covert channels can be categories into two categories:

- Covert storage channel: In covert storage channel, the sender and receiver use a shared variable where one person will insert covert data inside it and other person will read covert data from it. In network environment, fields of header will acts as shared variables.
- Covert Timing Channels: In a timing channel, the receiver and sender agree a priori on a timing interval and the starting protocol. During each time interval the sender either transmits a single packet or maintains silence. The receiver monitors each interval to determine whether a packet was received or not. Note that the raw data that flows across the channel is binary but the actual interpretation of the binary stream is up to the communicating parties.

2.2 TCP Steganography

TCP Header contains different fields for proper communication. Each field has its own properties and usage. The following figure 2 shows the TCP header. Covert fields can be useful to hide information. These fields act as a carrier for steganography. The Initial sequence number (ISN), generated by OS, vary from OS to OS. Author of [19] explained how OPEN BSD and Linux 2 0 will generate ISN. For data hiding purpose ISN field serves as a perfect medium for transmitting over the internet because of its size. Successful embedding steganographic data inside ISN is shown in [26]. Authors of [27] came up with improvement of Rowland scheme [26] with a kernel level module (NUSHU). Though this method solves the randomization problem but it has a drawback.

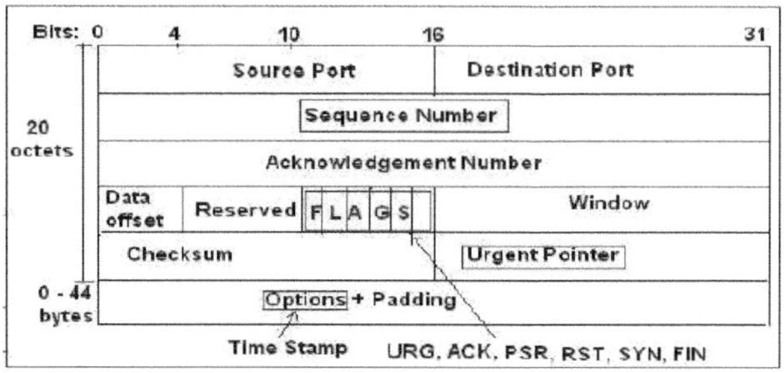

Fig. 2. TCP Header: The header fields marked with RED color represents possible covert channels exists in TCP

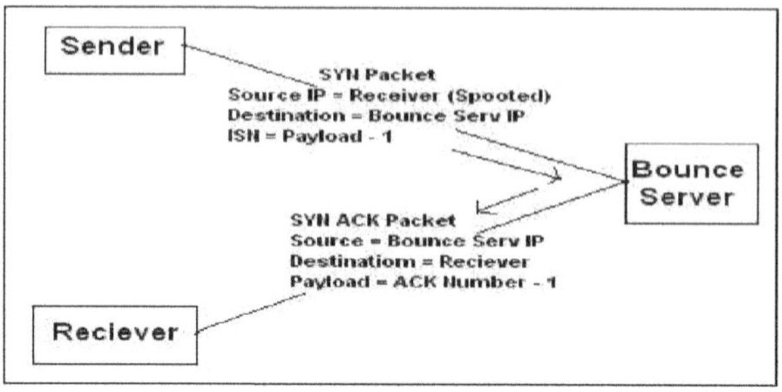

Fig. 3. ACK Bounce method: Before transmits the payload packet (SYN, the value of the payload (32 bit) is decremented by one and is written to the Sequence Number field of the TCP header

But the problem with this scheme is only one byte of information can be send for each connection. Apart from that, this module needs to take a lot of overhead to maintain connection. However, authors of [28] successfully detected the same using neural network.

In literature [26] the TCP header is used in the ACK Bounce Method. It provides relatively high anonymity over the cost of no backward communication. The following figure shows how ACK Bounce method works.

The important characteristics of this method:

1. The destination IP addresses of the payload packet is set to the IP address of the Bounce (Intermediate) Server.
2. The source IP address of the packet is set to the IP address of the receiving party.

TCP Reserved bits, TCP Flag bits, TCP Urgent Pointer, TCP Options (Timestamp) are also serves as a perfect medium for transmitting secret message over the internet as ISN. The features based on them can be found in literature [19].

2.3 IP Steganography

Like TCP, IP protocol also contains a number of fields in its header which helps in information hiding and detection. IP identification field, IP Flags, IP Fragment offset, IP Options field and IP Type of service in the IP header are used to hide information. many researchers came up with different type of hiding techniques based on above covert channels. Authors of [29] mentioned four data scenarios based on IP identification and DF bit.

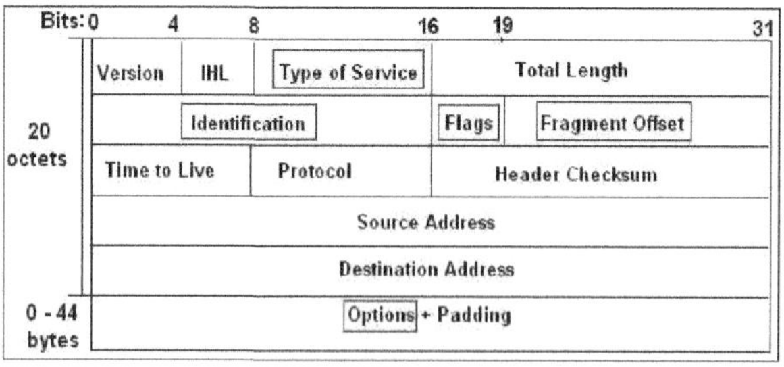

Fig. 4. IP Header: The header fields marked with RED color represents possible covert channels exists in IP

2.4 ICMP Steganography

Internet Control Message Protocol (ICMP) was designed to pass error notification and messages between network hosts and servers. ICMP packets are encapsulated inside IP datagrams. ICMP is implemented by all TCP/IP hosts. The following figure shows ICMP header.

Fig. 5. ICMP Header: The Type field of ICMP Header identifies the type of packet associated code is notified by the Code field

ICMP Echo Request, Echo Reply message probably have covert channel. A proof-of-concept library called Loki, which implemented ICMP echo request or reply based covert channels and provided authentication support (simple XOR or Blowfish), was developed which can be used to implement covertness in any application. Other popular implementations which are widely used are ICMP Tunnel, Ish, ITunnel and 007Shell which emulate a remote shell.

2.5 Datalink and Physical Layer Steganography

Like TCP and IP steganography, there exist steganography schemes which are based on data link layer and physical layer. Here, direct storage fields not exist but by utilizing the properties of these layers we can communicate covertly with others.

HICCUPS is a new covet communication in shared type network (LAN) is introduced in literature [20]. HICCUPS take an advantage of imperfection of transmission, noise in communication medium and interferences. The following figure 6 shows general HICCUPS scheme. This method offers high steganographic capacity but the implementation is more difficult than any of the other methods.

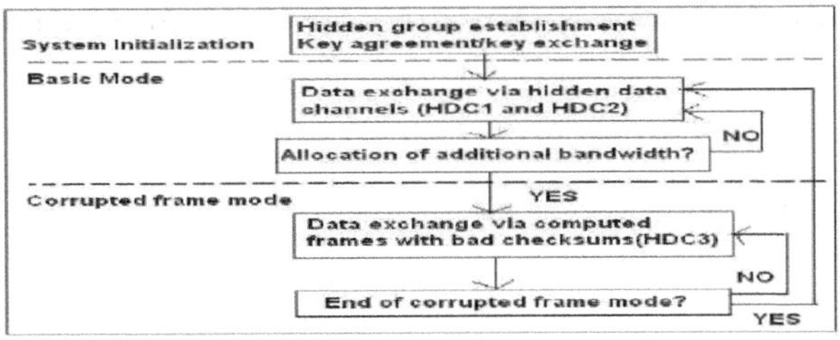

Fig. 6. HICCUPS MODEL: System initialization mode and Basic mode of this scheme are used for secrete key initialization and exchange the data based on cipher initialization (HDC1) and MAC addresses (HDC2). The data exchange in basic mode is very low approximately 1%.

3 Proposed Work

From the above survey, we identified that the headers of the packets cannot be modified or tampered as the detection becomes possible since the modification may not imitate the header properties. It is observed that the sequence number in the TCP header changes in all the packets and it obeys certain properties. We made an attempt to put the secret data in the TCP sequence number by following the properties of the TCP. This is done by adjusting the length of the TCP payload.

3.1 Embedding Secret in the TCP Sequence Number by Adjusting TCP Payload

Information or data is exchanged among work stations in a network in the form of packets. The payload part of packet depends upon the application layer. In the network, the maximum packet length will be MSS (maximum segment size which is known at negotiation time). The pattern of length of packets depends on the speed of the application transferring bytes to transport layer. A basic file transfer type application sends more bytes at a time to next layer. So the packet size will be maximum for certain time. Certain applications like TELNET send tiny packets. Communicating the secret data with the help of the varying length of packet is called as "length based steganography". The detection becomes hard if the packet traced imitates the normal network flow. This sort of technique belongs to "Modification of Packets" classification, discussed later. TCP connection between two stations is initiated by a 3 way handshake.

In our scheme, the application wants to send a file to another client. After establishing the TCP connection between the two stations, the sender station sends the file in chunks to the lower layer. The TCP divides these chunks into segments of maximum length. The last segment of the chunk will be a value less than maximum segment size. For sending the last segment, the TCP does not wait for any other data to come from the upper layer. We use this last segment for sending our secret data.

This proposed scheme will adjust the size of this last segment in such a way that it imitates the normal traffic. The rest of the TCP segments will have maximum segment size. As a result our scheme imitates the normal flow.

3.2 Liping's Algorithm

This scheme is a length based algorithm. In this scheme, the length of the packet is adjusted to send the secret data across the network. The Authors simulated a hidden channel on HTTP protocol and analyzed its security. For Liping's [30] scheme, Alice wants to exchange secret information with Bob. Wendy is the network administrator who analyzes all the packets that flow between them.

The model is shown in following figure 7.

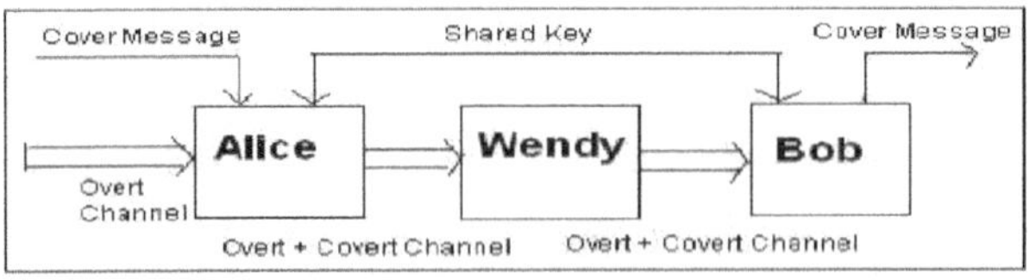

Fig. 7. Liping's Model in Consideration: The Type field of ICMP Header identifies the type of packet associated code is notified by the Code field

From the time series graph 8, it is understood that this scheme does not imitate the normal flow. It is observed that the correlation of the Normal and Stego is very less. Our new scheme can generate the stego traffic which resembles like the normal traffic.

3.2 Proposed Algorithm

In our proposed algorithm, we approach at sending secret information through a TCP data segments in the secret manner. We are using a file transfer application to send the secret information. We have used this, since TCP has a flow in sending data. We are imitating this flow and to send the secret information.

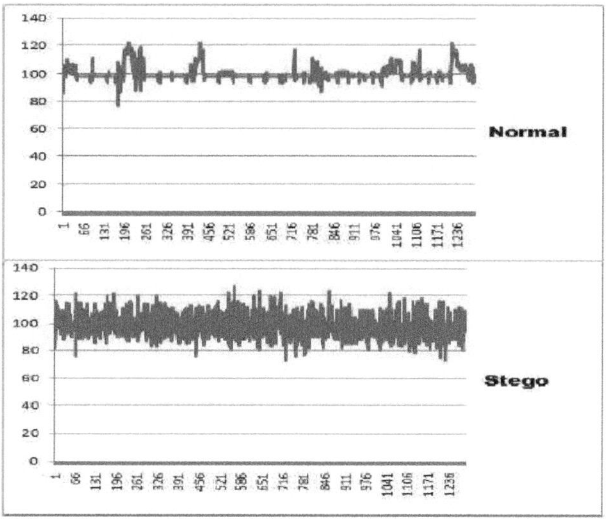

Fig. 8. Liping's Model In Consideration: A time series for a Cover and Stego for the Scheme by Liping

The algorithm proposed is divided into two sections, encoding algorithm and the decoding algorithm. Encoding algorithm is implemented at the sender side and the decoding algorithm is implemented at the sender side and the decoding algorithm is implemented in the receiver side. The encoding algorithm is used to send data to decode the same secret file.

In the encoding algorithm, we are using a file name "covert data" that is to be sent over the network in secret manner. For this, we are using another file, whose size is quite a big from "covert data", named as "sample data". This file will be send instead of "cover data". The Encoding algorithm adjusts the payload part of particular TCP segments based on the secret information present in "covert data" file. Through this, we can send secret information, i.e. covert data to the destination in the secret manner. The encoding algorithm is explained in details in the section 3.3.

The decoding algorithm is decoding the sent file, i.e. sample data, and checks the Sequence number field of those particular TCP data segment. With this Sequence number, it can regenerate the original secret file, i.e. "covert data". This is explained in detail in section 3.3.

Encoding Algorithm. The encoding algorithm is divided into two steps. In step 1, we are capturing the initial sequence number of TCP Connection. This sequence number will be used in calculating the initial length of the TCP data segment so that it represents the secret data file character in the next iteration. Further in step 2, we are calculating the amount of bytes that is to be sent, so that, it represents characters of secret data. Here, 'X' represents the value of the secret data file in some encoded format, say as ASCII (). The Temp variable represents the number of bytes to be adjust incoder to represent secret information in Sequence number field.

Then we calculate the number of bytes to be sent from sample data. This number of bytes is referred as N in the step 2. Further, we are sending this data and calculating a sequence variable that will be used in calculating of nest 'X'.

- Step 1: Capture ISN
  Sequence= (ISN+1)mod ASCII(MAX)
- Step 2: Repeat this until the entire file "covert.data" is transferred.
  X=Get ASCII(character from covert.data);
  N=Get Normal Bytes to be sent;
  K=N mod ASCII(MAX);
  Temp=X-Sequence;
  N=N+Temp;
- Step 3: Fetch N bytes of data from sample.data file and Send it.
  Sequence=X;

Decoding Algorithm. The decoding algorithm is used at the destination side. This is performed in one step and easy to implement. Here, it is capturing the sequence number of particular TCP segment and decode. This process will continue till the character extracted from the Sequence number represents EOF. The decoding algorithm is shown below:

- Step 1: Check for all the packets which are not having maximums segment size.
- Step 2: Accept the next packet;
  Character = (extract sequence from the packet) mod ASCII (MAX);
- Step 3: Store character in covert extract file;
- Step 4: If(character=ENCODING(EOF))
  Break;

Finally the extracted information from the Sequence number field be stored in covert extract file. Since, we are imitating the normal flow of TCP; the network administrator will not be able to detect the transfer of such data. We are showing the efficiency of the same algorithm implemented over 50 different samples in the next section.

4 Experimental Results

Till now there is no steganalysis scheme exits based on payload part of TCP. So we are going statistics analysis like correlation and auto correlation. And also we are comparing our results with the existing Liping's scheme [10].

To perform the analysis, 50 different file samples are taken and we applied our algorithm on it. A time series plot of one of the samples is shown in the figure 9.

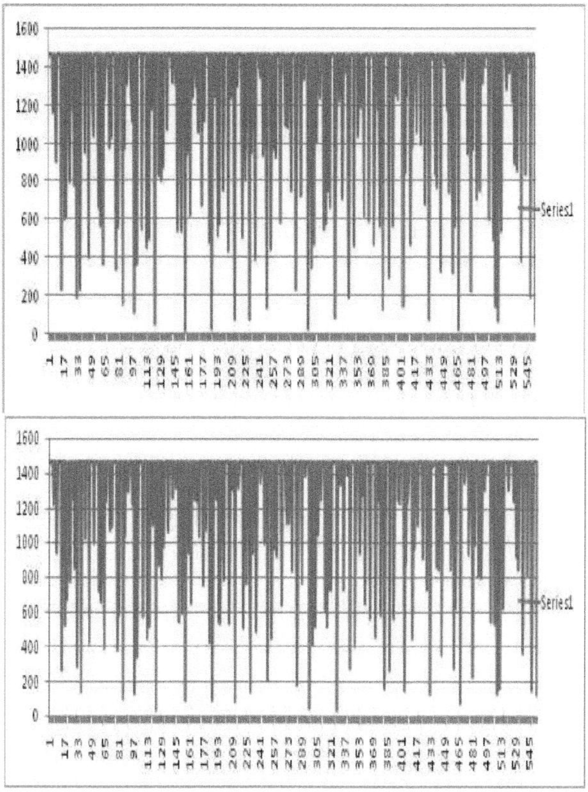

Fig. 9. Time Series Graph Of Normal And Stego

It is observed that the normal and the stego traffic is almost similar. The correlation coefficient between the normal and the stego traffic is 0.98. In comparison with the Liping scheme, our proposed algorithm provides a better correlation. The results are quite satisfactory.

5 Conclusion and Future Work

We have analyzed the various steganographic schemes in the network layers. In this paper, we identified that packet length based steganography has a huge potential to hide data. We discussed the latest length based steganographic scheme and proposed a better solution. Our novel steganographic scheme gives better result than the Liping's length based steganographic scheme.

Steganographic schemes can also be introduced which uses the fields of IPv6. In the future, all the communication in the IP layer will be done with IPv6 rather than IPv4.

References

1. Ahsan, K., Kundur, D.: Practical data hiding in TCP/IP. In: ACM Workshop on Multimedia and Security (2002), http://ee.tamu.edu/deepa/pdf/acm02.pdf
2. Lampson, B.W.: A note on the confinement problem. Commun. ACM 16(10), 613–615 (1973)
3. Szczypiorski, K.: A Performance Analysis of HICCUPS - a Steganographic System for WLAN. CoRR, vol. abs/0906.4217 (2003)
4. Murdoch, S.J., Steven, J., Lewis: Embedding Covert Channels into TCP/IP, University of Cambridge Computer Laboratory (July 25, 2005)
5. Girling, C.G.: Covert channels in LANs. IEEE Trans. Software Engineering SE-13(2), 292–296 (1987)
6. Rutkowska, J.: The implementation of passive covert channels in the Linux kernel. In: Chaos Communication Congress, Chaos Computer Club (2004), http://www.ccc.de/congress/2004/fahrplan/event/176.en.html
7. Padlipsky, M.A., Snow, D.W., Karger, P.A.: Limitations of end-to-end encryption in secure computer networks, Tech. Rep. ESD-TR-78-158, Mitre Corporation (August. 1978)
8. Rowland, C.H.: Covert channels in the TCP/IP protocol suite. First Monday, Peer Reviewed Journal on the Internet
9. Quan-zhu, Y., Peng, Z.: Coverting channel based on packet length. Computer Engineering, vol. 34(3) (February 2008)
10. Ji, L., Jiang, W., Dai, B., Niu, X.: A Novel covert channel based on length of messages. In: International Symposium on Information Engineering and Electronic Commerce, pp. 551–554 (2009)
11. Sellke, S.H., Wang, C., Bagchi, S., Shroff, N.B.: TCP/IP Timing Channels: Theory to Implementation, pp. 2204–2212 (2009), http://dblp.unitrier.de/db/conf/infocom/infocom2009.html
12. Ahsan, K., Kundur, D.: Covert Channel Analysis and Data Hiding in TCP/IP. M.A.Sc. thesis, Dept. of Electrical and Computer Engineering, University of Toronto (August 2002)
13. Nair, A.S., Sur, A., Nandi, S.: Network Steganography - A Brief Survey. In: National Workshop on Design and Analysis of Algorithms (2010)
14. Clarknet Dataset, http://ita.ee.lbl.gov/html/contrib/ClarkNet-HTTP.html
15. Mazurczyk, W., Smolarczyk, M., Szczypiorski, K.: Hiding information in retransmissions. CoRR, vol. abs/0905.0363 (2009)
16. Pfitzmann, B.: Information hiding terminology - results of an informal plenary meeting and additional proposals. In: Proceedings of the First International Workshop on Information Hiding, London, UK, pp. 347–350. Springer, Heidelberg (1996)
17. http://www.sans.org/reading-room/whitepapers/covert/677.php
18. Szczypiorski, K.: Steganography in tcp/ip networks. In: State of the Art and a Proposal of a New System - HICCUPS, Institute of Telecommunications, Warsaw University of Technology (November, 2003)

19. Murdoch, S.J., Lewis, S.: Embedding covert channels into tcp/ip. In: Barni, M., Herrera-Joancomartí, J., Katzenbeisser, S., Pérez-González, F. (eds.) IH 2005. LNCS, vol. 3727, pp. 247–261. Springer, Heidelberg (2005)
20. Szczypiorski, K.: Hiccups: Hidden communication system for corrupted networks. In: Proc. of The Tenth International Multi-Conference on Advanced Computer Systems ACS 2003, Miedzyzdroje, October 22-24, pp. 31–40 (2003)
21. Kundur, D., Ahsan, K.: Practical internet steganography: Data hiding in IP. In: Proc. Texas Workshop on Security of Information Systems (College Station, Texas) (April 2003)
22. Gianvecchio, S., Wang, H.: Detecting covert timing channels: an entropy-based approach. In: CCS 2007: Proceedings of the 14th ACM conference on Computer and communications security, pp. 307–316. ACM, New York (2007)
23. Servetto, S.D., Vetterli, M.: Communication Using Phantoms: Covert Channels in the Internet. In: Proc. IEEE International Symposium on Information Theory, p. 229 (2001)
24. Mazurczyk, W., Szczypiorski, K.: Steganography of voip streams. In: Chung, S. (ed.) OTM 2008, Part II. LNCS, vol. 5332, pp. 1001–1018. Springer, Heidelberg (2008)
25. U.D.: of Defense. Trusted Computer System Evaluation in The Orange Book. Publication DoD 5200.28-STD. Washington: GPO (1985)
26. Henry, P.A., Corporation, C., Rowland, C.H.: Covert channels in the tcp/ip protocol suite
27. Rutkowska, J.: Implementation of passive covert channels in the linux kernel
28. Tumoian, E., Anikeev, M.: Network based detection of passive covert channels in tcp/ip. In: LCN 2005: Proceedings of the The IEEE Conference on Local Computer Networks 30th Anniversary, pp. 802–809. IEEE Computer Society, Washington, DC, USA (2005)
29. Ashan, K.: Covert-channel analysis and datahiding in tcp/ip, in A thesis submitted in conformity with the requirements for the degree of Masters of Applied Science (2003)
30. Ji, L., Jiang, W., Dai, B., Niu, X.: A novel covert channel based on length of messages. In: International Symposium on Information Engineering and Electronic Commerce, pp. 551–554 (2009)

Intrusion Detection System Based on Real Time Rule Accession and Honeypot

Abhay Nath Singh, Shiv Kumar, and R.C. Joshi

Department of Electronics & Computer Engineering
Indian Institute of Technology, Roorkee, India-247667
abhay.iitr@yahoo.com
sk_agrawal10@yahoo.co.in
rcjosfec@iitr.ernet.in

Abstract. The Intrusion Detection System (IDS) used today suffer from several shortcomings in the presence of complex and unknown attacks. Intrusion detection system based on honeypot is proposed with Real Time Rule Accession (RTRA) capability. We make use of honeypot to prevent the attack and collect attack traffic on the network. Furthermore, in order to improve the detection performance of our IDS, the Apriori algorithm for association rule mining is used on the data logged by honeypot to generate rules which will be added to the Snort IDS dynamically. This is different from the previous method of off-line rule base addition. The experimental results show that the proposed intrusion detection system is efficient in detecting the attacks at the time of their occurrences even if the system was not equipped with rules to detect it.

Keywords: Intrusion detection system; Honeypot; Snort; Apriori Association rule mining; Real Time Rule Accession (RTRA).

1 Introduction

Security is a main concern for all networks in today's organization environment. To secure the network infrastructure and communication over the Internet, a lot of systems have been developed. Among them firewalls, encryption, virtual private networks etc are important.

"A honeypot is an information system resource whose value lies in unauthorized or illicit use of that resource" [4]. These are computer systems that are placed on a network to attract hackers, thus allowing the administrators to capture and examine current attack methodologies and use that information to secure their systems and networks. Theoretically, no traffic should be seen at the honeypot because it has no legitimate activity. This means if there is any interaction with a honeypot then it is most likely an illegal or malicious activity [5].

An attempt to compromise the integrity, confidentiality or availability of a resource is termed as intrusion. The process of identifying that a network or server is under attack after launch of the attack is called detection. A commonly used detection approach is either signature-based or anomaly-based. Signature-based approach checks the passing traffic and looks for matches against known attacks patterns.

D.C. Wyld et al. (Eds.): CNSA 2011, CCIS 196, pp. 292–301, 2011.

Whereas an anomaly based detection system observes the normal network behavior and finds for any type of deviation from the normal traffic. Most of existing anomaly based solutions [1]-[3] to detect and categorize attacks use volume based metrics. Their normal traffic models are mainly based on flow rates.

The main problem with Anomaly based approaches is that they need huge amount of offline data for training. It is very difficult to provide this kind of attack labeled data. Hence in this paper, we are proposing a scheme by which with the help of honeypot, rules are dynamically added in real time in Snort with the help of data mining technique. Hence we do not need any type of off line data to train data mining algorithm. Honeypot provides that real time online data.

The remaining part of this paper is organized as follows: Section 2 gives the background and the related work. Section 3 explains the system design and implementation. The experimentation results are discussed in section 4 and the paper concludes with challenges and future work in section 5.

2 Background and Related Work

The application of data mining techniques to IDS is a field of great potential. The problem of intrusion detection is reducible to classification of traffic to normal and different attacks accurately, which can be achieved by data mining. A number of research works have been proposed in this area.

MADAM ID [6] is an IDS which showed how data mining techniques can be used to construct IDS in a systematic and automated manner. ADAM [7], IDDM [8] and eBayes [9] uses anomaly detection techniques for intrusion detection. ADAM is a network based IDS which learns the behavior of network through normal attack free traffic and represents them in the form of association rules. Anomaly based techniques usually requires training data to learn normal behavior which is difficult to obtain. Clustering based approaches are also used in this field of research. Training data is not required here [10].

MINDS [11] project uses data mining techniques to automatically detect attacks. A score is assigned to each connection to determine how anomalous it is compared to normal traffic. They are successful in detecting various unknown intrusions that could not be identified by widely used tools like Snort.

Apart from the known attacks a lot of unknown types of attacks keep happening. A lot of machine intelligence techniques have been used in intrusion detection area to reduce its vulnerability to unknown attacks. If we talk about Fuzzy logic, [13] gives the fuzzy expert system based approach in which automated learning of fuzzy rules is done with the help of genetic algorithm. [14] gives the application of different data mining techniques for building data mining models. In this classification, association rule mining and link analysis are used as anomaly detection tools. Even Support vector machine (SVM) is also used in this area. After that outlier analysis, another data mining technique is used for detecting intrusion as an outlier. SPOT is used as an outlier algorithm. All these methods use off line data to train its algorithm.

If we talk about the statistical techniques used for building models to detect intrusions, the first model is proposed by [15]. Here Denning told the general model based on anomalies found in the user profiles developed by the statistical algorithms over a period of time. A lot of methods are taken from statistical signal theory to detect anomalies like Principal Component Analysis (PCA), covariance methods, Auto Regressive Moving Average (ARMA). Entropy is another tool for quantifying the information of network traffic and has been extensively studied for anomaly detection and prevention. But all these statistical techniques suffer from a fatal problem of huge network statistics for formulation of user profiles which is very difficult.

The intrusion detection/prevention systems such as IDSs, Snort, Honeypots, Firewalls etc provided a platform to identify intrusion activities with the help of distributed systems. In [12], it is accomplished by a protocol, named *Detection* making detection and prevention of any anomaly accurately. It uses service oriented approaches.

In [16], an IDS based on Fuzzy inferencing technique was given to detect misuse and unknown attacks. Some heuristics were used for faster association rule generation algorithm. This model was tested on off line data and also required training. A Snort based hybrid IDS was proposed in [17] that combines misuse detection system with anomaly detection systems. Snort is the basis of misuse detection module. Anomaly Detection Module (ADS) was constructed by using frequent episode rule and could detect the unknown attacks. Again here it suffers the problem of model construction of ADS. A model of IDS using honeypots was proposed in [18]. Here clustering technique and genetic algorithm are applied on honeypot logged data to find abnormal activities. This approach was not realized on any real time system.

To fill the research gaps discussed above we are proposing a Real Time Rule Accession (RTRA) technique with the help of association rule mining and honeypot. Also we have implemented and integrated it with Snort, a most famous open source IDS and tested it as well.

3 System Design and Implementation

System design includes major three modules. First is data collection by honeypot, second is mining the data to generate attack rules and last is the RTRA (real time rule accession) in Snort. But all these modules are incompatible. E.g. honeypot log file cannot be directly given as input to the mining algorithm. So to eliminate these problems, interfaces are designed in between these modules. Similar interface is designed for rules generated by Apriori and rules added in Snort. A log file is very large so in order to efficiently process these log files DBMS is used.

Honeypots are implemented using honeyd tool. The fake wired network and routing topology was created by writing a configuration file that honeyd used. A number of virtual systems were created. Each virtual system was shown as if it ran a particular operating system. The virtual systems were also provided with multiple scripts that ran on various ports. These faked the services on the virtual systems and would help in deceiving the attacker. Whenever attacker tries to attack this network the data is logged. The logged data is stored in Mysql database for efficient processing. For performing this, a python script is implemented because honeyd log contains some attributes which can be neglected like timestamp, operating system of attacker etc. Hence python script converts all these records into homogeneous form so that they can be added in Mysql.

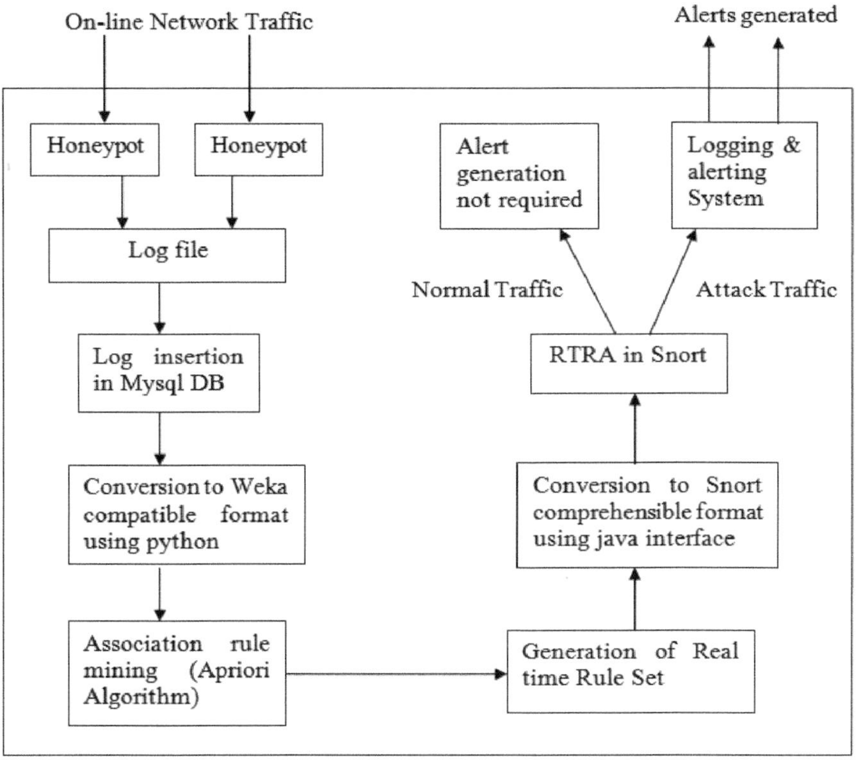

Fig. 1. System architecture of our Intrusion Detection System

Association rule mining algorithm is used to generate frequent item sets from that data. Weka tool is used for that algorithm. Weka takes a special file format named as arff as input. Hence Java program is deployed as an interface between Mysql and Weka. This program first discretizes each column of database because association rule mining can be applied only to categorical data. All the attributes are already in discrete form. But we cannot take all port numbers as different classes as it will make 65535 classes. So we found all distinct port numbers from database and assigned them as individual discrete classes. Same thing has been done with all other attributes. With the help of above procedure, the interface generates a compatible arff file for Weka. Weka employs various association rule mining algorithms like apriori, predictive apriori etc. We have employed apriori due to its less time complexity. It takes various parameters like support, confidence and their lower and upper bound value.

Rule set generated by Weka has to be converted into the form so that rules can be comprehended by Snort. For this another python script is implemented as an interface. Not all weka rules can be added to Snort because suppose if some of the weka rules doesn't have any protocol field then that rule is not added to Snort. Finally rules are added dynamically in Snort in real time. The traffic that enters the system is then matched against the attack patterns stored in our system. If it doesn't have a match then no alert is generated and it is bypassed. If a match is found then alerts are generated corresponding to the rules that match. These alerts can be used to take further action like blocking the traffic etc.

This processing cannot be done on whole honeypot log at once because log is increasing continuously. So we have decided to follow this process repeatedly on a certain number of records at a time. One main advantage of this design is that Snort continuously works in parallel to all this work. Hence no attack is missed which is already present in Snort rule base. But when rules are generated by our system, they are added in the rule base of Snort, and are used for detecting attack thereafter.

4 Experimental Results

The system was developed in Ubuntu 9.10. The various parameters used for experiment and analysis have been shown in Table 1.

Table 1. Various parameters used for system analysis

S.No	Parameter		Value
1	No. of virtual systems created in honeypot		10
2	No. of log records considered at a time		1000
3	Support value in Apriori	Upper bound	1.0
		Lower bound	0.05
4	Confidence value in Apriori	Upper bound	1.0
		Lower bound	0.01

We have to consider a number of records logged by honeypot to generate rules. As soon as it reaches 1000 the process of RTRA starts. It calls a shell script by which whole of this process is accomplished. We chose 1000 because the rules generated were sufficient as well as alert generation was quicker. We can choose number of records considered at a time, based on the intensity of attack traffic. Also, we can set timers to collect number of records; hence the system need not wait for 1000 records (as specified above). The system will produce the frequent item sets periodically. As every record logged by honeyd is significant, hence we chose a range starting from a very low value of support and confidence.

The shell script then generates a rule set which is added in Snort dynamically. After adding rules, Snort is restarted hence it is able to formulate a rule chain of newly added rules. This thing makes whole IDS capable of dynamic rule accession. This process continues until all log records are read. Output of association rule mining algorithm depends upon various parameters like support, confidence, upper and lower bound on support and confidence, number of rules required. System is tested on these different parameters which have been shown in results. Table 2 shows the log records of honeypot inserted in Mysql after processing of honeyd log by python script.

Table 2. Records of mysql database

Proto	S/E	Source IP	Source Port	Destination IP	Dest. Port	Size	Flags
tcp(6)	-	192.168.111.204	50953	192.168.111.103	53:	0	NULL
tcp(6)	-	192.168.111.204	50953	192.168.111.103	53:	0	NULL
…	…	…	…	…	…	…	…
tcp(6)	-	192.168.111.105	53	192.168.111.204	50953:	60	SA
tcp(6)	-	192.168.111.105	53	192.168.111.204	50953:	60	SA

S/E denotes the start and end of the packet for a particular connection established. In tcp(6), '6' denotes the protocol number. Source IP is the IP address of the attacker's system. Destination IP is the IP address of the virtual LAN created by honeyd. Size field denotes the packet size (data part) in bytes of corresponding protocol. Flags denote the various flags set in the packets. NULL flag indicates that packet is UDP or TCP having no flag set.

Frequent item sets generated by Apriori algorithm are shown in Table 3. Length of these large item sets are 7. Here 91 and 64 indicate the support of these item sets. We have analyzed the system on 6 and 7 length large item sets. Smaller the item sets larger will be redundancy.

Table 3. Frequent itemset generated by apriori

protocol=tcp(6) isStart=S SIP=192.168.111.204 SPort=50953 DIP=192.168.111.105 packSize=0 flags=NULL 91
protocol=tcp(6) isStart=- SIP=192.168.111.105 DIP=192.168.111.204 DPort=50953: packSize=60 flags=SA 64

Finally, Snort rules generated by these frequent item sets of Weka by java interface are shown in Table 4.

Table 4. Snort rules generated for rtra

alert tcp 192.168.111.204 50953 -> 192.168.111.105 any (msg: "HoneyPot Detected Attack" ; sid: 100005;)
alert tcp 192.168.111.105 any -> 192.168.111.204 50953 (msg: "HoneyPot Detected Attack" ; flags: SA; dsize: < 60 ; sid: 100024;)

First Snort rule means that generate the alert whenever there is a tcp packet from 192.168.111.204 and 50953 port to 192.168.111.105 tagged with 100005 id. Similarly flags field in second rule denoted the set flags in tcp packets. Sid is assigned to each rule of honeypot so that they can be uniquely identified. After adding these rules, Snort must be restarted so that changes can take effect. Snort is restarted using sending SIGHUP signal to process.

ZENMAP tool is used for attacking the honeyd. Slow comprehensive scan is used. With this UDP scan, TCP SYN/ACK scan, ICMP echo, ICMP timestamp, OS detection, version detection, etc. can be done.

The results shown by above experiments have been depicted using Fig.2 and Fig.3. Once a stream of records (1000) is considered, the frequent item sets generated by Weka and rules added to Snort are shown in the form of a graphs.

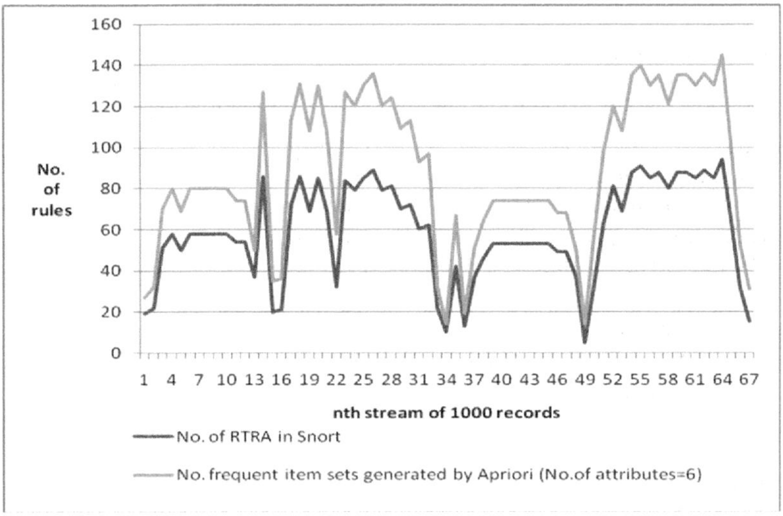

Fig. 2. Relationship between rules generated by Weka and accession in Snort against successive stream of attack records (number of attributes considered in frequent item set is 6)

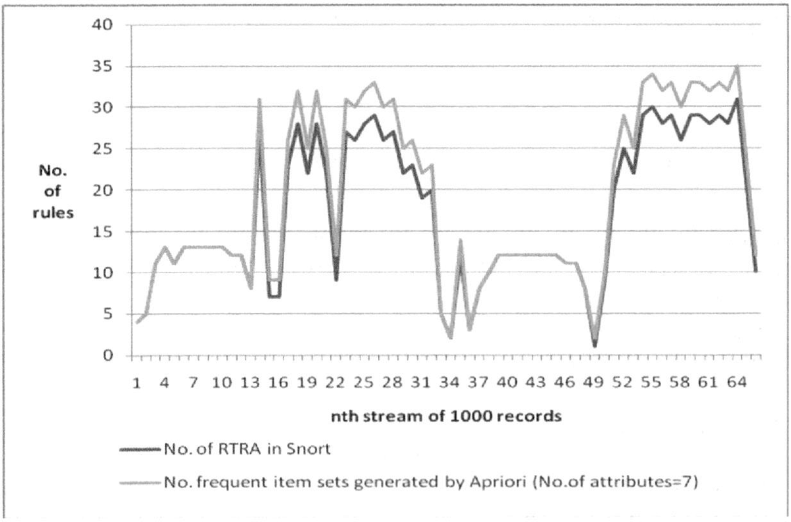

Fig. 3. Relationship between rules generated by Weka and accession in Snort against successive stream of attack records (number of attributes considered in frequent item set is 7)

Fig. 2 and Fig.3 show the values when number of attributes considered in frequent item sets in Apriori Algorithm is 6 and 7 respectively. The peaks in the graphs show the higher intensity attack while the troughs show lower intensity attack.

In each graph, the difference between number of frequent item set generated by Weka and number of rules added to Snort is due to the fact that we cannot convert all frequent item sets into Snort rules. For example, if any frequent item set does not contain any protocol field, we cannot convert that set to a meaningful Snort rule. Hence only meaningful sets can be converted to Snort rules.

The number of rules in Fig 2 is very higher than Fig 3. This variation in number of rules in the graphs is due to the difference in number of attributes considered in frequent sets. The relevant number of attributes logged by honeyd is seven. If we consider all the attributes the rules generated are less but of high value. While decreasing the number of attribute to six even though the number of rules increase but redundancy creeps in.

Alerts were generated in both the cases but numbers of rules fired in the case of seven attributes were less than the case of six attributes. Hence the efficiency of our IDS will be best when considering all seven attributes.

Table 5 shows a couple of alerts generated by our system corresponding to the rules in Table 4. These alerts show the timestamp when the attack was detected, the rule Id (100005 and 100024) and the rules. These alerts verify that our system is capable of detecting the attack with the help of RTRA. Hence, this shows that the rules added in real time in Snort rule base are actually detecting the attack. As honeypots are considered as pure attack capturing, thus new attacks will also be captured by it. This makes it capable of detecting novel attacks also.

Table 5. Alerts generated by our IDS

01/25-16:39:58.288325 [**] [1:100005:0] Snort Alert [1:100005:0] [**] [Priority: 0] {TCP} 192.168.111.204:50953 -> 192.168.111.105:1334
01/25-16:40:12.083140 [**] [1:100024:0] Snort Alert [1:100024:0] [**] [Priority: 0] {TCP} 192.168.111.105:42368 -> 192.168.111.204:50953

5 Conclusions

In this paper we presented an Intrusion Detection system developed using honeypots and association rule mining techniques which detected attack traffic in the network timely and effectively. The honeypot was used to create a virtual network topology with virtual systems running various services. This honeypot logged the various activities of attackers. The log was then processed using the Apriori association rule mining technique to generate various rules. The existing rule database of the Snort IDS was updated dynamically to generate alerts ahead. This was different from the previous method of off-line rule base addition.

The experimental results show that the proposed intrusion detection system is efficient in detecting the attacks at the time of their occurrences even if the system was not previously equipped with rules to detect it. Hence this system can be used to detect new type of attacks as well.

Acknowledgments. We wish to thank for useful comments and suggestions from faculty members of our institute. This research is supported by Internet Security Lab of Indian Institute of Technology-Roorkee. We wish to thank our colleagues at IIT-Roorkee.

References

1. Roesch, M.: Snort—Lightweight Intrusion Detection for Networks. In: Proceedings of LISA 1999 (1999)
2. Mirkovic, J., Prier, G., Reiher, P.: Attacking DDoS at the source. In: Proceedings of ICNP 2002, Paris, France, pp. 312–321 (2002)
3. Sardana, A., Gandhi, B., Joshi, R.C.: A Novel Framework for Characterization, Source Identification and Mitigation of DoS Attacks. In: Proceedings of ISCF-2006, pp. 99–108 (2006)
4. Spitzner, L.: Honeypots, Definition and value of honeypots (2003), `http://www.tracking-hackers.com/papers/honeypots.html`
5. `http://www.honeypots.net/`
6. Lee, W., Stolfo, S.J.: Data mining approaches for intrusion detection. In: Proc. Seventh USENIX Security Symposium, San Antonio, TX (1998)
7. Barbara, D., Couto, J., Jajodia, S., Wu, N.: Adam: Dtecting Intrusions by Data Mining. In: Proc. 2nd Annual IEEE Information Assurance Workshop, West Point, NY (2001)
8. Abraham, T.: IDDM: Intrusion Detection Using Data Mining Techniques. Technical report DSTO-GD-0286, DSTO Electronics and Surveillance Research Laboratory (2001)
9. Valde, A., Skinner, K.: Adaptive, model based monitoring for cyber attack detection. In: Recent advances on Intrusion Detection, pp. 80–93. Springer, France (2000)
10. Portnoy, L., Eskin, E., Stolfo, S.J.: Intrusion Detection with unlabelled data using clustering. In: Proceedings of ACM Workshop on Data Mining Applied to Security (2001)
11. Eetoz, L., Eilertson, E., Lazarevic, A., Tan, P., Dokes, P., Kumar, V., Srivastava, J.: Detection of Novel Attacks using Data Mining. In: Proc. IEEE Workshop on Data Mining and Computer Security (2003)
12. Rikhtechi, L., Roozbahani, A.R.: Creating a Standard Platform for All Intrusion Detection/Prevention Systems. In: Second International Conference on Computer Modeling and Simulation, ICCMS 2010, vol. 3, pp. 41–44 (2010)
13. Wang, Y.: Using Fuzzy Expert System Based on Genetic Algorithms for Intrusion Detection System. In: International Forum on Information Technology and Applications, IFITA 2009, vol. 2, pp. 221–224 (2009)
14. Wenke, L., Stolfo, S.J., Mok, K.W.: A data mining framework for building intrusion detection models. In: Proceedings of the 1999 IEEE Symposium on Security and Privacy, pp. 120–132 (1999)
15. Denning, D.E.: An Intrusion-Detection Model. IEEE Transactions on Software Engineering SE-13(2), 222–232 (1987)

16. Shanmugam, B., Idris, N.B.: Improved Intrusion Detection System Using Fuzzy Logic for Detecting Anamoly and Misuse Type of Attacks. In: International Conference of Soft Computing and Pattern Recognition, SOCPAR 2009, pp. 212–217 (2009)
17. Ding, Y., Xiao, M., Liu, A.: Research and implementation on snort-based hybrid intrusion detection system. In: International Conference on Machine Learning and Cybernetics, 2009, vol. 3, pp. 1414–1418 (2009)
18. Yang, Y., Mi, J.: Design and implementation of distributed intrusion detection system based on honeypot. In: 2nd International Conference on Computer Engineering and Technology (ICCET), vol. 6, pp. V6-260-V6-263 (2010)

Key Predistribution in 3-Dimensional Grid-Group Deployment Scheme

Samiran Bag

Applied Statistics Unit, Indian Statistical Institute, Kolkata-700108, India
samiran_r@isical.ac.in

Abstract. We propose one deterministic key distribution schemes for wireless sensor networks, where the nodes are deployed in a 3 dimensional grid like structure.We use combinatorial designs for key predistribution in sensor nodes. Here the deplyment region is a 3-D grid. The whole deployment region is divided into smaller cubic zones. The predistribution scheme has the advantage that all nodes within a particular region can communicate with each other directly and nodes which lie in a different regions can communicate via special nodes called agents which have more resources than the general nodes. The number of agents depend upon the construction.

In our key distribution scheme we have used within group key-distribution and one key distribution for inter-group communication. We use one existing key pre-distribution scheme for intra-group communication between nodes and for inter-group communication we use our proposed scheme.

1 Introduction

Wireless sensor networks consist of many tiny sensing devices, with very limited memory and power, and are scattered randomly in large numbers over a target area. The networks are used for both military and civilian purposes like seismic activity monitoring, military surveilence, oceanwater temperature monitoring, smoke detection, wild fire detection in forest etc. These sensor nodes communicate via radio waves within a certain range called Radio Frequency range. To achieve secure communication each pair of sensor nodes has to have a secret key. If two nodes(say a and b) don't have a common key then it is required to find a chain of nodes starting from the node a ending at node b such that two consecutive nodes in the chain of nodes have a common key. Whenever node a would like to communicate with node b it can generate a random key and can pass it securely to node b through the path of the node-chain. This randomly generated key can be used in secure communication of node a and b. Thus communication can be achieved between the nodes a and b through the chain of nodes.

There are many schemes that deals with establishment of common key between two parties. Among them Key pre distribution is one that is prefered most because of the low inherent cost of the protocol. Key pre-distribution means preloading the nodes into the sensors before deployment. Key pre-distribution in wireless sensor networks has three different steps. They are 1) Preloading the individual sensor nodes with certain number of keys.This is done prior to deployment of the sensor nodes in the target area 2) Shared key discovery: this is the process of establishing a common key between two sensor

D.C. Wyld et al. (Eds.): CNSA 2011, CCIS 196, pp. 302–319, 2011.

nodes who want to communicate between each other. 3) Path key establishment :this deals with the process of establishing a chain of paths (as mentioned above) between the first node and the second node. Key pre-distribution can both be probabilistic and deterministic. In Probabilistic scheme keys are drawn randomly from a key-pool and are placed into sensor nodes. In deterministic scheme as the name suggests a deterministic method is used for distributing the keys into the sensor nodes.

In this paper we discuss key pre-distribution scheme in a 3-D grid group deployment scheme. In case of grid group deployment sensor nodes are deployed such that they create a 3 dimensional grid(Fig. 1). 3–dimensional grid based deployment can be used in a big office building where sensors are deployed not only along the width and length of the deployment zone but also along the height of the same that gives rise to a 3–D structure called rectangular parallelepiped. This parallelepiped are further divided into smaller rectangular parallelepipeds(as in fig 1.) that contain sensor nodes that form a group among themselves. Communication between sensor nodes within the same group is usually much higher than two sensor nodes belonging to two different groups. This is driven by the fact that the communication between two close nodes are higher than two distant nodes.

In our scheme there are two types of pre-distribution schemes. One which is used for intra group communication or in other words communication between two nodes within the same group. We have previously stated that communication between the node in the same group is higher than the communication between two nodes from two different groups. The other key pre-distribution scheme is for communication between two different groups via some special nodes called agents. These agents have more computational power as well as more memory. For intra group key pre-distribution we use the Camptepe Yener scheme [9]. Since the amount of communication between two nodes within the same group is high, so using Camptepe Yener scheme would provide better efficient communication as in this scheme every pair of nodes do share a key. For inter group communication we use our proposed key pre-distribution scheme. Hence our work mainly focusses on inter group communication only.

Upto this point it is clear that our scheme is based on deployment knowledge of nodes. Schemes in which deployment knowledge has been used are [Du et al. 2004; Du et al. 2006; Yu and Guan 2005; 2008; Liu and Ning 2003; 2005; Younis et al. 2006; Zhou et al. 2006; Huang et al. 2004; Huang and Medhi 2007; Chan and Perrig 2005; Simonova et al. 2006], Ruj and Roy[2008].

2 Related Work

Key pre-distribution in wireless sensor networks was first introduced by Eschenaur and Gligor [15]. In this scheme there are a pool of keys out of which a certain number of keys are drawn at random each time and are placed in the individual nodes. nodes prior to deployment. In this scheme each and every pair of nodes may not have a common key. So, if any pair of nodes need to communicate then a path of nodes need to be established between them such that any two consecutive nodes in the chain have a shared key. Thus a path of nodes can be established from the source node to the destination node and a secret key can be passed from the source node to the destination

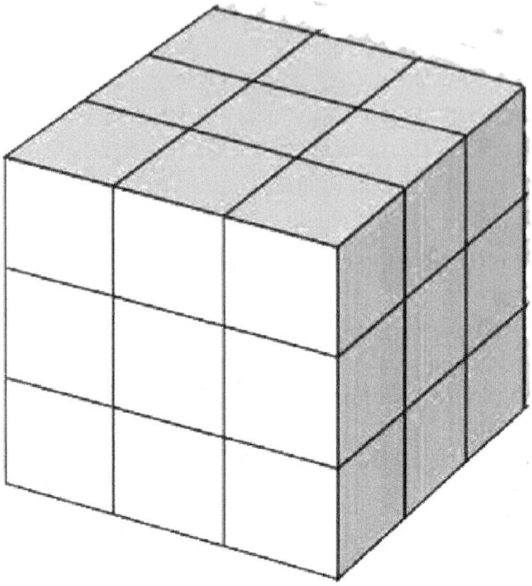

Fig. 1. A 3–D grid group deployment

node through the chain of nodes. Thereafter that key can be used by the two nodes for secret communication. These scheme was the first probabilistic scheme for key pre-distribution in wireless sensor networks. Many modifications of the same are avaiable. Other schemes include Camptepe Yener scheme [9], Lee Stinson scheme [11], Ruj and Roy scheme [39] etc to name a few. All these schemes were designed for homogenous wireless sensor networks where all the sensor nodes in the network is identical. These are key pre-distribution schemes that deal with homogenious networks. There are other schemes that deal with heterogenious networks. These schemes can be found in [30], [31], [32], [33], [34], [35], [36], [37], [38], [39]. These schemes mostly discuss of 2-dimensional grids where the deployment region is planar. Our scheme discusses about 3-dimensional grid.

3 Preliminaries

A **design** [5] is a pair $(X, \mathcal{A})$ such that the following properties are satisfied:

1. X is a set of elements called points.
2. $\mathcal{A}$ is a collection (i.e., multiset) of nonempty subsets of X called blocks.

A $(v, b, r, k; \lambda)$ balanced incomplete block design is a design $(X, \mathcal{A})$ with the following properties:

1. $|X| = v$, $|\mathcal{A}| = b$.
2. each block contains exactly k points.
3. every pair of distinct points is contained in exactly λ blocks.
4. each element in X is contained in exactly r blocks.

A $(v, b, r, k; \lambda)$ BIBD where $v = b$ is called a symmeric BIBD or SBIBD$(v, k; \lambda)$.

A *finite projective plane* [5] of order p is a $(p^2 + p + 1, p + 1, 1)$–BIBD with $p \geq 2$.

A transversal design TD$(k, n; \lambda)$ [5] is a triple $(X, \mathcal{G}, \mathcal{B})$ such that the following properties are satisfied:

1. X is a set of kn elements called points
2. $\mathcal{G}$ is a partition of X into k subsets of size n called groups
3. $\mathcal{B}$ is a set of k-subsets of X called blocks
4. any group and any block contain exactly one common point
5. every pair of points from distinct groups is contained in exactly λ block.

4 Proposed Scheme

As told earlier, our scheme is meant for a heterogenous wireless sensor networks. There are n^3 number of groups organized like a 3-dimensional structure as depicted in figure 1. In this figure a small cube represents a homogenous group of sensor nodes. Each group consists of equal or nearly equal number of nodes. We asume that the 3-dimensional grid consists of $n \times n \times n$ smaller groups(figure 1). So we can identify each group uniquely by their co-ordinate in the 3-dimensional space. Let the base of the cube be taken as the $X - Y$ plane and the axis parallel to the height of the cube be it's Z axis. So, each group will have a co-ordinate (i, j, k), where $i, j, k \in \{0, 1, \ldots, n - 1\}$. We use two separate key pre-distribution schemes in this context eg. for intra group key pre-distribution and for inter-group key pre-distribution. The intra-group key pre-distribution scheme is used for the sensor nodes within a group. On the other hand the inter group key pre-distribution scheme is meant for cross group communication. Now in our scheme the intra-group key-distribution is done using the Camptepe Yener scheme [9]. These means the key pre-distribution scheme There are less than $p^2 + p + 1$ nodes in a group. So keys to each node is distributed like scheme [9]. Our proposed scheme for inter-group key-distribution. We have stated that there are some special nodes called agents who are responsible for inter-group communication. These agents have more memory and are very less likely to be compromised. Any agent is a node of the group to which it belongs. Thus, like other sensors in the same group it contains some keys of the inter-group key pre-distribution scheme that allows it to establish secure connection with other nodes in the same group and vice-versa. Again since the same agent is a part of the inter-group key pre-distribution scheme, so it contains some keys of the inter-group key pre-distribution scheme. This enables an agent to securely communicate to the sensors within the same group as well as the agents of the other group.

Whenever two nodes belonging to two different groups want to communicate, they can do so by the help of agents. Let node $n^r_{i,j,k}$ belonging to group (i, j, k) wants to communicate to a node $n^s_{i',j',k'}$ belonging to group (i', j', k'). Since the nodes within a group use key pre-distribution scheme [9], so the node $n^r_{i,j,k}$ can establish a connection to an agent(say $A^u_{i,j,k}$) of the group (i, j, k) using the inter group key pre-distribution scheme [9]. Then the agent $A^u_{i,j,k}$ can establish a connection to the agent

$A^{v}_{i',j',k'}$ belonging to group (i', j', k') by means of the inter group key pre-distribution among agents. Finally the agent $A^{v}_{i',j',k'}$ can establish a secure connection with the node $n^{s}_{i',j',k'}$ via the inter-group key pre-distribution scheme.

Definition 1. *A key-path is a sequence of nodes* $\{n_1, n_2, \ldots, n_t\}$, *such that two consecutive nodes in the sequence do have a common key.*

4.1 First Scheme

For the purpose of key pre-distribution in the agents we use transversal design. Our transversal design is discussed below. In our design the set of keys are identified by $\mathcal{K} = \{(x, y) : x \in \{0, 1, \ldots, k-1\}, y \in \{0, 1, \ldots, p-1\}\}$ where p is a prime.

Therefore, there will be kp number of keys totally.

$X = \{(x, y) : x \in \{0, 1, \ldots, k-1\}, y \in \{0, 1, \ldots, p-1\}\}$

The groups are $G_r = \{(r, s)\} : r \in \{0, 1, \ldots, k-1\}\}$ for each $s \in \{0, 1, \ldots, p-1\}$

The blocks are

$A^{1}_{i,j,k} = \{(x, ix^2+jx+k \bmod p) : x \in \{0, 1, \ldots, p-1\}\}$ for $i, j, k \in \{0, 1, \ldots, n-1\}$.

$A^{2}_{i,j,k} = \{(x, jx^2+kx+i \bmod p) : x \in \{0, 1, \ldots, p-1\}\}$ for $i, j, k \in \{0, 1, \ldots, n-1\}$.

$A^{3}_{i,j,k} = \{(x, kx^2+ix+j \bmod p) : x \in \{0, 1, \ldots, p-1\}\}$ for $i, j, k \in \{0, 1, \ldots, n-1\}$.

Now, if $i \neq j \neq k$ let block $A^{t}_{i,j,k}$ be assigned to an agent t at the group (i, j, k) for $t = \{1, 2, 3\}$. So, that particular agent t will be containing other than it's own keys, all the keys in the block $A^{t}_{i,j,k}$ for $t = \{1, 2, 3\}$. If $i = j = k$, then $A^{1}_{i,j,k} = A^{2}_{i,j,k} = A^{3}_{i,j,k}$. So all the three agents along one main diagonal of the grid will have the same set of keys. It is evident that each agent will have p number of keys.

4.2 Key-Path Establishment

We used [9] for achieving a key pre-distribution within a group. So if two nodes from the same group want to communicate, they can find a shared key using the method described in [9]. Alternately, if two different nodes from two different groups want to communicate, they need to establish a key-path. Let node $n^{x}_{(i,j,k)}$ of group (i, j, k) wants to establish a key-path to node $n^{y}_{(x',y',z')}$ belonging to group (i', j', k'), then first of all we need to find a key-path between two agents of the two groups. If such a key-path is found starting at agent $A^{t}_{i,j,k}$ ending in agent $A^{w}_{i',j',k'}$, then the overall key-path will be $\{n^{x}_{(i,j,k)}, A^{t}_{i,j,k}, \ldots, A^{w}_{i',j',k'}, n^{y}_{(x',y',z')}\}$.

We discuss the key-path establishment method between two agents of the two groups below.

Case 1. If there exists a direct key between two groups. Let the two two groups be (i, j, k) and (i', j', k'). A direct key will be possible between any two agents if any two agents each from one group. In that case six subcases are possible

a. The first agents of both the groups can have a common key if. $ix^2 + jx + k = i'x^2 + j'x + k'$

Or, $(i - i')x^2 + (j - j')x + (k - k') = 0$

$$x = (-(j - j') \pm \sqrt{(j - j')^2 - 4(i - i')(k - k')})(2(i - i'))^{-1}$$

Hence, two shared key will exist if $i \neq i'$ and
$(j - j')^2 - 4(i - i')(k - k')$ is a quadratic residue under division *modulo* p.

b. The second agent of first group and the first agent of second group can find a direct key(if one exists)
$jx^2 + kx + i = i'x^2 + j'x + k'$
Or, $(j - i')x^2 + (k - j')x + (i - k') = 0$

$$x = (-(k - j') \pm \sqrt{(k - j')^2 - 4(j - i')(i - k')})(2(j - i'))^{-1}$$

Hence, two shared key will exist if $j \neq i'$ and
$(k - j')^2 - 4(j - i')(i - k')$ is a quadratic residue under division *modulo* p.

c. The 3rd agent of first group and the 1st agent of the second group can find a direct key(if one exists)
$kx^2 + ix + j = i'x^2 + j'x + k'$
Or, $(k - i')x^2 + (i - j')x + (j - k') = 0$

$$x = (-(i - j') \pm \sqrt{(i - j')^2 - 4(k - i')(j - k')})(2(k - i'))^{-1}$$

Hence, two shared key will exist if $k \neq i'$ and
$(i - j')^2 - 4(k - i')(j - k')$ is a quadratic residue under division *modulo* p.

d. The first agent of the first group and the second agent of the second group can find a direct key
$ix^2 + jx + k = j'x^2 + k'x + i'$
Or, $(i - j')x^2 + (j - k')x + (k - i') = 0$

$$x = (-(j - k') \pm \sqrt{(j - k')^2 - 4(i - j')(k - i')})(2(i - j'))^{-1}$$

Hence, two shared direct key will exist if $i \neq j'$ and
$(j - k')^2 - 4(i - j')(k - i')$ is a quadratic residue modulo p.

e. The second agent of the first group and the second agent of the second group can find a shared key between them like this;
$jx^2 + kx + i = j'x^2 + k'x + i'$
Or, $(j - j')x^2 + (k - k')x + (i - i') = 0$

$$x = (-(k - k') \pm \sqrt{(k - k')^2 - 4(j - j')(i - i')})(2(j - j'))^{-1}$$

Hence, two shared direct key will exist if $j \neq j'$ and
$(k - k')^2 - 4(j - j')(i - i')$ is a quadratic residue modulo p.

f. The third agent of the first group and the second agent of the second group can find a shared key between them like this;
$kx^2 + ix + j = j'x^2 + k'x + i'$
Or, $(k - j')x^2 + (i - k')x + (j - i') = 0$

$$x = (-(i - k') \pm \sqrt{(i - k')^2 - 4(k - j')(j - i')})(2(k - j'))^{-1}$$

Hence, two shared direct key will exist if $k \neq j'$ and
$(i - k')^2 - 4(k - j')(j - i')$ is a qudratic residue modulo p.

g. The first agent of the first group and the third agent of the second group can find a shared key between them like this;
$ix^2 + jx + k = k'x^2 + i'x + j'$
$(i - i')x^2 + (j - i')x + (k - j') = 0$

$$x = (-(j - i') \pm \sqrt{(j - i')^2 - 4(i - i')(k - j')})(2(i - i'))^{-1}$$

Hence, two shared keys will exist if $i \neq i'$ and
$(j - i')^2 - 4(i - i')(k - j')$ is a qudratic residue modulo p.

h. The second agent of the first group and the third agent of the second group can find a shared key between them like this;
$jx^2 + kx + i = k'x^2 + i'x + j'$
$(j - k')x^2 + (k - i')x + (i - j') = 0$

$$x = (-(k - i') \pm \sqrt{(k - i')^2 - 4(j - k')(i - j')})(2(j - k'))^{-1}$$

Hence, two shared keys will exist if $j \neq k'$ and
$(k - i')^2 - 4(j - k')(i - j')$ is a qudratic residue modulo p.

i. The third agent of the first group and the third agent of the second group can find a shared key between them like this;
$kx^2 + ix + j = k'x^2 + i'x + j'$
$(k - k')x^2 + (i - i')x + (j - j') = 0$

$$x = (-(i - i') \pm \sqrt{(i - i')^2 - 4(k - k')(j - j')})(2(k - k'))^{-1}$$

Hence, two shared keys will exist if $k \neq k'$ and
$(i - i')^2 - 4(k - k')(j - j')$ is a qudratic residue modulo p.

Thus there can be at most $3 \times 3 \times 2 = 18$ keys between every pair of agents from the two groups.

Case 2. We, now consider the case when the two groups won't have any direct key. Let $a_1 = (i, j, k)$ and $a_2 = (i', j', k')$ be such two groups where there are no pair of agents who share a common key. For communication between any two nodes from both of the groups we need another group a_3 such that a_1 establishes a key with group a_3 and a_3 establishes a key with a_2. Now a path will be established from a_1 to a_2 through a_3. Now any node in the group a_1 can send a randomly generated key to any node in the group a_2. Here do we show how it can be accomplished.

Here our assumption is $j \neq j'$. Let $a_3 = (i, j', k''), k'' \neq k'$. Now, we the first agent of first group can have a shared key with the first agent of a_3 like this;
$ix^2 + jx + k = ix^2 + j'x + k''$
Or, $jx + k = j'x + k''$
Or, $x = (k'' - k)(j - j')^{-1}$
If $j \neq j'$, then x exists and can be computed in $O(\log^2 p)$ time using extended eucleadian algorithm [40].

Now, we need to find a shared key between a_3 and a_2. The second agent of a_3 can find a shared key with the second agent of a_2 like this;
$j'x^2 + k''x + i = j'x^2 + k'x + i'$
$k'x + i = k'x + i'$
$x = (i' - i)(k'' - k')^{-1}$
If $k'' \neq k'$, then $(k'' - k')^{-1}$ exists and so does x. $(k'' - k')^{-1}$ can be calculated in $O(\log^2 p)$ time using Extended Eucleadian algorithm [40].

Case 3. Next, we will consider shared key discovery between two groups when the groups are in the same plane i.e. if the co-ordinates of the two groups be (i, j, k) and (i', j', k') then at least one of the following must hold (but not all):

1. $i = i'$
2. $j = j'$
3. $k = k'$

1. If $i = i'$ but $j \neq j'$, then the first agent of the first group can find a shared key with the first agent of the second group like this;
   $ix^2 + jx + k = i'x^2 + j'x + k'$
   $jx + k = j'x + k'$
   $x = (k' - k)(j - j')^{-1}$
   $(j - j')^{-1}$ will exist as $j \neq j'$ and can be computed in $O(\log^2 p)$ time by E.E. algorithm [40].
   Alternately, if $i = i'$ and $j = j'$, then $k \neq k'$. Then the second agents of both the groups will have a shared key given by $(0, i)$.

2. If $j = j'$ but $k \neq k'$, then the second agent of the first group and the second agent of the second group can find a shared key like this;
   $jx^2 + kx + i = j'x^2 + k'x + i'$
   $kx + i = k'x + i'$

$x = (i' - i)(k - k')^{-1}$
$(k - k')^{-1}$ will exist as $k \neq k'$ and can be computed in $O(\log^2 p)$ time by E.E. algorithm [40].
Alternately, if $j = j'$ and $k = k'$ then $i \neq i'$. Then the third agents of both the two groups will have a shared key given by $(0, j)$.

3. If $k = k'$ but $i \neq i'$, then the third agents of both groups can find a shared key between them like this;
$kx^2 + ix + j = k'x^2 + i' + j'$
Or, $ix + j = i'x + j'$
Or, $x = (j' - j)(i - i')^{-1}$
$(i - i')^{-1}$ will exist as $i \neq i'$ and can be computed in $O(\log^p)$ time by E.E. algorithm.
Alternately, if $k = k'$ and $i = i'$, then $j \neq j'$. Then the first agents of both the groups will have a shared key given by $(0, k)$.

5 Connectivity

We have seen that this scheme does not ensure that between each pair of group there will be a direct communication through the agents of the nodes. But in all cases there will be a path with at most one extra node in between the source group and destination group. It can be observed that two differen groups will have at least one common key if the co-ordinate of any axis of any group is same as the co-ordinate of any axis of the other group.

6 Alternate Design

We now propose our last scheme for key pre-distribution among different agents of the groups. Here, we shall use finite geometry over $\mathbb{Z}_q$.

6.1 Prelimineries

Finite geometry: A finte affine plane over a finite field $GF(q)$ consists of finite number of points and lines such that

- Given any two distinct points, there is exactly one line incident with both of them.
- Given any line L and a point p not on L, there exists exactly one line L through p that does not intersect L.
- There are four points such that no line is incident with more than two of them.

There are a number of methods of constructing affine planes. These are given in [29], [28], [27] We are describing one particular method of designing the same below. Let P be the set of points (x, y) where $x, y \in GF(q)$.

Let, $L_{\alpha,\beta,1} = \{(x, y, 1) : x, y \in GF(q) \ \& \ (x, y) \neq (0, 0)\}$,

$L_{1,\beta,0} = \{(1, y, 0) : y \in GF(q)\}$

and $L_{0,1,0} = \{(0, 1, 0)\}$

$L = L_{\alpha,\beta,1} \cup L_{1,\beta,0} \cup L_{0,1,0}$. Now, it can be proved that this set points P and the set of lines L form an affine plane $AG(2, q)$ over $GF(q)$.From the definition above, it is evident that $|L_{\alpha,\beta,1}| = q^2 - 1$, $|L_{1,\beta,0}| = q$, and $|L_{0,1,0}| = 1$. This gives rise to a totality of $q^2 + q$ number of lines in $AG(2, q)$.

Let (x, y) be a particular point in the construction of $AG(2, q)$ defined above. The set of distinct lines through (x, y) is $L_{(x,y)} = \{(a, b, c) : (a, b, c) \in L, ax + by = c\}$. Lets divide this to two parts:

$L_{(x,y)} = \{(a, b, 1) : (a, b, 1) \in L, ax+by = 1\} \cup \{(a, b, 0) : (a, b, 0) \in L, ax+by = 0\}$

$\Rightarrow L_{(x,y)} = \{(a, b, 1) : (a, b, 1) \in L_{\alpha,\beta,1}, ax + by = 1\} \cup \{(a, b, 0) : (a, b, 0) \in L_{1,\beta,0} \cup L_{0,1,0}, ax + by = 0\}$

$\Rightarrow |L_{(x,y)}| = |\{(a, b, 1) : (a, b, 1) \in L_{\alpha,\beta,1}, ax + by = 1\}| + |\{(a, b, 0) : (a, b, 0) \in L_{1,\beta,0} \cup L_{0,1,0}, ax + by = 0\}|$

Let, $m_1 = |\{(a, b, 1) : (a, b, 1) \in L_{\alpha,\beta,1}, ax + by = 1\}|$

and, $m_2 = |\{(a, b, 0) : (a, b, 0) \in L_{1,\beta,0} \cup L_{0,1,0}, ax + by = 0\}|$.

Case 1

If $(x, y) \neq (0, 0)$, then at least one of x and y is non-zero. Lets say $x \neq 0$ then,

$m_1 = |\{(a, b, 1) : (a, b, 1) \in L_{\alpha,\beta,1}, ax = 1 - by\}|$

Or, $m_1 = |\{(a, b, 1) : (a, b, 1) \in L_{\alpha,\beta,1}, a = (1 - by)x^{-1}\}|$

Now, for each $b \in GF(q)$, we will get exactly one a, or in other words, we will get q many solution pairs (a, b) such that $(a, b, 1) \in L_{\alpha,\beta,1}, ax + by = 1$

Hence, $m_1 = |\{(a, b, 1) : (a, b, 1) \in L_{\alpha,\beta,1}, ax + by = 1\}| = q$

$$m_2 = |\{(a, b, 0) : (a, b, 0) \in L_{1,\beta,0} \cup L_{0,1,0}, ax + by = 0\}|$$

$\Rightarrow m_2 = |\{(a, b, 0) : (a, b, 0) \in L_{1,\beta,0}, ax + by = 0\}| + |\{(a, b, 0) : (a, b, 0) \in L_{0,1,0}, ax + by = 0|$

$\Rightarrow m_2 = |\{(1, b, 0) : (1, b, 0) \in L_{1,\beta,0}, x + by = 0\}| + |\{(0, 1, 0) : (0, 1, 0) \in L_{0,1,0}, by = 0\}|$

If $y = 0$, then $x \neq 0$. Hence,

$$\{(1, b, 0) : (1, b, 0) \in L_{1,\beta,0}, x + by = 0\} = \phi$$

and, $\{(0, 1, 0) : (0, 1, 0) \in L_{0,1,0}, by = 0\} = \{(0, 1, 0)\}$ So, $m_2 = 1$

Whence, $L_{(x,y)} = m_1 + m_2 = q + 1$

Case 2

If $(x, y) = (0, 0)$, then

$$m_1 = |\{(a, b, 1) : (a, b, 1) \in L_{\alpha,\beta,1}, ax + by = 1\}| = 0$$

$m_2 = |\{(a,b,0) : (a,b,0) \in L_{1,\beta,0}, ax+by = 0\}| + |\{(a,b,0) : (a,b,0) \in L_{0,1,0}, ax+by = 0|$
$\Rightarrow m_2 = |\{(1,b,0) : (1,b,0) \in L_{1,\beta,0}, x + by = 0\}| + |\{(0,1,0) : (0,1,0) \in L_{0,1,0}, by = 0\}|$
Now, for all element $(1,b,0) \in L_{1,\beta,0}, x + by = 0$ Similarly, for all element $(0,1,0) \in L_{0,1,0}, by = 0$
So, $m_2 = |L_{1,\beta,0}| + |L_{0,1,0}| = q + 1$
So, $L_{(x,y)} = q + 1$

Hence, each point in $AG(2,q)$ is contained in $q+1$ lines [5]. It can be proven that every line contain equal number of points [5]. Let this number be r. Since there are q^2 points and each point passes through $q+1$ lines, so there are $q^2(q+1)$ many point-line intersections. Alternately, since there are q^2+q number of lines and each line contains exactly m points, so there are $m(q^2+q)$ number of point-line intersections. Equating them, we get
$m(q^2+q) = q^2(q+1) = q(q^2+q)$
Hence, $m = q$. So, each line contains precisely q many points.

6.2 Key Predistribution in Agents

$N_{x,y}$	node with id $(x,y), x, y \in \{0,1,\ldots,n-1\}$
$P_{x,y}$	set of lines/keys belonging to $N_{x,y}$
$K_{\alpha,\beta}$	the set of lines through the point (α,β) in $AG(2,q)$
$\mathcal{K}$	the set of q^2+q keys

Before we move on to the key pre-distribution of agents, we discuss the same key pre-distribution scheme in a group of n^2 nodes viz.

$$\begin{array}{ccccc} N_{0,0} & N_{0,1} & N_{0,2} & \cdots & N_{0,n-1} \\ N_{1,0} & N_{1,0} & N_{1,2} & \cdots & N_{1,n-1} \\ \vdots & \vdots & \vdots & \vdots & \vdots \\ N_{n-1,0} & N_{n-1,1} & N_{n-1,2} & \cdots & N_{n-1,n-1} \end{array}$$

We denote the set of keys belonging to a particular node $N_{x,y}$ by $P_{x,y}; \forall x, y \in \{0, 1, ..., n-1\}$. Let $\mathcal{K}$ be a set of q^2+q keys. Since the number of lines in $AG(2,q)$ is equal to $|\mathcal{K}|$, so we can have a one to one correspondence between the keys and the lines in $AG(2,q)$ and vice versa. In other words we can represent a key by a line in $AG(2,q)$. For the rest of this paper we will use them to bear same meaning.

Let, q be a prime number such that $q \geq 2n$. For any point (x,y) in $AG(2,q)$ let $K_{x,y}$ be the set of lines that pass through it.

$$P_{x,y} = K_{x,y} \cup K_{n+x,n+y} \forall x, y \in \{0,1,\ldots,n-1\}$$

So, node $N_{x,y}$ will get all the keys corresponding to the lines in $K_{x,y}$ and $K_{n+x,n+y}$

Theorem 1. *For any node* $N_{x,y}; x, y \in \{0,1,\ldots,n-1\}, |P(x,y)| = 2q+1$.

Proof. $P_{x,y} = K_{x,y} \cup K_{n+x,n+y} \forall x, y \in \{0, 1, \ldots, n-1\}$.
$P_{x,y} = |K_{x,y}| + |K_{n+x,n+y}| - |K_{x,y} \cap K_{n+x,n+y}| \forall x, y \in \{0, 1, \ldots, n-1\}$.
The number of lines through a particular point (x, y) in $AG(2, q)$ is $q+1$. So, $|K_{x,y}| = |K_{n+x,n+y}| = q+1$. The set $K_{x,y} \cap K_{n+x,n+y}$ contains the line(s) through (x, y) and $(n+x, n+y)$. Now there can be only a single line through any two points in $AG(2, q)$. Hence, $|K_{x,y} \cap K_{n+x,n+y}| = 1$.

Note that, $|P(x, y)|$ is the number of keys belonging to a node $N_{x,y}$. Since $2n \leq q \leq 2(n+1)$, $|P(x, y)| = O(n)$

Theorem 2. *For any two nodes,* $N_{\alpha,\beta}, N_{\delta,\gamma}; \alpha, \beta, \delta, \gamma \in \{0, 1, \ldots, n-1\}$,$1 \leq |P_{\alpha,\beta} \cap P_{\gamma,\delta}| \leq 4$.

Proof. From the way of distributing the points, among nodes, it is clear that (α, β), (δ, γ), $(n+\alpha, n+\beta)$, $(n+\delta, n+\gamma)$ are 4 distinct points. Let's consider the case when all 4 of them lie on a single line. In that case $P_{\alpha,\beta} \cap P_{\gamma,\delta}$ will consists of only a single line, i.e. the line through all of them.

On the other hand, if no three of the 4 points are collinear then the total number of common lines between $P_{\alpha,\beta}$ and $P_{\gamma,\delta}$ is the total number of lines passing through any point of $\{(\alpha, \beta), (n+\alpha, n+\beta)\}$ as well as any point of $\{(\delta, \gamma), (n+\delta, n+\gamma)\}$. This is equal to 2×2 or 4.

Note that, the number of common keys between two nodes $N_{\alpha,\beta}, N_{\delta,\gamma}; \alpha, \beta, \delta, \gamma \in \{0, 1, \ldots, n-1\}$ is equal to $|P_{\alpha,\beta} \cap P_{\gamma,\delta}|$.

This way, we create a key pre-distribution scheme having n^2 nodes, each node containing precisely $O(n)$ keys, and where, the number of common keys between any two nodes is 1 to 4.

Now, we proceed to map the same key pre-distribution scheme to the agents of the 3-D wireless sensor network. For this purpose, we divide the agents in the 3 dimensional grid containing n^2 groups like this

For a 3 dimensional cube, there are 3 planes viz. one parallel to the X-Y plane, another parallel to X-Z plane and the last parallel to the Y-Z plane intersect at a particular group whose co-ordinate is (x, y, z). We assign three agents to each of the n^3 groups. The agents corresponding to a group with co-ordinate (x, y, z) are $a^1_{x,y,z}, a^2_{x,y,z}, a^3_{x,y,z}$.

Let,for all $i \in \{0, 1, ..., n-1\}$ $S^1_i = \{a^1_{x,y,i} : x, y \in \{0, 1, ..., n-1\}\}$

Similarly, for all $i \in \{0, 1, ..., n-1\}$ $S^2_i = \{a^1_{x,i,z} : x, z \in \{0, 1, ..., n-1\}\}$

and, for all $i \in \{0, 1, ..., n-1\}$ $S^3_i = \{a^1_{i,y,z} : y, z \in \{0, 1, ..., n-1\}\}$

Thus, there are $3n$ number of sets $S^j_i, j \in \{1, 2, 3\}, i \in \{0, 1, ..., n-1\}$, each S^j_i containing n^2 agents.

Now, we move on to use the key pre-distribution scheme described in section VIII-B for key pre-distribution among the agents in each set S^j_i, separately for all $j \in \{1, 2, 3\}, i \in \{0, 1, ..., n-1\}$.

Let, q be a prime number such that $q \geq 2n$. For the time being we assume $j = 1, i = k$. So, our key distribution is for the set S^1_k.

$S^1_k = \{a^1_{x,y,k} : x, y \in \{0, 1, ..., n-1\}\}$.

We, select two points from the set of q^2 points and place all the lines passing through them into the agents in S_k^1. So, the points corresponding to agent $a^1_{x,y,k}$ is
$P^1_{x,y,k} = \{(x, y), (n + x, n + y)\}$.
This gives rise to a key pre-distribution in agents in S_k^1.
Similarly, we can have a key point-distribution among the agents in the set S_k^2.
$S_k^2 = \{a^2_{x,k,z} : x, y \in \{0, 1, ..., n-1\}\}$.
The points corresponding to agent $a^2_{x,k,z}$ is
$P^2_{x,k,z} = \{(x, z), (n + x, n + z)\}$.
Similarly, we can have a key point-distribution among the agents in the set S_k^3.
$S_k^3 = \{a^3_{k,y,z} : y, z \in \{0, 1, ..., n-1\}\}$.
The points corresponding to agent $a^3_{k,y,z}$ is
$P^3_{k,y,z} = \{(y, z), (n + y, n + z)\}$.

6.3 Key-Path Establishment

As mentioned earlier, given two nodes n_1 and n_s key-path establishment is the process of finding a chain of nodes $n_1, n_2, \ldots, n_s$ such that any two consecutive nodes in the chain do have a shared key. It is expected that there will be more than one such key-paths. So we need to find one key-path of minimum number of intermediate nodes in it.

Before we move into discussing the core algorithm, we first discuss a method for shared Key Discovery between two agents $a^r_{i,j,k}$ and $a^r_{i',j',k'}$ both belonging to the same S^r_m for any $r \in \{1, 2, 3\}$ and $i, j, k, i', j', k', m \in \{0, 1, 2, \ldots, n-1\}$.

Case I: If $r = 1$, then $i = i'$. Hence, the points belonging to $a^r_{i,j,k}$ is $\{(j, k), (n + j, n + k)\}$. Similarly, the points belonging to $a^r_{i',j',k'}$ is $\{(j', k'), (n + j', n + k')\}$. Let us denote $p_1 = (j, k)$, $p_2 = (n + j, n + k)$, $p_3 = (j', k')$ and $p_4 = (n + j', n + k')$.

Case II: If $r = 2$, then $j = j'$. Hence, the points belonging to $a^r_{i,j,k}$ is $\{(i, k), (n + i, n + k)\}$. Similarly, the points belonging to $a^r_{i',j',k'}$ is $\{(i', k'), (n + i', n + k')\}$. Let us denote $p_1 = (i, k)$,$p_2 = (n + i, n + k)$, $p_3 = (i', k')$ and $p_4 = (n + i', n + k')$.

Case III: If $r = 3$, then $k = k'$. Hence, the points belonging to $a^r_{i,j,k}$ is $\{(i, j), (n + i, n + j)\}$. Similarly, the points belonging to $a^r_{i',j',k'}$ is $\{(i', j'), (n + i', n + j')\}$. Let us denote $p_1 = (i, j)$,$p_2 = (n + i, n + j)$, $p_3 = (i', j')$ and $p_4 = (n + i', n + j')$.

The algorithm is as follows;

Note that both the agents $a^r_{i,j,k}$ and $a^r_{i',j',k'}$ execute the same code of the algorithm, so they end up finding the same key.

We have used [9] for key pre-distribution in the same group. So, the algorithm to find the shared key between two nodes in the same group can be found in [9]. This algorithm can be used to find a shared key between a node of any group and any agent of the same group.

The algorithm to find the key-path between two nodes $n^i_{(x,y,z)}$ and $n^j_{(x',y',z')}$ belonging to groups (x, y, z) and (x', y', z') respectively is written in Algorithm 2.

Algorithm 1. Algorithm to find common key between two agents

if $i + j + k \leq i' + j' + k'$ **then**
  Let $a_1x + b_1y = c_1$ is the line between p_1 and p_3
  $a_2x + b_2y = c_2$ is the line between p_1 and p_4
  $a_3x + b_3y = c_3$ is the line between p_2 and p_3
  and, $a_4x + b_4y = c_4$ is the line between p_2 and p_4
  if t be such that all keys (a_h, b_h, c_h) are compromised where $h < t \leq 4$ **then**
    OUTPUT (a_t, b_t, c_t).
  else
    OUTPUT No uncompromised common key.
  end if
else
  Let $\alpha_1x + \beta_1y = \gamma_1$ is the line between p_1 and p_3
  $\alpha_2x + \beta_2y = \gamma_2$ is the line between p_1 and p_4
  $\alpha_3x + \beta_3y = \gamma_3$ is the line between p_2 and p_3
  and, $\alpha_4x + \beta_4y = \gamma_4$ is the line between p_2 and p_4
  if t be such that all keys $(\alpha_h, \beta_h, \gamma_h)$ are compromised where $h < t \leq 4$ **then**
    OUTPUT $(\alpha_t, \beta_t, \gamma_t)$.
  else
    OUTPUT No uncompromised common key.
  end if
end if

Algorithm 2. Algorithm to find a key-path between two nodes $n^i_{(x,y,z)}$ and $n^j_{(x,y,z)}$

if $x = x'$ **then**
  the agents $a^1_{(x,y,z)}$ and $a^1_{(x,y',z')}$ in S^1_x have a common key(1).
  the key-path is $\{n^i_{(x,y,z)}, a^1_{(x,y,z)}, a^1_{(x,y',z')}, n^j_{(x',y',z')}\}$
else if $y = y'$ **then**
  the agents $a^2_{(x,y,z)}$ and $a^2_{(x',y,z')}$ in S^2_y have a common key(1)
  the key-path is $\{n^i_{(x,y,z)}, a^2_{(x,y,z)}, a^2_{(x',y,z')}, n^j_{(x',y',z')}\}$
else if $z = z'$ **then**
  the agents $a^3_{(x,y,z)}$ and $a^3_{(x',y',z')}$ in S^3_z have a common key(1)
  the key-path is $\{n^i_{(x,y,z)}, a^3_{(x,y,z)}, a^3_{(x,y',z')}, n^j_{(x',y',z')}\}$
else
  the key-path is
  $\{n^i_{(x,y,z)}, a^1_{(x,y,z)}, a^1_{(x,y',z')}, a^2_{(x,y',z')}, a^2_{(x',y',z')}, n^j_{(x',y',z')}\}$
  or,
  $\{n^i_{(x,y,z)}, a^2_{(x,y,z)}, a^2_{(x',y,z')}, a^3_{(x',y,z')}, a^3_{(x',y',z')}, n^j_{(x',y',z')}\}$
  or,
  $\{n^i_{(x,y,z)}, a^3_{(x,y,z)}, a^3_{(x',y',z)}, a^1_{(x',y',z)}, a^1_{(x',y',z')}, n^j_{(x',y',z')}\}$
end if

6.4 Resiliency

We have used $3n$ different sets of keys, for key pre-distribution in $3n$ number of S^i_j, $i \in \{1,2,3\}, j \in \{0,1,...n-1\}$ where each set contains q^2+q number of keys for a prime $q \geq 2n$. So, if an agent corresponding to a group gets compromised then this will affect only the links corresponding to a particular S^i_j to which the agent belongs. The links of other S^i_j's will remain unaffected.

It is observable that we could have assigned only one point rather than two points corresponding to an agent belonging to a particular S^i_j. In other words we could have used a key pre-distribution where in the set S^3_k,
We take a prime $q \geq n$
$S^3_k = \{a^3_{x,y,k} : x, y \in \{0,1,...,n-1\}\}$6.2.
and

$$P^3_{x,y,k} = \{(x,y)\}$$

Then each agent would get precisely $q+1$ many keys as there are $q+1$ number of lines through any point (x,y) in $AG(2,q)$. Now, if any agent(say $a^3_{x,y,k}$) gets compromised, then this would cause all the $q+1$ keys in it get exposed. Since each key correspond to a line in $AG(2,q)$ and a line passes through q many points. These q many points may correspond to q many nodes that shared the same key. Since that shared key is exposed, so $\binom{q}{2}$ number of links, one for every pair of nodes are broken. So, for one key $\binom{q}{2}$ number of links are broken. Hence for $q+1$ number of keys in that agent atmost $(q+1)\binom{q}{2}$ number of links get broken.

Alternately, if we use two points per agent, this will increase the number of links between two nodes. For example in our design the maximum number of links between two nodes is 4. So, if one link gets broken then also there can be more links in terms of uncompromised keys between two nodes. Further because of the memory constraint we can not increase the number of keys per node or in other words the number of points corresponding to a node.

Ruj & Roy [39] proposed a measure for resiliency of any key pre-distribution scheme. This measure is called $V(s)$. $V(s)$ is defined as the proportion of nodes disconnected, when s nodes are compromised. That is, if N is the total number of nodes in the network and t, the number of nodes disconnected when s nodes are compromised, then

$$V(s) = \frac{t}{N-s}$$

Theorem 3. *For any set $S^i_j, i \in \{1,2,3\}, j \in \{0,1,...,n-1\}$, if s number of agents belonging to that set S^i_j gets compromised then an uncompromised agent will have an unexposed link to any uncompromised node if $s < (q+1)/2$.*

Proof. Let $i=1$. Let $a^1_{(j,y_1,z_1)}, a^1_{(j,y_2,z_2)}, \ldots, a^1_{(j,y_s,z_s)}$ are the s agents of S^1_j. Let $a^1_{(j,y_t,z_t)}, t \notin \{1,2,\ldots,s\}$ be an uncompromised agent. There are two points (α_1,β_1), $(\alpha_2,\beta_2) \in AG(2,q)$ that correspond to $a^1_{(j,y_t,z_t)}$. There are $q+1$ number of lines through a point (α_1,β_1) corresponding to $a^1_{(j,y_t,z_t)}$.

There are at the most $2s$ distinct points in $a^1_{(j,y_1,z_1)}, a^1_{(j,y_2,z_2)}, \ldots, a^1_{(j,y_s,z_s)}$. Two points cannot be present together in more than one distinct line. So, there can be at most

$2s$ distinct lines that pass through (α_1, β_1) as well as each of the points in $a^1_{(j,y_1,z_1)}$, $a^1_{(j,y_2,z_2)}, \ldots, a^1_{(j,y_s,z_s)}$. If $2s < q+1$, then (α_1, β_1) will contain at least one line that does not pass through the compromised nodes. So $a^1_{(j,y_t,z_t)}$ will not be disconnected, if $s < (q+1)/2$.

This suggest that for our key pre-distribution scheme for any $S^i_j, i \in \{1,2,3\}, j \in \{0,1,...,n-1\}$, $V(s) = 0$ for all $s < (q+1)/2$.

7 Conclusion

In this paper, we have proposed two novel approaches for key pre-distribution in a heterogenous wireless sensor network. Here, we assumed the network is divided into a 3-dimensional grid consisting many small groups. For each group the sensor nodes inside it uses a different key pre-distribution scheme and they can directly communicate between each other. If any two nodes from two different groups want to communicate, they need to do so via some special nodes called agents. The schemes we developed focuses on the inter group key pre-distribution and we use an existing scheme for intra-group key pre-distribution. Each group contains three of such special nodes called agents. Now whenever two nodes want to communicate, they establish a key-path comprising two agents from two groups and some additional agents. We have discussed the key-path establishment procedure for each of the two schemes we discussed.

References

1. Steiner, J.G., Neuman, B.C., Schiller, J.I.: Kerberos: An authentication service for open network systems. USENIX Winter, 191–202 (1988)
2. Gura, N., Patel, A., Wander, A., Eberle, H., Shantz, S.C.: Comparing elliptic curve cryptography and RSA on 8-bit cpus. In: Joye, M., Quisquater, J.-J. (eds.) CHES 2004. LNCS, vol. 3156, pp. 119–132. Springer, Heidelberg (2004)
3. Malan, D.J., Welsh, M., Smith, M.D.: Implementing public-key infrastructure for sensor networks. TOSN 4(4) (2008)
4. Xu, D., Huang, J., Dwoskin, J., Chiang, M., Lee, R.: Re-examining probabilistic versus deterministic key management. In: Proceedings of the 2007 IEEE International Symposium on Information Theory (ISIT), pp. 2586–2590 (2007)
5. Street, A.P., Street, D.J.: Combinatorics of Experimental Design, Oxford U. P (Clarendon), p. 400+xiv (1987) ISBN 0198532563
6. Lee, J., Stinson, D.R.: On the construction of practical key predistribution schemes for distributed sensor networks using combinatorial designs. ACM Trans. Inf. Syst. Secur. 11(2) (2008)
7. Ruj, S., Roy, B.: Key predistribution using combinatorial designs for grid-group deployment scheme in wireless sensor networks. ACM Transaction on Sensor Networks 6(1), 14:1–14:28 (2009)
8. Chan, H., Perrig, A.: PIKE: peer intermediaries for key establishment in sensor networks. In: INFOCOM, pp. 524–535. IEEE, Los Alamitos (2005)
9. Çamtepe, S.A., Yener, B.: Combinatorial design of key distribution mechanisms for wireless sensor networks. In: Samarati, P., Ryan, P.Y.A., Gollmann, D., Molva, R. (eds.) ESORICS 2004. LNCS, vol. 3193, pp. 293–308. Springer, Heidelberg (2004)

10. Çamtepe, S.A., Yener, B.: Combinatorial design of key distribution mechanisms for wireless sensor networks. IEEE/ACM Trans. Netw. 15(2), 346–358 (2007)
11. Lee, J., Stinson, D.R.: A combinatorial approach to key predistribution for distributed sensor networks. In: IEEE Wireless Communications and Networking Conference, WCNC 2005, New Orleans, LA, USA, pp. 1200–1205 (2005)
12. Lee, J., Stinson, D.R.: Deterministic key predistribution schemes for distributed sensor networks. In: Handschuh, H., Hasan, M.A. (eds.) SAC 2004. LNCS, vol. 3357, pp. 294–307. Springer, Heidelberg (2004)
13. Ruj, S., Roy, B.: Key predistribution using partially balanced designs in wireless sensor networks. In: Stojmenovic, I., Thulasiram, R.K., Yang, L.T., Jia, W., Guo, M., de Mello, R.F. (eds.) ISPA 2007. LNCS, vol. 4742, pp. 431–445. Springer, Heidelberg (2007)
14. Chakrabarti, D., Maitra, S., Roy, B.: A key pre-distribution scheme for wireless sensor networks: Merging blocks in combinatorial design. In: Zhou, J., López, J., Deng, R.H., Bao, F. (eds.) ISC 2005. LNCS, vol. 3650, pp. 89–103. Springer, Heidelberg (2005)
15. Eschenauer, L., Gligor, V.D.: A key-management scheme for distributed sensor networks. In: Atluri, V. (ed.) ACM Conference on Computer and Communications Security, pp. 41–47. ACM, New York (2002)
16. Chan, H., Perrig, A., Song, D.X.: Random key predistribution schemes for sensor networks. In: IEEE Symposium on Security and Privacy, pp. 197–213. IEEE Computer Society, Los Alamitos (2003)
17. Blom, R.: An optimal class of symmetric key generation systems. In: Beth, T., Cot, N., Ingemarsson, I. (eds.) EUROCRYPT 1984. LNCS, vol. 209, pp. 335–338. Springer, Heidelberg (1985)
18. Blundo, C., Santis, A.D., Herzberg, A., Kutten, S., Vaccaro, U., Yung, M.: Perfectly-secure key distribution for dynamic conferences. In: Brickell, E.F. (ed.) CRYPTO 1992. LNCS, vol. 740, pp. 471–486. Springer, Heidelberg (1993)
19. Du, W., Deng, J., Han, Y.S., Varshney, P.K., Katz, J., Khalili, A.: A pairwise key predistribution scheme for wireless sensor networks. ACM Trans. Inf. Syst. Secur. 8(2), 228–258 (2005)
20. Mitchell, C.J., Piper, F.: Key storage in secure networks. Discrete Applied Mathematics 21, 215–228 (1988)
21. Chakrabarti, D., Maitra, S., Roy, B.: A key pre-distribution scheme for wireless sensor networks: merging blocks in combinatorial design. Int. J. Inf. Sec. 5(2), 105–114 (2006)
22. Blackburn, S.R., Etzion, T., Martin, K.M., Paterson, M.B.: Efficient key predistribution for grid-based wireless sensor networks. In: Safavi-Naini, R. (ed.) ICITS 2008. LNCS, vol. 5155, pp. 54–69. Springer, Heidelberg (2008)
23. Wei, R., Wu, J.: Product construction of key distribution schemes for sensor networks. In: Handschuh, H., Hasan, M.A. (eds.) SAC 2004. LNCS, vol. 3357, pp. 280–293. Springer, Heidelberg (2004)
24. Ruj, S., Roy, B.: Revisiting key predistribution using transversal designs for a grid-based deployment scheme. international Journal of Distributed Sensor Networks, (accepted)
25. Ruj, S., Roy, B.: Key predistribution using partially balanced designs in wireless sensor networks. International Journal of High Performance Computing and Networking (IJHPCN) (accepted)
26. M.A.S. Jr., Barreto, P.S., Margi, C.B., Carvalho, T.C.: A survey on key management mechanisms for distributed wireless sensor networks. Computer Networks 54(15), 2591–2612 (2010)
27. Stinson, D.R.: Combinatorial Designs: Constructions and Analysis. Springer, Heidelberg (2004)
28. Hirschfeld, J.: Projective Geometries Over Finite Fields, Oxford, U.K (1979)

29. Storme, L., Govaerts, P., Beule, J.D., Lemens, P.: Projective geometries (pg) share package for gap4. (2004), `http://cage.rug.ac.be/jdebeule/pg/` (last accessed October 2, 2010)
30. Du, W., Deng, J., Han, Y.S., Chen, S., Varshney, P.K.: A key management scheme for wireless sensor networks using deployment knowledge. In: INFOCOM, pp. 261–268 (2004)
31. Du, W., Deng, J., Han, Y.S., Varshney, P.K.: A key predistribution scheme for sensor networks using deployment knowledge. IEEE Trans. Dependable Sec. Comput. 3(1), 62–77 (2006)
32. Yu, Z., Guan, Y.: A key pre-distribution scheme using deployment knowledge for wireless sensor networks. In: IPSN, pp. 261–268. IEEE, Los Alamitos (2005)
33. Yu, Z., Guan, Y.: A key management scheme using deployment knowledge for wireless sensor networks. IEEE Transactions of Parallel and Distributed Systems 19(10), 1411–1425 (2008)
34. Liu, D., Ning, P.: Improving key predistribution with deploy- ment knowledge in static sensor networks. TOSN 1(2), 204–239 (2005)
35. Younis, M.F., Ghumman, K., Eltoweissy, M.: Location-aware combinatorial key management scheme for clustered sensor networks. IEEE Trans. Parallel Distrib. Syst. 17(8), 865–882 (2006)
36. Huang, D., Mehta, M., Medhi, D., Harn, L.: Location-aware key management scheme for wireless sensor networks. In: 2nd ACM Workshop on Security of Ad Hoc and Sensor Networks, SASN, Washington, USA, pp. 29–42 (2004)
37. Simonova, K., Ling, A.C.H., Wang, X.S.: Location- aware key predistribution scheme for wide area wireless sensor networks. In: Zhu, S., Liu, D. (eds.) SASN, pp. 157–168. ACM, New York (2006)
38. Chan, H., Perrig, A.: PIKE: peer intermediaries for key estab- lishment in sensor networks. In: INFOCOM, pp. 524–535. IEEE, Los Alamitos (2005)
39. Ruj, S., Maitra, S., Roy, B.K.: Key Predistribution Using Transversal Design on a Grid of Wireless Sensor Network. Ad Hoc & Sensor Wireless Networks 5(3-4), 247–264 (2008)
40. Stinson, D.R.: Cryptography: Theory and Practice, 3rd edn. CRC Press Inc, Boca Raton (2006)

Novel Methods for Montgomery Modular Multiplication for Public Key Cryptosystems

V.R. Venkatasubramani, M. Surendar, and S. Rajaram

Department of Electronics and Communication Engineering
Thiagarajar College of Engineering, Madurai, India

Abstract. Extension of Montgomery multiplication algorithms in GF(p) are studied and analyzed. The time and space requirements of various state-of-the-art algorithms are presented. We propose Modified Montgomery Modular Multiplication Algorithms that reduces the number of computational operations such as number of additions, memory reads and writes involved in the existing algorithms, thereby, saving considerable time and area for execution. Many design examples has been solved to prove the theoretical correctness of the proposed algorithms. Complexity analysis shows that Modified Coarsely Integrated Scanning (MCIOS) consume less space and time compared to other modified Montgomery Algorithms. To verify the logical correctness, the proposed MCIOS algorithm was implemented in Xilinx Spartan3E FPGA. The total memory for execution of 64 –bit operand is 135484 KB for MCIOS and 140496 KB for existing Coarsely Integrated Scanning (CIOS) method. Also, the proposed algorithm can be changed to be suitable for any arbitrary Galois field size with little modifications.

Keywords: Montgomery multiplication, Scalar multiplication, Elliptic curve cryptography (ECC), Field-programmable gate array (FPGA).

1 Introduction

It is widely recognized that security issues will play a crucial role in the majority of future computer and communication systems. A central tool for achieving system security is cryptographic algorithms. For performance as well as for physical security reasons, it is often advantageous to realize cryptographic algorithms in hardware. The RSA algorithm [8], the Diffie - Hellman key exchange scheme [2] require the computation of modular exponentiation, which is broken into a series of modular multiplications by the application of the binary or m-ary methods [5].The Elliptic curve cryptography (ECC) [11,12] require the computation of iterative modular multiplication.

In 1985, Neil Koblitz and Victor Miller independently proposed the elliptic curve cryptosystem, whose security rests on the discrete logarithm problem over points on an elliptic curve. Elliptic curve cryptography can be used to provide both a digital signature scheme and an encryption scheme. With the apparent advantage of high cryptographic strength relative to key size, elliptic curve cryptosystems [11, 12] have gained much popularity in the implementation of discrete logarithm based public key protocols. The shorter key size generally leads to improved computational efficiencies

D.C. Wyld et al. (Eds.): CNSA 2011, CCIS 196, pp. 320–330, 2011.

and smaller storage and bandwidth requirements. Although elliptic curve cryptosystem can be based on finite field of any characteristic, it is generally practical to implement within the prime or binary finite field. The algorithms presented are especially for prime finite field. However the algorithms can be easily extended to the binary finite field [10].

Implementation of Elliptic Curve Cryptosystems follows a layered hierarchical scheme [14]. The performance of the top layers of the hierarchy is greatly influenced by the performance of the underlying layers. It is therefore important to have efficient implementations of finite field operations such as additions, multiplications, reductions and inversion.

One of the most interesting and useful advances has been the introduction of Montgomery multiplication algorithm due to Peter L. Mongtomery [6] for finite field modular multiplication. This algorithm is still considered to be the high-speed and space-efficient algorithm for modular multiplication. This algorithm is used to speed up the modular multiplications and squarings required during the exponentiation process. The Montgomery algorithm computes

$$\text{MonPro}(a, b) = a \cdot b \cdot r^{-1} \pmod{n} \tag{1}$$

given $a, b < n$ and r such that $\gcd(n, r) = 1$. Even though the algorithm works for any r which is relatively prime to n, it is more useful when r is taken to be a power of 2. In this case, the Montgomery algorithm performs divisions by a power of 2, which is an intrinsically fast operation on general-purpose computers; this leads to a simpler implementation than ordinary modular multiplication [7].

In this paper, the existing Montgomery modular multiplication algorithms and modified Montgomery modular multiplication algorithms for computing MonPro (a, b) are compared and analyzed. Many design examples has been solved to prove the theoretical correctness of the proposed modified Montgomery modular multiplication algorithms. Complexity analysis shows that modified algorithms consume less space and time compared to existing Montgomery Algorithms [1]. Modified Montgomery modular multiplication algorithms reduces the number of computational operations such as number of additions, memory reads and writes involved in the existing algorithms, thereby, saving considerable time and area for execution. Reducing these operations will subsequently reduce the power consumption. We have considered the most used Separated Operand Scanning (SOS), Coarsely Integrated Operand Scanning (CIOS), and Finely Integrated Operand Scanning (FIOS) algorithms [1] for analysis and performance comparison with the modified Montgomery modular multiplication algorithms.

2 Montgomery Multiplication

Let the modulus n be a k-bit integer, i.e., $2^{k-1} \leq n < 2^k$, and let r be 2^k. The Montgomery multiplication algorithm requires that r and n be relatively prime, i.e., $\gcd(r, n) = \gcd(2^k, n) = 1$. This requirement is satisfied if n is odd. In order to describe the Mongtomery multiplication algorithm, we first define the n-residue of an integer $a < n$ as $\bar{a} = a \cdot r \pmod{n}$. It is straightforward to show that the set

$$\{a \,.\, r \bmod n \mid 0 \le a \le n\text{-}1\}$$

is a complete residue system, i.e., it contains all numbers between 0 and n -1. Thus, there is one-to-one correspondence between the numbers in the range 0 and n - 1 and the numbers in the above set. The Montgomery reduction algorithm exploits this property by introducing a much faster multiplication routine which computes the n-residue of the product of the two integers whose n-residues are given. Given two n-residues $\bar{a}$ and $\bar{b}$, the Montgomery product is defined as the n-residue

$$\bar{c} = \bar{a}.\bar{b}.r^{-1}(\bmod n)$$

Where r^{-1} is the inverse of r modulo n, i.e., it is the number with the property

$$r^{-1} \,.\, r = 1 \pmod n$$

The resulting number c is indeed the n-residue of the product $c = a \,.\, b \pmod n$, since

$$\bar{c} = \bar{a}.\bar{b}.r^{-1}(\bmod n)$$

$$= a \,.\, r \,.b \,.\, r \,.\, r^{-1} \pmod n$$

$$= c \,.\, r \pmod n$$

In order to describe the Montgomery reduction algorithm, we need an additional quantity, n', which is the integer with the property $r \,.\, r^{-1} - n \;\; n' = 1$. The integers r^{-1} and n' can both be computed by the extended Euclidean algorithm [5]. The computation of MonPro($\bar{a}$, $\bar{b}$) is achieved as follows:

Function MonPro($\bar{a}$, $\bar{b}$)
Step 1. $t := \bar{a} \,.\, \bar{b}$
Step 2. $u := (t + (t.\, n' \bmod r)\, n)/r$
Step 3. if $u > n$ then return $u - n$ else return u

Multiplication modulo r and division by r are both intrinsically fast operations, since r is a power of 2. Thus the Montgomery product algorithm is potentially faster and simpler than ordinary computation of $a.\ b$ mod n, which involves division by n. However, since conversion from an ordinary residue to an n-residue, computation of n', and conversion back to an ordinary residue are time-consuming, it is not efficient to use the Montgomery product computation algorithm when a single modular multiplication is to be performed. It is more suitable when several modular multiplications with respect to the same modulus are required. Such is the case when one needs to compute modular exponentiation in RSA and scalar multiplication in ECC. Using the binary method for computing the powers [5], the exponentiation operation is replaced by a series of square and multiplication operations modulo *n in RSA*. In ECC scalar multiplication operation is replaced by a series of point doubling and addition operations modulo n.

In typical implementations, operations on large numbers are performed by breaking the numbers into words. If w is the word size of the computer, then a number can be thought of as a sequence of integers each represented in radix $W = 2^w$. If these "multi-precision" numbers require s words in the radix W representation, then we take r as $r = 2^{sw}$.

In the following sections, we will give several algorithms for performing the Montgomery multiplication MonPro(a, b), and analyze their time and space requirements. The time analysis is performed by counting the total number of multiplications, additions (subtractions), and memory read and writes operations in terms of the input size parameter s. For example, the following operation

$$(C,S) := t[i+j] + a[j]*b[i] + C$$

is assumed to require three memory reads, two additions, and one multiplication since most microprocessors multiply two one-word numbers, leaving the two- word result in one or two registers. Multi-precision integers are assumed to reside in memory throughout the computations. Therefore, the assignment operations performed within a routine correspond to the read or write operations between a register and memory. They are counted to calculate the proportion of the memory access time in the total running time of the Montgomery multiplication algorithm. In our analysis, loop establishment and index computations are not taken into account. We assume the registers that are available are those to hold the carry C and the sum S as above (or equivalently, borrow and difference for subtraction). Obviously, in many microprocessors there will be more registers, but this gives a first-order approximation to the running time, sufficient for a general comparison of the approaches. Actual implementation on particular processors gives a more detailed comparison. The space analysis is performed by counting the total number of words used as the temporary space. However, the space required to keep the input and output values a, b, n, n_0' and u is not taken into account.

3 Existing Algorithms

There are a variety of ways to perform the Montgomery multiplication [1,4]. In all cases the algorithms are described as operations on multi-precision numbers. Thus it is straightforward to rewrite the algorithms in an arbitrary radix, e.g., in binary or radix-4 form for hardware. The five existing algorithms are:

- Separated Operand Scanning (SOS)
- Coarsely Integrated Operand Scanning (CIOS).
- Finely Integrated Operand Scanning (FIOS)
- Finely Integrated Product Scanning (FIPS)
- Coarsely Integrated Hybrid Scanning (CIHS)

A brief inspection of the SOS method for counting the number of operations, shows that it requires $(2s^2+s)$ multiplications, $(4s^2+4s+2)$ additions, $(6s^2+7s+3)$ reads, and $(2s^2+6s+2)$ writes. Furthermore, the SOS method requires a total of $(2s+2)$ word for temporary results, which are used to store the $(2s + 1)$-word array t and the one-word variable m. Other algorithms (CIOS, FIOS, FIPS and CIHS) are given in [1].

4 Proposed Algorithms

In this paper we modified Separated Operand Scanning (SOS), Coarsely Integrated Operand Scanning (CIOS) and Finely Integrated Operand Scanning (FIOS) algorithms to improve its time-space consumption. The modified algorithms are named as follows:

- Modified Separated Operand Scanning (MSOS)
- Modified Coarsely Integrated Operand Scanning (MCIOS).
- Modified Finely Integrated Operand Scanning (MFIOS)

CIOS is considered to be the most efficient one for FPGA implementation because of its comparatively less space-time requirement.

4.1 Modified Separated Operand Scanning (MSOS) Method

The MonPro(a, b) is calculated by computing the product $a.b$ first with an improvement using

```
(C,S) := a[0]*b[0]
t[0] := S
for j=1 to s-1
        (C,S) := a[j]*b[0]+C
        t[j] := S
t[s] := C
for i=1 to s-1
    C := 0
   (C,S) := t[i+j] + a[j]*b[i]
   t[i] := S
    for j=1 to s-1
       (C,S) := t[i+j] + a[j]*b[i] + C
       t[i+j] := S
   t[i+s] := C
```

Secondly, we compute u using the formula $u: = (t + m. n)/r$, where $m: = t .n'$ mod r. as like in SOS method but in an improved manner using

```
for i=0 to s-1
  C := 0
  m := t[i]*n'[0] mod W
(C,S) := t[i] + m*n[0]
  for j=1 to s-1
    (C,S) := t[i+j] + m*n[j] + C
     t[i+j] := S
ADD (t[i+s],C)
```

A brief inspection of the MSOS method, based on our techniques for counting the number of operations, shows that it requires $2s^2 +s$ multiplications, $4s^2 +2$ additions, $6s^2 +5s+3$ reads, and $2s^2 + 4s + 2$ writes.

4.2 Modified Coarsely Integrated Operand Scanning (MCIOS) Method

The Coarsely Integrated Operand Scanning (CIOS) method is the most efficient of all five algorithms, at least for the general class of processor [1]. This CIOS algorithm is further improved by modifying it using

```
for i=0 to s-1
   C: = 0
if (i = =0)
(C,S) :=  a[0]*b[0]
t[0]=S;
for j=1 to s-1
    (C,S) :=  a[j]*b[i] + C
    t[j] := S
t[s]=c
else
(C,S) := t[0]+ a[0]*b[0]
t[0]=S;
for j=1 to s-1
    (C,S) :=  t[j]+a[j]*b[i] + C
    t[j] := S
(C,S) := t[s] + C
 t[s] := S
 t[s+1] := C
 C: = 0
 m := t[0]*n'[0] mod W
 (C,S) := t[0] + m*n[0]
 for j=1 to s-1
     (C,S) := t[j] + m*n[j] + C
      t [ j-1] := S
(C,S) := t[s] + C
t[s-1] := S
if (i = = 0)
    t [s]=C
else
t[s] := t[s+1] + C
```

Modified Coarsely Integrated Operand Scanning (MCIOS) method consists of a few conditional statements, whose time consumption is very negligible compared to operations such as multiplication, addition, reads and writes. The MCIOS method requires $2s^2+s$ multiplications, $4s^2+2s+2$ additions, $6s^2+6s$ reads, and $2s^2+5s$ writes, including the final multi-precision subtraction, and uses $s + 3$ words of memory space. This shows a significant improvement over the CIOS method.

4.3 Modified Finely Integrated Operand Scanning (MFIOS)

FIOS method integrates the two inner loops of the CIOS method into one by computing the multiplications and additions in the same loop. The multiplications $a_j \cdot b_i$ and $m \cdot n_j$ are computed in the same loop, and then added to form the final t. Improvement in FIOS is made using

```
(C,S) := a[0]*b[0]
 t[1]=C
m := S*n'[0] mod W
 (C,S) := S + m*n[0]
for j=1 to s-1
          (C,S) := t[j] + a[j]*b[0] + C
         t[j+1]=C
          (C,S) := S + m*n[j]
         t[j-1] := S
(C,S) := t[s] + C
t[s-1] := S
t[s] :=  C
for i=1 to s-1
        (C,S) := t[0] + a[0]*b[i]
        ADD (t[1],C)
      m := S*n'[0] mod W
      (C,S) := S + m*n[0]
for j=1 to s-1
          (C,S) := t[j] + a[j]*b[i] + C
          ADD (t[j+1],C)
          (C,S) := S + m*n[j]
         t[j-1] := S
(C,S) := t[s] + C
t[s-1] := S
t[s] :=  C
t[s+1] := 0
```

The MFIOS method requires $2s^2+s$ multiplications, $5s^2+3s+2$ additions, $7s^2+5s+2$ reads, and $3s^2+4s+1$ writes, including the final multi-precision subtraction. From Table 5.2, FIOS requires about s^2 more additions, writes, and reads compared to MFIOS method. The total amount of temporary space required is $s + 3$ words.

5 Complexity Analysis

The complexity analysis for the existing CIOS method is given in [1]. The complexity analysis for the Modified CIOS (MCIOS) is presented as follows:

Calculating the operations of the MCIOS method:

STATEMENTS	Operations				Iterations
	Multiplications	Adds	Reads	Writes	
for *i=0* to *s-1*	-	-	-	-	-
C := 0	-	-	-	-	*s*
if (i = =0)					
*(C,S) := a[0]*b[0]*	*1*	-	2	-	*1*
t[0]=S;	-	-	-	*1*	*1*
for *j=1* to *s-1*	-	-	-	-	*1*
*(C,S) := a[j]*b[i] + C*	*1*	*1*	2	-	*(s-1)*
t[j] := S	-	-	-	*1*	*(s-1)*
t[s]=c	-	-	-	*1*	*1*
else					
*(C,S) := t[0]+ a[0]*b[0]*	*1*	*1*	*3*	-	*(s-1)*
t[0]=S;	-	-	-	*1*	*(s-1)*
for *j=1* to *s-1*	-	-	-	-	*(s-1)*
*(C,S) := t[j]+a[j]*b[i] + C*	*1*	2	*3*	-	$(s-1)^2$
t[j] := S	-	-	-	*1*	$(s-1)^2$
(C,S) := t[s] + C	-	*1*	*1*	-	*(s-1)*
t[s] := S	-	-	-	*1*	*(s-1)*
t[s+1] := C	-	-	-	*1*	*(s-1)*
C := 0	-	-	-	-	*(s-1)*
*m := t[0]*n'[0]* mod *W*	*1*	-	2	*1*	*(s-1)*
*(C,S) := t[0] + m*n[0]*	*1*	*1*	*3*	-	*(s-1)*
for *j=1* to *s-1*	-	-	-	-	*(s-1)*
*(C,S) := t[j] + m*n[j] + C*	*1*	2	*3*	-	$(s-1)^2$
t [j-1] := S	-	-	-	*1*	$(s-1)^2$
(C,S) := t[s] + C	-	*1*	*1*	-	*(s-1)*
t[s-1] := S	-	-	-	*1*	*(s-1)*
if (i = = 0)					
t [s]=C	-	-	-	*1*	*1*
else					
t[s] := t[s+1] + C	-	*1*	*1*	*1*	*(s-1)*
	$2s^2+s$	$4s^2-1$	$6s^2+4s-2$	$2s^2+4s-1$	-
Final subtraction	*0*	*2(s + 1)*	*2(s + 1)*	*s+ 1*	*1*
Total	$2s^2+s$	$4s^2+2s+1$	$6s^2+6s$	$2s^2+5s$	-

Comparing Time and space requirements of the various methods:

Method	Multiplications	Adds	Reads	Writes	Space
SOS	$2s^2+s$	$4s^2+4s+2$	$6s^2+7s+3$	$2s^2+6s+2$	$2s+2$
MSOS	$2s^2+s$	$4s^2+2$	$6s^2+5s+3$	$2s^2+4s+2$	$2s+2$
CIOS	$2s^2+s$	$4s^2+4s+2$	$6s^2+7s+2$	$2s^2+5s+1$	$s+3$
MCIOS	$2s^2+s$	$4s^2+2s+2$	$6s^2+6s$	$2s^2+5s$	$s+3$
FIOS	$2s^2+s$	$5s^2+3s+2$	$7s^2+5s+2$	$3s^2+4s+1$	$s+3$
MFIOS	$2s^2+s$	$4s^2+s+1$	$6s^2+3s+1$	$2s^2+3s+1$	s+3

6 Results and Discussions

The major bottleneck process in Elliptic curve cryptosystems is scalar multiplication which involves various group and field operations. The core of scalar multiplier is Montgomery modular multiplication algorithms. For performing this field modular multiplications SOS, CIOS and FIOS algorithms were used and also modified algorithms - MSOS, MCIOS and MFIOS were used for obtaining high efficiency. These design entry is done through verilog coding and implementation is done in Spartan 3 FPGA. The device chosen is 3s200ft256-5.

Table 1. Total Memory for the Execution

Method	Total Memory for the Execution of 64 bit inputs
CIOS	140496 kilobytes
MCIOS	135484 kilobytes

Table 2. Timing Detail

Method	Time for Execution of 64 bit inputs
CIOS	102.812ns (66.302ns logic, 36.510ns route) (64.5% logic, 35.5% route)
MCIOS	99.287ns (65.102ns logic, 34.185ns route) (65.6% logic, 34.4% route)

Comparing our modified MCIOS Montgomery modular multiplication to the existing CIOS method, the timing results shows about 3.6 percent improvement for the multiplication and 3.5 percent improvement in memory required for the execution of 64 bit inputs. Further, the Montgomery multiplication in a prime field can be easily extended to the binary extension field [10] by replacing the integers n, 2^k, a, b, *and* c with the polynomials $P(x)$, x^n, $A(x)$, $B(x)$, and $C(x)$, where $P(x)$ is an irreducible polynomial of degree n and $A(x)$, $B(x)$, $C(x)$ are polynomials whose degree is less than n. Then, (1) becomes

$$C(x) = A(x)\, B(x)\, x^{-n} \bmod P(x).$$

7 Conclusion

In this paper we proposed novel methods for efficient implementation of Montgomery Modular Multiplication Algorithms in prime finite fields. Complexity analysis shows that Modified Coarsely Integrated Scanning (MCIOS) consume less space and time. This resulted in lesser time and space requirements on a FPGA. Implementation results shows that our modified MCIOS Montgomery modular multiplication method improves by about 3.6 percent improvement for multiplication and 3.5 percent improvement in memory required for the execution of 64 bit inputs compared to the existing CIOS method. Further the algorithms can be changed to be suitable for any arbitrary Galois field size and can be easily extended to the binary extension field with little modifications.

References

1. Koc, C.K., Acar, T., Kaliski Jr, B.S.: Analyzing and Comparing Montgomery Multiplication Algorithms. IEEE Micro 16(3), 26–33 (1996)
2. Diffie, W., Hellman, M.E.: New Directions in Cryptography. IEEE Trans. Information Theory 22(11), 644–654 (1976)
3. Even, S.: Systolic modular multiplication. In: Menezes, A.J., Vanstone, S.A. (eds.) CRYPTO 1990. LNCS, vol. 537, pp. 619–623. Springer, Heidelberg (1991)
4. Kaliski Jr., B.S.: The Z80180 and big-number arithmetic. Dr. Dobb's Journal, 50–58 (1993)
5. Knuth, D.E.: The Art of Computer Programming: Seminumerical Algorithms, 2nd edn., vol. 2. Addison-Wesley, Reading (1981)
6. Montgomery, P.L.: Modular multiplication without trial division. Mathematics of Computation 44(170), 519–521 (1985)
7. Naccache, D., M'Raihi, D., Raphaeli, D.: Can Montgomery parasites be avoided? A design methodology based on key and cryptosystem modifications. Designs, Codes and Cryptography 5(1), 73–80 (1995)
8. Rivest, R.L., Shamir, A., Adleman, L.: A method for obtaining digital signatures and public-key cryptosystems. Communications of the ACM 21(2), 120–126 (1978)
9. Han, Y., Leong, P.-C., Tan, P.-C., Zhang, J.: Fast Algorithms for Elliptic Curve Cryptosystems over Binary Finite Field. In: Lam, K.-Y., Okamoto, E., Xing, C. (eds.) ASIACRYPT 1999. LNCS, vol. 1716, pp. 75–85. Springer, Heidelberg (1999)

10. KoH, G.K., Acar, T., Kaliski, B.S.: Montgomery Multiplication in GF(2^k). Designs, Codes and Cryptography 14(1), 57–69 (1998)
11. Koblitz, N.: Elliptic curve cryptosystems. Mathematics of Computation 48, 203–209 (1987)
12. Miller, V.: Use of elliptic curves in cryptography. In: Williams, H.C. (ed.) CRYPTO 1985. LNCS, vol. 218, pp. 417–426. Springer, Heidelberg (1986)
13. Guajardo, J., Paar, C.: Efficient algorithms for elliptic curve cryptosystems. In: Kaliski Jr., B.S. (ed.) CRYPTO 1997. LNCS, vol. 1294, pp. 342–356. Springer, Heidelberg (1997)
14. Hankerson, D., Menezes, A., Vanstone, S.: Guide to Elliptic Curve Cryptography. Springer, New York (2004)

Protection against Denial of Service and Input Manipulation Vulnerabilities in Service Oriented Architecture

Alwyn Roshan Pais, Deepak D.J., and B.R. Chandavarkar

Department of Computer Science and Engineering,
National Institute of Technology,
Karnataka (NITK), Surathkal, India
{alwyn.pais,deepak3884}@gmail.com, sai_srajan@yahoo.co.in

Abstract. Organizations are increasingly adopting Service Oriented Architecture (SOA) to build their distributed applications. SOA is a computing paradigm, emphasizing dynamic service discovery composition and interoperability. Web services are a technology that can be used to implement SOA and are increasingly becoming the SOA implementation of choice. Because a Web service relies on some of the same underlying HTTP and Web-based architecture as common Web applications, it is susceptible to similar threats and vulnerabilities. There are many vulnerabilities in web services such as SQL injection, Denial of Service, etc. that cannot be detected by web service standards and conventional firewalls. In this paper, we present a detailed design of XML firewall that can be used to prevent different vulnerabilities by validating the input xml documents before being processed by the web services. Also the XML firewall does the function of authentication, authorization and session management. We designed a modular architecture for XML firewall where each module checks for a particular vulnerability. We have also developed methods to detect and prevent SQL injection and Denial of Service vulnerabilities.

Keywords: Service Oriented Architecture, XML firewall, Web services, Input manipulation, Denial of service (DOS), XDOS, SQL Injection , SOAP, Web Service Security.

1 Introduction

A service-oriented architecture is essentially a collection of services. These services communicate with each other. Services are well-defined units of functionality that are accessible over the network via standard protocols [14]. They are invoked by software, and are not accessed by a human user. In other words, services are more like a remote procedure calls. The system that implements a service is called a provider, while the system that uses the service is called a consumer. The central standards relevant to service implementation and deployment are XML, SOAP, WSDL, and UDDI and services that conform to these standards are called web services.

D.C. Wyld et al. (Eds.): CNSA 2011, CCIS 196, pp. 331–343, 2011.

A web service is actually a collection of individual service operations, each of which can be thought of as an individual procedure.

As more businesses deploy web services over the internet that dynamically interact with various applications and data sources, the issue of how to secure them from intruders and possible threats becomes more important. According to OSVDB and NVD Input manipulation, Information disclosure and Denial of service vulnerabilities account for more than 90% of the total vulnerabilities found as on February 2009 [1].

2 Related Work

Web service security is an important part of Service Oriented Architecture environment since web service is the preferred choice of implementation of SOA. There are many research works are being done on Web service security. The proposed XML firewall is based Role Based Access Control (RBAC) model [5]. RBAC model is used in many of the security solutions provided in the distributed computing environment.

Previous work on web service security based on XML firewall was done by Haiping Xu et al. [4] which were based on Coloured Petri Nets (CPN). They proposed a formal XML firewall security model which consists of two major components, namely the application model and the XML firewall model, which are designed compositionally using colored Petri nets. They developed a compositional CPN model for XML firewall protected service-oriented systems. But the work did not give any details of how to detect and prevent different vulnerabilities [2].

Similar work on XML firewall was a SOA state XML firewall which gave a design of state based firewall architecture that supports role based access control detection of XML based attacks. The state-based XML firewall was designed as a software module with four functional components, namely client interface, RBAC processor, SOAP filter, and admin interface, which coordinate to protect the web services deployed on a web server. The access policies and the detection rules are modularized so that they can be dynamically updated without recompiling and reinstalling the XML firewall. The work explains the design of XML firewall but there were no implementation details and results regarding the performance and testing [15].

Denial of service attack on web services has been researched by few researchers like Gruschka et al. in his paper "Preventing Web Services Dos attack by SOAP message validation" [8], has presented a method to validate each incoming soap request for XML and schema validation , which in turn increases overhead of system. Another work in same area is done by Srinivas Padmanabhuni et al. [11] where he proposes a Patricia trie based representation so that schema and request message can be validated in efficient manner.

The research on SQL injection in web services was done by Nuno Antunes and Marco Vieira [18].The goal was to study the effectiveness of the scanners and to try to identify common types of vulnerabilities in web services environments. The results showed that many of the services tested were deployed without proper security testing as a large number of vulnerabilities were observed. They compared some of the existing web vulnerability scanners. They use a representative workload to exercise the services and understand the expected behavior and the typical responses in the presence of valid inputs. A Classification of SQL Injection attacks and the countermeasures to reduce them was given William G.J. Halfond et.al. They presented and analyzed existing detection and prevention techniques against SQL injection attacks.

Work on SQL injection in web services was done in the paper, "Comparing the Effectiveness of Penetration Testing and Static Code Analysis on the Detection of SQL Injection Vulnerabilities in Web Services" [19].Penetration testing and static code analysis are two well know techniques frequently used by web service developers to identify security vulnerabilities in their code. The work analyzed different penetration testers and static code analyzers and performed manual testing to confirm that the vulnerabilities identified by the tools do exist.

3 XML Firewall

3.1 Architecture of XML firewall

A typical Service Oriented Architecture system mainly consists of two parts namely web services which provide different services and web service clients which invoke the web services. The web services can be invoked by various applications at runtime, so web services should be able to interact with various applications concurrently. So in this type of environment, web services are vulnerable to different types of attacks. The developed XML firewall can be used between the web services and Web service client to protect the web services from different vulnerabilities by verifying each request coming to web service.

The XML Firewall consists of four components that act together to provide security. The components are Authentication and Authorization module, Session and Role verification module, SOAP validation module and Administrator Interface. The XML Firewall components are supported by three databases i.e. User Info database, State info database and Role database. Each request coming to web service has to pass through the XML firewall before accessing the web service. The user is first authenticated against the UserInfo database and only after successful authentication he is allowed to access other web services depending on his roles. After successful authentication, session is created for each user and corresponding role is assigned. The next request from the user is sent directly to the session and role verification module where the soap request is validated on parameter like whether the user session exist or not, whether user session is active or not and whether he is authorized to access that service or not. Then the request is sent to the SOAP validation module where the request is checked for various vulnerabilities in different modules.

3.2 Databases Used in XML Firewall

The Databases act a critical role in providing essential information to various modules of XML Firewall which is used to find out the different type of XML based attack. The architecture of XML firewall shows a database module containing three databases namely UserInfoDB, StateDB, and RoleDB.

- UserInfoDB database contains user credentials which are used to authenticate users and it also contains authorization details of different users.
- StateDB database contains user state, session state and web service state information tables.
- RoleDB database consists of the details of the access privileges of different Web services. Each user is allowed to access only a subset of services offered by different web services depending upon his roles.

The fig.1 shows the architecture of XML firewall which contains different modules.

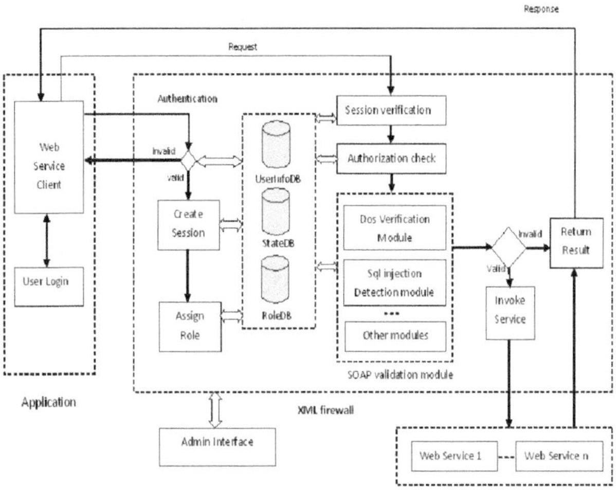

Fig. 1. Architectural model of XML Firewall

3.3 Authentication Module

The user is authenticated in the authentication block before accessing the web services where the basic username and password authentication mechanism is used. The UserInfoDB database contains all the usernames and passwords of the users; it also contains the roles information and trust level of the users. The user is authenticated only after verifying his username/password and trust level. Failing in any of these criteria, the user is denied access to the web service. The user is also assigned a role depending on his access privileges.

After authentication of the user, a session identifier (sessionID) is created for each user and maintained in the UserInfoDB database. If the user is fully authenticated and authorized, subsequent request and reply operations use this sessionID to maintain the session of the user.

Also the session start time and expiry time are added to the StateDB database. The sessionID is added to the SOAP message as part of the SOAP header and is used by user and web service client for future communication. The web service client has to add this sessionID to SOAP header of every request. Every request then passes through the session verification module. The sessionID is deleted from the database whenever the user logs out.

3.4 Session Verification and Role Authorization Module

After the authentication of the user, subsequent requests pass through the session verification module. In session verification module, the SOAP header field is extracted from the SOAP message and the sessionID is taken out of the header. This sessionID is verified using the SessionState database. Any request with wrong sessionID is rejected or not allowed to access the web service. If the session is valid, the session expiry time is renewed to a new value.

In the role authorization module, the request is checked if it has the permission to access the particular web service. Each user can access only a particular set of services depending on the role assigned to him. Information regarding the roles is present in the RoleDB database. After the successful authorization, the request is sent to the SOAP validation module where the input request is checked for vulnerabilities.

3.5 SOAP Validation Module

SOAP validation module is a collection of modules where each module checks for a particular vulnerability. In our architecture, we have added Denial of Service verification module and SQL injection detection module. Since the XML firewall architecture is modular and scalable, we can add many modules as and when they are developed.

3.6 DoS Identification and Verification Module

The DoS Identification and Verification block in SOAP validation module is used to maintain the availability of web service. As web services communicate through SOAP messages which are xml file, there is inherent vulnerability that is present in XML. Therefore web services have to face a new type of attack known as XML denial of service attack. In this attack malicious user send the SOAP messages infected with malicious content like Inline DTD's, CDATA element, external entities etc.

In the DoS Identification and verification block, DoS Identification detects the suspicious user with high frequency of request (the threshold frequency is determined by a number of steps described later), then the request is sent to the DoS Verification module to verify if the user is trying to do XDoS attack. In DoS verification module the request SOAP message is checked if the message length exceeds the normal SOAP message size, maximum allowed nesting depth in order to detect oversized or recursive payload attack and malicious content in the SOAP message. Malicious content could be CDATA element tag, external entities reference and entities expansion etc. We have used a modular approach so that it can be expanded for newer XDoS attack vectors.

The DoS verification module uses certain predefined pattern of malicious content to detect matched string in the SOAP message passed to the web service operation. If SOAP request is coming from a normal user whose request frequency is normal and has active session and authorization, it is immediately forwarded to the web services without going through the DoS verification module. When the web service invocation is complete, the result is forwarded back to the web service client and served to the user. The DoS Identification module also uses user's previous behaviors in order to detect the DoS attack. A user with low level of trust level is checked each time and if attack is found his trust level can be degraded further or even can be permanently blocked. If an attack is detected in DoS verification module the user is immediately logged out and his session is deleted along with degradation in trust level. Repeating the attack may result in permanent blocking of user.

To keep track of the web service availability, we periodically update the wsstate database (web service state) and userstate database. If the web service is busy (depends on the maximum number of requests that a web service can process in a given time interval), the threshold request frequency for each user goes down so as to reduce the load on web server and maintain its availability. To calculate the request frequency, we count the number of users that are currently online. To calculate the number of online user, we check the sessionstate database with active session. We then find out the frequency to make the web service state free (Usually one third to half of the number in busy state) and divide it by number of users online. By this we can easily find out which user is trying to do an attack and which is genuine. This frequency is changed once web service is free and, threshold of each user is increased. This way we can maintain the availability of web services and avoid the service inaccessibility to the genuine users.

3.6.1 Algorithm for DoS Identification and Verification

Step 1: Get the SOAP message from the Session veification and authorization module.

Step 2: Get the username from SOAP header and find his user frequency from userstate Database.

Step 3: Get the web service state and the current threshold frequency from wsstate database.

Step 4: If the user frequency less than threshold, go to step 7.

Step 5: If frequency is more than threshold, reduce trust level and forward SOAP request to DoS verification module.

Step 6: Check SOAP message for different XDoS vulnerability.

- Check the SOAP message for maximum length, if violated logout the user.
- Check the SOAP message for maximal depth, if violated logout the user.
- Check the SOAP message for malicious data, if malicious content found logout the user.

Step 7: Invoke the Web Service.

3.7 SQL Injection Detection Module

SQL injection detection module checks the SOAP requests for inputs which may contain attack strings and filters these attack strings before the request is sent to the web service.

In case of Service Oriented Architecture environment, the input data sent by the end user to the web application which hosts the web service client may not check the input data before sending it to the web service. Thus any malicious input which reaches the web service may cause SQL injection attack. The main cause for SQL injection vulnerability is insufficient validation of user input. To address this problem, developers have proposed a range of coding guidelines that promote defensive coding practices, such as encoding user input and input validation. There are many types of SQL injection attacks and countless variations of these basic types and the solution should be able to detect most of them [16].

SQL injection Detection module mainly takes care of SQL injection attack by checking the user input which will be in the form of SOAP request. In this paper, we have proposed a regular expression based solution for detection SQL injection attacks in web services.

3.7.1 Regular Expressions for SQL Injection Detection

It is very important to note that SQL injection attack strings may come from the end user who may enter the inputs through a browser or standalone application which hosts the web service client. The input validation logic should consider each and every type of input that originates from the user. Also if you discover too many alerts coming in from a signature that looks out for a single-quote or a semi-colon, it just might be that one or more of these characters are valid inputs in cookies created by your Web application. Therefore, there is a need to evaluate each of these signatures for your particular Web application where the web service is hosted.

A trivial regular expression to detect SQL injection attacks is to watch out for SQL specific meta-characters such as the single-quote (') or the double- dash (--). In order to detect these characters and their hex equivalents, the following java regular expression may be used:

((%27)|')|--|=|#

We first detect either the hex equivalent of the single-quote, the single- quote itself or the presence of the double-dash. These are SQL characters for MS SQL Server and Oracle, which denote the beginning of a comment, and everything that follows is ignored. Additionally, if you're using MySQL, you need to check for presence of the '#' or its hex-equivalent.

((%3d)|=)[^\n]*|((%27)|')|--|((%3b)|;)

This signature first looks out for the = sign or its hex equivalent (%3D). It then allows for zero or more non-newline characters, and then it checks for the single-quote, the double-dash or the semi-colon.

((%27)|')union|((%27)|')select|((%27)|')insert|((%27)|')update|((%27)|')delete|
((%27)|')drop

The use of the 'union' SQL query is also common in SQL Injection attacks against a variety of databases. If the earlier regular expression that just detects the single-quote or other SQL Meta characters results in too many false positives, you could further modify the query to specifically check for the single-quote and the keyword 'union'. This can also be further extended to other SQL keywords such as 'select', 'insert', 'update', 'delete', etc.

((%27)|('))((%6F)|o|(%4F))((%72)|r|(%52)) .

A typical SQL injection attempt of course revolves around the use of the single quote to manipulate the original query so that it always results in a true value. Most of the examples that discuss this attack use the string **1'or'1'='1**.

However, detection of this string can be easily evaded by supplying a value such as **1'or2>1--**. Thus the only part that is constant in this is the initial alphanumeric value, followed by a single-quote, and then followed by the word 'or'. The above signature also checks for the word 'or' with various combinations of its upper and lower case hex equivalents.

exec(\s|\+)+(s|x)p

If the back-end database is on an MS SQL server, the attacker will typically try to execute one of the many dangerous stored and extended stored procedures. These procedures start with the letters 'sp' or 'xp' respectively. The above signature is used to check this case.

Algorithm for Detecting SQL injection attack

Step 1: Get the input SOAP request from session verification and authorization module.
Step 2: Get each node from the body of the SOAP request.
Step 3: Check each node for SQL injection attack strings using the regular expressions given in section 4.6.1.

- If any of the input data matches with the regular expression,update the SQLDB database.
- If the number of attempts in current session is more than three and no previous attempts, then the user is logged off and trust level is reduced by 1.
- If the number of attempts in current session is more than three and if there are any previous attempts, then the user trust level is set to minimum i.e., permanent block state.

Step 4: Check whether the current node is the last child.

If it is not the last node, go to step 2.

Step 5: Request is allowed to invoke the service.

3.8 Administrator Interface

Administrator interface is present in XML firewall to view the real time operation happening inside firewall.

4 Implementation of XML Firewall

In this section we explain a sample XML Firewall developed and how it worked under different type of attacks scenario. A Service Oriented Architecture based application called Order Processing was developed in java. Order processing application is a collection of three web services, each providing a particular set of services. The developed application implements the order processing business process which contains three web services namely, sales order service, customer information service and product information service as shown in the figure. A web application was developed which hosts the web service client where the different services are invoked.

XML firewall was implemented using message handler interface provided by java web services. Message handlers are used for intercepting the SOAP messages in both the request and response of the Web Service.Two types of message handlers are SOAP handlers and logical handlers. In our application, we have used SOAP handlers to build the XML firewall. SOAP handlers can access the entire SOAP message, including the message headers and body. Thus we get the control over the SOAP requests coming from the web service clients. We can decide on the number of handlers (Handler Chain) and sequence of execution as shown in the fig 2. Using the message handler, we can access the required nodes and also we can modify it. The required nodes are extracted and then sent to the SOAP validation module for validation. Only the valid requests are allowed to invoke the services. In our implementation each handler works as a module of XML firewall since it follows modular architecture.

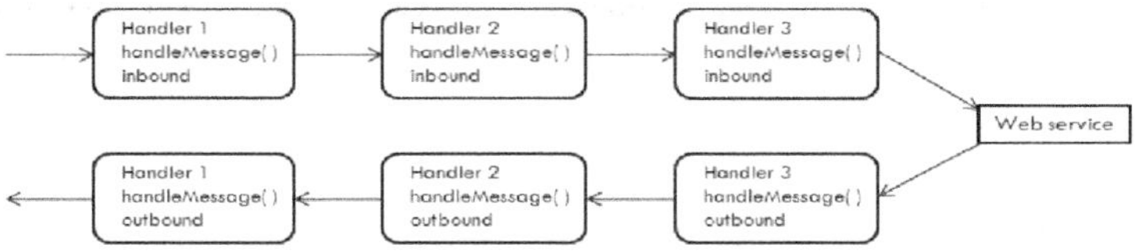

Fig. 2. Request Flow through Message Handlers

There are many handlers in XML firewall, each handler representing a module. Since it is a modular architecture, we can add as many modules as possible using the SOAP handler.The modules present in XML firewall are:

Security Message Handler: this handler is used to authenticate users before they access the web service. Apart from this, session information for each user is created and added to statedDB database.

Session check handler: This handler is responsible for session verification of every request. In XML Firewall after successful authentication, each request goes directly to the SessionCheckHandler. SOAP request contains session information of the user. After receiving SOAP request, the handler extracts the sessionID and username from the SOAP header. It is then verified against the sessionstate database that checks whether the session exists or not. Then the handler also checks that whether the session is active or not. If the session is active, session expiry time is increased by some constant value.

After session verification is done the handler verifies whether the user is authorized to access the web services. For this, the handler checks what web service operation the user is trying to invoke. It then checks the roleDB database to see if the web service operation could be invoked by the user. If the handler returns true, the SOAP request is forwarded to SOAP validation module.

Frequency Update Module: The Firewall monitors each and every request and prepares a different file for each user, web service and total request coming to XML firewall. We are then periodically calculating the request frequency of each of the user, firewall and web service. The time interval to check each of these attributes is predefined or decided by administrator. This method in turn reduces the over head on the XML Firewall as the frequencies are not calculated continuously. The frequency update module updates frequency after calculating the values and then writing it to the various state databases. Wsstate database and userstate database is being updated in this module. It also calculates the web service state by its frequency and thereby sets the threshold of the user.To calculate the threshold the module first get the current no of user online, this value is calculated by getting the number of user in the userstate database.

After this the wsstate frequency is calculated and web service state is decided, it could be busy, normal or free. If Web Service is in busy state the threshold for each user is decided by dividing the request frequency in Free State by number of user online. The threshold changes as WS State changes. Threshold is maintained such that web service doesn't become unavailable to any genuine user.The DoS identification module later in SOAP Filter uses this threshold to determine the attacks.

SOAP validation module: contains different modules, each checking the SOAP request for a particular vulnerability. In our implementation we have developed DoS identification and verification module and SQL injection detection module.

After successful session verification and authorization check, the request is forwarded to the DoS Identification and verification module. Here request frequency of user is checked and if any user with high request frequency is found, the request is sent to the DOS verification module where SOAP message is checked against the XDOS vulnerabilities. If any XDOS attack is detected, the user is immediately logged out and his trust level lowered. If no XDOS attack is found, his trust level is degraded as a warning.

After this, the request is forwarded to the SQL injection detection module. In this module, each SOAP request is checked for SQL injection attack strings. The regular expression given in section 3 is used to find Meta characters in SOAP request nodes which may cause SQL injection. Each node is traversed and checked for attack strings by matching the data with the regular expressions (signatures). If any attack is detected, the request is blocked and the trust level of the user is degraded.If the SOAP request through all these modules, then it is allowed to invoke the web service operations.

5 Results and Performance Analysis

To test the XML Firewall against various vulnerabilities, we deployed the XML firewall in front of web services and tested the web services for the response time it takes to serve the number of request. The web service client was hosted on other system with same configuration and the request was sent from the third system continuously.

First the response time was calculated for a large number of requests without Firewall after that we calculated the response time with firewall. The comparison graph is given below. As the complexity of web service increases the gap between the graph lines will become narrower (as firewall overhead is constant and significantly less).The results of the performance evaluation of the XML firewall are given in fig. 3. We also calculated overhead of a firewall separately by calculating the time taken by number of request inside firewall. Fig. 4 shows the overhead of firewall of 1 SQL operation web service.

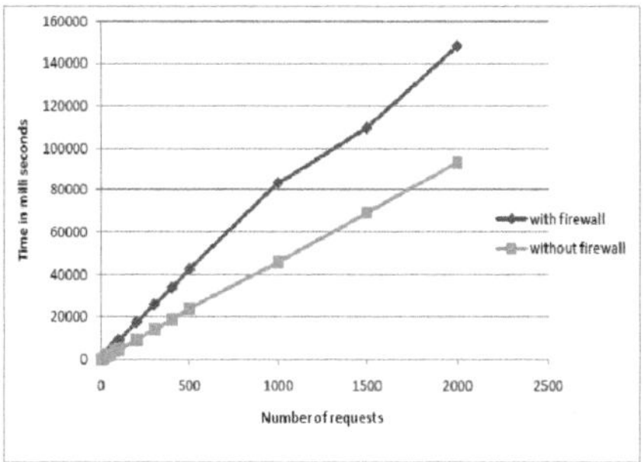

Fig. 3. Comparison graph between Web Service with Firewall and without Firewall

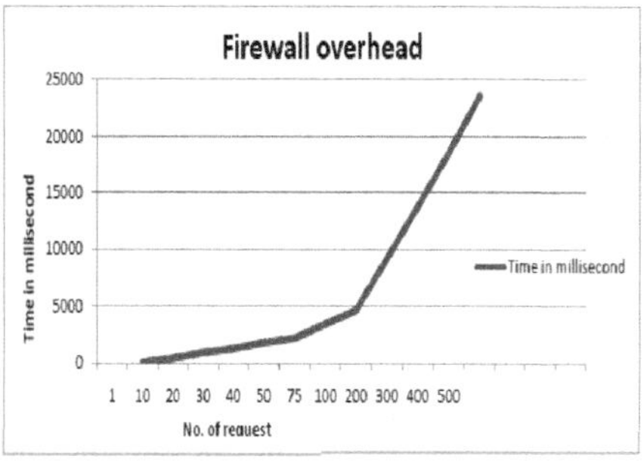

Fig. 4. Overhead caused due to XML Firewall on Order processing Web Service

We have also checked the firewall against different web services to prove that XML firewall takes constant time irrespective of web service. Fig. 5 gives the response time taken by two different web services.

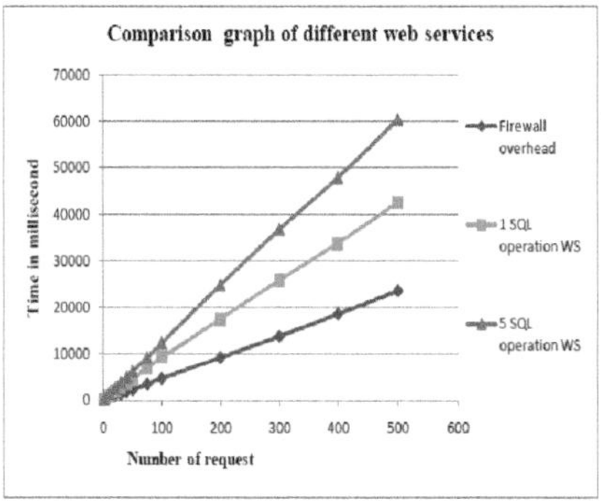

Fig. 5. Graph comparing different web services

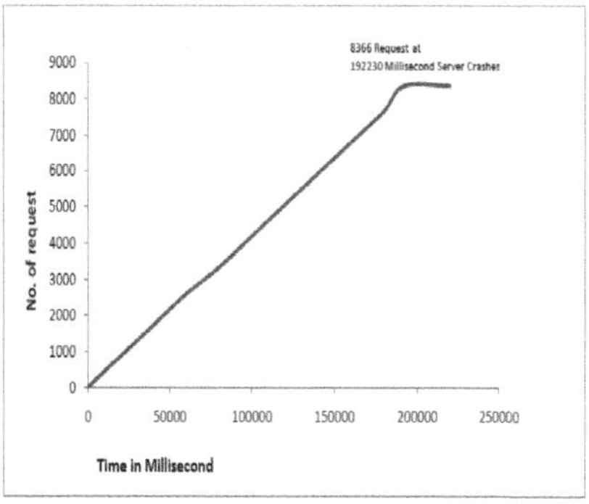

Fig. 6. Graph showing attack on web service

Web Service was also checked against the DoS attack, for this we send request from four terminals continuously until the web server stop responding request. The figure shown below describes the server response on attack.

To show the effectiveness of firewall we attack the firewall with two users online. The web service frequency was set to 200 for busy state and 150 for normal state. Hence the user frequency was automatically 75 if state is busy or normal. One user was idle while other user flood the web service with request packets. The graph in figure 6 clearly show that after 75 request threshold the user was logged out and not allowed to invoke the service. In graph we can see that after 90 request the attacker was logged out hence not allowed to Access the web service. Graph also shows the line when firewall is off (threshold is disabled) and compares the two scenario.

In figure 7 user is logged out at 90 instead of threshold value of 75. This is because in firewall, the frequency of user and firewall is updated every 1 second, so there is a chance of serving more request than threshold while firewall is setting the frequency.

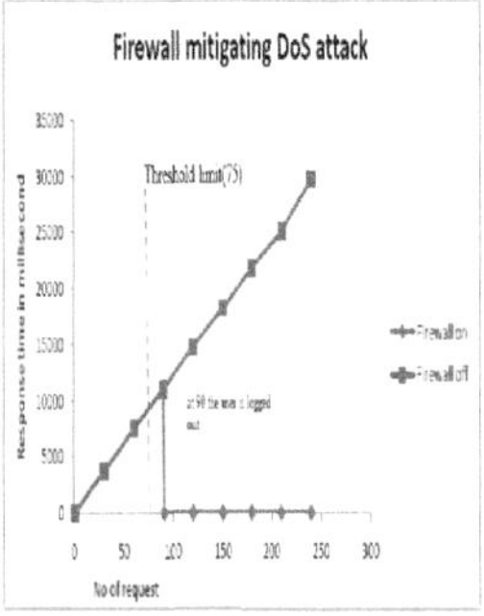

Fig. 7. Graph showing mitigation of attack through firewall

Table 1. SQL Injection attack with and without firewall

Web Operations	Without XML firewall		With XML firewall	
	No. of Attack Vectors	Successful Attacks	No. of Attack Vectors	Successful Attacks
Security	85	18	85	0
addCustomer	85	26	85	0
addProduct	85	26	85	0
cancelOrder	85	14	85	0
getOrderStatus	85	16	85	0
getProducInfo By Name	85	42	85	0

SQL injection detection module was tested using the penetration testing. The firewall was tested using WS digger tool which takes the WSDL file as input and scans the web services. It then gives all the operations along with the details of return type and input arguments of these operations present in the web service. The results are given in table 1.

6 Conclusion

The use of Service Oriented Architecture and web services are increasingly becoming popular in the IT industry and so are the threats and vulnerabilities. In this paper, we proposed an XML firewall architecture that protects the web services from different types of vulnerabilities. We have also developed a web services and the front end application used by the end user. We have also tested the firewall against SQL injection and DoS vulnerabilities and presented the results. The results show that our XML firewall architecture is effective in detecting most of the SQL injection vulnerabilities and mitigating the DoS vulnerabilities. Since we are using a modular approach in our design, new modules for detecting other types of vulnerabilities can be added easily.

References

[1] Marco, C., Ernesto, D.: An XML-Based Approach to combine Firewalls and Web services Security Specifications.
[2] Haiping, X., Mihir, A., Abhinay, R.: Formal modeling and analysis of XML firewall for service-oriented systems.
[3] Esmiralda, M., Anne, H.: Possible attacks on XML web services.
[4] Mihir, A.M., Haiping, X.: A Petri net based XMl Firewall security model for web services invocation.
[5] Sandhu Ravi, S., Coyne Edward, J., Fienstien Hal, L., Youman Chrles, E.: Role- Based Access Control. IEEE Computer 29(2), 38–47 (1996)
[6] Ramy, B., Hesham, S., Sherif-El, K., Youssef, H., Youssef, Y.: Nedgty-Web Services Firewall.
[7] Fernandez Eduardo, B.: Two pattern for web service security.
[8] Nils, G., Norbert, L.: Protecting web services from DoS Attacks by SOAP message Validation.
[9] Kanneganti, R., Chodavarapu, P.: SOA Security. Manning publication (2008)
[10] Service Oriented Architecture Security Vulnerabilities Web Services (July 2010), `http://www.nsa.gov/ia/_files/factsheets/SOA_security_vulnerabilities_web.pdf`
[11] Srinivas, P., Vineet, S., Senthil, K.K.M., Abhishek, C.: Preventing Service Oriented denial of Service (PreSODoS): A Proposed Approach. In: IEEE international Conference on Web Services (ICWS 2006) (2006)
[12] Xinfeng, Y.: Countering DDoS and XDoS Attacks against web Services. In: IEEE/IFIP International Conference on Embedded and Ubiquitous Computing (2008)
[13] Shreeraj, S.: Web 2.0 Security Defending Ajax, RIA and SOA. Charles river Media publication, Hingham
[14] Josuttis Nicolai, M.: SOA in Practice. O'Reilly publication, Sebastopol
[15] Abhinay, R., Haiping, X.: Securing Service-Oriented Systems Using State-Based XML Firewall
[16] Halfond William, G.J., Jermy, v., Alessandro, O.: A Classification of SQL Injection Attacks and Countermeasures.
[17] Kevin, S.: SQL Injection. White paper SPI Labs
[18] Nuno, A., Narco, V.: Detecting SQL Injection Vulnerabilities in Web Services. In: Fourth Latin-American Symposium on Dependable Computing (2009)
[19] Nuno, A., Narco, V.: Comparing the Effectiveness of penetration Testing and Static Code analysis pn the Detection of SQL Injection Vulnerabilities in Web Services. In: 15th IEEE Pacific Rim International Symposium on Dependable Computing (2009)
[20] Nuno, A., Narco, V., Nuno, L., Henrique, M.: Effective Detection of SQL/XPath Injection Vulnerabilities in Web Services. In: IEEE International Conference on services computing (2009)

Highly Resilient Key Predistribution Scheme Using Transversal Designs and Reed Muller Codes For Wireless Sensor Network

Samiran Bag[1], Amrita Saha[2], and Pinaki Sarkar[3]

[1] Applied Statistics Unit, Indian Statistical Institute, Kolkata-700108, India
samiran_r@isical.ac.in

[2] CSE Department, IIT Bombay, Mumbai-400076, India
amrita@cse.iitb.ac.in

[3] Mathematics Department, Jadavpur University, Kolkata-700032, India
pinakisark@gmail.com

Abstract. Resource constraints of the nodes make security protocols difficult to implement. Thus key management is an important area of research in Wireless Sensor Networks (WSN). Key predistribution (kpd) which involves preloading keys in sensor nodes, has been considered as the best solution for key management when sensor nodes are battery powered and have to work unattended. This paper proposes a method to fix some loophole in an existing key predistribution scheme thereby enhancing the security of messages exchanged within a WSN. Here we use a model based on Reed Muller Codes to establish connectivity keys between sensor nodes. The model is then utilized to securely establish communication keys and exchange messages in a WSN designed on basis of two schemes using transversal designs for key predistribution. The combination of the key predistribution scheme and the connectivity model gives rise to highly resilient communication model with same connectivity between nodes as the chosen key predistribution scheme.

Keywords: Connectivity, Communication, Reed-Muller Codes, Transversal Designs, Security.

1 Introduction

Wireless Sensor Network (WSN) consists of many tiny sensor nodes having very limited amount of storage, insufficient battery power, low computational power. They are scattered randomly or deterministically over a large target area. These sensors communicate between each other via radio frquency waves. These nodes gather sensitive information and they have widespread application in several civil and military purposes. These purposes include military surveilance, ocean-water monitoring, wild fire detection, temperature monitoring etc. to name a few. Since these sensors deal with very sensitive information, they must communicate securely so that no adversary can get hold of the information sent by them. To achieve this, cryptographic primitives have to be used for communication between sensors. Inevitably, this gives rise to usage of cryptographic keys.

D.C. Wyld et al. (Eds.): CNSA 2011, CCIS 196, pp. 344–355, 2011.

1.1 Related Works and Our Contributions

Cryptographic keys can be established between two parties in many ways. The conventional way using protocols like Kerberos [5] is expensive for sensor networks, which are resource constrained. The other method using public keys is being explored [11, 12] but not preferred because of costly operations involved. Key predistribution (kpd) is a method to preload cryptographic keys in sensor nodes, even before their deployment in the area of operation. It is a symmetric key approach, where two communicating nodes share a common secret key. The sender encrypts the message using the secret key and the receiver decrypts using the same key. Several key predistribution schemes that can be found in [3, 6–10]

In this paper we propose a connectivity model based on Reed Muller Codes that we use to enhance the security of two existing key predistribution scheme proposed by Lee Stinson scheme [6–8]. This combination of the two schemes give rise to a secure communication model for Wireless sensor networks.

2 Communication Model

Here, we shall be using two communication models proposed by Lee & Stinson. In both papers the authors used transversal design for key predistribution in Wireless sensor networks. A transversal design $TD(k, \lambda; n)$ is a triple (X, G, A) with the following properties:

1. X is a set of kn number of elements called varieties.
2. $G = G_1 \cup G_2 \cup \ldots \cup G_n$ is a partition of X where $|G_i| = k, \forall i \in \{1, 2, \ldots, n\}$.
3. $A = \{B_1, B_2, \ldots, B_b\}$ where $|B_j| = n, \forall j \in \{1, 2, \ldots, b\}$ and $|B_j \cap G_i| = 1, \forall j \in \{1, 2, \ldots, b\}, \forall i \in \{1, 2, \ldots, n\}$.
4. For any $x \in G_i, y \in G_j, i \neq j, |\{r : x, y \in B_r, 1 \leq r \leq b\}| = 1$.

The authors mapped the same design to key predistribution scheme in Wireless sensor networks. Their key predistribution scheme is described below.

2.1 Design 1

The details of the first design proposed by Lee Stionson can be found in [7, 8]. A brief outline is presented below:

Let p be a prime number and k be an integer such that $2 \leq k < p$.
There are p^2 number of nodes in the network. These nodes are given by

$$\begin{array}{ccccc} N_{0,0} & N_{0,1} & N_{0,2} & \cdots & N_{0,p-1} \\ N_{1,0} & N_{1,0} & N_{1,2} & \cdots & N_{1,p-1} \\ \vdots & \vdots & \vdots & \vdots & \vdots \\ N_{p-1,0} & N_{p-1,1} & N_{p-1,2} & \cdots & N_{p-1,p-1} \end{array}$$

Let, $X = \{(x, y) : 0 \leq x \leq k-1, 0 \leq y \leq p-1\}$ is the set of varities.
$G_i = \{(i, y) : 0 \leq y \leq p-1\} \forall i \in \{0, 1, \ldots, k-1\}$ are the groups of the design.

$A_{a,b} = \{(x, ax + b) : 0 \leq x \leq k - 1\}$ where $0 \leq a, b \leq p - 1$ are the block where all operations are done under modulo p.

Now , if each variety is mapped to a unique key and each block made to correspond to a node, then this will give rise to a key predistribution scheme. This is the key predistribution scheme of Lee Stinson. Here the set of keys is given by

$$\mathcal{K} = \{(x, y) : 0 \leq x \leq k - 1, 0 \leq y \leq p - 1\}$$

The keys belonging to node $N_{a,b}$ is

$$K_{a,b} = \{(x, ax + b \mod p) : 0 \leq x \leq k - 1\}$$

Now two nodes $N_{a,b}$ and $N_{a',b'}$ will have a common key if $K_{a,b} \cap K_{a',b'} \neq \phi$. Such a key will exist if $ax + b = a'x + b'$ has a solution under division modulo p or if $x = (b' - b)(a - a')^{-1}$ exists and lies in between 0 and $k - 1$. We shall get a solution for x if $a \neq a'$

2.2 Design 2

The second chosen kpd scheme was proposed in details by Lee Stionson in [6, 8]. Briefly recalling:

Again let p be a prime number and k be an integer such that $2 \leq k < p$. There are p^3 number of nodes in the network. These nodes are given by

$$\begin{array}{ccccc}
N_{0,0,0} & N_{0,0,1} & N_{0,0,2} & \cdots & N_{0,0,p-1} \\
N_{0,1,0} & N_{0,1,0} & N_{0,1,2} & \cdots & N_{0,1,p-1} \\
\vdots & \vdots & \vdots & \vdots & \vdots \\
N_{0,p-1,0} & N_{0,p-1,1} & N_{0,p-1,2} & \cdots & N_{0,p-1,p-1}
\end{array}$$

$$\begin{array}{ccccc}
N_{1,0,0} & N_{1,0,1} & N_{1,0,2} & \cdots & N_{1,0,p-1} \\
N_{1,1,0} & N_{1,1,0} & N_{1,1,2} & \cdots & N_{1,1,p-1} \\
\vdots & \vdots & \vdots & \vdots & \vdots \\
N_{1,p-1,0} & N_{1,p-1,1} & N_{1,p-1,2} & \cdots & N_{1,p-1,p-1}
\end{array}$$

$$\begin{array}{ccccc}
\vdots & \vdots & \vdots & \vdots & \vdots
\end{array}$$

$$\begin{array}{ccccc}
N_{p-1,0,0} & N_{p-1,0,1} & N_{p-1,0,2} & \cdots & N_{p-1,0,p-1} \\
N_{p-1,1,0} & N_{p-1,1,0} & N_{p-1,1,2} & \cdots & N_{p-1,1,p-1} \\
\vdots & \vdots & \vdots & \vdots & \vdots \\
N_{p-1,p-1,0} & N_{p-1,p-1,1} & N_{p-1,p-1,2} & \cdots & N_{p-1,p-1,p-1}
\end{array}$$

Let, $X = \{(x, y) : 0 \leq x \leq k-1, 0 \leq y \leq p-1\}$ be the set of varities. $G_i = \{(i, y) : 0 \leq y \leq p-1\} \forall i \in \{0, 1, \ldots, k-1\}$ are the groups of the design. $A_{a,b,c} = \{(x, ax^2 + bx + c) : 0 \leq x \leq k-1\}$ where $0 \leq a, b, c \leq p-1$ are the block where all operations are done under modulo p.

Now , if etch variety is mapped to a unique key and each block made to correspond to a node, then this will give rise to a key predistribution scheme. This is the key predistribution scheme of Lee and Stinson. Here the set of keys is given by:

$$\mathcal{K} = \{(x, y) : 0 \leq x \leq k-1, 0 \leq y \leq p-1\}$$

The keys belonging to node $N_{a,b,c}$ is

$$K_{a,b,c} = \{(x, ax^2 + bx + c \mod p) : 0 \leq x \leq k-1\}$$

Now two nodes $N_{a,b,c}$ and $N_{a',b',c'}$ will have a common key if $K_{a,b,c} \cap K_{a',b',c'} \neq \phi$. Such a key will exist if $ax^2 + bx + c = a'x^2 + b'x + c'$ has a solution under division modulo p or if $x = \{-(b-b') \pm \sqrt{(b-b')^2 - 4(a-a')(c-c')}\}/(2(a-a'))^{-1}$ exists and lies in between 0 and $k-1$. We shall get a solution for x if $(b-b')^2 - 4(a-a')(c-c')$ is a quadratic residue modulo p.

3 Weakness: Motivation of Our Work

We observe a weakness in the aforesaid key predistribution scheme. Here the node ids reveal the points inside a particular node. Let us say node $N_{i,j}$ and node $N_{i',j'}$ want to communicate securely. If they do share a key then it will have the id (x, y) where $x = (j' - j)(i - i')^{-1}, y = ix + j = i'x + j'$. For finding this key both the nodes must exchange their node-ids. An adversary, say Alice can tap the radio frequency channel and come to know the unencrypted node ids passing through them. She can then find the key ids of the shared key((x, y)) between the nodes in a manner similar to the nodes. Then she can find the node id of a node containing the key with id (x, y) in the following manner:

Let the id of the node be (r, s). If this node contains the key (x, y) then $y = rx + s$ or, $s = y - rx$. By fixing an r she can compute s thus finding the node id of a third node containing the shared key between node (i, j) and (i', j'). Thus enabling selective node attack. She can capture node (r, s) and get to know the actual key with id (x, y).

Similar attack can be done on design 2. Here, the common key between two nodes $N_{i,j,k}$ and $N_{i',j',k'}$ is given by (x, y), where
$x = \{-(j - j') \pm \sqrt{(j - j')^2 - 4(i - i')(k - k')}\}/(2(i - i'))^{-1}$
and $y = ix^2 + jx + k = i'^2 + j'x + k'$. Now, the adversary can find the id of a node (say $N_{a,b,c}$) containing the key (x, y) like the following;
$ax^2 + bx + c = y$
or, $c = y - ax^2 - bx$
by fixing a and b, the adversary will be able to compute c.

To counter this problem, we first differentiate the two aspects communication and connectivity of a WSN. Then like in [4], apply Reed Muller Codes to suitably model the connectivity aspect. The construction of the model is presented the in following section. The model can be made secure by using suitable cryptosystems.

As shall be later established the combination of the two ideas results in a highly resilient key predistribution scheme for WSN providing same connectivity amongst nodes as the initial models with virtually same communication overhead.

4 Proposed Connectivity Model

As stated above, Reed Muller codes will be utilized to structure the connectivity aspect of the WSN. These codes have been elaborately described in [2] and necessary notational changes have been highlighted by Sarkar et al. in [4, section IV]. We follow similar procedure as described in [4, section IV] baring some modification to be illustrated now.

Both the models will always have three tiers with the "Base Station" or "KDS" in the 1st or topmost tier. The second tier will consist of p & p^2 newly introduced cluster heads (CHs) for the first and second designs respectively. Each of these CHs will be assigned p many nodes in the 3rd tier in both the designs. Thus for 'Design 1' we introduce p many new CHs in the 2nd tier each having p 'ordinary nodes' under it. Whereas for 'Design 2' we allocate p^2 many CHs in the 2nd tier each having p 'ordinary nodes' under it. This ensures key storage for each CH is same (= O(p)) for both designs.

It is evident that current connectivity model is heterogeneous in nature having different number of nodes in various clusters. Other than this exactly here 3 tiers are required for connectivity model. These facts distinguishes present designs from the original design of Sarkar et al. [4, section IV].

Clusters between various tiers of the connectivity model are designed using first order Reed Muller codes. Connectivity of 1st & 2nd levels of 'Design 1' is given by a p complete graph. Whereas connectivity pattern of 1st & 2nd levels of 'Design 2' is a p^2 complete graph.

Consider $\mathbb{Z}_2[x_1, x_2, \ldots, x_m]$ where $m = p$ or p^2 for 'Design 1' and 'Design 2' respectively. Like in [4], the monomials x_i will represent the bit pattern of length $2^{\lceil \frac{q}{4} \rceil}$ having 2^{i-1} 1's followed by 2^{i-1} 0's where $1 \leq i \leq m$ where m is mentioned above. Sample connectivity pattern for a cluster containing KDS & 3 CHs (meant for 'Design 1') and another pattern with KDS & $4 = 2^2$ CHs (meant for 'Design 2') are presented in the following matrix below:

$$\begin{bmatrix} \mathbf{KDS} & 1\,1\,1\,1\,1\,1\,1\,1 \\ \mathbf{CH_1} & 1\,0\,1\,0\,1\,0\,1\,0 \\ \mathbf{CH_2} & 1\,1\,0\,0\,1\,1\,0\,0 \\ \mathbf{CH_3} & 1\,1\,1\,1\,0\,0\,0\,0 \end{bmatrix} \tag{1}$$

$$\begin{bmatrix} \mathbf{KDS} & 1\,1\,1\,1\,1\,1\,1\,1\,1\,1\,1\,1\,1\,1\,1\,1 \\ \mathbf{CH_1} & 1\,0\,1\,0\,1\,0\,1\,0\,1\,0\,1\,0\,1\,0\,1\,0 \\ \mathbf{CH_2} & 1\,1\,0\,0\,1\,1\,0\,0\,1\,1\,0\,0\,1\,1\,0\,0 \\ \mathbf{CH_3} & 1\,1\,1\,1\,0\,0\,0\,0\,1\,1\,1\,1\,0\,0\,0\,0 \\ \mathbf{CH_4} & 1\,1\,1\,1\,1\,1\,1\,1\,0\,0\,0\,0\,0\,0\,0\,0 \end{bmatrix} \tag{2}$$

Matrices like the above one are used for construction of Reed Muller codes. In particular the first matrix (meant for 'Design 1') has been referred to as $R(1;3)$ in [2]. Here

1 means the degree of the monomials is '1' and 3 stands for the number of variables. The significance of the entries 1 and 0 in the first matrix ($R(1;3)$) is the presence and absence of a connectivity link at that row and column position respectively. Thus for connectivity of two any entities (KDS or CHs or ordinary nodes), both of them should have a 1 in the same column for at least one column. Each column is assigned a separate connectivity key immaterial of them using the same radio frequency channel.

The connectivity pattern between of each of the clusters of the 2nd and 3rd level is meant to be a 2 complete graph having $m = p$ variables (for both designs) in the matrix. Each node is assigned a row. Thus we look at $\mathbb{Z}_2[x_1, x_2, \ldots, x_p]$ as was similarly done in [4, section IV, subsection B] Connectivity matrix for a cluster having 1 CH & 3 nodes and 1 CH & 4 nodes for the respective designs are as follows:

$$\begin{bmatrix} \mathbf{CH} & 1 & 0 & 0 & 1 & 0 & 1 & 1 & 1 \\ \mathbf{N_1} & 1 & 0 & 1 & 0 & 1 & 0 & 1 & 0 \\ \mathbf{N_2} & 1 & 1 & 0 & 0 & 1 & 1 & 0 & 0 \\ \mathbf{N_3} & 1 & 1 & 1 & 1 & 0 & 0 & 0 & 0 \end{bmatrix}$$

$$\begin{bmatrix} \mathbf{1} & 1 & 0 & 0 & 0 & 0 & 0 & 1 & 0 & 0 & 0 & 1 & 0 & 1 & 1 & 1 \\ \mathbf{x_1} & 1 & 0 & 0 & 0 & 0 & 1 & 0 & 0 & 0 & 1 & 0 & 1 & 0 & 1 & 0 \\ \mathbf{x_2} & 1 & 0 & 0 & 0 & 1 & 0 & 0 & 0 & 1 & 0 & 0 & 1 & 1 & 0 & 0 \\ \mathbf{x_3} & 1 & 0 & 0 & 1 & 0 & 0 & 0 & 0 & 1 & 1 & 1 & 0 & 0 & 0 & 0 \\ \mathbf{x_4} & 1 & 0 & 0 & 1 & 0 & 1 & 1 & 1 & 0 & 0 & 0 & 0 & 0 & 0 & 0 \end{bmatrix}$$

The construction of second matrices of respective designs from first can be found in [4, Section IV, Subsection B]. There is a broadcast channel and a provision for special link meant only for communication of the CH with KDS. CH need not be present in the inter-nodal links. Here also 1 means presence of connectivity link & 0-its absence.

Figure 1 give an lively example of 9 nodes under $p = 3$ CHs constructed using 'Design 1'. While in Figure 2, a small network example with 8 nodes under $p^2 = 2^2 = 4$ CHs have been constructed using 'Design 2'. As was earlier stated both the models have 3 tier with KDS in topmost, CHs in 2nd & nodes in 3rd. The line joining CH-1 and node 2, CH-2 and node 5, CH-3 and node 8 are bent to symbolize they do not interfere with other links.

5 Deployment

There can be various methods for node deployment. We discuss one of them here as an example. At the time of deployment, we shall drop the CHs along with the nodes of its cluster. Clearly instead of totally random deployment, we are deploying in small groups where exact position of nodes may still be unknown. Thus we adopt a kind of *pseudo-random* deployment technique. This ensures that all the clusters are formed according to the model. However in an unlikely event of some nodes falling out of position, we adopt the following key re-scheduling technique.

Assume some node of one cluster A falls into another cluster B. In such a case, CH of cluster B broadcasts the node id or I.P. address of the misplaced node amongst all the

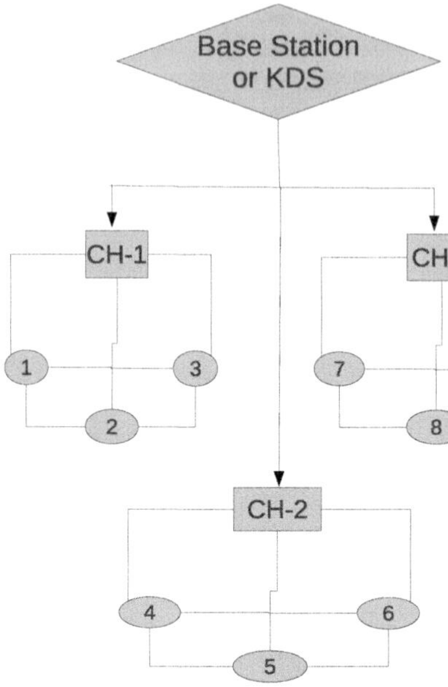

Fig. 1. Network structure for $p = 3$ has $p = 3$ CHs in 2nd & $N = p^2 = 9$ nodes in 3rd tier using Design 1

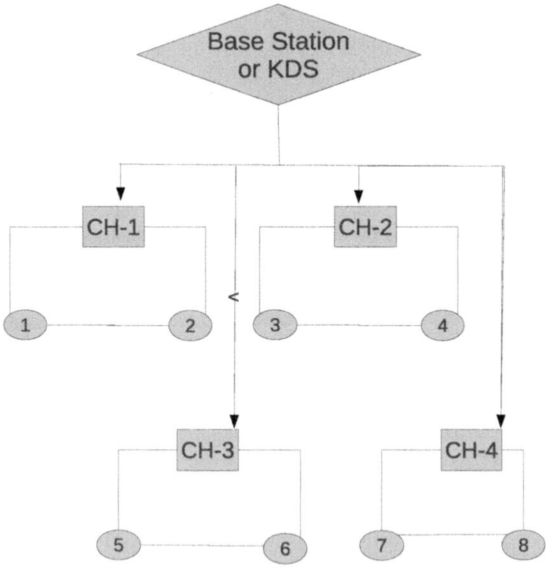

Fig. 2. Network structure for $p = 2$ has $p^2 = 4$ CHs in 2nd & $N = p^3 = 8$ nodes in 3rd tier using Design 2

CHs to find out the actual cluster where it should have been placed. On seeing the I.P. address or node id of this node, the CHs respond whether or not the misplaced node belongs to their cluster. Since this node was supposed to be in cluster A, its CH is the only who responds with 'YES'. Using the secure link between CH of cluster A and cluster B, the connectivity key corresponding to this sensor and CH of cluster A is transmitted to the CH of cluster B. This key is used to set up a secure connectivity link between the CH of cluster B and the misplaced. Depending on the requirements and practical hazards, CH of cluster B decides on the exact connectivity for this misplaced node in its cluster. Clearly a redistribution of connectivity keys may be required. In case this is not possible, still the node remains connected to the network but all communication will involve CH of B. It is clear that in this scenario, there is a process of node addition in cluster B and node deletion at cluster A. These processes have been described in [4] We would like to remark that instead of interconnectivity (clique connectivity) of sensor at the base level, one may desire to have just the connection with the CHs. This will enable better security, make (connectivity) key distribution easier and also reduce the importance of simple nodes at the bottommost level. In such a case the 2nd tier CHs may have to be powerful to ensure security.

6 Communication Key Establishment

We now describe how one can utilize the secure connectivity model for communication key establishment. As mentioned earlier node ids can be used for this purpose.

Every node encrypts its node id using the connectivity key that it shares with its CH and sends the encrypted node id to its CH. On receiving these encrypted ids, the CHs decrypts them and circulates them securely amongst themselves using the connectivity keys of one another.For each incoming node id pairs (i, j) , the CHs immediately form the linear equation $ix + j$ for each pair. These equations are then solved as described in section 2 for the key ids of the corresponding node. Once the key ids are obtained, common keys are immediately traced and informed back to the node via the same secure channels.

Clearly when the nodes send their ids we utilize the connectivity model of last two tiers. Whereas when the node ids are being circulated at the CH level, we use the connectivity keys corresponding to 1st and 2nd level. Surely, if required one can make use of different cryptosystems for various clusters of 2nd & 3rd tiers and certainly for KDS-CH tier (i.e. 1st & 2nd tier) of our connectivity model.

Thus instead of the nodes, CHs get to know other nodes' id and equating the resulting linear equations. Then the nodes are securely informed about the common key by the CHs. Hence any attack on the resultant system during key establishment would require capture of some CH or somehow read the encrypted node ids. Considering both capturing CH or decrypting the encrypted node is high unlikely during key establishment, we are ensured of extremely secure key establishment of the resultant system.

7 Message Sending Protocol

Suppose a message has to be sent from node $N_{i,j}$ to node $N_{i',j'}$ for some fixed $0 \leq i, j, i', j' \leq p - 1$. Then the following protocol is to be executed.

Choose one common communication key μ between $N_{i,j}$ and $N_{i',j'}$.
$N_{i,j}$ encrypts the message with this key μ.
if $N_{i,j}$ and $N_{i',j'}$ share a connectivity key **then**
  The message encrypted with com. key is again encrypted with the shared con. key and send directly to node $N_{i',j'}$.
  $N_{i',j'}$ decrypts outer encryption done using the con. key of the common CH.
else
  node $N_{i,j}$ uses the con. key that it shares with its Cluster Head and send the doubly encrypted message to its CH.
  if node $N_{i',j'}$ lies in the same cluster **then**
    After decrypting with $N_{i,j}$'s con. key and encrypting with $N_{i',j'}$'s con. key, the common CH directly send it to node $N_{i',j'}$.
  else
    the doubly encrypted message from $N_{i,j}$ is decrypted using $N_{i,j}$'s con. key at the CH of $N_{i,j}$.
    It is re-encrypted at CH of $N_{i,j}$ using the con. key shared with Cluster Head of $N_{i',j'}$.
    Send the doubly encrypted message to the CH of $N_{i',j'}$.
    Cluster Head of $N_{i',j'}$ then decrypts it with the con. key shared with the cluster head of $N_{i,j}$.
    CH of $N_{i',j'}$ encrypts it using the shared con. key with $N_{i',j'}$.
    Send the doubly encrypted message to $N_{i',j'}$.
  end if
  $N_{i',j'}$ will first decrypt the outer encryption done using the con. key of its CH (not $N_{i,j}$'s).
end if
Finally $N_{i',j'}$ uses the chosen common com. key μ shared with $N_{i,j}$ to decrypt and read the message.

8 Resilience

A hypothetical intrusion (i.e. attack) detection mechanism informs the KDS, CHs & subsequently the nodes about compromise of any node(s) as and when it occurs. For capture of a node X_1, connectivity keys sacrificed are its broadcast key, keys between X_1 & remaining nodes in its cluster and the exclusive key shared by X_1 & its CH.

Based on this information the concerned nodes and CH delete all the (above) connectivity keys ensuring that the captured node gets thoroughly delinked from the network. This deletion process has been elaborately described in [4, section V, subsection B]. In fact the beauty of this process is that after deletion of required connectivity links due to capture of some node(s), the other nodes in that cluster remains connected in much the same way as they would without the compromised node(s).

Remark: It should be noted that at any stage the communication keys are not known to the CH. Thus for affecting the resiliency of the network, definitely some nodes have to be captured.

Introduction of a secure connectivity model enables doubly encryption of message while transmitting. The second encryption involves connectivity of the nodes & CHs. Nodes contain only the con. keys concerned to itself. Connectivity keys of all nodes in a cluster can only be found in CH of that particular cluster (not even in other CHs or KDS). This automatically implies to affect the communication of any node in the network, its CH must be captured. Thus while calculating the effect of the system when some nodes are captured, we must ensure some CHs are also captured. In practice capturing a CH is quite infeasible.

9 Experimental Results

Experimental results have been tabulated in Table 1. N and k are as defined in section 2. In the table, "Exp." stands for experimental, "Thry." means theoretical results for current scheme. "LS Exp" is used as an abbreviation for Lee Stinson's experimental results as presented in [7] corresponding to 'Design 1'. The tabulated values compares our results with [7].

Table 1. Simulation & comparative results for $E(s,t)$ for Design 1 with $p = 47$, hence $N = p^2$ where s nodes & t CHs are captured

k	N	s	t	Our Exp. $E(s,t)$	LS. Exp. $E(s,t)$
30	2209	2	1	0.00851	0.4000
30	2209	4	2	0.01901	0.4469
30	2209	6	3	0.02852	0.4469
30	2209	8	3	0.02992	0.4689
30	2209	10	4	0.04171	0.4901

10 Conclusion

A secure connectivity model has been utilized to make key establishment secure and then enhance message exchange of two pre-existing key predistribution schemes. Both the scheme were designed by Lee and Stinson in their works [7] and [8]. Both these scheme are based on Transversal designs meant to support p and p^2 nodes respectively for a prime p. Significance of choosing a prime p is that the authors of [7] and [8] focused on the finite field$\mathbb{Z}_p$. We have pointed out in section 2 how one can extend their idea to a general finite field $\mathbb{F} - p$.

While designing our connectivity model, we have used a novel technique introduced by Sarkar, Saha and Chowdhury [4]. Like them, we have also utilized 1st order Reed Muller Codes for generating the connectivity patterns in each cluster. However ours is an heterogeneous model as compared to homogeneous model of theirs as has been explained in 4 . Another point of distinction specially for 'Design 2' is that we have exactly 3 tiers with unequal nodes/CHs in various clusters.

As has been elaborately explained in section 7, if these two nodes are in 'radio frequency range' of each other (and share a connectivity key), doubly encrypted messages can be exchanged directly. In case they are not in each other's 'radio frequency range' or don't have any common connectivity key, they are supposed to communicate through their CHs. However these CHs can not decrypt the encryption done with communication key shared by the nodes. To the best of our knowledge proposing a secure connectivity model, then using it for secure establish and later for enhancing the security during message exchange was first proposed by [4].

Experimental results presented in section 9 exhibit the amount of improvement in resilience as compared the original key predistribution scheme proposed by Lee and Stinson. Though Sarkar et al. provided theoretical bounds of resiliency, experimental results were not mentioned. Other than this, they didn't indicate any particular deployment strategy. Thus how exactly the connectivity model was achieved in the target area was not clear. Section 5 has been devoted to address the deployment issue. From the discussion in section 5, it is clear that no physical movement of a node is required as long as there is some CH in its 'radio frequency range' after deployment. Considering the hazards of deployment of nodes in a target area of WSN, this observation can be pretty useful to set up a network.

11 Future Work

Several future research directions stems out of our current work. The chosen key predistribution scheme does not guarantee direct node-to-node communication. Thus even though the connectivity is path connected graph, the resultant system does not have full connectivity.

The number of keys vary from 2 to $p^r - 1$. For better connectivity, we need the number of keys to be closer to p^r. This number is rather high and prove dangerous when a node is captured. Thus we must seek a scheme having lesser keys per node with O(1) keys shared between any pair of nodes. Then one can perhaps apply the connectivity model in a suitable way to get promising results.

Repeated enciphering and deciphering has been suggested at each CH in between two communicating nodes of different clusters. Certainly some communication cost will be reduced if one develops a system avoiding this. In this regard, it may be fascinating to see if one can apply any other Mathematical tools.

Acknowledgement

Firstly we want to express our gratitude to University Grants Commission of India for financially supporting the doctoral program of Mr. Pinaki Sarkar. This work is meant to be a part of the doctoral thesis of Mr. Pinaki Sarkar.

We would like to thank Dr. Goutam Paul of Jadavpur University, Kolkata and Mr. Sumit Kumar Pandey of Indian Statistical Institute, Kolkata for discussing the paper and critically analyzing it. A special word of appreciation goes to Dr. Brijesh Kumar

Rai of Indian Institute of Technology, Bombay for his constant motivation and active participation in preparation of the paper.

References

[1] Bag, S., Ruj, S.: Key Distribution in Wireless Sensor Networks using Finite Affine Plane. Accepted for publication in AINA-2011
[2] Cooke, B.: Reed Muller Error Correcting Codes. MIT Undergraduate Journal of Mathematics (1999)
[3] Ruj, S., Roy, B.: Key predistribution using partially balanced designs in wireless sensor networks. In: Stojmenovic, I., Thulasiram, R.K., Yang, L.T., Jia, W., Guo, M., de Mello, R.F. (eds.) ISPA 2007. LNCS, vol. 4742, pp. 431–445. Springer, Heidelberg (2007)
[4] Sarkar, P., Saha, A., Chowdhury, M.U.: Secure Connectivity Model in Wireless Sensor Networks Using First Order Reed-Muller Codes. In: WSNS 2010 in conjunction with MASS 2010, pp. 507–512 (complete it 2010)
[5] Steiner, J.G., Neuman, B.C., Schiller, J.I.: Kerberos: An authentication service for open network systems. USENIX Winter, 191–202 (1988)
[6] Lee, J., Stinson, D.R.: Deterministic Key Predistribution Schemes for Distributed Sensor Networks. In: Handschuh, H., Hasan, M.A. (eds.) SAC 2004. LNCS, vol. 3357, pp. 294–307. Springer, Heidelberg (2004)
[7] Lee, J., Stinson, D.R.: A combinatorial approach to key predistribution for distributed sensor networks. In: IEEE Wireless Communications and Networking Conference, WCNC 2005, vol. 2, pp. 1200–1205. IEEE Communications Society, New Orleans (2005)
[8] Lee, J., Stinson, D.R.: On the construction of practical key predistribution schemes for distributed sensor networks using combinatorial designs. ACM Trans. Inf. Syst. Secur. 11(2) (2008)
[9] Çamtepe, S.A., Yener, B.: Combinatorial design of key distribution mechanisms for wireless sensor networks. In: Samarati, P., Ryan, P.Y.A., Gollmann, D., Molva, R. (eds.) ESORICS 2004. LNCS, vol. 3193, pp. 293–308. Springer, Heidelberg (2004)
[10] Chakrabarti, D., Maitra, S., Roy, B.: A key pre-distribution scheme for wireless sensor networks: Merging blocks in combinatorial design. In: Zhou, J., López, J., Deng, R.H., Bao, F. (eds.) ISC 2005. LNCS, vol. 3650, pp. 89–103. Springer, Heidelberg (2005)
[11] Gura, N., Patel, A., Wonder, A., Eberle, H., Shantz, S.C.: Comparing Elliptic Curve Cryptography and RSA on 8-BIT CPUs. In: Joye, M., Quisquater, J.-J. (eds.) CHES 2004. LNCS, vol. 3156, pp. 119–132. Springer, Heidelberg (2004)
[12] Malan, D.J., Welsh, M., Smith, M.D.: Implementing public-key infrastructure for sensor networks. TOSN 4 (2008)
[13] Xu, D., Huang, J., Dwoskin, J., Chiang, M., Lee, R.: Re-examining probabilistic versus deterministic key management. In: Proceedings of the 2007 IEEE International Symposium on Information Theory (ISIT), pp. 2586–2590 (2007)

Improving Fairness in Network Traffic by Controlling Congestion and Unresponsive Flows

M. Azath[1], R.S.D. Wahida Banu[2], and A. Neela Madheswari[3]

[1] Assistant Professor & Head, Department of Computer Science and Engineering, MET'S School of Engineering, Thrissur, India
mailmeazath@gmail.com
[2] Professor & Head, Department of Electronics and Communication Engineering, Government College of Engineering, Salem, India
drwahidabanu@gmail.com
[3] Associate Professor & Head, Department of Information Technology, KMEA Engineering College, Aluva, India
neela.madheswari@gmail.com

Abstract. Traffic engineering is the task of handling the traffic flows in the back bone networks in order to provide maximum network resource utilization. The key characteristics are redirecting the traffic flows to avoid congestion, applying constraint based shortest path first, providing the ISPs to get more control for the management of traffic flows. Fairness measures or metrics are used in traffic engineering to determine whether users or applications are receiving a fair share of system resources. In this work, the fairness measure considered is congestion control and the control of unresponsive flows.

Keywords: Traffic engineering, congestion, unresponsive flows, fairness.

1 Introduction

Computer networks are used very widely starting from the end users of small institutions to huge performance computing environments. Mainly the networks are used for transfer the data across the systems widely. The network providers provide the users with their specified constraints and access for the resources and transfer of data.

The process of managing the allocation of network resources to carry traffic subject to constraints is known as traffic engineering. It is concerned with the performance optimization of networks. It addresses the problem of efficiently allocating resource in the network so that user constraints are met and operator benefit is maximized. It can be performed automatically or through manual intervention, and is required at a variety of timescales. Traffic engineering still performs a useful function for network operators and customers. Enabling it to be performed in an efficient and consistent manner is valuable [3].

Network operators must have control over the flow of traffic into, out of, and across their networks. The border gateway protocol does not facilitate common traffic engineering tasks, such as balancing load across multiple links to a neighboring node

D.C. Wyld et al. (Eds.): CNSA 2011, CCIS 196, pp. 356–363, 2011.

or directing traffic to a different neighbor. Solving these problems is difficult because the number of possible changes to routing policies is too large to exhaustively test all possibilities, some changes in routing policy can have an unpredictable effect on the flow of traffic and the border gateway protocol decision process implemented by router vendors limits an operator's control over path selection [5].

2 Motivation

In 1986, Internet first faces the congestion when too much network traffic caused a series of Internet meltdowns and the entire network getting down. During October 1986, Internet began to experience a serious of congestion collapses. So many computers were piling their traffic on to the network at the same time that the network came to grinding halt and no one got any meaningful throughput. During mid 1987, Van Jacobson gave the solution.

With millions of consumers on the Internet today with a competent appetite for multi-gigabyte videos, the Internet is facing its congestion crisis. While the network is not completely melting down, it is completely unfair because fewer than 10% of all Internet users using P2P hogs roughly 75% of all network traffic at the expense of all other Internet users.

The basic traffic engineering problem is how to set up explicit routers to meet bandwidth demands between the edge nodes of the network and at the same time to optimize the network performance. Two mathematical formulations are proposed with the objective of minimizing congestion and maximizing potential for traffic growth [1].

Unresponsive flows are the flows that increase their load on the network and subject to packet drops. The malicious attacks like DDoS (Distributed Denial of Service) and worms will generate unresponsive flows to the Internet traffic. To avoid a congestion collapse, network flows should adjust their sending rates. Adaptive flows adjust the sending rates while unresponsive flows do not respond to congestion and keep sending packets. Unresponsive flows waste resources by taking their share of the upstream links of a domain and dropping packets later when the downstream links are congested. A congestion control algorithm is evaluated using both adaptive and unresponsive flows [4].

The unresponsive flows to the network congestion control are dangerous to the network equilibrium and quality of service. In some certain scenarios, the limited network resource can be occupied by the unresponsive flows easily, which results in reduction of quality. A new AQM algorithm is proposed in order to strengthen the robustness of Internet against unresponsive flows [9].

Application based network fairness is proposed in [7]. The impact on server-side fairness judgment caused by non-subjective factors and providing the fairness scheduling mechanism of server based on network measurement are analyzed with its feasibility and validity primarily proved through an actual implementation.

Unresponsive flows are flows that do not use end-to-end congestion control and in particular, that do not reduce their load on the network when subject to packet drops.

This unresponsive behavior result in both unfairness and congestion collapse in network. There are several ways to detect the presence of unresponsive flows. It is suggested that routers monitor flows to detect whether it is responsive to congestion or not. If a flow is not responsive to congestion, it is penalized by discarding packets to a higher rate at the router. It does not help to save bandwidth at the upstream if the flow sees congestion at the downstream because this solution does not propagate the congestion information from downstream to upstream [2].

A rate based dropping policy is proposed for unresponsive flows. This policy uses the difference in traffic arrival patterns of responsive and unresponsive flows and discards more packets from unresponsive flows. The dropping probability of an arriving packet at the router is determined by the temporal arrival rate of the router at that time and the router does not need to identify the flow to which the packet belongs [6].

3 System Model

Simulation provides the powerful way to measure performance before the system under study has not actually been implemented. Such simulation can capture the dynamic interaction between applications and parallel architectures. Also it offers flexibility as one can make modifications to the simulation model and check their effect easily [8]. Hence to study the congestion control and unresponsive flows, a simulation system environment is considered that is assumed to have four nodes, in which one of them serves as a server.

4 Congestion Avoidance and Unresponsive Flow Control

In network, one system is considered as server and all other nodes are considered as clients. The server handles the congestion control and unresponsive flows. The nodes here are considered as edge routers which had forward and backward feedback mechanisms. The exchange of feedback between routers at the borders of a network in order to detect and restrict unresponsive traffic flows before they enter the network, thereby preventing congestion within the network.

Users are certified by the server to enter into the network to prevent the unauthorized users access the server. After getting authentication by the server, the user gives the request for retrieving file and gets the file from the server. If the server communicates with another user also, the server acts as a supervisor between those users. The users share the files from the server.

Based on the user defined query, server searches the corresponding file in the database and sends that file to the particular user. The server responds to the request send by the client with its IP address and port number. The packets which are sent by the server may vary from different speeds. If the speed varies, congestion or collision or packet loss may occur.

(A) Feedback control algorithm

An algorithm has been followed to avoid the congestion or collision while transfer of packets varies in different speeds. A feedback algorithm is followed to check the various speeds of the packets and finds which packet speed has to be reduced. Normally packets are traversed in various speeds and hence there is a chance of congestion or occurrence of packet loss. To overcome this problem, feedback control algorithm is followed which is used to find the speed of the per-flow of packets.

(B) Rate control algorithm

After finding the feedback, the rate has been reduced by the router near the end point of the network router. It is insisted that the packet rate has to be reduced and controlled. After finding the feedback, if it is found to be faster the threshold rate, then the speed of the packet should be controlled and thus the congestion is reduced. The rate control algorithm also regulates the rate at which each flow is allowed to enter the network.

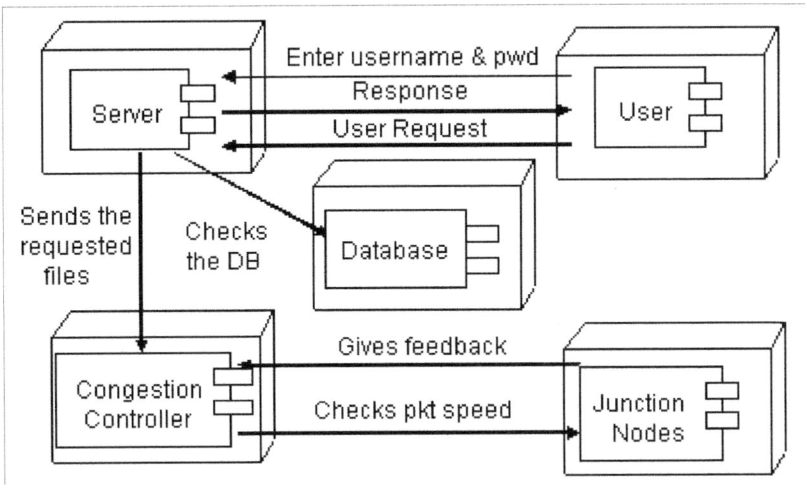

Fig. 1. Deployment diagram for congestion control and unresponsive flows

5 Experimental Results

The server is activated initially. The request for file is given from the client to the server. The figure 2 shows the simulation run of the server with the details of congestion control and rate control algorithms.

After authenticating from the server, the client can give the request for required file transfer. The list of files and directories available from the server is also shown in the window. The user can select the requested file. It is shown in figure 3.

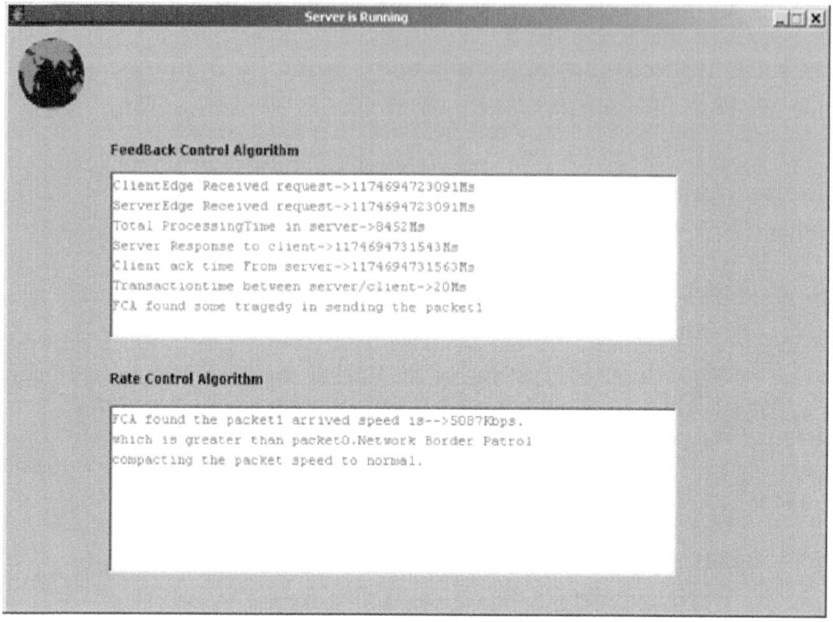

Fig. 2. Server running the algorithm and showing the status

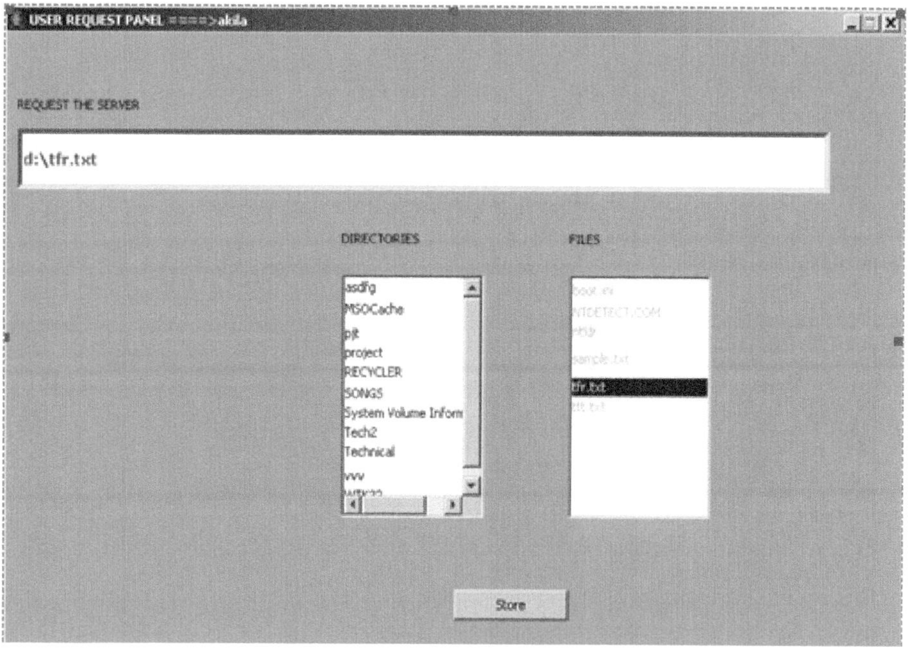

Fig. 3. User request for file in the server

For rate control algorithm, the packet speed must be reduced. Hence for a specified request, the packet speed sending for the first time is 5087 bits/second and during the second time, it is reduced to 5000 bits/second. The sample window is shown in figure 4.

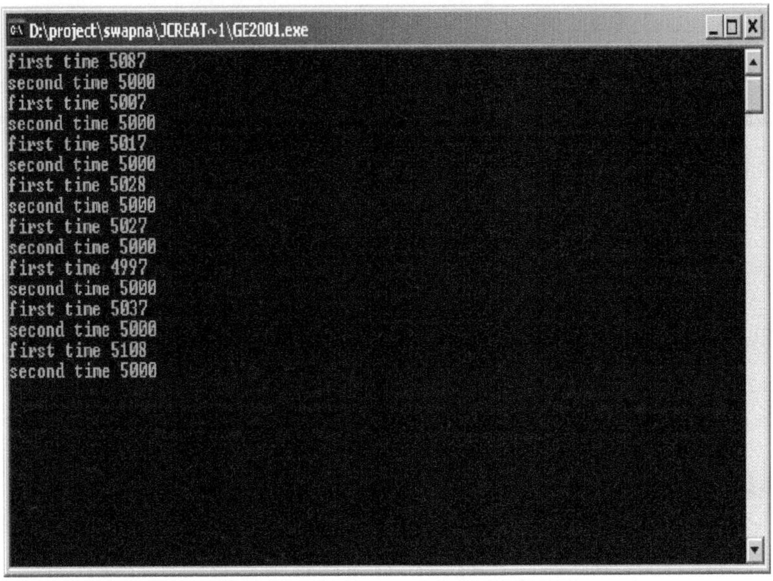

Fig. 4. Server controls the packet speed

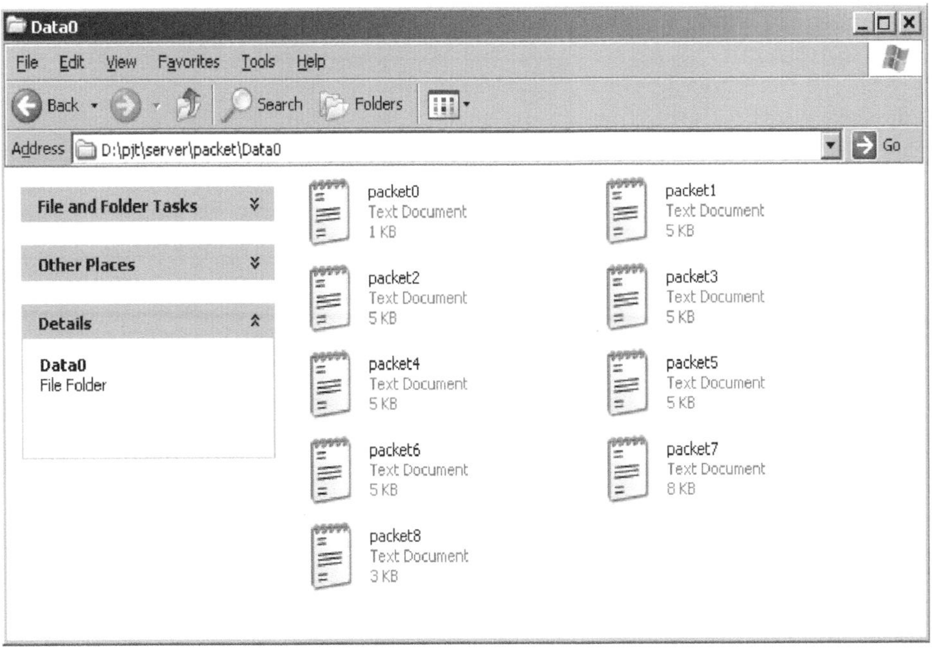

Fig. 5. Server splits the file into packets (i.e. to separate files)

For transfering the file, the server first splits the file into number of packets and then send one after another. Figure 5 shows the file spliting for a requested file from a sample client.

After sending all the packets, the client also receive the file in correct form. It is shown in figure 6.

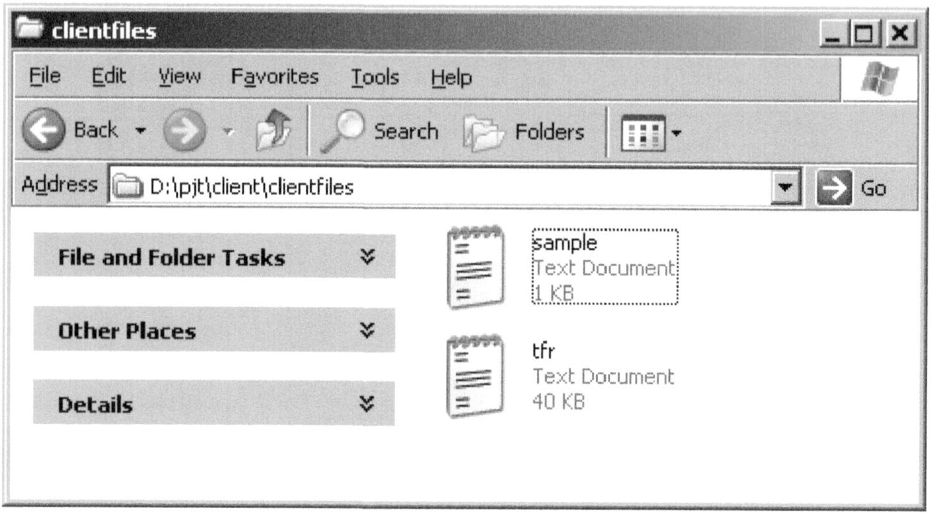

Fig. 6. Received files at the clients

6 Conclusion

Nowadays network utilization is very essential for any kind of end user usage. There are various factors that affect the fairness of the networks. The main factors to be considered in this work for unfairness for networks are congestion collapse and unresponsive flows. There are many solutions that are focused towards either the congestion control or the control of unresponsive flows. This work is focusing on both the problems and giving the solution. For that, the main file transfer between the server and clients are simulated. The resultant observation shows that the unresponsive flows are controlled and at the same time, congestion is also avoided. For future work, other factors are to be considered for improving the fairness of the networks.

References

1. Wang, Y., Wang, Z.: Explicit routing Algorithms for Internet Traffic Engineering. In: Proceedings of eighth International Conference on Computer Communications and Networks (October 1999)
2. Floyd.S, Fall.K, Promoting the use of end-to-end congestion control in the Internet. In: IEEE/ACM Transactions on Networking (August. 1999)
3. Mortier, R.: Internet Traffic Engineering, Technical Report (April 2002)

4. Juan, S., Rico, P.: Network Tomography-based unresponsive flow detection and control. In: Ninth IEEE Workshop on Future Trends of Distributed Computing Systems (May 2003)
5. Feamster, N., Borkenhagen, J., Rexford, J. In: ACM SIGCOMM Computer Communication Review (October 2003)
6. Yeom, I.: A rate based dropping policy for punishing unresponsive flows. Computer Communications 29(10) (June 2006)
7. Wang, X., Zhang, X., Yang, S.: Design of a fairness guarantee mechanism based on network measurement. In: Tenth High Assurance Systems Engineering Symposium (December 2007)
8. Chhabra, A., Singh, G., kumar, G.: Simulated Performance analysis of multiprocessor dynamic space-sharing scheduling policy. International Journal of Computer Science and Network Security 9(2) (Febraury 2009)
9. Thiruchelvi, G., Raja, J.: An adaptive congestion control mechanism for unresponsive flows. In: IEEE International Conference on Internet Multimedia Services Architecture and Applications (December 2009)

Authenticated Routing for Ad-Hoc On-Demand Distance Vector Routing Protocol

Preeti Sachan and Pabitra Mohan Khilar

Department of Computer Science and Engineering,
National Intitute of Technology Rourkela, Odisha, India
preetischn@gmail.com, pmkhilar@nitrkl.ac.in

Abstract. Mobile ad hoc network (MANET) is a collection of mobile hosts without any existing infrastructure or centralized access point such as a base station. MANET is an emerging research area because of their self configuration and self maintenance capabilities. However the wireless ad-hoc network is more vulnerable to security than conventional wired and wireless networks due to its characteristics like open medium, lack of centralized monitoring, wireless and dynamic nature. Routing security is an important issue in MANET. The primary function of a routing protocol is to establish a secure and efficient route between communicating nodes so that data may be delivered correctly. Existing routing protocols need security mechanism to guard against external and internal attacks but it is very difficult to find a general idea that can prevent efficiently all types of attacks, as each attack has its own distinct characteristics. In this paper, we proposed a method that is based on ad hoc on-demand routing (AODV) protocol and can efficiently prevent the attacks from member of the network including black hole, modifying routing information and impersonation attacks. The proposed method uses only hash function and thus provides fast message verification and sender as well as intermediate nodes authentication. Simulation result shows that in the presence of malicious node, the proposed method performs better than the original AODV protocol.

Keywords: Mobile ad hoc network (MANET), Routing security, AODV, Black hole, Impersonation, Hash function, Authentication.

1 Introduction

MANET is an autonomous system of mobile nodes without any existing infrastructure or centralized access point such as a base station [6]. MANET is an emerging research area because of their self configuration and self maintenance capabilities. The applications of MANET are found in the areas such as personal area networking, meeting rooms and conferences, robot data acquisition, military environments, disaster relief and emergency operations etc. due to their easy deployment. However, a MANET presents a greater security problem than conventional wired and wireless networks due to its fundamental characteristics of open medium, dynamic topology, absence of centralized access point, distributed cooperation, lack of association [21]. Authorized and malicious nodes

D.C. Wyld et al. (Eds.): CNSA 2011, CCIS 196, pp. 364–373, 2011.

both can access the wireless channel. Nodes are portable devices that make them vulnerable to compromises or physical capture. Routing algorithm needs mutual trust between nodes and absence of centralized access point prevents use of monitoring agent in the system. The limitation of wireless network and mobile nodes such as bandwidth of wireless channel, frequent disconnection of link, partition of network, short battery life time and limited computation capability poses an important challenge for implementation of cryptographic algorithms for providing security to these networks. Routing security is an important issue in MANET [4, 5]. A malicious node can perform many types of routing attacks such as routing table overflow, routing table and cache poisoning [15]. Routing protocols must be robust against routing attack in order to establish correct and efficient route between pair of nodes.

The rest of the paper is organized as follows. Section 2 discusses network security attacks and related works in MANET. Section 3 summarizes the basic operations of AODV routing protocol and its security flaws. We propose a security mechanism to protect routing messages based on AODV protocol. In section 4, we analyze simulation result of proposed method. Finally, we conclude and address the related future works in section 5.

2 Security Attacks and Related Work

MANET is vulnerable to various types of attack in the presence of malicious nodes. Attacks can be classified as passive attacks and active attacks [4, 5, 12, 15, 23]. Passive attacks typically involve eavesdropping, snooping or traffic analysis. Active attacks involve actions performed by adversaries such as data modification, gain authentication, replication or deletion of data, inserting false packets etc. Furthermore, active attacks can be divided into external attacks and internal attacks. External attacks are caused by nodes that are not a member of network while internal attacks are more severe as malicious nodes are already members of network. Some of the active attacks are denial of service, blackhole [5], wormhole [8], impersonation, resource consumption, information disclosure, routing attacks etc. The five major security services that need to be addressed in order to prevent above mentioned attacks are: Availability, Confidentiality, Authentication, Integrity and Non-repudiation [2, 14]. However ad hoc network routing protocols do not need *confidentiality* as routing messages need to be processed by intermediate nodes before forwarding in the network.

Many researchers have addressed security issues with routing [4, 5, 6, 15, 21, 23]. They have studied the vulnerabilities of ad hoc networks against attacks and proposed solution to combat the attack [3, 8, 9, 16]. Hu, Johnson and Perrig proposed Secure Efficient Ad hoc Distance Vector (SEAD) [7] protocol that is based on the design of DSDV [17]. SEAD is designed to prevent attacks such as DoS and resource consumption attacks. SEAD uses one way hash function for authenticating the updates that are received from malicious nodes and non-malicious nodes. This protocol is very efficient and can be easily implemented. The protocol is robust against multiple uncoordinated attacks but would not be able to prevent the attacker who uses the same metric and sequence number which were used by the recent update message. Ariadne [10], by the same authors, is based on basic operation of DSR [11]. Ariadne provides security against one compromised node and also prevents many types of denial-of-service attacks. Ariadne uses message authentication code (MAC) and secret key shared between two parties to ensures point-to-point authentication of a routing message. However, it relies on the TESLA [19] broadcast authentication protocol for secure authentication of a routing message which requires loose time synchronization. Security-aware routing (SAR) [13] is an on demand routing protocol based on AODV [18]. SAR defines level of trust as a metric for routing. The main drawback of SAR is that during the path discovery process, encryption and decryption is done at each hop which increases the power consumption. The protocol also requires different keys for different level of security which leads to increase in number of keys required when the number of security levels used increases. K. Sanzgiri et al [20] developed authenticated routing for ad hoc networks (ARAN), which is based on AODV. In ARAN, each node has a certificate signed by a trusted server whose public key is known to all legal nodes in the network. ARAN provides authentication, non repudiation and message integrity but needs a small amount of prior security coordination among nodes. The keys are generated a priory and distributed to all the nodes by the server. The ARAN prevents unauthorized participation, message modification attacks but prone to replay attacks if nodes do not have time synchronization. The ARAN uses asymmetric cryptography computation which causes higher cost for route discovery. Zapata and Asokan [22] proposed Secure AODV (SAODV), another protocol designed to secure AODV. The idea behind SAODV is to use a digital signature to authenticate the non-mutable fields of messages and hash chains to secure the hop count information. The SAODV is based on asymmetric key cryptographic operation therefore the nodes in MANET are unable to verify the digital signatures quickly enough as they have limited battery life and processing power. Moreover if a malicious node floods messages with invalid signatures then verification can be very expensive.

3 Proposals of Authentication Mechanisms

3.1 Ad-Hoc On-Demand Distance Vector Routing (AODV) Protocol

Ad hoc on-demand distance vector routing (AODV) protocol is a reactive routing protocol. Each node maintains a routing table, which contains information about the route to particular destination. AODV allows mobile nodes to establish routes quickly for new destinations as well as to respond to changes in network topology and link failure. AODV protocol works in two phases a) route discovery process and b) route maintenance process. Route discovery process uses route request (RREQs) and route reply (RREPs) messages where as route maintenance is performed with two additional messages: Hello and RRER messages. Sequence number is used for route freshness, loop prevention and faster convergence. AODV protocol does not provide any security mechanisms to guard against attack. The major vulnerabilities present in AODV protocol are: An attacker can impersonate a node by forging a RREQ/RREP with its IP address as IP address of that node. Hop count or sequence number can be modified in routing message. A malicious node can also forge RRER message. AODV routing protocol requires at least two security services: Data origin authentication at each receiving node and routing message integrity. Message integrity is of the most concern in routing. Modification of routing information may lead to inconsistency in network. Routing table may contain false information about network topology. Change in sequence number may result in routing loops etc.

3.2 Assumption and Notation

The proposed method is based on shared secret key technology. We assume a mechanism to set up a pairwise shared secret keys. A total number of $n.(n-1)/2$ pairwise shared keys will be maintained in the network; if n is the number of nodes in the network. Both source and destination nodes are not compromised. AODV assumes bidirectional links. The following notation is used to describe cryptography operations:

- S and D are source node and destination node respectively.
- $K_{SD}\,(or K_{DS})$ denotes the secret key shared between node S and D.
- Each node holds the HMAC (message authentication code) algorithm [15] .
- MACm defined by $HMAC\,(K_{SD}, M)$ denotes the computation of the message authentication code of message M using secret key K_{SD} between nodes S and D.

3.3 Proposed Method

In AODV protocol, routing messages RREQ or RREP have two types of information: Mutable and Non Mutable. The hop count is only mutable field as intermediate node increment the hop count field while forwarding the RREQ. The rest fields such as sequence number or IP address are non mutable fields as they remain unchanged. The proposed method uses two mechanisms to secure the AODV messages: $HMAC\,(K_{SD}, M)$ is used to authenticate the non-mutable fields of the routing messages M and one way HMAC key chains is used to secure the hop count information. We assume that HMAC function takes a variable number of arguments by simply concatenating them and computes the message authentication code. The propagation of the route request (RREQ) and route reply (RREP) messages is described in Figure 1, where $*$ denotes a local broadcast and $HMAC_{K_X}(.)$ denotes HMAC code generated using shared secret key K_X. The message P is extended route request packet (RREQ) containing the following fields : < RREQ, MAC_m , HMAC chain, intermediate node list >, where

RREQ is original route request message. Here route request packet has been extended (denoted as message P) to hold three more fields MACm, HMAC chain and intermediate node list. As shown in Figure 2(a), source node S first compute $MAC_m = HMAC_{K_{SD}}(RREQ)$ using secret key K_{SD} shared between itself and destination node D. The source node uses fields such as sequence number; source and destination IP address except the hop count of RREQ packet and compute message authentication code MACm by simply concatenating them. The sender node compute $h0 = HMAC_{K_{SD}}(S, N)$ and initialize the intermediate node list to empty list. Here S is source IP address and N is time varying component known as nonce. Nonce is used to prevent replay attack. We can use route request broadcast id or source sequence number as nonce since each time a source node broadcast a new route request message, it monotonically increases its RREQ broadcast id or source sequence number. When any intermediate node for example node A receives a packet P it modifies packet P by appending IP address of previous node S (from which it receives the packet P) to the intermediate node list and replacing the HMAC chain field with $h1 = HMAC_{K_{AD}}(A, h0)$ where K_{AD} is shared secret key between intermediate node A and destination node D. In the proposed method, the intermediate node only forwards the route request packet P by broadcasting it and does not send the route reply packet to the source node S. For the destination node D, if a packet P is received, it checks the following three conditions:

- **Condition 1:** Check $MAC_m = HMAC_{K_{SD}}(RREQ)$.

Destination node D checks integrity of received RREQ message. Destination node D first computes message authentication code from RREQ and then compare with received MACm.

- **Condition 2:** Check $h_3 = HMAC_{K_{CD}}(C, HMAC_{K_{BD}}(B, HMAC_{K_{AD}}(A, HMAC_{K_{SD}}(S, N))))$.

Destination node obtains intermediate node list (S, A, B, C) which contains the IP address of intermediate nodes. It computes HMAC chain using intermediate node list and verify h3. If h3 is verified it means that received node list (S, A, B, C) is correct and malicious node hasn't removed any intermediate node from node list.

- **Condition 3:** Check the hop count field i.e. Number of intermediate nodes in node list (including source node) = Hop count value in RREQ message.

If the three above-mentioned conditions are all satisfied, then received RREQ message is regarded as a valid message. If the destination node determines that the RREQ is valid, it unicast route reply packet P back along the reverse path to the source, containing following fields : $<$ RREP, MAC_m , HMAC chain, intermediate node list $>$. In same way, the source node can authenticate the destination node as well as can check integrity of RREP message. The whole procedure will be same but instead of route request message (RREQ), route reply (RREP) message is used.

The RREQ process is illustrated below:

$S: \quad MAC_m = HMAC_{K_{SD}}(RREQ), h_0 = HMAC_{K_{SD}}(S, N)$
$\quad P =< RREQ, MAC_m, h_0, () >$
$S->*: \quad P$
$A: \quad h_1 = HMAC_{K_{AD}}(A, h_0), P =< RREQ, MAC_m, h_1, (S) >$
$A->*: \quad P$
$B: \quad h_2 = HMAC_{K_{BD}}(B, h_1), P =< RREQ, MAC_m, h_2, (S, A) >$
$B->*: \quad P$
$C: \quad h_3 = HMAC_{K_{CD}}(C, h_2), P =< RREQ, MAC_m, h_3, (S, A, B) >$
$C->*: \quad P$
$D: \quad \text{receives} \quad P =< RREQ, MAC_m, h_3, (S, A, B, C) >$

The RREP process is illustrated below:

$D: \quad MAC_m = HMAC_{K_{SD}}(RREP), h_0 = HMAC_{K_{SD}}(D, N)$
$\quad P =< RREP, MAC_m, h_0, () >$
$D->*: \quad P$
$C: \quad h_1 = HMAC_{K_{CS}}(C, h_0), P =< RREP, MAC_m, h_1, (D) >$
$C->*: \quad P$
$B: \quad h_2 = HMAC_{K_{BS}}(B, h_1), P =< RREP, MAC_m, h_2, (D, C) >$
$B->*: \quad P$
$A: \quad h_3 = HMAC_{K_{AS}}(A, h_2), P =< RREP, MAC_m, h_3, (D, C, B) >$
$A->*: \quad P$
$S: \quad \text{receives} \quad P =< RREP, MAC_m, h_3, (D, C, B, A) >$

Fig. 1. The sequence of secure routing message exchange in proposed method

3.4 Security Analysis

Our proposed scheme provides an efficient way to verify the message authentication and message integrity. The receiver node can authenticate the sender of message using shared secret key between receiver and sender node. The receiver can verify each fields of the RREQ or RREP message. No malicious node can remove IP address of intermediate node from intermediate node list in the RREQ or RREP as they do not know the secret key shared between pairs of node. The receiver node can authenticate the intermediate nodes using MAC key shared between itself and intermediate node. Since a one-way hash function prevents a compromised node from removing a node from the node list, the receiver node can verify the hop count fields in RREQ or RREP message using the intermediate node list. In proposed method, Only HMAC is used to protect the integrity of message so computation is very efficient, and even affordable for low-end devices such as small sensor nodes. However, an HMAC can be verified only by the intended receiver, so that we can not apply this technique to verify and authenticate broadcast message such as RRER messages having a big amount of mutable information. In the proposed method, only the destination node is permitted to initiate route reply message therefore the delay involved in the route discovery process increases as the size of the network increases. Moreover with increase in network size, a node needs more memory space to store shared secret key. Besides, the proposed method uses pairwise shared secret key, so establishing the secret key between any two nodes is an expensive operation.

4 Performance Analysis

We used network simulator tool (NS2) [1]. Network Simulator (NS2) is an event driven simulator tool and designed specifically to study the dynamic nature of wireless communication networks. To evaluate the performance of proposed method, we compared it with original AODV protocol in the presence of one malicious node that performs black hole attack. The malicious node does this by assigning a high sequence number and small hop count to the route reply message (RREP). Network traffic and scenario are configured according to Table 1. To analyze the effect of mobility, pause time is varied from 0 seconds (high mobility) to 600 seconds (no mobility) and the maximum number of connection (source-destination pairs) is 20. We consider the following performance metrics to evaluate and compare the performance of proposed method with AODV routing protocol : Packet delivery ratio, Time delay and Normalized control packet overhead.

Table 1. Simulation Parameters

Simulator	NS2 (v-2.34)
Simulation Time	600 sec
Number of Nodes	50
Area Size	1000m * 1000m
Transmission Range	250m
Maximum Speed	0-20 m/s
Pause Time	0, 100, 200, 300, 400, 500, 600
Maximum Number of Connection	20
Application Traffic	CBR
Packet Size	512 bytes
Traffic Rate	4 packets/sec
Node Mobility Model	Random Way-point Model

4.1 Packet Delivery Ratio

Packet Delivery Ratio = Total Packets Received / Total Packets Sent. The ratio of the number of data packets successfully delivered to the destinations to those generated by CBR sources. Packet delivery ratio describes the loss rate. It reflects the completeness and the accuracy of the routing protocol. Figure 2(b) shows the impact of mobility of node on packet delivery ratio when there is one malicious node in the network. It is clear that packet delivery ratio decreases with increase in mobility as the packet drop at such a highly change in network topology is much high. In case of original AODV protocol, packet delivery ratio is very less than proposed method because AODV protocol has no security mechanism to guard against malicious attacks so very few of data packets reach the destination node.

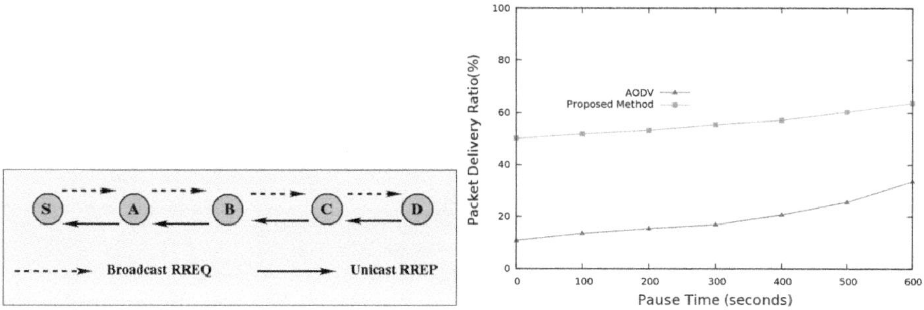

Fig. 1. (a) Message Exchange in AODV (b) Pause Time Vs Packet Delivery Ratio

4.2 Time Delay

Time delay of data packet is the difference between the time when the first data packet is received by the destination node and the time when the source node broadcasts a RREQ message. Figure 3(a) shows that time delay is more in case of proposed method . In proposed method, only destination node can send route reply message so more time is required to establish particular route. But at some pause time, the delay in AODV protocol is same when compared to the proposed method. This happens when source node selects the route where malicious node may present thus data packet takes more time to reach the destination node.

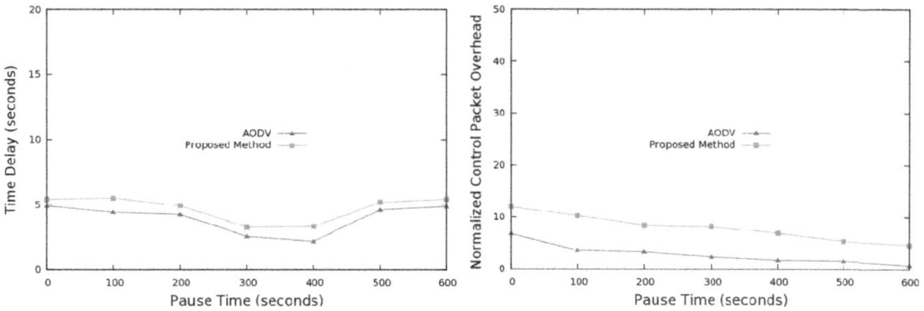

Fig. 2. (a) Pause Time Vs Time delay(b) Pause Time Vs Control Packet Overhead

4.3 Normalized Control Packet Overhead

Normalized Control Packet Overhead = (Routing Packets Sent * Size of Routing Packet) / (Received Data Packets * Size of Data Packet).

The number of routing packets transmitted per data packet delivered at the destination. Each hop wise transmission of a routing packet is counted as one routing packet. Figure 3(b) shows the impact of the mobility speeds of nodes on control packet overhead. The overhead increases with increase in mobility since higher speed of nodes leads to more link failure which will result in more route discoveries thus increases the routing packet overhead. In proposed method, routing or control packets use extra bytes to store hashes and intermediate node address therefore overhead is more in compared to AODV protocol.

5 Conclusion and Future Work

In this paper we studied the security requirements in MANET and proposed a method based on AODV protocol that can effectively prevent internal attack from member of this network including black hole and impersonation attacks. The proposed method uses a one-way hash function and does not involve any asymmetric cryptographic operation and thus provides fast message verification and nodes authentication. The proposed method uses pairwise shared secret key, so establishing the secret key between any two nodes is an expensive operation. Moreover the proposed method cannot verify and authenticate broadcast message such as RRER message. Our next work will be how to solve this problem.

References

[1] Ns-2, the ns manual (formally known as ns documentation), `http://www.isi.edu/nsnam/ns/doc`
[2] Stallings, W.: Cryptography and Network Security: Principles and Practices, 3rd edn. Prentice Hall, Englewood Cliffs (2003)
[3] Castelluccia, C., Montenegro, G.: Protecting aodv against impersonation attacks. ACM SIGMOBILE Mobile Computing and Communication Review 6(3), 108–109 (2002)
[4] Djenouri, D., Khelladi, L., Badache, N.: A survey of security issues in mobile ad hoc and sensor networks. IEEE Communications Surveys and Tutorials Journal 7(4), 2–29 (2005)
[5] Deng, H., Li, W., Agrawal, D.P.: Routing security in wireless ad hoc networks. IEEE Communications Magzine 40(10), 70–75 (2002)
[6] Hu, Y.C., Perrig, A.: A survey of secure wireless ad hoc routing. IEEE Security and Privacy 2(3), 28–39 (2004)
[7] Hu, Y., Johnson, D.B., Perrig, A.: Sead: Secure efficient distance vector routing for mobile wireless ad hoc networks. In: Proceedings of the IEEE Workshop on Mobile Computing Systems and Applications (WMCSA), pp. 3–13 (June 2002)
[8] Hu, Y., Perrig, A., Johnson, D.B.: Packet leashes: A defense against wormhole attacks in wireless ad hoc networks. In: Proceedings of IEEE INFOCOM 2003, vol. 3, pp. 1976–1986 (April 2003)

[9] Hu, Y., Perrig, A., Johnson, D.B.: Rushing attacks and defense in wireless ad hoc network routing protocols. In: ACM Workshop Wireless Security WiSe 2003, pp. 1–10 (September 2003)
[10] Hu, Y.C., Johnson, D.B., Perrig, A.: Ariadne: A secure on-demand routing protocol for ad hoc networks. In: Proc. 8th Ann. Intl Conf. Mobile Computing and Networking (MobiCom 2002), pp. 12–23. ACM Press, New York (2002)
[11] Johnson, D.B., Maltz, D.A.: The dynamic source routing protocol in ad hoc wireless networks. In: Mobile Computing, vol. 353, pp. 153–181. Kluwer Academic Publishers, Dordrecht (1996)
[12] Kannhavong, B., Nakayama, H., Nemoto, Y., Kato, N.: a survey of routing attacks in mobile ad hoc networks. IEEE Wireless Communications, 85–91 (October 2007)
[13] Kravets, R., Yi, S., Naldurg, P.: A security-aware routing protocol for wireless ad hoc networks. In: Proceedings of ACM MOBIHOC 2001, pp. 299–302 (October 2001)
[14] Menezes, A.J., Oorschot, P.V., Vanstone, S.: Handbook of applied cryptography. CRC press, Boca Raton (1996)
[15] Murthy, C.S.R., Manoj, B.: Ad hoc wireless networks: Architectures and Protocols. Prentice Hall, Englewood Cliffs (2004)
[16] Papadimitratos, P., Haas, Z.J.: Secure routing for mobile ad hoc networks. In: Proceedings of the SCS Communication Networks and Distributed Systems Modeling and Simulation Conference (CNDS 2002), pp. 1–13 (January 2002)
[17] Perkins, C.E., Bhagwat, P.: Highly dynamic destination-sequenced distance-vector routing (dsdv) for mobile computers. In: Proceeding of ACM SIG-COMM, vol. 24, pp. 234–244 (August 1994)
[18] Perkins, C.E., Royer, E.M.: Ad hoc on-demand distance vector (aodv) routing. In: Proceeding of IEEE Workshop on Mobile Computing system and applications, pp. 90–100 (February 1999)
[19] Perrig, A., Canetti, R., Song, D., Tygar, D.: Efficient and secure source authentication for multicast. In: Network and Distributed System Security Symposium, NDSS 2001 (February 2001)
[20] Sanzgiri, K., Dahill, B., Levine, B.N., Shields, C., Royer, E.M.B.: A secure routing protocol for ad hoc networks. In: Proceedings of IEEE ICNP, pp. 78–87 (November 2002)
[21] Yang, H., Luo, H., Ye, F., Lu, S., Zhang, L.: security in mobile ad hoc networks: challenges and solutions. IEEE of Wireless Communications 11, 38–47 (2004)
[22] Zapata, M.G., Asokan, N.: Securing ad hoc routing protocols. In: Proc. ACM Workshop on Wireless Security(WiSe), pp. 1–10. ACM Press, New York (2002)
[23] Zhou, L., Haas, Z.J.: Securing ad hoc networks. IEEE Network 13(6), 24–30 (2009)

Passblot: A Usable Way of Authentication Scheme to Generate One Time Passwords

Sainath Gupta, Pruthvi Sabbu, Siddhartha Varma, and Suryakanth V. Gangashetty

IIIT – Hyderabad, Gachibowli, Hyderabad, India 500032
{sainath.guptapg08,pruthvireddy.sabbu,siddhartha.varma}
@research.iiit.ac.in, svg@iiit.ac.in

Abstract. User authentication is necessary to secure the data and process on internet or mobile communications. Most commonly employed system for said purpose is Static alpha-numeric password based authentication system. But they are susceptible to various types of active and passive attacks. One of the promising alternatives is Graphical password based authentication systems which if implemented properly are secure but not as easy to understand or learn.

In this paper we propose a varied version of inkblot authentication [1] graphical password system which is secure as well as usable. It generates pseudo random one time passwords using a set of inkblots unique to the user. Properties of one time passwords ensures the resistance towards replay, phishing, shoulder surfing, active and dictionary attacks. We also analyze the results from two experiments we have conducted to confirm that this system is easy to learn and password memorability is high, thus making it a promising authentication mechanism.

Keywords: Usable security, Authentication, One-time passwords, Cueing, Interfaces.

1 Introduction

Computer users generally have multiple user accounts for which they tend to use different passwords. People tend to forget their passwords [8, 9] due to human memory's fallibility and need reminders or replacements. Cost of replacement is anything but negligible and has to be funded. Garner [16] claims that a single replacement costs anywhere between \$30 and \$15. They estimate that on an average each employee will call about 5 times a year (since they have passwords for multiple systems). Also, this causes users to use unsafe practices like writing down, saving it in email drafts, reusing the same password across multiple sites, or frequently reinitializing passwords upon failure to authenticate [10, 11, 12, 13].

Further, due to various types of successful dictionary attacks, system providers are forced to implement new password schemes of adding a special character, a capital and a number which has further worsened the scenario. In addition, static alpha numeric passwords authentication systems are prone to replay attacks, session hijacking, shoulder surfing attack, dictionary attack, key logger attack and replay attack.

D.C. Wyld et al. (Eds.): CNSA 2011, CCIS 196, pp. 374–382, 2011.

One of the promising alternatives for authentication systems is Graphical password systems which often have the advantage that they are significantly more secure with respect to both writing down and verbal disclosure. Many Graphical Authentication systems [1, 2, 4] have been proposed as an alternative. However, they are susceptible to replay attacks and as well shoulder surfing attack. The advent of technology has made capturing, analysis and deciphering of data very easy. The users may be frustrated if these systems are erroneous in their implementation. To address the above issues, we propose a modified inkblot based graphical password system, known as Passblot which is resistant to most of the attacks mentioned above. Passblot has the following salient features.

i. Immune to replay, dictionary attacks and key loggers
ii. Unique password at every login. It acts as one-time password.
iii. Robust against brute-force and blind attacks.
iv. Scalable.
v. Can also be used to overcome session hijacking attack.

In this paper, we review Stubblefield's Inkblot authentication [1] in Section 2. In Section 3, proposed scheme is introduced and methodology followed is explained. User study on our scheme is explained in Section 4. Section 5 outlines the results and analysis and Section 6 presents the conclusion.

2 Related Work

Two phase protocol is a common practice to grant access to restricted digital space. This involves identification followed by authentication. The major problem with this practice is that it tends to fail most of the times due to fallible human memory or insecure communication channels. In the face of fallible human memory and insecure communication channels which tend to fail, passwords have to be often replaced, which poses problems.

The ideal process would be for a suitable cueing mechanism to be identified which could help users to remember their passwords thus reducing the incidence of password replacements. The cueing mechanism should be ideal enough to help users to remember their passwords easily.

2.1 Cueing Mechanisms

A cue can be defined as: a) A reminder or prompting, or b) A hint or suggestion [18].But, in an authentication system, this mechanism should easily be understood for a lay-man to use.

Hertzum [5] proposes that users specify particular password characters which will be displayed at password entry in order to jog their memory. This idea was tested and concluded that even though it worked, the passwords were often weak and some kind of cueing mechanism is required for stronger passwords. The proposed inkblot cues rely on the fact that there is strong evidence that pictures are more memorable than words because of the picture superiority effect [6].

Since, a purely representational image will not work because what one really needs is an image that elicits a different textual association from different users so that malicious users cannot confidently guess textual associations within the required strikes allowed before a lockout.

Stubblefield and Simon [1] experimented with inkblots, to assist users to form a semantic association with the textual password, which could be used as a reminder. They displayed 10 inkblots in a particular sequence. For each blot the user was required to enter two characters (the starting and ending character of their inkblot description). They had some success in trials of this mechanism, achieving entropy of 4.09 bits per character. Here, the user is encouraged to create a password more resilient to dictionary attacks, rather than simply making dictionary attacks more difficult.

2.2 Problems Associated with Inkblot Authentication System

Inkblot Authentication system [1] solves only one problem associated with regular passwords, which is being prone to dictionary attack. It is still susceptible to all the attacks associated with static password systems like shoulder surfing, replay attack & most types of active attacks. Moreover, even if one session is compromised, the whole system gets compromised, forcing the user to register another set of images, which is very resource intensive for user.

3 Our Proposal

Authentication in Passblot is based on the inkblots similar to the scheme introduced in [1], but has enhanced security. Even though we can generate inkblots on the fly, we chose to use ten inkblot-like random images taken from inkblot authentication website [7] with the required permissions.

During registration, a user registers using their respective email ids as usernames. They were given the selected 10 inkblots one by one as shown in Fig. 1 and asked to think of a description for each inkblot. And then type the first and last letters of the description which can be referred as an association to that inkblot or hash of the

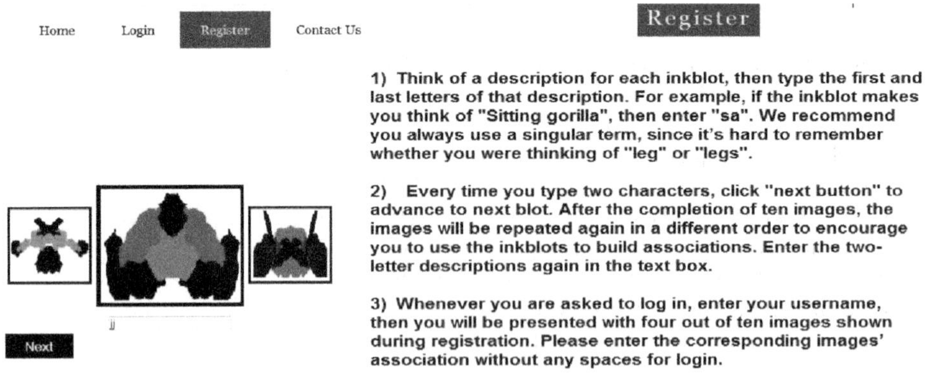

Fig. 1. Registration page for Passblot

description. After that, the users were again shown the same inkblots in a different order to confirm the corresponding associations and as well to prevent them from forming their own associations.

In the authentication phase, when the user inputs his username, the user is shown only four inkblots out of the ten inkblots he was shown during the registration phase and is asked to input the corresponding associations. The process is as shown in Fig. 2. The Authentication system authenticates the user if any of the three out of four associations are valid.

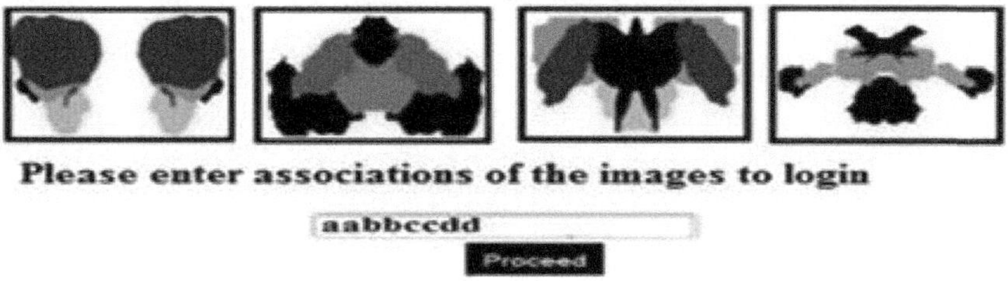

Fig. 2. Login for Passblot

For example, let the associations made during the registration phase to the inkblot images Inkblot 1, Inkblot 2, Inkblot 3, Inkblot 4(shown in Fig 2) be aa, bb, cc, dd respectively. Then the password for this particular session will be aabbccdd. Since the user is authenticated even if one of the association is wrong, the following associations i.e., xxbbccdd or aaxxccdd or aabbxxdd or aabbccxx are also authorized associations to login to the system.

We have conducted a user study to analyze our system's security, ease of use. The analysis is discussed in the following section.

4 User Study

A total of 1000 inkblots were given by Jeremy Elson of Microsoft Corporation of which we used only 10 images for the experiment, which are shown in Fig 3. The abstract inkblot images can also be generated on the fly during registration process to give each user as well as each registration a unique set of inkblots.

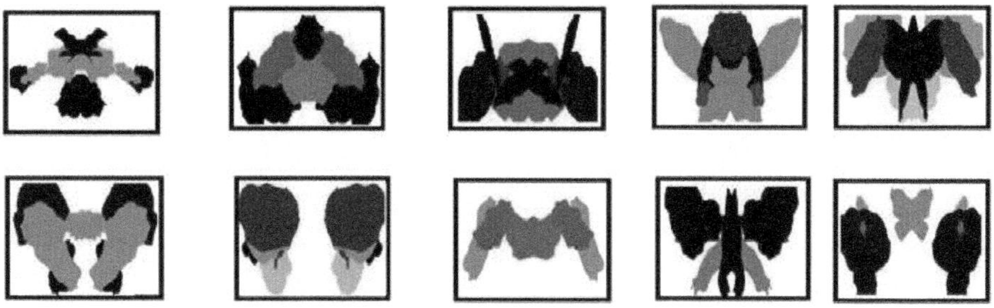

Fig. 3. Ten inkblot images used in the experiment

We conducted the user study on two platforms (i.e., on personal computers and smart phones) conducting three different experiments in total.

i. The first experiment was conducted on 30 volunteers using their Personal Computers in their own work space as we wanted to keep the experiment close to the real-life conditions. Both registration and login phase were conducted as discussed in Section 3.
ii. The second experiment was conducted to analyze the experience on smart phones. This experiment involved five users, using smart phones with Wi-Fi access and QWERTY keyboard. In this experiment, users were encouraged to carry out the registration phase on the Personal Computers to avoid the effect of vexation on the process, caused due to slightly extended time-consuming registration method. And the complete login phase is conducted normally on the smart phones.
iii. The third experiment happened in parallel with the first experiment where six volunteers were asked to use the standard text based password authentications.

A total of 41 undergraduate students and Research Associates volunteered for the prototype testing. 16 of the volunteers are female & rest 25 of them were male, with ages between ranging 18 to 31, there median age being 23.

Users were sent an email with complete instructions and a link to the website. The set of instructions are also shown in the login page as shown in figure 1. Users were also shown a demo of the concept before the experiment.

The experimental procedure has the following phases:

i. **Registration:** The users were asked to register using their respective email ids as usernames. They were initially shown 10 inkblots one by one as shown in Fig 1, and asked to enter an association to that inkblot. After that, the users were again shown the same inkblots in a jumbled order to confirm whether they associated properly and as well to prevent them from forming their own associations. There was no time constraint placed on the whole process to analyze the ease with which the user is using the system. After the registration, the users had to login twice to get familiarized with the system (these logins were not used in our analysis).
ii. **Authentication:** During login phase, the user is asked to enter his user name. Once the system confirms his username, it shows 4 inkblots randomly chosen out of the 10 inkblots, as shown in Fig 2, that were used in registration phase by that particular user. The user then enters the unique 8 character pass-phrase (concatenation of the 4 inkblots' associations). Login success rate and time taken to complete the process were recorded.

The users were also asked to login in three sessions to check how good the system works in long-time usage as shown below.

Session 1:	Twice after 1 hour of registration
Session 2:	Once the next day
Session 3:	Once next week

Users could also request a re-registration from the website administrator by email if the password had been forgotten. All accesses were logged to facilitate analysis. Experimental analysis and their results are presented in the following section.

5 Analysis and Results

Results shown in Table 1 show us that most of the users where able to login in session 1 & session 2, but for session 3, the users had problem with remembering the associations. Since, there was not much difference between pc & mobile users login we clubbed them both. There were a total of 137 successful logins (Mean time (M): 23.737, Standard Deviation (SE): 9.438).

Table 1. Login Success rate

Session	No of successful logins	No of users with first Attempt failed
Session 1	70	1
Session 2	34	3
Session 3	33	6

Another interesting finding that we found was that some of the people associated the inkblots in their native language like French, Hindi & Telugu. This might increase the entropy of the inkblots' associations than their regular 4 bits per character.

Authentication mechanisms, must try to maximize both security and ease of use with neither taking the upper hand. The following two sub sections will consider our findings of Passblot assisted authentication in terms of these perspectives. The main aim of these experiments is to determine whether the level of cognitive processing required in using Passblot was acceptable to users. In addition to the quantitative analysis of logging records, we also analyzed responses to a questionnaire given to the website users.

5.1 Security

Here, we report the key outcomes of the analysis. First, our scheme provides much better security against many types of active and passive attacks than many other authentication schemes. We describe some of the general password attacks and resistance of our scheme against them.

5.1.1 Immune to Replay Attack, Dictionary Attack, Key Loggers, Brute Force and Blind Attacks

Replay attack involves intercepting a stream of messages between two parties and replaying the stream as is to one or both ends. Our system requires a unique pass phrase for each login session to authenticate which makes it immune to replay attacks.

Dictionary attacks use a targeted technique of successively trying all the words in an exhaustive list called a dictionary. As of now, no such dictionary exists which can work on inkblot system. Even if somebody attempts to make a dictionary for the attack it is very resource intensive with a less chance of success. Hence, dictionary attack cannot be successful.

Key-logger is a software program or hardware device that monitors each keystroke user types on a keyboard. Attacks involving key-loggers will not succeed against our system, due to the usage of a one-time password for each login session.

For a successful login, at least 6 characters out of 8 characters have to be correct. Since, there are 26 possibilities for each character in the pass-phrase and there are 10_{P_4} possibilities for the different permutations of the inkblot image queries. Hence the probability for blind or brute force attack to succeed is $1/\,(26^6 * 10_{P_4})$.

5.1.2 Resistant to Shoulder Surfing Attack

Shoulder surfing is using direct observation techniques, such as looking over someone's shoulder, to get information. Due to advent of cheap and good resolution cameras it has become very easy for a malicious user to capture data, which is big threat for both static password system and graphical password.

Even though an attacker observes or records one successful authentication passphrase, he gets only partial information on the associations. The worst case scenario where 3 consecutive login pages contain all the 10 inkblots is the best chance for the attacker to know all the inkblot's associations. Given, the probability that two consecutive sets of 4 inkblots are the same is $1/10_{C_4}$, the attacker usually have to be successful for minimum of 3 times which makes it more robust compared to other authentication schemes.

5.1.3 Session Hijacking Attack

Since, every login produces a unique 8 alpha numeric character phrase, which can be used as a seed to generate session key with long random variable or as well it can be used as encryption key to encrypt the data being communicated with the server, any or combination of both of the methods can be effectively used to thwart the session hijacking by a malicious user.

5.1.4 Social Engineering Attack

In a social engineering attack, someone attempts to obtain your password, while masquerading as a support technician or other authorized individual who needs your login information, relying on social engineering. The inherent feature of this system's inability to share password data makes this attack infeasible.

5.1.5 Resistant to Intercepting

Packet sniffers and other tools that monitor network traffic can easily capture passwords transmitted over the network in unencrypted form. In our system, as the pass phrase generated is a one-time password, even if one session's password is sniffed by an attacker he can't possibly use it to authenticate next session. Also, since the key is almost like pseudo random character code of length 8, it can be used as symmetric key between user and server to safe guard in man in middle attacks and as well against phishing attack.

5.2 Ease of Use

In this section we focus on the results and the feedback gathered from our experiment to measure the user's experience while using our system when compared to the traditional password system.

We start at the logical beginning and discuss our registration procedure. Although it is often glossed over, the registration of a system can play a vital role in forming the user's initial perspective of the system. During our experiment, there was no time restraint placed upon registration process. As many users never used graphical passwords before the experiment, we found that many users spent considerable amount of time during the registration phase (Mean time M: 210.257 s, Standard Deviation SE: 80.343 s).

This can be viewed as a positive or negative effect depending on the reader's point of view. It clearly makes the registration less stressful, which is a good thing and is likely to lead to more memorable passwords but increases the registration time.

We continue our discussion by considering the mean length of time (measured in seconds) required to login for successful sessions. This measurement was taken from the moment the user enters his username to the point when the login session is completed. This may also include more than one login attempt, if users were unsuccessful at first.

We found that there was a significant difference between Passblot (M: 23.737 s, SE: 9.438 s) and normal text passwords (M: 12.5455 s, SE: 3.3626 s). This value includes any additional time it would have taken for the user's browser to download and display the image representing the inkblot. During the course of the experiment there were a total of 137 successful login sessions for Passblot and 22 successful login sessions for static passwords. Also, the users didn't login strictly on time.

The questionnaire revealed that while most users felt that they understood how to use the Passblot, at least half found it hard to describe their inkblots, and to retain their description. But, almost all of them appreciated the enhanced security of the system. There is an implicit understanding that any authentication mechanism teeters between security and usability and a weakening of the one will lead to a strengthening of the other. This is also the case when Passblot was used.

6 Conclusion

In this paper, we propose Passblot to develop an authentication scheme with enhanced network security with people in mind. This work contributes design of a modified graphical password authentication system that extends the challenge-response paradigm to resist various attacks. The user study and interviews support the overall concept but requires improvement to enhance usability and reduce risks.

Further, Passblot is scalable as it seamlessly matches the conventional text-based passwords and can accommodate various lengths of textual passwords, which requires minimal-efforts for network administrators to migrate their existing passwords to Passblot. However, there are still some minor drawbacks in this system similar to other graphical password schemes such as a complicated and longer login processes. Hence, we feel that this system is best implemented where there is a need of enhanced security like in Bank transactions or in places where network cannot be trusted.

We plan to design a modified version of Passblot which is immune to shoulder-surfing attack and has a better ease of use in our future work.

Acknowledgement

I would like to thank Mr. Jeremy Elson of Microsoft for giving us the images for the experiment, Rohit A Khot for being an inspiration for my research.

I would also like to thank Mrs. Kirti Garg, Mr. Uday Kiran, Dr. Guru Prasad, Dr. Saras Chandra, Mr. Satya Aditya and Mr.Bajibabu B for their support in writing this paper, and also all the volunteers that participated/helped in the user study for spending their time & giving us valuable feedback on the system.

References

1. Stubblefield, A., Simon, D.: Inkblot authentication. Technical Report MSR-TR-2004-85 (August 2004)
2. Real User Corporation. The science behind Passfaces (2001), `http://www.realusers.com`
3. Weinshall, D.: Cognitive authentication schemes safe against spyware. In: Proc. IEEE Symp. Sec. and Privacy (May 2006)
4. Dhamija, R., Déjà vu, P.A.: A User Study Using Images for Authentication. In: Proceedings of the 9th USENIX Security Symposium (2000)
5. Hertzum, M.: Minimal-feedback hints for remembering passwords. Interactions, 38–40 (2006)
6. Paivio, A.: representations: A dual coding approach. Oxford University Press, Oxford (1986)
7. Inkblot Authentication system, `http://www.inkblotpassword.com`
8. Ensor, B.: How Consumers Remember Passwords. Forrester Research Report (June 2, 2004)
9. Florencio, D., Herley, C.: A large-scale study of web password habits. In: Proceedings of the International Conference on World Wide Web (WWW 2007), pp. 657–666 (2007)
10. Adams, A., Sasse, M.A.: Users are not the enemy. In: Communications of the ACM (CACM 1999), pp. 40–46 (December 1999)
11. Adams, A., Sasse, M.A., Lunt, P.: Making passwords secure and usable. In: Proceedings of HCI on People and Computers XII (HCI 1997), pp. 1–19 (1997)
12. BBC News. UN warns on password 'explosion'., `http://news.bbc.co.uk/2/hi/technology/6199372.stm`
13. Gaw, S., Felten, E.: Password management strategies for online accounts. In: Proceedings of the Symposium on Usable Privacy and Security (SOUPS 2006), pp. 44–55 (2006)
14. Ives, B., Walsh, K.R., Schneider, H.: The domino effect of password reuse. In: Communications of the ACM (CACM 2004), pp. 75–78 (April 2004)
15. Morris, R., Thompson, K.: Password security: A case history. In: Communications of the ACM (CACM 1979), pp. 594–497 (November 1979)
16. Witty, R.J., Brittain, K.: Automated password reset can cut IT service desk costs, Gartner Report (2004)
17. Paik, M.: Stragglers of the Herd Get Eaten: Security Concerns for GSM Mobile Banking Applications. In: HotMobile 2010: The Eleventh International Workshop on Mobile Computing Systems and Applications. ACM, Maryland (2010)
18. Renaud, K.: Password Cueing with Cue (ink) blots., `http://www.mcbryan.co.uk/papers/cueblots.pdf`

Safeguarding Web Services Using Self-Adaptive Schema Hardening Algorithm

Vipul Patel, Radhesh Mohandas, and Alwyn Pais

Information Security Research Lab,
National Institute of Technology Karnataka, India
{vip04pat,radhesh,alwyn.pais}@gmail.com

Abstract. Web Services in production often evolve over time due to changes in business and security requirements. Often various Web Service standards such as WS-Security, WS-Trust, WS-Routing etc. are introduced or revoked. Such changes alter the structure of an input message accepted by web services. Message validation mechanism becomes in-effective if schemas in use are not updated in line with aforementioned changes. Also, Web Services become prone to different attack vectors if the schemas are loosely defined. Here, we present algorithms that help fine tune schemas by the process of iterative deduction. Also, our work helps to identify patterns of attack vectors that demarcate themselves from genuine messages. Our adaptive schema refining algorithm classifies logged requests into set of schema classes based on a measure of similarity. This classification of messages in to schema classes enables us to tighten the schemas to prevent bad requests or expand the schemas to accommodate newer requests.

Keywords: Schema Hardening, Schema Refining, Adaptive Algorithm, SOAP Message Validation, XSD Signature.

1 Introduction

A Web Service is used as a basic building block for the implementation of Service Oriented Architecture (SOA) based system. Growing importance of Web Services has enticed attackers. To safeguard web services from attackers, an extra layer of security is deployed at server side which checks for various vulnerabilities such as large payload size, well-formed message structure, XML Injections and many more. An easier way to hamper web services is by sending malformed messages that do not adhere to expected message structure. These kinds of messages either bring down the server or cause unintended operations on the server side. The best way to safeguard against such issues is to use message validation before the request is supplied to the business logic. A Simple Object Access Protocol (SOAP) message validator assures that messages adhere to the prescribed schema and discards messages if they appear to be malformed. Often such validators rely on Xml Schema Definitions (XSD) derived from Web Service Description Language (WSDL) document or hand coded by programmers.

The use of standards such as WS-Security, WS-Addressing, WS-Routing, WS-Trust, WS-SecureConversation etc. requires change in the structure of input SOAP messages as their use may introduce additional elements which were not present before. In the same way if the use of any such standard is revoked then the

D.C. Wyld et al. (Eds.): CNSA 2011, CCIS 196, pp. 383–392, 2011.

message structure can change significantly. Also, schemas used by validators may be loosely defined which may cause bad messages to pass through. These kinds of changes demand significant modifications to the schema being used for validation. Manual un-guided schema updates that completely rely on the skills of a programmer may make validator susceptible to attacks.

In this paper, we propose a solution to deduce groups of schema classes by the process of iteratively learning from the logged SOAP requests. This kind of classification provides clear demarcation between kinds of messages encountered by the server. Schema classes pertaining to good requests are used to tighten schemas and schema classes pertaining to bad requests are used to expand schemas. The act of fine tuning schemas based on the deduced schemas is called "Schema Hardening Process" that would increase the efficacy of the validation mechanism. It is adaptive in nature because schema classes are formed by learning message patterns.

Section 2 reviews related work pertaining to SOAP message schema validation and a mechanism of schema comparison. In section 3, we have discussed the overall architecture of our solution. Section 4 details an operation of our solution by describing working of each stage of an algorithm. Section 5 lists future work and then section 6 concludes the paper.

2 Related Work

Gruschka, N [4] has elucidated a need of message validation to thwart an attack on Web Services. They have shown the use of schema validation mechanism to counter the Denial of Service attack (DoS). DoS attack often relies on sending a message with large number of nested XML elements that would consume considerable server resources and keep it busy. Their work has shown a way to detect such oversized payload by validating them against hardened schema. Also, they have outlined a process of deriving schema from WSDL file. Web Services can also be compromised through XML signature wrapping attacks [5]. XML structure of SOAP messages affected by signature wrapping attacks differ significantly from the normal message structure. Our work leverages upon a similarity among XML schema to deduce schema classes. We have adapted algorithms discussed in [2] and [3] to calculate a measure of difference between candidate schemas. This schema comparison algorithm has its seed in the dynamic programming algorithm given in [1] that uses edit graph to determine a sequence of operations that would transform one schema tree in to another with minimum cost. Nierman and Jagadish [3] have described a notion of allowable sequence of edit operations by which an overall cost of comparison can be lowered significantly. The reduction in computation cost is achieved by means of graft costs and prune costs computations that they calculate for every sub tree of a schema tree. If a sub-tree of one schema tree is present in other schema tree then the cost of inserting/deleting whole sub-tree is taken into account and not just the cost of inserting/deleting every individual node of a sub-tree.

3 Overview of Adaptive Schema Hardening

All incoming SOAP request messages are intercepted by the message validator that validates them against schemas available in the schema repository. Initially, this repository would hold schemas derived from the WSDL files or the hand coded schemas. Messages are logged once they are subjected to the validation logic. The Schema Hardening algorithm then operates on logged messages and fine tunes schemas in the repository. The SOAP messages exhibiting common features shall fall into same bucket. It is difficult to capture common features if SOAP messages are compared in an XML domain. Our algorithm analyses XSDs generated from SOAP messages and produces as an output the set of schema classes. Subset of these schema classes would represent good messages while remaining schema classes may represent potentially dangerous messages probably instances of attack vectors. The reference schemas of repository are then updated in line with schema classes pertaining to good messages.

3.1 Stages of Algorithm

In this section, we shall give you an overview of the stages of our algorithm. It starts by deriving XSDs from the logged SOAP requests. As shown in Fig. 1, entities of the form M_is represent logged SOAP requests. Derived schemas are denoted by S_is. Next, it traverses through the generated XSDs and constructs schema trees out of it which are denoted by N_is which are in the form that facilitates an easier schema comparison. Having obtained the schema tree, we calculate the tree signature that helps us identify each schema tree uniquely and hence the corresponding XSD that it represents. If the currently generated tree signature does not match the tree signature of any of the previously generated schema trees then we consider this schema tree to represent a new class of schema not observed before.

The second stage constitutes comparing the generated schema tree against the reference schema tree (being used for validation). An attempt to find equivalence between these two trees gives a scalar quantity that signifies an extent to which two schemas differ. Here, we introduce a notion of a 'Bucket'. A bucket is capable of holding multiple schema trees provided all schema trees share the same measure of difference (scalar quantity) with respect to the reference schema tree. Two schema trees belonging to the same bucket need not be equivalent though they have same measure of difference with the reference schema. As shown in Fig. 2, two schema trees have been placed in the Bucket 1 because their measure of difference with respect to the reference schema is same. Incidentally, these two schema trees are also equivalent because a measure of difference between them would be evaluated to zero. We can observe that data types of an element 'no2' are compatible and hence both schema trees are equivalent. The schema trees of Bucket 2 share the same measure of difference with the reference schema. However, these two schema trees are not equivalent because they differ in name of elements ('no3' and 'no4'). There can be other reasons also that make them non-equivalent such as incompatible data types, disparity in element cardinality. Such differences would not result in a zero measure of difference between them.

Without bucketing and tree signatures, we would have to find out equivalence against all generated XSDs to deduce the final schema classes. The use of schemas in a repository as a reference narrows down the scope of comparison. Only similar schemas in a bucket need to be checked for equivalence so that they can be merged to form a new schema class.

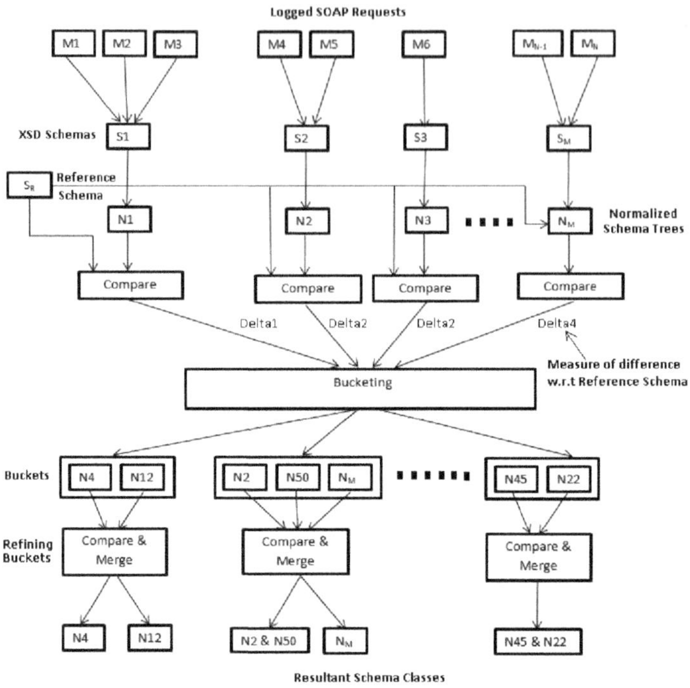

Fig. 1. Stages involved in generating schema classes

```
<soap:Envelope>
  <soap:Body>
    <Add xmlns="http://tempuri.org/">
      <no1>10</no1>
      <no2>30</no2>
      <name>Who am i</name>
    </Add>
  </soap:Body>
</soap:Envelope>

|->Envelope, element,
   |->Body, element,
      |->Add, element,
         |->no1, element, unsignedByte
         |->no2, element, unsignedByte
         |->name, element, string

Signature: 5943F21304C15E9A9B15B8ED491772EC
```

```
<soap:Envelope>
  <soap:Body>
    <Add xmlns="http://tempuri.org/">
      <no1>2</no1>
      <no2>30.55</no2>
      <name>Who am i</name>
    </Add>
  </soap:Body>
</soap:Envelope>

|->Envelope, element,
   |->Body, element,
      |->Add, element,
         |->no1, element, unsignedByte
         |->no2, element, decimal
         |->name, element, string

Signature: BDA245919E4185705E42B2F627BB9367
```

Fig. 2. Schema Trees of Bucket 1 which are equivalent

```
<soap:Envelope>
  <soap:Body>
    <Add xmlns="http://tempuri.org/">
      <no1>10</no1>
      <no2>30</no2>
      <name>Who am I</name>
      <no3>44</no3>
    </Add>
  </soap:Body>
</soap:Envelope>

|->Envelope, element,
   |->Body, element,
      |->Add, element,
         |->no1, element, unsignedByte
         |->no2, element, unsignedByte
         |->name, element, string
         |->no3, element, unsignedByte

Signature: 75814BFBF3DEB2F4878AF7F481AA319C
```

```
<soap:Envelope>
  <soap:Body>
    <Add xmlns="http://tempuri.org/">
      <no1>10</no1>
      <no2>30</no2>
      <name>Who am I</name>
      <no4>44</no4>
    </Add>
  </soap:Body>
</soap:Envelope>

|->Envelope, element,
   |->Body, element,
      |->Add, element,
         |->no1, element, unsignedByte
         |->no2, element, unsignedByte
         |->name, element, string
         |->no4, element, unsignedByte

Signature: 13DC9EF281D44941F4BB73104CB01E28
```

Fig. 3. Schema Trees of Bucket 2 which are not equivalent

At this stage, each schema tree within a bucket is a separate schema class. The third stage attempts to reduce the total number of schema classes by merging together likely equivalent schema trees within a bucket. It does so by merging together a subset of schema trees within a bucket whose measure of difference turns out to be zero. The measure of difference is calculated between the candidate schema trees selected from the bucket rather than comparing them with reference schema in this run. If they are found to be equivalent then they are merged together and replaced with a new schema class. This process is repeated until no more merging is possible within a bucket. This process is carried out across all buckets. Finally, each bucket is left with the minimal set of schema trees. Now, the schema trees spanned across all the buckets form the final set of schema classes. Some of these schema classes represent genuine SOAP messages while some of these schema classes represent instances of different attack vectors.

4 Self Adaptive Schema Hardening

In this section, we describe the stages of our algorithm at length.

4.1 Normalized Schema Tree and XSD Tree Signature

Direct comparison of XSDs is cumbersome. Hence, we need to transform XSD in to a tree representation that is consistent for the purpose of comparison. We accomplish this by traversing through the generated XSD and introducing a node for each XSD element encountered. Mlynkova has described the methodology in [2] to construct a normalized tree representation of a XSD schema. They take into consideration various structural as well as semantic equivalence features. We use relatively simpler approach to construct the schema tree. Each node of the schema tree has following attributes:

Name: Name of a node
Node Type: It can be Element, Attribute, Restriction, Extension etc.
Data Type: Data type of a node
Cardinality: Depicts MinOccurs and MaxOccurs

Having derived the schema tree from the XSD, we compute a tree signature to be associated with each one of the schema tree that uniquely identifies a particular schema (XSD). We compute tree signature as follows:

```
Algorithm: ComputeTreeSignature(IN XsdTree)
1. PreOrderTrace = PreOrderTraverse(XsdTree->Root)
2. PostOrderTrace = PostOrderTraverse(XsdTree->Root)
3. TreeTrace = Concat(PreOrderTrace, PostOrderTrace)
4. Signature = MD5(TreeTrace)
5. Return Signature
```

```
Algorithm: PreOrderTraverse(IN Node)
1.  NodeStamp = Concat(Node->Name, Node->Type,
                Node->DataType, Node->Cardinality)
2.  Foreach ChildNode of Node
3.       ChildStamp = PreOrderTraverse(ChildNode)
4.       NodeStamp = Concat(NodeStamp, ChildStamp)
5.  Return NodeStamp
```

```
Algorithm: PostOrderTraverse(IN Node)
1. SubTreeStamp = NULL
2. Foreach ChildNode of Node
3.    ChildStamp = PostOrderTraverse(ChildNode)
4.    SubTreeStamp = Concat(SubTreeStamp, ChildStamp)
5. NodeStamp = Concat(Node->Name, Node->Type,
               Node->DataType, Node->Cardinality)
6. NodeStamp = Concat(SubtreeStamp, NodeStamp)
7. Return NodeStamp
```

Pre-Order and Post-Order trace taken together provides unique representation of the tree. We leverage upon this property to generate such a traversal trail of the schema tree and compute the fixed length MD5 hash over it. This computed value serves as a signature of the schema tree. Any two SOAP messages that share exactly the same structure would have the same XSD and hence the same tree signature. Associated with every XSD is a hit count; i.e. the number of SOAP requests that resulted in this particular XSD. This hit count then becomes associated with the schema tree and hence the tree signature.

4.2 Schema Tree Equivalence: Measure of Difference

Bucketing similar messages together translates to a problem of grouping together likely similar schemas. Hence, if we are given 'N' schema trees then we would have to perform roughly N(N-1)/2 tree comparisons which is expensive. Instead, we compare 'N' candidate schemas against reference schema obtained from the repository which is currently being used for the validation. We have adapted an algorithm discussed in [2] to suit our requirement. This algorithm is based on dynamic programming and gives as output a scalar quantity depicting an extent to which the two schemas differ. It computes a minimum cost associated with transforming one schema tree into another through sequence of operations. It's based on a computation of graft cost and prune cost. The graft cost of a node corresponds to a cost of inserting a node while prune cost refers to a cost associated with deleting a node. Similarly graft costs and prune costs for a sub tree refer to a cost of inserting and deleting a sub tree. The algorithm takes as input two trees Tx and Ty.

Below algorithm first computes the cost of inserting every single sub tree of schema tree Ty followed by cost of deleting every single sub tree of schema tree Tx.

```
Algorithm: FindSimilarity (IN Tx, IN Ty)
    GraftCost = ComputeCost(Ty->Root)
    PruneCost = ComputeCost(Tx->Root)
    return GetMeasureOfDifference(Tx, Ty, GraftCost, PruneCost)
```

```
Algorithm: ComputeCost(IN r)
    sum0 = GetNodeWeight(r)
    for all child of r do
        ComputeCost(child)
        sum0 += Cost(child)
    end for
    sum1 = Infinity
    if ContainedIn[r] is not
                    empty then
        sum1 = 1
    end if
    Cost(r) = Min(sum0, sum1)
    Return Cost
```

```
Algorithm: CreateContainedInLists(IN Tx, IN r)
    for all child of r do
        CreateContainedInLists(Tx, child);
    end for
    ContainedIn[r] = FindSimilarNodes(Tx, r);
    for all child of r do
        ContainedIn[r]=
        FilterLists(ContainedIn[r],
                    ContainedIn[child]);
    end for
    return
```

We have slightly changed the "ComputeCost" algorithm mentioned in [2] to take in to account a type of the node while determining a cost to insert/delete it. A weight is assigned to a node based on its type. Typically, a node of a type 'element' would have more weightage than a node representing 'attribute'. This prevents two non-equivalent schema trees from falling into same bucket by co-incidence. With respect to Fig. 4, both the schema trees, Schema Tree 1 and Schema Tree 2 have one additional node than the reference schema. Without a node weightage, a measure of difference with respect to the reference schema tree would have been the same for both the candidate schema trees and they would have ended up in the same bucket and their un-equivalence would have been determined in the next stage while attempting to merge them. Considering node weight while computing cost of insertion/deletion would result in a different measure of difference for both the schema trees. Hence, the overall cost of comparison has been reduced by putting them in separate buckets.

```
|->Envelope, element,
   |->Body, element,
      |->Add, element,
         |->no1, element, int
         |->no2, element, int
         |->name, element, string
```

Reference Schema

```
|->Envelope, element,
   |->Body, element,
      |->Add, element,
         |->no1, element, unsignedByte
         |->no2, element, unsignedByte
         |->name, element, string
         |->no3, element, unsignedByte
```

Schema Tree 1

```
|->Envelope, element,
   |->Body, element,
      |->Add, element,
         |->no1, element, unsignedByte
         |->no2, element, unsignedByte
         |->name, element, string
         |->no3, attribute, unsignedByte
```

Schema Tree 2

Fig. 4. Two Non-Equivalent Schema Trees w.r.t Reference Schema

Before computing graft and prune costs, a 'ContainedInList' is created for every node in both trees. This list for node 'X' points to nodes in another tree that are likely similar to node 'X'. Two nodes are said to be likely similar if they have node name and node type in common and the following condition is also satisfied:

(0.5 * Cardinality Similarity + 0.5 * Data Type Coefficient) > Threshold

Here, Cardinality Similarity is computed as follows:

CardSim(X, Y)
= 0 if (XMaxOccur < YMinOccur) OR (YMaxOccur < XMinOccur)
= 1 if XMaxOccur, YMaxOccur = Infinity AND XMinOccur = YMinOccur
= 0.9 if XMaxOccur, YMaxOccur = Infinity AND XMinOccur!=YMinOccur
= 0.6 if XMaxOccur = Infinity OR YMaxOccur = Infinity

Data Type Co-Efficient shows an extent to which one data type can be substituted for another one. For example Integer, Short and Byte are compatible data types. Below we demonstrate dynamic programming algorithm discussed by Neirman and Jagdish in [3] that computes measure of difference between two schema trees.

Initially, we invoke this algorithm 'N' times; each time passing reference schema tree and candidate schema tree as parameters. This way, we will end up with 'N' scalar quantities denoting measure of difference with respect to reference schema.

```
Algorithm: GetMeasureOfDifference(IN Tree A, IN Tree B,
                IN GraftCost, IN PruneCost)
 M = Degree(A)
 N = Degree(B)
 Dist = new Int[0..M][0..N]
 If ((A->Name = B->Name) & (A->Type = B->Type))
 Then           Dist[0][0] = 1
 Else           Dist[0][0] = 0
 EndIf
 for (j = 1; j <= N; j++)
    Dist[0][j] = Dist[0][j-1] + GraftCost(Bj)
 for(int i = 1; i <= M; i++)
    Dist[i][0] = Dist[i-1][0] + PruneCost(Ai)
 for(int i = 1; i <= M; i++)
    for(int j = 1; j <= N; j++)
          Dist[i][j] = Minimum{
             Dist[i-1][j-1] +
             GetMeasureOfDifference(Ai, Bj),
          Dist[i][j-1] + GraftCost(Bj),
          Dist[i-1][j] + PruneCost(Ai)}
 return Dist[M][N]
```

4.3 Initial Bucketing of Schemas

Tree signatures of two schema trees Tx and Ty may not be same but their measure of difference with reference schema tree may still be same which means they can be combined together.

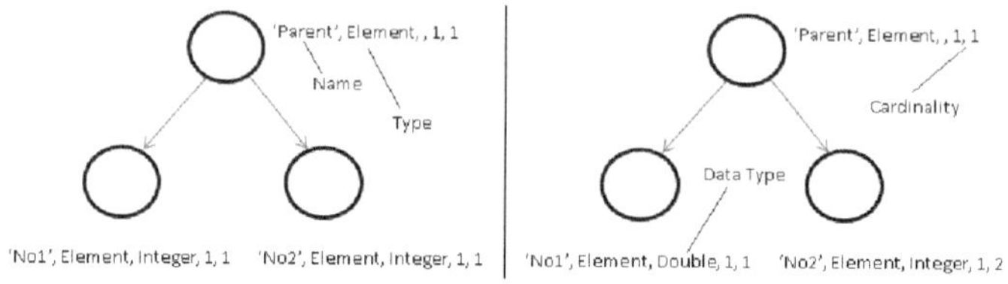

Fig. 5. Sub tree of Schema tree

Fig. 5 shows part of schemas of two different schema trees. Corresponding schema trees shall have different tree signature value but their measure of difference with respect to reference schema would be same because data type co-efficient of element 'No1' would yield a value likely over threshold; also cardinality similarity measure would also be above threshold. Hence, all schemas sharing same measure of difference with reference schema tree shall fall in to same bucket initially. That means, 'N' candidate schema trees will end up in 'B' buckets such that B <= N with B=N being the worst case.

4.4 Grouping within Buckets through Merging

As presented in previous sections, buckets are created based on a measure of difference between the schema trees and the reference schema tree. A schema class represents each of the schema trees in the bucket. Some subset of these schema trees of the same bucket can be merged together if they fall into an equivalent class. Now, we will calculate a measure of difference between schema trees in the same bucket using a dynamic programming algorithm 'GetMeasureOfDifference' described earlier in section 4.2. Let T_{XB} and T_{YB} be two schema trees belonging to bucket 'B'. If the measure of difference between these two trees turns out to be zero then they are of an equivalent class. We merge these two schema trees together and form a new tree which effectively replaces the previous two schema trees of the bucket. The new schema tree would incorporate features of both the previous schema trees. The resultant schema tree is then compared against other schema trees of the same bucket. We continue this process until no two schema trees in a bucket can be merged. At this stage, we are left with the minimal set of schema classes in the bucket. Each of the schema trees in the bucket represents a separate class. Below shown is the algorithm used to deduce schema classes from the bucket. We have used a variation of the bubble sort algorithm to group together equivalent schema classes within the bucket. The bubble sort swaps elements when first element is larger than second one (while sorting in ascending order). Instead of swapping, our algorithm merges two schema trees when they are found to be equivalent. The second schema tree is incorporated into the first schema tree and the second schema tree is removed from the bucket. We get a new schema class after every pass of the outer loop in the algorithm.

```
Algorithm: RefineBucket(IN Bucket)
1. For(i = 1, i < Bucket->Count, i++)
2.    For(j = i + 1, j <= Bucket->Count, j++)
3.        If Bucket->SchemaTrees[i] and
             Bucket->SchemaTrees[j] are
             equivalent
4.        Then   Incorporate Bucket->SchemaTrees[j] into
                   Bucket-> SchemaTrees[i]
5.                    Remove Bucket->SchemaTrees[j]
6.                 j = j - 1
7.        EndIf
8. Return Bucket->SchemaTrees
```

We process all buckets in a similar way. At the end, schema trees of all these buckets are final schema classes. Some of these classes shall represent a set of acceptable messages while some of these classes represent a pattern corresponding to an attack messages. Each of the resultant schemas would contain a resultant schema that was obtained as a result of merging multiple schemas during bucket refining step. Also, a schema class contains a stack of SOAP requests whose XSDs were merged together to obtain a resultant schema that this schema class represents. Corresponding to every SOAP request, we have a tree signature that identifies corresponding XSD from which schema tree used for comparison was generated. Whenever a specific schema class is chosen to be incorporated or discarded, a list of tree signatures residing within that schema class is added to the version control system. This facilitates keep track of changes that reference schema has undergone over a time. Changes are applied to the reference schema in accordance with the schema classes marked for inclusion.

5 Future Work

Our current solution forms schema classes in an automated way by iteratively learning similarity among SOAP requests. However human inspection is needed to decide which of the schema classes are to be incorporated into the reference schema used for the validation. In the next release, we plan to develop heuristics to facilitate automated decision making reducing if not eliminating the human inspection.

6 Conclusion

The solution we have proposed takes advantage of equivalence of XML schemas. Our algorithm initially categorizes candidate schemas by placing them in buckets to reduce total number of schema comparisons. It then iteratively groups together similar schemas contained within a bucket to form schema classes. A set of schema classes belonging to genuine messages are used to refine and tighten schemas used for validation so as to increase an overall efficacy of the validation mechanism. Also, the schema classes corresponding to attack vectors provide insight into the kind of attacks experienced by the deployed Web Services and this knowledge can be used to tighten security mechanism on the server side.

References

1. Chawathe, S.: Comparing Hierarchical Data in External Memory. In: VLDB 1999 Proceedings of the 25th International Conference on Very Large Data Bases, pp. 90–101. Morgan Kaufmann Publishers, San Francisco (1999)
2. Mlynkova, I.: Equivalence of XSD Constructs and its Exploitation in Similarity Evaluation. In: Proceedings of the OTM 2008 Confederated International Conferences, CoopIS, DOA, GADA, is, and ODBASE 2008. LNCS, pp. 125–1270. Springer, Monterrey (2008)
3. Nierman, A., Jagadish, H.: Evaluating Structural Similarity in XML Documents. In: Proceedings of the Fifth International Workshop on the Web and Databases WebDB 2002, Citeseer, Wisconsin, USA, pp. 61–66 (2002)
4. Gruschka, N., Luttenberger, N.: Protecting Web Services from DoS Attacks by SOAP Message Validation. In: IFIP International Federation for Information Processing, pp. 171–182. Springer, Boston (2006)
5. McIntosh, M., Austel, P.: XML signature element wrapping attacks and countermeasures. In: Proceedings of the 2005 Workshop on Secure Web Service, pp. 20–27. ACM, New York (2005)
6. Lee, M., Yang, L., Nick, J., Hsu, W., Yang, X.: XClust: Clustering XML Schemas for Effective Integration. In: Proceedings of the Eleventh International Conference on Information and Knowledge Management, pp. 292–299. ACM, New York (2002)
7. Inferring Schemas from XML Documents, `http://msdn.microsoft.com/en-us/library/xz2797k1.aspx`

Modeling and Performance Analysis of QAM System

T.P. Surekha[1], T. Ananthapadmanabha[2], C. Puttamadappa[3], and A.P. Kavya[4]

[1] Research Scholar and Assistant Professor, Dept. of E&CE,
Vidyavardhaka College of Engineering, Mysore, India
tpsuriramesh@gmail.com
[2] Professor, Dept. of E&EE, National Institute of Engineering, Mysore, India
and
Honorary secretary of IEI, Mysore local center, Mysore, India
drapn2008@yahoo.co.in
[3] Professor and Head, Dept. of E&CE, S.J.B. Institute of Technology, Bangalore, India
puttamadappa@gmail.com
[4] Project student, Dept. of E&CE, Vidyavardhaka College of Engineering, Mysore, India

Abstract. One of the most common forms of modulation used in wire and wireless system are QAM system. Quadrature amplitude modulation (QAM) has been widely used in adaptive modulation because of its efficiency in power and bandwidth. Adaptive modulation system is one of the important techniques in building a mobile communication network. Such as WLAN (wireless local area Networks) and WIMAX (Worldwide Inter-oprability for Microwave Access) according to IEEE 802.16 standard. In this paper, a Simulink based simulation system is designed and the details of the simulation is implemented using AWGN Channel. Simulation study helps us to visualize Eye-diagram and scatter plot both at the transmitter and at the receiver and also to observe Spectrum scope. performance analysis is done by comparing the simulated BER with theoretical plot using BER tool. The BER curve for a Communication system illustrates the relationship between power in the transmitted signal in terms of SNR and the resulting BER for the system.

Keywords: AWGN, BER, E_b/No, GUI, QAM, RRC filter, SNR.

1 Introduction

In any digital communication systems a symbol is defined by the rate at which information is sent over the link in the form of pulses at baseband. A symbol is always a phase state (BPSK and QPSK) or a phase and amplitude state (QAM). Popular modulations that transmit more than one bit per symbol are QPSK(Quadrature phase shift Keying) (2bits/symbol) and QAM (upto 10 bits/ symbol). QPSK is widely used in satellite links including direct broadcast satellite television. QAM is used in high speed modems designed for telephone lines to send a high bit rate in a small bandwidth. In m-ary modulation by allowing the amplitude to vary with the phase, QAM is obtained, QAM is a modulation that combines the four phase states of QPSK with multiple pulse amplitude as in m-ASK. The purpose of this paper is to illustrate some important aspects on analysis and simulations of 16_QAM system operating over an

D.C. Wyld et al. (Eds.): CNSA 2011, CCIS 196, pp. 393–401, 2011.

Additive White Gaussian Noise (AWGN) channel. All the modeling and simulation is carried out using Simulink. In the simulation model, Error rates of QAM systems versus the SNR are used to evaluate the system performance analysis.

The basic description of QAM system is as shown in fig. 1. It consists of Data signal generator , Transmitter, Channel, Receiver and a Bit sink.

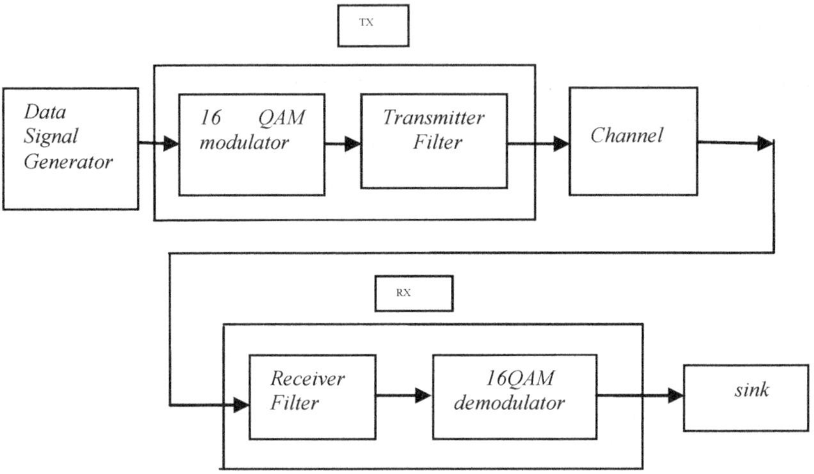

Fig. 1. The basic QAM system

1.1 Data Signal generator

Data signal generator generates a stream of information bits to be transmitted by the transmitter, specifically Bernoulli binary generator is employed as a data signal generator.

1.2 Transmitter

The transmitter converts the bits into QAM symbols and applies optional pulse shaping and up-conversion. As with many digital modulation techniques, the QAM modulation helps to visualize the constellation diagram. Complex modulation schemes are best viewed using a scatter diagram. The scatter diagram allows us to visualize the real and the imaginary (in-phase and quadrature) component of the complex signal. Pulse shaping is an important consideration in the design of a system. The pulse shape filter must make efficient use of bandwidth and also have limited duration in time. A pulse too wide in time will overlap into adjacent symbol periods and cause inter symbol interference(ISI). This filtering can be performed by using Root-Raised cosine (RRC) filters. The eye diagram allows us to understand the time domain characteristic of a signal and its susceptibility to symbol timing error.

1.3 Channel

Communication channels introduce noise, fading, interference, and other distortions to the transmitted signals. Simulating a communication system involves modeling a channel based on mathematical descriptions of the channel. Several different channels are possible, the one being used here is AWGN channel. It is assumed that while passing electromagnetic waves through air or other mediums, there is an additive noise introduced to the transmission. Thus channel simply adds white Gaussian noise to the signals as shown in fig. 2.

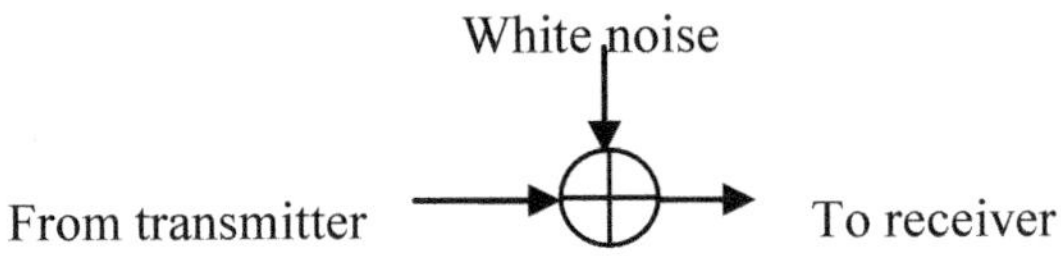

Fig. 2. An AWGN channel

1.4 Receiver

The receiver is the most complex part in the system. It performs the reverse process of the transmitter. Receiver block takes the output from the channel, estimates timing and phase offset, and demodulates the received 16- QAM symbols into information bits, which are fed to the bit sink. In a simulation condition, the bit sink counts the number of errors that occurred to-gather statistics used for investigating the performance of the system.

1.5 Sink

The Error Rate Calculation block compares a transmitted data stream with a receive data stream to calculate the Bit error rate of a system. It also outputs the number of error events that have occurred, and the total number of bits or symbols compared.

2 Implementation

2.1 Methodology

Modeling and simulating of QAM system is implemented in this paper. The bits are mapped onto corresponding QAM symbols using Gray coding, as shown in Fig.3.

The constellation of 16-QAM is as shown in Fig. 3. The constellation consists of a square lattice of signal points. The general form of an M-ary signal can defined as [1] as shown in Fig.3

$$Si(t)= \sqrt{\frac{2Emin}{Ts}}\, a_i \, Cos\, (2\pi f_c t) + \sqrt{\frac{2Emin}{Ts}}\, b_i \, sin\, (2\pi f_c t)$$

$$0 \leq t \leq Ts \quad \text{Where} \quad i = 1,2\text{----}M \tag{1}$$

Where E_{min} is the energy of the signal with the lowest amplitude and a_i and b_i are a pair of independent integers according to the location of the particular signal point. f_c is the carrier frequency and T_s is the symbol period.

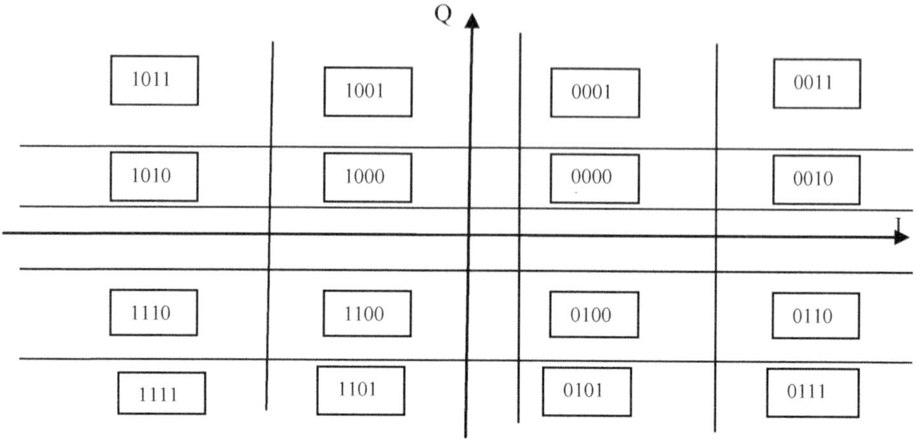

Fig. 3. Constellation diagram for 16-QAM

If rectangular pulse shapes are assumed, $S_i(t)$ may be expanded in terms of a pair of basis functions.

$\Phi_1(t)$ and $\phi_2(t)$ are the basis functions defined by

$$\phi_1(t)=\sqrt{2/T_s}\ \mathrm{Cos}\ (2\pi f_c t) \quad 0\leq t\leq Ts\text{-------} \qquad \text{--- (2)}$$

$$\phi_2(t)=\sqrt{2/T_s}\ \mathrm{Sin}\ (2\pi f_c t) \quad 0\leq t\leq Ts\text{ -----} \qquad \text{--- (3)}$$

The first basis function is used as the in-phase component of the signal and the second as the quadrature component of the signal. The average probability of bit error in the additive white Gaussian noise (AWGN) channel is obtained as

$$Pe,\ QAM=4\left(1-\frac{1}{\sqrt{M}}\right)Q\left(\sqrt{\frac{2Emin}{N_O}}\right)\text{------------} \qquad \text{----(4)}$$

Where Emin is the energy of the signal and N_o is the noise.

2.2 Simulation Model

Simulink, developed by the Mathworks, is an tool for multi-domain simulation and Model-based Design for dynamic and Communication systems. Communication Blockset of Simulink is helpful in simulating the modeling. The simulation model of16- QAM system is as shown in Fig. 4.

QAM Specifications:
Upsample Factor =8,
Pulse shaping Filter $\alpha = 0.2$
Group Delay = 4

All signal sources in the signal processing and communication 's can generate frame based data. In this work, the signal is frame based and samples are propagated through a model and multiple samples are processed in batches. Frame – based

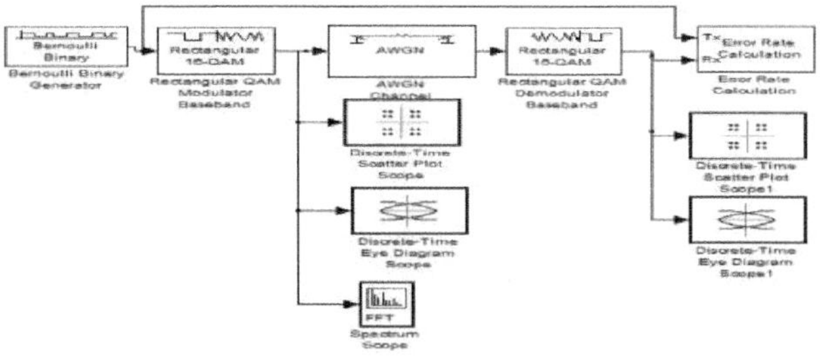

Fig. 4. The QAM simulation model

processing takes advantage of Simulink matrix processing capabilities to reduce overhead. Complex modulation scheme are best viewed using a scatter diagram. The scatter diagram allows us to visualize the real and imaginary (in-phase and quadrature) component of the complex signal. Thus Fig.5 shows the Scatter plot of QAM system in the transmitter and Fig.6 shows the Scatter plot of QAM system in the receiver. Fig. 7 shows the Spectrum scope. The power spectral density (PSD) embodies the frequency- domain properties of a process.

An Eye diagram is a convenient way to visualize a shaped signal in the time domain, which indicates that the ‘eye’ is most widely opened, and use that point as the decision point when de-mapping a demodulated signal to recover a digital message as shown in Fig. 8 which shows the eye diagram at the transmitter and Fig.9 shows the eye diagram at the receiver.

Using the Root-raised Cosine (RRC) filters at the transmitter and the receiver, a slight amount of phase and magnitude distortion can be seen at the output of the transmitting filter. To verify that the model was built properly, Error rate Calculation block compares a transmitted data stream with a receive data stream to calculate the error rate of a system. It also outputs the number of error events that have occurred, and the total number of bits or symbols compared. The block can output the error statistics as a variable in the displayed port.

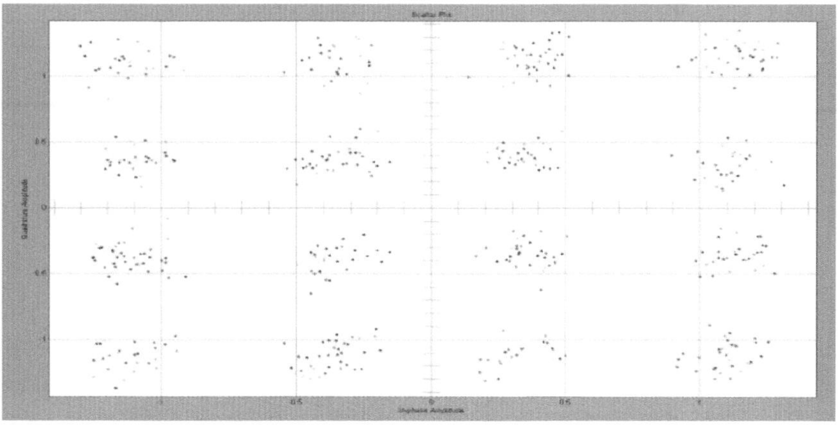

Fig. 5. Scatter plot of QAM system in the transmitter

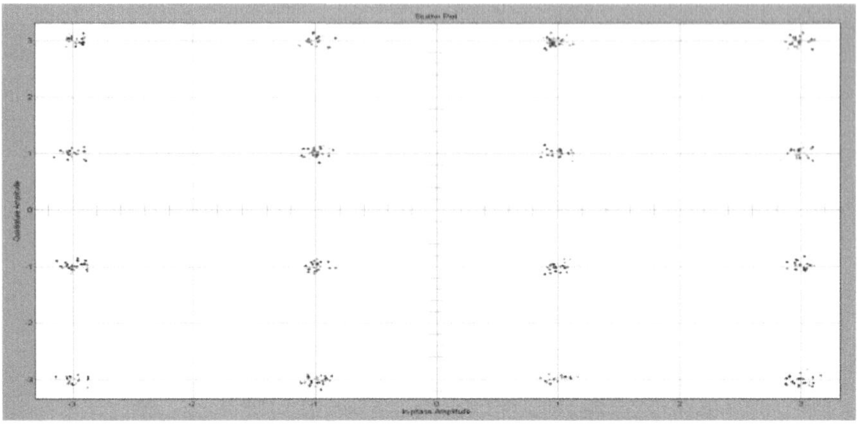

Fig. 6. Scatter plot of QAM system at the Receiver

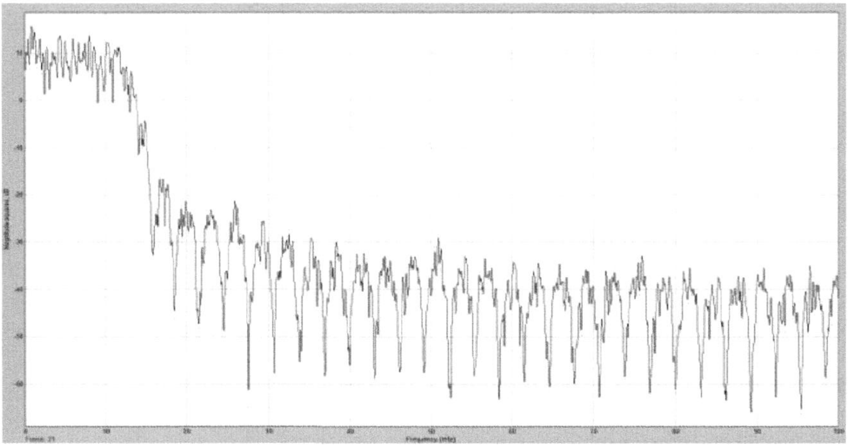

Fig.7. Spectrum scope of QAM system

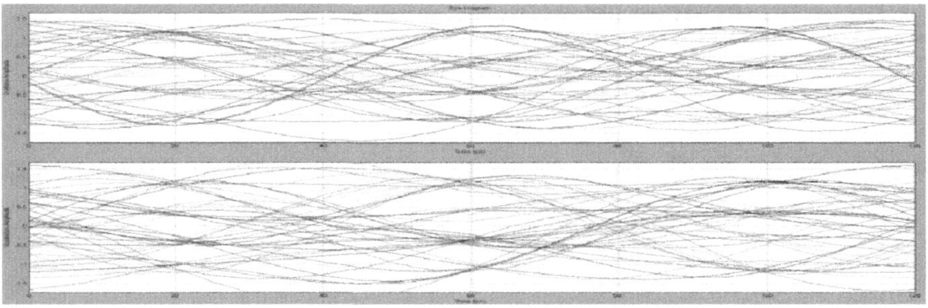

Fig. 8. Eye diagram of QAM Transmitter

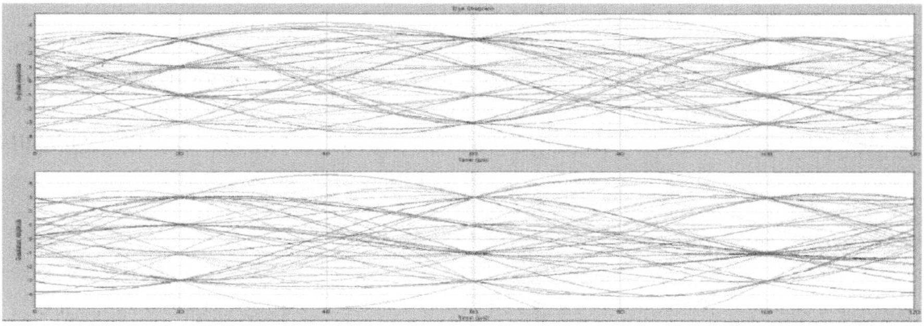

Fig. 9. Eye diagram of QAM Receiver

2.3 System Analysis

Characterizing the performance of a communication system under noisy conditions is an important part of the design process. Noise, interference, fading, and other types of distortion affecting the transmitted signal can cause incorrect decisions to be made by the receiver, resulting in bit errors. The ratio of bit errors to received bits is called the bit error rate (BER). The BER curve illustrates the relationship between power in the transmitted signal in terms of signal-to-noise ratio (SNR) and the resulting BER for the system. By analyzing the BER curve for a given system, we can find the minimum SNR that is required to achieve a particular BER. Thus bit error rate is computed by simulating the 16- QAM system as shown in Fig.10 and the same is compared with theoretical plot as shown in Fig.11. Performing such simulation for a range of SNR value results in the BER curve.

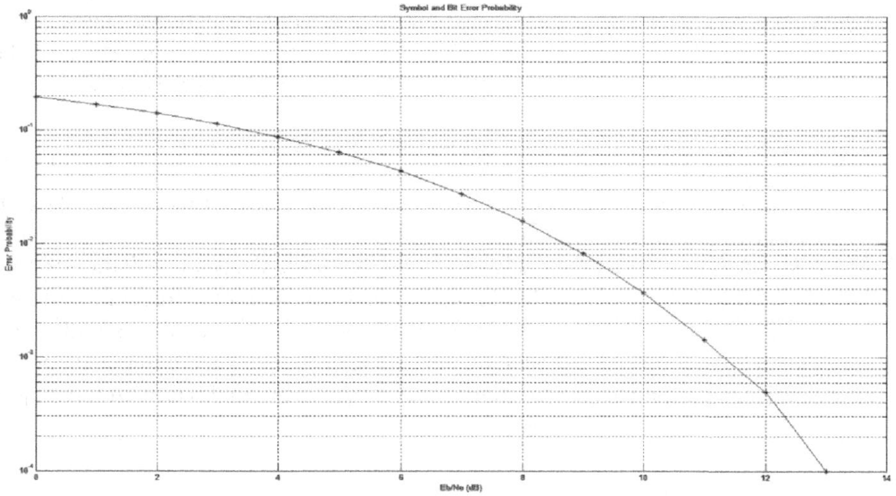

Fig. 10. Bit error rate as a function of E_b/No for QAM curve

3 Results and Conclusion

Fig.10. shows BER curve with Monte-carlo simulation is compared with BER Tool curve to display theoretical BER plot as shown in Fig. 11. BER Tool is a Graphical User Interface (GUI) for analyzing bit error - error - rate statistics of a communication model. BER Tool helps us to generate and analyze the BER data for a given system with theoretical plot.

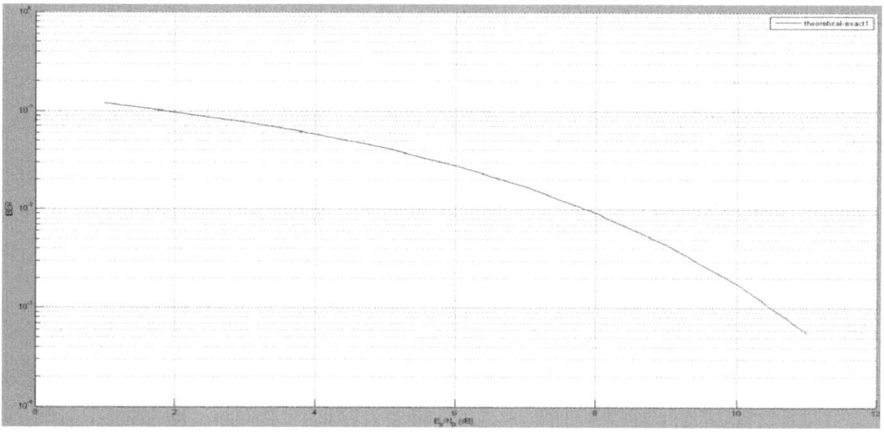

Fig. 11. Bit error rate as a function of E_b/No with theoretical plot

The results can be concluded by comparing Fig.10 with Fig. 11.Fig.10 shows E_b/N_o ranges from 1:13. that is specified, collects the BER data from the simulation and creates a plot. The second plot is Theoretical technique, which computes the bit error rate by using a bertool which varies E_b/N_O ranges from 1:11.as shown in Fig.11. The second plot provides closer results compared to simulated result. Thus BER tool plays an important role in Characteristic performance analysis of QAM system.

Acknowledgments

The authors are very grateful to the Management of Vidya vardhaka College of Engineering, Mysore, Karnataka, India. The National Institute of Engineering, Mysore ,Karnataka India. S J B I T, Kengeri, Bangalore, Karnataka, India. for their constant encouragement, and Motivation during their work.

References

[1] Li, X.: Simulink – based Simulation of quadrature Amplitude Modulation System. In: Proceedings of International Conference IAJC – IJME 2008 (2008)
[2] Sakla, T., Jain, D., Gautham, S.: Implementation of Digital QPSK modulator by using VHDL/MATLAB. International Journal of Engineering and Technology 2(9)
[3] Pratt, T., Bostian, C., Allnutt, J.: Satellite Communication, 2nd edn. John Wiley and Sons, Chichester

[4] Rappaport, T.S.: Wireless Communications, Principles and Practice, 2nd edn. Prentice – Hall of India Private Limited, Englewood Cliffs
[5] Sharma, S.: Wireless and Cellular Communications. S.K. Kataria and Sons,
[6] Jeruchim, M.C., Balaban, P., Sam shanmugan, K.: Simulation of Communication System Modeling, Methodology and Techniques, 2nd edn. Kluwer Academic Publishers, Dordrecht (2000)

Biographies

T.P. Surekha, received the B.E degree from Mangalore University, Mangalore. And M.Tech degree from Visvesvaraya Technological University, Belgaum. Presently she is working as Asst professor in the department of Electronics and Communication Engineering, Vidyavardhaka College of Engineering, Mysore. Her research interest include Power-line communication System, Automation and Simulation of Communication System in Power System. Modeling and Simulation of Communication systems.

T. Ananthapadmanabha received the B.E. degree, M.Tech degree and Ph.D. degree from the University of Mysore, Mysore. Presently, he is working as Professor and Head in the Department of Electrical Engineering, The National Institute of Engineering, Mysore. He is also Honorary Secretary of Institute of Engineers, (India), Mysore Local Centre, Mysore. His research interest include voltage stability, distribution automation and AI applications in power system. Simulation of Power and Communication System.

C Puttamadappa, received the B.E degree from Mysore University, Mysore. And M. E degree from Bangalore University, Bangalore. Ph.D degree from Jadvapur University, Kolkatta. Presently he is working as professor and Head in the department of Electronics and Communication Engineering, S J B institute of Technology, Kengeri, Bangalore, His research interest include Power Electronics, Simulation of communication systems, and Mobile Wireless Networks.

A.P. Kavya, is an undergraduate student in the department of Electronics and Communication Engineering at Vidyavardhaka College of Engineering, Mysore, India. She is pursuing her project, and her area of Interest include modeling and simulation of communication system.

An IDS Evaluation-Centric Taxonomy of Wireless Security Attacks

Khalid Nasr, Anas Abou El Kalam, and Christian Fraboul

INPT-ENSEEIHT, IRIT, Université de Toulouse, Toulouse, France
{khalid.nasr,anas.abouelkalam,christian.fraboul}@enseeiht.fr

Abstract. Wireless technology has become a very popular alternative to wired technology in recent years. However, wireless communication faces several security threats. Consequently, several security efforts have been exerted to make wireless communication systems invulnerable to attacks, but unfortunately complete attack prevention is not realistically attainable. Thus, the emphasis on detecting intrusions through a second line of defense, in the form of Intrusion Detection System (IDS), is increasing. But the question that arises is what IDS is more suitable for our systems? The answer necessarily should take the IDSs evaluation into account. However, to consider all possible cases and contexts, the classification of wireless attacks seems necessary. Dealing with this challenge, this paper proposes a holistic taxonomy of wireless security attacks from the perspective of the IDS evaluator. The proposed taxonomy includes all relevant dimensions of wireless attacks and helps to extract the attack test cases that are used for managing unbiased evaluations. Finally, we present our benchmark of two popular wireless IDSs.

Keywords: Taxonomy, intrusion detection system, wireless attacks.

1 Introduction

To meet the growing demand on communication at a distance easily and efficiently, numerous telecommunication techniques and protocols have been proposed and implemented, especially for wireless networks. Flexibility in dealing with these protocols and their vulnerabilities creates a problem of poor security. Although several security-defense systems have been developed such as firewalls, encryption, authentication, and VPNs, most of the wireless systems are still susceptible to attacks. Unfortunately, complete attack prevention in wireless networks is not realistically attainable due to the openness of wireless medium, system complexity, configuration and administration errors, abuse by authorized users, lack of centralized monitoring and management points, dynamically changed network topologies, etc. [1]. Using a second line of defense based on Intrusion Detection System (IDS) seems thus necessary in this context. Basically, IDS monitors the system activities to identify unauthorized use, misuse, or abuse, and then alerts the complementary prevention part to hinder the intrusion attacks. Although IDSs are incontestably crucial elements in network security, their efficiency and performance are sometimes not satisfying in practice. Thus, evaluating IDSs is a pressing necessity.

D.C. Wyld et al. (Eds.): CNSA 2011, CCIS 196, pp. 402–413, 2011.

By evaluation we mean a systematic assessment that measures ability of an IDS to meet the intended security and performance. This task naturally necessitates taking into account all possible attacks to fairly evaluate the IDSs. While this is operationally impossible, it seems necessary to develop an attack classification that groups the common characteristics, techniques, and objectives of attacks under expressive categories or dimensions. This helps to minimize the attack test cases and facilitates the election of the representative attack samples. It is worth mentioning that there is a great lack of IDSs evaluation in wireless networks. In this paper, we will holistically study and classify the wireless attacks from the perspective of the IDS-evaluator, and then extract the valid test cases of attacks.

The rest of this paper is organized as follows. To better understand our context, Section 2 presents the main purposes of the attack classification and the requirements of a satisfactory taxonomy. Section 3 gives the basis of our work by discussing some previous works concerned with attack classifications. After that, Section 4 presents our proposed taxonomy and the methodology of classification. Afterward, Section 5 presents an application of our taxonomy in an evaluation test of two popular wireless IDSs. Finally, section 6 presents our conclusions and future work.

2 Background

In the network security domain, we believe that the classification of security attacks can be directed according to one of the following two purposes: 1) security defense or 2) security countermeasure evaluation.

In the first direction, the attacks are classified from the perspective of the security defender. The considered taxonomy is created by extracting the attack signs or signatures from all possible attacks and assembling the common attack signs under representative dimensions. These taxonomy dimensions are suggestive of techniques and mechanisms that can be followed by the security-defender to prevent the attacks. This taxonomy is called *defense-centric taxonomy*.

In the second direction, the attacks are classified from the perspective of the security-countermeasure evaluator. Dimensions of this taxonomy are suggestive of attack generation and help for extracting the attack test cases. In this taxonomy, the evaluator generally describes the main phases of compromising and hacking processes; scanning-phase, exploiting-phase and infecting-phase, in addition to recruiting-phase that is mainly used to avoid tracing and discovering the attack origin. This taxonomy is called *evaluation-centric taxonomy*.

Several attempts of attack classification were developed, but most of them concerned about wired networks. Besides, some taxonomies focused on the security flaws [2], others focused on the exploited vulnerabilities, and others just listed the terms and types of attacks [3, 4, 5]. But, to our knowledge, there is no a holistic taxonomy that covers all necessary and sufficient dimensions of attack classification in wireless networks, especially from the perspective of the security-countermeasure evaluator. We thus concern in this paper about developing an IDS evaluation-centric taxonomy of wireless attacks.

Before defining our classification attributes, it is important to first define some important requirements of a satisfactory and holistic taxonomy:

- *Objectivity*: the objective of classification must be clearly determined and defined; defense-centric or evaluation-centric.
- *Completeness/Exhaustive*: the taxonomy should take into account all possible attacks and provide the categories accordingly.
- *Determinism*: the procedure of classification must be clearly defined.
- *Mutually exclusive*: each attack should only be classified into one category.
- *Repeatable*: the classification procedure should ensure that an attack is always placed in the same category.
- *Unambiguous*: each taxonomy dimension must be clear and precise.

3 Related Work

This section presents some of the previous works related to the attack classification. We will study and categorize these taxonomies according to the security-defense and security-evaluation as mentioned in the previous section. Many of the proposed taxonomies, that have been originally developed to help the security defender, have followed the direction of the security-evaluation.

3.1 Defense-Centric Taxonomies

Kumar in [6] proposed an attack taxonomy that seems as a defense-centric one. This classification was based on inspection of attack signatures, to help ultimately in designing and building a signature-based IDS. He classified the attack signatures under the following dimensions: *Existence*, *Sequence, Regular Expression patterns*, and *other patterns* which contain all other intrusion signatures that cannot be represented directly in one of the earlier categories. Existence patterns look for evidence that may have been left behind by an intruder. For Sequence patterns, some attacks manifest themselves as a sequence of events. Regular expression patterns include events that often specify several activities to be done jointly.

Killourhy et al. in [7] classified the attacks from the perspective of the anomaly-based IDS defender. Their classification was based on observing the anomalies of attack manifestation: *Foreign Symbol, Minimal Foreign Sequence, Dormant Sequence*, and *Non-Anomalous Sequence.* In foreign symbol, the attack manifestation contains a system call which never appears in the normal record. For minimal foreign sequence, the attack manifestation contains a system call sequence which never appears in the normal record, although all subsequences appear in the normal record. In dormant sequence, a sequence of system calls in the attack manifestation matches a subsequence in the normal record, but does not match the full sequence. In non-anomalous sequence, the attack manifestation entirely matches the normal sequence without anomaly.

3.2 Evaluation-Centric Taxonomies

In this section, we will study the attack taxonomies that followed one step or more towards the evaluation-centric taxonomy.

The taxonomies presented by Wood and Stankovic in [8] and Howard in [9] followed closed methodologies and dimensions. Due to space limitations, we couldn't list all dimensions of these taxonomies. These taxonomies can be adapted to become a complete evaluation-centric taxonomy; by deleting some unuseful redundant dimensions and adapting others according to the evaluator's point of view.

Gad El Rab et al. in [10] proposed an attack taxonomy that seems helpful for the IDS evaluation process. This taxonomy has five dimensions; (1) *Firing source*: indicates the launching place of the attack, (2) *Privilege escalation*: indicates whether the attack results in raising the privilege level, (3) *vulnerability*: specifies the exploited vulnerability, (4) *Carrier*: describes the means by which the attack reaches the victim, either via network traffic or through a local action, (5) *Target*: indicates the objectives of attack. Although this taxonomy is interesting, it does not cover all dimensions of attacks according to the IDS evaluation, especially in wireless networks. In particular, it needs some details about the attack techniques.

In the next section, we treat the shortcomings of the previous attempts of attack classification in the direction of the security-evaluation; and accordingly, we develop a new taxonomy of wireless attacks.

4 Our Proposed Taxonomy

In this section, we propose the necessary and sufficient dimensions to create a holistic and satisfactory taxonomy of wireless attacks from the perspective of the IDS-evaluator. Basically, these dimensions can be extracted from the conception of attack generation. The logical sequence of this process begins by determining what does the attacker want? i.e., *attack objectives*. According to the *network mode* and *access privileges*, the *attack objectives* can be achieved through exploiting *network vulnerabilities* using certain *attack techniques and mechanisms*. In the following subsections, we will explain the importance of each dimension in our taxonomy which is summarized in Figure 1.

4.1 Network Modes

The first dimension in our taxonomy focuses on determining the wireless network mode which is considered as the foundation of the attack test cases in wireless environments. It helps in determining the manifestation and launching point of attack. Based on the wireless network mode, we differentiate between two main types; wireless infrastructure and ad-hoc networks.

Infrastructure Network. In infrastructure network, wireless nodes associate themselves through a wireless access point (AP) which is connected to a wire line network that solves centralized network management function.

Ad-hoc Network. A wireless Ad-hoc network is a collection of autonomous wireless nodes that communicate with each other by forming a multi-hop radio network and maintaining connectivity in a decentralized manner, without need to a base station or central access point.

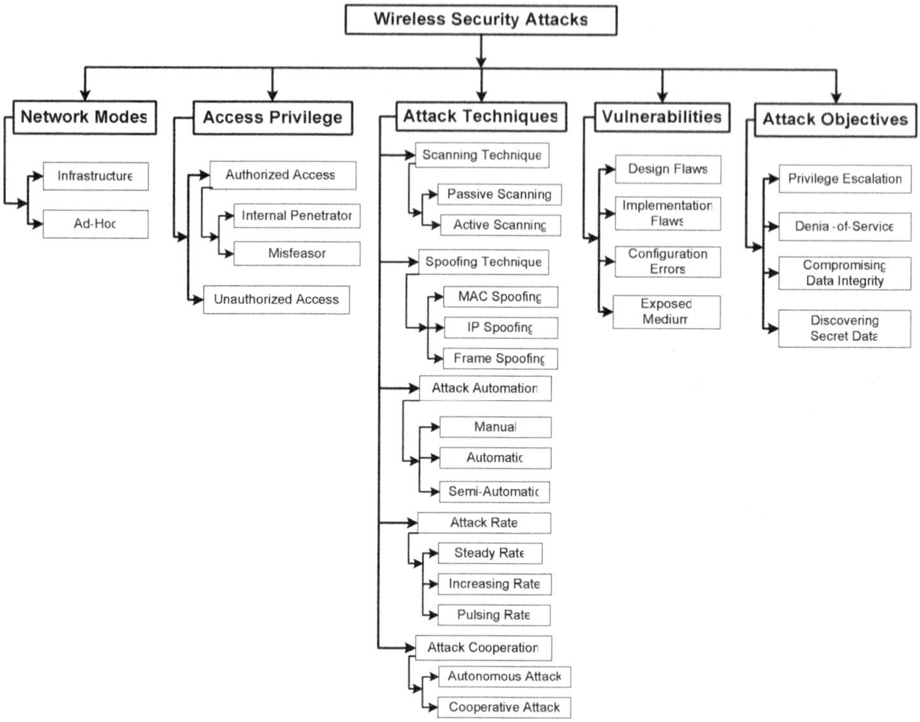

Fig. 1. IDS Evaluation-Centric taxonomy of wireless security attacks

4.2 Access Privileges

Each of them, the user and administrator, has a determined access privilege to perform his assigned tasks. Based on access privilege, we differentiate between authorized and unauthorized access.

Authorized Access. Two sorts of attackers can have an authorized access privilege; internal penetrator and misfeasor.

Internal Penetrator. Refers to a malicious user which is authorized to access a certain determined network resources, but not authorized to access another ones. The internal penetrator tries to hack the prohibited network area by exploiting the security breaches.

Misfeasor. Refers to a misuse by an administrator of his authorized access privilege to the network devices, resources and databases.

Unauthorized Access. This category related to the unauthorized users that try to gain access and escalate the access privilege using several compromising and hacking techniques.

4.3 Attack Techniques and Mechanisms

Attack techniques and mechanisms clarify the tactics that can be followed to prepare and execute the attack. Based on attack techniques and mechanisms, we differentiate between scanning techniques, spoofing techniques, degree of attack automation, attack rate organization, and attack cooperation.

Scanning Techniques. The premier intuitive procedure in the preparation process of wireless attacks is the scanning phase. It helps to locate the vulnerable services, wireless stations, access points, in addition to discovering the secret data, passwords, and so on. Based on scanning techniques, we differentiate between passive and active scanning.

Passive Scanning. In wireless networks, an attacker can use the radio channels in radio frequency (RF) monitor mode to listen to or sniff the wireless network traffic broadcast through the wireless medium. Basically, each wireless access point (AP) advertises its presence several times per second by broadcasting beacon frames that carry service set identifier (SSID). The attacker exploits this process to sniff beacons. After detecting the SSID, the attacker can take steps to passively scanning and collecting MAC addresses.

Active Scanning. Even though the attacker gathers considerable amount of information regarding a wireless network through passive scanning, without revealing his presence at all, there are data that may still be missing. The attacker then sends artificially constructed packets to the target to trigger useful responses [11]. This activity is known as active scanning or probing.

Spoofing Techniques. Through spoofing techniques, the attacker forges his identity to masquerade as another one, or even creates multiple illegitimate identities. The attacker may resort to use this technique to avoid detection by the security-defense systems, impersonate another network device, gain unauthorized access, or falsely advertise services to wireless clients. In our context, we will focus on MAC, IP, and Frame spoofing.

MAC Address Spoofing. MAC address is a layer 2 unique identifier, and it has already been embedded in the device or the network card during manufacturing. Using MAC address spoofing the attacker may be able to bypass the access control mechanisms. Typical APs control access by permitting only those stations that have known MAC addresses from an assigned address-set. The attacker may either compromise a legitimate station that already exists in the MAC address-set or spoof one with a legitimate MAC address.

IP Address Spoofing. IP spoofing refers to the creation of IP packets with a forged source IP address. An IP address is usually assigned by the network administrator as a static address or by internet service provider (ISP) as a dynamic one every time the device connects to the network. It is conceptually different than MAC spoofing; where it may use any arbitrary IP address.

Frame Spoofing. Basically, frame spoofing allows an attacker to insert unauthorized contents into the frames. Wireless frames themselves are not authenticated. So when a frame has a spoofed source address, it cannot be detected unless the address is wholly bogus [11].

Attack Automation. Depending on the system immunity, exploited vulnerabilities, and attack objectives, one or more of the attack phases; scanning-phase, exploiting-phase, recruiting-phase, and infecting-phase can be executed either manually, automatically, or semi-automatically.

Manual. It refers to executing all phases of attack manually. The attacker manually scans the system vulnerabilities and exploits them to reach the intended objectives.

Automatic. On the contrary, using automatic attack techniques all phases of attack are performed automatically. All attack features such as attack type, duration, and victim addresses are preprogrammed in the fired attack code.

Semi-Automatic. Semi-automatic attack merges between both manual and automatic techniques. For example, in the distributed DoS (DDoS) attack, the attacker may perform scanning, exploiting, and recruiting phases automatically and infecting phase manually by specifying the attack type, onset, and duration [12].

Attack Rate Organization. Attack rate can be organized according to the analysis of the real-time state of the targeted system. The attack may be managed at steady rate, increasing rate, or pulsing rate.

Steady Rate. Using several tools, the attacker can be able to generate a steady number of attack packets during the attack interval. An attack with high steady rate can exhaust the victim resources.

Increasing Rate. Typical successful attack resorts to many tactics to avoid the attack detection. One of these tactics is the generation of attack at a gradually increasing rate. This can lead to a slow exhaustion of the victim resources, as aimed by some flooding attacks, and thus delay the early detection of the attack [12].

Pulsing Rate. Another successful tactic with low probability of attack revealing is the generation of attack at an intermittent or pulsing rate. With the pulsing rate tactic, the attacker generates an attack during a certain interval (on-state), and holds it during another alternate interval (off-state). At the end of off-state, the attacker resumes the attack again and so on. The attacker adjusts the on and off intervals according to the real-time state of the victim. As well as, during on-state, the attack may use steady constant rate or gradually increasing rate.

Attack Cooperation. Based on the attack cooperation, there are two strategies to prepare and perform the attack; autonomous or cooperative attack. This dimension can be used to measure the ability of an IDS to distinguish between the autonomous and cooperative attacks, to facilitate tracing and combating the source of attack.

Autonomous Attack. In autonomous attack, each attacker prepares and launches an attack independently without any contribution or help from any other entity.

Cooperative Attack. Cooperative attack has two forms. First, cooperation between autonomous attackers to achieve a common goal. Second, one attacker can compromise multiple agents (centrally controlled) to be cooperated to launch an intended attack against a certain victim. DDoS attack is a clear example of this tactic.

4.4 Vulnerabilities

A vulnerability is a weakness or fault in system security procedures, design, implementation, or communication medium that could be accidentally triggered or intentionally exploited and result in a security breach [13]. Basically, we can identify two main categories of wireless vulnerabilities; physical vulnerabilities and logical vulnerabilities. Physical vulnerabilities which are exploited by tampering and vandalism attacks are outside the IDS evaluation interest. Therefore, we will focus only on the logical vulnerabilities, which exist in the network services, protocols and applications, and can be exploited by logical attacks. In this section, we classify the logical vulnerabilities into four main categories.

Design Flaws. Design flaw refers to using a protocol to violate the assumptions of normal behavior in the network, while conforming the protocol specification design. For example, an attacker can exploit the vulnerability in the TCP protocol design to perpetrate a TCP-SYN flooding attack. The attacker violates the three-way handshake operation of TCP connection making a half-open connection that ties up the server's allocated resources.

Implementation Flaws. Refer to errors in hardware construction or software coding due to the unfamiliarity with the programming language or the ignorance of security issues. For example, inadequate boundary checking which may result in a buffer overflowing with attacker-controlled contents [8].

Configuration Errors. Configuration errors are the result of improper settings of a particular environment or threat model, programs/utilities that are installed in a wrong place, or incorrect installation of program/utilities parameters [14].

Exposed Medium. Due to the openness of the exposed wireless medium, the attacker can easily access the wireless network with poor authentication. However, most of wireless networks are not configured securely and usually only MAC address spoofing is required to gain full access.

4.5 Attack Objectives

Attack objectives are the ultimate goals of attack. They can be classified into four main categories; privilege escalation, denial of service, compromising data integrity and information disclosure.

Privilege Escalation. A malicious user may intend to climb or elevate the access privilege of a trusted user, e.g., user-to-root privilege escalation. Usually, this task is considered as a penultimate goal that is used to reach another ultimate goal.

Denial-of-Service. Denial-of-service goal can be achieved by hindering a targeted system from serving the legitimate users. DoS attacks intend to disrupt the normal operation of the system by exhausting its resources (CPU time, memory, band-width, battery power, etc.).

Compromising Data Integrity. This goal can be achieved by altering the network traffic. However, the attacker may intend to modify the transmitted packet or inject complete created packets into the data stream.

Discovering Secret Data. Due to the exposed wireless medium and other network vulnerabilities, an attacker is able to sniff or probe the wireless beacon frames and discover the secret information.

In the following section, we will apply our proposed taxonomy in an experimental test of wireless IDSs evaluation.

5 Wireless IDSs-Evaluation Test

In this section, we use our taxonomy for extracting the attack test cases for a simple experimental evaluation of two popular wireless IDSs (WIDSs): Kismet and AirMagnet. Using Classification Tree Editor (CTE) tool [15], we have extracted 5184 test cases, which are the all possible test cases according to our taxonomy. But, not all these test cases are valid. According to our study of nearly 85 wireless attacks, we found that most of wireless attacks respect the following rule: [(Infrastructure + Adhoc Network) * Unauthorized * Passive * (MAC+IP) * (Manual + Semi-Automatic) * (Steady + Pulsing Rate) * Autonomous * Vulnerabilities * (DoS + Compromising Data Integrity + Discovering Secret Data)]. Note that in CTE, "*"represents the AND logic operator, and "+" means OR. This rule generates nearly 35 valid test cases. But, for the test presented in this section, we have constructed a wireless infrastructure network as an evaluation test bed as shown in Figure 2. Our corresponding CTE-based rule is: [Infrastructure * Unauthorized * Passive * (MAC + IP) * (Manual+ Semi Automatic) * (Steady + Pulsing) * Autonomous * Design * (DoS + Compromising Data Integrity + Discovering Secret Data)]. This rule generates 12 valid test cases as shown in Figure 3. We have selected the first five test cases to evaluate the two WIDSs. The corresponding attacks for these test cases are chopchop, fragmentation, ARP Replay, deauthentication flooding, and rogue AP attacks. In this test, we have used wireless adapter Alfa-AWUS036H [16], and access point Linksys-WRT54G [17], as well as the aircracking [18] and Backtrack [19] tools.

Fig. 2. Evaluation Test Bed

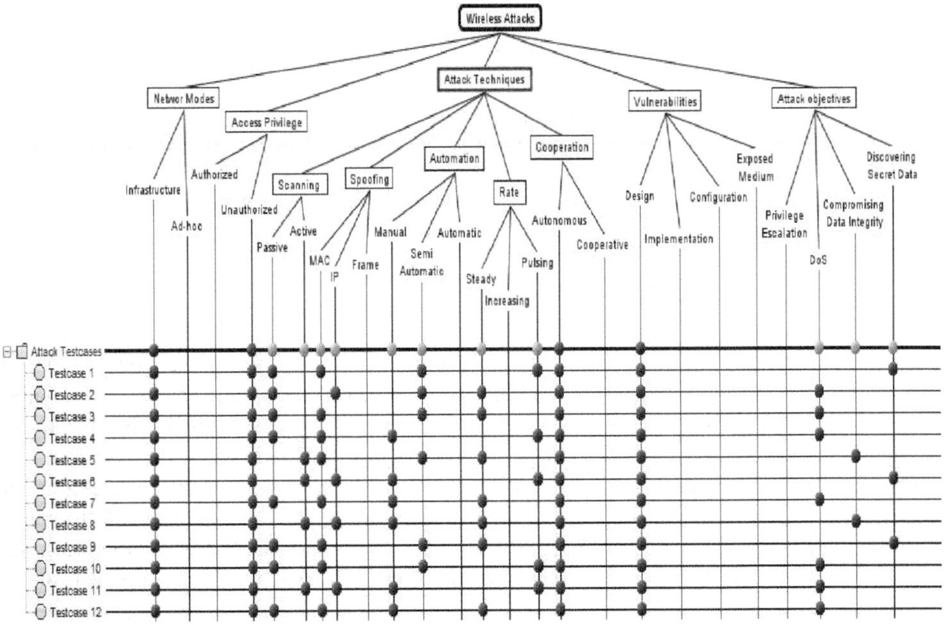

Fig. 3. Attack Test Cases

The benchmarking results are drawn in Table 1, where "?" designates "bad detection". The results show that each of them, Kismet and AirMagnet, was able to detect some specific attacks, but not able to detect others. Of course our experiment does not completely validate our work but it gave us a starting point with a good practical background. We are thus currently adapting this test to manage a more fair and unbiased evaluation of wireless IDSs.

Table 1. WIDSs-Evaluation Results

WIDS	Discovering Secret Data	Compromising data integrity	DoS	Score
Kismet	?	√	√	8
AirMagnet	√	?	√	7

6 Conclusions

This paper has proposed a holistic taxonomy of wireless attacks from the perspective of the IDS evaluator. Our proposed taxonomy followed the requirements of the satisfactory taxonomy, taking into account all the sufficient and necessary dimensions of wireless attacks. As a result, this taxonomy gives a guide-line to IDS-developers, network administrators and security analysts to be able to evaluate the WIDSs, and manipulate any drawbacks for the new design. We have used our taxonomy to generate the valid attack test cases to evaluate two of WIDSs (Kismet and AirMagnet) in a wireless infrastructure network. In the future work, we will extend our test using OPNET simulator with a real experimental test, as well as some auxiliary tools to evaluate the security and performance of WIDSs in different network modes, and according to quantitative measurement metrics.

Acknowledgement. This work was partially supported by Feel@Home and IMAP projects.

References

1. Robert, J.B.: Wireless Threats and Attacks. Handbook of Information Security. John Wiley & Sons, Chichester (December 2006)
2. Landwehr, C.E., Bull, A.R., McDermott, J.P., Choi, W.S.: A taxonomy of computer program security flaws. ACM Computing Surveys 26(3), 211–254 (1994)
3. Cohen, F.: Information System Attacks: A Preliminary Classification Scheme. Computers & Security 16, 29–46 (1997)
4. Cohen, F.: Protection and Security on the Information Superhighway. John Wiley & Sons, Chichester (March 1995)
5. Icove, D., Seger, K., VonStorch, W.: Computer Crime: A Crimefighter's Handbook, 1st edn. O'Reilly & Associates, Sebastopol (September 1995)
6. Kumar, S.: Classification and Detection of Computer Intrusions. Ph.D. thesis, Purdue University (August 1995)
7. Killourhy, K.S., Maxion, R.A., Tan, K.M.C.: A Defense-Centric Taxonomy Based on Attack Manifestations. In: Proceedings of International Conference on Dependable Systems and Networks (DSN 2004), Florence, Italy, June 28 - July 01, pp. 102–111 (2004)
8. Wood, A.D., Stankovic, J.A.: A Taxonomy for Denial-of-Service Attacks in Wireless Sensor Networks. Handbook of Sensor Networks, Compact Wireless and Wired Sensing Systems. CRC Press, Boca Raton (2004)

9. Howard, J.D.: An Analysis of Security Incidents on The Internet 1989-1995. PhD thesis, Department of Engineering and Public Policy, Carnegie Mellon University (April 1997)
10. Gad El Rab, M., Abou El Kalam, A., Deswarte, Y.: Execution Patterns in Automatic Malware and Human-Centric Attacks. In: IEEE International Symposium on Network Computing and Applications (IEEE NCA 2008), Cambridge, MA USA, July 10 - 12 (2008)
11. Bidgoli, H.: Hacking Techniques in Wireless Networks. Handbook of Information Security, 1st edn. John Wiley & Sons, Chichester (December 2005)
12. Mirkovic, J.: D-WARD: Source-End Defense against Distributed Denial-of Service Attacks. Ph.D. Thesis, Computer Science Department, University of California (2003)
13. Stoneburner, G., Goguen, A., Feringa, A.: Risk Management Guide for Information Technology Systems. NIST Special Publication 800-30, Washington, DC (2001)
14. Aslam, T.: A Taxonomy of Security Faults in the UNIX Operating System. Master thesis, Purdue University (August 1995)
15. CTE, http://systematic-testing.com/functional_testing/cte_main.php?cte=1
16. Alfa, http://www.alfa.com.tw/in/front/bin/ptdetail.phtml?Part=AWUS036H&Category=0
17. Linksys, http://www.linksysbycisco.com/EU/en/products/WAP54G?lid=LearnMore
18. Aircrack-ng, http://www.aircrack-ng.org/
19. BackTrack, http://www.backtrack-linux.org/

Rational Secret Sharing with Honest Players over an Asynchronous Channel

William K. Moses Jr. and C. Pandu Rangan

Department of Computer Science and Engineering,
Indian Institute of Technology Madras, Chennai, India
{wkmjr3,prangan55}@gmail.com

Abstract. We consider the problem of rational secret sharing introduced by Halpern and Teague [5], where the players involved in secret sharing play only if it is to their advantage. This can be characterized in the form of preferences. Players would prefer to get the secret than to not get it and secondly with lesser preference, they would like as few other players to get the secret as possible. Several positive results have already been published to efficiently solve the problem of rational secret sharing but only a handful of papers have touched upon the use of an asynchronous broadcast channel. [3] used cryptographic primitives, [11] used an interactive dealer, and [14] used an honest minority of players in order to handle an asynchronous broadcast channel.

In our paper, we propose an m-out-of-n rational secret sharing scheme which can function over an asynchronous broadcast channel without the use of cryptographic primitives and with a non-interactive dealer. This is possible because our scheme uses a small number, $k+1$, of honest players. The protocol is resilient to coalitions of size up to k and furthermore it is ε-resilient to coalitions of size up to $m-1$. The protocol will have a strict Nash equilibrium with probability $Pr(\frac{k+1}{n})$ and an ε-Nash equilibrium with probability $Pr(\frac{n-k-1}{n})$. Furthermore, our protocol is immune to backward induction.

Later on in the paper, we extend our results to include malicious players as well.

We also show that our protocol handles the possibility of a player deviating in order to force another player to get a wrong value in what we believe to be a more time efficient manner than was done in Asharov and Lindell [2].

1 Introduction

1.1 Background

The classical problem of m-out-of-n secret sharing deals with distributing information about a secret to several players and then having them cooperate and work together in order to reconstruct that secret. More specifically, if m or more players come together, then no matter which players they are, they should be able to correctly reconstruct the secret. However, if less than m players come

D.C. Wyld et al. (Eds.): CNSA 2011, CCIS 196, pp. 414–426, 2011.

together, then they should not be able to reconstruct the secret. A solution to this problem came in the form of Shamir secret sharing [15]. Suppose we wanted it such that a minimum of at least m players must come together in order for a secret to be reconstructed. Then what we would do is construct a polynomial, $\mathcal{F}(x)$, of degree $m-1$ and make $\mathcal{F}(0)$ the secret. We would then distribute a pair of values $(y, \mathcal{F}(y))$ to each player where y is a different value for each player. If at least m players participate in the protocol, then by Lagrange's interpolation formula, they can reconstruct the secret.

The rational version of this classical problem alters the type of players involved in the game. In the classical version, players were either honest or malicious. However, in the rational version, players are rational, which means that they will only play the game if it is in their best interests to do so. In this scenario, we make a few assumptions about the players. First, that players prefer to learn the secret rather than not learn it. Secondly, that players prefer as few others as possible to learn the secret. With these two assumptions in mind, the problem ceases to be one of merely protecting honest players from the trickery of malicious players, and starts to be one of protecting every player from every other player and moreover, incentivizing every player to participate. With this new setting, we need a new solution concept in order to judge the effectiveness of protocols. This concept comes in the form of Nash equilibrium. A game is in Nash equilibrium if every player is playing her best response to every other player's best response.

In the rational setting, Shamir's scheme, which previously worked, proves unsuccessful as shown below. Suppose that m^* players actually play an m-out-of-n Shamir secret sharing game.

If $m^* < m$, then Nash equilibrium. But the secret is not reconstructed.
If $m^* = m$, then not a Nash equilibrium. At this point, if a player decides not to send her share, then she ends up with everyone else's share and is able to reconstruct the secret while the others cannot.
If $m^* > m$, then Nash equilibrium. Even if a player does not send her share, the remaining players would. However, this is unstable because if enough people decide not to send their share, then this case degenerates to the previous case where $m^* = m$, which is not a Nash equilibrium.

Due to the unstable Nash equilibrium when $m^* > m$ and non-Nash equilibrium when $m^* = m$, it is ill advised to use Shamir's secret sharing as is in the rational setting. Several protocols have been devised to solve this problem [5,4,1,11,10,9,8,7,12,14,2,3], but only a handful have actually dealt with rational secret sharing using an asynchronous broadcast channel. These include Maleka et al.'s result [11] and Fuchsbauer et al.'s result [3], and Ong et al.'s result [14]. However, we contest that we can remove the interactive dealer [11] and cryptographic primitives [3] at the cost of assuming that a few of the participating players must be honest, but we believe that this is a reasonable assumption when the number is small, as in our scheme. This idea of assuming a small minority of honest players with a rational majority was first introduced by Ong et al. [14] and enabled them to obtain very strong results in rational secret sharing.

They were able to also address the use of asynchronous broadcast channels, however their method differs from ours. Also, our protocol is able to handle coalitional deviations, which is one of the future directions of work mentioned in [14].

A rational secret sharing scheme consists of two algorithms, the dealer's algorithm and the player's algorithm. The dealer's algorithm is used to distribute shares to each of the players. In our scheme, the dealer's algorithm is only used once before the start of play. The player's algorithm is used by the players in order to interpret the information of their own shares as well as the information sent by other players and prescribes a set of actions to follow in order to progress the game. When we refer to the protocol in our paper, we are referring to the player's algorithm for the most part.

1.2 Our Results

Our protocol is an m-out-of-n secret sharing scheme which utilizes an asynchronous broadcast channel, involves a non-interactive dealer, and does not use any cryptographic primitives. Depending on the number of honest players $k+1$ participating in the protocol, the protocol is resilient to coalitions of size up to and including k and furthermore it is ε-resilient to coalitions of size up to and including $m-1$. Choosing the right value of k really depends on how many honest players you believe to be active in the network and allows for a good trade-off, more the number of players you believe play honestly, better the protection against coalitions.

In Asharov and Lindell's work [2], they talked about the concept of U_i^f-independence of any player i and it's impossibility in the case of synchronous and asynchronous networks. U_i^f of a player refers to the utility gained by the player i when deviating in order to force another player to obtain a wrong value as the secret. U_i^f-dependence reflects how well a protocol deals with this utility of a player i. In order to handle U_i^f-dependence in non-simultaneous channels, they proposed a mechanism wherein they add a number of completely fake rounds to the protocol. In the case of 2-out-of-2 secret sharing using their mechanism, if the second player tries to deviate and achieve U_i^f in a completely fake round, the first player will know and hence both players will achieve their respective U_i^-, i.e. the utility gained when a player does not get the secret. In this scenario, the second player stands to gain nothing from deviating in a completely fake round and the fact that she does not know which rounds are completely fake acts as a deterrent to her. The probability of deviating and fooling the other player becomes $\frac{E(r)-f}{E(r)}$, where f is the number of completely fake rounds and $E(r)$ is the expected number of rounds (including the completely fake rounds). To achieve better protection, we need to increase the number of completely fake rounds in the protocol. This leads to a longer expected time. In our protocol, we can achieve the same sort of deterrent because despite a player's deviation, the honest players will always reveal the game to be real or fake. The only way that this will fail is if the deviating player manages to beat the authentication of the message. For information theoretic message authentication which uses $\log \frac{1}{\beta}$ bits, the probability of beating the authentication is β. By trading off between linear time and logarithmic number of bits, we are able to handle the U_i^f-dependence of any player i while reducing the expected running time of the protocol.

Furthermore, our protocol is immune to backward induction.

1.3 Organization

Section 2 discusses work related to this paper. Section 3 provides a background of the area with required definitions and assumptions made. Section 4 provides a detailed explanation and analysis of the proposed protocol. Section 5 extends our work to include malicious players. Section 6 wraps up the paper with some proposed lines of research to pursue.

2 Related Work

Work has already been done in the area of asynchronous broadcast by [11], [3], and [14].

In [11], the authors suggested that by modifying their protocol and using repeated games with an interactive dealer, it was possible to have a working protocol for asynchronous broadcast. Our protocol makes use of repeated games, however it does not require an interactive dealer.

In [3], the authors proposed a working protocol for synchronous broadcast using cryptographic primitives and also extended their results to asynchronous broadcast as well by modifying their protocol. Our protocol does not require any cryptographic primitives but is instead information theoretically secure.

In [14], the authors proposed a working protocol for synchronous broadcast using the idea of an honest minority with rational majority and in the process obtained very good results both in terms of expected number of rounds taken to finish the protocol as well as in terms of the equilibrium used. They further extended this model to asynchronous broadcast, still maintaining good results. However, in their protocol, it is required that the subset of honest players is a random subset of $k = \omega(\log n)$, where n, the total number of players, is sufficiently large. Our protocol only places the restriction that $k < m < n$, where $k + 1$ players are honest in an m-out-of-n secret sharing scheme. The difference between the schemes is that in order for theirs to work properly, n must be sufficiently large, but ours will work for small groups of players as well as large groups. Furthermore, they gained an exact notion of equilibrium ($\varepsilon = 0$) at the cost of having an approximate notion of fairness, i.e. there is a negligible probability that the honest players may fail to compute the secret correctly if they follow the prescribed protocol. Our protocol however achieves an exact notion of fairness. Also, with regards to our equilibrium notion, we achieve ε-Nash equilibrium in most cases, but as the number of honest players involved in the reconstruction protocol increases, so does the probability of obtaining a strict Nash equilibrium. Finally, one of the future directions of work mentioned in [14] was to find a solution concept which would be resilient to coalitional deviations. An earlier version of their paper [13] showed coalition-proofness against stable coalitions in a model simpler than their fail-stop one. Our protocol is resilient to coalitions of size $\leq k$ and furthermore ε-resilient to coalitions of size up to and including $m-1$.

3 Definitions and Assumptions

3.1 Definitions

In order to understand the work done in subsequent sections of this paper, we must first define a few important terms. Please note that definitions 3.1 to 3.7 are taken from Kol and Naor's paper [8] with slight modifications. Please note especially that the term game as used in their definitions has been changed to set of games in our definitions. This is done in order avoid confusion, due to the fact that we use repeated games in our paper.

Definition 3.1. The utility function u_i of a player is defined as a function which maps a player's actions to a payoff value in such a way that preferred actions result in higher payoff values.

Definition 3.2. We say that a player retrieves the designated value (the secret or $F(x)$) when outcome o is reached, if according to o the player quits and outputs the right value. Let o and o' be two possible outcomes of the set of games, and let $retrieve(o)$ be the set of players retrieving the value when o is reached. If the following condition holds, then we say that the nature of the utility function is learning preferring: $u_i(o) > u_i(o')$ whenever $i \in retrieve(o)$ and $i \notin retrieve(o')$ (players prefer to learn).

Definition 3.3. Note that we call a vector of players' strategies a strategy profile, and use the following notations: $\alpha_{-i} = (\alpha_1, ..., \alpha_{i-1}, \alpha_{i+1}, ..., \alpha_n)$, $(\alpha_{-i}, \alpha_i') = (\alpha_1, ..., \alpha_{i-1}, \alpha_i', \alpha_{i+1}, ...\alpha_n)$, and $u_i(\sigma) = \mathcal{E}_{o \sim \mathcal{O}(\sigma)}[u_i(o)]$ where $\mathcal{O}(\sigma)$ denotes the probability distribution over outcomes induced by the protocol σ. Now, a behavioural strategy profile σ for a protocol is said to be a Nash equilibrium if for every $i \in N$ and any behavioural strategy σ_i', it holds that $u_i(\sigma_i, \sigma_{-i}) \geq u_i(\sigma_i', \sigma_{-i})$.

Definition 3.4. A behavioural strategy profile σ for a set of repeated games is said to be a strict Nash equilibrium if for every $i \in N$ and any behavioural strategy σ_i', it holds that $u_i(\sigma_i, \sigma_{-i}) > u_i(\sigma_i', \sigma_{-i})$.

Definition 3.5. A behavioural strategy profile σ for a set of repeated games is said to be a ε-Nash equilibrium if for every $i \in N$ and any behavioural strategy σ_i', it holds that $u_i(\sigma_i, \sigma_{-i}) + \varepsilon \geq u_i(\sigma_i', \sigma_{-i})$, where ε is a negligible value.

Definition 3.6. A coalition is a subset of the players who are active during the reconstruction phase.

Definition 3.7. A protocol is said to be resilient to coalitions of size t if even a coordinated deviation by a coalition of that size or less won't increase the utility of any of the players of the coalition. According to the prescribed strategy, each player of the coalition, $i \in C$, plays the strategy σ_i and the remaining players play σ_{-i}. Let the player's deviating strategy be σ_i^d. Then the protocol is said to be resilient to coalitions of size t if $\forall i \in C, \forall |C| \leq t$, it holds that $u_i(\sigma_i, \sigma_{-i}) > u_i(\sigma_i^d, \sigma_{-i})$.

Definition 3.8. We say that a protocol is ε-resilient to a coalition of size t if no member of the coalition can gain more than ε in the process of a coordinated deviation by the coalition. According to the prescribed strategy, each player of the coalition, $i \in C$, plays the strategy σ_i and the remaining players play σ_{-i}. Let the player's deviating strategy be σ_i^d. Then the protocol is said to be ε-resilient to coalitions of size t if $\forall i \in C, \forall |C| \leq t$, it holds that $u_i(\sigma_i, \sigma_{-i}) + \varepsilon \geq u_i(\sigma_i^d, \sigma_{-i})$, where ε is a negligible value.

Definition 3.9. We define the utility U_i^f of a player i as the utility she gets if she is able to trick the other players into believing that a non-secret is the secret. U_i^f-dependence refers to how well the protocol deals with this utility for any player i.

Definition 3.10. Backward induction can be described as follows. If we know that the last round of a game is r, then we choose not to broadcast information in that round in order to gain in utility (if other players broadcast while we do not, then we gain the secret while others may not). Since each player thinks like this, common knowledge states that we all know that no one will broadcast in round r, and hence round $r - 1$ effectively becomes the last round. Similarly, everyone will not broadcast in $r - 1$ because it is now the last round and since that becomes common knowledge, round $r - 2$ becomes the last round. This type of thinking continues until at last we don't broadcast in any of the rounds. Similarly, if we are dealing with repeated games, as in this paper, if we know when the last game of the protocol will be played, then if we know when the last round (in our case, stage) of the last game is to be played, we can choose not to play that game and effectively the previous game becomes the last game.

Definition 3.11. In our protocol to reconstruct the secret, we use repeated games. In that context, we refer to the true game as the game, which upon completion, will reveal the actual secret.

3.2 Assumptions

As for the assumptions made, we follow several of those made in Fuchsbauer et al.'s paper [3] when it comes to an asynchronous broadcast channel.

1. We consider that an Asynchronous Broadcast Channel is present and connects all the n players such that a message sent from one player will be received by all the remaining players.

2. All players broadcast their values simultaneously.
3. Any message sent will eventually be received, even if it is at time ∞.
4. Rational and malicious players may schedule the message delivery. In other words, players who are not honest may schedule message delivery to benefit themselves.

4 Our Protocol

At the heart of our protocol is a 2-stage game which is repeated a number of times depending on a geometric distribution. First we describe the 2-stage game and then we describe how it is used.

The information shared in stage 1 and stage 2 of the game correspond to the 2 stages in [2]. In stage 1, we broadcast player i's share of $R_j \otimes S_j$ where R_j is a random number used in game j and S_j is the possible secret used in game j. We also broadcast information theoretic authentication information about the stage 1 information as done in [8]. In stage 2, we broadcast player i's share of R_j as well as i's share of a boolean indicator, which indicates whether the current game is the true game or not. Here as well, we broadcast information theoretic authentication information for stage 2. Note that we choose the value of k according to the number of honest players "$k + 1$" participating in the protocol.

The game is played as follows. Initially everyone broadcasts their share of $R_j \otimes S_j$ and it is reconstructed using m-out-of-n Shamir secret sharing. Once every player's share has been received and is verified, stage 2 commences. Now, every player broadcasts their share of R_j and a boolean indicator. Both these values are reconstructed using k-out-of-n Shamir secret sharing. The value of $R_j \otimes S_j$ Xored with R_j produces the possible secret and the reconstructed boolean indicator tells us whether this game was the true game or not. In stage 2, it is guaranteed that at least k people broadcast (even though $k + 1$ people are honest players, one of them may be the short player and this may be the true game, in which case k other long players are required to reconstruct the secret). So, whether or not this game was the true game can be determined except in the very rare case that a player manages to break the information theoretic authentication check and pass off a forged stage 2 share. This would only happen with a negligible probability ε which can be lowered by increasing the bit size on the security checking "tag" and "hash" values.

This game is repeated $O(\frac{1}{\beta})$ times until the short player (the player who has less number of games to play) finishes playing all her games. At this point the short player should ideally broadcast $\perp$, which would be a message understood by all parties to signify that the player has finished playing all her games. For our purposes, we may assume that $\perp$ is represented by the value zero.

Protocol Analysis

We now analyze the protocol in some detail. First, we review the impact of using honest players. Then we move on to why we are able to obtain a strict

Table 1. Dealer's share allotment protocol

Dealer(y, β)
Let $\mathcal{F} = GF(p)$ where $p \geq |Y|$ prime, and associate each element of the secret set Y with an element of $\mathcal{F}$. Denote by $\mathcal{G}(\beta)$ the geometric distribution with parameter β.

- **Create the list of possible secrets and random numbers:**
  - Choose $l, d \sim \mathcal{G}(\beta)$ such that $L = l + d - 1$ is the size of the full list of possible secrets.
  - Select a random ordering of the possible secrets such that the lth secret is the actual secret y.
  - Generate a list of size L of random numbers.
- **Create shares:** Create n shares. One share will contain $l - 1$ cells and the remaining shares will contain L cells. The player who gets the share with less number of cells is deemed the short player and the remaining players are deemed the long players. The values in each cell of the short player are the same as the values in the corresponding cells in the long players. The lth cell of the long players is considered the true game and the secret revealed after playing the game will be the real secret. Each cell corresponds to a 2-stage game and consists of the following information:
  Stage 1 information:
  - **Masked Secret:** An m-out-of-n Shamir share of $R_j \otimes S_j$, where R_j is a randomly generated number for game j and S_j is a possible secret for game j.
  - **Authentication Information:** Information theoretic security checking as done in [8]. A "tag" to prove the authenticity of the masked secret and "hash values" to check the authenticity of other players' tags.

  Stage 2 information:
  - **Mask:** A k-out-of-n Shamir share of R_j.
  - **Indicator:** A k-out-of-n Shamir share of a boolean value indicating whether this game reveals the true secret or whether the game should be repeated.
  - **Authentication Information:** A "tag" to prove the authenticity of stage 2 information for this game and "hash values" to verify the authenticity of other players' tags.
- **Add one more half cell (containing only stage 1 info) to each share.**
- **Assign shares:** Randomly allot the shares to the players.

Nash equilibrium and an ε-Nash equilibrium with given probabilities. Next we show why our protocol is immune to backward induction and finally we explain how the protocol handles the U_i^f-dependence of a player i.

The key to our protocol is the honest players. An honest player disregards her utilities and plays the game exactly as it is specified. Because of them, we can guarantee that some players will follow the protocol. Because of this assurance we have more control and can guarantee good results as was done in [14]. Also, if we look at previous results in the field of rational secret sharing, we come across [2], which basically said that if we make secret sharing a two stage process wherein we first share the Xor of a random number and the secret using m-out-of-n secret sharing and then follow that up by sharing the random number using l-out-of-n secret sharing, where l is any number less than m, then we could provide an incentive to players to not act maliciously, because even if they did, they would never benefit from it. This was analyzed for simultaneous secret sharing and proven in the paper. However, in the cases of synchronous broadcast and asynchronous broadcast, the incentive falls through and the idea cannot be used as is. [14] used another approach coupled with a small minority

Table 2. Player i's reconstruction protocol

Player$_i$($share$)
Set secret_revealed ← FALSE and cheater_detected← FALSE.
Repeat the following until secret_revealed is TRUE or cheater_detected is TRUE:

- **If the player's share ended (the player is at the final half cell containing only stage 1 info):**
  - If this is stage 1 of the game:
    - Broadcast the player's stage 1 tag and the player's share of $R_j \otimes S_j$.
    - If anyone's message did not pass the authentication check, set cheater_detected←TRUE.
  - If this is stage 2 of the game:
    - Broadcast $\perp$.
    - If at least k people have broadcasted and their messages passed the authentication check, set secret_revealed←TRUE and leave the game.
    - If anyone's message did not pass the authentication check, set cheater_detected←TRUE.
- **If the player's share did not end:**
  - If this is stage 1 of the game:
    - Broadcast the player's stage 1 tag and the player's share of $R_j \otimes S_j$.
    - If anyone's message did not pass the authentication check, set cheater_detected ← TRUE.
    - After the player has received all $n - 1$ of the other shares.
      - If they all passed the authentication check, proceed to stage 2.
      - Else leave the game.
  - If this is stage 2 of the game:
    - Broadcast the player's stage 2 tag and the player's share of the random number and indicator.
    - If anyone's message did not pass the authentication check, set cheater_detected ← TRUE.
    - If at least $k - 1$ people have broadcasted and their messages passed the authentication check:
      - If the reconstructed indicator shows that this game revealed the true secret, then set secret_revealed ← TRUE and leave the game.
      - If the reconstructed indicator shows that this game did not reveal the true secret and someone broadcasted $\perp$ in stage 1 or in stage 2, then set cheater_detected ← TRUE and leave the game.
    - After other messages have arrived, if all have passed authentication check, then proceed to next game in share. Else, leave the game.
- **Leave the game:** If secret_revealed is TRUE, then the secret can be reconstructed as follows. First reconstruct the masked secret using shares broadcasted in stage 1 of the game. Then construct the mask using shares broadcasted in stage 2 of the game. Xor the mask and the masked secret to get the secret. Quit and output the possible secret. If secret_revealed is FALSE, then the real secret was not obtained.

of honest players in order to obtain good results for synchronous broadcast. By using the idea of [2] coupled with honest players, we are able to obtain results for asynchronous broadcast.

As to our protocol having a strict Nash equilibrium with probability $Pr(\frac{k+1}{n})$ and an ε-Nash equilibrium with probability $Pr(\frac{n-k-1}{n})$, the reason for this rests solely with who the short player is. When the short player is honest, we can guarantee that she will not join a coalition or try to forge a fake secret during the true game. In that case, due to the way in which we choose β, it is strictly better for all the players involved to follow the protocol than to deviate. However, if the short player is not an honest player, then she may try to forge a secret and may succeed with a negligible probability of ε. Hence, when the short player is honest, we have a strict Nash equilibrium, else we have an ε-Nash equilibrium. The short player will be an honest player with a probability of $Pr(\frac{k+1}{n})$.

Our protocol is immune to backward induction because it maintains the property that after any history that can be reached by the protocol, the protocol is still a strict Nash equilibrium with probability $Pr(\frac{k+1}{n})$ and an ε-Nash equilibrium with probability $Pr(\frac{n-k-1}{n})$. This is because one player is short while the others are long. No one knows if they are the short player or the long player and hence they are forced to keep playing. Furthermore, the honest players will always play irregardless of utility.

An idea also discussed in [2] is that of the U_i^f-dependence of a player i. It basically deals with the fact that a player may have something to gain by forcing other players to think they have the correct secret when in fact they don't, essentially making those players obtain a *fake secret*, and asks if it is possible to create a protocol where the desire to force others to obtain such a fake secret may be counteracted. Our protocol deals with this by intrinsically assuming that a possible secret is false until proven true. That is to say that even if a party i aborts early in order to achieve a gain of U_i^f, we don't assume the secret has been gained until and unless the secret is proven to be the true secret by the honest players, using a boolean indicator. By the same token, one might consider the possibility of a player, who somehow manages to discover which game reveals the true secret, trying to make it appear to be a fake secret by sending an incorrect message. Our protocol is designed to detect this trickery using information theoretic authentication and will correctly determine whether the current possible secret is indeed the true secret with a negligible error probability of ε, where the information theoretic authentication of the messages uses $\log \frac{1}{\beta}$ bits and β is the parameter used for the geometric distribution in the dealer's protocol.

The values of β_0 and c_0: We now need to calculate two values before we proceed to formulate our theorem. This analysis is present in Kol and Naor's paper [8] and will be repeated below (with slight tweaks) for the sake of understanding. We first define the utility values for a player i as follows:

- U_i is the utility of a player i when she obtains the secret along with at least one player not belonging to any coalition of which she is a part.
- U_i^+ is the utility of a player i when she obtains the secret and no player, other than those belonging to her coalition, obtains the secret.
- U_i^- is the utility of a player i when she does not obtain the secret.

Now, if the set of secrets Y follows a distribution D, then let us assume that $b \in Y$ is the secret with the highest probability of being the actual secret according to D. In other words, $\forall x \in Y, \mathcal{D}(b) \geq \mathcal{D}(x)$. Let the probability that a player i can guess the secret given the distribution $\mathcal{D}$ and her share be g.

If the player follows the protocol, then she will get U_i. If she deviates and gets the secret, then she will get a utility of U_i^+. If she deviates but does not get the secret, with a probability of $1-g$, then she stands to get a utility of U_i^-. Now, it matters to us to ensure that the expected utility from following the protocol is more than the expected utility from deviating from the protocol. So, the following must hold true:

$$\text{Expected utility (deviating)} < \text{Expected utility (following protocol)}$$

$$g * U_i^+ + (1-g) * U_i^- < U_i$$
$$g * (U_i^+ - U_i^-) < U_i - U_i^-$$
$$g < \frac{U_i - U_i^-}{U_i^+ - U_i^-}$$

Let us call the ratio $\frac{U_i - U_i^-}{U_i^+ - U_i^-}$ for a player i, c_i. Since every player has learning preferring utilities, it follows that $U_i^- < U_i \leq U_i^+$ and hence $c_i > 0$ for every player i. So, for a given player i to follow the protocol, we must ensure that the chance of her deviating and getting the secret is less than c_i. In order for the protocol to work for every player, we must ensure that the probability of deviating and getting the correct secret is less than all players' c_i's. For a set of players N, we require

$$g < min_{i \in N} c_i$$

We call the value $min_{i \in N} c_i$ as c_0. Since every player's guess is at least as good as $\mathcal{D}(b)$ we should require $\mathcal{D}(b) < c_0$.

In our theorem we use β_0 to cap the value of β, which is the parameter of the geometric distribution used in the dealer's algorithm. For now, we state that the value of β_0 is $min_{i \in N}\{\frac{c_i - \mathcal{D}(b)}{c_i - \mathcal{D}(b) + 2*z*n+1}\}$ where $z = |Y|$. The reason for this value lies in the proof of Theorem 1. However, do note that since we require $c_0 > \mathcal{D}(b)$, it follows that $c_i > \mathcal{D}(b)$ which implies that $\beta_0 > 0$ and hence this is a valid cap of β.

Theorem 1. *Let Y be a finite set of secrets with distribution $\mathcal{D}$, and let each rational player have learning preferring utilities. If $\mathcal{D}(b) < c_0$, then for $\beta < \beta_0$ and for all $2 \leq m \leq n$, the scheme described above is, for Y,*

- *an asynchronous strict rational m-out-of-n secret sharing scheme with probability $Pr(\frac{k+1}{n})$,*
- *an asynchronous ε-rational m-out-of-n secret sharing scheme with probability $Pr(\frac{n-k-1}{n})$,*
- *immune to backward induction,*
- *and handles U_i^f-dependence of any player i in a time efficient manner.*

Depending upon the number of honest players $k+1$, where $2 \leq k \leq m-1$, participating in the k-out-of-n secret sharing stage of each game, the protocol will be resilient to coalitions of size $\leq k$ and furthermore ε-resilient to coalitions of size up to and including $m-1$. The scheme has expected round complexity of $O(\frac{1}{\beta})$ and expected share size of $O(\frac{1}{\beta} \log \frac{1}{\beta})$.

Proof. Please see full version [6].

5 Addition of Malicious Players

A malicious player is someone who disregards her utility values and whose only goal is to disrupt the game. They can do this by causing the game to stop early, misleading others to believe that they have the right secret when they don't, or causing some players to get the secret and others not to. A step in the direction of dealing with malicious players was made by Lysyanskaya and Triandopoulos in [9], where they dealt with a situation where both rational and malicious players were involved in a game. They concluded that it was possible to play such a game but they were unable to prevent early stoppage. Our protocol is also able to function properly even with malicious players, but it cannot prevent early stoppage. It can, however, prevent the other two problems mentioned above. However, **Theorem 1.** needs to be modified in order to incorporate this new element.

Theorem 2. *Let Y be a finite set of secrets with distribution $\mathcal{D}$, and let each rational player have learning preferring utilities. If $\mathcal{D}(b) < c_0$, then for $\beta < \beta_0$ and for all $2 \leq m \leq n$, the scheme described above is, for Y,*

- *an asynchronous strict rational m-out-of-n secret sharing scheme with probability $Pr(\frac{k+1}{n})$,*
- *an asynchronous ε-rational m-out-of-n secret sharing scheme with probability $Pr(\frac{n-k-1}{n})$,*
- *immune to backward induction,*
- *and handles U_i^f-dependence of any player i in a time efficient manner.*

Let t players be the number of malicious players actively involved in the protocol. Depending upon the number of honest players $k+1$, where $2 \leq k \leq m-1$, participating in the k-out-of-n secret sharing stage of each game, the protocol will be resilient to coalitions of size $\leq k-t$ and ε-resilient to coalitions of size up to and including $m-1-t$. The scheme has expected round complexity of $O(\frac{1}{\beta})$ and expected share size of $O(\frac{1}{\beta}\log\frac{1}{\beta})$.

This change in the theorem occurs because one way the malicious players can disrupt the game is by sending their shares to one player, through a side channel, but not to others. In order to avoid this, we must reduce the size of coalitions so that even if all malicious players send their shares to members of a coalition, that coalition will still not be able to reconstruct the secret on their own.

The proof for this theorem follows in the same vein as that of Theorem 1.

6 Conclusion and Future Work

In this paper, we have proposed an m-out-of-n RSS protocol for the case of asynchronous broadcast, which makes use of a small number of honest players in order to achieve information theoretic security and protect against coalitions to a given extent. Further directions of work include:

- Probing the case of asynchronous point to point communication through the lens of information theoretic security.

- Further improving the coalition resilience for the asynchronous broadcast scenario.
- Further improving the communication complexity for the asynchronous broadcast scenario.

References

1. Abraham, I., Dolev, D., Gonen, R., Halpern, J.: Distributed computing meets game theory: robust mechanisms for rational secret sharing and multiparty computation. In: PODC 2006: Proceedings of the Twenty-Fifth Annual ACM Symposium on Principles of Distributed Computing, pp. 53–62. ACM, New York (2006)
2. Asharov, G., Lindell, Y.: Utility dependence in correct and fair rational secret sharing. In: Halevi, S. (ed.) CRYPTO 2009. LNCS, vol. 5677, pp. 559–576. Springer, Heidelberg (2009)
3. Fuchsbauer, G., Katz, J., Naccache, D.: Efficient rational secret sharing in standard communication networks. In: Micciancio, D. (ed.) TCC 2010. LNCS, vol. 5978, pp. 419–436. Springer, Heidelberg (2010)
4. Gordon, S.D., Katz, J.: Rational secret sharing, revisited. In: De Prisco, R., Yung, M. (eds.) SCN 2006. LNCS, vol. 4116, pp. 229–241. Springer, Heidelberg (2006)
5. Halpern, J., Teague, V.: Rational secret sharing and multiparty computation: extended abstract. In: STOC 2004: Proceedings of the Thirty-Sixth Annual ACM Symposium on Theory of Computing, pp. 623–632. ACM, New York (2004)
6. Moses Jr., W.K., Pandu Rangan, C.: Rational secret sharing with honest players over an asynchronous channel. Cryptology ePrint Archive, Report 2011/068 (2011), http://eprint.iacr.org/
7. Kol, G., Naor, M.: Cryptography and game theory: Designing protocols for exchanging information. In: Canetti, R. (ed.) TCC 2008. LNCS, vol. 4948, pp. 320–339. Springer, Heidelberg (2008)
8. Kol, G., Naor, M.: Games for exchanging information. In: STOC 2008: Proceedings of the 40th Annual ACM Symposium on Theory of Computing, pp. 423–432. ACM, New York (2008)
9. Lysyanskaya, A., Triandopoulos, N.: Rationality and adversarial behavior in multi-party computation. In: Dwork, C. (ed.) CRYPTO 2006. LNCS, vol. 4117, pp. 180–197. Springer, Heidelberg (2006)
10. Maleka, S., Shareef, A., Pandu Rangan, C.: The deterministic protocol for rational secret sharing. In: SSN 2008: The 4th International Workshop on Security in Systems and Networks, pp. 1–7 (2008)
11. Maleka, S., Shareef, A., Pandu Rangan, C.: Rational secret sharing with repeated games. In: Chen, L., Mu, Y., Susilo, W. (eds.) ISPEC 2008. LNCS, vol. 4991, pp. 334–346. Springer, Heidelberg (2008)
12. Micali, S., Shelat, A.: Purely rational secret sharing (extended abstract). In: Reingold, O. (ed.) TCC 2009. LNCS, vol. 5444, pp. 54–71. Springer, Heidelberg (2009)
13. Ong, S.J., Parkes, D.C., Rosen, A., Vadhan, S.P.: Fairness with an honest minority and a rational majority (April 2007), http://people.seas.harvard.edu/~salil/research/Fairness-abs.html
14. Ong, S.J., Parkes, D.C., Rosen, A., Vadhan, S.P.: Fairness with an honest minority and a rational majority. In: Reingold, O. (ed.) TCC 2009. LNCS, vol. 5444, pp. 36–53. Springer, Heidelberg (2009)
15. Shamir, A.: How to share a secret. Commun. ACM 22, 612–613 (1979)

Agent Based Cross Layer Intrusion Detection System for MANET

V. Anjana Devi[1] and R.S. Bhuvaneswaran[2]

[1] St. Joseph's College of Engineering
anjanadevi_anne@yahoo.com
[2] Anna University, Chennai – 600 025
bhuvan@annauniv.edu

Abstract. Due to the development of in the field of computer networks, Mobile ad hoc network (MANET) has emerged as a technology to provide anywhere, anytime communication. Due to its deployment nature, MANETs are more vulnerable to malicious attack. Authentication and encryption techniques can be used as the first line of defense for reducing the possibilities of attacks. However, these approaches have several drawbacks and they are designed for a set of well known attacks. These techniques cannot prevent newer attacks. Hence there is a critical need for cross layer detection technology. This paper proposes efficient cross layer intrusion detection architecture to discover the malicious nodes and different types of DoS. This proposed approach implements a fixed width clustering algorithm for efficient detection of the anomalies in the MANET traffic and also generated different types of attacks in the network. In the association process, the Fast Apriori algorithm is utilized in association process; it increases efficiency of detecting intrusion in MANET

Keywords: Intrusion Detection System (IDS), Mobile ad hoc network (MANET), Ad Hoc On-Demand Distance Vector (AODV), Fixed Width Clustering Algorithm.

1 Introduction

MANETs are subjected to different types of threats like any other radio-based networking technology [13]. These threats include outside attackers as well as misbehaving entities on the inside. Therefore, many different information assurance technologies need to be applied to protect these kinds of networks, such as data encryption, access control, identity management, and intrusion detection [11]. Unfortunately, many of the well established intrusion detection approaches and implementations are not immediately transferrable from infrastructure-based IP networks, since there are many extensive implications to the usage of radio links and the mobility of the respective devices. Not only has the attack surface for broadband and smart jamming been enlarged, but the danger of impersonation and MITM (man-in-the-middle) attacks in the network has also increased. Due to the possibility of unsuccessful transfer of protocol packets, the probability for false alarms and false accusations of nodes in the networks is very significant. This possibility increases with physical motion in

D.C. Wyld et al. (Eds.): CNSA 2011, CCIS 196, pp. 427–440, 2011.

the network which leads to interruption of transmissions and fluctuation of routes. Moreover, there are no key locations in the network, where all relevant traffic may be observed and analyzed in order to detect malicious behavior, which was the case for routers, switches, and firewalls in wired IP networks.

To overcome these problems, a novel Intrusion Detection System (IDS) based on cross layers are proposed in this paper. These will helps in detecting the abnormalities occurred in the wireless networks. For the linkage between the OSI protocol stack and the IDS module, the association algorithm is implemented in this paper. This paper uses fast apriori algorithm in order to perform the association algorithm faster. The fixed width clustering algorithm is applied in this paper in order to detect the intrusion efficiently in the adhoc network.

In MANET, in order to implement end-to-end communication along dynamic paths composed by multi-hop wireless links, a set of interacting nodes should cooperatively implement routing functions. Several multi-hop routing protocols have been proposed for MANET, and most popular ones include:

- Dynamic Source Routing (DSR),
- Optimized Link-State Routing (OLSR),
- Destination-Sequenced Distance-Vector (DSDV) and
- Ad Hoc On-Demand Distance Vector (AODV).

These protocols mostly rely on the assumption of a trustworthy cooperation among all participating devices; unfortunately, this may not be a realistic assumption in real systems. Malicious nodes could exploit the weakness of MANET to launch various kinds of attacks.

2 Related Works

Hong *et al.,* [1] proposed a Real-time cooperation intrusion detection system for MANETs. It is very common that lot of intrusion detection systems are required for mobile ad hoc networks (MANETs) [16]. In recent times, Real-time Intrusion Detection for Ad hoc Networks (RIDAN) has been proposed to detect malicious activity which is less error prone than other detection techniques, such as the behavior-based. But, RIDAN lacks central monitor and cooperation function; the nodes couldn't share information with each other. In this paper, the author proposes an improved RIDAN based on cooperative idea, Real-time Cooperation Intrusion Detection system for MANETs (RCID MANET). The simulation results show that the RCID MANET achieves more detecting accuracy and success than the RIDAN.

Identification of critical nodes for MANET intrusion detection systems is presented by Karygiannis *et al.,* [2]. The general design goal of reactive, proactive, and hybrid ad hoc routing protocols is to faithfully route packets from a source node to a destination node while maintaining a satisfactory level of service in a resource-constrained environment. Detection of malicious nodes in an open ad hoc network in which participating nodes have no previous security associations presents a number of challenges which are not faced by traditional wired networks. Traffic monitoring in wired networks is generally executed at switches, routers and gateways, but an ad hoc network does not have these types of network elements where the intrusion detection system (IDS) [5, 6] can collect and analyze audit data [7] for the entire network. A number of neighbor-monitoring, trust-building, and cluster-based voting techniques have been proposed in the research to enable the detection and reporting of malicious activity in ad hoc networks. The resources utilized by ad hoc network member nodes to monitor, detect, report, and diagnose malicious activity, however, may be greater than simply rerouting packets through a different available path. This paper proposes a method for determining conditions under which critical nodes should be monitored, describes the details of a critical node test implementation, presents experimental results, and offers a new approach for conserving the limited resources of an ad hoc network IDS.

Cabrera *et al.,* [3] put forth infrastructures and methodologies for distributed anomaly-based intrusion detection in mobile ad-hoc networks. This paper addresses one aspect of the problem of defending mobile ad-hoc networks (MANETs) [9] against computer attacks, namely, the development of a distributed anomaly-based intrusion detection system [20]. In a general sense, the proposed system is a co-located sensor network, in which the monitored variable is the health of the network being monitored. A three level hierarchical system for data collection [8], processing and transmission is described. Local IDSs (intrusion detection systems) are attached to each node of the MANET, collecting raw data of network operation, and computing a local anomaly index measuring the difference between the current node operation and a baseline of normal operation. Anomaly indexes from nodes which belong to a cluster are periodically transmitted to a cluster head, which fuses the node indexes producing a cluster-level anomaly index. In the same way, cluster heads periodically transmit these cluster-level anomaly indexes to a manager node, which fuses the cluster-level indexes into a network-level anomaly index. Due to network mobility, cluster membership and cluster heads are times varying. The paper describes:

- Clustering algorithms to update cluster centers;
- Machine learning approaches for computing the local anomaly indexes;
- A statistical technique for fusing the anomaly indexes at the cluster heads and at the manager.

The statistical technique is formally shown to increase detection accuracy under idealized assumptions. These approaches were implemented and tested under the following conditions. Routing techniques: AODV (ad-hoc on demand distance vector routing) and OLSR (optimized link state routing); mobility patterns: random walk mobility model and reference point group mobility at various speeds; types of attacks: traffic flooding denial-of-service and black hole. The ROC (receiver operating characteristics) for several operational conditions at the nodes, cluster heads and manager is determined for the performance evaluation. The overall results shows the effectiveness of the infrastructures and algorithms described in the paper, with detection accuracy generally improving as it move up in the hierarchy, i.e. detection accuracy at the cluster level is very higher than at local level, while network-level detection outperforms cluster-level detection.

A fully distributed intrusion detection system for MANET is provided by Puttini *et al.,* [4]. The entire distribution of the intrusion detection process is the prominent feature of this proposition: distribution is not restricted to data collection but also applied to execution of the detection algorithm and alert correlation [17]. Each node in the Mobile Ad hoc Network runs a local IDS (LIDS) that cooperates with others LIDS. A mobile agent framework is used to protect the autonomy of each LIDS while providing a flexible technique for exploring the natural redundancies in MANET to compensate for the dynamic state of wireless links between high mobility nodes. The proposed approach has been validated by actual implementation, which is described in the paper. Three attacks are presented as illustrative examples of the IDS mechanisms [18]. Attack detection is officially described by specification of data collection, attack signatures associated with such data and alerts generation and correlation.

3 Methodology

3.1 Cross Layer Technique in IDS

For efficient intrusion detection, we have used cross layer techniques in IDS. Generally, routing is considered in a routing layer and medium access in MAC layer whereas power control and rate control are sometimes considered in a PHY and sometimes in a MAC layer. If there is no cross layer inter action then the routing can select between several routes and have no information about congestion or malicious nodes. As a result, it selects a congested route or it selects a route that includes malicious nodes. With the help of cross layer interaction, the routing forwards possible route choices to MAC and MAC decides the possible routes using congestion and IDS information as well as returns the result to the routing. The selection of correct combination of layers in the design of cross layer IDS is very critical to detect attacks targeted at or sourced from any layers rapidly. It is optimal to incorporate MAC layer in the cross layer design for IDS as DoS attack is better detected at this layer. The routing protocol layer and MAC layer is chosen for detecting routing attacks in an efficient way. Data with behavioral information consisting of layer specific information are collected from multiple layers and forward it to data analysis module which is located in an **optimal location**. This cross layer technique incorporating IDS leads to an escalating detection rate in the number of malicious behavior of nodes increasing the true positive and reducing false positives in the MANET.

It also alleviates the congestion which can adapt to changing network and traffic characteristics. In order to evade congestion and reroute traffic, MAC and routing layers have to cooperate with each other with the IDS in order to avoid insertion of malicious nodes in the new routes. The physical layer collects various types of communication activities including remote access and logons, user activities, data traffics and attack traces. MAC contains information regarding congestion and interference. The detection mechanism for misbehaving nodes interacts with routing layer for the detection process as MAC layers also help in detection of certain routing attacks. MAC also interacts with the physical layer to determine the quality of suggested path. By combining cross layer features, attacks between the layers inconsistency can be detected. Furthermore, these schemes provide a comprehensive detection mechanism for all the layers i.e attacks originating from any layers can be detected with better detection accuracy.

3.2 Association Module

Once association rules are extracted from multiple segments of a training data set, they are then aggregated into a rule set. The feature sets consist of control and data frames from MAC frames and control packets like RREQ, RREP and RERR including data packets of IP packets from network layer. All the control packets are combined into one category as routing control packet and IP data packet as routing data packet. So, the payloads in MAC data frames contain either a routing CtrlPkt or routing DataPkt. The feature set is foreshortened by associating one or more features from different layers to specific MAC layer feature so that the overhead of learning is minimized. The characteristics are assorted based on dependency on time, traffic and other features.

The association rules that we consider here allows a consequent to have more than one item. Initially basic generalized algorithm is provided and the fast algorithm for association mining is provided.

To generate rules, for every large itemset l, all non-empty subsets of l are found out. For every such subset a, a rule of the form a ⇒ (l - a) is generated if the ratio of support (l) to support (a) is at least minconf. Then the subsets of l are considered to generate rules with multiple consequents. Since the large itemsets are stored in hash tables, the support counts for the subset itemsets can be found efficiently.

The above procedure can be improved by generating the subsets of a large itemset in a recursive depth-first fashion. . For example, given an itemset ABCD, the subset ABC is considered initially, then AB, etc. Then if a subset a of a large itemset l does not generate a rule, the subsets of a need not be considered for generating rules using l. For example, if ABC ⇒ D does not have enough confidence, it is not necessary to check whether AB ⇒ CD holds. No rule is missed because the support of any subset of a must be as great as the support of a. Therefore, the confidence of the rule $\tilde{a} \Rightarrow (l - \tilde{a})$ cannot be more than the confidence of a ⇒ (l - a). Hence, if a did not yield a rule involving all the items in l with a as the antecedent, neither will$\tilde{a}$. The following algorithm embodies these ideas:

// Simple Algorithm
forall *large itemsets* l_k, $k \geq 2$ *do*
    call *genrules(*l_k, l_k*);*
// The genrules generates all valid rules $\tilde{a} \Rightarrow (l_k - \tilde{a})$ *, for all* $\tilde{a} \subset a_m$
procedure genrules(l_k*: large k-itemset,* a_m*: large m-itemset)*
1) A = *{(m-1)-itemsets* a_{m-1} / $a_{m-1} \subset a_m$*};*
2) ***forall*** $a_{m-1} \in A$ ***do begin***
3) conf = support(l_k*)/support(*a_{m-1}*);*
4) ***if*** *(conf ≥ minconf)* ***then begin***
7) ***output*** *the rule am-1* ⇒ *(*$l_k - a_{m-1}$*), with confidence = conf and support = support(*l_k*);*
8) ***if*** *(m - 1 > 1)* ***then***
9) ***call*** *genrules(*l_k, a_{m-1}*); // to generate rules with subsets of* a_{m-1} *as the antecedents*
10) ***end***
11) ***end***

Faster Algorithm

It is shown earlier that if a ⇒ (l - a) does not hold, neither does $\tilde{a} \Longrightarrow (l - \tilde{a})$ for any $\tilde{a} \subset a$. By rewriting, it follows that for a rule (l - c) ⇒ c to hold, all rules of the form $(l - \tilde{c}) \Longrightarrow \tilde{c}$ must also hold, where $\tilde{c}$ is a non-empty subset of c. For example, if the rule AB ⇒ CD holds, then the rules ABC ⇒ D and ABD ⇒ C must also hold.

Consider the above property that for a given large itemset, if a rule with consequent c holds then so do rules with consequents that are subsets of c. This is similar to the property that if an itemset is large then so is all its subsets. From a large itemset l, therefore, initially all rules are generated with one item in the consequent. The consequents of these rules are used and the function apriori-gen is used to generate all possible consequents with two items that can appear in a rule generated from l, etc. An algorithm using this idea is given below. The rules having one-item consequents in step 2 of this algorithm can be found by using a modified version of the preceding genrules function in which steps 8 and 9 are deleted to avoid the recursive call.

3.2.1 Apriori Candidate Generation

The apriori-gen function takes as argument L_{k-1}, the set of all large (k-1)-itemsets. It returns a superset of the set of all large k-itemsets. The function works as follows. First, in the join step, we join L_{k-1} with L_{k-1}:

```
// Faster Algorithm
1) forall large k-itemsets l_k, k ≥ 2 do begin
2) H_1-{ consequents of rules derived from l_k with one item in the consequent};
3) call ap-genrules(l_k, H_1);
4) end
procedure ap-genrules(l_k: large k-itemset, H_m: set of m-item consequents)
if (k > m+ 1) then begin
H_{m+1} = apriori-gen(H_m);
forall h_{m+1} ∈ H_{m+1} do begin
conf = support(l_k)/support(l_k - h_{m+1});
if (conf ≥ minconf) then
output the rule (l_k - h_{m+1}) ⇒ h_{m+1} with confidence _ conf and support _
support(l_k);
else
delete h_{m+1} from H_{m+1};
end
call ap-genrules(l_k, H_{m+1});
```

As an example of the advantage of this algorithm, consider a large itemset ABCDE. Assume that ACDE ⇒ B and ABCE⇒ D are the only one-item consequent rules derived from this itemset that have the minimum confidence. If the simple algorithm is used, the recursive call genrules(ABCDE, ACDE) will test if the two-item consequent rules ACD ⇒ BE, ADE ⇒ BC, CDE ⇒ BA, and ACE ⇒ BD hold. The first of these rules cannot hold, because E ⊂ BE, and ABCD ⇒ E does not have minimum confidence. The second and third rules cannot hold for similar reasons.

The call genrules(ABCDE, ABCE) will test if the rules ABC ⇒ DE, ABE ⇒ DC, BCE ⇒ DA and ACE ⇒ BD hold, and will find that the first three of these rules do not hold. In fact, the only two-item consequent rule that can possibly hold is ACE ⇒ BD, where B and D are the consequents in the valid one-item consequent rules. This is the only rule that will be tested by the faster algorithm.

3.3 Intrusion Detection Module

The data mining techniques is used in intrusion detection module in order to improve the efficiency and effectiveness of the MANET nodes. It if found out that among all the data mining intrusion detection techniques [18], clustering-based intrusion detection is the most potential one because of its ability to detect new attacks. Many traditional intrusion detection techniques are limited with collection of training data from real networks and manually labeled as normal or abnormal. It is very time consuming and expensive to manually collect pure normal data and classify data in wireless networks.

The association algorithm such as Fast Apriori is used which can be utilized to achieve traffic features which is then followed by clustering algorithm. It is previously observed that a good efficiency and performance is obtained with association algorithm and clustering algorithm. The association rule and clustering are used as the root for accompanying anomaly detection of routing and other attacks in MANET. The proposed IDS architecture is shown in fig. 1 is shown below.

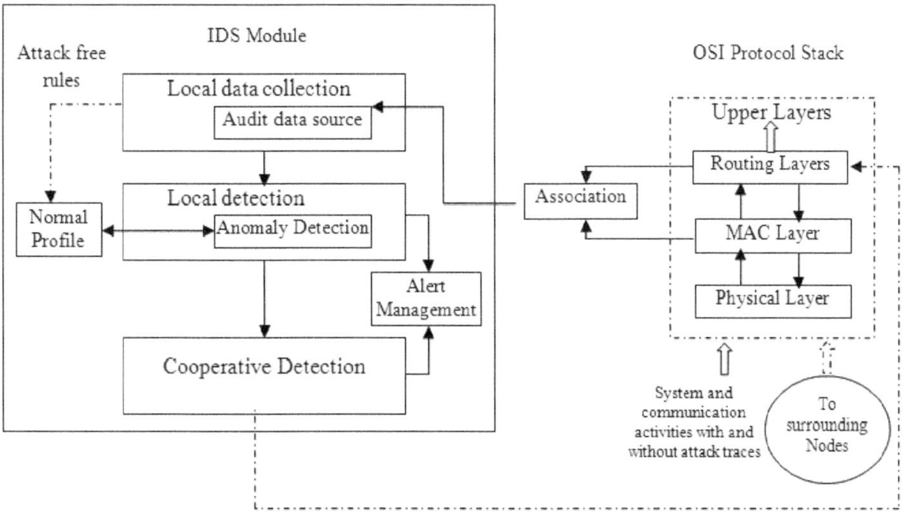

Fig. 1. Proposed IDS Architecture in MANET

3.3.1 Local Data Collection

The local data collection module collects data streams of various information, traffic patterns and attack traces from physical, MAC and network layers via association module. The data streams can include system, user and mobile nodes' communication activities within the radio range.

3.3.2 Local Detection

The local detection module consists of anomaly detection engine. The local detection module analyzes the local data traces gathered by the local data collection module for evidence of anomalies. A normal profile is an aggregated rule set of multiple training data segments. New and updated detection rules across ad-hoc networks are obtained from normal profile. The normal profile consists of normal behavior patterns that are computed using trace data from a training process where all activities are normal. During testing process, normal and abnormal activities are processed and any deviations from the normal profiles are recorded. The anomaly detection distinguishes normalcy from anomalies as of the deviation data by comparing with the test data profiles with the expected normal profiles. If any detection rules deviate beyond a threshold interval and if it has a very high accuracy rate it can determine independently that the network is under attack and initiates the alert management.

3.3.3 Cooperative Detection

When the support and confidence level is low or intrusion evidence is weak and inconclusive in the detecting node then it can make collaborative decision by gathering intelligence from its surrounding nodes via protected communication channel. The decision of cooperative detection is based on the majority of the voting of the received reports indicating an intrusion or anomaly.

3.3.4 Alert Management

The alert management receives the alert from the local detection or co-operative detection depending on the strength of intrusion evidence. It collects them in the alert cache for t seconds. If there are more abnormal predictions than the normal predictions then it is regarded as "abnormal" and with adequate information an alarm is generated to inform that an intrusive activity is in the system.

3.4 Anomaly Detection Mechanism in Manet

The anomaly detection system creates a normal base line profile of the normal activities of the network traffic activity. Then, the activity that diverges from the baseline is treated as a possible intrusion. The main objective is to collect set of useful features from the traffic to make the decision whether the sampled traffic is normal or abnormal. Some of the advantages of anomaly detection system are it can detect new and unknown attacks, it can detect insider attacks; and it is very difficult for the attacker to carry out the attacks without setting off an alarm. The process of anomaly detection comprises of two phases: training and testing. The basic framework for normal behavior is constructing by collecting the noticeable characteristic from the audit data. The data mining technique is used for building Intrusion detection system to describe the anomaly detection mechanism.

3.4.1 Construction of Normal Dataset

The data obtained from the audit data sources mostly contains local routing information, data and control information from MAC and routing layers along with other traffic statistics. The training of data may entail modeling the allotment of a given set of training points or characteristic network traffic samples. The few assumptions have to be done so that the traced traffic from the network contains no attack traffic:

- The normal traffic occurs more frequently than the attack traffic.
- The attack traffic samples are statistically different from the normal connections.

Since, two assumptions are used; the attacks will appear as outliers in the feature space resulting in detection of the attacks by analyzing and identifying anomalies in the data set.

3.4.2 Feature Construction

For feature construction, an unsupervised method is used to construct the feature set. The clustering algorithm is used to construct features from the audit data. The feature set is created by using the audit data and most common feature set are selected as essential feature set which has weight not smaller than the minimum threshold. A set of considerable features should be obtained from the incoming traffic that differentiates the normal data from the intrusive data. Few and semantic information is captured which results in better detection performance and saves computation time. In case of feature construction, the traffic related features as well as non-traffic related features which represent routing conditions are collected. Some of the features are used for detecting DoS attacks and attacks that manipulate routing protocol. The number of data packets received is used to detect unusual level of data traffic which may indicate a DoS attack based on a data traffic flood.

3.4.3 Training Normal Data Using Cluster Mechanism

Fixed-width clustering algorithm is implemented in this paper as a technique for anomaly detection. Fixed-width clustering algorithm is shown. It calculates the number of points near each point in the feature space. In fixed width clustering technique, set of clusters are formed in which each cluster has fixed radius w also known as cluster width in the feature space. The cluster width w is chosen as the maximum threshold radius of a cluster.

(1) Fixed width algorithm

A set of network traffic sample ST are obtained from the audit data for training purpose. Each sample s_i in the training set is represented by a d-dimensional vector of attributes. In the beginning, the set of clusters as well as the number of clusters are null. Since, there is significant variation in each attribute. While calculating the distance between points, normalization is done before mapping into the feature space to ensure that all features have the same outcome. It is obtained by normalizing each continuous attribute in terms of the number of standard deviations from the mean. The first point of the data forms the centre of the new cluster. A new cluster $\psi 1$ is formed having centroid ψ_1* from sample s_i. For every succeeding point, the distance of each traffic sample s_i to the centroid of each cluster ψ_1* that has been generated by the cluster set Ψ is measured. If the distance to the nearest cluster ψ_n is within w of cluster center, then the point is assigned to the cluster, and the centroid of the closest cluster is updated. The total number of points in the cluster is incremented. Else, the new point forms the centroid of a new cluster. Euclidean distance as well as argmin is used because it is more convenient to have items which minimizes the functions. As a result, the computational load is decreased. Moreover, the traffic samples are not stored and only one pass is required through the traffic samples. In the final stage of training, labeling of cluster is done based on the initial assumptions like ratio of the normal traffic is very small than attack traffic and the anomalous data points are statistically different to normal data points. If the cluster contains less than a threshold τ % of the total set of points then it is considered as anomalous. Besides, the points in the dense regions will be higher than the threshold; the points that are outliers are only considered.

Fixed width clustering Algorithm:

Training samples S_T-$\{s_i, i$-$1, 2,\ldots N_T\}$
where each sample has dimension d, $s_i = <x_1, \ ,x_d>$

Initial set of clusters $\Psi := \{\}$, *the number of clusters* $C:=0$
Normalizing S_T,
For each training samples $s_i \in S_T$
If $C=0$ *then*
Make new cluster Ψ_1 *with centroid* Ψ_1^* *from* s_i
$\Psi_1 := \{s_1\}, \Psi_1^* = s_i, \Psi := \{\Psi_1\}, C=C+1$
Else
Find the nearest cluster Ψ_n *to* s_i
$n := argmin_k\{Distance(s_i, \Psi_1^*)\}$, *where* $k=1,\ldots,C$
If *distance to nearest cluster* $Distance(s_i, \Psi_1^*)<w$ *then*
Add s_i *to cluster* Ψ_n *and update cluster centroid* Ψ_1^*
$\Psi_n := \{s_i\} U \Psi_n$

Else
Make new cluster Ψ_{C+1} *with centroid* Ψ_{C+1}^* *from* s_i
$\Psi_{C+1} := \{s_i\}, \Psi_{C+1}^* := s_i, \Psi := \{\Psi_{C+!}\} U \Psi,$
$C:=C+1$
For each cluster Ψ_k
Find the outermost point s_{max} *in cluster* Ψ_k
$s_{max} := argmin_i\{Distsnce(s_i, \Psi_k{}^*)\}$, *where* $s_i \in \Psi_k$ *and* $i=1,\ldots,N_T$
Set width w_k *of cluster* Ψ_k
$w_k := Distance(s_{max}, \Psi_k^*)$
Cluster Labeling:
If $|\Psi_k|/N_T <$ *classification threshold* τ *then*
Label Ψ_k *as anomalous*
Else
Label Ψ_k *as normal*

4 Experiment Results

The proposed technique is experimented with 25 similar wireless mobile nodes and attack is provided with single node. The routing protocol used for all the nodes is AODV routing protocol. The experiment s carried in the campus with the area of 800m x 800m. AODV routing protocol is used here because of its low message overhead. The experiment is carried for around 350 seconds.

Table 1 shows the simulation statistics used for the proposed technique.

Table 1. Simulation Statistics

Statistics	Value
Scenario Size	800m X 800m
802.11b Data Rate	11 Mbps
Transmission Range	<250 meter
Power of each Node	0.005 W
Simulation Time	350 seconds
No. of Mobile Nodes	25
Mobility	Random Waypoint, Random Direction Mobility

In the proposed association model, the common control packets and data packets from MAC and network layer are combined into single category as either routing control packets or routing data packets using association rules. For evaluating the Intrusion Detection, the packets are sent to IDS module. The fixed width algorithm included in IDS module is helpful in detecting the anomalous behavior. The normal traffic behavior is considered as normal profile and if the traffic abnormal, the packets are processed for intrusion detection.

For evaluation, the source, destination and attacker node is considered. At the same time, other nodes have their own purpose. In order to train the system with normal traffic, the attacker node is disabled during the training phase.

The streaming multimedia UDP data traffic sent by the source to the destination node along with the anomalous traffic is shown n figure 3. The red color in figure 3 indicates the UDP data traffic. The attacker starts to send the custom anomalous unidirectional traffic to the same destination node at around 3 minutes. This anomalous traffic consists of high request count and tries to increase the normal traffic at the destination node. The destination node receives the normal multimedia traffic from 20 seconds but at around 3 minutes it receives abnormal data traffic till the end of the simulation. These data traffic are collected and then sent to IDS specification where the data traffics are compared with the normal behavior of the normal profile. If the traffic samples at the destination does not match with the normal traffic generated by the fixed width algorithm and lies in the sparse region then an irregularity is detected. If any deviation is found from the normal behavior then an anomaly is observed and an alarm is generated indicating intrusive behavior. In the proposed method, the anomaly is detected and IDS treats this anomalous activity as an intrusive behavior.

In the figure 4, during the testing process, the abnormal behavior can be seen in the wireless data traffic received after 3 minutes interval time. The simulation is run in two setups, one with attacker node and other without the attacker node. The red color in the figure indicates the data traffic without the attacker node while the blue one is in the presence of the attacker node. In this case, there is a deviation between the normal and abnormal traffic in the destination node and the anomalous traffic is regarded as malicious behavior so an alarm is generated.

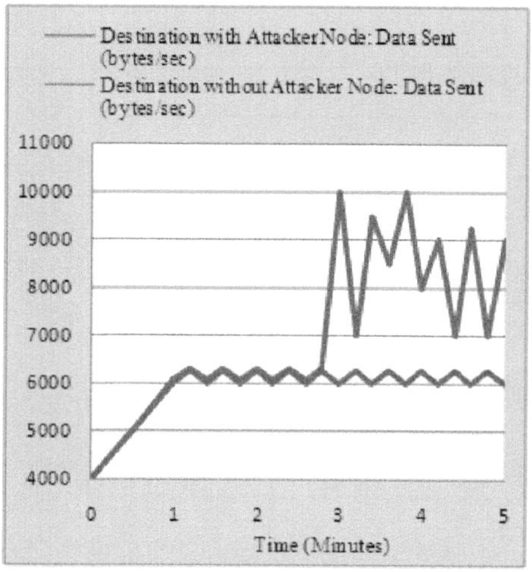

Fig. 3. UDP traffic analysis in destination node

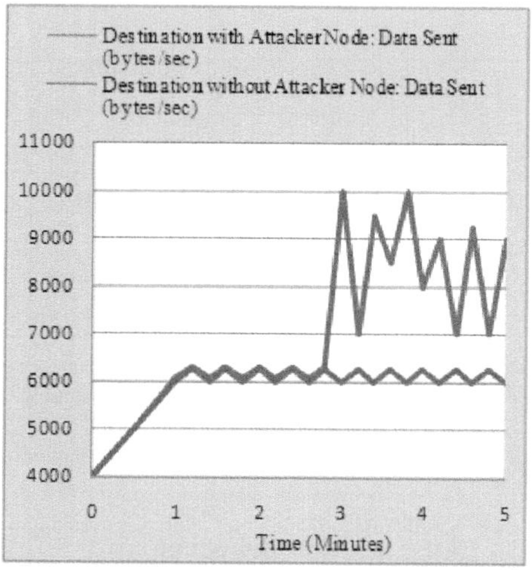

Fig. 4. Wireless LAN Data Traffic Received in bits/sec

From these 25 nodes, node 3 is chosen for consideration. The traffic is introduced in the network and the performance of the proposed technique is evaluated. Figure 5 shows the AODV routing traffic for the existing technique, proposed technique

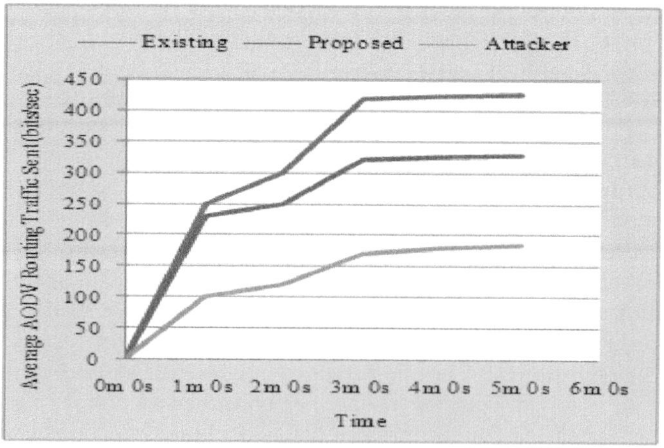

Fig. 5. Time-Average in AODV Routing Traffic Sent

and the traffic introduced by the attacker. From the figure, it can be clearly observed that the AODV routing traffic for the proposed technique is lesser when compared to the AODV routing traffic produced in the existing technique. This case continues even after the introduction of traffic in the wireless network. This clearly indicates that the proposed technique for intrusion detection will yield only lesser traffic when compared to the conventional techniques.

5 Conclusion

Designing of Intrusion detection system for MANETs is challenging task because these networks change their topologies dynamically due to node mobility, lack concentration points where traffic can be analyzed for intrusions, utilize self-configuring multi-party infrastructure protocols that are susceptible to malicious manipulation and rely on wireless communications channels that provide limited bandwidth and are subject to noise and intermittent connectivity. The Intrusion detection systems for MANETs based on cross layers which satisfy these challenges are proposed in this paper. This paper utilizes clustering and data mining techniques for detecting the occurrence of intrusion. The proposed technique implements the fixed width algorithm for clustering process. The usage of fixed width algorithm helps in finding the DoS attacks and sink hole attack at different layers of the protocol stack. The proposed techniques will make use of fast apriori algorithm for the association process. This helps in increasing in speed for detecting the intrusion occurred in the network when compared to the conventional techniques. The various types of UDP flooding attack can also be detected efficiently using the proposed Intrusion detection system. The experimental results shows that the proposed technique undergoes lesser traffic when the intrusion is included in the network than the traffic occurred in the existing Intrusion detection systems.

References

1. Ding, H., Xu, X.: Real-time cooperation intrusion detection system for MANets. In: IET International Conference on Wireless, Mobile and Multimedia Networks, pp. 1–4 (2006)
2. Karygiannis, A., Antonakakis, E., Apostolopoulos, A.: Detecting critical nodes for MANET intrusion detection systems. In: Second International Workshop on Security, Privacy and Trust in Pervasive and Ubiquitous Computing, pp. 9–15 (2006)
3. Cabrera, J.B.D., Gutierrez, C., Mehra, R.K.: Infrastructures and algorithms for distributed anomaly-based intrusion detection in mobile ad-hoc networks. In: IEEE Military Communications Conference, pp. 1831–1837 (2005)
4. Puttini, R., Percher, J.M., Me, L., de Sousa, R.: A fully distributed IDS for MANET. In: Ninth International Symposium on Computers and Communications, pp. 331–338 (2004)
5. Endorf, C., Schultz, E., Mellander, J.: Intrusion Detection & Prevention. McGraw-Hill, New York (2004)
6. Esposito, M., Mazzariello, C., et al.: Evaluating Pattern Recognition Techniques in Intrusion Detection Systems. In: The 7th International Workshop on Pattern Recognition in Information Systems, pp. 144–153 (2005)

7. Ye, N., Li, X., et al.: Probabilistic Techniques for Intrusion Detection Based on Computer Audit Data. IEEE Transactions on Systems, Man, and Cybernetics, 266–274 (2001)
8. Florez, G., Bridges, S.M., Vaughn, R.B.: An Improved Algorithm for Fuzzy Data Mining for Intrusion Detection. In: The North American Fuzzy Information Processing Society Conference, New Orleans, LA (2002)
9. Mishra, A., Nadkarni, K., Patcha, A.: Intrusion Detection in Wireless Ad Hoc Networks. IEEE Wireless Communications 11(1), 48–60 (2004)
10. Zhang, Y., Lee, W., Huang, Y.: Intrusion Detection Techniques for Mobile Wireless Networks. Wireless Networks Journal (ACM WINET) 9(5), 545–556 (2003)
11. Zhang, Y., Lee, W.: Intrusion detection in wireless ad-hoc networks. In: The 6th Annual International Conference on Mobile Computing and Networking, pp. 275–283 (2000)
12. Bo, S., Kui, W., Pooch, U.W.: Towards adaptive intrusion detection in mobile ad hoc networks. In: IEEE Global Telecommunications Conference, pp. 3551–3555 (2004)
13. Yang, H., Luo, H.Y., et al.: Security in Mobile Ad Hoc networks: challenges and solutions. In: IEEE Wireless Communications, pp. 38–47 (2004)
14. Anantvalee, T., Wu, J.: A Survey on Intrusion Detection in Mobile Ad Hoc Networks. Book Series Wireless Network Security, pp. 170–196. Springer, Heidelberg (2007)
15. Albers, P., Camp, O., et al.: Security in Ad Hoc Networks: a General Intrusion Detection Architecture Enhancing Trust Based Approaches. In: Proceedings of the 1st International Workshop on Wireless Information Systems, pp. 1–12 (April 2002)
16. Sterne, D., Balasubramanyam, P., et al.: A General Cooperative Intrusion Detection Architecture for MANETs. In: Proceedings of the 3rd IEEE International Workshop on Information Assurance, pp. 57–70 (2005)
17. Sun, B., Wu, K., Pooch, U.W.: Alert Aggregation in Mobile Ad Hoc Networks. In: ACM Workshop on Wireless Security in conjuction with the 9th Annual International Conference on Mobile Computing and Networking (MobiCom 2003), pp. 69–78 (2003)
18. Krugel, C., Toth, T.: Applying mobile agent technology to intrusion detection. In: ICSE Workshop on Software Engineering and Mobility (2001)
19. Ramanujan, R., Kudige, S., Nguyen, T., Takkella, S., Adelstein, F.: Intrusion-Resistant Ad Hoc Wireless Networks. In: Proceedings of MILCOM (2002)
20. Kachirski, O., Guha, R.: Effective Intrusion Detection Using Multiple Sensors in Wireless Ad Hoc Networks. In: Proceedings of the 36th Annual Hawaii International Conference on System Sciences (2003)

Evaluating Machine Learning Algorithms for Detecting DDoS Attacks*

Manjula Suresh and R. Anitha

Department of Mathematics and Computer Applications,
PSG College of Technology, Coimbatore, India
manjuasmi3@gmail.com, anitha_nadarajan@mca.psgtech.ac.in

Abstract. Recently, as the serious damage caused by DDoS attacks increases, the rapid detection of the attack and the proper response mechanisms are urgent. Signature based DDoS detection systems cannot detect new attacks. Current anomaly based detection systems are also unable to detect all kinds of new attacks, because they are designed to restricted applications on limited environments. However, existing security mechanisms do not provide effective defense against these attacks, or the defense capability of some mechanisms is only limited to specific DDoS attacks. It is necessary to analyze the fundamental features of DDoS attacks because these attacks can easily vary the used port/protocol, or operation method. Also lot of research work has been done in detecting the attacks using machine learning techniques. Still what are the relevant features and which technique will be more suitable one for the attack detection is an open question. In this paper, we use the chi-square and Information gain feature selection mechanisms for selecting the important attributes. With the selected attributes, various machine learning models, like Navies Bayes, C4.5, SVM, KNN, K-means and Fuzzy c-means clustering are developed for efficient detection of DDoS attacks. Then our experimental results show that Fuzzy c-means clustering gives better accuracy in identifying the attacks.

Keywords: Classifier, Navies Bayes, SVM, C4.5, K-NN, K-means, Fuzzy c-means.

1 Introduction

Distributed Denial of Service (DDoS), is a relatively simple, yet very powerful technique to attack Internet resources as well as system resources. Distributed multiple agents consume some critical resources at the target within the short time and deny the service to legitimate clients. As a side effect, they frequently create network congestion on the way from source to target, thus disrupting normal Internet operation and denying the services to many legitimate users.

DDoS is a large-scale, coordinated attack on the availability of services of a victim system or network resources, launched indirectly through many compromised computers called zombies on the internet. Using client/server technology, the

* This work is a part of the Collaborative Directed Basic Research on Smart and Secure Environment project, funded by NTRO and AISRF.

D.C. Wyld et al. (Eds.): CNSA 2011, CCIS 196, pp. 441–452, 2011.

perpetrator is able to multiply the effectiveness of the attack significantly by using the resources of many unwitting accomplished zombies which serve as attack platforms. The zombies carry out the actual attack by increasing the traffic to a victim machine significantly. As a result, the victim machine loses all its computing and communication resources.

Many researchers have analyzed DDoS attacks and contributed some defense mechanisms. The widely used defense techniques are detection, filtering and traceback.

Detection suffers from efficiently differentiating the normal stream and abnormal stream of traffic. Filtering clogs up during heavy traffic whereas traceback can only be effective under subsidized traffic, so performed mostly after the closing of the attack. Most of the existing detection mechanism have limited success because of the following challenges (i) the attack itself often uses legitimate requests to flood the target and this makes it hard to distinguish an attack traffic from legitimate traffic (ii) fast real time detection is difficult because of huge amount of data involved in current computer networks.

Abnormal changes in the resource usage due to DDoS attack could be detected using statistical methods. The problem with statistics based detection is that it is not possible to find out the normal network packet distribution. Rather, it can only be simulated as a uniform distribution [10]. Some methods which apply data mining techniques, can obtain a high correction rate in detecting the attack. However, these methods usually can't be used in real-time computing [14]. Some research papers suggest the usage of clustering methodology to formulate the normal patterns. One of the advantages of clustering methods over statistical methods is that they do not rely on any prior known data distribution. There are many variables that can be used to identify normal network patterns [10]. But extracting the important and relevant attributes from huge network is crucial for modeling network behaviors so that attack behaviors can be differentiated clearly from normal one. In this paper, based on a comprehensive analysis for the current research challenges in DDoS, evaluating machine learning algorithms for detecting DDoS is presented, which includes feature extraction, classification and comparison. Within this evaluation, some recently developed machine learning methods for detecting DDoS are applied and their performances are evaluated based on experiments on public benchmark datasets such as CAIDA [20]. Although various hybrid approaches may be employed, it is illustrated that these evaluation results of research challenges are mainly suitable for machine learning methods. Finally among various machine learning algorithms, fuzzy c-means clustering technique provides better performance over many of the existing methods. A brief report of this work is available in [1].

The rest of the paper is organized as follows. Section 2 summarizes related studies in the area of DDoS attack detection. Next, in section 3, the proposed method for the detection of DDoS attacks is described in detail. Section 4 presents the data collected and the experimental results. Finally, in section 5, we conclude our work with directions of further studies.

2 Related Work

Two important and challenging research problems in detecting DDoS attacks are:

1. extracting a valid and sufficient subset of features that can be used to build efficient models to identify a DDoS attack; and

2. ranking the efficacy of the various machine-learning techniques that have been utilized in the detection process.

For most problem domains, the process of feature reduction which involves extracting the most significant and relevant attributes or features prior to applying modeling techniques (such as machine learning and statistical techniques) can lead to a major improvement in the time required in training and testing the model. However, in comparison with other problem domains, extracting a set of features that characterize Internet traffic to the point of being able to distinguish normal traffic from anomalous traffic is particularly difficult. One problem, for example, is that nodes in the Internet experience widely differing traffic flux densities caused by the large variations in the number of users seen at each node. This makes it difficult to decide as to what constitutes "normal" traffic on the Internet. Another problem, and one that can be seen from the discussion on the detection techniques already presented, is that there are potentially a large number of variables that can be used to characterize network traffic patterns. Nevertheless extracting the important and relevant attributes from network traffic is crucial for modeling network behaviours so that attack behaviours can be differentiated clearly from normal behaviour. This feature-extraction problem has been studied by a number of groups. For example Xu et. al. [4] selected eight relative values as features that are independent from the network flow. Zargar et. al. [24] propose and investigate the identification of effective network features for probing attack detection using the principal component analysis (PCA) method to determine an optimal feature set. Jin et al. [5] discussed the application of multivariate correlation analysis to DDoS detection and proposed a covariance analysis model for detecting flooding attacks. They used all of the flag-bits in the flag field of the TCP header as features in the covariance analysis model. The authors have demonstrated the successful use of the proposed method in detecting SYN flooding attacks which is an important form of DDoS attacks. However, the method has the major limitation that there is no guarantee that the 6 flags are valid or sufficient features to detect all forms of DDoS attack with consistent accuracy.

A widely diverse range of statistical methods and machine learning techniques could be used to detect abnormal changes in the resource usage that are indicative of a DDoS attack. However both approaches have their limitations. For example one identifiable problem with statistics based detection is that it is not possible to find out the normal network packet distribution. Rather, it can only be simulated as a uniform distribution. Some research papers suggested that this problem may be resolved by using clustering methodologies to formulate the normal patterns, since one of the advantages of clustering methods over statistical methods is that they do not rely on any prior known data distribution. While machine learning techniques, typically drawn from the allied field of data mining, have been shown to produce a high degree of accuracy in detecting DDoS attacks, they also have their own limitations. For example these techniques require a lengthy learning period and hence currently these methods can't operate in real-time.

Despite these current limitations, a solution to the problem of reliable DDoS detection will come from either or both these domains and considerable research effort continues to be directed to this end. For example Seo et al. [17] have used a multiclass SVM classification model to detect DDoS attack. In the work of Xu et al. [18], a group of new features was also introduced including the composition of relative values as part of an expanded set of detection information. They also proposed a new approach of using attack intensity to detect a DDoS event. In [15], Paruchuri et. al. proposed a new probabilistic packet marking (PPM) scheme called TTL-based PPM scheme, where each packet is marked with a probability inversely proportional to the distance traversed by the packet so far, enabling a victim source to traceback the attack source. In [3], Cheng et. al. proposed a novel algorithm to detect DDoS attacks using IP address feature values using support vector machine (SVM) classification. Nguyen et. al. [14] have developed an Anti-DDoS framework for detecting DDoS attack proactively utilising K-NN Classifier. They used the k-nearest neighbour method to classify the network status into each phase of DDoS attack. However, while the K-NN approach is excellent in attack detection, the detector is computationally expensive for real-time implementation when the number of processes simultaneously increases. As has been indicated previously the problem of computational intensity is critical in the DDoS problem as it is in other applications of data mining where large databases are analysed.

One of the key resources used to evaluate the performance of DDoS detection techniques is the KDD dataset. The set contains 14 attacks which is used for testing and model creation. Several methods have been proposed to extract useful features from this dataset and a wide range of classifiers drawn from areas such as statistics, machine learning and pattern recognition have been evaluated against this dataset. For example in Kim et. al. [7], the 1999 KDD data set was pre-processed followed by learning and testing process. In the learning process they used polynomial, kernel functions linear, and radial bias function (RBF). A classification accuracy of 93.56% was achieved. A SVM based one-class classifier is also used to perform anomaly detection in [4]. The training data in the feature space was mapped into a new feature space. Yuan et. al. [23] used the cross-correlation analysis to capture the traffic patterns and then to decide where and when a DDoS attack may possibly arise.

3 Proposed Work

The following study discusses the extraction of a feature set from two different sources of datasets of Internet traffic. These are the public-domain CAIDA Dataset [20] and traffic collected on the smart and secure environment (SSE) Network. Various types of DDoS attacks are studied to select the traffic parameters that change unusually during such attacks. Twenty-three features are collected and ranking the twenty-three features is done with Information Gain and Chi-Square statistic which reduces the number of features to eight. All the features used in this paper are calculated at an interval of 1 second. Since these classes are well divided as attack and normal, it is possible to apply various machine learning algorithms for the detection. The approach considered is to use the feature selection mechanism discussed previously and build the classifier using various machine learning algorithms such as SVM, K-NN, Naive Bayesian, Decision Tree, K-means and Fuzzy c-means clustering. This phase of the study is an evaluation of the performance of the selected set of machine learning algorithms in detecting DDoS attacks. The performance measures are the receiver operating characteristic (ROC) curve and F-measure. An important conclusion drawn from the experimental results is that, of the various methods used, Fuzzy c-means clustering is very efficient in detecting DDoS attacks.

3.1 Feature Extraction

For the first phase of the study, the following lists of 23 features are extracted.

Table 1. Basic Features

SNo	Feature	Description
1	OnewayRatio	The ratio of one way connection packets to all packets.
2	AverageLengthIPFlow	Number of Ip packets by Number of Ip flows
3	RatioofInOut	Ratio between incoming and outgoing packets
4	Entropyflowlength	Entropy of IP flow length
5	Entropyprotocols	Entropy of the packet ratios of the three protocols TCP, UDP and ICMP
6	Ratiotcp	Ratio of TCP Protocol
7	Ratioudp	Ratio of UDP Protocol
8	Ratioicmp	Ratio of ICMP Protocol
9	Datalength	Number of data bytes from source to destination
10	Dstdatalength	Number of data bytes from destination to source
11	Urg	Number of packets where urg flag is set
12	Service	Destination port mapped to service
13	Prototype	Connection protocol (tcp,udp,icmp)
14	Land	Number of connection is from/to the same host/port
15	Wrongfrag	Number of wrong fragments
16	Segmenterror	Number of connections that have SYN errors
17	Srccnt	Number of connections to the same service
18	Dstcnt	Number of connections having the same destination host
19	Syncnt	Number of packets where syn flag is set
20	Fincnt	Number of packets where fin flag is set
21	Ackcnt	Number of packets where ack flag is set
22	Pshcnt	Number of packets where psh flag is set
23	Rstcnt	Number of packets where rst flag is set

Chi square and Information Gain are applied to measure the importance of each feature. The Information gain of a given attribute X with respect to the class Y is the reduction in uncertainty about the value of Y, after observing values of X. The uncertainty about the value of Y is measured by its entropy defined as

$$H(Y) = -\sum_i P(y_i) \log_2(P(y_i)) \tag{1.1}$$

where $P(y_i)$ is the prior probabilities for all values of Y. The uncertainty about the value of Y after observing values of X is given by the conditional entropy of Y given X defined as

$$H(Y|X) = -\sum_j P(x_j \sum_i P(y_i|x_j) \log_2(P(y_i|x_j)\log_2(P(y_i|x_j)) \tag{1.2}$$

where $P(y_i|x_j)$ is the posterior probabilities of Y given the values of X. The information gain is thus defined as

$$IG(Y|X) = H(Y) - H(Y|X) \tag{1.3}$$

By calculating information gain, the correlations of each attribute can be ranked to the class. The most important attributes can then be selected based on the ranking.Chi-square [22] measures the lack of independence between a feature X and a cluster Y. It can be compared to the chi-square distribution with one degree of freedom to judge extremeness:

$$\chi^2 = \sum_{i=1}^{r} \sum_{j=1}^{k} \frac{(A_{ij} - E_{ij})^2}{E_{ij}} \tag{1.4}$$

where r is the number of feature and k is number of clusters, A_{ij} is number of instances for which the value of a feature is i and the value of the cluster is j, E_{ij} is the expected number of instances of A_{ij}. The larger the χ^2 value, the more important the feature is to the cluster. Thus ranking the importance of each feature with respect to the clusters based on the value of χ^2 for the proposed work is considered.

Based on the χ^2 value and information gain rank, eight features are considered as the important features. Table 2 gives the ranking of the features based on chi-square and information gain.

Table 2. Feature ranking

Features	Chi-square Rank	Information gain Rank
Ratio ICMP	1	1
Land	2	2
Ratio UDP	3	3
One way Ratio	4	4
Ratio TCP	5	5
Protocol Type	6	6
AverageLengthIPFlow	7	8
Ratio of In/Out Packets	8	7

Based on Chi-square and information gain the following eight features are selected for the detection of DDoS attacks.

a) One Way Connection Density (OWCD):

An IP packet without a corresponding reverting packet composes a One-Way Connection (OWC). In a sampling interval T, the ratio of OWC packets to the all packets is called One-Way Connection Density (OWCD).

$$OWCD = \frac{\sum OWC\ Packets}{\sum IP\ Packets} * 100 \tag{1.5}$$

b) Average Length of IP Flow (L_{ave_flow}):

IP Flow, a concept which is used widely in network analysis area, means that a packets set has a same five-element-group (source IP address, source port, destination IP address, destination port and protocol). Length of IP flow means the number of packets belong to certain IP flow.

$$L_{ave\_flow} = \frac{\sum IP\ Packets}{\sum IP\ flows} \tag{1.6}$$

c) Incoming and Outgoing Ratio of IP packets (R_{io}):

Normally the ratio between incoming and outgoing packets is steady. But in DDoS attack, quickly R_{io} increases.

$$R_{io} = \frac{\sum incoming\ IP\ packets}{\sum outgoing\ IP\ Packets} \tag{1.7}$$

d) Ratio of TCP Protocol (R_t):

$$R_t = \frac{\sum TCP\ packets}{\sum IP\ Packets} \tag{1.8}$$

e) Ratio of UDP Protocol (R_u):

$$R_u = \frac{\sum UDP\ packets}{\sum IP\ Packets} \tag{1.9}$$

f) Ratio of ICMP Protocol (R_i):

$$R_i = \frac{\sum ICMP\ packets}{\sum IP\ packets} \tag{1.10}$$

g) Land:The number of packets having the source ip address same as the destination ip address.

h) Protocol-type: Type of the Protocol, eg: TCP, UDP, ICMP etc.

All the above mentioned features except Land have been selected based on the principles mentioned in Xu et al.[18], are used to classify the network status. Each variable is normalized to eliminate the effect of difference between the scales of the variables, as proposed by Lee et al. [6]. With normalization, variables become

$$z = \frac{x-\overline{x}}{\sigma} \quad (1.11)$$

where x, $\overline{x}$, and $\boldsymbol{\sigma}$, denote the value of each feature, the mean of the sample dataset, and the standard deviation, respectively.

The first step is to extract these eight features from the dataset consisting of both normal and attack data patterns. In the experiments a sampling frequency of one second is used. The next step is to train the machine learning techniques with these datasets. In the detection phase, the same set of eight features are computed for the given network traffic and the traffic is labeled as attack or normal based on the majority of the values computed by the machine learning classifiers.

3.2 Machine Learning Algorithms

In this section, we briefly describe the various machine learning algorithms employed in the proposed framework.

Naive Bayes

The Naïve Bayes is a simple probabilistic classifier [13]. It assumes that the effect of a variable values on a given class is independent of the values of other variables. This assumption is called class conditional independence.

C4.5

C4.5 algorithm which was developed by Quinlan is the most popular tree classifier. This algorithm is based on the ID3[2] algorithm that tries to find small decision tree.

K-Mean Clustering

In K-Mean clustering [2], assignment of the data points to clusters depends upon the distance between cluster centroid and data point.

SVM

In classification and regression, Support Vector Machines are the most common and popular method for machine learning tasks [21]. In this method, a set of training examples is given with which each example is marked belonging into one of two categories. Then, by using the Support Vector Machines algorithm, a model that can predict whether a new example falls into one categories or other is built.

k-NN Classifier

The k-NN algorithm [14] is a similarity-based learning algorithm and is known to be highly effective in various problem domains, including classification problems. Given a test element dt, the k-NN algorithm finds its k nearest neighbors among the training elements, which form the neighbourhood of dt. Majority voting among the elements in the neighborhood is used to decide the class for dt.

FCM Clustering

Fuzzy c-means (FCM) [2] is a method of clustering which allows one piece of data to belong to two or more clusters. This method (developed by Dunn in 1973 and improved by Bezdek in 1981) is frequently used in pattern recognition. It is based on minimization of the following objective function:

$$J_m = \sum_{i=1}^{N}\sum_{j=1}^{C} u_{ij}^{m} \left\| x_i - c_j \right\|^2 , \qquad 1 \le m < \infty$$

where m is any real number greater than 1, u_{ij} is the degree of membership of x_i in the cluster j, x_i is the ith of d-dimensional measured data, c_j is the d-dimension center of the cluster, and ||*|| is any norm expressing the similarity between any measured data and the center.

4 Experimental Results

The CAIDA Dataset [20] is used in the experiments as the attack component. Data collected on the SSE network provided the normal traffic component. Classification of attack and normal traffic is done using an open-source tool called KNIME (Konstanz Information Miner) version 3 [8]. Table 3 shows details of the CAIDA dataset and the normal traffic collected on the SSE network. Table 4 shows the correct classification and the attack detection time. Table 5 shows the F-measure details and Figure 1 shows the evaluation results using ROC curves for the selected machine learning techniques. Based on the results of these experiments, the Fuzzy C-means based classification gives the best result in detecting DDoS attacks.

Table 3. Samples collected

Network Data	Data Type	Total Number of Packets
Trained	Attack (CAIDA)	945372
	Normal	110535
Untrained Test Data	Attack (CAIDA)	324098
	Normal	36485

Table 4. Classification results

Method Used	Correct Classification %	Detection Time (in seconds)
Fuzzy C Means	98.7	0.15
Naive Bayesian	97.2	0.52
SVM	96.4	0.23
KNN	96.6	0.26
Decision Tree	95.6	0.25
K-Means	96.7	0.20

Table 5. F-Measure details of classifiers

Method	TP	FP	TN	FN	F-Measure
Fuzzy C Means	298	2	270	3	0.987
Naive Bayesian	290	10	256	17	0.972
KNN	280	20	243	30	0.969
SVM	282	18	253	20	0.964
K-Means	285	15	273	0	0.9669
Decision Tree	278	22	218	55	0.956

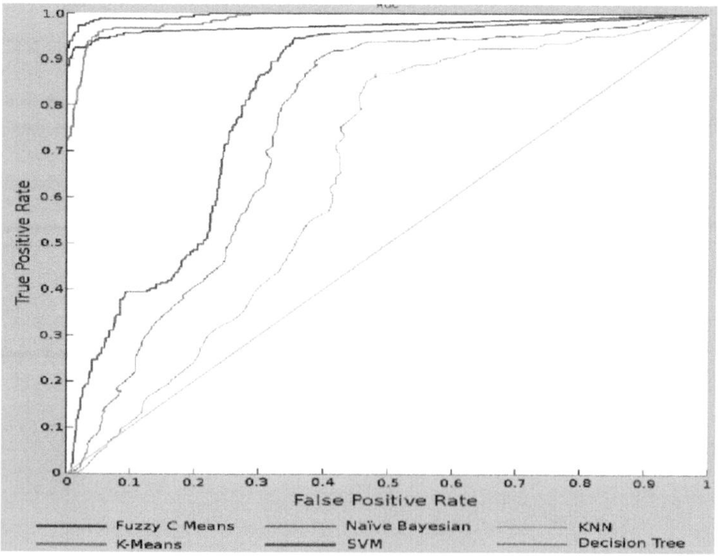

Fig. 1. False vs true positive rate

5 Conclusion

This paper, deals with the evaluation of machine learning algorithms for effectively detecting the DDoS attacks. CAIDA data set is used as the attack data and based on chi-square and information gain ranking, relevant features have been selected. Experimental results show that Fuzzy c-means clustering gives better classification and it is fast compared to the other algorithms.

References

1. Anitha, N.: An Investigation into the detection and Mitigation of Denial of Service (DoS) Attacks, Monograph. Springer, Heidelberg (in press, 2011)
2. A Tutorial on Clustering Algorithms, `http://Clustering-FuzzyC-means.htm`
3. Cheng, J., Yin, J., Liu, Y., Cai, Z., Li, M.: DDoS Attack Detection Algorithm Using IP Address Features. In: Deng, X., Hopcroft, J., Xue, J. (eds.) FAW 2009. LNCS, vol. 5598, pp. 207–215. Springer, Heidelberg (2009)
4. Erskin, E., Arnold, A., Prerau, M., Portnoy, L.: A Geometric Framework for Unsupervised Anomaly Detection: Detecting Intrusions in Unlabeled Data. In: Barbará, D., Jajodia, S. (eds.) Applications of Data Mining in Computer Security, pp. 77–102. Kluwer, Dordrecht (2002)
5. Jin, S., Yeung, D.S.: A covariance analysis model for ddos attack detection. In: Proceedings of IEEE International Conference on Communications, June 20-24, vol. 4, pp. 1882–1886. IEEE, Los Alamitos (2004)
6. Jang, J.-S.R., Sun, C.-T., Mizutani, E.: Data Clustering Algorithms. In: Neuro-Fuzzy and Soft Computing – A Computational Approach to Learning and Machine Intelligence. ch.15, pp. 423–433. Prentice-Hall, Inc., Englewood Cliffs (1997)
7. Kim, D., Park, J.: Network-Based Intrusion Detection with Support Vector Machines. In: Kahng, H.-K. (ed.) ICOIN 2003. LNCS, vol. 2662, pp. 747–756. Springer, Heidelberg (2003)
8. KNIME, `http://www.knime.org (accessed February 7, 2011)`
9. Jalil, K.A., Masrek, M.N.: Comparison of Machine Learning Algorithms Performance in Detection Network Intrusion. In: International Conference on Networking and Information Technology, pp. 221–226. IEEE, Los Alamitos (2010)
10. Lee, K., Kim, J., Kwon, K.H., Han, Y., Kim, S.: DDoS Attack Detection Method using Cluster Analysis. Expert Systems with Applications 34, 1659–1665 (2008)
11. Panda, M., Patra, M.R.: Evaluating Machine Learning Algorithms for Detecting Network Intrusions. International Journal of Recent Trends in Engineering 1(1), 472–477 (2009)
12. Kim, M., Na, H., Chae, K., Bang, H., Na, H.: A Combine Datamining Approach for DDoS Attack Detection. In: Kahng, H.-K., Goto, S. (eds.) ICOIN 2004. LNCS, vol. 3090, pp. 943–950. Springer, Heidelberg (2004)
13. Mitchell, T.: Machine Learning. McGraw Hill, New York (1997)
14. Nguyen, H.V., Choi, Y.: Proactive Detection of DDoS Attacks Utilizing K-NN Classifier in an Anti-DDos Framework. International Journal of Electrical and Electronics Engineering 4(4), 247–252 (2009)
15. Paruchuri, V., Durresi, A., Chellappan, S.: TTL based Packet Marking for IP Traceback. In: Proceedings of the IEEE Global Telecommunications Conference, November 30 - Decmber 4, pp. 2552–2556. IEEE, LA (2008)

16. Kabiri, P., Zargar, G.R.: Category-Based Selection of Effective Parameters for Intrusion Detection. IJCSNS International Journal of Computer Science and Network Security 9(9) (September 2009)
17. Seo, J., Lee, C., Shon, T., Cho, K.H., Moon, J.: A New DDoS Detection Model Using Multiple SVMs and TRA. In: Enokido, T., Yan, L., Xiao, B., Kim, D.Y., Dai, Y.-S., Yang, L.T. (eds.) EUC-WS 2005. LNCS, vol. 3823, pp. 976–985. Springer, Heidelberg (2005)
18. Xu, T., He, D., Luo, Y.: DDoS Attack Detection Based on RLT Features. In: Proceedings of the International Conference on Computational Intelligence and Security, China, December 15-19, pp. 697–701 (2007)
19. Xu, T., He, D.K., Zheng, Y.: Detecting DDoS Attack Based on One-Way Connection Density. In: Proceedings of IEEE International Conference on Communications, Singapore, pp. 1–5 (October 2006)
20. UCSD Network Telescope – Code-Red Worms Dataset. The Cooperative As-sociation for Internet Data Analysis (2001), `http://www.caida.org/data/passive/codered_worms_dataset.xml:` (accessed February 7, 2009)
21. Vapnik, V.: The Nature of Statitical Learning Theory. Springer, Heidelberg (1995)
22. Wang, W., Gombault, S.: Efficient detection of DDoS attacks with important attributes. In: Proceedings of the Third International Conference on Risks and Security of Internet and Systems, pp. 61–67 (October 2008)
23. Yuan, J., Mills, K.: Monitoring the Macroscopic Effect of DDoS Flooding Attacks. IEEE Transactions on Dependable and Secure Computing 2, 324–335 (2005)
24. Zargar, G.R., Kabiri, P.: Identification of effective network features for prob-ing attack detection. In: Proceedings of the First International Conference on Networked Digital Technologies, pp. 392–397 (July 2009)

Insecure Query Processing in the Delay/Fault Tolerant Mobile Sensor Network (DFT-MSN) and Mobile Peer to Peer Network

Rahul Johari[1] and Neelima Gupta[2]

[1] USIT, GGSIP University, Kashmere Gate, Delhi
[2] Department of Computer Science, University of Delhi, Delhi

Abstract. The Delay/Fault Tolerant Mobile Sensor Network (DFT- MSN) and Mobile Peer to Peer network (MP2PN) have evolved at a tremendous rate in the last couple of years. As the networks are evolving so is the rate at which the queries are exchanged in between these net- work and the number of database accesses that need to be performed. The queries are getting complex due to the mobile nature of the nodes in these network and their eagerness to get the response accurately in short span of time because of their limited energy resources. In this paper we not only propose a set of SQL/TIQL queries that are exchanged between the pair of nodes in the DFT-MSN and MP2PN, but also portrays their execution on Oracle 9i Enterprise Edition Release 9.2.0.1.0 Production and expose how these queries are vulnerable to the SQL Injection attack which can either be launched manually or through the various propri- etary and open source SQL Injection tools.

Keywords: DFT-MSN, MP2PN.

1 Introduction

The Delay/Fault Tolerant Mobile Sensor Network (DFT-MSN) are established on adhoc basis without any pre-defined configuration. The DFT-MSN comprises of a wearable sensor nodes (source node) and the high end sink node(HES) [1].The source node takes the responsibility of the gathering data from its envi- ronment and relaying it to the high end sink node through direct transmission if the sink node is one hop away or through the multi-hop transmission if the high end sink node is distant away. This situation is similar to the Mobile Peer to Peer network(MP2PN) where the resource management and the network communi- cation is multi hop [3].The High end Sink node are then further inter-connected to each other [7] or they can be connected to backbone access point where the received information is then filtered, processed and the analysed for decision making process [8] [9]. The analysed data are then stored in the in the local copy of the database at the high end sink node and the final results are stored in the global copy of the database stored at server which is

D.C. Wyld et al. (Eds.): CNSA 2011, CCIS 196, pp. 453–462, 2011.

connected via the backbone network access point or access point with sink node. The Source nodes can either be wore by human or they can be attached or plugged in via Crossbow imotes [10] or injected by means of a chip in animals (without injuring them) depending on whether the data to be gathered is from human populace or from animal habitation. Sun Spots [11] from SunMicroSystem is another recently in- troduced hardware device that is immensely popular in gathering information about neighborhood environment. Various Analytic models with several data delivery schemes (including direct transmission, Zebranet [12], South African Village [13]model Replication based Data delivery schemes) and nodal mobil- ity patterns(such as uniform and power law distributions) have been proposed and implemented [13]. One of the pertinent question often posed in DFT-MSN type of network is that whether the Source node and Sink node is mobile or stationary, one of the pertinent answer is can be that it purely depends on the application in which they are deployed.

2 Related Work

[5] is concerned with query processing in sensor networks. Researchers world- wide have noted the advantages of a query processor-like interface to wireless sensor networks and the need for sensitivity to limited power and computational resources.[4] suggests that the in-network query processing paradigm in sensor networks involves the concept that a query is routed among sensors and collects the answers from the sensors on its tra jectory. It works for static and connected sensor networks. However, when the network consists of multiple number of mo- bile sensors and is sparse, a different approach is needed. The author presents a idea that a query processing method uses cooperative caching. To cope with communication bandwidth and storage constraints, the method prioritizes the data-items in terms of their value, as reflected by supply and demand.

The method of prioritization has been further taken on in [3] where in the author presents an architecture for Tactical Information Middleware for band- width constrained information management. The author further proposes an idea of rank-based data dissemination, and the use of a SQL(Structured Query Lan- guage)/TIQL(Tactical information management query language) which would be responsible for the exchange of the data or information between the nodes.

The author proposes a new application called CarTel [2] that they deployed on a set of six cars running on a small scale in Boston and Seattle for over a year. It has been used to analyze commute times, analyze metropolitan Wi- Fi deployments and for automotive diagnostics. CarTel applications run on the portal using a delay tolerant continuous query processor ICEDB to specify how the mobile nodes should summarize, filter and dynamically prioritize data. The portal and the mobile nodes use a delay tolerant network stack, CafNet to communicate.

3 Model

We propose to establish two networks of dimension 100mx100m and 500mx500m as depicted in figure 1 and figure 2 respectively. In the former type of network , entire region is classified into several unit or zones each possessing one source sensor node responsible to capture the data and at the edge of the zones we keep one high end sink nodes.

The model visualize the process of direct transmission where in the sink node are strategically located so that it is just one hop away from the source node.

The second network is one where single sink node caters to all the sensor node and all the sensor node are responsible to transmit the data to high end sink node.The real problem that arises is when the data is exchanged between these either from source to sink node or from one sensor node to another sensor node.

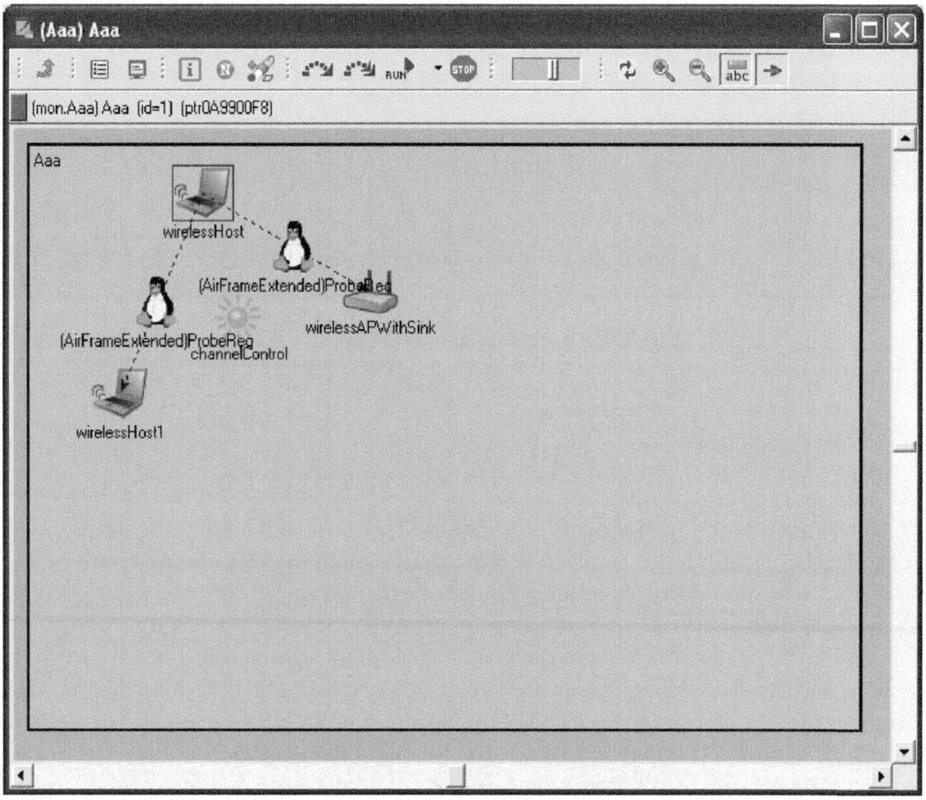

Fig. 1. Network with dimension 100m x 100m

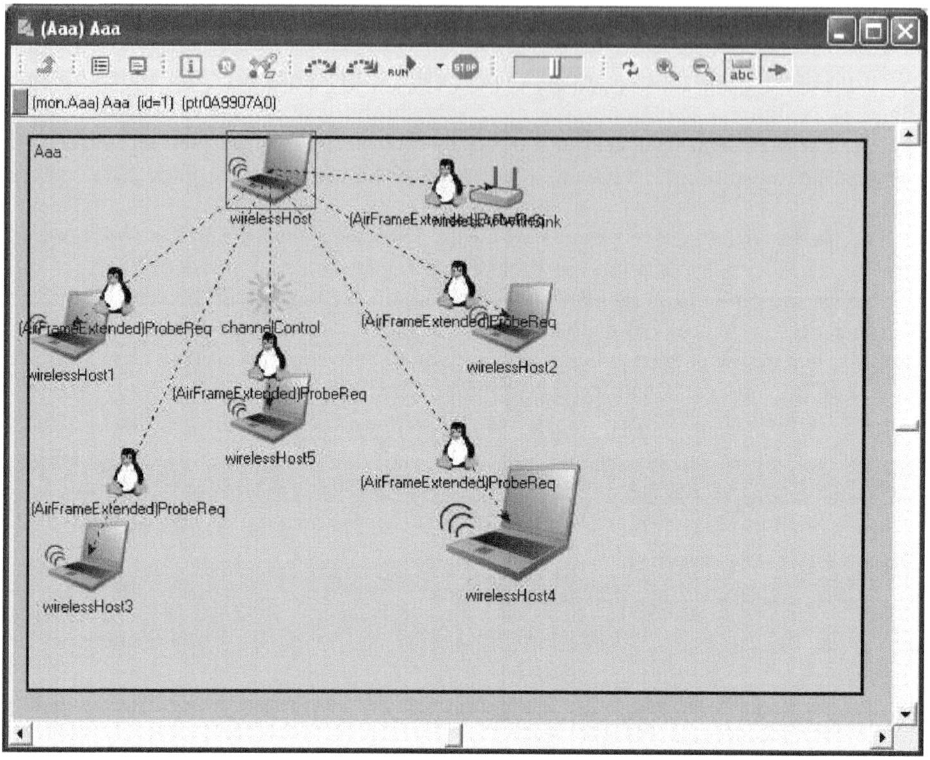

Fig. 2. Network with dimension 500m x 500m

Let m = total no of sensor nodes
n = no of sink node
pxq = dimension of the network cell

Our work is based on Tactical Information Management Middleware architec- ture proposed in [3] . In these models when the nodes share the MIO (comprising of pay-load and metadata) during the query to data or data to query commu- nication mode then during this short duration of request - response paradigm the SQL(or TIQL [3]) queries are exchanged. For better management of the query transition between the Source node to Sink Node it is proposed to ex- tends the Tactical Information Management Middleware architecture [3] first by incorporating the concept if In-Network Query Processing [4] and then further strengthening the exchange of the SQL queries it up by suggesting mechanism to handle the SQL injection types of attack. The idea of In-Network Query Pro- cessing involves the process of request - response paradigm wherein the multiple SQL or TIQL [3] queries are exchanged between the two mobile nodes who needs to share the data with each other. The queries in Wireless Sensor Network can be classified into following categories [5]:-

1. Monitoring Queries:- The Queries that request the value of one or more attributes continuously and periodically are known as Monitoring queries. Example:- Reporting the status of the no of queries received and queries replied after every 10 seconds.
2. Network Health Queries:- The queries that are concerned with the monitoring the status of the network after regular periodic intervals say after 10 seconds are known as Network Health queries .Example :- The Query for determining the current battery level of the node.
3. Exploratory Queries:- The one-stroke queries that determines the status of a particular node or set of nodes at any given point in time are known as Exploratory queries. These queries generally use the ONCE in the end. Example the query no 9(specified later) can be refined as :- select * from metadata where LocationTimeStamp =A ONCE;
4. Nested Queries :- Many SQL based languages like Tiny DB language does not currently support SQL-style nested queries, because the semantics of such queries are some what ill defined in a streaming environment. Also their exist no clarity that till what level the nesting is allowed to exist in the network.

4 Database Schema

The Database Schema, fig. 3, that is designed to handle these queries comprises of four tables whose DDL(Data Definition Language) is as follows:-

1. Metadata(ID,Description,CTS[CreationTimeStamp], TS[LocationTimeStamp], Topic)
2. Query[QID, Lifetime, Priority, Rank, AggerationAllowed, NID[NetworkID])
3. Payload(QueryId,Data)
4. Node(ID,Bandwidth,BatteryPower)

5 SQL Clauses

In a DFT-MSN and MP2PN we propose the set of various queries which are exchanged between the sensor node and sink node are as follows :-

1. If we want to fetch those queries whose lifetime is greater than 500 seconds and whose rank is more than four then the resultant SQL is :
   select * from query where lifetime <=500 and rank >4;
2. If we want to fetch the information about those nodes whose battery power is greater than 3 milliwatt then the query is as:-
   select * from node where batterypower > `3mw';
3. If we want to fetch all the records from metadata where topic is like document then the SQL Queries is as :-
   select * from metadata where topic like d`ocument';
4. If we want to fetch all the records from metadata where creation time stamp is greater than 8 am hrs.
   select * from metadata where cts >' 08 : 00 : 00';

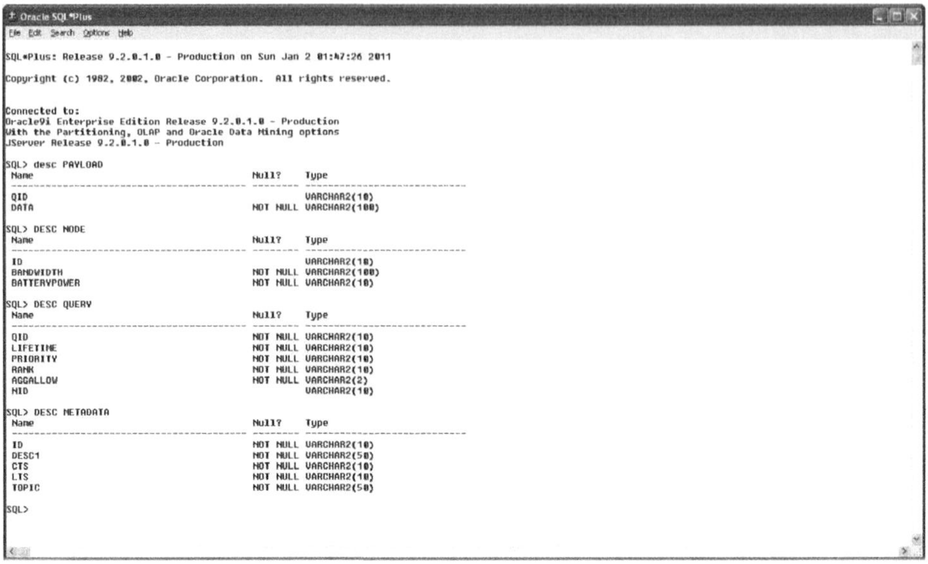

Fig. 3. Database Schema

5. If we want to fetch all the records from query and payload where rank is greater than three then the command is :-
   select * from query, payload where rank > 3 and query.qid=payload.qid
6. If we want to fetch all the records from query where priority is high and the aggregation of the queries is allowed to happen at the sensor node before it is relayed to the sink node
   select * from query where priority=H` igh' and Aggallow=Y` ';
7. If we want to fetch all the records from node table where bandwidth is greater than 64 Mb
   select * from node table where Bandwidth > 64;
8. If we want to fetch those records from the table metadata whose LocationTimeStamp is equal to Z`one A'
   select * from metadata where LocationTimeStamp =A` ';

Prospective results of the queries are mentioned in fig 4.

To the query/data that is being relayed from sensor node to sink node the query/data stands vulnerable to SQL injection attack, which to our knowledge is the first paper to investigate impose the SQL injection attacks. SQL Injection attack is defined as A` code injection technique that exploits a security vulnerability occurring in the database layer of an application. The vulnerability is present when user input is either incorrectly filtered for string literal escape characters embedded in SQL statements or user input is not strongly typed and thereby unexpectedly executed [14]. A successful SQL injection exploit can read sensi- tive and critical data from the database, modify(Insert/Update/Delete) database data if need be and execute administration operations on the database (such as shutdown the DBMS), recover the content of a given file present on the DBMS file system and in some remote cases issue commands to the operating system [26]. The different types of the SQL injection techniques are Authorization by- pass, using the select command, using the insert command and using the SQL Server stored procedures. The insert and select command perform their usual meanings where as authorization bypass is performed by passing log on forms.

The SQL injection in Oracle can be performed as follows:

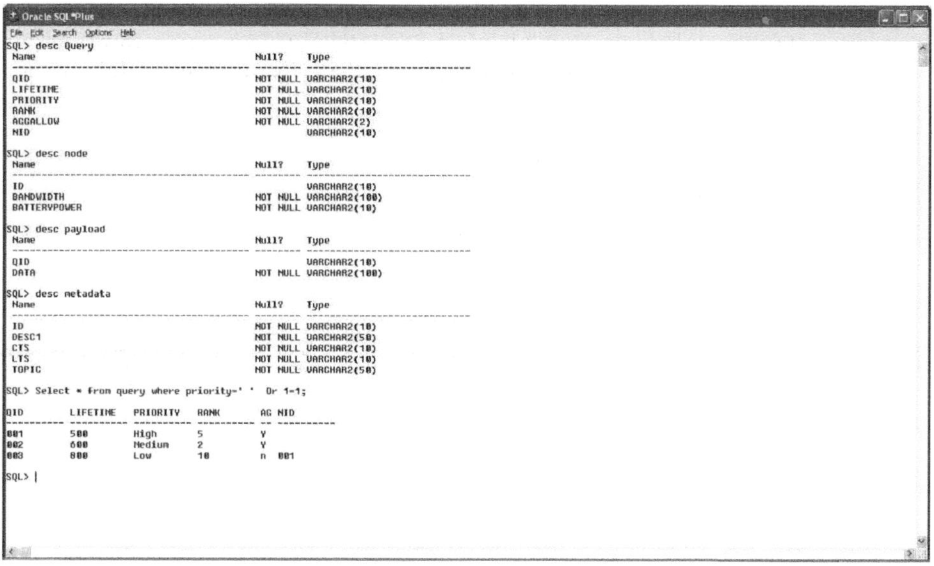

Fig. 4. Results of query

1. Unions can be added to the existing statement to execute a second statement.
2. SubSelects can be added to existing statements.
3. DDL(Data Definition Language) statements can be injected if DDL is used in SQL String.
4. Insert/Update and delete are also injected.
5. Anonymous PL/SQL blocks in procedures.

Hacker breaks into the system by injecting the malformed SQL statement into SQL query. For example, in SQL Query no. 7, select * from query where pri- ority=H` igh' and Aggallow=Y` '; after SQL injection attack is imposed the query is rewritten as:- select * from query where priority=`' or 1=1 and Aggallow=`'; Such a query when fired from sensor node to high end sink node or from high end sink node to access point actually got translated to :- Select * from query where priority=' ' Or 1=1 because the pair of hyphens (—) designates the beginning of comments in SQL, and such queries can result in devastating effect as when the same query was executed on Oracle 9i Enterprise Edition Release 9.2.0.1.0 Production it displayed all the records of the Query table where priority was either high, medium or low .

In a typical DTN [6] Scenario when the source node transmits the query(bundled as a part of application data unit) to the destination node and if the manipu- lated query(query after the SQL injection attack) is received successfully by the minimum reception group of the endpoint then the query would be believed to be successfully delivered to the destination node even though it is a mal- formed query. Besides an effective SQL injection in database queries various SQL injection Automated tools(Proprietary and Open Source) for effective and coordinated SQL injection attacks, are available, the summarized information of some of widely accepted tools is given in Table1.

Table 1. Table depicting different types of Automated SQL Injection tools

S.No	Tool Name	Description
1	SQLdict[15]	It is an dictionary attack tool for an SQL Server
2	SQLExec[16]	This tool executes the command on the compromised Microsoft SQL servers by using xp$_c$*mdshellstoredprocedure*
3	Sqlbf[17]	This tool is used to audit the strength of the Microsoft SQL Servers password offline.The tool can be used either in BruteForce mode or Dictionary attack mode.
4	SQLSmack[18]	It is a Linux based Remote Command Execution for MSSQL
5	SQL2[19]	IT is a UDP buffer overflow Remote Exploit Hacking tool.
6	Sqlmap [20]	This SQL injection tool developed in Python supports two SQL injection techniques :- Blind SQL injection and Inband SQL injection also known as SQL UNION query SQL injection
7	Sqlninja [21]	It is a tool to exploit SQL injection vulnerabilities on a web application
8	SQLier [22]	It takes a vulnerable URL and attempts to determine all necessary information to exploit SQL injection vulnerability by itself requiring no user interaction
9	Automagic SQL injector[23]	It is an SQL injection tool designed to save time in penetration testing. It is designed to work with Vanilla Microsoft SQL injection holes where errors are returned.
10	Absinthe[24]	It is a GUI based tool that automates the process of downloading the schema and the contents of the database that is vulnerable to blind SQL injection.
11	Blind SQL Injection [25]	It is a hacking method that allows an unauthorized attacker to access a database server.

In order to avoid the SQL injection various measures have been proposed including developing the traditional hashing method for handling the SQL in- jection but here we focus more on the two techniques as suggested by The Open Web Application Security Pro ject(OWASP) [26] which has proved to be success- ful methods of mitigating SQL Injection attacks:- a) By developing SQL Queries using bound, typed parameters(b) by writing SQL queries that makes use of parameterized stored procedures. For Example to make SQL Query no 7 SQL injection foolproof the query can be re-written in Java as Select * from query where priority=' ?' and Aggallow=' ?'; and the values of priority as high and Ag- gallow as Yes passed in the two placeholders dynamically at the run time which could provide protection against SQL injection attacks.

6 Conclusions

As seen from above the task of sharing the information between the node in- volving SQL/TIQL queries is a complex one and one the aforesaid mentioned SQL injection tools if deployed on the active source node, on the intermediate node or high end sink node they can tamper with of the exchange of the queries resulting in the malformed queries resulting in the undesired result. The tools can also be deployed from remote location through remote procedure call (port no 111).So the need is to develop and adopt strong and effective SQL Injection Countermeasures so as to ensure the safe passage of the SQL queries between the nodes in the DFT-MSN/MP2PN.It is further proposed that the same set of SQL Queries be executed on TinyDB which is a declarative database for Wire- less Sensor Networks, including the DFT-MSN and runs on MICA motes [10]. The future work can also be extended to do broad comparative study regarding the performance and security of the SQL queries when executed on the Oracle 9i Enterprise Edition Release 9.2.0.1.0 with the Tiny DB engine v 2.92 installed on TinyOS.

Acknowledgments. The authors wishes to express sincere thanks to the ad- ministration of the GGSIP University and Delhi University for providing the academic environment to pursue the research activities.

References

1. Wang, Y., Wu, H.: Delay/Fault-Tolerant Mobile Sensor Network(DFT-MSN): A new Paradigm for Pervasive Information Gathering. IEEE Trans. Mob. Comput. 6(9), 1021–1034 (2007)
2. Hull, B., Bychkovsky, V., Zhang, Y., Chen, K., Goraczko, M., Shih, E., Balakrishnan, H., Madden, S.: CarTel: A Distributed Mobile Sensor Computing System. In: 4th International Conference on Embedded Networked Sensor System, pp. 125–138. ACM, New York (2006)
3. Xu, B., Linderman, M., Madria, S., Wolfson, O.: A Tactical Information Management Middleware for Resource- constrained Mobile P2P Networks. In: 29th IEEE International Symposium on Reliable Distributed Systems, New Delhi, pp. 303–307 (2010)
4. Xu, B., Vafaee, F., Wolfson, O.: In-Network Query Processing in Mobile P2P Databases. In: 17th ACM SIGSPATIAL International Conferences on Advances in Geographic Information Systems, pp. 207–216. ACM, New York (2009)
5. Madden, S.R., Franklin, M.J., Hellerstein, J.M., Hong, W.: TinyDB: An Acqui- sitional Query Processing System for Sensor Networks. ACM Trans.Database Syst. 30(1), 122–173 (2005)

6. Cerf, V., Hooke, A., Torgerson, L., Durst, R., Scott, K., Burleigh, S., Fall, K., Weiss, H.: RFC 4838, Delay-Tolerant Networking Architecture. IRTF DTN Research Group (2007)
7. Omnet++ User Manual Version 4.1. Andrs Varga and OpenSim Ltd, (2010), http://www.ncbi.nlm.nih.gov
8. Omnet++ Installation Guide Version 4.1. Andrs Varga and OpenSim Ltd (2010)
9. INET Framework for OMNeT++ Manual (2010)
10. http://www.xbow.com/pdf/Imote2_press_release.pdf
11. http://www.sunspotworld.com
12. http://www.servopack.de/support/zebra/ZebraNet-Wireless.pdf
13. Jain, S., Fall, K., Patra, R.: Routing in Delay Tolerant Network. In: ACM SIGCOMM 2004, Portland Oregon USA, August 30-September (2004)
14. http://en.wikipedia.org/wiki/SQL_injection
15. http://www.ntsecurity.nu/toolbox/sqldict
16. http://www.msdn.microsoft.com/en-us/library/ms188332.aspx
17. http://www.econsultant.com/spyware-database/s/sqlbf.html
18. http://www.securiteam.Com/tools/5GP081P75C.html
19. http://www.sqlcourse2.com
20. http://www.sqlmap.sourceforge.net
21. http://www.sqlninja.sourceforge.net/download.html
22. http://www.nixbit.com/cat//security/sqlier
23. http://www.darknet.org.uk/../pangolin-automatic-sql-injection-tool/
24. http://www.0x90.org/releases/absinthe/download.php
25. http://www.sqlmap.sourceforge.net/
26. http://www.owasp.Org/index.php/Guide_to_SQL_Injection

Financial Time Series Volatility Forecast Using Evolutionary Hybrid Artificial Neural Network

Anupam Tarsauliya, Rahul Kala, Ritu Tiwari, and Anupam Shukla

Soft Computing & Expert System Laboratory, ABV-IIITM,
Gwalior- 474010, India
{anupam8391,rkala001,drritutiwari,dranupamshukla}@gmail.com

Abstract. Financial time series forecast has been classified as standard problem in forecasting due to its high non-linearity and high volatility in data. Statistical methods such as GARCH, GJR, EGARCH and Artificial Neural Networks (ANNs) based on standard learning algorithms such as backpropagation have been widely used for forecasting time series volatility of various fields. In this paper, we propose hybrid model of statistical methods with ANNs. Statistical methods require assumptions about the market, they do not reflect all market variables and they may not capture the non-linearity. Shortcoming of ANNs is their process of identifying inputs insignificantly through which network produces output. The attempt for hybrid system is to outperform the forecast results and overcome the shortcomings by extracting input variables from statistical methods and include them in ANNs learning process. Further genetic algorithm is used for evolution of proposed hybrid models. Experimental results confirm the lesser root mean square error (RMSE) results obtained from proposed evolutionary hybrid ANN models EANN-GARCH, EANN-GJR, EANN-EGARCH than conventional ANNs and statistical methods.

Keywords: Evolutionary, Hybrid, ANN, GA, GARCH, EGARCH, GJR.

1 Introduction

Financial forecasting has been challenging problem due to its non-linearity and high volatility [1]. Forecasting assumes that some aspects of past patterns will continue in future. Past relationship of it can be discovered through study and observation of data. Main idea behind forecasting has been to devise a system that could map a set of inputs to set of desired outputs [2]. There has always been risk involved with investment in financial market. ANNs have widely been used for the forecasting purpose because of their ability to learn linear and complex data [3]. ANNs is trained such as a set of inputs maps a set of desired output. These networks can hence automatically assume any shape that carries forward the task of determination of the outputs to the presented input.

The ANNs by their basic architecture represent the human brain [4]. They consist of a set of artificial neurons. The task of any fundamental artificial neuron may be divided into two parts. The first part does the weighted addition of the inputs presented to it.

D.C. Wyld et al. (Eds.): CNSA 2011, CCIS 196, pp. 463–471, 2011.

The second part of the neuron consists of an activation function. The weighted addition of the first part is passed through the activation function. This is the final output of the system [5]. Statistical methods such as GARCH, EGARCH and GJR also have been used extensively for volatility forecasting. GARCH model reflects the non-linear dependence of the conditional variance of the time series, which indicates the non-linear time series characteristics are from the conditional second-order moment of the distribution [6]. EGARCH model, which express conditional variance equation in the logarithm form, and relax the nonnegative restrictions on the parameters [7] . Genetic Algorithms (GA) can be used to optimize various parameters and to solve many problems in real time [8]. GA as a solution for optimization problems based on natural selection keeps an initial population of solution candidates and evaluates the quality of each solution candidate according to a specific cost function. Over successive generations, the population evolves toward an optimal solution [9].

2 Algorithms and Methods

2.1 Artificial Neural Network

General Backpropagation (BPA) Neural Network architecture as shown in figure 1, includes input layer, hidden layer and output layer. Each neuron in input layers are interconnected with neurons in hidden layers and each neuron of hidden layer in interconnected with output layer neuron with weights assigned to the connection [10]. On providing learning data to the network, the learning values are passed through input to hidden and finally to output layer where response for input data is obtained. For optimizing the error obtained, the error values are back propagated to make changes in weights of input to hidden layer and hidden to output layer. With error back propagation input response are made converged to desired response.

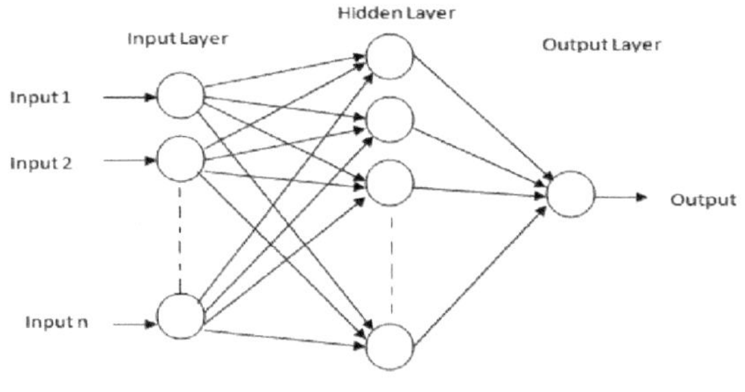

Fig. 1. General architecture of a Backpropagation Neural Network

BPA uses supervised learning in which trainer submits the input-output exemplary patterns and the learner has to adjust the parameters of the system autonomously, so that it can yield the correct output pattern when excited with one of the given input patterns [11].

2.2 Genetic Algorithm

Genetic algorithms (GA) function by optimizing an objective function. They exploit the structure of the error surface. GAs does not assume that the error surface is uni-modal, or even that its derivative exists [12]. A genetic algorithm performs a parallel stochastic search. It is parallel in the sense that many solutions in the population are considered simultaneously and the fittest solutions are chosen for reproduction. It is stochastic in the sense that the solutions are randomly selected for refinement and the likelihood of a solution being selected is enhanced by the quality of the solution or its fitness, and the search direction is also chosen randomly. Genetic Algorithm evolves ANNs by fixing the values and the weights and biases of the various nodes i.e. the GA optimizes the network parameters for better performance.

Steps followed for evolution of ANN are problem encoding, creation of random initial state, fitness evaluation, and genetic operator including selection, crossover, mutation and elite, generate next generation, testing and verification [13] are shown below in figure 2 below.

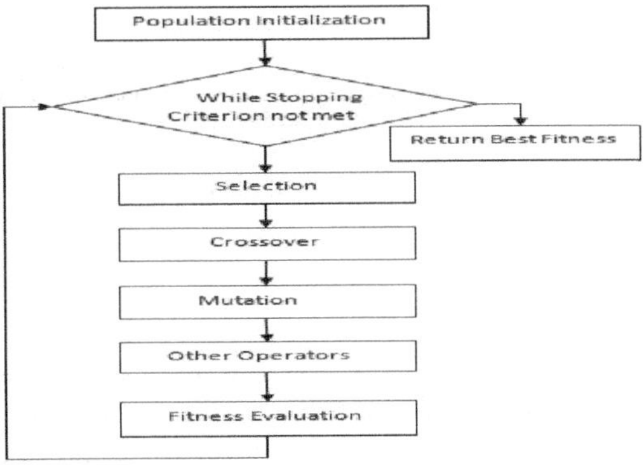

Fig. 2. Flow Chart of a working of Genetic Algorithm

3 Proposed Evolutionary Hybrid Neural Networks

3.1 EANN-GARCH

GARCH stands for generalized autoregressive conditional heteroscedasticity. It is a mechanism that includes past variances in the explanation of future variances. More specifically, GARCH is a time series technique used to model the serial dependence of volatility. The general GARCH (P, Q) model [14], [16] for the conditional variance of innovations is

$$\sigma_t^2 = k + \sum_{i=1}^{P} G_i \sigma_{t-i}^2 + \sum_{j=1}^{Q} A_j \varepsilon_{t-j}^2 \tag{1}$$

With constraints: $\sum_{i=1}^{P} G_i + \sum_{j=1}^{Q} A_j < 1$, k > 0, $G_i \geq 0$, $A_j \geq 0$

The basic GARCH (P, Q) model is a symmetric variance process, in that it ignores the sign of the disturbance [15]. ANN-GARCH model can be created by extracting the input variables based on above variables. After including these variables in ANN learning process, model can be used to forecast volatility. The newly extracted variables are as follows:

$$\sigma'^2_{t-1} = \sum_{i=1}^{P} G_i \, \sigma^2_{t-i} \qquad \varepsilon'^2_{t-1} = \sum_{j=1}^{Q} A_j \, \varepsilon^2_{t-j}$$

3.2 EANN-GJR

The general GJR (P, Q) model [16] for the conditional variance of innovations with leverage terms is

$$\sigma_t^2 = k + \sum_{i=1}^{P} G_i \, \sigma^2_{t-i} + \sum_{j=1}^{Q} A_j \, \varepsilon^2_{t-j} + \sum_{j=1}^{Q} L_j S_{t-j} \, \varepsilon^2_{t-j} \tag{2}$$

Where $S_{t-j} = 1 \; if \; \varepsilon_{t-j} < 0, S_{t-j} = 0 \; otherwise$

With constraints

$$\sum_{i-1}^{P} G_i + \sum_{j-1}^{Q} A_j + \frac{1}{2} \sum_{j-1}^{Q} L_j < 1$$

$$k \geq 0, \; G_i \geq 0, \; A_j \geq 0, \; A_j + L_j \geq 0$$

The lag lengths P and Q, and the magnitudes of the coefficients Gi and Aj, determine the extent to which disturbances persist. These values then determine the minimum amount of pre-sampled data needed to initiate the simulation and estimation processes. ANN-GJR model can be created by extracting the input variables based on above variables. After including these variables in ANN learning process, model can be used to forecast volatility. The newly extracted variables are as follows:

$$\sigma'^2_{t-1} = \sum_{i=1}^{P} G_i \sigma^2_{t-i}, \qquad \varepsilon'^2_{t-1} = \sum_{j=1}^{Q} A_j \, \varepsilon^2_{t-j}, \qquad \varepsilon''^2_{t-1} = \sum_{j=1}^{Q} L_j S_{t-j} \, \varepsilon^2_{t-j}$$

3.3 EANN-EGARCH

The general EGARCH (P, Q) model [15], [16] for the conditional variance of the innovations, with leverage terms and an explicit probability distribution assumption is

$$\log \sigma_t^2 = k + \sum_{i=1}^{P} G_i \log \sigma^2_{t-1} + \sum_{j=1}^{Q} A_j \left[\frac{\varepsilon_{t-j}}{\sigma_{t-j}} - \sqrt{\frac{2}{\pi}} \right] + \sum_{j=1}^{Q} L_j \left(\frac{\varepsilon_{t-j}}{\sigma_{t-j}} \right) \tag{3}$$

EGARCH models are fundamentally different from GARCH and GJR models in that the standardized innovation, serves as the forcing variable for both the conditional variance and the error. EANN-EGARCH model can be created by extracting the input variables based on above variables. After including these variables in ANN learning process, model can be used to forecast volatility. The newly extracted variables are as follows:

$$\log\sigma'^2_{t-1} = \sum_{i=1}^{P} G_i \log\sigma^2_{t-1}$$

$$Levergae\ Effect = \sum_{j=1}^{Q} A_j \left[\left|\frac{\varepsilon_{t-j}}{\sigma_{t-j}}\right| - \sqrt{\frac{2}{\pi}}\right]$$

$$Levergae = \sum_{j=1}^{Q} L_j \left(\frac{\varepsilon_{t-j}}{\sigma_{t-j}}\right)$$

4 Experiment and Results

4.1 Research Data

We have used two different data (un-normalized) have been collected from Prof. Rob J Hyndman's website http://robjhyndman.com/TSDL/ . Data sets analyzed are as: Daily closing price of IBM stock, Jan. 01 1980 - Oct. 08 1992. [17], Daily S & P 500 index of stocks, Jan. 01 1980 - Oct. 08 1992. [17].

Table 1. Time Series Data Sets Description

Time Series	Standard Deviation	Mean	Count
Daily IBM	28.76493	105.6183	3333
Daily S&P	97.01113	236.1225	3333

4.2 Methodology

We analyze the above discussed statistical forecasting models (P=1, Q=1) and extract the best suited input variables of these models. We divide the dataset into training and testing dataset. A random dataset division is followed to result 80% of dataset as training dataset and remaining 20% as testing dataset.

Supervised learning is followed for learning of the neural network with target prediction series given. Artificial neural network thus obtained is evolved using genetic algorithm. Genetic algorithm optimizes the weights and biases of neural network based on the given training dataset for better accuracy forecast.

Testing dataset thus obtained is used for simulating the evolutionary neural network, checking the error or accuracy of the trained network. We compare the output data as given by the network with the testing data set with the target dataset.

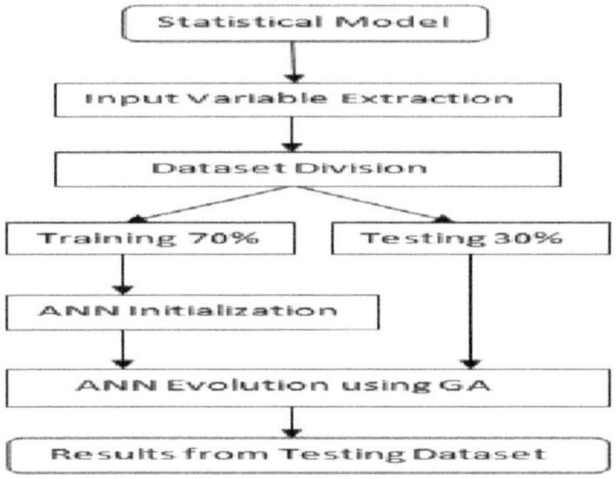

Fig. 3. Flow Chart of used Methodology

4.3 Empirical Results

Table 2. Results Obtained for Time Series

Methodology	Daily IBM (Mean RMSE)	Daily S&P (Mean RMSE)
BPA-ANN	0.00232	0.0027
EANN-GARCH	0.000287	0.000312
EANN-GJR	0.000242	0.000253
EANN-EGARCH	0.000198	0.000217

4.4 Graphical Analysis

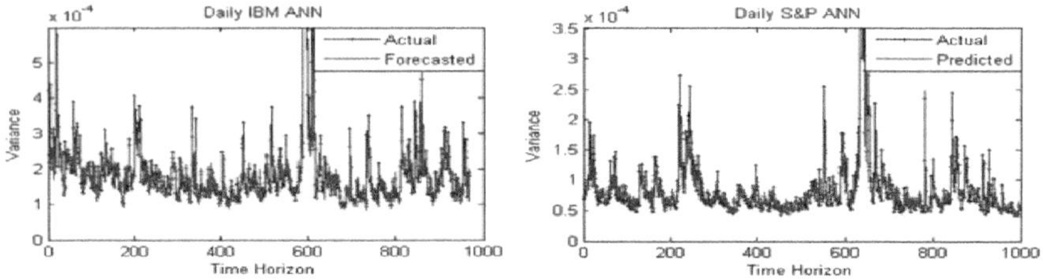

Fig. 4. Graphs for Actual and Predicted Values for Daily IBM and Daily S&P using traditional Backpropagation Algorithm with variance value is taken on Y-Axis and Day of Index is on X-Axis, with mean RMSE = 0.00232 and 0.0027 respectively

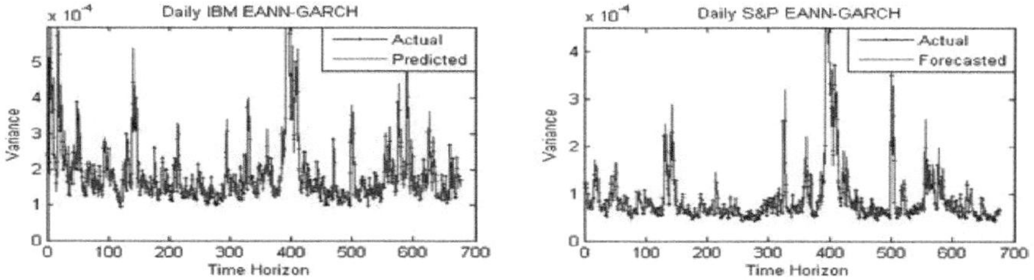

Fig. 5. Graphs for Actual and Predicted Values for Daily IBM and Daily S&P using EANN-GARCH with variance value is taken on Y-Axis and Day of Index is on X-Axis, with mean RMSE = 0.000287 and 0.000312 respectively

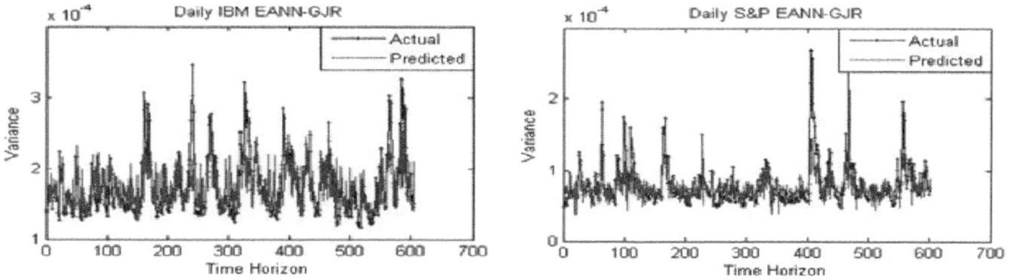

Fig. 6. Graphs for Actual and Predicted Values for Daily IBM and Daily S&P using EANN-GJR with variance value is taken on Y-Axis and Day of Index is on X-Axis, with mean RMSE = 0.000242 and 0.000253 respectively

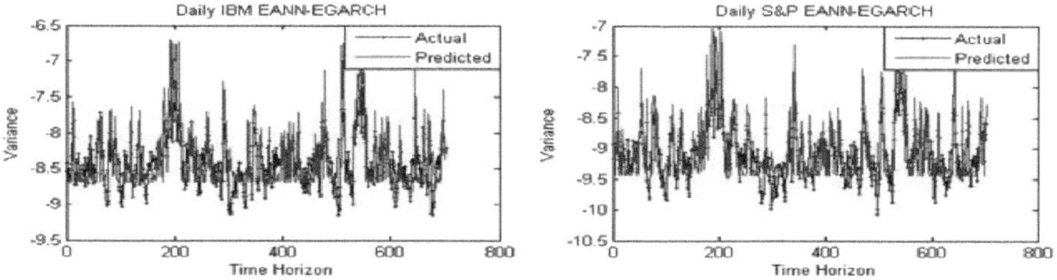

Fig. 7. Graphs for Actual and Predicted Values for Daily IBM and Daily S&P using EANN-EGARCH with variance value is taken on Y-Axis and Day of Index is on X-Axis, with mean RMSE = 0.000198 and 0.000217 respectively

5 Conclusions

The Evolutionary Hybrid Artificial Neural Network has been proposed in order to improve the financial forecast accuracy. It is based on the hybridization concept of using best features of different models for better result. We have extracted the input variables out of statistical forecast models GARCH, GJR and EGARCH, which optimizes the best input variable feed for artificial neural network initialization and learning. A hybrid model thus obtained from statistical model and artificial neural network is evolved using genetic algorithm. Genetic algorithm optimizes the artificial neural network parameters such as weights and biases as per the given training dataset, in order to improve the forecast accuracy of hybrid model. Accuracy results and plotted comparison graph of actual and predicted values shows the better performance by these proposed evolutionary hybrid artificial neural network over conventional artificial neural network forecasting. Order of performance can be adjudged as EANN-EGARCH > EANN-GJR > EANN-GARCH > ANN.

References

1. Yixin, Z., Zhang, J.: Stock Data Analysis Based on BP Neural Network. In: Second International Conference on Communication Software and Networks, ICCSN, pp. 396–399 (2010)
2. Marzi, H., Turnbull, M., Marzi, E.: Use of neural networks in forecasting financial market. In: IEEE Conference on Soft Computing in Industrial Applications, SMCia 2008, June 25-27, pp. 240–245 (2008)
3. Eng, M.H., Li, Y., Wang, Q.-G., Lee, T.H.: Forecast Forex with ANN Using Fundamental Data. In: Information Management, Innovation Management and Industrial Engineering, ICIII 2008, December 19-21, vol. 1, pp. 279–282 (2008)
4. Ram Kumar, P., Ramana Murthy, M.V., Eashwar, D., Venkatdas, M.: Time Series Modeling using Artificial Neural Networks. Journal of Theoretical and Applied Information Technology, JATIT 4(12), 1259–1264 (2005)
5. Zhao, Z., Xin, H., Ren, Y., Guo, X.: Application and Comparison of BP Neural Network Algorithm in MATLAB. In: International Conference on Measuring Technology and Mechatronics Automation 2010, March 13-14, vol. 1, pp. 590–593 (2010)
6. Zhao, H., Zhou, Y.: A joint model of chaos and GARCH effect in China's stock markets. In: 2nd International Conference on Power Electronics and Intelligent Transportation System (PEITS), December 19-20, vol. 3, pp. 220–223 (2009)
7. Ning, L., Dong-ping, H.: Emipirical Research on Term Structure of Buy-Back Rates Based on EGARCH Model. In: Second International Symposium on Electronic Commerce and Security, ISECS 2009, May 22-24, vol. 1, pp. 112–115 (2009)
8. Etemadi, H., Rostamy, A.A.A., Dehkordi, H.F.: A genetic programming model for bankruptcy prediction: Empirical evidence from Iran. Expert Systems with Applications 36(2), part 2, 3199–3207 (2009)
9. Yang, C.-X., Zhu, Y.-F.: Using genetic algorithms for time series prediction. In: Sixth International Conference on Natural Computation (ICNC), August 10-12, vol. 8, pp. 4405–4409 (2010)
10. Shukla, A., Tiwari, R., Kala, R.: Real Life Application of Soft Computing. CRC Press, Boca Raton (2010)
11. Lee, T.-L.: Back-propagation neural network for the prediction of the short-term storm surge in Taichung harbor. Engineering Applications of Artificial Intelligence 21(1), 63–67 (2008)
12. Shopova, E.G., Vaklieva-Bancheva, N.G.: BASIC–A genetic algorithm for engineering problems solution. Computers & Chemical Engineering 30(8), 1293–1309 (2006)
13. Altunkaynak, A.: Sediment load prediction by genetic algorithms. Advances in Engineering Software 40(9), 928–934 (2009)

14. Basrak, B., Davis, R.A., Mikosch, T.: Regular variation of GARCH processes. Stochastic Processes and their Applications 99(1), 95–115 (2002)
15. Wang, J., Wu, X., Zhong, M.: Empirical Analysis of the Market Risk of Chinese Open-Ended Funds Based on GARCH-VaR Models. In: International Joint Conference on Computational Sciences and Optimization, April 24-26, vol. 1, pp. 979–982 (2009)
16. Shamiri, A., Hassan, A.: Modeling and Forecasting Volatility of the Malaysian and the Singaporean stock indices using Asymmetric GARCH models and Non-normal Densities. Econometrics 0509015, EconWPA (2005)
17. Hipel, McLeod: Time Series Modelling of Water Resources and Environmental Systems. Elsevier, Amsterdam (1994)

Data Security in Free Roaming Mobile Agents

G. Geetha[1] and C. Jayakumar[2]

[1] Assistant Professor , Jerusalem college of Engineering, Chennai, India
gee_dgl@yahoo.com
[2] Professor, RMK Engineering college , Chennai, India
cjayakumar2007@gmail.com

Abstract. Mobile agents are software programs that live in computer networks, performing their computations and moving from host to host as necessary to fulfill their goals. Mobile agents are especially useful in electronic commerce, for both wired and wireless environments. In this research work, both chain relation and TTP(trusted host) has used for protecting data of free roaming mobile agents which is called Trusted host by Knowledge Based System(TKBS). Using Knowledge based system, trusted host list is maintained. In trusted Host agent may not clone. By using chain relation with trusted host, redundancy will be reduced and efficiency will be improved.

Keywords: Mobile agent, TKBS, security.

1 Introduction

Mobile agents migrate from originating hosts to intermediate servers to generate and collect data, and return to the originators to submit results after completing scheduled tasks.

Free roaming mobile agents are free to choose their respective next hops dynamically based on the data they acquired from their past journeys. Free-roaming agents have no pre-defined migration paths. They select their next hop at each hop they visit based on initial requirements and current conditions.

There are many security issues to be addressed in Data security in Free Roaming Mobile Agents for example data confidentiality, non reputability, insertion defense and truncation defense etc.

Generally security issues in mobile agents as

1. Protection of the host from malicious code
2. Protection of the agent from a malicious host trying to tamper the code and the agent data.

Agent Security is divided into code security (tampering attack, etc) and data security. Methods used to protect data in mobile agents count on move forms. The move forms of agent are pre defined itinerary and free roaming.

Security in free roaming agents is especially hard to achieve when the mobile code is executed in hosts that may behave maliciously. Data security in free roaming agent

D.C. Wyld et al. (Eds.): CNSA 2011, CCIS 196, pp. 472–482, 2011.

without itinerary information may face more complex attacks. This paper focus on Data Security in free roaming mobile agents.

1.1 Mobile Agent Work Flow

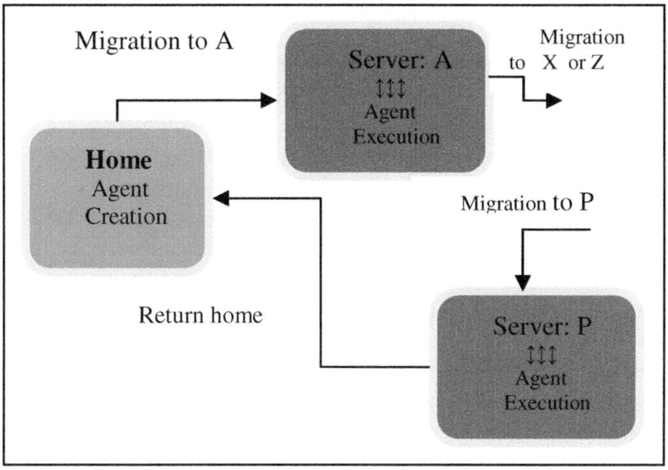

Fig. 1. The Mobile Agent Workflow

1.2 Related Works

Mobile agent's security problems divided into three threats: the mobile agent's transfer security problems, mobile agent platform's security problems and mobile agent security issues in malicious platform. Mobile agent security issues in malicious platform are very difficult to solve because agent's run-time code, data and communications are fully exposed to the host which agent running.

Mobile agents must have strong security properties to protect themselves and the collected data while leaving their homes and migrating to other potentially malicious server. A malicious server may expose, modify, insert or truncate data the agent collected from other previously visited servers to benefit it self .This problem is serious for free roaming mobile agents .

The mechanism used to protect data of free roaming mobile agents can be mainly divided in to two categories. Detecting mechanism and avoiding mechanism. Sorting Detecting Mechanism into

(i) TTP (Trusted Thirty Party)
(ii) Using Chain relation
(iii) Multi agent co-operation

We use TTP to record itinerary information directly or indirectly. The main problem is that we need one TTP at least, and the mobile agent need to communicate with it, so the TTP will become a bottleneck and even cause single-point failure. It is not easy to find a TTP in the open internet.

In chain relation we form a chain relation among previous and following hosts' computing data generated by the mobile agent. They can detect the modification made on the data by malicious hosts with this chain relation. Different chain relations decide different mechanisms and also decide their ability in detecting colluded truncation attacks.

Reference [1] has designed a trust model TAMAP. The model obtains trust score through interaction between hosts. Mobile agent adjusts its implementation according to trust score. The model is mainly consists of protection agreements, trust estimation mechanism and dynamic self-adaptive process, which can resist colluded truncation attack. Compared with other models, TAMAP has an advantage of simplifying complex, costly infrastructure, such as reputation database. But TAMAP is modeled on a real-world trust reputation mechanisms to achieve network security, need strong network management as support, no matter how sophisticated the design, how thoughtful the consideration it is difficult to be applied in practice.

Reference [2] uses partial result encapsulation for chain association certification, use digital signatures and Hash function to form association between results of two hosts adjacent. Through this association the mechanism can prevent data changed maliciously, but it cannot resist colluded truncation attack.

Reference [3] is an improvement of reference [2]. Data generated by agent on each host have relationship with data generated on consecutive two hosts before and after. The mechanism can resist two or noncontiguous multi-hosts' colluded truncation attack, but cannot resist contiguous multi-hosts' colluded truncation attack.

In reference [4] agent copies itself in each host, then the copy reach next host and test the host is malicious or not if not, the host become next hop, otherwise, agent chooses another host, but the mechanism cannot resist multi-hosts' colluded truncation attack

2 Trust Host BY Knowledge Based System

To solve the data security problems of free roaming mobile agent, we establish following model

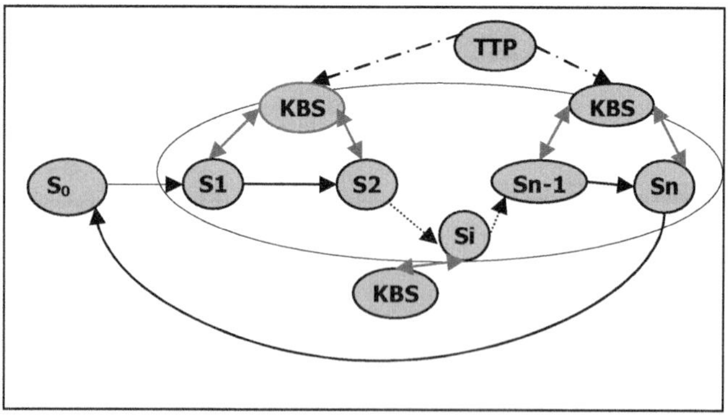

Fig. 2. Agent Migration With TKBS

As shown in fig 1, S_0, S_1, S_2....., S_n are network hosts, So is a task Sponsor or initiator or Originator or creator . Agent starts from So, chooses its next hop according to certain principles and on the new host it collects data , then chooses next hop, This process continues until the completion of scheduled tasks and return to S_0.

Now let's assume mobile agent's route is S1, S2 ......Sn. Among these hosts some malicious hosts may exist, and even there are multiple malicious hosts, which conspire with each other to modify, cut off data collected by agent to achieve their attack purpose.

Based on model above, we established TKBS on the following premises

Premise 1: Malicious hosts have impact on mobile agent's choosing its next hop if mobile agent is running on it. Even worse, malicious hosts can control its next hop.

Premise 2: On non-malicious hosts, mobile agent's choosing its next hop mainly depends on current network environment and so on but not depend on current host. We can assume that each host has equal possibility of being next hop.

Premise 3: We have established public key certificate system. Each host has its public and private key.

Premise 4: Mobile agent's route is generated dynamically TKBS should not only have ability to resist colluded truncation attack, but also meet following security requirements:

(1) Data confidentiality: only S0 can obtain data without encryption generated by hosts which agent chooses.
(2) Non-repudiation: No host which agent has run on can deny data results generated on them and agent's passing through.
(3) Anonymity: for some certain purpose, No host knows the task sponsor and mobile agent's migration path.
(4) Integrity: if malicious host modify other hosts' data mechanism can detect illegal alteration.
(5) Anti-insertion-attack: any host cannot have the data to insert redundant data.

2.1 The Basic Idea

General idea TKBS of is based on encryption, decryption and Signature Verification Principle. In TKBS, data was encrypted into a divisible whole for protection. Getting identity information from trusted third party via KBS to find whether the next hop is trusted host or not. If it is trusted host, verification and summarization of previous offers are done. If it is not a trusted host offer collected according to security policies to resist colluded truncation attack.

When agent reaching a host, it concatenates the data generated on it with data carried by agent then encrypts them and verifying identity information. TKBS gets identity information from the trusted third party periodically. When agent comes back to host after completes its work without any attack.

2.2 Model Description

We descript TKBS through 5 stages.

1. Task sponsor S0 generates MA
2. MA migrates to host S1
3. MA migrates to host Si with help of TKBS
4. MA reaches Task sponsor
5. MA finds results at Task sponsor

In 5 stages , MA is a agent, who finishes the task through migration among hosts. KBS is a host which gives trust information to MA. With KBS information, MA chooses its next host.

2.2.1 Symbol Description

Table 1. Symbols used in system model

S_0	Mobile agent's task sponsor
S_i	The no.i host
MA	Mobile Agent, an mobile agent to finish the task
third party	third party
d_0	S_0's logo, generated by S_0
d_i	Data collected on host S; without encryption
D_i	Data produced by agent running on host S; with
H	Hash operation
(Pri,Pbi)	s private key and public key in pair
$Enc_{PbS0}(m)$	Encrypt message m using S_0's public key
$Sig_{pr}(m)$	Sign message musing S_i 's private key
$Dec_{PrS0}(m)$	Decrypt message m using S_0's private key
A->B: m	A sends message m to B

2.3 The Proposed Algorithm

1. S_0 generates Mobile agent MA

Task sponsor (initiator) is S_0, who generates MA. S_0's logo is d_0. S_0 determines its next hop S_1 according to current network environment and counts:

$D_0 = Enc_{pbS0} (S_0 \| S_1 \| d_0 \| Sig_{pr0} (d_0))$

S_0 uses its private key to sign on d0, which then be encrypted to form D0.

$h_0 = H (S_0 \| S_1 \| d_0 \| Sig_{pr0}(d_0))$
$D_0' = D_0 \| h_0$
TA migrates to S_1 with D_0'.
$S_0 \rightarrow S_1 = D_0'$

2. MA migrates to host S_i

When reaches host S_i with data D_{i-1}, MA generates original data d_i through computation on host Si then chooses its next hop S_{i+1} according to current environment. S_i signs on d_i with its private key, concatenate d_i. S_i, S_{i+1} and D_{i-1} to form:

$D_i = Enc_{pbS0} (S_i \| S_{i+1} \| d_i \| Sig_{pri} (d_l) \| D_{i--1}')$

Then compute Hash value:

$h_i = H(S_i \| S_{i+1} \| d_i \| Sig_{prl}(d_i) \| D_{i-1}')$
$D_i' = D_i \| h_i$

MA migrates to next hop with encrypted data D_i':

$Si \rightarrow S_{i+1}: D_i'$

Meanwhile, Si sends its identity information to task initiator S_0:

$Si \rightarrow SA: Enc_{pbS0} (Sig_{pri} (S_i) \| S_i)$

S_0 can obtain Si's identity through decryption and certificating signing when receives data above:

$Dec_{prSA} (Enc_{pbSA} (Sig_{prl} (S_i) \| S_i))$

3. MA migrates to Trust host Si

We assume that MA to migrates to Trust host Si after passing through n hosts. In trust host agent has two works.

1. Verify and collect all the previous host's data
2. Current host data collection

To verify, MA needs S0 's private key . So that trust host gives request to S_0, And gets its private key .Now MA is carrying with data D_n'.

$D_n' = D_n \| h_n$.

$D_n \| h_n = Enc_{pbSA}(S_n \| SA \| d_n \| Sig_{prn}(d_n) \| D_{n-1}) \| H(S_n \| SA \| d_n \| Sig_{pm}(dn) \| D_{n-1})$

$= \ldots$

In trust host MA retrieves D_n and h_n through D_n'. MA decrypts D_n using its private key. Operate hash function on decryption result, then compare hash value with h_n. If they are same to each other, we can be sure that data has not been damaged on host

S_n. Then MA decrypt D_{n-1}, continue to this proceed. If hash value is different from corresponding h_i, that is to say, data has been damaged. After finishing the decryption, MA can obtain data collection data and address collection add1.

$$data = \{d_0, d_1 \ldots d_n\}$$
$$add1 = \{S_1, S_2 \ldots S_n\}$$

After steps above, if all the data has not been illegally modified through verify, MA encrypts original data and sends them to S_0, otherwise sends information to show damage .

We use 1 bit to express data received by MA is reliable or not. Bit 1 represents success (data received by S_0 is correct), 0 means failure (data received by S_0 has been damaged). Sending information as below when data has been transmitted correctly:

$$S_i \rightarrow S_0: Enc_{pb0} (1 \| Sig_{prsi} (S_i) \| d_i \| d_2 \| \cdots \| d_n)$$

Sending information as below when data has been damaged:

$$S_i \rightarrow S_0: Enc_{pbo} (0 \| Sig_{prSi} (S_i) \| S_j \| \ldots \| S_j)$$

Si...., Sj; are malicious hosts judged by S_0.

When receiving Trust host Si's data, agent sponsor decrypts the data with its private key then decide what the results mean according to the one bit 1 or 0.

Trust host S_i determines its next hop S_{i+1} according to current network environment, and counts similar at S_0:

$$D_i = EncpbSi (Si \| S_{i+1} \| d_i \| Sig_{pri} (d_i))$$

That is to say, Si uses its private key to sign on d, which then be encrypted to form D_i. Then count:

$$h_i = H(S_i \| S_{i+1} \| d_i \| Sig_{pri}(d_i))$$
$$D_i' = D_i \| h_i$$

TA migrates to S_i with D_i'.

$$S_i \rightarrow S_{i+1} = D_i'$$

4 MA returns to Task Sponsor S_0

We assume that MA returns to task sponsor after passing through n hosts. Now MA is carrying with data D_n'.

$$D_n' = D_n \| h_n. = Enc_{pbSA}(S_n \| S_{n-1} \| d_n \| Sig_{prn}(d_n) \| D_{n-1}) \| H(S_n \| S_{n-1} \| d_n \| Sig_{pm}(dn) \| D_{n-1}) = \ldots$$

MA retrieves D_n and h_n through D_n'. MA decrypts D_n using its private key. Operate hash function on decryption result, and then compare hash value with h_n. If they are same to each other, we can be sure that data has not been damaged on host S_n.

Then MA decrypt D_{n-1}, continue to this proceed. If hash value is different from corresponding h_i, that is to say, data has been damaged. After finishing the decryption, SA can obtain data collection data and address collection add1

$data = \{d_o, d1 \ldots d_n\}$
$add1 = \{S_1, S2 \ldots Sn\}$

Meanwhile, S_0 receives identity information from hosts agent passed:

$Enc_{pbSA}(Sig_{prl}(S_1) \| S_1)$, $Enc_{pbSA}(Sig_{pr2}(S_2) \| S_2)$,... $Enc_{pbSA}(Sig_{pm}(S_n) \| S_n)$

Through decryption and certificate signing on data above,S_0 can obtain address collection add2:

$add2 = \{S_1, S_2, \ldots S_i \ \ldots S_n\}$

If add2 is the same as add1, damage has not occurred, otherwise data has been damaged.

5 MA Finds Final Result at S_0

After steps above, if all the data has not been illegally modified through verify, MA encrypts original data and sends them to S_0, otherwise sends information to show damage.

We use 1 bit to express data received by MA is reliable or not. Bit 1 represents success (data received by S_0 is correct), 0 means failure (data received by S_0 has been damaged). Sending information as below when data has been transmitted correctly:

S_0: $Enc_{pb0}(1 \| Sig_{prsi}(S_i) \| d_i \| d_2 \| \cdots \| d_n)$

Sending information as below when data has been damaged:

S_0: $Enc_{pbo}(0 \| Sig_{prSi}(S_i) \| S_j \| \ldots \| S_j)$

Si. ... ,Sj; are malicious hosts judged by SA.

When receiving S_i's data, agent sponsor decrypts the data with its private key then decide what the results mean according to the one bit 1 or 0.

3 Explanation and Analysis

3.1 Realization of Trusted Third Party (KBS)

As mentioned above, KBS is the main factor of success. There are many methods of choosing n trust host. For example, analysis and improvement on a secure threshold group signature scheme, which can resist colluded attack and forge signature attack; Reference [9] designed and realized a trusted computer program based on embedded way. The program embeds ESM (Embedded Security Module) on General-purpose computer motherboard to achieve more complete security architecture.

3.2 Efficiency of TKBS

We assume there are n hosts those agents passing through in TKBS. It will need 2n+2 encryptions (include signature) and 2n+2 decryptions (include signature verification).

The efficiency of encryption and decryption times is O(n) if no single Trust host is not exit. If n trust nodes are avail, we need less than 2n+2 encryptions and decryptions. The efficiency of encryption and decryption times is less O (n) if n trust host is available in a chain.

4 Security Analysis

We analyze security of TKBS as below:

- General security analysis

(a) Data confidentiality: data D_i' carried by agent passing through host Si is encrypted in S_0's Public Key, So only S_0 can decrypt Di' in its private key to get original data. S_0 can obtain the original data by Trust host $S_{i.}$ However, other hosts in agent's migration can only know original data generated by it because of lacking S0's private key.

(b) Non-repudiation: host S_i uses its private key to sign on original data d_i generated on it, that is $Sig_{pri}(S_i)$,these signature information will be certified on S_i. So other hosts cannot deny data generated on it.

(c) Anonymity: in data D_i, any information about identity is encrypted in S_0's public key, so only S_0 can obtain hosts' identity through decryption. Other hosts cannot know which host MA has passed except its last hop, Trust host and next hop. Similarly, other hosts don't know the task sponsor S_0

(d) Integrity: if a malicious host S_{k+i} modifies data D_{k-1}' carried by MA, S_0or trust host can testify whether the data was damaged or not because the data has been encrypted in S_0's public key. When the data returns to S0, S0 can retrieve $D_{k-1}$and h_{k-1} through decryption. If D_{k-1} and h_{k-1} is different, that shows attack has happened.

5 Conclusion

To resolve the problem of mobile agent's security, especial on attacks on mobile agent data, paper analyzed current protection mechanism and put forward KBS to enforce its security., The analysis shows that TKBS can protect data of free roaming mobile agent effectively and realize some security needs such as data confidentiality, integrity, and anonymity.

Acknowledgment

I wish to express my sincere gratitude to my beloved Panel member **Dr.A.Kannan,** Professor, Computer Science &Engineering ,Anna University Chennai and **Dr.N.Sreenath ,**Professor Computer Science &Engineering ,Pondicherry University, Chennai for providing an opportunity and extending his timely assistance.

I am very much indebted to **Dr.P.Narayanasamy**, Director, Anna university of Technology, Chennai for extending his timely assistance and kind co-operation for this Work.

I take immense pleasure in expressing my sincere gratitude to **Dr.C.Jayakumar ,** Professor, Department of Computer Science & Engineering ,RMK Engineering college ,Kavarai Pettai,Chennai for his constant encouragement, valuable guidance and personal support during the work period, without which this work would not have attained completion.

Finally, I would like to express my sincere thanks to **my Family** without whom this work would not have been completed successfully.

References

1. Hacini, S., Guessoum, Z., Boufaida, Z.: TAMAP: a new trust-based approach for mobile agent protection. Journal of Compute Viro 1 3, 267–283 (2007)
2. Yao, M., Foo, E., Dawson, E.P., Pengo, K.: An Improved Forward integrity Protocol for Mobile Agents. In: Chae, K.-J., Yung, M. (eds.) WISA 2003. LNCS, vol. 2908, pp. 272–285. Springer, Heidelberg (2004)
3. Xu, D., Ham, L., NarasimhanAn, M., Junzhou, L.: Improved Free-Roaming Mobile Agent Security Protocol again Colluded Truncation Attacks. In: Proceedings of the 30th Annual (COMPSAC 2006), vol. 2, pp. 309–314. IEEE Computer Society, Los Alamitos (2006)
4. Jiang, Y.c., Xia, Z.Y., Zhong, Y.P., Zhang, S.Y.: Defend mobile agent against malicious hosts in migration itineraries. Microprocessors And Microsystems 28, 531–546 (2004)
5. Green, S., Hurst, L.: Software Agents: A Review. Trinity College Dublin Broadcom Eireanm Research Ltd., (I997)
6. Yunyong, Z., Jinde, L.: Mobile agent technology. Tsinghua University Press, Beijing (2003)
7. Balfe, S., Gailery, E.: Mobile Agents and the Deus Ex Machina 21st International Conference on Advanced Information Networking and Applications Workshops (AINAW 2007), pp. 486–492 (2007)
8. Shuiqing, W., Guocai, W., Jian, Y.: Analysis and improvement on Secure thresholdgroup signature scheme. Computer Engineering And Applications 44(26), 113–115 (2008)
9. Jing, X., Chao, Y.: Design and Implementation of a Trusted Computer System. Journal of Wuhan University of Technology 29(7), 1671–4431 (2007)
10. Silva, F., Popsecu-Zeletin, R.: mobile agent-based transaction In open environments. IEICE/IEEE JOINT Special Issue Autonomous De-centralized Systems E83-B(5), 973–987 (2000)
11. Breugst, M., Busses, I., Covaci, S., Magdanz, T.: Grasshopper- A Mobile agent platform for IN based service environments. In: Proc. IEEE Intelligent Networks Workshop, Bordeaux, France, pp. 279–290 (May 1998)
12. Eiter, T., Erdem, E., Faber, W.: Plan reversals for recovery in Execution monitoring. In: Non-monitoring Reasoning (2004)
13. Fedoruk, A., Deters, R.: Improving fault-tolerance by Replicating Agents. In: AAMAS 2002, pp. 737–744. ACM Press, New York (2002)
14. Morley, D., Myers, K.: The SPARK agent framework. In: AAMAS 2004, NY (2004H)

15. Pears, S., Xu, J., Boldyreff, C.: Mobile agent fault tolerance for information retrieval application: An exception handling Approach. In: The Sixth international Symposium on Autonomous Decentralized Systems (2003)
16. Unrh, A., Harjadi, H., Bailey, J.: Semantic-Compensation-Based recovery in Multi-Agent Systems. In: IEEE (2005)

G. Geetha received her B.E computer science and engineering from Bharathiar University and her M.E computer science from sathayabama university .Now she is working as Assistant professor in Jerusalem College of Engineering, Chennai, and doing research in Anna University Chennai

Professor **C. Jayakumar** received his M.E computer Science and PhD from Anna University Chennai. Now he is working as Professor in CSE, RMK Engineering College Chennai.

End-to-End Security for At-Home Medical Monitoring

Mohanavalli Seetha Subramanian[1] and Sheila Anand[2]

[1] Tagore Engineering College, Chennai, India
[2] Rajalakshmi Engineering College, Chennai, India
{ssmvalli,sheila.anand}@gmail.com

Abstract. Body Sensor Networks have helped to achieve continuous remote monitoring of the physiological parameters of patients without the need for hospitalization. However the confidentiality and integrity of the medical data that is sensed, collected and transmitted to the remote hospital server has to be ensured in order to protect patient privacy. This paper proposes an end-to-end security mechanism for the At-Home architecture used for monitoring patients in the comforts of their home. Biometrics and cryptography are combined to provide data confidentiality and patient authentication.

Keywords: Biometric, fingerprint, key generation, end-to-end security, medical data, confidentiality, authentication.

1 Introduction

Body Sensor Network (BSN) provides a workable solution towards continuous monitoring of critical vital signs to determine the state of health of patients. [1]. Patients requiring post-operative care or geriatric care can receive proper medical care without the need and expense of hospitalization, by remotely monitoring their physiological parameters within their home environment.

Such sensitive medical information must be secured against unauthorized access and fraudulent use. Securing the sensor data poses several challenges such as the well-known threats that are natural to wireless communication and the minimal available resources inherent to the sensors that limit the processing, computational, memory and communication capability of the sensors. Therefore there is a need to guarantee the privacy and confidentiality of the patient's medical information.

In our earlier work, we had proposed security architecture for monitoring patients in their home environment. [2]. The persons to be monitored would be fitted with multiple sensors to measure the body parameters like ECG, oxygen saturation, body temperature etc. The patient is equipped with a Wearable Data Acquisition Unit (WDAU) that collects the sensed data and transmits to a base station at home. The base station would then transmit the patient data to the remote Hospital Monitoring Station (HMS) for processing, analysis and appropriate care by medical professionals. We had also proposed a cryptographic solution to secure the data transferred within the confines of the home.

This paper extends the previous work to provide end-to-end security for data transferred between WDAU and HMS. The proposed solution combines the

D.C. Wyld et al. (Eds.): CNSA 2011, CCIS 196, pp. 483–488, 2011.

advantages of both biometrics and cryptography to provide patient authentication and data confidentiality. Section 2 discusses related work pertaining to the use of biometrics for medical data security. Section 3 deals with proposed solution, the choice of biometrics and how it is used to provide confidentiality of data and patient authentication, section 4 concludes the paper.

2 Related Work

Biometrics is based on physiological parameters measured or the behavioral characteristics of the individual [3]. Biometric recognition forms a strong link between a person and their identity, because biometric traits cannot be shared, lost, or easily duplicated and hence is considered superior and more resistant to attacks than the conventional methods of recognition. This section discusses some of the work done in securing communication of patient medical data and patient authentication using biometrics.

Much work has been done towards using biometrics for secure cryptographic key distribution among the sensor nodes forming the BSN. Cherukuri et al [4] have suggested the use of physiological parameters, like blood glucose, blood pressure etc. for securely distributing a crypto key. They propose a system to encrypt the symmetric key using a key (K_{commit}) derived from a biometric trait. The receiving node measures the same biometric trait, derives (K_{commit}) and decrypts to obtain the symmetric key. C.Y.Poon et al [5] propose the use of inter pulse interval (IPI) to provide a higher level of entropy and a greater degree of randomness to protect against invaders guessing the coded trait. However, the same biometric trait measured at different parts of the body at the same time would vary. Cherukuri et al have employed a fuzzy commitment scheme to adjust for the errors in the measured values [4].

Bui and Hatzinakos [6] propose the use of physiological measurements for resource-efficient key management towards secure key distribution within a BSN. It assumes that the cryptographic key is generated independent of biometrics. Instead of sending the entire key, a check code alone is transmitted. The receiving node regenerates the key with the locally measured biometric and verifies it using the check code. They have also suggested a novel data scrambling method to secure data transmitted within a BSN.

G.H.Zhang et al [7] in their paper propose a solution for generation of cryptographic key using biometric traits for use in telemedicine systems. They discuss a method to generate three keys which are to be used for secure data transmission between the sensors forming the BSN, between BSN and server and between server and physicians in telemedicine systems. This paper assumes that the physiological data used to generate the keys, is already available and is not measured real-time.

Malasri and Wang [8] propose a Sensor Network for Assessment of Patients (SNAP) architecture which deals with key exchange, patient authentication and a query mechanism for accessing the patient medical data. A mote that contains a finger print scanner or a finger vein scanner captures the unique signature of the patient and transmits the signature to the base station. The base station validates the signature by comparing with a stored database of valid patient signatures. However, since the patient signature is not encrypted, it can be prone to eavesdropping and attack by malicious persons.

G.H.Zhang et al [9], propose a method to secure the communication between intra BSN nodes and between BSN and the remote server using the key generated from heart rate, ECG or PPG of the patient.

Sarier [10] proposes a model for multi-factor user authentication wherein biometric template extraction method of bipartite biotokens is used to transform and separate into stable and non stable parts of the biometric. The stable part is encrypted using the public key of the user and stored in the authenticating server. Authentication of the user is done using the smart card that stores in plaintext the non stable part of the biometric. The private key of the user is however not needed by the server as the authentication decision is made in the encrypted domain. The advantage of this system is that the compromise of the secret key does not affect the security of authentication. However, this paper assumes that the attacker does not have simultaneous access to both the sensor and smart card of the user.

Zhang et al. [11] propose a method to generate keys from measured physiological signals. They also discuss a method to generate an authentication key from the patient's fingerprint.

In this paper, we present an approach that combines biometrics and cryptography for encryption of the medical data transmitted from the patients at home to the server which could also be used for remote patient authentication by server.

3 Proposed Solution

In our earlier work [2], we had proposed a security architecture for at-home monitoring of aged persons and patients requiring continuous monitoring. The security architecture is replicated is Figure 1.

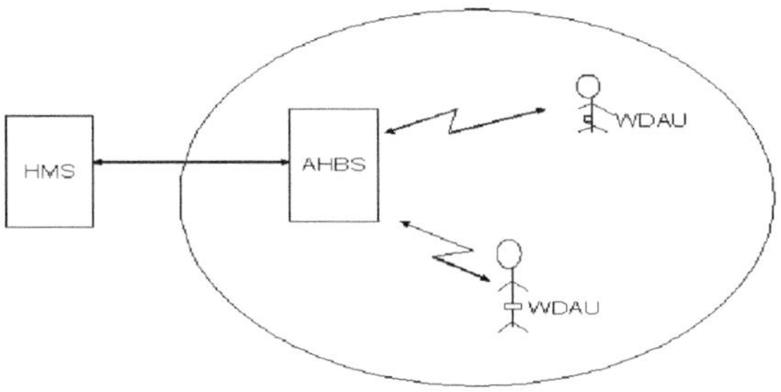

Fig. 1. At-Home Architecture

The patients to be monitored would be fitted with multiple sensors to measure their physiological parameters and a Wearable Data Acquisition Unit (WDAU) to collect the values recorded by the sensors. WDAU aggregates the data and sends it to At-Home Base Station (AHBS) using wireless communication. AHBS would then transmit the patient data to the Hospital Monitoring Station (HMS) for processing and follow-up by the medical professionals. We had also given a solution for securing the wireless transmission of patient medical data between WDAU and AHBS.

This paper is a continuation of the previous work and addresses security between WDAU and the remote server. AHBS will forward the encrypted data packets sent by WDAU and the same will be decrypted by HMS. Medical data will not be transmitted or stored in plaintext either in WDAU or AHBS.

While various features of the individual can be used for authentication, we have suggested the use of fingerprints as being more effective and less intrusive for the patients. Fingerprints have been used for personal identification for many decades. The accuracy of the fingerprint recognition systems is adequate for authentication in systems where there are only a few hundred users [12]. It is also a popular and an acceptable method for asserting an individual's identity.

When the patient is first issued the WDAU device at the hospital, the fingerprint is recorded using a fingerprint sensor and stored in HMS. Each patient is equipped with a WDAU that also has a fingerprint sensor, which is used to generate a cryptographic key that is used to encrypt data sent by WDAU to HMS. HMS will derive the key from the stored fingerprint to decrypt the data. Since this key is derived from a biometric trait unique to the patient it can also serve to authenticate the patient.

A hash function is applied to the fingerprint to generate the cryptographic key $K_{enc.}$ The fingerprint data of the patient is constant and hence the hash function would always produce the same key. We propose the use of an Initialization Vector (IV) to ensure that a random key is generated from the constant fingerprint data. If the key were to be compromised, it would be possible to generate and use a different key for encrypting the medical data. The block diagram for key generation is given in Figure 2.

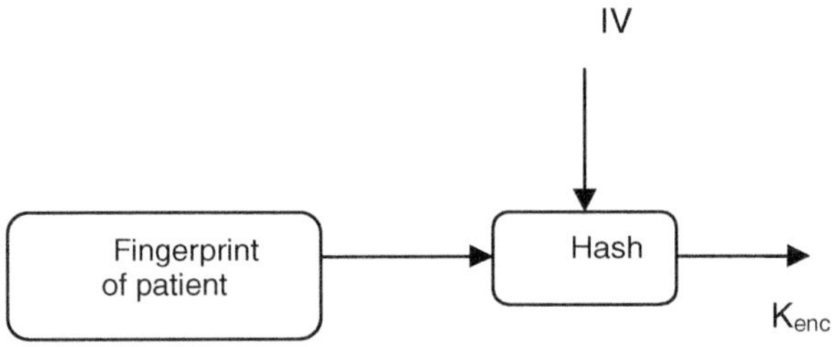

Fig. 2. Key Generation using Fingerprint

The patient fingerprint is captured using the fingerprint scanner in WDAU. The fingerprint image would be converted into a binary matrix and used by the one-way hash function to generate the cryptographic key K_{enc} . This key is used to encrypt all medical data transmissions from WDAU to HMS. At the receiving end, HMS would generate K_{enc} using IV and the stored fingerprint of the patient. K_{enc} is used to decrypt the data sent by WDAU. The IV can be generated by HMS or WDAU and exchanged using the well known Diffie–Hellman exchange.

The hash of these fingerprints was determined using SHA-1 hash algorithm. An initialization vector (IV) was used to randomize the hash value and obtain a different key from the same fingerprint data.

The data transmitted between WDAU and HMS is secured in two layers. First the medical data is encrypted at WDAU using K_{enc}. This encrypted data is once again encrypted using a secret key shared between WDAU and AHBS. As the transmission of data between AHBS and HMS is in the public domain and there is no scarcity of resources at AHBS or HMS, conventional public and private key pairs can be used to provide secure transmission between AHBS and HMS.

It should be noted that in the proposed solution, the fingerprint data is never stored either at WDAU or AHBS. The fingerprint is captured from the patient whenever a new key is to be generated. Further at AHBS, the patient medical data is present only in encrypted form and not in clear text and the key for decrypting the medical data is also not stored / available at AHBS.

To further enhance the security, we recommend the key be changed once every 12 hours. The fingerprint would be collected from the patient once every 12 hours which would also serve to authenticate the patient at regular intervals. If HMS suspects that the key has been compromised then it can initiate a new key generation.

4 Conclusion

Our proposed solution provides end-to-end security for the patient's medical data. Three keys shared between WDAU, AHBS and HMS provides two layers of security, guaranteeing confidentiality and integrity of the physiological data measured from the patients. To completely compromise the system all the three keys need to be known to the attacker. The security is further enhanced by generating a new key at periodic intervals. The proposed security architecture provides a robust solution against malicious attacks both at home and in the public domain.

References

1. Falck, T., Espina, J., Ebert, J.-P., Waterman, D.D.: BASUMA - The sixth sense for chronically ill patients. In: International Workshop on Wearable and Implantable Body Sensor Networks (2006)
2. Mohanavalli, S.S., Anand, S.: Security Architecture for At-Home Care using Sensor Network, In: International Conference on Sensor Networks, Information and Ubiquitous Computing, Singapore (March 2010). Foster, I., Kesselman, C.: The Grid: Blueprint for a New Computing Infrastructure. Morgan Kaufmann, San Francisco (1999)
3. Matyas, V., Riha, Z.: Security of biometric authentication systems Grid. IEEE, Los Alamitos (2010)
4. Cherukuri, S., Venkatasubramanian, K., Sandeep, Gupta, K.S.: BioSec: A Biometric based Approach for Securing Communication in Wireless Networks of Biosensors Implanted in the Human Body. In: International Conference on Parallel Processing Workshops (2003)
5. Poon, C.Y., Zhang, Y.-T.: A Novel Biometric Method to Secure Wireless Body Area Sensor Networks for Telemedicine and M-Health. IEEE Communications Magazine (2006)
6. Bui, F.M., Hatzinakos, D.: Biometric methods for secure communications in body sensor networks: resource-efficient key management and signal-level data scrambling. EURASIP Journal on Advances in Signal Processing (2008)

7. Zhang, G.H., Poon, C.Y., Li, Y., Zhang, Y.T.: A biometric method to secure telemedicine systems. In: Proceedings of 31st Annual International Conference of IEEE EMBS (2009)
8. Malasri, K., Wang, L.: Addressing Security in Medical Sensor Networks. In: Proceedings of HealthNet (2007)
9. Zhang, G.H., Poon, C.C.Y., Li, Y., Zhang, Y.T.: A biometric method to secure telemedicine systems. In: Proceedings of Annual International Conference of IEEE EMBS (2006)
10. Sarier, N.D.: Practical multi-factor biometric remote authentication. IEEE, Los Alamitos (2010)
11. Zhang, G.H., Poon, C.Y., Zhang, Y.T.: A Biometric based security solution for encryption and authentication in tele- healthcare systems. IEEE, Los Alamitos (2009)
12. Jain, A.K., Ross, A., Pankanti, S.: BIOMETRICS: A Tool for Information Security. IEEE Transactions on Information Forensics and Security 1(2) (2006)

Web Mining Research and Future Directions

G. Dileep Kumar and Manohar Gosul

Department of Computer Science & Engineering, SR Engineering College, Warangal
dileep.gdk@gmail.com, manohar_gosul@rediffmail.com

Abstract. Web is a collection of inter-related files on one or more Web servers. Web mining is one of the mining technologies, which applies data mining techniques in large amount of web data to improve the web services. Wide Web provides every internet citizen with access to an abundance of information, but it becomes increasingly difficult to identify the relevant pieces of information. Research in web mining tries to address this problem by applying techniques from data mining and machine learning to Web data and documents. The Web Mining is an application of Data Mining. Without the internet, life would have been almost impossible. The data available on the web is so voluminous and heterogeneous that it becomes an essential factor to mine this available data to make it presentable, useful, and pertinent to a particular problem. Web mining deals with extracting these interesting patterns and developing useful abstracts from diversified sources. The present paper deals with a preliminary discussion of WEB mining, few key computer science contributions in the field of web mining and outlines some promising areas of future research.

Keywords: Web mining, content mining, structure mining, usage mining, Hubs, attributes, page ranks.

1 Introduction

With the explosive growth of information sources available on the World Wide Web it has become increasingly necessary for users to utilize automated tools in order to find, extract, filter, and evaluate the desired information and resources. Two different approaches were taken in initially defining Web mining. First was a 'process-centric view', which defined Web mining as a sequence of tasks. Second was a 'data-centric view', which defined Web mining in terms of the types of Web data that was being used in the mining process. In this paper we follow the data-centric view, and refine the definition of Web mining as, Web mining is the application of data mining techniques to extract knowledge from Web data, where at least one of the structures (hyperlink) or the usage (Web log) data is used in the mining process (with or without other types of Web data). Web mining is a new research issue under dispute which draws great interest from many communities. Currently, there is no agreement about Web mining yet. It needs more discussion among researchers in order to define what it is exactly. In this paper we present a preliminary discussion about Web mining and future directions.

D.C. Wyld et al. (Eds.): CNSA 2011, CCIS 196, pp. 489–496, 2011.

2 Web Mining Taxonomy

Web Mining can be broadly divided into three distinct categories, according to the kinds of data to be mined.

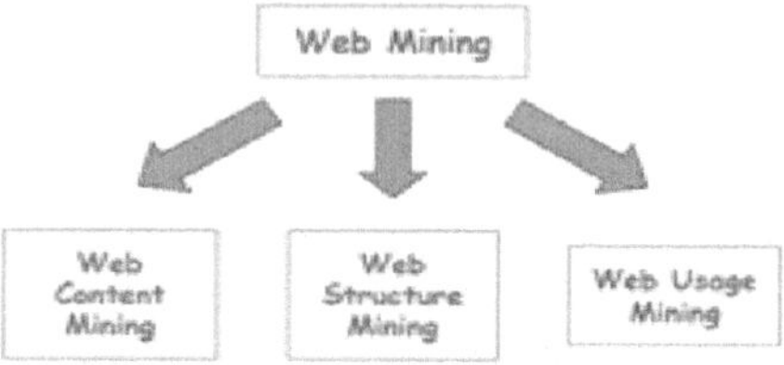

Fig. 1. Classification of web mining

2.1 Web Content Mining

Web Content Mining is the process of extracting useful information from the contents of Web documents. It may consist of text, images, audio, video, or structured records such as lists and tables. Research activities in this field also involve using techniques from other disciplines such as Information Retrieval (IR) and Natural Language Processing (NLP). While there exists a significant body of work in extracting knowledge from images - in the fields of image processing and computer vision - the application of these techniques to Web content mining has not been very rapid. The primary Web resources that are mined in Web content mining are individual pages.

2.2 Web Structure Mining

Web structure mining usually operates on the hyperlink structure of Web pages. Mining focuses on sets of pages, ranging from a single Web site to the Web as a whole. Web structure mining exploits the additional information that is (often implicitly) contained in the structure of hypertext. Therefore, an important application area is the identification of the relative relevance of different pages that appear equally pertinent when analyzed with respect to their content in isolation. For example, hyperlink-induced topic search analyzes hyperlink topology by discovering authoritative information sources for a broad search topic. This information is found in authority pages, which are defined in relation to hubs: Hubs are pages that link to any related authorities. Similarly, the search engine Google17 owes its success to the PageRank algorithm, which states that the relevance of a page increases with the number of hyperlinks to it from other pages, and in particular from other relevant pages. The structure of a typical Web graph consists of Web pages as nodes, and hyperlinks as edges connecting between two related pages.

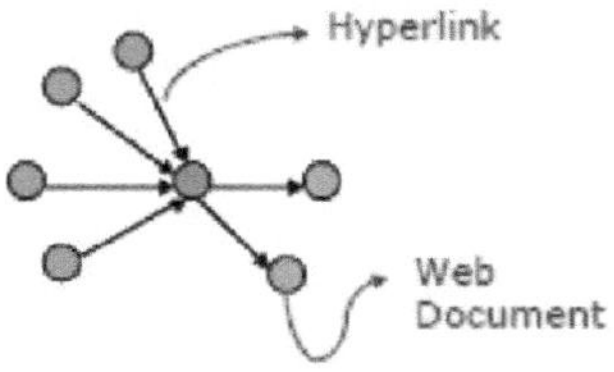

Fig. 2. Web Graph Structure

2.3 Web Usage Mining

Web Usage Mining is the application of data mining techniques to discover interesting usage patterns from Web data, in order to understand and better serve the needs of Web-based applications. Usage data captures the identity or origin of Web users along with their browsing behavior at a Web site Web Usage mining results from user interactions with a Web server, including Web logs, click streams and database transaction at a Web site or a group of related sites. Web usage mining introduces privacy concern and is currently the topic of extensive debate.

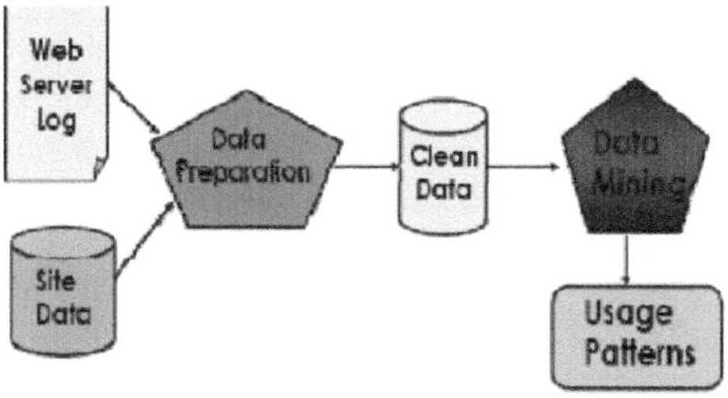

Fig. 3. Web Usage Mining process

3 Key Accomplishments

This section briefly describes the key new concepts introduced by the Web mining research community.

3.1 Page Ranking Metrics

Page Rank is a metric for ranking hypertext documents that determines the quality of these documents. The key idea is that a page has high rank if it is pointed to by many highly ranked pages. So the rank of a page depends upon the ranks of the pages pointing to it. This process is done iteratively till the rank of all the pages is determined.

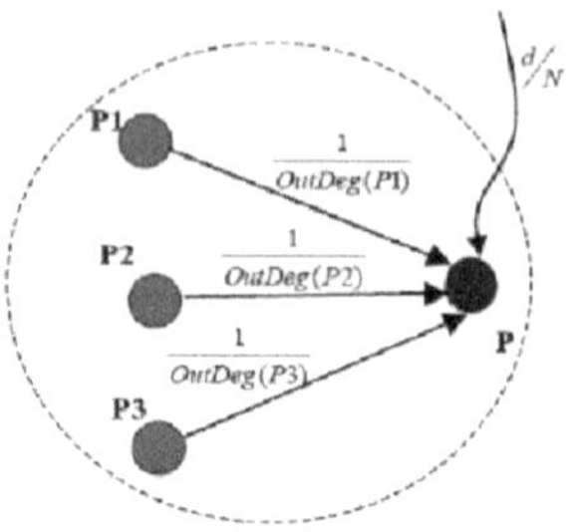

Fig. 4. Example for Page Rank

The rank of a page p can thus be written as:

$$PR(p) = d/n + (1-d) \sum_{(q,p)\in G} \left(\frac{PR(q)}{Outdegree(q)}\right)$$

Here, n is the number of nodes in the graph and OutDegree(q) is the number of hyperlinks on page q. Intuitively, the approach can be viewed as a stochastic analysis of a random walk on the Web graph. The first term in the right hand side of the equation corresponds to the probability that a random Web surfer arrives at a page p out of nowhere, i.e. (s)he could arrive at the page by typing the URL or from a bookmark, or may have a particular page as his/her homepage. d would then be the probability that a random surfer chooses a URL directly - i.e. typing it, using the bookmark list, or by default - rather than traversing a link1 . Finally, 1/n corresponds to the uniform probability that a person chooses the page p from the complete set of n pages on the Web. The second term in the right hand side of the equation corresponds to factor contributed by arriving at a page by traversing a link. 1- d is the probability that a person arrives at the page p by traversing a link. The summation corresponds to the sum of the rank contributions made by all the pages that point to the page p. The rank contribution is the PageRank of the page multiplied by the probability that a particular link on the page is traversed. So for any page q pointing to page p, the probability that the link pointing to page p is traversed would be 1/Outdegree(q), assuming all links on the page is chosen with uniform probability.

The PageRank Algorithm

```
Set PR ← [r1, r2, …..rN], where ri is some initial rank
of page I, and N the number of Web pages in the graph;
d ←0.15; D←[1/N…….1/N]T;
A is the adjacency matrix as described above;
do
PR i+1←AT*PRi;
PR i+1← (1-d)*PRi+1+ d*D; δ←|| PR i+1-PRi ||1
while δ< ε, where ε is a small number indicating the
convergence threshold return PR.
```

3.2 Hubs and Authorities

Hyperlink-induced topic search (HITS) is an iterative algorithm for mining the Web graph to identify topic hubs and authorities. "Authorities" are highly ranked pages for a given topic; "hubs" are pages with links to authorities. The algorithm takes as input, search results returned by traditional text indexing techniques, and filters these results to identify hubs and authorities. The number and weight of hubs pointing to a page determine the page's authority. The algorithm assigns weight to a hub based on the authoritativeness of the pages it points to. For example, a page containing links to all authoritative news servers (CNN, CNBC, and so on) is a powerful news hub.

3.3 Robot Detection and Filtering - Separating Human and Non Human Web Behavior

Web robots are software programs that automatically traverse the hyperlink structure of the World Wide Web in order to locate and retrieve information.

First of all, e-commerce retailers are particularly concerned about the unauthorized deployment of robots for gathering business intelligence at their Web sites. In addition, Web robots tend to consume considerable network bandwidth at the expense of other users. Sessions due to Web robots also make it more difficult to perform click-stream analysis effectively on the Web data. Conventional techniques for detecting Web robots are often based on identifying the IP address and the user agent of the Web clients. While these techniques are applicable to many well-known robots, they may not be sufficient to detect camouflaging and previously unknown robots. Experimental results have shown that highly accurate classification models can be built using this approach.

3.3.1 Information scent - Applying Foraging Theory to Browsing Behavior

Information scent is a concept that uses the snippets and information presented around the links in a page as a "scent" to evaluate the quality of content of the page it points to and the cost to access such a page. The key idea is a user at a given page "foraging" for information would follow a link with a stronger "scent". The "scent" of the pages will decrease along a path and is determined by network flow algorithm called spreading activation. The snippets, graphics, and other information around a link are referred as "proximal cues". The user's desired information is expressed as a weighted keyword vector. The similarity between the proximal cues and the user's information need is computed as "Proximal Scent". With the proximal cues from all the links and the user's information need vector a "Proximal Scent Matrix" is generated. Each element in the matrix reflects the extent of similarity between the link's proximal cues and the user's information need. If enough information is not available around the link, a "Distal Scent" is computed with the information about the link described by the contents of the pages it points to. The "Proximal Scent" and the "Distal Scent" are then combined to give the "Scent" Matrix. The probability that a user would follow a link is decided by the "scent" or the value of the element in the " Scent" matrix. Figure 3.3(c) depicts a high level view of this model. Chi et al [CPCP2001] proposed two new algorithms called Web User Flow by Information Scent (WUFIS) and Inferring User Need by Information Scent (IUNIS) using the theory of information scent based on Information foraging concepts. WUFIS tends to predict user actions based on user needs and IUNIS infers user needs based on user actions.

4 Future Directions

As the Web and its usage grows, it will continue to generate ever more content, structure, and usage data, and the value of Web mining will keep increasing. Outlined here are some research directions that must be pursued to ensure that we continue to develop Web mining technologies that will enable this value to be realized.

4.1 Web Metrics & Measurements

From an experimental human behaviorist's viewpoint, the Web is the perfect experimental apparatus. Not only does it provide the ability of measuring human behavior at a micro level, it (i) eliminates the bias of the subjects knowing that they are participating in an experiment, and (ii) allows the number of participants to be many orders of magnitude larger. However, we have not even begun to appreciate the true impact of a revolutionary experimental apparatus. The Web Lab of Amazon is one of the early efforts in this direction. It is regularly used to measure the user impact of various proposed changes - on operational metrics such as site visits and visit/buy ratios, as well as on financial metrics such as revenue and profit - before a deployment decision is made. Research needs to be done in developing the right set of Web metrics, and their measurement procedures, so that various Web phenomena can be studied.

4.2 Process Mining

Mining of 'market basket' data, collected at the point-of-sale in any store, has been one of the visible successes of data mining. However, this data provides only the end result of the process, and that too decisions that ended up in product purchase. Click-stream data provides the opportunity for a detailed look at the decision making process itself, and knowledge extracted from it can be used for optimizing the process, influencing the process, etc. Underhill has conclusively proven the value of process information in understanding users' behavior in traditional shops. Research needs to be carried out in (i) extracting process models from usage data, (ii) understanding how different parts of the process model impact various Web metrics of interest, and (iii) how the process models change in response to various changes that are made – changing stimuli to the user.

4.3 Fraud and Threat Analysis

The anonymity provided by the Web has led to a significant increase in attempted frauds, from unauthorized use of individual credit cards to hacking into credit card database for blackmail purposes. Yet another example is auction fraud, which has been increasing on popular sites like eBay. Since all these frauds are being perpetrated through the Internet, Web mining is the perfect analysis technique for detecting and preventing them. Research issues include developing techniques to recognize known frauds, and characterize and then recognize unknown or novel frauds, etc.

5 Conclusion

As the Web and its usage continue to grow, so does the opportunity to analyze Web data and extract all manner of useful knowledge from it. The past five years has seen the emergence of Web mining as a rapidly growing area, due to the efforts of the research community as well as various organizations that are practicing. In this paper we have briefly described the key computer science contributions made in this field, the prominent successful applications, and outlined some promising areas of future research.

References

[1] Berners-Lee, T., Cailliau, R., Loutonen, A., Nielsen, H., Secret, A.: The World- Wide Web. Communications of the ACM 37(8), 76–82 (1994)

[2] Albert, R., Jeong, H., Barabasi, A.-L.: Diameter of the World-wide web. Nature 401, 130–131 (1999)

[3] Androutsopoulos, I., Paliouras, G., Michelakis, E.: Learning to filter unsolicited commercial e-mail. Technical Report NCSR Demokritos (March 2004)

[4] Berendt, B.: Using site semantics to analyze, visualize, and support navigation. Data Mining and Knowledge Discovery, 37–59 (2002)

[5] Berendt, B., Hotho, A., Stumme, G.: Towards semantic web mining. In: Horrocks, I., Hendler, I. (eds.) ISWC 2002. LNCS, vol. 2342, pp. 264–278. Springer, Heidelberg (2002)

[6] Srivastava, J., Mobasher, B.: Panel discussion on Web Mining: Hype or Reality? In: The 9th IEEE International Conference on Tools With Artificial Intelligence (ICTAI 1997), Newport Beach, CA (1997)

[7] Cooley, R., Mobasher, B., Srivastava, J.: Web Mining: Information and Pattern Discovery on the World Wide Web. In: Proceedings of the 9th IEEE International Conference on Tools With Artificial Intelligence (ICTAI 1997), Newport Beach, CA (1997)

[8] Kosala, R., Blockeel, H.: Web Mining Research: A Survey. SIGKDD Explorations 2(1) (July 2000)

[9] Desikan, P., Srivastava, J., Kumar, V., Tan, P.-N.: Hyperlink Analysis – Techniques & Applications. Army High Performance Computing Center Technical Report (2002)

[10] Moh, C.-H., Lim, E.-P., KeongNg, W.: DTDMiner: A Tool for Mining DTD from XML Documents. In: WECWIS 2000, pp. 144–151 (2000)

[11] Srivastava, J., Cooley, R., Deshpande, M., Tan, P.-N.: Web Usage Mining: Discovery and Applications of usage patterns from Web Data. SIGKDD Explorations, 1(2) (2000)

[12] Page, L., Brin, S., Motwaniand, R., Winograd, T.: The Page Rank Citation Ranking: Bringing Order to the Web. Stanford Digital Library Technologes, 1999-0120 (January 1998)

[13] Brin, S., Page, L.: The anatomy of a large-scale hypertextual Web search engine. In: The 7th International World Wide Web Conference, Brisbane, Australia (1998)

[14] Kohavi, R.: Mining E-Commerce Data: The Good, the Bad, the Ugly. Invited Industrial Presentation At The ACM SIGKDD Conference, San Francisco, CA (2001)
[15] Tan, P.-N., Kumar, V.: Discovery of Web Robot Sessions based on their Navigational Patterns. DMKD 6(1), 9–35 (2002)
[16] Masand, B., Spiliopoulou, M., Srivastava, J., Zaiane, O. (eds.): Proceedings of "WebKDD 2002 – Web Mining for Usage Patterns and User Profiles, Edmonton, CA (2002)
[17] Ford Jrand, L.R., Fulkerson, D.R.: Maximal Flow through a network. Canadian J. Math. 8, 399–404 (1956)

About the Authors

G .Dileep Kumar received the B.Tech degree in Computer Science & Engineering from JSN College of Engineering & Technology, Kaghaznagar, India and M.Tech degree in Software Engineering from Ramappa Engineering College, warangal, India. Currently he is an Assistant Professor in the department Computer Science & Engineering, SR Engineering College, Warangal, India. His research interests include Data mining, web mining and Mobile Adhoc Networks.

Manohar Gosul received the B.Tech degree in Computer Science & Engineering from Poojya Doddappa Appa Engineering College, Gulbarga, India and M.Tech degree in Computer Science & Engineering from Poojya Doddappa Appa Engineering College, Gulbarga, India. Currently he is an Associate Professor in the department Computer Science & Engineering, SR Engineering College, Warangal, India. His research interests include Data Mining, Advance Databases.

Difference between Intrusion Detection System (IDS) and Intrusion Prevention System (IPS)

Asmaa Shaker Ashoor[1] and Sharad Gore[2]

[1] Pune University, Department Computer Science, India
[2] Pune university, Department Statistics, India
asmaa_zaid218@yahoo.com, sdgore@stats.unipune.ernet.in

Abstract. This paper discusses difference between Intrusion Detection system and intrusion Prevention System (IDS/IPS) technology in computer networks. The differences between deployment of these system in networks in which IDS are out of band in system, means it cannot sit within the network path but IPS are in-line in the system, means it can pass through in between the devices.IDS generates only alerts if anomaly traffic passes in network traffic, it would be false positive or false negative, means IDS detects only malicious activities but no action taken on those activities but IPS has feature of detection and prevention with auto or manual action taken on those detected malicious activities like drop or block or terminate the connections. Here IDS and IPS systems stability, performance and accuracy wise result are comparing in this paper.

Keywords: IDS, IPS, threats, malicious activities, alerts.

1 Introduction

Intrusion is a set of actions aimed at compromising the basic network security goals like confidentiality, integrity, availability of a computing/networking resource.

Intrusion detection systems (IDS) are basically identifying intrusion threats, attacks and malicious activities in a network and generate alerts. The limitation of IDS is they cannot resolve network attacks; it passes in network for only watches network traffic like packet sniffing. The IDS are basically analyses the copied packets on the network segment for detecting attacks or attack has already taken place, this to alert network admin for what is happening in network.

Intrusion prevention system (IPS) is the process of both detecting intrusion activities or threats and managing responsive actions on those detected intrusions and threats throughout the network. IPS are monitoring real time packet traffic with malicious activities or which match specific profiles and will trigger the generation of alerts and it can drop, block that traffic in real time pass through in network. The mainly IPS counter measures is to stop an attack in progress.

"In simple terms, IDS may be perfectly suited for network attack monitoring and for alerting administrators of emerging threats. But its speed, performance and passive limitations have opened the door for IPS to challenge it as the proactive defense weapon of choice." *[http://www.infoworld.com/article/03/04/04/14ips-sb_1.html, April 04, 2003]*

D.C. Wyld et al. (Eds.): CNSA 2011, CCIS 196, pp. 497–501, 2011.

2 IDS and IPS Terms under Network Security

In network security the firewall serves main purpose of security but it allows network traffic on specified ports to either in or out of the network. The firewalls cannot do to detect this network traffic sent on a particular port or legitimate port or part of an intrusion attempts or attacks.

If, for example, allow remote access to an internal web server through allowing inbound access on TCP port 80, then an attacker could use this port to attack the Web server. In this case the IDS can distinguish traffic between the allowed connections to Web server or attempted attack to Web server by comparing the signature of the traffic to a database of known attack signatures. The IDS will notify such an attack enabling and generate alert for take appropriate action and IPS, on the other hand, take action on that detected attacked connections or drop / close this connection.

Intrusion Detection and Intrusion Prevention Systems, IDS and IPS respectively, are network level defences deployed in thousands of computer networks worldwide. The basic difference between these two technologies are lies in how they provide protection for network environments with respect to detection and prevention terms. IDS generate only alerts or logs after threats or malicious activities are occurred. Intrusion Detection Systems simply detect possible intrusions and report this to network administrators.

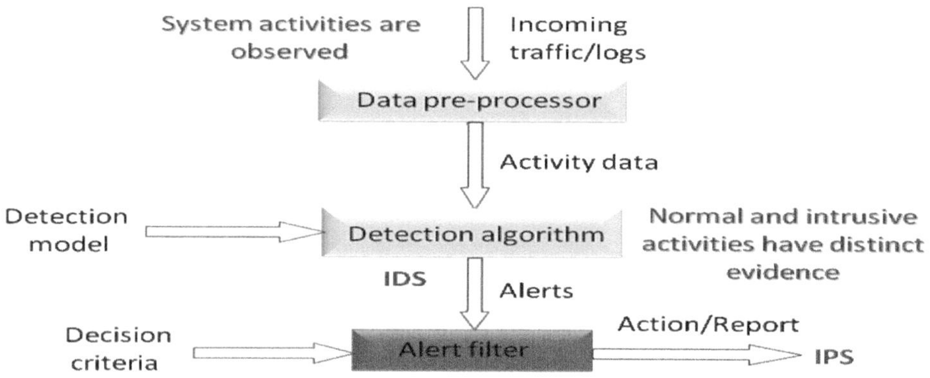

Role of IDS and IPS technology in network security

The actual role of IDS and IPS in network security shows in above diagram with details. How this detection algorithm and alert filter works with predefined rule sets for generating activity data or alerts for take an appropriate action on intrusive activities.

Intrusion Prevention Systems, IPS, perform the same analysis as Intrusion Detection Systems are detected because they are deployed in-line in the network, between other network components, they can take action on that malicious activity. Intrusion Prevention Systems will not only detect the intrusions but will take actions to like terminating the connection.

3 Difference between IDS and IPS Systems

IDS and IPS are originally developed for addressing requirements of lacking in most firewalls. IDS are basically used to detecting the threats or intrusions in network segment. But IPS is focused on identifying those threats or intrusions for blocking or dropping their activities.

The IDS and IPS are list of similar functions like packet inspection, stateful analysis, TCP segment reassembly, deep packet inspection, protocol validation, and signature matching.

The best example of security gate in term of difference of IDS and IPS is, An IDS works like a patrol car within the border, monitoring activities and looking for abnormal situations. But an IPS operates like a security guard at the gate of allowing and denying access based on credentials and some predefined rule set, or policy. No matter how strong the security at the gate is, the patrols continue to operate in a system that provides its own checks.

IDS

The IDS is software or an appliance that detects a threat, unauthorized or malicious network traffic. IDS has their own predefined rule sets, through that it can inspect the configuration of endpoints to determine whether they may be susceptible to attack (this is known as host-based IDS), and also it can record activities across a network and compare it to known attacks or attack patterns (this is called network-based IDS). The purpose of intrusion detection is to provide monitoring, auditing, forensics, and reporting of network malicious activities.

- Preventing network attacks
- Identifying the intruders
- Preserving logs in case the incident leads to criminal prosecution

IPS

The IPS are not only detect the bad packets caused by malicious codes, botnets, viruses and targeted attacks, but also it can take action to prevent those network activity from causing damage on network. The attacker's main motive is to take sensitive data or intellectual property, through that they interested in whatever they can get from customer data like employee information, financial records etc. The IPS is specified to provide protection for assets, resources, data, and networks.

- IPS stops the attack itself
- IPS changes the security environment

Objective	IPS		IDS	
	In-line, Automatic Block	Priority	Out-of-band, Human Alert	Priority
Stability	› Crash is catastrophic – network goes down	1	› Crash is annoying to security analysts who lose visibility – but no impact on network or apps	4
Performance	› Processing designed for peak network load (Gbps) › Small memory buffers (μsecs of latency) › Above required for interior network deployment and application transparency	2	› Processing designed for average network loads › Large memory buffers to absorb traffic bursts, creating seconds to minutes of latency › Above okay since out-of-band and well within human response time	3
Accuracy - False Positives	› False blocks @ Gbps rates and thousands of filters – kills applications	3	› Burdens security analysts with chasing false alarms	2
Accuracy - False Negatives	› Preventing automatic blocking of good traffic trumps failure to detect anomalies	4	› Missed anomalies may be missed attacks (information is power)	1

[Source: A Spire Research Report – March 2004 by Spire Security]

4 The Differences of IDS and IPS Are Categorized in Four Objectives as:

Network Stability and Performance

The IDS are deployed out of band in network means it passes all network traffic to this system but not through in between devices, the processing capability is matching with average network load. The latency between capture and reporting can range from a few seconds to minutes, but also it also depends on human response time. The IDS are a logging device, the large memory buffers to absorb traffic bursts & average network loads.

The IPS are deployed in-line in network means, it passes through in between the devices and which works in peak network load with large memory buffers to absorb traffic bursts is unacceptable. The latency is in microseconds which give the faster application response time with higher processing capacity.

Accuracy- False Positives:

There are three basic rules to find accuracy with false positives in IDS and IPS:

- The IDS has minimizes false positives but an IPS have no false positives. This changes dramatically the writing and testing of the alert filters.
- The IDS false positive alerts on an intrusion that it can be or cannot be – succeed, but IPS false positive blocks legitimate traffic.
- The anomaly filters cannot be used for blocking.

Accuracy- False Negatives

The accuracy of false negatives is simply a missed attack. The goal of this type of system is based on coverage of high priority attacks. The IDS may become overwhelmed with traffic beyond its capacity, dropping packets needed to detect the attack and an IPS is overwhelming the device causes traffic to be blocked or dropped preventing the attack from succeeding to detect anomalies.

Data log analysis

The IDS and IPS devices are gives a comprehensive logs and data collection, its without actionable alerts, the data gathered from these devices and sensors throughout the network can be used for event correlation and network forensics in a post-attack scenario. This type of data is critical for analysis during and after attacks and can help for organization with both incident response and compliance audits.

5 Conclusion

Intrusion types of systems are put in place to serve a business needs for meeting an objective of network security. The IDS and IPS are to provide a foundation of technology meets to tracking, identifying network attacks to which detect through logs of IDS systems and prevent an action through IPS systems. If the host with critical systems, confidential data and strict compliance regulations, then it's a great to use of IDS, IPS or both in network environments.

The basic benefits of IDS and IPS systems are as:

- Normal and intrusive malicious activities detected
- Proactive protection of network security infrastructure
- Operational efficiencies to reduced need to react to event logs for protection
- Increased coverage against packet attacks and zero-day attacks

The deterministic intrusion detection or prevention is the next generation firewall with deep packet inspection and sniffing in network. But it is not a silver bullet, to become a basic at the border and deeper in the network for "Defense in Depth."

References

1. Jabbusch, J.: IDS vs. IPS: How to know when you need the technology (November 22, 2010)
2. Smith, B.: IPS vs. IDS
3. Drum, R.: IDS & IPS Placement for network protection. CISSP (March 26, 2006)
4. Lindstrom, P., Director, R.: Intrusion prevention systems (IPS): Next generation firewalls, A Spire Research Report – by Spire Security (March 2004)
5. IPS vs. IDS: Similar on the Surface, Polar Opposites Underneath white paper by Tipping point

Conditional Proxy Re-Encryption - A More Efficient Construction

S. Sree Vivek[1,⋆], S. Sharmila Deva Selvi[1], V. Radhakishan[2], and C. Pandu Rangan[1,⋆]

[1] Department of Computer Science and Engineering, Indian Institute of Technology Madras
{sharmila,svivek,prangan}@cse.iitm.ac.in
[2] National Institute of Technology Trichy, India
vrkishan@gmail.com

Abstract. In a proxy re-encryption (PRE) scheme, Alice gives a special information to a proxy that allows it to transform messages encrypted under Alice's public key into a encryption under Bob's public key such that the message is not revealed to the proxy. In [14], Jian Weng and others introduced the notion of conditional proxy re-encryption (C-PRE) and proposed a system using bilinear pairings. Later, a break for the same was published in [17] and a new C-PRE scheme with bilinear pairings was introduced. In C-PRE, the proxy also needs to have the right condition key to transform the ciphertext (associated with a condition set by Alice) under Alice's public key into ciphertext under Bob's public key, so that Bob can decrypt it. In this paper, we propose an efficient C-PRE scheme which uses substantially less number of bilinear pairings when compared to the existing one [17]. We then prove its chosen-ciphertext security under modified Computational Diffie-Hellman (mCDH) and modified Computational Bilinear Diffie-Hellman (mCBDH) assumptions in the random oracle model.

Keywords: Random Oracle Model, Proxy Re-Cryptography, Conditional Proxy Re-encryption, Chosen Ciphertext Security.

1 Introduction

Encryption is used as a building block of any application requiring confidentiality. Let pk_i and pk_j be two independent public keys. As pointed out by Mambo and Okamato in [15], it is a common situation in practice where a data encrypted under pk_i is required to be encrypted under pk_j $(j \neq i)$. When the holder of sk_i is online, $E_i(m)$ is decrypted using sk_i and then message m is encrypted under pk_j giving $E_j(m)$. But in many applications like encrypted mail forwarding, secure

⋆ Work supported by Project No. CSE/05-06/076/DITX/CPAN on Protocols for Secure Communication and Computation sponsored by Department of Information Technology, Government of India.

D.C. Wyld et al. (Eds.): CNSA 2011, CCIS 196, pp. 502–512, 2011.

distributed file systems, and outsourced filtering of encrypted spam, when the holder of sk_i is not online, this has to be done by an untrusted party.

In 1998 Blaze, Bleumar, and Strauss [9] introduced the concept of proxy re-encryption (PRE). A re-encryption key ($rk_{i,j}$) is given to a potentially untrusted proxy so that the proxy can transform a message m encrypted under public key pk_i into an encryption of the same message m under a different public key pk_j without knowing the message. A PRE scheme can be of two types - unidirectional and bidirectional. The former is a scheme in which a re-encryption key ($rk_{i\rightarrow j}$) can be used to transform from pk_i to pk_j but not vice versa and the latter is a scheme in which the same re-encryption key ($rk_{i\leftrightarrow j}$) can be used to transform from pk_i to pk_j and vice versa. The re-encryption algorithm can be of two types - single hop, in which the re-encrypted ciphertext cannot be further re-encrypted and multi hop, in which the re-encrypted ciphertext can be further re-encrypted.

PRE can be used in many applications, including simplification of key distribution [9], key escrow [13], multicast [19], distributed file systems [3,5], security in publish/subscribe systems [4], secure certified email mailing lists [20,23], the DRM of Apple's iTunes [22], interoperable architecture of DRM [21], access control [11], and privacy for public transportation [7]. Hohenberger and others published a result of securely obfuscating re-encryption [16], which is the first positive result for obfuscating an encryption functionality. Shao and Cao have proposed a unidirectional PRE scheme without pairing [2]. Matthew Green and Giuseppe Ateniese have proposed a PRE scheme for ID-based cryptosystems [18].

Ran Canetti and Susan Hohenberger proposed a definition of security against chosen-ciphertext attacks for PRE schemes and presented a scheme that satisfied the definition [1]. In 2009, Jian Weng and others [14] introduced the concept of C-PRE, whereby Alice has a fine-grained control over the delegation. As a result, Alice can flexibly assign Bob the decryption capability based on the conditions attached to the messages using a proxy. For example, suppose Alice is on a vacation. She can make Bob to read only those messages which have the keyword "urgent" in their subject. This flexible delegation is obviously not possible with PRE schemes. In this paper, two separate keys are used - a partial re-encryption key and a condition key. The message can be delegated by the proxy only if both the keys are known.

Later in 2009, Jian Weng and others published a break of the scheme in [14] and gave a new scheme for C-PRE [17], which combines the re-encryption key and the condition key into a single key, which is then used for re-encryption. Also Cheng-Kang Chu and others in [8] introduced a generalized version of C-PRE named conditional proxy broadcast re-encryption (CPBRE), in which the proxy can re-encrypt the ciphertexts for a set of users at a time.

In this paper, we propose an efficient C-PRE scheme (single-hop and unidirectional) which uses significantly less number of bilinear pairings when compared to the existing schemes in [14] and [17]. Our scheme, as in [14], uses two separate keys for re-encryption.

1.1 Our Results

Let us briefly describe a C-PRE scheme. A C-PRE scheme involves a delegator (say user U_i), a delegatee (say user U_j) and a proxy. A message sent to U_i with condition w is encrypted by the sender using both U_i's public key and w. To re-encrypt the message to U_j, the proxy is given the re-encryption key ($rk_{i \to j}$) and the condition key ($ck_{i,w}$) corresponding to w. Both the keys can be generated only by U_i. These two keys form the secret trapdoor to be used by the proxy to perform translation. Proxy will not be able to re-encrypt cipher texts for which the right condition key is not available. Thus U_i can flexibly assign U_j the decryption rights by setting condition keys properly. The scheme works in practice as follows: the message encrypted for U_i is first handled by proxy and under appropriate conditions the proxy transforms the ciphertext into a ciphertext for U_j. However, proxy will obtain no information about the original message. While it is some what easier to design a PRE without pairing, designing C-PRE requires pairing based operations crucially. We have used a few constructions from [12] which drastically reduces the number of bilinear pairings. Table 1 compares the number of bilinear pairings and exponentiations between the scheme in [17] and our scheme.

Table 1. Computational Complexity Comparison

Algorithm	Scheme in [17]		Our Scheme	
	BP	EXP	BP	EXP
Encryption case 1	1	4	0	0
Encryption case 2	1	3	1	6
Re-Encryption	3	4	1	3
Decryption case 1	3	3	1	4
Decryption case 2	1	1	0	6
Total	9	15	3	19

BP - Bilinear Pairings, EXP - Exponentiations.

Encryption case 1 refers to the encryption without the condition. Encryption case 2 refers to the encryption with the condition. Decryption case 1 refers to the decryption of the re-encrypted ciphertext (first level ciphertext) and Decryption case 2 refers to the decryption of the encrypted ciphertext (second level ciphertext).

Although the number of exponentiations in our scheme is slightly more, it is insignificant when compared to the reduction in number of bilinear pairings. Thus, our scheme is more efficient than the existing one. We then formally prove the security of our scheme. We have slightly modified the security model in [14], as discussed in Section 3.

The C-PRE scheme in [14] has a break as given in [17]. Scheme in [17] has combined the two keys into a single key. Having the keys separate has an advantage. The delegation power of the proxy can be controlled. One of the two keys can be given to the proxy for partial re-encryption and the other key can be given to a third party for full re-encryption. Since the scheme in [14] has a break, our scheme is the only existing scheme having this unique property.

2 Preliminaries

Bilinear Groups and Bilinear Pairings: Let $\mathbb{G}$ and $\mathbb{G}_T$ be two cyclic multiplicative groups with the same prime order q. A bilinear pairing is a map $e : \mathbb{G} \times \mathbb{G} \rightarrow \mathbb{G}_T$ with the following properties.

- Bilinearity: We have $\hat{e}(g_1^a, g_2^b) = \hat{e}(g_1, g_2)^{ab}$ $\forall$ g_1,$g_2 \in \mathbb{G}$ and $\forall$ a,$b \in \mathbb{Z}_q^*$;
- Non-degeneracy: There exist $g_1, g_2 \in \mathbb{G}$ such that $\hat{e}(g_1, g_2) \neq 1$;
- Computability: There exists an efficient algorithm to compute $\hat{e}(g_1, g_2)$ $\forall$ g_1,$g_2 \in \mathbb{G}$.

Modified Computational Diffie-Hellman Problem. Let $\mathbb{G}$ be a cyclic multiplicative group with a prime order q. Let g be the generator of $\mathbb{G}$, The mCDH problem in $\mathbb{G}$ is as follows:

Given $(g, g^{\frac{1}{a}}, g^a, g^b)$ for some $a, b \in \mathbb{Z}_q^*$, compute $W = g^{ab} \in \mathbb{G}$. An algorithm $\mathcal{A}$ has an advantage ϵ in solving mCDH in $\mathbb{G}$ if

$$Pr[\mathcal{A}(g, g^{\frac{1}{a}}, g^a, g^b) = g^{ab}] \geq \epsilon$$

where the probability is over the random choice of $a, b \in \mathbb{Z}_q^*$, the random choice of $g \in \mathbb{G}$ and the random bits of $\mathcal{A}$.

Modified Computational Bilinear Diffie-Hellman Problem. Let $\mathbb{G}$ and $\mathbb{G}_T$ be two cyclic multiplicative groups with the same prime order q. Let $e : \mathbb{G} \times \mathbb{G} \rightarrow \mathbb{G}_T$ be an admissible bilinear map and let g be the generator of $\mathbb{G}$, The mCBDH problem in ($\mathbb{G}$,$\mathbb{G}_T, e$) is as follows:

Given $(g, g^{\frac{1}{a}}, g^a, g^b, g^c)$ for some $a, b, c \in \mathbb{Z}_q^*$, compute $W = \hat{e}(g, g)^{abc} \in \mathbb{G}_T$. An algorithm $\mathcal{A}$ has an advantage ϵ in solving mCBDH in $(\mathbb{G}, \mathbb{G}_T, e)$ if

$$Pr[\mathcal{A}(g, g^{\frac{1}{a}}, g^a, g^b, g^c) = \hat{e}(g, g)^{abc}] \geq \epsilon$$

where the probability is over the random choice of $a, b, c \in \mathbb{Z}_q^*$, the random choice of $g \in \mathbb{G}$ and the random bits of $\mathcal{A}$.

3 Security Model of Conditional Proxy Re-Encryption

We give the definitions and security notions for C-PRE systems in this section.

3.1 Definition of C-PRE Systems

A unidirectional C-PRE scheme consists of seven algorithms which are described as follows:

Global Setup(λ): The global setup algorithm takes a security parameter λ as input and outputs the global parameters *param*. The parameters in *param* are implicitly given as input to the following algorithms.

KeyGen(i): The key generation algorithm takes the user index i as input and generates a public key(pk_i) and a secret key(sk_i) for user U_i.

ReKeyGen(sk_i,pk_j): The partial re-encryption key generation algorithm takes a secret key sk_i and another public key pk_j as input and outputs the partial re-encryption key $rk_{i \to j}$. This algorithm is run by U_i. Here sk_j is not taken as input which indeed makes the scheme unidirectional.

CKeyGen(sk_i,w): The condition key generation algorithm takes a secret key sk_i and a condition w as input and outputs the condition key $ck_{i,w}$. This algorithm is run by U_i.

Encrypt(pk, m, w): The encryption algorithm takes a public key pk, a message m and a condition w as input and outputs the ciphertext ζ associated with w under pk. Here $m \in \mathcal{M}$ where $\mathcal{M}$ denotes the message space.

ReEncrypt($rk_{i \to j}$,$ck_{i,w}$,ζ_i): The re-encryption algorithm takes a partial re-encryption key $rk_{i \to j}$, a condition key $ck_{i,w}$ associated with condition w and a ciphertext ζ_i under the public key pk_i as input and outputs the re-encrypted ciphertext ζ_j under the public key pk_j. This algorithm is run by the proxy.

Decrypt(sk, ζ): The decryption algorithm takes a secret key sk and a ciphertext ζ as input and outputs either a message $m \in \mathcal{M}$ or the error symbol $\perp$.

Correctness: For any $m \in \mathcal{M}$, any condition w, any (pk_i,sk_i)←KeyGen(i), (pk_j,sk_j)←KeyGen(j), and ζ_i=Encrypt(pk_i, m, w),

$\Pr[\text{Decrypt}(sk_i,\zeta_i) = m] = 1$, and
$\Pr[\text{Decrypt}(sk_j,\text{ReEncrypt}(rk_{i,j},ck_{i,w},\zeta_i))= m] = 1$.
while for any other condition w' and user j' with $w' \neq w$ and $j' \neq j$, we have
$\Pr[\text{Decrypt}(sk_j,\text{ReEncrypt}(rk_{i,j},ck_{i,w'},\zeta_i))= \perp] = 1\text{-neg}(\lambda)$
$\Pr[\text{Decrypt}(sk_j,\text{ReEncrypt}(rk_{i,j'},ck_{i,w},\zeta_i))= \perp] = 1\text{-neg}(\lambda)$

3.2 Security Notions

The following game between an adversary $\mathcal{A}$ and a challenger $\mathcal{C}$ is used to define the semantic security of our C-PRE scheme against chosen ciphertext attacks.

Setup. $\mathcal{C}$ takes a security parameter λ and runs the algorithm GlobalSetup(λ) and gives the resulting global parameters *param* to $\mathcal{A}$.

Phase 1. $\mathcal{A}$ adaptively issues queries q_1,...,q_m where q_i is one of the following:

- *Uncorrupted key generation query*: $\mathcal{C}$ first runs algorithm KeyGen(i) to obtain the public/secret key pair (pk_i,sk_i), and then gives pk_i to $\mathcal{A}$.
- *Corrupted key generation query*: $\mathcal{C}$ first runs algorithm KeyGen(j) to obtain the public/secret key pair (pk_j,sk_j), and then gives (pk_j,sk_j) to $\mathcal{A}$.
- *Partial re-encryption key generation query* (pk_i,pk_j): $\mathcal{C}$ runs the algorithm ReKeyGen(sk_i,pk_j) and returns the generated re-encryption key $rk_{i \to j}$ to $\mathcal{A}$. Here sk_i is the secret key corresponding to pk_i.
- *Condition key generation query* (pk_i,w): $\mathcal{C}$ runs the algorithm CKeyGen(sk_i,w) and returns the generated condition key $ck_{i,w}$ to $\mathcal{A}$.

- *Re-encryption query* (pk_i,pk_j,w,ζ_i): $\mathcal{C}$ runs the algorithm ReEncrypt(ReKeyGen(sk_i,pk_j), CKeyGen(sk_i,w),ζ_i) and returns the generated ciphertext ζ_j to $\mathcal{A}$.
- *Decryption query* (pk,w,ζ) or (pk,ζ): $\mathcal{C}$ runs the algorithm Decrypt(sk,ζ) and returns its result to $\mathcal{A}$. Here (pk,w,ζ) and (pk,ζ) are queries on original ciphertexts and re-encrypted ciphertexts respectively.

For the last four queries it is required that pk, pk_i and pk_j are generated beforehand by the KeyGen algorithm.

Challenge. Once $\mathcal{A}$ decides Phase 1 is over, it outputs a target public key pk_{i^*}, a target condition w^* and two equal-length plaintexts $m_0, m_1 \in \mathcal{M}$. $\mathcal{C}$ flips a random coin $\delta \in \{0,1\}$, and sets the challenge ciphertext to be ζ^*=Encrypt(pk_{i^*},m_δ,w^*), which is sent to $\mathcal{A}$.

Phase 2 : $\mathcal{A}$ adaptively issues queries as in Phase 1, and $\mathcal{C}$ answers them as before.

Guess : Finally, $\mathcal{A}$ outputs a guess $\delta' \in \{0,1\}$ and wins the game if $\delta' = \delta$. Adversary $\mathcal{A}$ is subject to the following restrictions during the above game.

1. $\mathcal{A}$ cannot issue corrupted key generation queries on (i^*) to obtain the target secret key sk_{i^*}.
2. $\mathcal{A}$ can issue decryption queries on neither (pk_{i^*},w^*,ζ^*) nor (pk_j,ReEncrypt($rk_{i^*\to j}$,ck_{i^*,w^*},ζ^*)).
3. $\mathcal{A}$ cannot issue re-encryption queries on $(pk_{i^*},pk_j,w^*,\zeta^*)$ if pk_j appears in a previous corrupted key generation query.
4. $\mathcal{A}$ cannot obtain the partial re-encryption key $rk_{i^*\to j}$ if pk_j appears in a previous corrupted key generation query.

We refer to the above adversary $\mathcal{A}$ as an IND-CPRE-CCA adversary. $\mathcal{A}$'s advantage in attacking our CPRE scheme is defined as $Adv_{C-PRE,\mathcal{A}}^{IND-CPRE-CCA}$=|Pr[$\delta' = \delta$] - 1/2|, where the probability is taken over the random coins consumed by the adversary and the challenger. As in [14], we also distinguish between two types of IND-CPRE-CCA adversaries as follows:

- Type I IND-CPRE-CCA adversary: In the game, adversary $\mathcal{A}$ does not obtain the re-encryption key $rk_{i^*\to j}$ with pk_j corrupted.
- Type II IND-CPRE-CCA adversary: In the game, adversary $\mathcal{A}$ does not obtain both the condition key ck_{i^*,w^*} and the re-encryption key $rk_{i^*\to j}$ with pk_j corrupted.

4 An Efficient C-PRE Scheme

Here we present our efficient C-PRE scheme and then prove its security.

4.1 Construction

Our proposed scheme consists of the following seven main algorithms and one auxiliary algorithm for checking the validity of the ciphertext.

Global Setup(λ) : This algorithm takes the security parameter λ as input. Then two primes p and q are chosen such that $q \mid p-1$ where q is a λ bit prime. Then the algorithm generates $(q, \mathbb{G}, \mathbb{G}_T, e)$ where $\mathbb{G}$ and $\mathbb{G}_T$ are two cyclic groups with prime order q and e is a bilinear pairing $e : \mathbb{G} \times \mathbb{G} \rightarrow \mathbb{G}_T$. Let g be the generator of group $\mathbb{G}$, which is a subgroup of $\mathbb{Z}_q^*$ with order q. Choose hash functions as follows: $H_1 : \{0,1\}^{l_0} \times \{0,1\}^{l_1} \rightarrow \mathbb{Z}_q^*$, $H_2 : \{0,1\}^* \rightarrow \mathbb{Z}_q^*$, $H_3 : \mathbb{G} \rightarrow \{0,1\}^{l_0+l_1}$, $H_4 : \{0,1\}^* \rightarrow \mathbb{Z}_q^*$, $H_5 : \mathbb{G} \rightarrow \mathbb{Z}_q^*$, $H_6 : \{0,1\}^* \times \mathbb{G} \times \mathbb{G} \rightarrow \mathbb{G}$ and $H_7 : \mathbb{G}_T \rightarrow \{0,1\}^{l_0+l_1}$.

param$=((q, \mathbb{G}, \mathbb{G}_T, e), g, H_1, ..., H_7)$. l_0 and l_1 are determined by λ and the message space $\mathcal{M}$ is $\{0,1\}^{l_0}$.

KeyGen(i) : This algorithm randomly picks $sk_i = (x_{i,1}, x_{i,2} \xleftarrow{\$} \mathbb{Z}_q^*)$ and sets $pk_i = (g^{x_{i,1}}, g^{x_{i,2}})$.

ReKeyGen(sk_i,pk_j) : The re-encryption key $rk_{i \rightarrow j}$ is generated as follows:

1. Pick $h \xleftarrow{\$} \{0,1\}^{l_0}$ and $\pi \xleftarrow{\$} \{0,1\}^{l_1}$ and compute $v = H_1(h, \pi)$.
2. Compute $V = g^v$ and $W = H_3(pk_{j,2}^v) \oplus (h \parallel \pi)$.
3. Compute $rk_{i \rightarrow j}^{(1)} = \frac{h}{x_{i,1}H_5(pk_{i,2}) + x_{i,2}}$ and return $rk_{i \rightarrow j} = (rk_{i \rightarrow j}^{(1)}, V, W)$.

CKeyGen(sk_i, w) : This algorithm outputs the condition key $ck_{i,w} = H_6(w, pk_i)^{\frac{1}{x_{i,1}}}$.

Encrypt(pk_i, m, w) : This algorithm encrypts a message m with condition w for pk_i as follows:

1. Pick $s, z \xleftarrow{\$} \mathbb{Z}_q^*$ and compute $B = pk_{i,1}^s$ and $D = pk_{i,1}^z$.
2. Pick $r' \xleftarrow{\$} \{0,1\}^{l_1}$. Compute $r = H_2(m, r', pk_i, w)$ and $A = (pk_{i,1}^{H_5(pk_{i,2})} pk_{i,2})^r$.
3. Compute $C = H_3(g^r) \oplus (m \parallel r') \oplus H_7(\hat{e}(g, H_6(w, pk_i))^s)$.
4. Compute $E = s + zH_4(A, B, C, D)$ mod q.
5. Output the ciphertext $\zeta_i = (A, B, C, D, E)$.

Validity() : This algorithm implicitly takes all the inputs of the calling algorithm as its input and works as follows:

If $pk_{i,1}^E \neq B.D^{H_4(A,B,C,D)}$ return $\perp$.

ReEncrypt($rk_{i \rightarrow j}$, $ck_{i,w}$, ζ_i, pk_i, pk_j) : This algorithm re-encrypts ζ_i to ζ_j as follows:

1. Return $\perp$ if Validity() returns $\perp$.
2. Compute $A' = A^{rk_{i \rightarrow j}^{(1)}}$ and $C' = C \oplus H_7(\hat{e}(B, ck_{i,w}))$.
3. Output the transformed ciphertext as $\zeta_j = (A', C', V, W)$.

Decrypt (sk_i, ζ_i) : Parse the ciphertext ζ_i. Decryption of ζ_i is done as follows:

- ζ is the original ciphertext in the form $\zeta = (A, B, C, D, E)$.
  1. Return $\perp$ if Validity() returns $\perp$.
  2. Compute$(m \parallel r')= C \oplus H_3(A^{\frac{1}{x_{i,1}H_5(pk_{i,2})+x_{i,2}}}) \oplus H_7(\hat{e}(B, H_6(w, pk_i))^{\frac{1}{x_{i,1}}})$.
  3. If $A = (pk_{i,1}^{H_5(pk_{i,2})} pk_{i,2})^{H_2(m,r',pk_i,w)}$ holds, return m; else return $\perp$.
- ζ is the re-encrypted ciphertext in the form $\zeta = (A', C', V, W)$.
  1. Compute $(h \parallel \pi) = W \oplus H_3(V^{sk_{i,2}})$ and $(m \parallel r') = C' \oplus H_3(A'^{\frac{1}{h}})$.
  2. If $V = g^{H_1(h,\pi)}$ and $A' = g^{hH_2(m,r',pk_i,w)}$ hold, return m; else return $\perp$.

Correctness: The proxy must have both the right re-encryption key and the condition key to re-encrypt a ciphertext to the delegatee. Otherwise, the delegatee will not be able to decrypt the ciphertext with non-negligible probability. Suppose a proxy has the re-encryption key $rk_{i \to j}$ and the condition key $ck_{i,w'}$ $(w' \neq w)$, he will generate the re-encrypted ciphertext $\zeta_j = (A', C', V, W)$ as

$$\begin{aligned}
A' &= g^{rh} \\
C' &= H_3(g^r) \oplus (m \parallel r') \oplus H_7(\hat{e}(g, H_6(w, pk_i))^s) \oplus H_7(\hat{e}(B, ck_{i,w'})) \\
&= H_3(g^r) \oplus (m \parallel r') \oplus H_7(\hat{e}(g, H_6(w, pk_i))^s) \oplus H_7(\hat{e}(g^{sx_{i,1}}, H_6(w', pk_i)^{\frac{1}{x_{i,1}}})) \\
&= H_3(g^r) \oplus (m \parallel r') \oplus H_7(\hat{e}(g, H_6(w, pk_i))^s) \oplus H_7(\hat{e}(g, H_6(w', pk_i))^s) \\
V &= g^v \\
W &= H_3(pk_{j,2}^v) \oplus (h \parallel \pi).
\end{aligned}$$

Note that the two H_7 terms do not cancel each other implying that $C' \oplus H_3(A'^{\frac{1}{h}})$ in the decryption algorithm will not reveal the message m with overwhelming probability. The resulting value will also not pass the condition checks. Hence the delegatee cannot decrypt the re-encrypted ciphertext with high probability.

Security intuitions : It is impossible for the adversary to manipulate the ciphertext. This is because the validity of the original ciphertext can be publicly verified by the Validity() algorithm. Thus our scheme can ensure chosen-ciphertext security. Even if the conditional key w is changed to another value w' by the adversary, the scheme is secure because w is a parameter for H_2 and when w changes the value of r also changes.

4.2 Security

The proposed C-PRE scheme is IND-CPRE-CCA secure in random oracle model. This follows directly from Theorem 1 and Theorem 2.

Theorem 1. Our scheme is IND-CPRE-CCA secure in the random oracle model, assuming the mCDH assumption holds in group $\mathbb{G}$ and the Schnorr signature is EUF-CMA secure. Concretely, if there exists a Type I adversary $\mathcal{A}$, who asks at most q_{H_i} random oracle queries to H_i with $i \in 1, 2, ..., 7$, and breaks the $(t, q_u, q_c, q_{rk}, q_{ck}, q_{re}, q_d, \epsilon)$-IND-CPRE-CCA of our scheme, then, for any $0 < \psi < \epsilon$, there exists

1. either an algorithm $\mathcal{B}$ which can break the (t', ϵ')-mCDH assumption in $\mathbb{G}$ with

$$t' \leq t + (q_{H_1} + q_{H_2} + q_{H_3} + q_{H_4} + q_{H_5} + q_{H_6} + q_{H_7} + q_u + q_c + q_{rk} + q_{ck} + q_{re} + q_d)\mathcal{O}(1) + (2q_c + 2q_u + 6q_{rk} + q_{ck} + (q_{re} + 1)(2q_d + (2q_{H_2} + 2q_{H_3})q_d))t_{exp} + (q_{re} + q_d)t_p$$

$$\epsilon' \geq \frac{1}{q_{H_3}}\left(\frac{\epsilon - \psi}{\hat{e}(1+q_{rk})} - \frac{q_{H_2} + q_{H_4} + (q_{H_2} + q_{H_3})(q_{re} + q_d)}{2^{l_0+l_1}} - \frac{2(q_{re} + q_d)}{q}\right)$$

   where t_{exp} denotes the running time of an exponentiation in group $\mathbb{G}$ and t_p denotes the running time of a pairing in groups $(\mathbb{G}, \mathbb{G}_T)$.
2. or an attacker who breaks the EUF-CMA security of the Schnorr signature with advantage ψ within time t'.

Theorem 2. Our scheme is IND-CPRE-CCA secure in the random oracle model, assuming the mCBDH assumption holds in groups $\mathbb{G}$,$\mathbb{G}_T$ and the Schnorr signature is EUF-CMA secure. Concretely, if there exists a Type II adversary $\mathcal{A}$, who asks at most q_{H_i} random oracle queries to H_i with $i \in 1, 2, ..., 7$, and breaks the $(t, q_u, q_c, q_{rk}, q_{ck}, q_{re}, q_d, \epsilon)$-IND-CPRE-CCA of our scheme, then, for any $0 < \psi < \epsilon$, there exists

1. either an algorithm $\mathcal{B}$ which can break the (t', ϵ')-mCBDH assumption in $\mathbb{G}$ with

$$t' \leq t + (q_{H_1} + q_{H_2} + q_{H_3} + q_{H_4} + q_{H_5} + q_{H_6} + q_{H_7} + q_u + q_c + q_{rk} + q_{ck} + q_{re} + q_d)\mathcal{O}(1) + (2q_c + 2q_u + 6q_{rk} + q_{ck} + (q_{re} + 1)(2q_d + (2q_{H_2} + 2q_{H_3})q_d))t_{exp} + (q_{re} + q_d)t_p$$

$$\epsilon' \geq \frac{1}{q_{H_7}}\left(\frac{\epsilon - \psi}{e(1+q_{rk})} + \frac{\epsilon - \psi}{e(1+q_{ck})} - \frac{q_{H_4}}{2^{l_0+l_1}} - \frac{(q_{H_2}q_{H_3} + q_{H_3}q_{H_7} + q_{H_7}q_{H_2})(q_{re} + q_d)}{4^{l_0+l_1}} - \frac{(q_{H_2} + q_{H_3} + q_{H_7})(q_{re} + q_d)}{2^{l_0+l_1-1}} - \frac{3(q_{re} + q_d)}{q}\right)$$

   where t_{exp} denotes the running time of an exponentiation in group $\mathbb{G}$ and t_p denotes the running time of a pairing in groups $(\mathbb{G}, \mathbb{G}_T)$.
2. or an attacker who breaks the EUF-CMA security of the Schnorr signature with advantage ψ within time t'.

The formal and rigorous proofs for these theorems are given in the full version of the paper.

5 Conclusion

In this paper, we proposed a more efficient CCA secure unidirectional C-PRE scheme with less number of bilinear pairings. The scheme is more elegant when compared to its counterparts. We have proved the security of the scheme in the random oracle model under appropriate security definitions. There are still many open problems to be solved, such as designing CCA secure C-PRE scheme in the standard model, C-PRE in other settings like identity based and certificateless cryptography.

References

1. Canetti, R., Hohenberger, S.: Chosen-ciphertext secure proxy re-encryption. In: ACM Conference on Computer and Communications Security 2007, pp. 185–194 (2007)
2. Shao, J., Cao, Z.: CCA-Secure Proxy Re-encryption without Pairings. In: Jarecki, S., Tsudik, G. (eds.) PKC 2009. LNCS, vol. 5443, pp. 357–376. Springer, Heidelberg (2009)
3. Ateniese, G., Fu, K., Green, M., Hohenberger, S.: Improved proxy re-encryption schemes with applications to secure distributed storage. In: Internet Society (ISOC): NDSS 2005, pp. 29–43 (2005)
4. Khurana, H., Koleva, R.: Scalable security and accounting services for content-based publish subscribe systems. International Journal of E-Business Research (2006)
5. Ateniese, G., Fu, K., Green, M., Hohenberger, S.: Improved proxy re-encryption schemes with applications to secure distributed storage. ACM Transactions on Information and System Security (TISSEC), 1–30 (2006)
6. Coron, J.-S.: On the Exact Security of Full Domain Hash. In: Bellare, M. (ed.) CRYPTO 2000. LNCS, vol. 1880, pp. 229–235. Springer, Heidelberg (2000)
7. Heydt-Benjamin, T.S., Chae, H., Defend, B., Fu, K.: Privacy for public transportation. In: Danezis, G., Golle, P. (eds.) PET 2006. LNCS, vol. 4258, pp. 1–19. Springer, Heidelberg (2006)
8. Chu, C.-K., Weng, J., Chow, S.S.M., Zhou, J., Deng, R.H.: Conditional Proxy Broadcast Re-Encryption. In: Boyd, C., González Nieto, J. (eds.) ACISP 2009. LNCS, vol. 5594, pp. 327–342. Springer, Heidelberg (2009)
9. Blaze, M., Bleumer, G., Strauss, M.: Divertible protocols and atomic proxy cryptography. In: Nyberg, K. (ed.) EUROCRYPT 1998. LNCS, vol. 1403, pp. 127–144. Springer, Heidelberg (1998)
10. Schnorr, C.-P.: Efficient Identification and Signatures for Smart Cards. In: Brassard, G. (ed.) CRYPTO 1989. LNCS, vol. 435, pp. 239–252. Springer, Heidelberg (1990)
11. Talmy, A., Dobzinski, O.: Abuse freedom in access control schemes. In: AINA 2006, pp. 77–86 (2006)
12. Weng, J., Chow, S.S.M., Yang, Y., Deng, R.H.: Efficient Unidirectional Proxy Re-Encryption. Cryptology ePrint Archive, Report 2009/189 (2009), `http://eprint.iacr.org/`
13. Ivan, A., Dodis, Y.: Proxy cryptography revisited. In: Internet Society (ISOC): NDSS 2003 (2003)
14. Weng, J., Deng, R.H., Ding, X., Chu, C.-K., Lai, J.: Conditional proxy re-encryption secure against chosen-ciphertext attack. In: ASIACCS, pp. 322–332 (2009)
15. Mambo, M., Okamoto, E.: Proxy Cryptosystems: Delegation of the Power to Decrypt Ciphertexts. IEICE Trans. Fund. Elect. Communications and CS, E80-A/1:54-63 (1997)
16. Hohenberger, S., Rothblum, G.N., Shelat, A., Vaikuntanathan, V.: Securely obfuscating re-encryption. In: Vadhan, S.P. (ed.) TCC 2007. LNCS, vol. 4392, pp. 233–252. Springer, Heidelberg (2007)
17. Weng, J., Yang, Y., Tang, Q., Deng, R.H., Bao, F.: Efficient Conditional Proxy Re-encryption with Chosen-Ciphertext Security. In: Samarati, P., Yung, M., Martinelli, F., Ardagna, C.A. (eds.) ISC 2009. LNCS, vol. 5735, pp. 151–166. Springer, Heidelberg (2009)

18. Green, M., Ateniese, G.: Identity-Based Proxy Re-encryption. In: Katz, J., Yung, M. (eds.) ACNS 2007. LNCS, vol. 4521, pp. 288–306. Springer, Heidelberg (2007)
19. Chiu, Y.-P., Lei, C.-L., Huang, C.-Y.: Secure multicast using proxy encryption. In: Qing, S., Mao, W., López, J., Wang, G. (eds.) ICICS 2005. LNCS, vol. 3783, pp. 280–290. Springer, Heidelberg (2005)
20. Khurana, H., Hahm, H.-S.: Certified mailing lists. In: ASIACCS 2006, pp. 46–58 (2006)
21. Taban, G., C'ardenas, A.A., Gligor, V.D.: Towards a secure and interoperable drm architecture. In: ACM DRM 2006, pp. 69–78 (2006)
22. Smith. Tony. Dvd jon: buy drm-less tracks from apple itunes (2005), `http://www.theregister.co.uk/2005/03/18/itunespymusique`
23. Khurana, H., Slagell, A., Bonilla, R.: Sels: A secure e-mail list service. In: ACM SAC 2005, pp. 306–313 (2005)

Study of Malware Threats Faced by the Typical Email User

Anthony Ayodele, James Henrydoss, Walter Schrier, and T.E. Boult

Department of Computer Science,
University of Colorado at Colorado Springs
Colorado Springs, CO, USA
vast@uccs.edu

Abstract. Understanding malware behavior will help in implementing robust intrusion detection and prevention systems. In this paper, we studied the behavioral characteristics of different malware types affecting the Internet and other enterprise email systems. This research was carried out on spam email data received by a single user's test email account collected over a period of six months. A sandbox test environment platform using virtual machines was built to perform this research and simulate real-life malware behavior and determine its signature at the point of execution for proper analysis. Analysis of email data using the sandbox setup helps to produce a comprehensive data analysis about botnet behavior. We described in detail the design and implementation of sandbox test environment including the challenges faced in building this test environment. As a cost saving measure, we used VMware based virtual platforms built on Linux PC-class hardware. We present results of our behavioral measurement of the most active botnets. Our study discovered that for a single email user for a period of six months, two active Trojans contributed around 20 percent of the total identified malwares received within this time period and the remaining 80 percent of malware binaries were distributed over many different types of botnets; the email malware shows a classic long-tail distribution. During this experiment, we also discovered very strong polymorphic behaviors exhibited by these malware samples, ostensibly intended to help the malware authors and hackers to penetrate and bypass the enterprise intrusion detection systems. Finally, we are releasing the repository of malware collected as a data set for evaluation by other researchers.

Keywords: Malware, Intrusion Detection, Botnet.

1 Introduction

Malware is a malicious software agent that runs hidden using a secret communication channel to communicate with its Command and Control (C&C) center which is typically a server using either Internet Relay Chat (IRC) or web based access to control the remote machines. There is a quest to find mechanisms to protect the current and next generation Internet against botnets and their malicious fraudulent activities [15]. A bot is a compromised machine which can be controlled by C&C servers remotely,

D.C. Wyld et al. (Eds.): CNSA 2011, CCIS 196, pp. 513–525, 2011.

and the main intent is to inflict damage to the target client or end user for fraudulent purposes. The term bot and malware will be used interchangeably in this paper, even though some consider malware as the software and bots as malware infested machines. The name 'bot' is derived from the term 'robot' which means an automatic worker and refers to a single malware agent, functions automatically and autonomously. 'Botnet' refers to a collection of bots or a group of software agents. It is a network of malicious computers also known as zombies, which are remote machines hacked, compromised, and controlled over the Internet by its command, and control (C&C) servers called 'botmasters'. Botnets spread often infecting tens of thousands of computers that lie dormant until commanded to action by the attacker via the botmaster. The attacker is the main malware originator who instructs the bots or zombie army to carryout various malicious activities on remote machines and then report back to the command centers. The remote computer's owner is completely unaware of these bot agents who hide their behavior. Botnet infected machines open up a backdoor to listen for command and control issued by attackers. By sending command, the botmaster can take control of all or part of the infected systems, and direct them to perform tasks such as distribution of spam, spying computers for stealing the identity and personal information, launching attack on other computers using distributed DoS (Denial of Service), SYN attacks and other advertising commercial activities (i.e., adware). In addition, these compromised machines can also be used by attackers to launch attacks on newer machines by seeding newer bots, scanning for new victims, stealing confidential information from users, performing DDoS (Distributed Denial of Service) attacks, hosting web servers and phising content and propagating updates to the botnet software itself [1],[4].

1.1 Malicious Activities

The following summarizes the malicious activities performed by the malwares on the compromised machines: Denial of Service (DoS) attacks, TCP SYN attacks, DDoS attacks with distributed framework, phising for fraudulent activities (e.g., Identity theft, credit card fraud and e-fraud), coordinated spam attacks, recruiting other bots, zombies and upgrading the existing software by malware authors for polymorphic behavior. Even though majority of the bots are inflicting damage, there are few bots that can be used for good purposes and business use. Google bot, the web crawler which finds and retrieves the internet search pages on web before handling them off to the Google Indexer is categorized as a good bot [4], and does not infect end user machines.

1.2 Propagation Method

Bots can automatically scan their environment and propagate themselves using vulnerabilities and weak passwords. The more vulnerability a bot can scan and propagate thru, the more valuable it becomes to the botnet controller community. The process of stealing computing resources as a reason to attack a computer system being joined to a botnet is sometimes referred to as "scrumping". The bots typically spread through the following mechanisms: Internet and email downloads and attachments, software installations from un-trusted sources, scan exploit and planting, IM, twitter and social networking sites (e.g., Face book, Twitter and Skype), SMS, MMS and mobile emails target smart phones (e.g., Blackberry, I -phone and Android based phones).

1.3 Types of Bots

Malwares come in different disguised shapes and formats such as annoying pop-up ads, spyware and viruses that can be used to steal your identity or for tracking your activities[1].There are many different types of malwares and they can be categorized based on the method it used to propagate in the Internet or how they communicate. Bots can use various topologies such as centralized, peer-2-peer (P2P) or randomized and can operate on different communication protocols such as HTTP, IRC, and P2P. These popular methods are used for controlling and issuing commands to a large number of bots at a time via various kinds of controlling mechanisms [3],[4],[5].

Internet Relay Chat (IRC) Bots

Internet Relay Chat (IRC) is a popular web chatting system based on the Internet Engineering Task Force (IETF) standard 1459. IRC is based on a client server model and enables communication between server and clients. IRC enables direct communication between clients (bots) and C&C server using command and control method. IRC bot is based on centralized server architecture. These bots can be very large and powerful consisting of thousands of bots in their network. Since it is large, makes it increases its vulnerability for detecting and destroying. The communication between bots and the C&C server are often encrypted e.g., darknet.org, cyberarmy.net, eggdrop and winbot. The eggdrop (Open Source IRC bot) and Win bots (Windows Bots) were built for good purposes and not for fraudulent activities [2].

Point-to-Point (P2P) Bots

P2P is a new and emerging technology for bot communication. These bots are based on distributed network and smaller traffic patterns compared to large IRC bots. This makes it very difficult to detect and destroy e.g., Nugache and Sinit. These bots communicate with each other using P2P protocol methodology. The P2P bots only use the TCP or UDP server ports for opening a connection between bots and the C&C servers [4].

Web based HTTP Bots

Web based bots are primarily used for launching DDoS attacks using http protocol. These http botnets use html over http to communicate between the C&C server and the client bots. They naturally try to blend into the normal Internet web traffic and so detecting these bots is a daunting task. They form the basis of the next generation botnet architecture, providing 'botnet 2.0' for the herders. They are more accessible for those who didn't grow up with IRC. Examples include Machbot, Barracuda, and BlackEnergy [4].

Rest of this paper has been organized as follows. In section 2 we cover the relevant research work. In section 3, we cover the sandbox test setup environment used for this experiment. In section 4, we provide a detailed analysis and findings of this research work. In section 5, we summarize the work presented in this paper and in section 6 we discuss potential future directions of this work.

2 Related Work

Botlab gathers multiple real-time streams of information about botnets taken from distinct perspectives. By combining and analyzing these streams, Botlab produces accurate, timely, and comprehensive data about spam botnet behavior [1]. The Honeypot project is yielding a rich source of new malware samples analyzing methods [15]. Our current implementation does not follow the real-time streaming of these, but rather focuses on email malware analysis. The design and architecture of malware analysis environments employ an effective malware analysis lab environment to explore possibilities beyond the traditional two or three system VM-based lab [11]. The Nepenthes platform is a framework for large-scale collection of information on self-replicating malware in the wild. Using this platform several other organizations were able to greatly broaden the empirical analysis of self-replicating malware and provide thousands of samples of previously unknown malware to anti-virus system vendors [7].

3 Experiments

This section provides a detailed explanation about the sandbox test environment set up, and how we collected the malware sample binaries along with the test results.

3.1 Malware Sample Collection

Malware samples used for this research were collected using a single user account created in the lab email system, with the goal being to see the types of malware a single user faces. Apache open source spam filter "Spam Assassin" was used to collect the spam files from the email-MTA (Mail Transfer Agent) systems which runs on a Windows mail server, and filters the spam before it reaches user's mailbox [9]. We used the spam folder of this dedicated test email account to collect six months] of spam email binaries in zipped form for analysis [i.e. January - June 2010]. Each month's binary malware data is stored in a separate month_name.zip file for further malware processing. This method has been selected in lieu of using a honeypot set up to collect spam emails received by a real email user. The honeypot automatically feeds the spam data directly from the Internet but it does not provide the filtered email only traffic for our analysis which focuses on spam messages received by a single email user. Most users use email; few run unprotected machines as honeypots.

3.2 Experiment Setup

A closed network with reverse firewall functionality was used in this research for better analysis of malware behavior. This closed network called "sandboxes" consist a total number of five machines; one gateway machine, and four user assigned test machines. This sandbox test environment was built using VMware virtual machines running on UBUNTU 10 Linux operating system on single server hardware. The malware analysis platforms used for testing the malware binaries were installed with Windows XP. These virtual machines, running multiple virtual operating systems simultaneously on a single physical computer was useful for real time analysis of malware that seeks to interact with other systems, perhaps for the purpose of leaking data, obtaining instructions from the attacker, or upgrading itself. Since the testing and execution of the malware was restricted to a single machine, protecting the machines from network interaction was very controlled and isolated. In addition, virtualization reduces the number of physical boxes needed to conduct the research and in turn makes the research effort more affordable in terms of cost. By adopting this approach, we were able to run the malware on different virtual machines for easy analysis and monitoring of the malware behavior. The figure (Fig. 2) below provides a detailed view about the sandbox test setup.

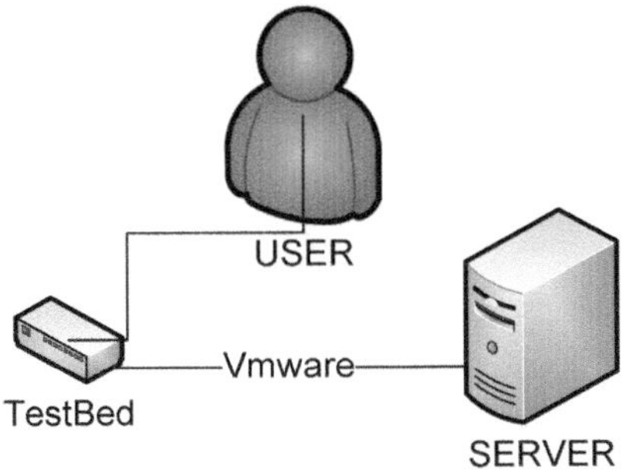

Fig. 1. Test Bed Using VMware Servers

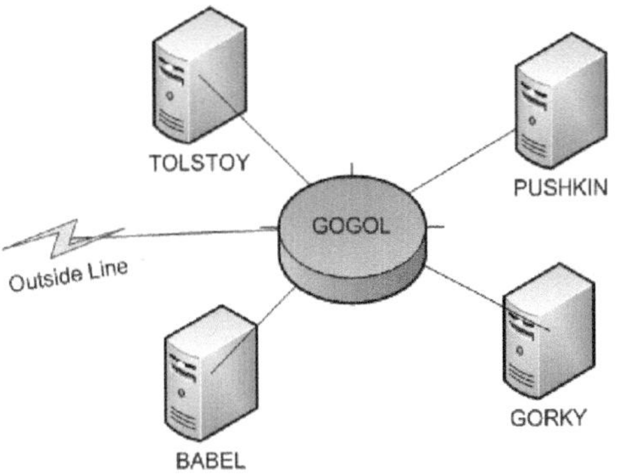

Fig. 2. Sandbox Test Environment

The main purpose of gateway machine, GOGOL is to filter the traffic to and from the network with the exception of passing in specific user IPs by implementing firewall IP filtering to thwart any unwanted access from outside the network. GOGOL utilizes Open BSD to close traffic and to pass the user IPs to the user's assigned test machine. TOLSTOY, PUSHKIN, BABEL and GORKY are the malware analyzing sandbox test machines used in this research work and built on Linux machines. Each test machine BABEL, GORKY, PUSHKIN, and TOLSTOY utilizes UBUNTU 10 as the primary OS and contains a virtual machine via VMware for user testing purposes. Figure 1 and 2 represents how each user machine has a test bed via VMware and each user interaction is directly with the test bed. In addition each computer acted as a local web server in order to allow the use of custom designed Hypertext Preprocessor (PHP) script that contained commands for VMware operating system reload and trace capture files upload. We have disabled the external Internet access from these servers to block any accidental spread of malware via Internet access during testing as a precautionary measure by using a reverse firewall. The web server installation allowed any captured data, reports to be 'uploaded' to the main server where the VM (i.e., Virtual Machine hosted on VMware Server) is hosted on and then revert the image of the VM back to a clean state. This helped the test machines to revert back to the original image after infected with malware binaries under test before moving on to the next test. Also GORKY acted as an FTP server to allow transfer of test data or any other data and software to be passed from host to the VM. The VM on each test bed hosts Windows XP operating system for purposes of testing malware in a windows environment. The VM also has a defined IP that allows it to be on the same network as the main host machines to allow the user traffic to reach the machine and to facilitate data transfer between host and VM. Wire Shark network monitoring tool on each VM was used to capture traffic data generated by each malware for each test run.

3.3 Data Collection Procedures

The malware data processing started with a user connecting via remote desktop client to GOGOL where each user utilizes a unique port, for example <GOGOL.ip: port>. The gateway GOGOL then checks the source IP address to make sure that this address is pre-defined IP and belonging to one of the individual test bed machines. If it matches, then it will route the traffic to appropriate IP of the test bed via its host. The user logs on to the VM and performs data collection on an individual malware file. This involves launching Wire Shark, releasing the malware, and then saving the Wire Shark report. Utilizing as web browser to access the custom PHP script allows the user to upload the Wire Shark report to host machine and then to revert the image of VM to a clean state. Finally, the whole process is repeated for each malware file.

4 Analysis

The following section explains the results of dynamic malware behavior that was studied using the sandbox infrastructure set up at our lab. This study includes all malware samples collected from the incoming email spam binaries for a period of six months at the lab email MTA servers received using a test account specifically created for this study.

4.1 Behavioral Characteristics

To study the malware behavior and its malicious, fraudulent activities, each and every malware collected from the spam folder were run on our sandbox analysis platform. The malware behavior was logged into Wire Shark, a network analysis tool which is used to log the messages sent out by the active bots from the analysis platform to outside network, its Command and Control (C&C) centers. First, we examined the actions of malware binaries run on the sandbox to understand the dynamic behavior while recording the outgoing email, Internet or any other relay chat accesses. Briefly this research work analyzed the following malware behaviors: networking characteristics, activity duration, polymorphic and correlation analysis between the malware activity and polymorphic behaviors. This paper focuses only on the dynamic malware behaviors of malware. The static behavior which involves studying the code and reverse engineering the malware binary is out of the scope of this research work and will be performed in future phases.

4.2 Malware Identification Method

Clam-AV software tool kit installed on virtual Windows XP platforms helped us to identify the malware types. It helped us to categorize the malwares into groups, and discard the unknown suspect types. By using antivirus software engine which is a shared library, the Clam-AV directly accepted the malware samples and using its internal shared library, it could identify the malware types. In addition to malware identification, MD5 checksum was run on all the malware binaries to verify its software instances [16]. We used approximately 396 source email binaries spanning over a period of six months for our testing. A total of 214 Trojan malware binaries were identified using Clam-AV antivirus software. The toolkit could not identify approximately 179 malware binary signatures and these unidentified malwares were tagged as suspects. We have shortlisted a total of 42 types of active malware Trojans that were active during this six months period. Based on the collected data, we found that the malware received by an individual email user is very distributed and none of the malwares exhibited a dominant behavior except Agent-165149 (23 attacks/ six months) and Generic FakeAV (25 attacks/six months). In our detailed analysis we have shortlisted the following list of fourteen Trojans which made significant contribution in affecting email users. These 14 malwares selected from the list of 214 identified samples showed significant contribution in term of average malware contribution (i.e., 5 % and above malware attacks in six month period) to the single email users and has been used for further analysis and reporting. The following data summarizes the Trojans indentified to be making significant monthly contribution to the email user: Agent165149 -23, Agent165380-8, Downloader 93419-8, Downloader Bredolab 1414-8, Downloader Bredolab 1415-7, Downloader Bredolab 1416-7, Downloader Bredolab 1417-11, Downloader Bredolab 1418-8, Downloader Bredolab 1419-10, Downloader Bredolab 1420-9, Downloader Bredolab 1421-11, Downloader Bredolab 1423-11, Downloader Bredolab 1424-7 and Generic FakeAV25.

4.3 Monthly Malware Attacks

We have summarized the number of malware attacks per month which includes both the malware binaries identified to be Trojans and suspects. The suspects list consists of binary that does not match the malware signature database of Clam-AV tool kit. A single email user received an average of 66 malware hits per month in their spam folders as identified to be Trojans. The data below provides only the malwares identified to be Trojans, but the actual number received by a single user is approximately twice the table values because this would have both identified and unidentified malware. Total Malware Attacks/Month is summarized as follows: Jan- 27 hits, Feb-160 hits, Mar-41 hits, Apr-46 hits, May – 46 hits and June -76 hits.

The highest numbers of malware attacks were received during the month of February and June compared to other four month period within the total six months window. Based on our findings, this high volume of malware traffic for February can be attributed to the highest number of spam activities during Valentine's Day [13]. Malware authors exploit the high volume of email activity during the Valentine's Day period to mix up the malware emails along with regular emails to the users. Though we confirm the highest numbers of email malware attacks during the month of February, we are unable to confirm the exact digital signatures of both the Waledac and Storm with our email data received during the month of February. This could be due to the fact that the malware authors change the malware signatures once detected to penetrate the intrusion detection systems by changing the code to come up with a new signature which has been referred to polymorphic behavior of the malwares [13].

4.4 Average Contribution

Even though we identified close to 42 types of malware using Clam AV, the monthly malware attacks were very evenly distributed. Two malwares, Agent-165149 and Generic Fake AV, were contributing over 20 percent of the overall malware attacks for the six months period and rest of the malware data is very distributed. The data below summarizes the average malware contribution for a single user in six months time period: Agent-165149 – 11 %, Generic FakeAV – 12%, Other Malwares – 77%.

4.5 Active Duration

One of the key behavioral characteristics of malware is the number of days/months a particular malware is active and spamming the email user's account. This characteristic measures how long a particular malware was in the active state and attacking the Internet by spamming malware messages regularly. We found out that the following four malwares were active for longer period of time compared to other malwares selected for detailed analysis: Trojan Agent-165149 (141 days / 4 months and 20 days), Downloader Bredolab-1417 (79 days / 2 months and 19 days), Downloader Bredolab-1419 (121 days / 4 months 1 day), Generic FakeAV (64 days/ 2 months 4 days). It is very straightforward to derive the activity behavior of Trojan Agent-165149 (4 and ½ months) and Generic Fake AV (2 months) from the Figure 8 to be active for longer duration to send frequent spam emails. These two malwares exhibited active characteristics and produced a large volume of email malware spam with Agent 165149 (141 attacks) and Generic Fake AV (64 attacks). It can be seen that from these figures, the Trojan Agent 165149 produced 141 attacks in its recorded activity time period of 4 ½ months with an average of one spam a day (i.e., 141 spam/135 days= 1.04 spam/day). In the case of Generic Fake AV, also we recorded an average of one spam a day (i.e., 64 spam/30 days =1.06 spam/day), but over a shorter period. In the case of Downloader.Bredolab-1417, which had been active for 2½ months and Dowonloader.Bredolab-1419 active for 4 months exhibited a very dormant behavior. Since these two Trojans were active for long periods without sending frequent spam emails, they are considered to be exhibiting dormant characteristics.

4.6 C&C Server Identification

We recorded all the networking behaviors exhibited by the malwares using the tool Wire Shark. Initially these malwares send domain name query (DNS) to resolve the IP address of its command & control centers. The table below (Table 1.) summarizes the networking behavior of the active Trojan Agent 165149 and Generic Fake AV malwares. These initial queries were sent over the regular UDP/IP packets. The malwares analyzed did not exhibit relay chatting and P2P behaviors.

Table 1. Networking Behavior by Malware Type

Malware Name	# of Instance	Command & Control Center Access	Access Protocol & discovery method	Discovery Method
Trojan.Agent 165149	7	hulejusoops.ru finderea.org mircosoft.com olgashelest.ru	NBNS Name Query	Static DNS Name
Trojan.Generic.FakeAV	9	msn.com, google.com, yahoo.com, postfolkovs.ru, Secureplaze.biz, designfolkov.ru	NBNS Name Query	Static DNS Name

4.7 Polymorphic Behavior

In the context of malware analysis, polymorphism refers to the same behavior exhibited by malwares with different signatures to evade anti-virus and anti-spam programs (e.g., Norton, Symantec and McAfee). Malware authors change the malware source code and its attributes to make it undetectable by signature and behavior-based antivirus and intrusion detection defenses implemented in corporate firewall and malware detection engines. Typical morphing methods include change of malware filenames and change of compression and encryption methods by using different keys. Polymorphic malware is very destructive and intrusive computer programs. This self-mutating malwares constantly change its signature to penetrate the detection engines. Since it is frequently morphing i.e., changing signature, filename etc, makes it very difficult for anti-malware programs to detect these attacks. Even though the appearance of the code in polymorphic malware varies with each mutation, the main function of the software usually remains the same. In our malware analysis, we recorded polymorphic nature of all the malware binary instances collected during the six months period. The following six malwares exhibited strong polymorphic behavior: Generic Fake AV, Downloader Bredolab1423, Downloader Bredolab1421, Downloader Bredolab1419, Downloader Bredolab1417 and TrojanAgent165149. We recorded the polymorphic behavior in table 2. The rank (i.e., number of polymorphic instances) of polymorphic behavior for these six malware is ranging between three and nine. The highest polymorphic behavior was exhibited by Generic Fake AV and Trojan Agent165149 which also results in more number of days active and spamming the maximum number of Trojan attacks to a single email user. Our research confirms that if a botnet does not exhibit polymorphic behavior, it is possible to be removed from the network by identifying the source and its activities [12],[13].

Table 2. Polymorphic Malware Instance and Checksum Signature

Identified Malware Name	# of Binary Instances	MD5 - Checksum
Trojan.Agent-165149	1	671ddabffd1aa0af81ec473997d27da8
	2	753f471d81f7a8bb98c45c8ec92f6153
	3	84fc51805858 1ca2702f5a48d5041cb8
	4	86f4fb71d03f7cce6a488985d46d8186
	5	8efcba93aa9ccd15266982ca2d925b27
	6	9c0147ee3b6abd19ebdf36933328c262
	7	c13a1fcc57fe3a196d55b6106479bc99
Trojan.Generic.FakeAV	1	d0bbdb80dc4c0802bf0560f99893380b
	2	d1da19076736f695c3c9282c58d1bf0c
	3	d3b3b663204209acbbe9c649623f1371
	4	daf85e2b0308351a00fd9b29211e6b6a
	5	dcf3a471e78636766fddfc62863e7d18
	6	df39e909d1ccfa918f401c87fa778d53
	7	e1aaa4c118ea9a9f8a072d294fec29fa
	8	e3d65f444114f5ed771b4fa91add5761
	9	e4efec9070d45a31061b7a588e876666

By exhibiting polymorphic behaviors malwares come up with many alternate signatures and attacks users even though it is destroyed from one location by spreading the bots around. The following data provides the number of polymorphic instances exhibited by the Malware within that six month periods: Trojan Agent-165149-7, Downloader Bredolab1417–4, Downloader Bredolab1419-5, Downloader Bredolab1421 -3, Downloader Bredolab1423 -5 and Generic FakeAV – 9. Table 2 provides the polymorphic malware and its different digital signatures. We found that the malwares identified to be polymorphic were sent out using a different email file name/subject line name, with different MD5 checksum had different signature and were part of the same malware groups identified by the Clam AV engine used in this research.

4.8 Correlation Analysis

A correlation analysis has been performed using the two selected active malwares, Trojan Agent 165149 and Generic Fake AV which are the two malwares that contributed around twenty percent of the overall malware attacks to a single user. In case of Trojan Agent 165149, it was detected with initial signature during the month of January and then it was dormant for about five months relating to the problems in the active behavior of the malware. It came back with different malware signature by exhibiting polymorphic behavior and was active during the entire month of June. Also Trojan Agent 165149 generated many hits to the single email user while changing only the file names and not the signatures. Eventually, the polymorphic behavior demonstrated by this malware was changing both the binary signature and file names. In the case of Generic Fake AV, we recorded a very unique polymorphic characteristic using file name and binary signature. This malware poses a serious threat to the Intrusion detection engines by changing the file name, binary digital signatures every time it is sent to the user's email account.

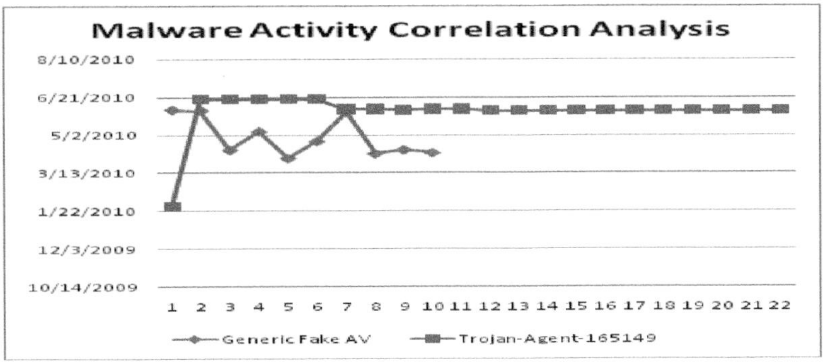

Fig. 3. Malware Activity Correlations

4.9 Unidentified Malwares

The Clam-AV tool kit could not identify approximately 174 malware binaries that we suspect are Trojans. Figure 4 shows a detailed data about the number of suspect/unidentified malware binaries versus number of occurrences.

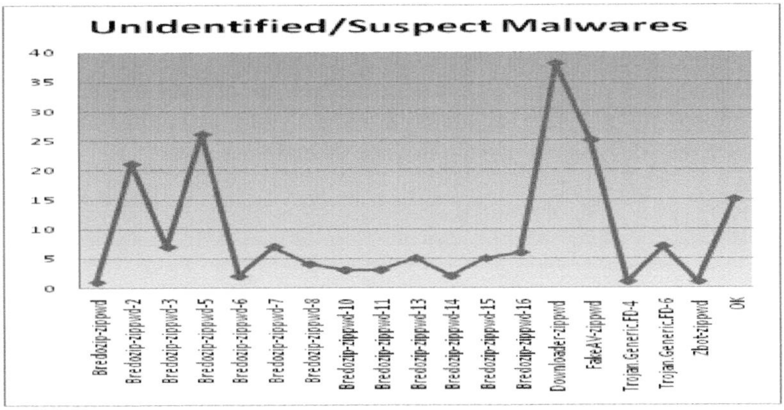

Fig. 4. Unidentified Malware Chart

This non-identification can also be due to shortcomings in the open source tool kit Clam AV; however this has not been verified. This alarming number of unidentified malware within short time periods for a single user email account emphasizes the importance of further malware study and need for in-depth analysis of malware signatures. These malware behaviors could not be analyzed and so further investigation needs to be done to verify these signatures.

5 Conclusion

In this work, we have studied the malware behavioral characteristics using its binary signature from the spam email collected for a period of six months by means of an experimental sandbox test environment. The key aspect of this design is that by using this malware sandbox testing environment, we can analyze the dynamic behavioral characteristics of the spam binaries directly received from the corporate email MTA servers comprehensively. We identified approximately 42 types of malware using Clam AV tool kit. Our study finds that during this six months period only two active Trojans, Agent-165149 and Generic Fake AV are contributing around 20 percent of the malwares received and rest of the 80 percent email spam are evenly distributed over many different types of botnets. In addition to that a strong surge of spam activity was recorded during the month of February and June. This study also recorded a strong polymorphic behaviors exhibited by the malwares to overcome the up-to-date malware detection mechanisms employed by the corporate email security firewalls and Intrusion detection systems.

6 Future Work

One dimension of future work is to expand the malware data coverage to a maximum of one year period to record a complete picture of the malware behavior over an extended period of time. In addition, this research work needs to be extended to multiple email users with automated data feed mechanism and measurement method for processing large volume of malware samples in real time. We want to use malware static code analysis tools to study both static and dynamic behavioral characteristics at the same time. This will help to improve the analyzing technique, and in turn help build a better malware signature and intrusion detection engines.

References

1. John, P., Alexander, M., Steven, G., Arvind, K.: Studying Spamming Botnets using Botlab. In: NSDI:6th USENIX Symposium on Networked Systems Design and Implementation (2009)
2. Holz, T., Steiner, M., Dahl, F., Biersack, E., Freiling, F.: Measurements and Mitigation of Peer-to-Peer-based Botnets: A Case Study on Storm Worm. In: First USENIX workshop on Large Scale Exploits and Emergent Threats. USENIX (2008)
3. Lu, W., Tavallaee, M., Rammidi, G., Ghorbani, A.: BotCop: An Online Botnets Traffic Classifier. In: Proceedings of the 7th Annual Conference on Communication Networks and Services Research (CNSR 2009), Moncton, New Brunswick, Canada, May 11 - 13, pp. 70–77 (2009)
4. Botnet - An Overview, CERT - In white paper CIWP 2005-05
5. Lu, W., Ghorbani, A.: Botnets Detection Based on IRC-Community. In: Proceedings of the IEEE Global Communications Conference (GLOBECOM 2008), New Orleans, LA, USA, November 30 - December 4, pp. 2067–2071 (2008)

6. Karasaridis, A., Rexroad, B., Hoeflin, D.: Wide-Scale Botnet Detection and Characterization. In: Proceedings of the First Workshop on Hot Topics in Understanding Botnets (2007)
7. Baecher, P., Koetter, M., Holz, T., Dornseif, M., Freiling, F.: The nepenthes platform: An efficient approach to collect malware. In: Zamboni, D., Krügel, C. (eds.) RAID 2006. LNCS, vol. 4219, pp. 165–184. Springer, Heidelberg (2006)
8. Lu, W., Tavallaee, M., Ghorbani, A.: Automatic Discovery of Botnet Communities on Large-Scale Communication Networks. In: Proceedings of the 2009 ACM Symposium on Information, Computer and Communications Security, ASIACCS 2009, Sydney, Australia, March 10-12, pp. 1–10. ACM, New York (2009)
9. Apache Spam Assassin Project, Open Source Windows Spam Filter, `http://spamassassin.apache.org`
10. Sanabria, A.: Malware Analysis Environment Design Architecture, SANS Institute, SANS Institute InfoSec Reading Room, (January 18, 2007)
11. Higgins, K.: DDos Botnets, Thriving and Threatening, `http://www.darkreading.com/security/vulnerabilities/208803800/index.html`
12. Polymorphic Malware: A Threat That Changes on the Fly -Polymorphic malware changes shape to fool detection schemes, `http://www.csoonline.com/article/221190/polymorphic-malware-a-threat-that-changes-on-the-fly`
13. Malware Writers Use Multiple Botnets to Spread Valentine's Day Heartache, `http://www.eweek.com/c/a/Security/Malware-Writers-Use-Multiple-Botnets-to-Spread-Valentines-Day-Love/`
14. HoneyNet Project, Know Your Enemy Tracking Botnets, `http://www.honeynet.org/papers/bots/`
15. The Crime ware Landscape: Malware, Phishing, Identity Theft and Beyond, A Joint Report of the US Department of Homeland Security –SRI International Identity Theft Technology Council and the Anti-Phishing Working Group (October 2006), `http://www.antiphishing.org/reports/APWG_CrimewareReport.pdf`
16. Clam anti virus tool kit, `http://www.clamav.net`

Sequential Multi-Clustering Protocol Using a Node Deployment Protocol for Efficient Multi-Clustering in Wireless Sensor Networks

Pradipta Ghosh, Joydeep Banerjee, Swarup Kumar Mirta, Souvik Kumar Mitra, and Mrinal Kanti Naskar

Dept. of Electronics & Tele-Communication Engineering, Jadavpur University, Kolkata-700032, WB, India
{Iampradiptaghosh,swarup.subha,souvikmitra.ju}@gmail.com, jogs.1989@rediffmail.com, mrinalnaskar@yahoo.co.in

Abstract. A cluster-based wireless sensor network (WSN) can enhance the whole network lifetime. In each cluster, the cluster head (CH) plays an important role in aggregating and forwarding data sensed by other common nodes. So a major challenge in the WSN is the appropriate cluster head selection approach while maintaining all the necessary requirement of the WSN. Lack of sufficient power and bandwidth makes the task of clustering much more challenging. In this paper we have introduced a new clustering approach termed as Sequential Multi-Clustering Protocol (SMCP).This ensures message complexity and number of clusters formed much smaller compared to the other clustering algorithms. Moreover along with the message efficient multi-clustering we also proposed a node deployment protocol which enhances the lifetime of the network. The effectiveness of these proposed methods is presented in this paper in form of simulation results.

Keywords: Expanded Ring algorithm, Persistent algorithm, Rapid algorithm, Sequential Multi-Clustering Protocol, Node deployment protocol.

1 Introduction

Wireless sensor network (WSN) technology finds its applications in diverse fields–military, environmental monitoring, health, smart households and offices. Wireless sensor networks possess certain characteristics such as rapid deployment, fault tolerance etc. which makes them suitable for use in military communication and intelligence systems. In the field of healthcare, sensor nodes have been deployed to monitor the condition of patients [1]. Sensor nodes have also been deployed for cattle ranch monitoring [2], cattle control [3], zebra herd monitoring [4], etc. Efficient flood forecasting systems utilizing wireless sensor network technology are also being developed [5, 6]. They have an enormous potential to minimize the devastations caused by severe floods in rural and developing regions. With the growing use of wireless sensor networks the size and complexity of the networks will increase. The sensor nodes are essentially low-cost, low-power devices capable of communicating in short distances

D.C. Wyld et al. (Eds.): CNSA 2011, CCIS 196, pp. 526–536, 2011.

and processing some data. These sensor nodes are generally densely deployed in the concerned region either in a regular or irregular manner. Wireless sensor networks could get exposed to adverse environments [7] e.g.-wireless sensor networks used for disaster monitoring. Therefore these networks should have a self organizing capability and immune to node failures. Thus it becomes necessary to prevent single points of failure which in turn calls for distributed algorithms. The self-organizing property of wireless sensor networks requires network decomposition into clusters of specific sizes. The main aim should be to minimize the message complexity of the clustering algorithms and to ensure the cluster formed attain the specific bound with minimum number of clusters. Lack of sufficient power in the nodes and limited bandwidth of the wireless medium [1] makes the task of clustering more challenging.

The very first clustering algorithm was the expanding ring algorithm by Ramamoorthy et al. [8]. However the no. of messages used by the algorithm in case of dense topologies is too large. Rajesh Krishnan and David Storobinski [9] suggested message-efficient algorithms, based on allocation of local growth budget to neighbors. The two algorithms suggested were the Rapid and Persistent approach. Both are far more efficient in terms of message complexity than the expanding ring approach. The Rapid algorithm generally uses fewer messages than the persistent approach but very often fails to achieve the specified cluster size. The second algorithm is an improved version of the Rapid approach as it persistently tries to produce a cluster of the specific size in exchange of some extra messages.

This paper includes a protocol for multi clustering of the WSN which we have termed as Sequential Multi-Clustering Protocol (SMCP). This protocol mainly focuses upon reduction of message complexity and to maintain the number of cluster within a range along with no of elements in each cluster within desired value while clustering the entire WSN. The effectiveness of this method is justified by a set of simulations using three clustering algorithms and the results are presented in this paper. We have also incorporated a realistic and adaptive node distribution protocol for ensuring the wireless connection between each nodes and energy saving by keeping one of the node in sleep mode if two node senses data of somewhat the same region. We have used the latest network programming tool - NS 2.33 in evaluating the performance along with MATLAB 7.8 for the other relevant experimentations.

The rest of the paper is organized as follows. Section 2 presents previous work in the field of wireless sensor networks regarding clustering. Section 3 describes our proposed works. Section 4 provides the simulation results. Section 5 concludes our manuscript.

2 Related Works

The clustering algorithms should be able to form bounded-size clusters with few messages. The no. of nodes in a cluster should always be as close as possible to the specified bound. However the early clustering algorithms treated size as a secondary factor. Ramamoorthy et al. [8] applied an expanding ring approach which requires an initiator and proceeds in rounds with continuously increasing hop limits. In each round the nodes at a distance of the hop limit for that round get clustered. Eventually on most occasions, the cluster size exceeds the specified bound. Extra nodes were un-clustered using additional message. This approach however could lead to a larger number of messages.

Heinzelman et al. [10] proposed a clustering-base approach, called LEACH (Low Energy Adaptive Clustering Hierarchy) with 2 main assumptions: existence of a unique base station and ability of all sensors to communicate directly with the base station. The LEACH protocol selects a certain no. of cluster-heads, which then communicate directly with the base station whereas other nodes send data to the base station through the cluster-heads. Also the LEACH protocol allows different nodes to be cluster-heads at different times, thus allowing conservation of energy. Other work related to LEACH includes the PEGASIS protocol [11] in which nodes form a chain to facilitate further energy conservation. The LEACH protocol is a very important work in the field of wireless sensor networks. But our work substantially differs from it. Subramanium and Katz [12] proposed general architectural guidelines for wireless sensor networks and also explained the superiority of multi-hop communication over single-hop communication. They also proposed a clustering approach quite similar to the Expanding Ring algorithm of Ramamoorthy et al [8]. The only difference is that the initiator increases its power rather than the hop count. For each round the initiator sends message and all the sensors within the initiator's communication range respond to it and get clustered. At the end of each round the initiator increases its power and hence its communication range. This process continues till the cluster size attains a value between a certain minimum and maximum bound. It has been already shown that the message efficiency of this approach can be very low but the energy of the node that becomes an initiator on any round loses its power exponentially and hence affects the lifetime of the network.

Rajesh Krishnan and David Starobinski [9] proposed two clustering algorithms namely Rapid and Persistent both of which have a far lower message complexity compared to the Expanding Ring approach especially in case of dense topologies. In the same paper Rajesh Krishnan and David Starobinski [8] showed the worst case message complexities of the clustering algorithms. They proved that the worst case message complexity of the Rapid and the Persistent algorithms are B and $2B^2$ respectively where B is the specified cluster bound.

3 Proposed Work

We have segregated our proposed work into two sections. Firstly we have described the node deployment protocol and then we introduce our Sequential Multi-Clustering Protocol.

3.1 Deployment Protocol

The Wireless Sensors are spatially distributed in a certain topology to co-operatively monitor physical or environmental conditions. But this spatial distribution must follow certain pattern. Here we also propose a justifiable protocol for distribution of sensors for increasing the energy saving efficiency in a given network. We have used the discrete radio model [13] in framing this protocol. Our intension is to make the motes to operate at the lowest possible power level considering the power level definitions as in [13]. Moreover there is no meaning to place two sensors at some nearby regions as both of them would collect the same data. For an efficient and economic approach one must optimize the deployment of sensors. This is the part of deployment protocol. For achieving this we divide the field in n squares of edge length ‘a/√n’ for the deployment of ‘n’ sensor motes in a square field of edge length ‘a’. This is shown in Figure 1. The nodes are deployed within each such sub squares on a randomly occupying position in those regions. For explanation we deployed two motes in one sub square and it can be seen that the sensing region of those nodes are overlapping at the lowest possible power level. Thus there is no need to place two sensors within such close proximity or in more generalized way in same such square block. But if it is so it would be more power saving to switch one of the sensors off while the other does not get exhausted in terms of power. Now it can be also seen in Figure 2 that by following this protocol each sensor has eight sensors surrounding its sensing region. Now two particular sensors communicate at the lowest power level settings and hence the message transmit cost will also be low and hence enhances the lifetime of the network. As per the above theory it is clear that a single sensor can communicate with at the most of 8 sensors to a minimum of 1.

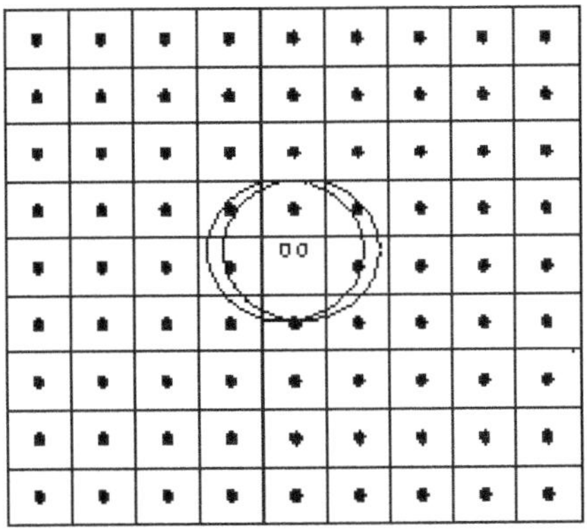

Fig. 1. Representation of sensor deployment protocol to be adopted for enhancement of lifetime in wireless sensor network

3.2 Our Proposed Sequential Multi-Clustering Protocol (SMCP)

In this section we will present the clustering protocol proposed by us. Ours method is a sequential clustering method. So in our method, at a moment only one cluster can be generated. That means until the previous cluster formation is complete next cluster cannot be generated. The most important thing of clustering is proper selection of cluster heads which is the primary focus of any clustering method. We must also keep in mind the available energy, message complexity and most of the important parameters regarding any WSN.

In our proposed method, the first cluster head is selected randomly from the entire set of available nodes. After the cluster formation is complete, the last hop of the formed cluster marks their available (i.e. un-clustered) neighbor nodes so that they cannot be selected as cluster head. Also from simple reasoning one can infer that all the nodes that are already clustered cannot be selected as cluster heads either. So they are marked as well. After the first cluster is formed, we have to select next cluster head. Now there are two types of selection is offered in our algorithm for selecting the next cluster head.

- Case 1: Previously we have provided a method of marking the neighbor nodes of previously clustered nodes. We have stated that the un-clustered neighborhood nodes of the respective last hops of the clusters, that are formed already, are marked. Now one of these nodes, that are marked for not to be selected as cluster head, is randomly chosen. The chosen node checks its immediate neighborhood for nodes available and unmarked (i.e. Unclustered and eligible of being selected as a cluster head) for selection of next cluster head. If there is a number of nodes are available, then any one of them can be selected as cluster head. So we have adopted a randomized approach toward selection of cluster head i.e. one of the sorted out nodes is selected randomly. This is shown in figure 2.

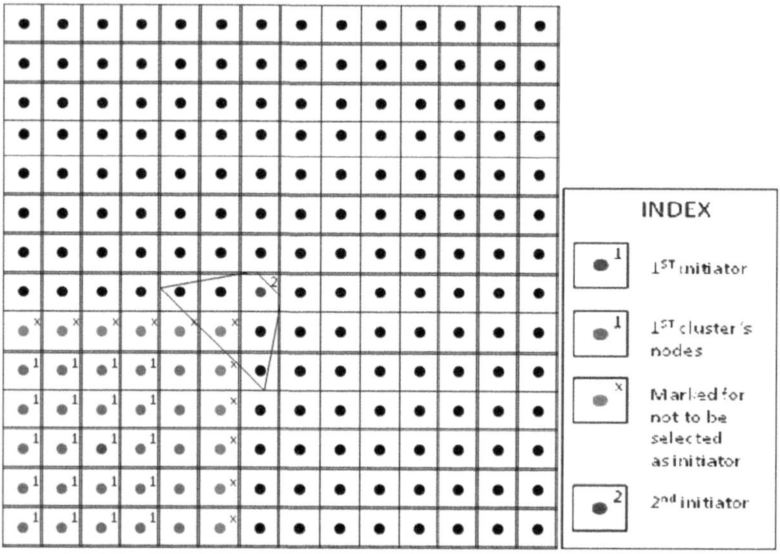

Fig. 2. Representation of cluster head selection protocol for case 1

- Beside the first method of selection, another approach towards head section is given equal priority. This approach mainly focuses upon reduction of the message count in course of selection of cluster heads. We have a set of nodes that cannot be selected as cluster head. So we can easily select any one node among the rests (i.e. nodes not included in that set) as cluster head. This approach is also randomized. So any one of the nodes, available for selection as cluster head, is selected randomly as the next cluster head. This is shown in figure 3.

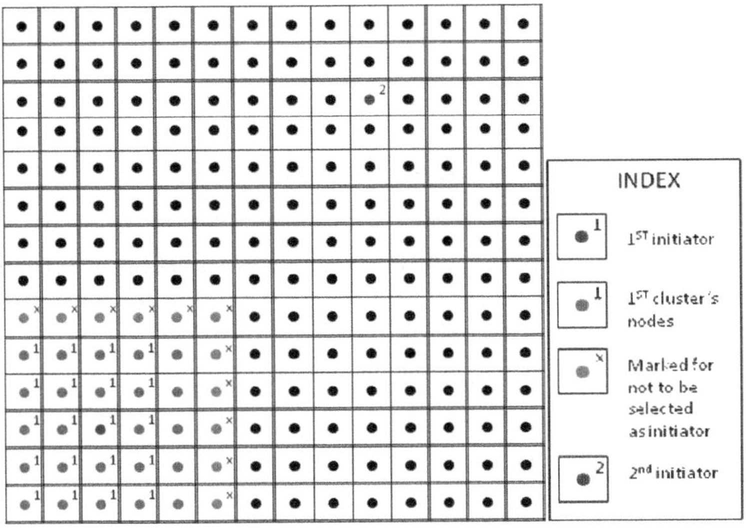

Fig. 3. Representation of cluster head selection protocol for case 2

These two types of selection method are given probability of 0.5. If both of these methods fail, then we check for nos. of un-clustered and unmarked nodes. If the number is high enough our algorithm will select one of these left-out nodes as cluster head in the high density region.

After selection of every cluster head the clustering is performed. After the next cluster is formed, previously describes steps are repeated again and again until most of the nodes are clustered.

It is observed that by using our method 1-3 nodes are left out after the clustering is complete. So we have included another mechanism to include them also. They are included to their nearest cluster at the expenses of one or two extra overhead.

4 Observations

We have first observed by computations the suitability of the node deployment protocol. In Figure 4 we have shown the energy expense in one cluster formation for varying edge length. The energy required for formation of cluster of 500 nodes by expanded ring algorithm using the node deployment protocol is much less a s compared to random deployment and hence justifies its suitability for clustering and even employing routing algorithms for wireless sensor network.

For checking the applicability of our SMCP method at first we have created the WSN network topology over which all the algorithms are run in NS 2.33. The average outcomes of the simulation are given here for two different topologies.

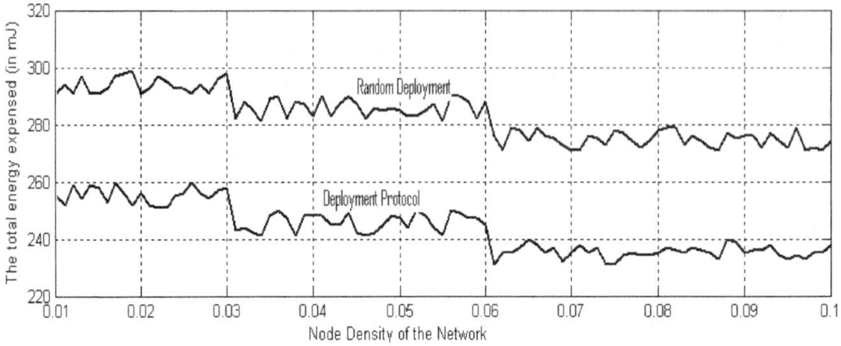

Fig. 4. Comparison graph of the energy required for cluster formation of 500 nodes by using deployment protocol and random deployment

- Topology 1

In the table 1, we presented the results over the topology 1 with the corresponding parameters as follows.

Length of the square 2-D area over which the network is created in meter = 100
Total number of nodes in the network = 500

The range of the nodes in meter = 7.5

Max no of nodes in a the cluster = 25

So, No of Desired Cluster = 20

Table 1. Results of simulation over topology 1

TOPOLOGY 1	Expanding Ring	Rapid	Persistent
No of Clusters	22	29	22
No. Messages exchanged	1005	886	558
Avg. No. of un-clustered nodes	2	3	1

- Topology 2

In the table 2, we presented the results over the topology 2 with the corresponding parameters as follows.

Length of the square 2-D area over which the network is created in meter = 200
Total number of nodes in the network = 1000

The range of the nodes in meter = 7.5

Max no of nodes in a the cluster = 25

So, No of Desired Cluster = 40

Table 2. Results of simulation over topology 2

TOPOLOGY 2	Expanding Ring	Rapid	Persistent
No of Clusters	44	55	43
No. Messages exchanged	1620	1543	1146
Avg. No. of un-clustered nodes	3	5	2

From Table 1 and Table 2 we can see that our proposed multi cluster algorithm performs well for all the clustering algorithms. We can also see that the nos. of clusters and nos. of message exchanged for each of the algorithms are as per our assumptions. Number of clusters is the highest for rapid and for rest of the algorithms it is almost same. No of message is highest for expanding ring algorithm. We can also see that the average no of left-out nodes is very small i.e. within 5 or both the cases. These results are obtained from simulations based on NS 2.33. The average values are taken over 25 runs.

Now for generalized experimentation we have done the simulation in MATLAB over a varied number of nodes. In Figure 5, 6 and 7 we have shown the number of clusters formed when the number of nodes in the network is varied from 200 to 1000 for each of the algorithms that are expanded ring, rapid and persistent respectively for a cluster bound of 25 nodes for a square field of edge 200m. Thus we have indirectly varied the node density from 0.005 to 0.025. Three individual runs were made to compute the actual number of clusters formed for each number of nodes varying from 200 to 1000 and we have taken the linear average of the three. These simulations were performed in MATLAB 7.8 and it had taken nearly a day to compute this data for each algorithm on a 3 Giga hertz processor and 4 GB RAM machine. From figure 5 and 7 we see that for expanded ring and persistent the number of cluster formed is nearly same as the expected number of clusters formed which is shown by the plot resembling like box function 2 dimensional plots as shown in the figures. The maximum variation from the ideal number of cluster formed in expanded ring is 12.9% where as it is 9.7% for persistent. On the other hand for rapid algorithm the cluster bound in never reached so we get a slightly higher number of cluster in many cases which is depicted in the comparative plot of Figure 6.The method applied by [9] produced the 1.97 times the number of expected number of clusters for expanded ring and 1.76 and 3.6 times the number of cluster for persistent and rapid respectively, Thus our algorithm proves sufficient enough to reduce the number of clusters formed in the network which in turn reduces the energy consumption per round of data transfer for the network.

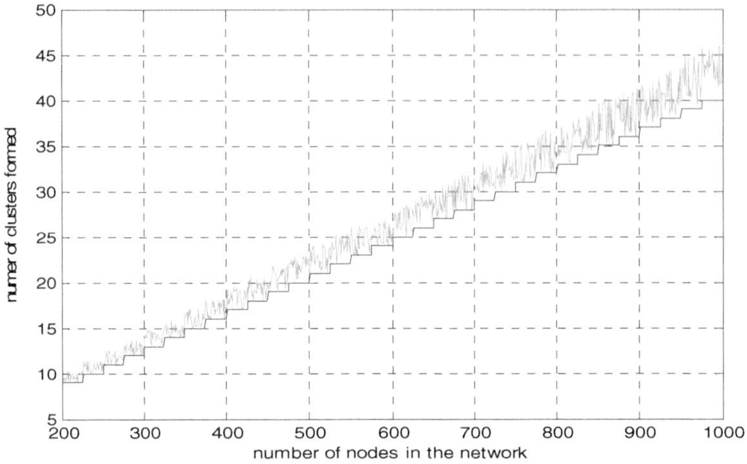

Fig. 5. The number of cluster formed for Expanded Ring Algorithm for a varying number of nodes

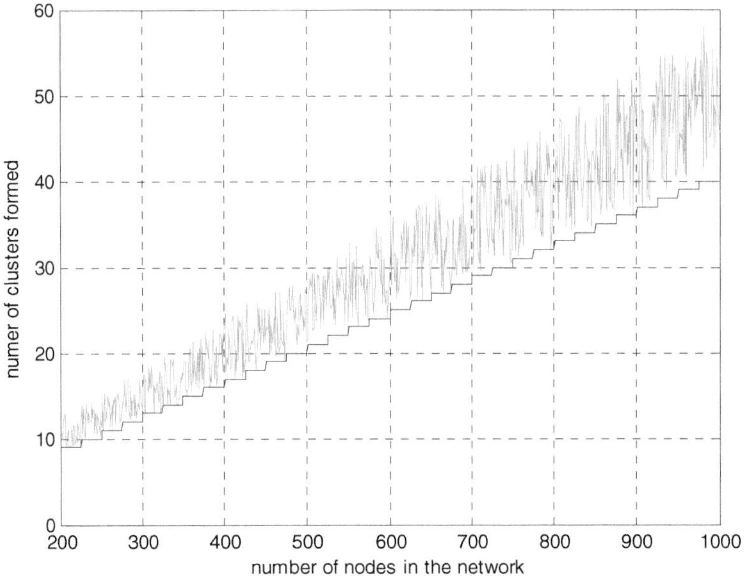

Fig. 6. The number of cluster formed for Rapid Algorithm for a varying number of nodes

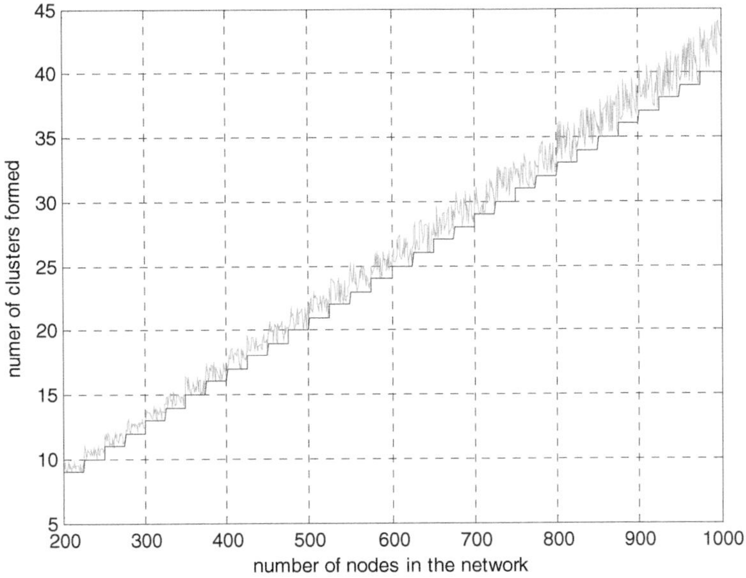

Fig. 7. The number of cluster formed for Persistent Algorithm for a varying number of nodes

5 Conclusions and Future Work

We have proved that our proposed SMMCP is very efficient in terms of energy awareness, message count, nos. of formed cluster etc. Moreover the node deployment protocol assist in the improvement in the performance of our algorithm to a greater extend. There are also scopes of modification in SMMCP. We have implemented sequential clustering in this paper. Our further work will be focused on implementing a simultaneous clustering protocol i.e. all the cluster should form simultaneously for time saving.

References

1. Akyildiz, et al.: Georgia Institute of Technology,, A Survey on Sensor Networks. IEEE Comunication Magazine (August 2002)
2. Sikka, P., Corke, P., Valencia, P., Crossman, C., Swain, D., Bishop-Hurley, G.: Wireless adhoc sensor and actuator networks on the farm. In: IPSN 2006: Proceedings of the 5th International Conference on Information Processing in Sensor Networks, pp. 492–499. ACM Press, New York (2006)
3. Butler, Z., Corke, P., Peterson, R., Rus, D.: From robots to animals: Virtual fences for controlling cattle. Int. J. Rob. Res. 25(5-6), 485–508 (2006)
4. Zhang, P., Sadler, C.M., Lyon, S.A., Martonosi, M.: Hardware design experiences in ZebraNet. In: SenSys 2004: Proceedings of the 2nd International Conference on Embedded Networked Sensor Systems, pp. 227–238. ACM Press, New York (2004)

5. Hughes, D., Greenwood, P., Blair, G., Coulson, G., Pappenberger, F., Smith, P., Beven, K.: An intelligent and adaptable grid-based flood monitoring and warning system. In: Proceedings of the 5th UK eScience All Hands Meeting (2006)
6. Basha, E.A., Ravela, S., Rus, D.: Model-Based Monitoring for Early Warning Flood Detection. In: SenSys 2008, November 5-7. ACM Press, Raleigh (2008)
7. Sterbenz, J.P.G., Krishnan, R., Hain, R.R., Jackson, A.W., Levin, D., Ramanathan, R., Zao, J.: Survivable mobile wireless networks: issues, challenges, and research directions. In: ACM Workshop on Wireless Security (WiSe), Atlanta, GA, USA, September 28, vol. 1, pp. 31–40 (2002)
8. Ramamoorthy, C.V., Bhide, A., Srivastava, J.: Reliable Clustering techniques for large, mobile packet radio networks. In: Proceedings of the 6th Annual Joint Conference of the IEEE Computer and Communications Societies(INFOCOM 1987), San Francisco, CA, USA, March 31 April 2, vol. 1, pp. 218–226 (1987)
9. Krishnan, R., Starobinski, D.: Efficient clustering algorithms for self-organizing wireless sensor networks. Ad-Hoc Networks 4, 36–59 (2006)
10. Heinzelman, W., Chandrakasan, A., Balakrishnan, H.: Energy-efficient communication protocols for wireless micro sensor networks. In: Proceedings of the 33rd Hawaiian International Conference on Systems Science (HICSS-33), Maui, HI, USA, January 4–7 (2000)
11. Lindsey, S., Raghavendra, C.S.: PEGASIS: Power Efficient Gathering in Sensor Information Systems. In: Proceedings of IEEE Aerospace Conference, Big Sky, MT, USA, March 9–16, vol. 3, pp. 3-1125–3-1130 (2002)
12. Subramanian, L., Katz, R.H.: An architecture for building self-configurable systems. In: Proceedings of the 1st ACM International Symposium on Mobile Ad Hoc Networking and Computing, Boston, MA, USA, pp. 63–73 (2000)
13. Mallinson, M., Drane, P., Hussain, S.: Dsicrete Radio Power Level Consumption Model in Wireless Sensor Network. In: IEEE International Conference on Mobile Ad-Hoc and Sensor Systems MASS 2007, pp. 1–6 (2007)

Online Based Fuzzy Analyzer for Arrhythmia Detection

K.A. Sunitha[1], N. Senthil Kumar[2], S.S. Dash[3], and k. prema[1]

[1] Assistant professor, Instrumentation and Control Engineering Department, SRM University
[2] Professor, Mepco schlenk Engineering College, Sivakasi
[3] Professor, EEE Department, SRM University
sunithasrm@yahoo.in, {nsk_vnr,munu_dash_2k}@yahoo.com,
premsb4u@gmail.com

Abstract. Due to changing trends, there is an increasing risk of people having Cardiac Disorders. This is the impetus behind, for developing a system which can diagnose the cardiac disorder and also risk level of the patient, so that effective medication can be taken in the initial stages. In this paper, Atrial rate, Ventricular rate, QRS Width and PR Interval are extracted from ECG signal, so that arrhythmia disorders- Sinus tachycardia (ST), supra-ventricular tachycardia (SVT), ventricular tachycardia (VT), junctional tachycardia (JT), ventricular and Atrial fibrillation (VF & AF) have been diagnosed with their respective risk levels. So that the system acts as an risk analyzer, which tells how far the subject is prone to arrhythmia. LabVIEW signal express is used to read ECG and for analysis this information is passed to the Fuzzy Module. In the Fuzzy module Various "If-then rules" have been framed to identify the risk level of the patient. The Extracted information is then published to the client from the server by using a Online publishing tool. After passing the report developed by the system to the doctor,he or she can pass the medical advice to the server, i.e. generally the system where the patient ECG is extracted and analyzed.

Index Terms: LabVIEW, Arrhythmia- Sinus tachycardia (ST), supra-ventricular tachycardia (SVT), ventricular tachycardia (VT), junctional tachycardia (JT), ventricular and Atrial fibrillation (VF & AF), Online publishing tool, QRS width, trial rate,ventricular rate.

1 Introduction

According to the World Health Organization (WHO) heart disease and stroke kills around 17 million people a year, which is almost one-third of all deaths globally. By 2020, heart disease and stroke will become the leading cause of both death and disability worldwide. So, it is very clear that proper diagnosis of heart disease is important for patients to survive. Electrocardiogram (ECG) is an important tool for Diagnosis of heart diseases .But it has some drawbacks such as:

1) Special skill is required to administer and interpret the results of ECG.
2) Cost of ECG equipment is high.
3) Limited availability of ECG equipment.

D.C. Wyld et al. (Eds.): CNSA 2011, CCIS 196, pp. 537–544, 2011.

Due to these drawbacks, telemedicine contacts were mostly used for consultations between special telemedicine centres in hospitals and clinics in the past. More recently, however, providers have begun to experiment with telemedicine contacts between health care providers and patients at home to monitor conditions such as chronic diseases [1].

LabVIEW (Laboratory Virtual Instrument Engineering Workbench) is a graphical programming environment suited for high-level or system-level design. As it has been proven that LabVIEW based telemedicine system does have the following features.

1) It replaces multiple stand-alone devices at the cost of a single instrument using virtual instrumentation and its functionality is expandable [2].
2) It facilitates the extraction of valuable diagnostic information using embedded advanced biomedical signal processing algorithms [2].
3) It can be connected to the internet to create an internet –based telemedicine infrastructure, which provides a comfortable way for physicians to communicate with friends, family and colleagues [3].

Several systems had been developed on acquisition and analysis of ECG [4]-[8] using labVIEW . Some systems [9] and [10],[11] also deals with identifying the cardiac disorder but it lacks , identifying the risk levels of the patient for the cardiac disorder and the online publishing system.

In this paper, we developed a program not only to access the patient's data but also we had tried to diagnose the heart abnormalities, which can be a reference to the doctor or physician for further procedure. This can be taken up from anywhere if an internet connection is available. And a fuzzy system is developed to identify the risk level of the patient. . Fuzzy system is more accurate than the normal controller because instead of being either true or false, a partial true case can also be declared. The risk scores can be accurately and exactly calculated for specific records of a person.

2 Proposed System

Figure 1. Shows the proposed Fuzzy analyser with online System.

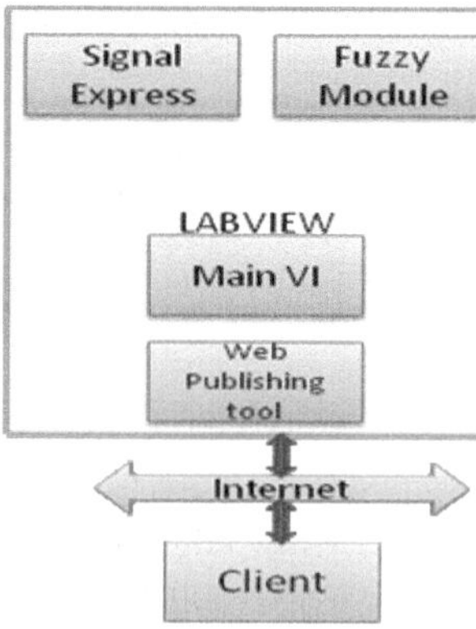

Fig. 1. Proposed system

The ECG waveforms are obtained from MIT-BIH Database.LabVIEW signal express is used to read and make analysis of the ECG and pass the information to the Fuzzy Module, in the Fuzzy module Various "If-then rules " have been written to identify the risk level of the patient.

The Extracted information is then published to the client from the server by using a Online publishing toolkit. To prevent unauthorized access, a username and password is provided to the client. Client refers to the Doctor`s Computer.

After passing the information the doctor can pass the medical advice to the server, i.e. generally the system where the patient ECG is extracted and analyzed.

A. *Internet based System*

The internet is used as a to and fro vehicle to deliver both the virtual medical instruments, medical data and prescription from the doctor in real time .An internet-based telemedicine system is shown in fig:2. This work involves an internet –based telemonitoring system, which has been developed as an instance of the general client-server architecture presented in fig:.

The client server architecture is defined as follows: the client application provide visualization, archiving, transmission, and contact facilities to the remote user (i.e., the patient). The server, which is located at the physicians end takes care of the incoming data, and organizes patient sessions.

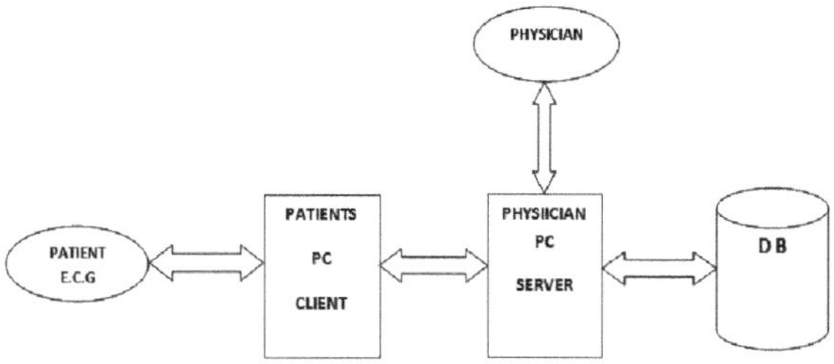

Fig. 2. Internet based system

B. *LABVIEW*

LabVIEW is a graphical programming language developed by National instruments. Programming with LabVIEW gives a vivid picture of data flow by the graphical representation in blocks. labview is used here for getting the ECG waveform and also for analyzing the parameters like PR interval, QRS width, heart rates which are later passed to the fuzzy system.

LabVIEW offers modular approach and parallel computing , which makes easier for developing complex systems. Debugging tools like probes, Highlight execution are handy in analyzing where actually the error occurred.

C. *Fuzzy system*

Fuzzy controllers are the widely employed as they are efficient controllers when working with the vague values. A Fuzzy controller has a rule base in "IF-THEN" fashion, which is used for identification of the risk level of disease using the weight.

A Fuzzy system is generally given by Fig 3.

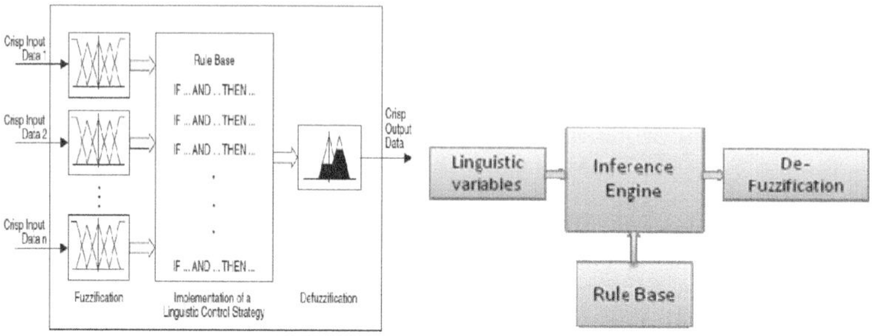

Fig. 3. Fuzzy system

A. Fuzzification

In this system we are considering the atrial and ventricular heart rates, QRS complex width and PR interval values as the input linguistic variables, which are passed to the inference engine.

Based on the rule base and linguistic variables, the fuzzy system output is obtained.

B. Defuzzification

The defuzzified values are the risk levels high risk, medium risk, low risk which are obtained according to the weights of fuzzy variables.

C. Relation between input and output variables

The relationship between input and output is shown by a 3-Dimensional figure 4. shown below

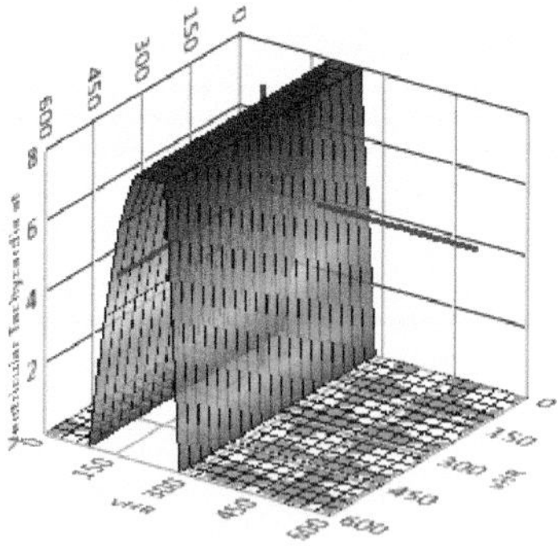

Fig. 4. Relation between input and output

D. Fuzzy Rules

In this Fuzzy system we are using the centre of area method as the fuzzificaton method. The rule base of the fuzzy system consists of rules in the form of "If-Then". The risk levels are dependent on the number of conditions are met by the input variables for the respective cardiac disorder. As there is no particular rule of identifying the arrhythmia based on heart rate, since it can differ from patient to patient and so this system thus is more accurate in determining the arrhythmia since it is not based only on heart rate.

Fuzzy rule base is acts like a database of rules for selecting the output, basing on the input quantities. Some of the rules are:-

1. IF 'PR interval' IS 'Normal' AND 'vHR' IS '30,40' AND 'aHR' IS '60,75' THEN 'First Degree Block' IS 'No ' ALSO 'Third Degree block' IS 'Medium Risk'
2. IF 'PR interval' IS 'Normal' AND 'vHR' IS '30,40' AND 'aHR' IS '75,90' THEN 'First Degree Block' IS 'No ' ALSO 'Third Degree block' IS 'Medium Risk'
3. IF 'PR interval' IS 'Normal' AND 'vHR' IS '30,40' AND 'aHR' IS '90,100' THEN 'First Degree Block' IS 'No ' ALSO 'Third Degree block' IS 'High Risk'.
4. IF 'vHR' IS '150,180' AND 'QRS Width' IS 'Narrow QRS' THEN 'Ventricular Tachycardia at' IS 'Low risk' ALSO 'Junctional Tachycardia at' IS 'Low Risk' ALSO 'Supra Ventricular Tachy at' IS 'High Risk'
5. IF 'vHR' IS '180,210' AND 'QRS Width' IS 'Normal QRS' THEN 'Ventricular Tachycardia at' IS 'Low risk' ALSO 'Junctional Tachycardia at' IS 'High Risk' ALSO 'Supra Ventricular Tachy at' IS 'Low Risk'

In this manner, based upon the PR interval,QRS width, atrial and Ventricular heart rates a Fuzzy system is developed to identify the Cardio disorder as well as its level of risk.

3 Online Publishing

One of the Unique feature of this system is its ability to publish or pass the extracted information to the Client, usually to a doctor`s computer. This helps in implementing a telediagnosis system. The doctor will be able to see the diagnosis result along with risk levels and then pass the information to the doctor for further advice. Since internet issued for passing the values to the doctor ,This becomes immensely help for immediate action to be taken. This will cater to the need of public health care centres rural areas where it is difficult to have cardiologists. And also this system can be used to assist the doctor in monitoring the patient's heart during surgery.

Results

This system is able to measure the arrhythmias accurately and also publish it online.

In the above Fig 5 block diagram , it perform the function of passing the HR value obtained from the signal express to the fuzzy system .

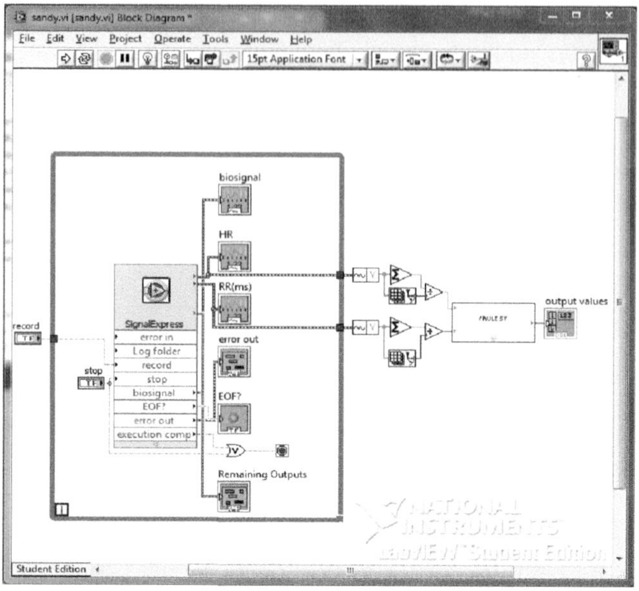

Fig. 5. Block Diagram for extracting ECG waveform

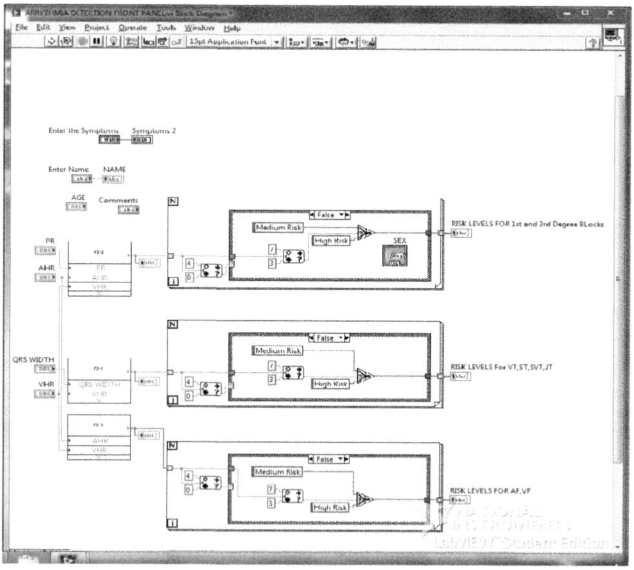

Fig. 6. Block diagram for calling fuzzy system in labVIEW

Above figure 6. Shows the block diagram of risk level detection , we show how we called the fuzzy system into the main panel for diagnosing and risk level indication.

Fig 7 shows the Front panel which is developed from the fuzzy system ,and is sent to the doctor using web publishing tool for the second advice .System also have a database to save the details of patient like Name, Age, Sex, Symptoms which can used for the next time..

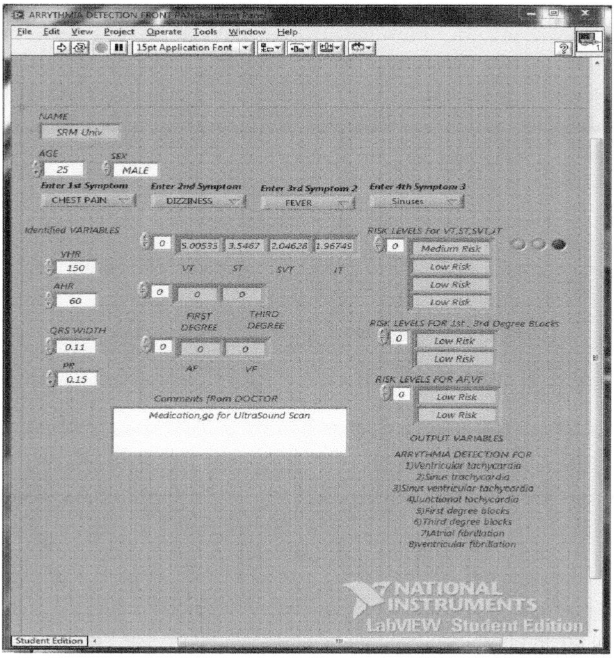

Fig. 7. Front panel

4 Conclusion

In this way we had developed a fuzzy system with good accuracy in determining the cardiac disorders with risk levels when compared to the normal system considering the atrial and ventricular heart rates, QRS complex width and PR interval values as the input linguistic variables using labVIEW. This report is successfully sent to the doctors system using web publising tool for the second advice.

References

[1] Noury, N., Pilichowski, P.: A telematic system tool for home health care. In: Proc. IEEE 14th Annu. Int. Conf. EMBS, Paris, pp. 1175–1177 (October 1992)

[2] Guo, Z., Moulder, J. c.: An internet based Telemedicine system. IEEE transactions (2000)

[3] Hrusha, V., Osolinskiy, O., Daponte, P., Grimaldi, D.: Distributed Web-based Measurement system. In: IEEE Workshop on Intelligent Data and Advanced Computing System Technology and Applications, pp. 5–7 (2005)

[4] Zhang, L., Jiang, X.: Acquisition and Analysis System of the ECG Signal Based on LabVIEW

[5] Cohen, K.P., Tompkins, W.J., Djohan, A., Webster, J.G., Hu, Y.H.: Qrs Detection Using A Fuzzy Neural Network
[6] Classification of ECG Arrhythmias using Type-2 Fuzzy Clustering Neural Network
[7] Robust techniques for remote real time arrhythmias classification system
[8] Zarei Mahmoodabadi, S., Ahmadian, A., Abolhassani, M.D., Alireazie, J., Babyn, P.: ECG Arrhythmia Detection Using Fuzzy Classifiers
[9] Chowdhury, E., Ludeman, L.C.: Discrimination of Cardiac Arrhythmias Using a Fuzzy Rule-Based Method
[10] Zong, W., Jiang, D.: Automated ECG Rhythm Analysis Using Fuzzy Reasoning
[11] Usher, J., Campbell, D., Vohra, J., Cameron, J.: Fuzzy Classification of Intra-Cardiac Arrhythmias

A Novel Autonomic Design Pattern for Invocation of Services

V.S. Prasad Vasireddy[1], Vishnuvardhan Mannava[1], and T. Ramesh[2]

[1] Department of Computer Science and Engineering, KL University, Vaddeswaram, 522502, A.P., India
vasireddy.vvs@gmail.com, vishnu@klce.ac.in
[2] Department of Computer Science and Engineering, National Institute of Technology, Warangal, 506004, A.P., India
rmesht@nitw.ac.in

Abstract. According to a definition rolled out from the Workshop on Adaptable and Adaptive Software[1] *"A program is called adaptive if it changes its behaviour automatically according to its context."*Within this context, we restrict our research domain to the automatic runtime adaptation of existing behaviours. In this paper, we propose an Autonomic Design Pattern which is an amalgamation of chain of responsibility and visitor patterns that can be used to analyze or design self-adaptive systems.We harvested this pattern and applied it on unstructured peer to peer networks and Webservices environments.Representation of an operation to be performed on the elements of an object structure is taken from the Visitor pattern and to reduce the coupling between the sender of a request to its receiver by giving more than one object a chance to handle the request is adopted from Chain of responsibility.

Keywords: Autonomic Computing, Design Patterns, WebService, JXTA, Peer-to-peer computing.

1 Introduction

Advances in software technologies and practices have enabled developers to create larger, more complex applications to meet the ever increasing user demands. In today's computing environments, these applications are required to integrate seamlessly across heterogeneous platforms and to interact with other complex applications[9]. The unpredictability of how the applications will behave and interact in a widespread, integrated environment poses great difficulties for system testers and managers. Autonomic computing proposes a solution to software management problems by shifting the responsibility for software management from the human administrator to the software system itself. It is expected that autonomic computing will result in significant improvements in terms of system management, and many initiatives have begun to incorporate autonomic capabilities into software components.

D.C. Wyld et al. (Eds.): CNSA 2011, CCIS 196, pp. 545–551, 2011.

On the other hand as applications grow in size, complexity, and heterogeneity in response to growing computational needs, it is increasingly difficult to build a system that satisfies all requirements. and design constraints that it will encounter during its lifetime. Furthermore, many of these systems are required to run continuously, disallowing downtimes while code is modified[8]. As a result, it is important for an application to self-adapt in response to changing requirements and environmental conditions. Autonomic computing has been proposed to meet this need, where a system manages itself based on high-level objectives from a systems administrator. Due to their high complexity, adaptive and autonomic systems are difficult to specify, design, verify, and validate. In addition, the current lack of reusable design expertise that can be leveraged from one adaptive system to another further exacerbates the problem.

To address these concerns, researchers have built adaptation-enabling frameworks, middleware, and language-based support. These approaches, however, may be tightly coupled with specific domains or technologies, possibly limiting their applicability across different domains. In contrast, design patterns work at the modeling and design level of abstraction, thus facilitating design reuse. The pattern proposed is a generic solution that can be easily adapted to specific situations.

Our paper is organized as follows. Section 2 presents the original design pattern. Section 3 presents the proposed pattern. In section 4 we have discussed a case study by applying it on unstructured peer to peer networks developed using JXTA with performance results. Lastly, in Section 5 we draw our conclusion sketching the path for future work.

2 Related Work

In literature there are some patterns proposed but they are not applied on computers field [4] and some outlined the challenges in implementing p2p systems[3]. Gamma et al[5]. introduced a set of design patterns for dynamically reconfiguring specific types of software architectures.

These design patterns leverage the concept of dynamic change management by specifying the behavior required to dynamically reconfigure master/ slave, server/client, centralized, and decentralized architectures[4]. Most importantly, Gamma et al.'s[5] reconfiguration patterns identify when it is safe to perform a reconfiguration based on the application's architecture.

A survey conducted by the authors[2] reveals different Web Service composition techniques.In particular the authors[6] proposed an architecture to address the issues encountered in a flexible and scalable P2P network.According to them the ultimate vision for eBusiness is an Internet-based global market place, accessible to all enterprises, regardless of size and geographical location, where automatic cooperation and integration among firms are allowed and enhanced.

A powerful mean for these purposes is represented by sharing, reusing and composing value-added services made available on the Web, i.e. Web services. In this scenario, by making the Web content machine accessible and understandable, semantic Web services aim to provide efficient and effective Web service automatic discovery, selection, and composition.

2.1 Visitor Pattern

Indent

- Represent an operation to be performed on the elements of an object structure. Visitor lets you define a new operation without changing the classes of the elements on which it operates.
- The classic technique for recovering lost type information.
- Do the right thing based on the type of two objects.
- Double dispatch

Structure

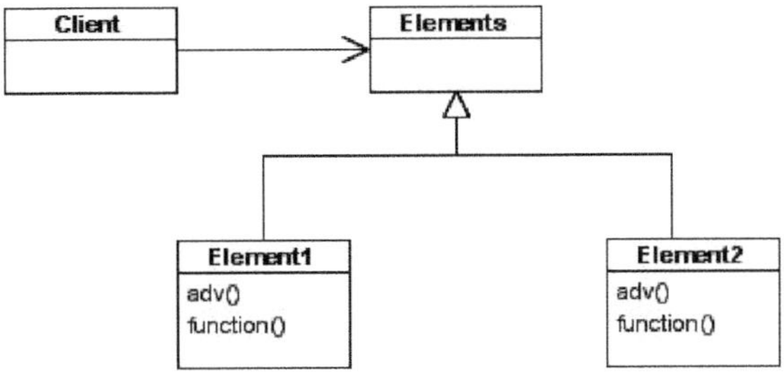

Fig. 1. UML class diagram of Visitor Pattern

2.2 Chain of Responsibility

Indent

- Avoid coupling the sender of a request to its receiver by giving more than one object a chance to handle the request. Chain the receiving objects and pass the request along the chain until an object handles it.
- Launch-and-leave requests with a single processing pipeline that contains many possible handlers.
- An object-oriented linked list with recursive traversal.

Structure: The pattern proposed in this paper is derived by fusing the Visitor and Chain of Responsibility patterns by Gamma et al[5].

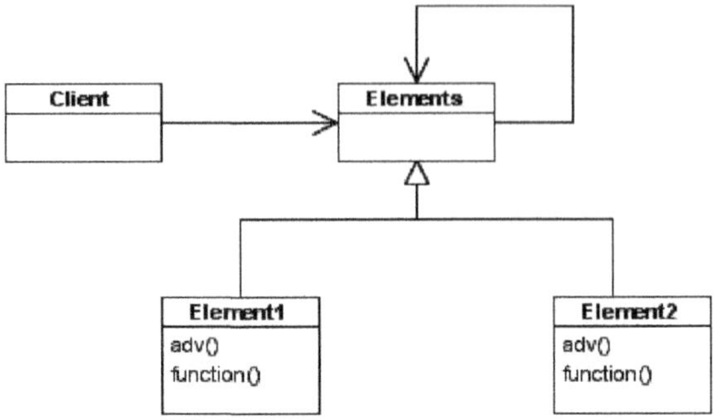

Fig. 2. UML Class diagram for Chain of Responsibility pattern

3 Proposed Pattern

Indent

- Represent an operation to be performed on the elements of an object structure.
- Lets you define a new operation without changing the classes of the elements on which it operates.
- Avoid coupling the sender of a request to its receiver by giving more than one object a chance to handle the request.
- Chain the receiving objects and pass the request along the chain until an object handles it.
- Launch-and-leave requests with a single processing pipeline that contains many possible handlers.

Structure

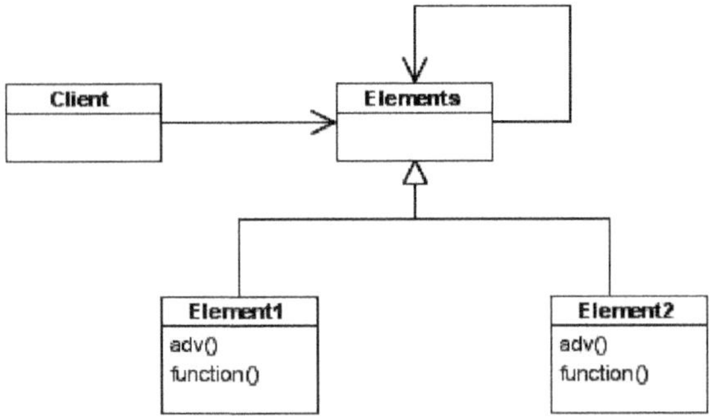

Fig. 3. UML class diagram of proposed pattern

Sequence Diagram

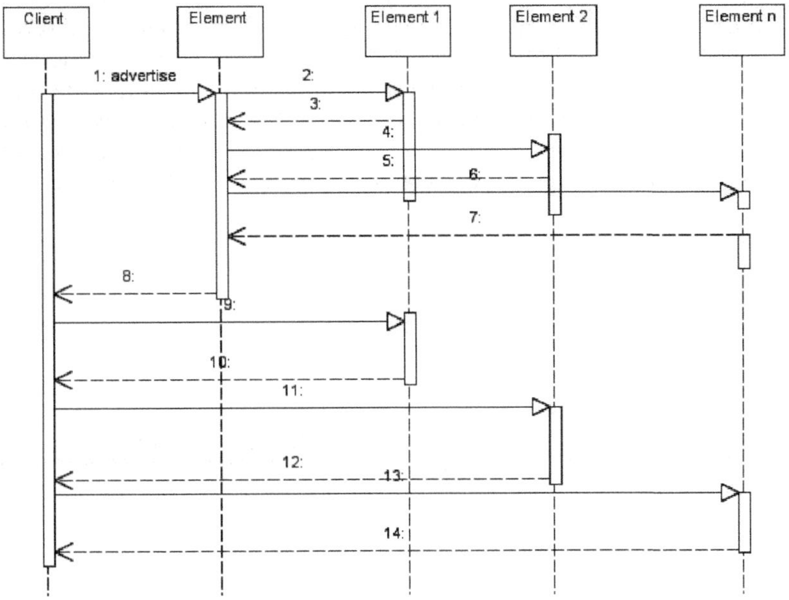

Fig. 4. Sequence diagram for the proposed autonomic design pattern

4 Case Study

To demonstrate the usefulness of this pattern this is applied to overlay environment using JXTA[7] package.In this application the client will make use of the visitor pattern to make an announcement and the peers that have the requested service will make an advertisement accordingly.Now the client peer will make use of the Chain of Responsibility pattern to find out the optimal service that serves its need and best suits in the budget.We have made the client to make an announcement for a movie and all the peers that has this movie has made an advertisement, now the client has checked for the best quality of the requested movie exploiting the Chain of Responsibility pattern and then the client has invoked the file transfer service from the resulting peer.

The following code snippet is used to create a Socket pipe advertisement with pre-defined pipe Id and to return a Socket PipeAdvertisement.This method is exploited by the client and makes use of the visitor pattern embedded in our proposed pattern to make a call to all peers that can offer the requested service.

```
public static PipeAdvertisement makeSocketAdvertisement() {
    PipeID socketID = null;
    try {

        socketID =(PipeID)IDFactory.fromURI(new URI(SOCKETIDSTR));
    } catch (URISyntaxException use) {
        use.printStackTrace();
    }
    PipeAdvertisement advertisement = (PipeAdvertisement)
     AdvertisementFactory.newAdvertisement(
     PipeAdvertisement.getAdvertisementType());
    advertisement.setPipeID(socketID);
    advertisement.setType(PipeService.PropagateType);
    advertisement.setName("Make Advertisement");
    return advertisement;
}
```

Here in our context, a service can be a method with respect to Object Oriented Paradigm, Functionalities that a peer offers and even a webservice also.We have applied it to all these domain successfully.We are presenting the profiling results taken for ten runs without applying this pattern and after applying this pattern using the profiling facility available in the Netbeans IDE.The graph is plotted taking the time of execution in milliseconds on Y-axis and the run count on the X-axis.The graph has shown good results while executing the code with patterns and is shown in Figure 5.This can confirm the efficiency of the proposed pattern. We have applied this proposed design pattern to webservice environment also and found a dynamic change in the invocation time.The class diagram of the same is shown in figure 6.

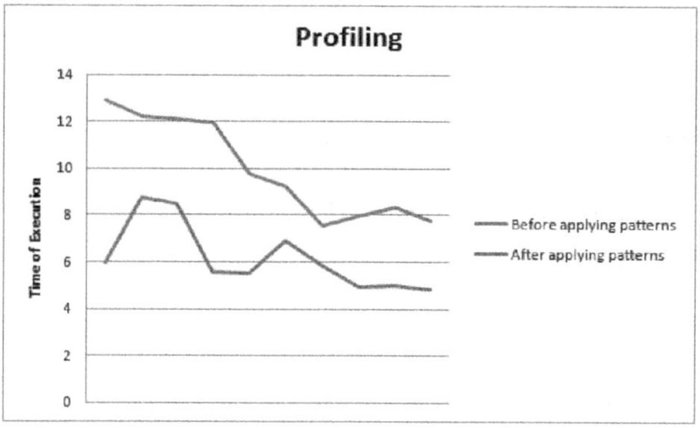

Fig. 5. Profiling data

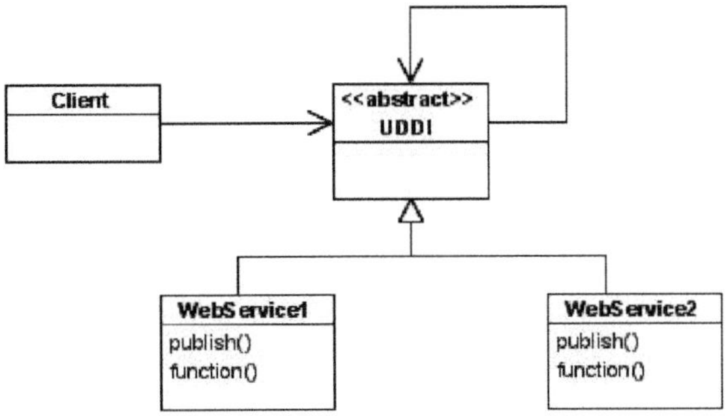

Fig. 6. UML class diagram for WebService Scenario

5 Conclusion

In this paper we have proposed a pattern to facilitate the ease of developing autonomic applications that make decisions.Several future directions of work is possible.We are examining how these design patterns can be inserted into a non-adaptive application through the use of aspect-oriented techniques. we are exploring the use of evolutionary computation techniques to determine how adaptation design patterns can be automatically instantiated and integrated into legacy systems to meet adaptation needs. We are making a generic decision making and reconfiguration infrastructure so that any application that needs dynamic adaptability can make use of them.

References

1. Aubert, O., Beugnard, A.: Adaptive strategy design pattern (2001)
2. Demian Antony D'Mello, V., Salian, S.: A review of dynamic web service composition techniques. In: Meghanathan, N., Kaushik, B.K., Nagamalai, D. (eds.) CCSIT 2011, Part III. Communications in Computer and Information Science, vol. 133, pp. 85–97. Springer, Heidelberg (2011)
3. Ekaterina Chtcherbina, M.V.: P2p patterns results from the europlop 2002 focus group. EuroPLoP 2002 focus group (2002)
4. Ferscha, A., Hechinger, M., Mayrhofer, R., Chtcherbina, E., Franz, M., Rocha, M.D.S., Zeidler, A.: Bridging the gap with p2p patterns
5. Gamma, E., Helm, R., Johnson, R., Vlissides, J.: Design patterns: elements of reusable object-oriented software. Addison-Wesley Professional, Reading (1995)
6. Mandreoli, F., Perdichizzi, A.M., Penzo, W.: A p2p-based architecture for semantic web service automatic composition
7. Microsystems, S.: Project jxta: An open, innovatice collaboration. Tech. rep. Sun Microsystems Inc., (2001)
8. Ramirez, A.J.: Design Patterns for Developing Dynamically Adaptive Systems. Master's thesis, Michigan State University, East Lansing, Michigan (August 2008)
9. Ramirez, A.J., Cheng, B.H.C.: Design patterns for developing dynamically adaptive systems. In: Proceedings of the ICSE Workshop on Software Engineering for Adaptive and Self-Managing Systems SEAMS 2010, pp. 49–58. ACM, New York (2010), `http://doi.acm.org/10.1145/1808984.1808990`

A Novel Way of Providing Dynamic Adaptability and Invocation of JADE Agent Services from P2P JXTA Using Aspect Oriented Programming

Vishnuvardhan Mannava[1], T. Ramesh[2], and V.S. Prasad Vasireddy[1]

[1] Department of Computer Science and Engineering, KL University,
Vaddeswaram 522502, A.P., India
vishnu@klce.ac.in, vasireddy.vvs@gmail.com
[2] Department of Computer Science and Engineering, National Institute of Technology,
Warangal, 506004, A.P., India
rmesht@nitw.ac.in

Abstract. Rapid development of the Internet and increasing number of available Web services has generated a need for tools and environments facilitating automated composition of atomic Web services into more complex Web processes. JADE is an agent development environment where Web services and agents can be linked together to enable semantic Web applications. However, the current JADE message transportation protocols do not allow agent communication through firewalls and network address translators (NAT-s). Fortunately, the firewall/NAT issue can be solved by using the current JXTA implementation for agent communication. In this paper we describe our efforts to incorporate JXTA protocols into JADE for facilitating inter-agent communication over the Internet. We also describe the design and implementation of an agent-based Web service composition environment, where service registration and discovery are resolved using the JXTA advertisements. By combining the capabilities of JADE and JXTA, agent-based Web service applications can be supported in JADE at a higher level of abstraction. In this paper we are using Aspect oriented programming (AOP) to enable dynamic adaptation at the time of invoking Agent web services in P2P network. We propose an approach to implement dynamic adaptability especially in existing Agent Services, p2p JXTA-WS programs and Aspect weaving in P2P JXTA using AOP. We have used AspectJ; Java based language to create aspects in Eclipse supported framework.

Keywords: Dynamic adaptation, AspectJ, Automated Web service composition, Multi-Agent systems, JADE, WSIG, P2P networks, and JXTA.

1 Introduction

A software application is adaptable if it can change its behavior dynamically (at run time) in response to transient changes in its execution environment or to permanent changes in its requirements. Recent interest in designing adaptable software is driven in part by the demand for autonomic computing. Autonomic computing [24] refers to self-managed, and potentially self-healing, systems that require only high-level

D.C. Wyld et al. (Eds.): CNSA 2011, CCIS 196, pp. 552–563, 2011.

human guidance. Autonomic computing is critical to managing the myriad of sensors and other small devices at the wireless edge, but also in managing large-scale computing centers and protecting critical infrastructure (e.g., financial networks, transportation systems, power grids) from hardware component failures, network outages, and security attacks. Developing and maintaining adaptable software are nontrivial tasks. An adaptable application comprises functional code that implements the business logic of the application and supports its imperative behavior, and adaptive code that implements the adaptation logic of the application and supports its adaptive behavior.

JADE is a FIPA compliant agent development environment which facilitates the implementation of multi-agent systems. Since Web services middleware has been integrated into JADE, agents implemented in JADE can exploit Web services as computational resources. A Web service can be published as a JADE agent service and an agent service can be symmetrically published as a Web service endpoint. Invoking a Web service is just like invoking a normal agent service. In addition, Web services' clients can also search for and invoke agent services hosted within JADE containers.

The Web Services Integration Gateway (WSIG) uses a Gateway agent to control the gateway from within a JADE container. Interaction among agents on different platforms is achieved through the Agent Communication Channel (ACC). Whenever a JADE agent sends a message and the receiver lives on a different agent platform, a Message Transport Protocol (MTP) is used to implement lower level message delivery procedures [3]. There are two main MTPs available today to support this inter-platform agent communication - CORBA IIOP-based and HTTP-based MTP.

JXTA peers advertise their services within advertisements, which enable other peers on the network to learn how to connect to, and interact with peer's services. The advertisements are XML-based documents composed of a series of hierarchically arranged elements. The JXTA's Peer Discovery Protocol (PDP) is used to discover any published resources, both on client and server sides.

In this paper we describe how to provide dynamic adaptability, reusability using AOP and how to invoke JADE Agent Services from P2P JXTA network as web services using AOP.

Our paper is organized as follows. We review related work in section 2. Section 3 describes AOP paradigm. In we describe 4, we describes Communication between JADE Agent and P2P JXTA using AOP. Try to show the Efficiency of AOP by CPU Profiling in section 5. Section 6, Try to show the affect of 'Aspects' on application through Eclipse's Aspect Visualizer. We conclude the paper in section 7 and possible future directions.

2 Related Work

Previous work has been done by Yang [19] to implement a system which performs dynamic adaptation using AOP. This approach uses join points to specify where the adaptation should take place, and a set of rules to specify the conditions when an adaptation should occur. Another solution to achieve adaptation in applications using AspectJ is proposed by Dantas et al [20]. An adaptation framework developed by Pierre-Charles David et al [21] is implemented using the Fractal component model. Peers in peer-to-peer networks are usually considered uniform in resources. There are several articles related to automated Web service composition. Ontology-Driven Web Services Composition Platform [23] aims to generate a composite service out of semantically described existing services. In this work, the possible automatic compositions are obtained through interface-matching, which checks semantic similarities between interfaces of individual services. Different services can be integrated to satisfy user requirements.

Within this body of literature, conflicting opinions as to the relationship between these two developing technologies are given including the following [22, 23]: JXTA complements Web Services, JXTA extends Web Services, JXTA supersedes Web Services, and JXTA and Web Services will converge.

So far, there is proposal for Services deployed in JXTA or Agent Web Services Environment to be able to find each other and communicate using JSDL like WSDL. Yet, they are not able to provide communication between JXTA and JADE AGENT each other. Integration of Agent Web services with p2p networks has been extensively examined in the sense of using a p2p infrastructure to enhance the various web service activities. In METEOR-S [12], a JXTA-based p2p network is utilized to organize web service registries, in order to facilitate the tasks of service publication and discovery. Yet, to the best of our knowledge, there is no approach other than the one presented in this paper, which attempts to integrate the web service and p2p worlds in terms of unified service discovery.

At the end of the paper we will present an experimental evaluation of the performances of JXTA, by comparing it with the JADE-JXTA-WS with AOP and without AOP. To this aim we adopted the performance model introduced where the authors study the JXTA rendezvous protocol performances, by comparing it with the policy of older versions of JXTA, and by using a JXTA subproject benchmark suite [16].

Here, we are successfully providing communication between JADE, p2p JXTA and Web Services in novel way using AOP. To our best knowledge, there is no related work of providing dynamic adaptability and calling Agent Services from p2p JXTA using Aspect Oriented Programming.

3 Aspect Oriented Programming (AOP)

Aspect Oriented Programming (AOP) is a program development methodology proposed by Gregor Kiczales in "Aspect-Oriented Programming"[2], published in 1997. In AOP, the requirements (requests) of the program are termed ‘concerns’. Concerns are divided into core concerns and crosscutting concerns. An example that is used most frequently to explain core and cross-cutting concerns is the Distributed Auction system. In a system, core concerns are the main functions of the Auction System, which are to set the product for auction, set minimum bid, set current bid etc. However, other features required by a distributed system, such as logging, distribution, profiling and tracing are cross-cutting concerns. Although object oriented programming is currently the most widely used methodology for dealing with core concerns, it comes up short in processing crosscutting concerns. This becomes more so for complex applications. AOP is a new methodology that enables separation of crosscutting concerns and their implementation through a new module termed the ‘aspect’. Figure 1 displays the weaving process of application code with aspect.

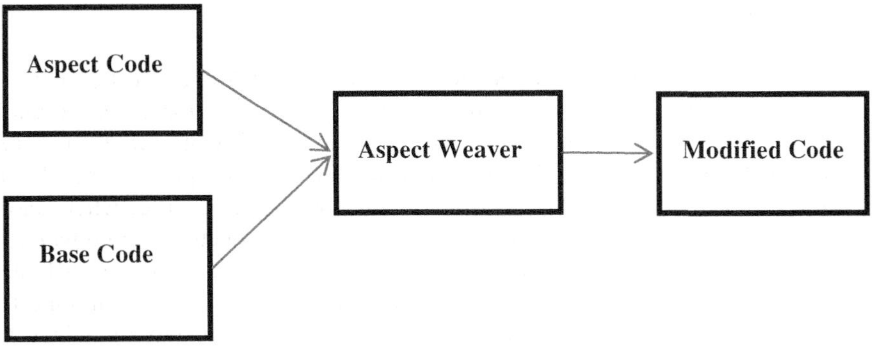

Fig. 1. Weaving of Aspect on Source Code

3.1 AspectJ

AspectJ, originally from Xerox PARC, but now part of the Eclipse initiative supported by IBM, is currently the most widely adopted programming language supporting AOP and was also used for our case studies which are described in following sections. AspectJ is built on top of the programming language Java [17, 18]. It provides mechanisms to modularize crosscutting concerns as explained above. In AspectJ programs, Java classes are used to implement the core characteristics, and aspects (understandable as pseudo classes) are used to implement crosscutting concerns in a modular fashion. In an AspectJ application, everything revolves around join points. These are points in the control flow graph of a compiled program, where crosscutting concerns are woven in. According to AspectJ's terminology there are two types of crosscutting:

Static crosscutting describes crosscutting that influences the interfaces of the involved types and does not modify the execution behavior of the system. AspectJ provides the following two mechanisms to achieve this kind of influence:

Introduction introduces changes to the classes, aspects and interfaces of the system.

Compile-time Declaration adds compile time warnings and error messages for the case that certain occurrences of patterns are captured.

Dynamic crosscutting describes crosscutting that influence the execution behavior of an application.

AspectJ provides the following two languages constructs to achieve this kind of influence:

Pointcut is a constructor that selects join points and collects the context at those points based on different conditions. This construct is an aggregation of execution join points and object join points.

Advice declares a method which will be executed before, after or around join points in execution flow of application picked up by a pointcut whenever a match is occurred with signature of defined join points. With these additional constructs, there are two execution object pointcut designators: this () and target () as defined in [17]. The Java developer can add new functionality in the system without changing any code in the core modules (classes). AspectJ retains all the benefits of Java and is therefore platform-independent. As far as compatibility is concerned it is important to note that

- Every syntactically correct Java program is also a syntactically correct AspectJ program, and
- Every successfully compiled AspectJ program can be executed on a standard Java Virtual Machine.

After these preliminary explanations, we present experimental study of applying aspects in P2P JXTA-JADE Agent Services after performs Aspect weaving in Object Oriented program, especially on providing dynamic adaptation between peer to peer communication, and also try to provide Reusability in JXTA-JADE Agent services using AOP.

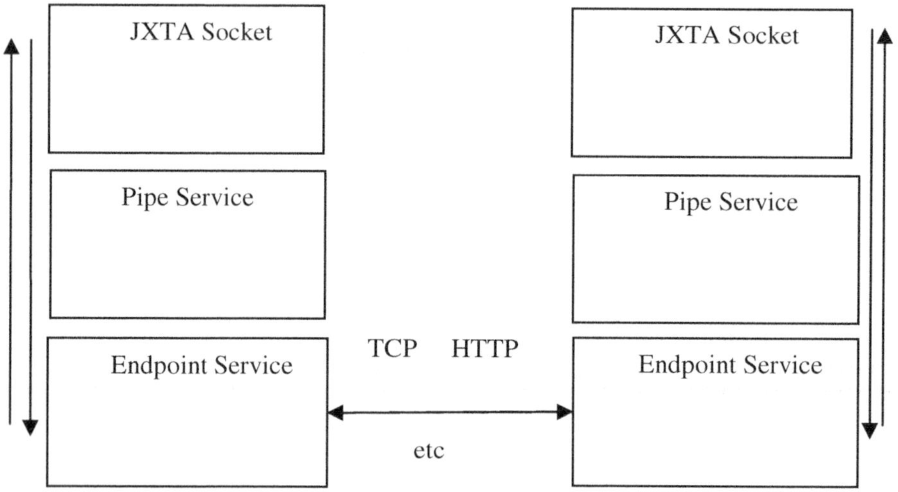

Fig. 2. Stack of JXTA communication protocol

In the above figure 2, peers are communicating using TCP and HTTP protocols. JXTA socket are necessary to discover peer service and to advertise about peer group services. By using end point service peers can easily communicate with each other.

4 Communication between JADE AGENT and P2P JXTA Using AOP

We are using Web Service Integration Gateway (WSIG) to access agent services as web services. Here, we are requesting particular agent service from P2P JXTA network. Any peer can request for agent service like traditional web service.

Here we placed agent service invocation details in AOP. So, we can change Agent Service invocation details dynamically and everyone can reuse this AOP. Dynamic changes means; if specified agent not available at run time then we can pass request to another available agent to get response. AOP will support run time changes dynamically without restarting their application. AOP dynamically adapt changes in user environments when run time changes occur.

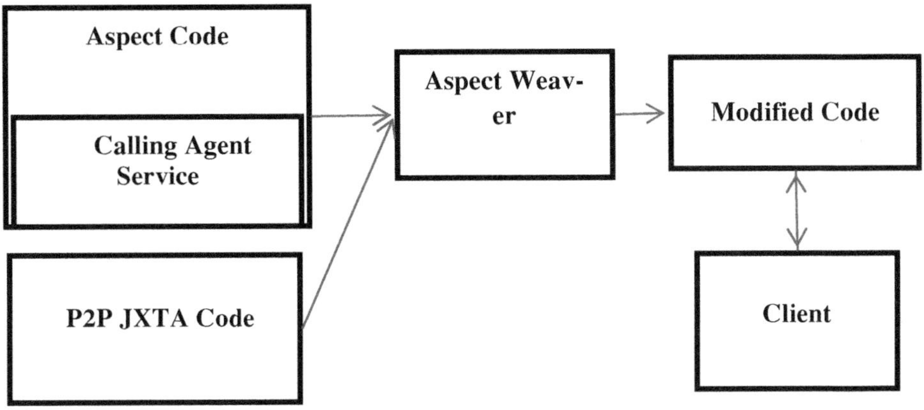

Fig. 3. Dynamic Changes in JADE-JXTA services using AOP

In the above figure 3, Calling Agent Service using AOP. Aspect weaver will weave the P2P JXTA code and Aspect code then generate a class file which is referred as modified code as shown in figure 3.Client can access Agent service by running modified code. If we change Agent Service invocation details in AOP, it will adapt those changes dynamically without restart the application or communication between peers.

4.1 Calling a Agent Service Using AOP

This example illustrates how to invoke JADE Agent Services from p2p JXTA network using AOP.

In the following examples, we are using the traditional JXTA code of sun JXTA 2.5 tutorial. We are converting that code into dynamic adaptable code using AOP.

- **AgentWSPeer.java:**

```
//Traditional JXTA code which is used to pass the values
to Agent services

public class AgentWSPeer {
public Float callWebService(Float a,Float b) throws
IOException {
//Aspect crosscutting placed Here
return 0.0F;
```

```
}
public static void main(String args[])
{
NetworkManager manager = null;
manager = new NetworkMan-
ager(NetworkManager.ConfigMode.ADHOC, "HelloWorld", new
File(new File(".cache"), "HelloWorld").toURI());
  System.out.println("Starting JXTA");
  manager.startNetwork();
  System.out.println("JXTA Started");
BufferedReader br = new BufferedReader(new InputStream-
Reader(System.in));
float a=0.0F,b=0.0F;
//Defining inputstream to take user input
System.out.println("Enter the First Number");
a =(float)br.read();
System.out.println("Enter the Second Number");
b=(float)br.read();
AgentWSPeer ag=new AgentWSPeer();
ag.callWebService(a,b);
boolean connected= man-
ager.waitForRendezvousConnection(12000);
System.out.println(MessageFormat.format("Connected :{0}",
connected));
manager.stopNetwork();
}}
```

- **AgentJxtaWS.aj:**

```
//Providing Dynamic adaptability and calling Agent Ser-
vice using AOP
public aspect AgentJxtaWS
{
//Crosscutting the method using pointcut and joinpoints
pointcut invoke(AgentWSPeer w,float firstElement,float
secondElement):call (* AgentWSPeer.callWebService(..))
      && target(w)
      && args(firstElement,secondElement);
//Weaving additional code into cross cut method using be-
fore advice
before(AgentWSPeer w,float firstElement,float secondEle-
ment):
invoke(w,firstElement,secondElement)
{
Agent.MathFunctionsService service = new
Agent.MathFunctionsService();
Agent.MathFunctionsPort port = ser-
vice.getMathFunctionsPort();
//process result here
```

```
float result = port.sum(firstElement, secondElement);
System.out.println("Result = "+result);
}}}}
```

In the above code, AgentWSPeer indicates that a traditional P2P JXTA code which is used to provide p2p communication, getting the input values from user and pass those values to JADE Agent services which is located in Aspect Oriented Program. Here, AgentJxtaWS is an AOP code. AOP code crosscut the callWebService method of AgentWSPeer class. In the before advice, we are weaving the Agent service calling details and then print the results to user.

Here, we can change Agent service invocation address details at run time; means if we are identifying specified agent is not available or not working then we can change Agent address at run time. Here AOP will adapt that run time changes dynamically without inconvenience to users.

Everyone can reuse this AOP code by cross cut their class and method using point cuts. We are using before advice to run additional implementation to callWebService method. Hence, we strongly say that AOP always support Dynamic adaptability and reusability in existing programs. To prove all above specified things, we are using Eclipse supported framework. Output Screen is as follows.

Output Screen

```
Mar 25, 2011 10:47:21 AM org.apache.catalina.startup.HostConfig deployDirectory
INFO: Deploying web application directory ProfileEval
Mar 25, 2011 10:47:21 AM org.apache.catalina.startup.HostConfig deployDirectory
INFO: Deploying web application directory ROOT
Mar 25, 2011 10:47:21 AM org.apache.catalina.startup.HostConfig deployDirectory
INFO: Deploying web application directory uddi-portlets
Mar 25, 2011 10:47:24 AM org.apache.catalina.startup.HostConfig deployDirectory
INFO: Deploying web application directory WebRoot
Mar 25, 2011 10:47:24 AM org.apache.coyote.http11.Http11AprProtocol start
INFO: Starting Coyote HTTP/1.1 on http-8088
Mar 25, 2011 10:47:24 AM org.apache.coyote.ajp.AjpAprProtocol start
INFO: Starting Coyote AJP/1.3 on ajp-8009
Mar 25, 2011 10:47:24 AM org.apache.catalina.startup.Catalina start
INFO: Server startup in 42455 ms
25 Mar 2011 10:47:45,758 --> WSDL request arrived (http://localhost:8088/wsig/ws
/MathFunctions)
25 Mar 2011 10:47:45,773 --> WSDL request for service MathFunctions
25 Mar 2011 10:47:47,286 --> WSIG SOAP request arrived, start elaboration...
25 Mar 2011 10:47:48,612 --> Request service: MathFunctions
25 Mar 2011 10:47:48,612 --> Request operation: sum
25 Mar 2011 10:47:48,753 --> Jade Action: (sum :firstElement 52.0 :secondElement
 13.0)
Mar 25, 2011 10:47:48 AM jade.wrapper.gateway.DynamicJadeGateway execute
INFO: Requesting execution of command com.tilab.wsig.agent.WSIGBehaviour@19550a8

Mar 25, 2011 10:47:48 AM jade.wrapper.gateway.GatewayBehaviour action
INFO: ControlWSIG-Container started execution of command com.tilab.wsig.agent.WS
IGBehaviour@19550a8
Mar 25, 2011 10:47:48 AM jade.wrapper.gateway.GatewayBehaviour releaseCommand
INFO: ControlWSIG-Container terminated execution of command com.tilab.wsig.agent
.WSIGBehaviour@19550a8
25 Mar 2011 10:47:48,940 --> operationResult: 65.0, type BO_Float
25 Mar 2011 10:47:49,065 --> WSIG SOAP response sended, stop elaboration.
```

Fig. 4. Agent Service invocation through WSIG information

5 Efficiency of AOP by CPU Profiling

In some cases, flexibility and reusability of the design comes with the price of decreased efficiency. At the same time, performance is often a key quality attribute of distributed applications. It is therefore beneficial to investigate whether AOP may influence performance of applications. The comparison of the differences between AOP and OOP shows results that indicates influence of application quality, especially performance. To demonstrate this JADE Agent Service calling is applied and the CPU profiling data is collected. It took 4.81 ms to execute the program without AOP and 3.46 ms to execute when AOP is applied.

5.1 Profiling Statistics before Applying AOP

The main method execution took 4.81 ms with 1 invocation. The below figure 5 shows that the complete details of the invocations and time spent by the processor in each time.

5.2 Profiling Statistics after Applying AOP

The main method execution took 3.96 ms with 1 invocation of each method defined. The below figure 5 shows that the complete details of the invocations and the time spent by the processor in each method. By comparing these two call tree graphs we can say that the code having the AOP cross cutting is more efficient in terms of computation power usage. These both resulted has the same for memory usage.

Here, we have observed practically that execution time analysis comparison of JADE Agent Service invocation without AOP and With AOP by run the above code seven times shows in Fig 5. Both result the same for memory usage.

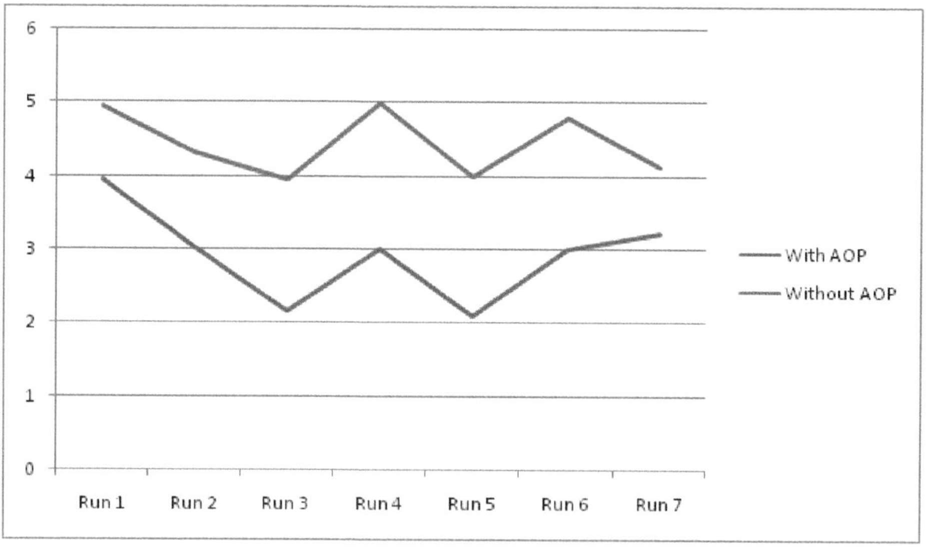

Fig. 5. Execution Time analysis for JADE Agent Service invocation without AOP and with AOP

6 Eclipse's Aspect Visualiser

Aspect Visualiser is an extensible plugin that can be used to visualize anything that can be represented by bars and stripes. It began as the Aspect Visualiser, which was a part of the popular AspectJ Development Tools (AJDT) plug-in. It was originally created to visualize how aspects were affecting classes in a project. As in Figure 6 we have shown the member view of distribution, tracing, and profiling aspects with class, p2p JXTA-JADE Agent Service calling. Here bars represent classes and aspects in AOP code and black colored stripes represent advised join points in the execution flow of AOP code, which were matched with defined pointcuts in various aspects.

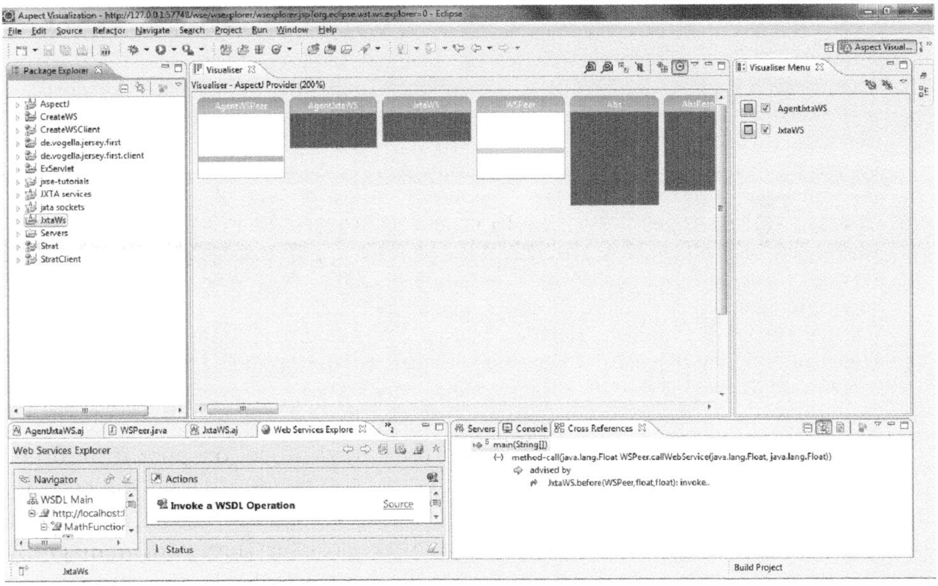

Fig. 6. Aspect Visualizer member view

7 Conclusion

In this paper, we demonstrates dynamic adaptability and reusability in JADE Agent Services and p2p JXTA Services using Aspect Oriented Programming that supports reuse of existing programs in new, dynamic environments even though the specific characteristics of such new environments were not necessarily anticipated during the original design of the programs. In particular, many existing programs, not designed to be adaptable, are being ported to dynamic wireless environments, or hardened in other ways to support autonomic computing. In future we will address how to integrate p2p JXTA and Web Services using AOP.

References

1. Gradecki, J.D.: Mastering JXTA: Building Java Peer-to-Peer Applications, 528 pages. John Wiley & Sons, Chichester (2002)
2. Kiczales, G., Lamping, J., Mendhekar, A.: Aspect-oriented programming. In: Aksit, M., Auletta, V. (eds.) ECOOP 1997. LNCS, vol. 1241, pp. 220–242. Springer, Heidelberg (1997)
3. Cortese, E., Quarta, F., Vitaglione, G., Vrba, P.: Scalability and Performance of the JADE Message Transport System. Analysis of Suitability for Holonic Manufacturing Systems, exp. 3(3), 52–65 (2002)
4. Gradecki, J.D.: Mastering JXTA: Building Java Peer-to-Peer Applications, 528 pages. John Wiley & Sons, Chichester (2002)
5. Paolucci, M., Soudry, J., Srinivasan, N., Sycara, K.: A Broker for OWL-S Web Services. In: Proceedings of the First International Semantic Web Services Symposium, AAAI 2004, March 22-24. Spring Symposium Series, pp. 92–99. AAAI Press, Menlo Park (2004)
6. Ponnekanti, S.R., Fox, A.: SWORD: A Developer Toolkit for Web Service Composition. In: Proceedings of The Eleventh World Wide Web Conference (Web Engineering Track), Honolulu, Hawaii, USA, May 7-11, pp. 83–107 (2002)
7. Sycara, K., Paolucci, M., Ankolekar, A., Srinivasan, N.: Automated Discovery, Interaction and Composition of Semantic Web Services. Journal of Web Semantics 1(1), 27–46 (2003)
8. Thakkar, S., Knoblock, C.A., Ambite, J.L., Shahabi, C.: Dynamically Composing Web Services from On-line Sources. In: Proceeding of 2002 AAAI Workshop on Intelligent Service Integration, Edmonton, Alberta, Canada (2002)
9. Wu, D., Parsia, B., Sirin, E., Hendler, J., Nau, D.: Automating DAML-S Web Services Composition Using SHOP2. In: Fensel, D., Sycara, K., Mylopoulos, J. (eds.) ISWC 2003. LNCS, vol. 2870, pp. 195–210. Springer, Heidelberg (2003)
10. Zhu, Y., Wang, H., Hu, Y.: A Super-Peer Based Lookup in Structured Peer-to-Peer Systems. In: ISCA PDCS, pp. 465–470 (2003)
11. Jiang, N., Schmidt, C., Matossian, V., Parashar, M.: Enabling Applications in Sensor-based Pervasive Environments. In: Proceedings of the 1stWorkshop on Broadband Advanced Sensor Networks, BaseNets 2004 (2004)
12. jxta-meteor official web site: `https://jxta-meteor.dev.java.net/`
13. Kato, D.: GISP: Global Information Sharing Protocol A Distributed Index for Peer-to-Peer Systems. In: Proceedings of the 2nd International Conference on Peer-to-Peer Computing (P2P 2002), p. 65 (2002.d)
14. Ratnasamy, S., Francis, P., Handley, M., Karp, R., Schenker, S.: A scalable content-addressable network. In: Proceedings of the 2001 conference on Applications, technologies, architectures, and protocols for computer communications, pp. 161–172 (2001)
15. Halepovic, E., Deters, R.: The Costs of Using JXTA. In: Third International Conference on Peer-to-Peer Computing (P2P 2003), p. 160 (2003)
16. jxta-benchmarking official web site: `https://jxtabenchmarking.dev.java.net/`
17. Clement, A., Harley, G., Webster, M., Colyer, A.: Eclipse AspectJ: aspect oriented programming with AspectJ and the Eclipse AspectJ development tools. Addison Wesley Prof, Reading (2005)
18. Avgustinov, P., Christensen, A.S., Hendren, L., Kuzins, S., Lhoták, J., Lhoták, O., deMoor, O.: An Extensible AspectJ Compiler. In: Proceedings of the 4th International Conference on Aspect-Oriented Software Development, pp. 87–98. ACM Digital Library, New York (2005)
19. Yang, Z.: An Aspect-Oriented Approach to Dynamic Adaptation. In: WOSS 2002 (2002)

20. Dantas, A., Borba, P.: Adaptability Aspects: An Architectural Pattern for Structuring Adaptive Applications with Aspects. In: Proceedings of SugarloafPLoP 2003 Conference (2003)
21. David, P., Ledoux, T.: Towards a Framework for Self-Adaptive Component-Based Applications. In: Proceedings of FMOODS/DAIS 2003 (2003)
22. Goff, M.: Jini Network Technology, JXTA and Web Services, `http://developer.java.sun.com/developer/onlineTraining/webcasts/20plus/mgoff.html`
23. Koman, R.: XTRA JXTA: The P2P/Web Services Connection (2001-10-24), `http://www.onjava.com/pub/a/onjava/2001/10/24/jxta.html`
24. Kephart, J.O., Chess, D.M.: The vision of autonomic computing. IEEE Computer 36(1), 41–50 (2003)

A Novel Way of Providing Dynamic Adaptability in P2P JXTA Multicast Sockets and P2P JXTA-WS Using Aspect Oriented Programming

Vishnuvardhan Mannava[1], T. Ramesh[2], and Bangaru Babu Kuravadi[1]

[1] Department of Computer Science and Engineering,
KL University, Vaddeswaram 522502, A.P., India
vishnu@klce.ac.in, bngrbbk@gmail.com
[2] Department of Computer Science and Engineering, National Institute of Technology,
Warangal, 506004, A.P., India
rmesht@nitw.ac.in

Abstract. The need for adaptability in software is growing, driven in part by the emergence of autonomic computing. In many cases, it is desirable to enhance existing programs with adaptive behavior, enabling them to execute effectively in dynamic environments. The peer-to-peer (p2p) paradigm is attracting increasing attention from both the research community and software engineers, due to potential performance, reliability and scalability improvements. P2P model has opened many new avenues for research and applications within the field of distributed computation, so performance evaluation is unavoidable.Existing web service invocation and adaptation mechanisms are limited only to the scope of web service choreography in terms of web service selection. Such a scope hardly leaves ground for a participating service in a choreographed flow to re-adjust itself in terms of changed non functional expectations.In this paper we are using Aspect oriented programming (AOP) to enable dynamic adaptation at the time of invoking web services in P2P Systems. We propose an approach to implement dynamic adaptability especially in existing p2p JXTA-WS programs and Aspect weaving in p2p JXTA Multicast sockets using AOP. We have used AspectJ; Java based language to create aspects in Eclipse supported framework.

Keywords: Dynamic adaptation, AspectJ, Web Services, P2P networks, and JXTA.

1 Introduction

A software application is adaptable if it can change its behavior dynamically (at run time) in response to transient changes in its execution environment or to permanent changes in its requirements. Recent interest in designing adaptable software is driven in part by the demand for autonomic computing. Autonomic computing[1] refers to self-managed, and potentially self-healing, systems that require only high-level human guidance. Autonomic computing is critical to managing the myriad of sensors

D.C. Wyld et al. (Eds.): CNSA 2011, CCIS 196, pp. 564–576, 2011.

and other small devices at the wireless edge, but also in managing large-scale computing centers and protecting critical infrastructure (e.g., financial networks, transportation systems, power grids) from hardware component failures, network outages, and security attacks. Developing and maintaining adaptable software are nontrivial tasks. An adaptable application comprises functional code that implements the business logic of the application and supports its imperative behavior, and adaptive code that implements the adaptation logic of the application and supports its adaptive behavior.

JXTA is a set of open protocols for P2P networking. The JXTA protocols enable developers to build and deploy P2P applications through a unified medium. The main JXTA concepts include peers, peer groups, pipes, advertisements, and JXTA services [3]. A JXTA peer is any networked device that implements one or more of the JXTA protocols. Several peers can self-organize into peer groups, which provide a common set of services. Pipes are bound to specific endpoints at runtime, such as a TCP port and an associated IP address. The supported objects for transmission are binary code, data strings and Java-based objects.

Web service is a new paradigm to deliver application services on Web and enables a programmable Web, not just an interactive Web. Web service is the third generation in the Web evolution after static HTML and interactive Web development such as PERL, ASP, JSP, and others. Web services are typical black box–reusable building block components in the distributed computing. Following Fig. 1 shows Web Services Architecture. There are three important components in Web services architecture.

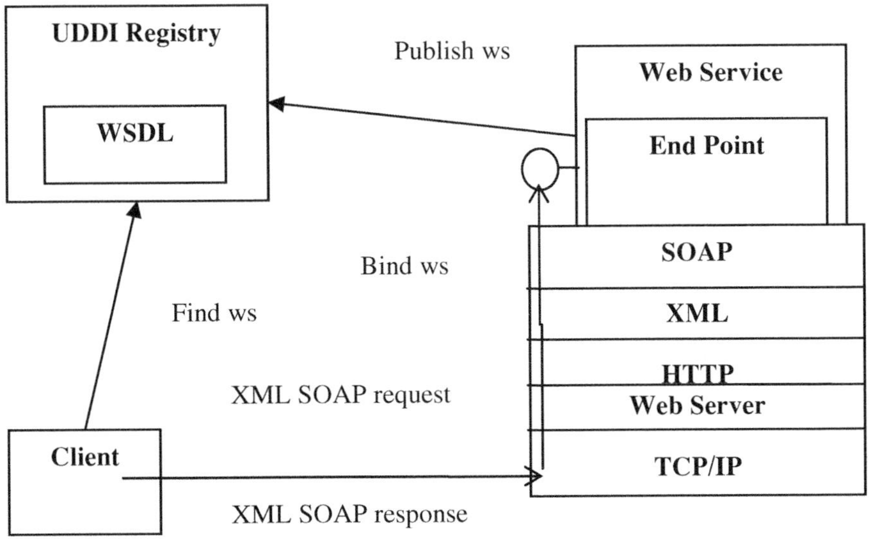

Fig. 1. Web Services Architecture

Figure 1 shows the Web service requester (simplified client) on the left, the Web service provider on the right, and the Web service registry on the top.

A Web services provider must publish/register its services with a Universal Description, Discovery, and Integration (UDDI) registry so that it can be accessed by any Web services requester globally. It just looks like a phonebook, where all businesses register their phones there for customers to look up services. A customer must look up the phonebook either on-line or by phonebook unless a customer knows the phone number before.

In this paper we describe how to provide dynamic adaptability, reusability using AOP and how to invoke p2p JXTA-WS AOP.

Our paper is organized as follows. We review related work in section 2. Section 3 describes AOP paradigm. In section 4, 5 we describes AOP p2p JXTA-WSinvocation and p2p JXTA Multicast socket communication respectively. Try to show the Efficiency of AOP by CPU Profiling in section 6. We conclude the paper in section 7 with possible future directions.

2 Related Work

Previous work has been done by Yang [19] to implement a system which performs dynamic adaptation using AOP. This approach uses joinpoints to specify where the adaptation should take place, and a set of rules to specify the conditions when an adaptation should occur. Another solution to achieve adaptation in applications using AspectJis proposed by Dantas et al [20]. An adaptation framework developed by Pierre-Charles David et al [21] is implemented using the Fractal component model. Peers in peer-to-peer networks are usually considered uniform in resources.

Within this body of literature, conflicting opinions as to the relationship between these two developing technologies are given including the following [23]: JXTA complements Web Services, JXTA extends Web Services, JXTA supersedes Web Services, and JXTA and Web Services will converge.

So far, there is proposal for Services deployed in JXTA or Web Services Environment to be able to find each other and communicate using JSDL like WSDL. Yet, they are not able to provide communication between JXTA and Web Services each other.

Integration of web services with p2p networks has been extensively examined in the sense of using a p2p infrastructure to enhance the various web service activities.In METEOR-S [6], a JXTA-based p2p network is utilized to organize web service registries, in order to facilitate the tasks of service publication and discovery. Yet, to the best of our knowledge, there is no approach other than the one presented in this paper, which attempts to integrate the web service and p2p worlds in terms of unified service discovery.

At the end of this paper we will present an experimental evaluation of the performances of JXTA, by comparing it with the JXTA-WS with AOP and without AOP. To this aim we adopted the performance model introduced in [9], where the authors study the JXTA rendezvous protocol performances, by comparing it with the policy of older versions of JXTA, and by using a JXTA subproject benchmark suite [16].

Here, we are successfully providing communication between p2p JXTA and Web Services in novel way using AOP. To our knowledge, there is no related work of providing dynamic adaptability and calling Web Services from p2p JXTA-WS using Aspect Oriented Programming.

3 Aspect Oriented Programming (AOP)

Aspect Oriented Programming (AOP) is a program development methodology proposed by Gregor Kiczales in "Aspect-Oriented Programming"[2], published in 1997. In AOP, the requirements (requests) of the program are termed 'concerns'. Concerns are divided into core concerns and crosscutting concerns. An example that is used most frequently to explain core and cross-cutting concerns is the Distributed Auction system. In a system, core concerns are the main functions of the Auction System, which are to set the product for auction, set minimum bid, set current bid etc. However, other features required by a distributed system, such as logging, distribution, profiling and tracing are cross-cutting concerns. Although object oriented programming is currently the most widely used methodology for dealing with core concerns, it comes up short in processing crosscutting concerns. This becomes more so for complex applications. AOP is a new methodology that enables separation of crosscutting concerns and their implementation through a new module termed the 'aspect'. Figure 2 displays the weaving process of application code with aspect.

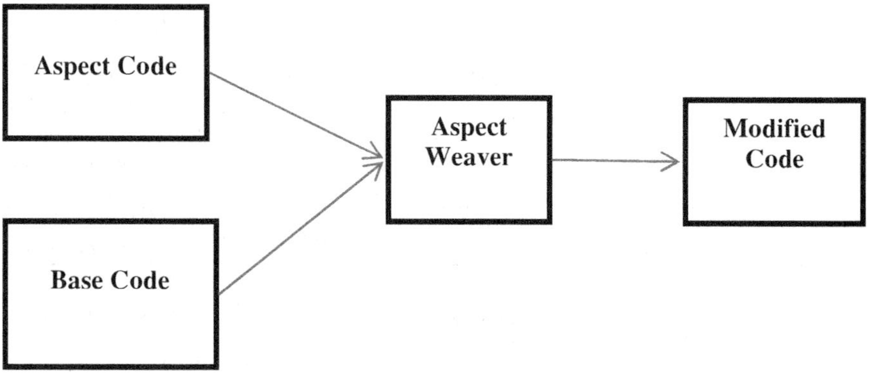

Fig. 2. Weaving of Aspect on Source Code

In the below figure 3, peers are communicating using TCP and HTTP protocols. JXTA socket are necessary to discover peer service and to advertise about peer group services. By using end point service peers can easily communicate with each other.

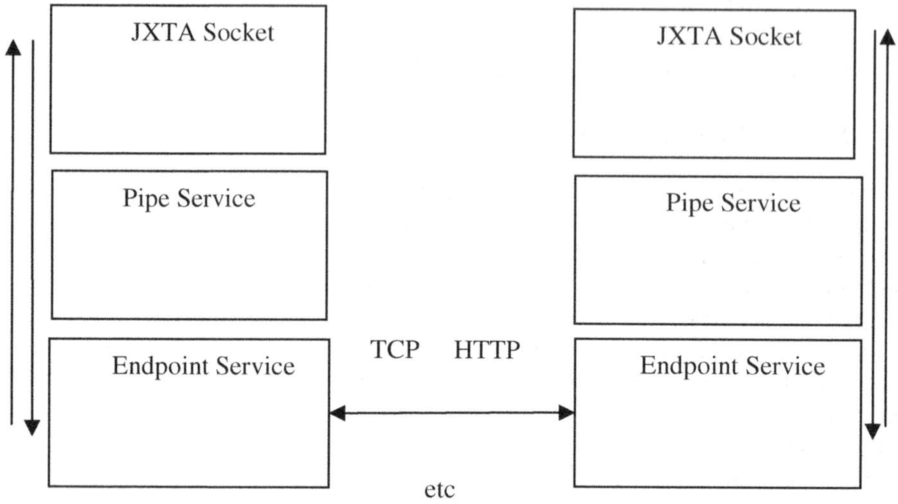

Fig. 3. Stack of JXTA communication protocol

4 P2P JXTA-WS Services Using AOP

In the below figure 4, Calling Web Service using AOP which is after referred as JXTA-WS. Aspect weaver will weave the P2P JXTA code and Aspect code then generate a class file which is referred as modified code as shown in figure 3.Client can access peer service by running modified code only. If we change JXTA service details in AOP code, it will adapt that change dynamically without restart the application or communication between peers.

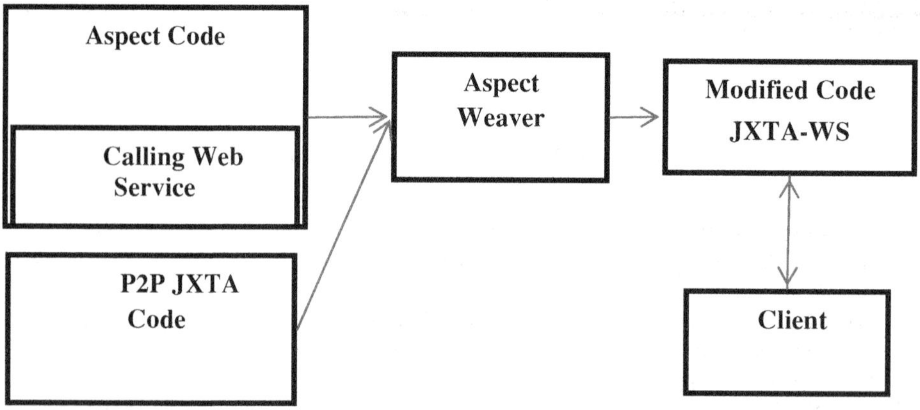

Fig. 4. Dynamic Changes in JXTA service using AOP

4.1 Calling a JXTA-WS Using AOP

This example illustrates how to invoke a web service in p2p JXTA systems using AOP.

In the following examples, we are using the traditional JXTA code of sun JXTA 2.5 tutorial. We are converting that code into dynamic adaptable using AOP.

- **WSPeer.java:**

```
//Traditional JXTA code which is used to pass the values
to web services
public class WSPeer {
    public static void main(String args[]) {
      NetworkManager manager = null;
      manager = new
      NetworkManager(NetworkManager.ConfigMode.ADHOC,
      "HelloWorld", new File(new File(".cache"),
      "HelloWorld").toURI());
      manager.startNetwork();
      BufferedReader br = new BufferedReader(new
      InputStreamReader(System.in));
      float a=0.0F,b=0.0F;
      System.out.println("Enter the First Number");
      a =(float)br.read();
      System.out.println("Enter the Second Number");
      b=(float)br.read();
      WSPeer w=new WSPeer();
      w.callWebService(a,b);
      boolean connected =
      manager.waitForRendezvousConnection(12000);
      manager.stopNetwork();}
      public Float callWebService(Float a,Float b) throws
      IOException {
      //Aspect crosscutting code will be placed here
      return 0.0F;}}

//Providing Dynamic adaptability and calling WS using AOP
public aspect JxtaWS{
//Crosscutting the method using pointcut and joinpoints
      pointcut invoke(WSPeer w,float firstElement,float
      secondElement):call (* WSPeer.callWebService(..))
      && target(w)
      && args(firstElement,secondElement);
//Weaving additional code into cross cut method using
before advice
```

```
before(WSPeer w,float firstElement,float
secondElement):invoke(w,firstElement,secondElement)
{ Agent.MathFunctionsService service = new
Agent.MathFunctionsService();
Agent.MathFunctionsPort port =
service.getMathFunctionsPort();
//process result here
float result = port.diff(firstElement,
secondElement);
System.out.println("Result = "+result);}}}
```

In the above code, WSPeer indicates that traditional JXTAcode which is proviode p2p communication, getting the input values from user and passes those values to web services which is locates in Aspect Oriented Program. Here JxtaWS is an AOP code. It crosscut the callWebService method of WSPeer class. In the before advice, we are weaving the web service calling details and then print the results to user.

Here, we can change web service invocation address details at run time; means if we are identifying specified end point address is not available or not working then we can change address at run time. Here AOP will adapt that run time changes dynamically without inconvenience to users.

Everyone can reuse this AOP code by cross cut their class and method using point cuts. We are using before advice to run additional implementation to callWebServicemethod. Hence, we strongly say that AOP always support Dynamic adaptability and reusability in existing programs. To prove all above specified things, we are using Eclipse supported framework. Output Screen is as follows.

Output Screen

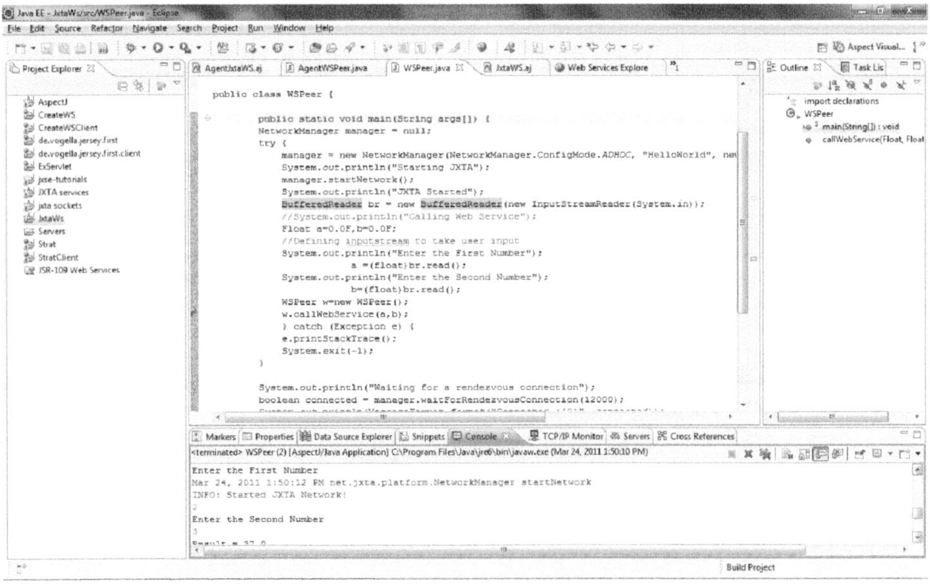

Fig. 5. Web Service invocation from P2P JXTA network using AOP

5 P2P JXTA Multicast Socket Using AOP

A JxtaMulticastSocket is a sub-class of a java.net.MultiscastSocket, the difference being, is how it is bound. A java.net.MultiscastSocket is bound by a multicast address and a port number, where a JxtaMulticastSocket is bound by PeerGroup and PipeAdvertisement. Its having following steps to construct JxtaMulticaseSocket communication between peers.

- Construction and use of a JxtaMulticastSocket
- Joining a virtual JXTA multicast group
- Sending/receiving datagrams

5.1 Basic Operations

- Construct a JxtaMulticastSocket with precreated pipe ID
- Send/Receive a datagram
- Stop the JXTA network

5.2 Caveats

- A JxtaMulticastSocket operates over a propagated pipe, the scope of propagation is governed by the network topology, and the role of the node (Ad-Hoc, Edge, Rendezvous).
- Datagram size is limited by the TcpTransportMulticastSocketSize, where multicast is utilized, and MTU size where a relay is utilized.
- By default the example operates in Ad-Hoc mode. The configuration must be altered in order to operate differently.

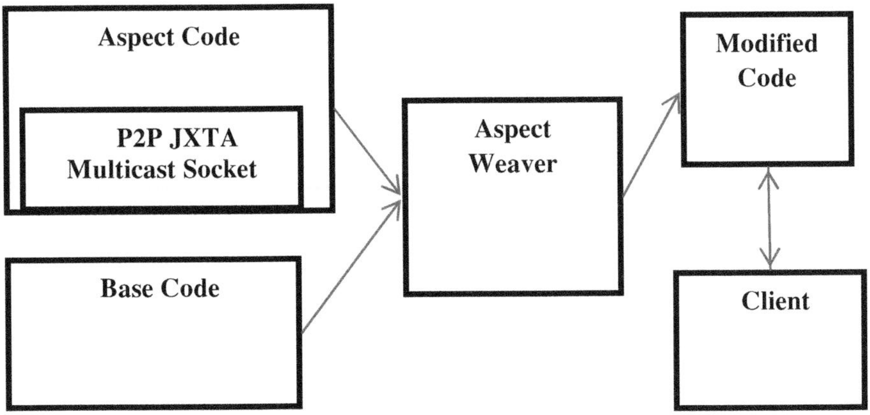

Fig. 6. Dynamic Adaptability in JXTA Multicast Sockets using AOP

In the following examples, we are using the traditional JXTA code of sun JXTA 2.5 tutorial. We are converting that code into dynamic adaptable using AOP.

5.3 Serverside p2p JXTA Multicast Socket Using AOP

In the following code read method of JxtaMulticastSocket* class will cross cut by read pointcut. It will get one input parameter from the base class and will start the network based on parameter NetworkManager. We can change the server functionalities dynamically. Here * indicates that class name should start with JxtaMulticastSocket. Here we are creating multicast socket using JxtaMulticastSocket to send the messages to multiple peers.

```
  publicaspectAspectJxtaMulticastSocketServer {
  // private static PeerGroupnetPeerGroup = null;
  publicfinalstatic String SOCKETIDSTR = "urn:jxta:uuid-
59616261646162614E5047205032503393B5C2F6CA7A41FDB0F890173
088E79404";
  pointcut read(NetworkManager m) :call(public  *
  JxtaMulticastSocket*.read(..))
  &&args(m);
  before(NetworkManager m) : read(m) {
  System.out.println("Creating JxtaMulticastSocket");
  JxtaMulticastSocketmcastSocket = null;
  try {mcastSocket = newJxtaMulticast-
Socket(m.getNetPeerGroup(), getSocketAdvertisement());
  System.out.println("LocalAddress :" + mcast-
Socket.getLocalAddress());
  System.out.println("LocalSocketAddress :" + mcast-
Socket.getLocalSocketAddress());
  } catch (IOException e)
{e.printStackTrace();System.exit(-1);}
  byte[] buffer = newbyte[16384];
  String ten4 = "Ten 4";
  DatagramPacket packet = newDatagramPacket(buffer,
buffer.length);
  try {// wait for a datagram. The following can be put
//into a loop
  mcastSocket.receive(packet);
  String sw = newString(packet.getData(), 0,
packet.getLength());
  System.out.println("Received data from :" +
packet.getAddress());
  System.out.println(sw);
  // unicast back a response back to the remote
  DatagramPacket res = newDatagramPacket(ten4.getBytes(),
ten4.length());
  res.setAddress(packet.getAddress());
  mcastSocket.send(res);   } catch (IOException e){
e.printStackTrace();}}
  publicstaticPipeAdvertisementgetSocketAdvertisement(){
```

```
  PipeIDsocketID = null;
  try {socketID = (PipeID) IDFactory.fromURI(new
URI(SOCKETIDSTR));}
  catch (URISyntaxException use){use.printStackTrace();}
  PipeAdvertisement advertisement = (PipeAdvertisement)
AdvertisementFactory.newAdvertisement (PipeAdvertise-
ment.getAdvertisementType ()); advertisement.setPipeID
(socketID);    // set to type to //propagate
  advertisement.setType(PipeService.PropagateType);
  advertisement.setName("Socket tutorial");
  return advertisement;}}
```

5.4 Clientside p2p JXTA Multicast Socket Using AOP

In the following code, w* method will cross cut by write pointcut and get one input parameter from the base class. It will discover the service and send the data to desired peer service. Here w* indicates that method starting letter should be w and remaining can be letters anything to cross cut.

```
  publicaspectAspectJxtaMulticastSocketClient {
  pointcut write(NetworkManager m) :
call(publicvoidJxtaMulticast*.w*(..))&&args(m)  ;
  before(NetworkManager m) : write(m) {
  PeerGroupnetPeerGroup = m.getNetPeerGroup();
  JxtaMulticastSocketmcastSocket = null;
  try {mcastSocket = newJxtaMulticastSocket(netPeerGroup,
AspectJxtaMulticastSocket-
Server.getSocketAdvertisement());  } catch (IOException
e) {  e.printStackTrace();
  System.exit(-1);}Date date = new
Date(System.currentTimeMillis());
  String hello = "Hello on : " + date.toString();
  try { DatagramPacket packet = newDatagram-
Packet(hello.getBytes(), hello.length());
  mcastSocket.send(packet);
  byte[] res = newbyte[1638467];
  DatagramPacketrpacket = newDatagramPacket(res,
res.length);
  // It's likely we'll receive 2 packets a loopback and a
response
  // loopback
  mcastSocket.receive(rpacket);
  // server response
  mcastSocket.receive(rpacket);
  String sw = newString(rpacket.getData(), 0,
rpacket.getLength());
  System.out.println("Received data from :" +
rpacket.getAddress());
```

```
System.out.println(sw);
// stop the platform
m.stopNetwork();} catch (IOException e) {
e.printStackTrace();          }}}
```

Both Serverside multicast socket and client side sockets are reusable and dynamic adaptable at run time. AOP will changes the user changes at run time class file base class, so, the changes are automatically effect to application without restarting the application.

6 Efficiency of AOP by CPU Profiling

The comparison of the differences between AOP and OOP shows results that indicates influence of application quality, especially performance. To demonstrate this Web Service invocation and JXTA Multi Socket Communication is applied and the CPU profiling data is collected using IDE. The below figure 7 shows the complete details of the invocations and Multi Socket Communication time differences with AOP and Without AOP.

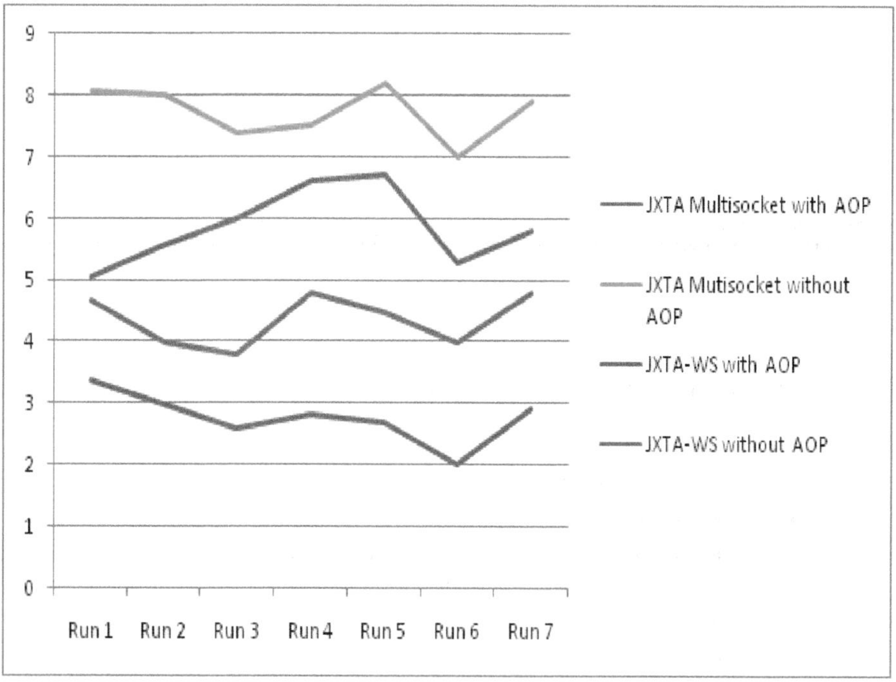

Fig. 7. Execution time analysis for JXTA-WS and Multi Socket without AOP and with AOP

7 Conclusion

In this paper, Aspect Oriented Programming supports reuse of existing programs in new, dynamic environments even though the specific characteristics of such new environments were not necessarily anticipated during the original design of the programs. In particular, many existing programs, not designed to be adaptable, are being ported to dynamic wireless environments, or hardened in other ways to support autonomic computing. Here we practically proved above mentioned things that dynamic adaptability and reusability in p2p JXTA-WS Services. In future we will address how Agent based java program communicates with p2p JXTA-WS Service using AOP.

References

1. Kephart, J.O., Chess, D.M.: The vision of autonomic computing. IEEE Computer 36(1), 41–50 (2003)
2. Kiczales, G., Lamping, J., Mendhekar, A.: Aspect-oriented programming. In: Aksit, M., Auletta, V. (eds.) ECOOP 1997. LNCS, vol. 1241, pp. 220–242. Springer, Heidelberg (1997)
3. Gradecki, J.D.: Mastering JXTA: Building Java Peer-to-Peer Applications, 528 pages. John Wiley & Sons, Chichester (2002)
4. Paolucci, M., Soudry, J., Srinivasan, N., Sycara, K.: A Broker for OWL-S Web Services. In: Proceedings of the First International Semantic Web Services Symposium, AAAI 2004, March 22-24. Spring Symposium Series, pp. 92–99. AAAI Press, Menlo Park (2004)
5. Ponnekanti, S.R., Fox, A.: SWORD: A Developer Toolkit for Web Service Composition. In: Proceedings of The Eleventh World Wide Web Conference (Web Engineering Track), Honolulu, Hawaii, USA, May 7-11, pp. 83–107 (2002)
6. Verma, K., Sivashanmugam, et al.: METEOR-S WSDI: A Scalable Infrastructure of Registries for Semantic Publication and Discovery of Web Services. Journal of Information Technology and Management 6(1), 17–39 (2005)
7. Sycara, K., Paolucci, M., Ankolekar, A., Srinivasan, N.: Automated Discovery, Interaction and Composition of Semantic Web Services. Journal of Web Semantics 1(1), 27–46 (2003)
8. Thakkar, S., Knoblock, C.A., Ambite, J.L., Shahabi, C.: Dynamically Composing Web Services from On-line Sources. In: Proceeding of 2002 AAAI Workshop on Intelligent Service Integration, Edmonton, Alberta, Canada (2002)
9. Junginger, M., Lee, Y.: The Multi-Ring Topology-High-Performance Group Communication in Peer-to-Peer Networks. In: 2nd International Conference on Peer-to-Peer Computing (P2P 2002), pp. 49–56. IEEE Computer Society, Linköping (2002)
10. Zhu, Y., Wang, H., Hu, Y.: A Super-Peer Based Lookup in Structured Peer-to-Peer Systems. In: ISCA PDCS, pp. 465–470 (2003)
11. Jiang, N., Schmidt, C., Matossian, V., Parashar, M.: Enabling Applications in Sensor-based Pervasive Environments. In: Proceedings of the 1stWorkshop on Broadband Advanced Sensor Networks, (BaseNets 2004) (2004)
12. jxta-meteor official web site: `https://jxta-meteor.dev.java.net/`
13. Kato, D.: GISP: Global Information Sharing Protocol a Distributed Index for Peer-to-Peer Systems. In: Proceedings of the 2nd International Conference on Peer-to-Peer Computing (P2P 2002), p. 65 (2002.d)

14. Ratnasamy, S., Francis, P., Handley, M., Karp, R., Schenker, S.: A scalable content-addressable network. In: Proceedings of the 2001 conference on Applications, Technologies, Architectures, and Protocols for Computer Communications, pp. 161–172 (2001)
15. Halepovic, E., Deters, R.: The Costs of Using JXTA. In: Third International Conference on Peer-to-Peer Computing (P2P 2003), p. 160 (2003)
16. jxta-benchmarking official web site: https://jxtabenchmarking.dev.java.net/
17. Clement, A., Harley, G., Webster, M., Colyer, A.: Eclipse AspectJ: aspect oriented programming with AspectJ and the Eclipse AspectJ development tools. Addison Wesley Prof., Reading (2005)
18. Avgustinov, P., Christensen, A.S., Hendren, L., Kuzins, S., Lhoták, J., Lhoták, O., deMoor, O.: An Extensible AspectJ Compiler. In: Proceedings of the 4th International Conference on Aspect-Oriented Software Development, pp. 87–98. ACM Digital Library, New York (2005)
19. Yang, Z.: An Aspect-Oriented Approach to Dynamic Adaptation. In: WOSS 2002 (2002)
20. Dantas, A., Borba, P.: Adaptability Aspects: An Architectural Pattern for Structuring Adaptive Applications with Aspects. In: Proceedings of SugarloafPLoP 2003 Conference (2003)
21. David, P., Ledoux, T.: Towards a Framework for Self-Adaptive Component-Based Applications. In: Proceedings of FMOODS/DAIS 2003 (2003)
22. Arpinar, B., Aleman-Meza, B., Zhang, R., Maduko, A.: Ontology-Driven Web Services Composition Platform. In: 2004 IEEE International Conference on E-Commerce Technology (CEC 2004), July 6-9, pp. 146–152. IEEE Computer Society Press, San Diego (2004)
23. O'Hearne, B.S.: Web Services and JXTA: Companion Technologies (April 2002), http://www.devx.com/javaSR/articles/ohearne/ohearne-1.asp
24. Kilmer, R.: Peering beyond the PC: Where P2P Meets the Wireless Web (May/June 2002), http://dsonline.computer.org/0205/features/w3icon.htm

Intelligent Energy Efficient Routing for Ad-Hoc Sensor Network by Designing QCS Protocol

Debaditya Ghosh[1], Pritam Majumder[1], and Ayan Kumar Das[2]

[1] Department of ComputerScience & Engineering,
Calcutta Institute of Engineering and Management, Kolkata, India
debadityaghosh94@yahoo.com, pritmajumder@rocketmail.com
[2] Department of Information Technology,
Calcutta Institute of Engineering and Management, Kolkata, India
ayandas24114057@yahoo.co.in

Abstract. In today's world Wireless Ad-hoc sensor network, which consists of many small sensor nodes having limited resources, has a great potential to solve problems in various domain like disaster management, military field etc. In this paper a new protocol "QCS-protocol" has been introduced which is the backbone of our Intelligent Energy Efficient Ad-hoc Sensor Network. Two other protocols "Final Broadcast-Petrol Flow" protocol and "Irregular Information Transfer" protocol are designed to help the QCS protocol to run the system properly and make the network more energy efficient and perfect. The challenges in Ad-hoc sensor network are limited node power, Ad-hoc organization of network and reliability. Most of the existing approaches have done by addressing the problems separately, but not in a totality. This paper shows how the network can have unlimited life and all time readiness with overall stability to send information to the base station with minimum power dissipation with the help of multimode same type sensor nodes and type categorization of generated information.

Keywords: Information categorization, Multimode Sensor Nodes, Stability monitoring, Network longevity, All time readiness.

1 Introduction

Wireless sensor networks present Ad-hoc networks [5], [3] consisting of a large number of sensor nodes which collaborate to perform a shared mission. There is a wide range of promising applications for these networks, such as, environment monitoring, health-care and battlefield operations. Energy efficiency in communication is one of the major challenges for designing the above described networks. This paper work is done emphasizing on the energy efficiency of the nodes so as the entire network, which will definitely add a positive effect on the stability of the established network. We have introduced a new concept starting from the establishing of the network (QCS) and categorized the node-to-node signal depending upon their signal-type, i.e. regular, irregular or devastating.

D.C. Wyld et al. (Eds.): CNSA 2011, CCIS 196, pp. 577–586, 2011.

2 A Brief Review of Existing Routing Protocols and Comparative Measures

Routing in mobile ad hoc sensor networks [9] faces additional problems and challenges, when compared to routing in traditional wired networks with fixed infrastructure. There are several well known protocols in that have been specifically developed to cope with the limitations imposed by ad hoc networking environments. Most of the existing routing protocols follow two different design approaches to handle the inherent Characteristics of ad hoc networks: the table-driven and the source-initiated on-demand approaches [2].

2.1 Table-Driven Routing Protocols

Table-driven ad hoc routing protocols maintain all times routing information regarding the connectivity of every node to all other nodes. It is also known as proactive routing and these protocols allow every node to have a clear and consistent view of the network topology by propagating periodic updates.

2.1.1 Destination-Sequenced Distance-Vector Routing (DSDV)

DSDV [2] is based on traditional Bellman-Ford routing algorithm and it is a routing table-based protocol. Each node in an operation must be stored in a routing table, which records all the possible links with the nodes and the distance like the number of hops, routing table within each record which also contains a sequence number and is used to determine any older path in order to avoid routing table generation.

2.1.2 Cluster head Gateway Switch Routing (CGSR)

CGSR [6] is build from the DSDV routing protocol, using a cluster head to manage a group of nodes. The action is divided into a group of a group of nodes, each having a head, namely cluster head. Through a gateway the nodes are connected to each other, into a hierarchical structure. Whether a link between nodes within a cluster, or a link between each cluster head, are based on DSDV routing.

2.1.3 Wireless Routing Protocol (WRP)

Wireless Routing Protocol makes use of the routing table maintained at each node to complete the routing, and DSDV with CGSR difference is that, WRP require each node to operate four tables, namely distance table, routing table, link-cost table, message retransmission list table. WRP can effectively improve the distance-vector routing possible count-to-infinity problem.

2.2 Source - Initiated on-Demand Routing Protocols

An alternative approach is the source-initiated on-demand routing, also known as Reactive routing protocol. According to this approach, a route is created only when the source node requires a route to a specific destination. A route is acquired by the initiation of a route discovery function by the source node.

2.2.1 Ad-Hoc On-Demand Distance Vector Routing (AODV)

Ad-Hoc On-Demand Distance Vector Routing [11], [5] uses distance-vector concept. AODV does not maintain a routing table, but when a node needs to communicate with another node only on demand it maintains routing table. AODV protocol is a mixture of both DSR and DSDV protocols. It keeps the basic route-discovery and route-maintenance of DSR and uses the hop-by-hop routing sequence numbers and beacons of DSDV.

2.2.2 Dynamic Source Routing (DSR)

Dynamic Source Routing uses the concept of source routing, the routing information that is directly recorded inside of each packet. In DSR protocol the agent checks every data packet for source-route information. The packets are then forwarded depending on the routing information.

2.2.3 Temporally Ordered Routing Algorithm (TORA)

TORA [4] is a highly adaptive loop-free distributed routing algorithm based on the concept of link reversal. The key design concept of TORA is the localization of control messages to a very small set of nodes near the occurrence of a topological change. TORA is proposed to operate in a highly dynamic mobile networking environment, source-initiated and provides multiple routes for any desired source pair.

3 Proposed Work

3.1 Basic Methodology

One of the most important features of our approach to "Mobile Ad Hoc Sensor Network" - solution is "Generated Information Type" categorization. Depending on the type of information generated on a particular node or signal transmitted from a particular node to other node can be of three types- a) Regular information, b)Irregular Information, c)Devastating – Immediate Response Information. Our proposed network goes through mainly three stages – Nodes placing, Node activation and Node communication. In this regard we have designed a basic "QCS protocol" which stands for "QUERY-CHECKED-SOURCE" protocol. According to this protocol all the Nodes of this network are of same type but all of them can behave in three different categories of node – QUERY NODE, CHECKED NODE and SOURCE NODE, depending on the situation.

3.2 Data Dictionary

Table 1. Variables list

Q-node	Query Node
C-node	Checked Node
S-node	Source Node
Type-1 flag	This flag is set in a sensor node when the sensor node senses some irregular type of information through its sensor nodes.

Table 1. (*Continued*)

Type-2 flag	This flag is set in a sensor node when the sensor node senses some devastating type of information through its sensor nodes.
T-time period	This is the time period for which a C node will be in sleeping mode.
I	Local variable to run the for loop
N	No. of reply coming from neighbor nodes.
Node_id	Unique identification of a node to indentify the node separately.
REP[n]	Reply packets those are received by a node is saved in REP[n] array.
N_Type	Reply send by the nodes on query about its condition "ok" or "not ok".

3.3 Procedure in Short

All the nodes we consider in this network are of same type and Signals are categorized into three types, 1.regular, 2.irregular & 3.devastating depending upon the sensed value by the sensor. Network Initialization is done in the following way-

A node is activated as "Q" node(Query node) randomly from all nodes in the network. The one non adjacent node of "Q" is chosen and denoted as "Q". This procedure continues until all the nodes nonadjacent to each other are chosen and denoted as "Q". Query node will query first and those nodes which will answer be the "C" nodes, i.e. checked nodes. At the next moment (after the time period "T") "C" nodes turn into "Q" and will repeat the procedure. The above procedure is true for type 1 &type2 signals. The type3 signal will be flooded following Final Broad Cast-Petrol Flow protocol only, as it is an emergency & make all adjacent as "S" &continue.

3.3.1 Regular Information with Regular Network Behavior

3.3.1.1 Objective. Maintain overall network stability & readiness to serve unusual /devastating events [7] and reduce power consumption with "Q-C-S" protocol by checking each node status like node power, temperature, pressure etc. and regular update of network condition to base station.

3.3.1.2 Explanation. Regular information includes current position of the nodes (longitude & latitude), node status variables' values (like node- power remained, environmental variable's status, node's component status etc.), current neighbor list etc. One node queries when its status is "Q" i.e. Query flag is set, it asks others "whether you are well or not & I am fine", when some nodes replies it, will be included into the neighboring list. At the next instance this node will remain idle for one instance. Idle means it will not query to anyone, but will do its analysis on data got from its own sensors or from other node signals. This process is equally valid for all the nodes. This is how after some instances base-station will also come to know that "Network is fine".

Now whenever any type of agitation occurs into the network which exceeds the upper-bound condition of being regular, Type1 or/and Type2 flag is/are set into the header of the sending signal if it is querying at that moment, otherwise checking mode node is converted into querying node and Type1 or/and Type2 flag is/are set.

3.3.2 Network Behavior with Irregular Information

3.3.2.1 Objective. To maintain network integrity by node replacement and network status check and to analyze irregular events and to provide service for irregular event like unusual pressure, temperature etc and sending information of power failure, node damage etc. to Base station by an optimized network path way.

3.3.2.2 Explanation. The Type1flag in the header of the signal is set, means there is some abnormal situation occurred in one or more nodes. Our intension is to track those nodes and find the shortest path to convey the information to the base station as early as possible, with minimum power dissipation, so that corrective measures can be taken quickly. Thus when Type1 flag is set we switch to another algorithm "Irregular Information Transfer" protocol which will handle all these things and again make all the nodes ready for devastating situations. In this irregular case path optimization to reach the base-station is not only saves time but also it saves power, because it doesn't involves all the nodes in the network.

3.3.3 Network Behavior with Devastating Information

3.3.3.1 Objective. To protect mankind from various natural Disaster like Forest fire, Tsunami and To send this information to base Station by any means very fast.

3.3.3.2 Explanation. Information flooded to base stations following "Final Broad cast-petrol flow" network protocol. In this situation the node which will get the signal will be converted into "S" i.e. source node and immediately it will start broadcasting that signal to others , and it will go on in a recursive manner , no node will reply to this signal .

4 Design of Protocols

"QCS" protocol is the backbone protocol of our proposed network. This protocol has two subsections – one is for network initialization and 2nd is for after initialization of network. Two other protocols namely "Irregular Information Transfer" and "Final Broad Cast – Petrol Flow" are designed to help "QCS" protocol.

4.1 Algorithm for QCS protocol

4.1.1 Network Initialization

Step1. Begin.
Step2. Place the nodes and activate nodes during node placing.
Step3. Activate any one node as "Q" node.
Step4. Activate all its neighboring nodes as "C" node.
Step5. Activate another "Q" node which is not a neighbor of previous "Q" node.
Step6. Repeat Step3 to Step4 until every node on the network are activated properly.
Step7. End.

4.1.2 After Initialization

Step1. Begin
Step2. "Q" node sends Query to its neighboring nodes by broadcasting the query
Step3. Replies from neighbor nodes are stored in REP [N] array.
Step4. For i=0 to n
If (Type1 flag = = Node_id&& Tpye2 flag = = Null &&N_type = "Not Ok")
Go to "REGULAR INFORMATION TRANSFER" protocol routine.
Else If (Type1 flag = = Node_id&& Tpye2 flag = = Node_id&&N_type =="Not Ok")
Go to "Final Broadcast - Petrol Flow" protocol routine.
Else If (Type1 flag = = Null && Tpye2 flag = = Null &&N_type == "Ok")
Step4.1. Set "ACK" packet sender as "C" node put it into sleep for "T" time period.
Step4.2. After "T" time period "C" node automatically wakes up and became "Q" node and start Querying. [At the sleeping time "C" node won't any querying service.]
Step4.3. Go to Step4.
Step5. End.

4.2 Algorithm for Irregular Information Transfer protocol

Step1. Begin.
Step2. Sender of "ACK" packet become "S" by sensing its own sensor value and processing them.
Step3. i^{th}, node will locate sender node address through passive GPS system. [Here, Base station location is used as reference to find the location of the "S" node.]
Step4. "S" node sends query packet to its neighbor and receives "ACK" packets from neighbor nodes.
Step5. Choose a node among the replying nodes which has maximum existing power and location is closest to the Base Station.
Step6. Set the node as "S" node by sending signal to that very node setting its flags.
Step7. Repeat Step4 to Step6 until Base Station receives the signal.
Step8.Action is taken by the Base Station depending on the problem.
Step9. End.

4.3 Algorithm for Final Broad Cast– Petrol Flow Protocol

Step1. Begin.
Step2.Senderof "ACK" packet become "S" by sensing its own sensor values.
Step3. Broadcast that "ACK" packet to every direction.
Step4. Set Type1, Type2 flag of every receiving nodes and make them "S" node.
Step5. Repeat Step3 to Step4.
Step6. Signal will be received by Base Station and necessary action will be taken.
Step7. Reinitialize the network by making neighbor nodes of the Base Station as "Q" node and it start its usual job by resetting Type1 andType2 flags.
Step8. End.

5 Case Study

5.1 Network Behavior with Regular Information

In this case of network instance query nodes "Q" generates queries and send to checked nodes and base stations with its present status and overall network status. Checked node(c) works in power saving mode to reduce overall network station consumption. It sends ack. Packet with regular sensor information. Base stations regularly monitors network status and stores information and take necessary actions if needed. It is following above explained "Q-C-S" protocol.

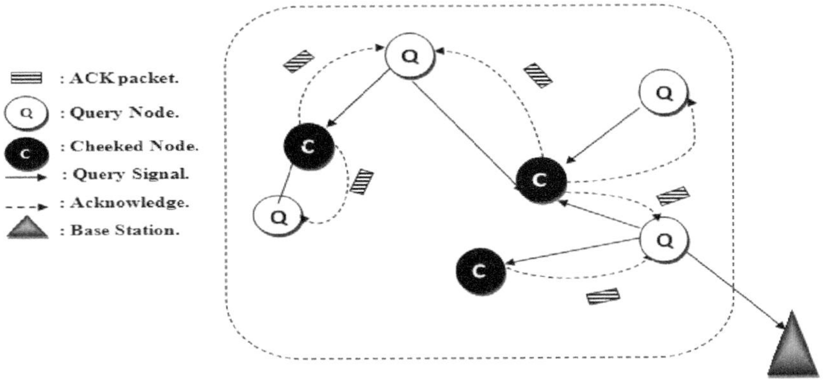

Fig. 1. Network Instance for regular information propagation

5.2 Network Behavior with Irregular Information

Here in this case "S" node is generated with setting Type-1flag. Following "Irregular Information Transfer" protocol, choosing optimized path, signal of irregular events like power failure, temperature change etc. has reached to base station. As it chooses optimized path based on maximum power and minimum distance from base station it consumes very less power and gives a fast action.

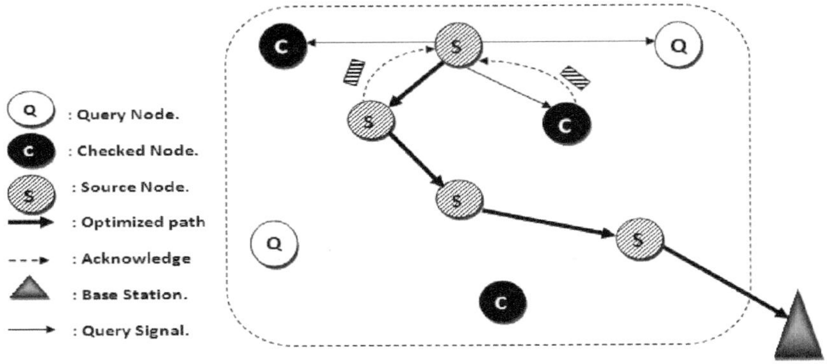

Fig. 2. Network Instance for irregular information propagation

5.3 Network Behavior with Devastating Information

Here, Type-2 flag is set to source node "S" to denote devastating situation. Information flooded to base stations following "Final Broad cast-Petrol Flow" network protocol.

Finally the message is reached to the base station. As information is flowing like fire with petrol i.e. in every possible direction with very fast speed propagation of message is to base station is very much quick and assured.

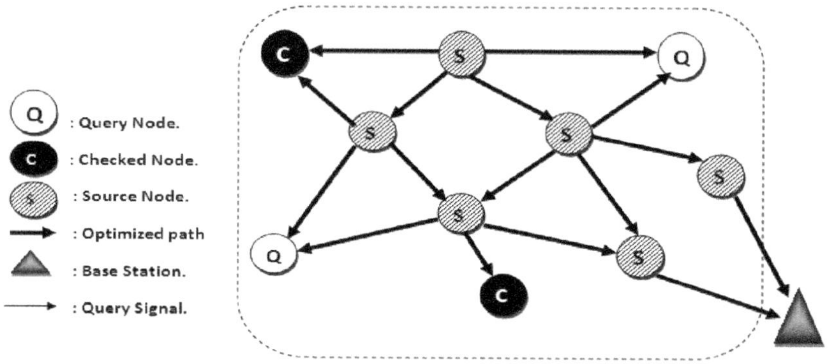

Fig. 3. Network Instance for devastating information propagation

6 Performance Analysis

To analyze the performance of the algorithm designed in this paper multiple operations of message propagation have been done on sensor nodes of the proposed network while simulating the network behavior under various possible situations explained above. After completion of the operations power consumed by the nodes has measured and a graph of node power vs. no. of operations has been drawn from that result. In the simulation procedure initial power of all the nodes are set as 50 units and network is initialized according to the QCS protocol, designed in this paper.

Multiple operations are done by making a node as "S" node to check the performance of the network behavior in case of hazardous conditions. After completion of ten such operation power consumption by the nodes are measured and from them five of the node are chosen randomly to draw the performance graph.

The graph shows that the power dissipation of all these five nodes is of similar range and it is between 50-48 units. From this result it can be said that amount of power dissipation of nodes in the network is uniform in nature and stability of the network is sustained. Thus power consumption of nodes is almost linear with time.

This network also provide guarantee of all time readiness as the network integrity and stability is maintained automatically by the nodes following QCS protocol with the help of base station. If any node loses its power or get damaged by any means the information will propagate to the base station for necessary action to be taken to maintain the readiness of the aforesaid network.

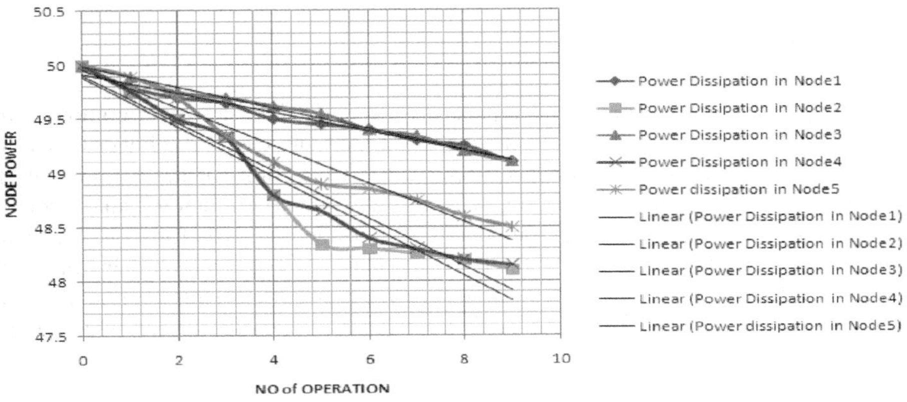

Fig. 4. Shows the node power vs. no. of operations graph with smaller division of Y-axis

Another important feature of this network, unlimited network life is achieved by the intelligence imposed on the nodes following QCS protocol. Here, network itself manages its stability and in case of any problem or hazard like node damage, power failure etc. the base station is informed by the network. Base station will then replace the node or take other necessary action to maintain network integrity and stability, thus overall network will achieve an unlimited life.

7 Conclusion

In this paper many important aspects of an ideal wireless Ad-hoc sensor network are considered to build the network proposed here as efficient as possible from the point of view of energy, stability, durability of network, readiness and speed of message propagation. Intelligence is introduced in this sensor network by information type categorization and recognition of those types. By designing a new protocol-QCS with its associate protocol namely Irregular Information Transfer protocol it is shown here how stability of an Ad-hoc sensor network can be maintained automatically by the network resources itself. Once the network is installed and activated by following QCS protocol network resources start communicating among themselves automatically and they take care of the network life by sensing any unusual event and sending that message to the base station for action. Thus, the life of the network proposed in this paper will be unlimited. It is also shown here that how network can always be ready for devastating hazards with its full efficiency, i.e. all time readiness along with very fast propagation of devastating information to the base station.

References

1. Kazi, A.S., Aouad, G., Baldwin, A.: An architecture for decision support in ad hoc sensor Networks (June 2009)
2. AbdRahman, A.H., Zukarnain, Z.A.: Performance Comparison of AODV, DSDV and I-DSDV Routing Protocols in Mobile Ad Hoc Networks. European Journal of Scientific Research 31(4), 556–576 (2009)

3. Shih, K.-P., Chen, H.-C., Liu, B.-J.: Integrating Target Coverage and Connectivity for Wireless Heterogeneous Sensor Networks with Multiple Sensing Units (2007)
4. Giannoulis, S., Antonopoulos, C., Topalis, E., Koubias, S.: ZRP versus DSR and TORA: A comprehensive survey on ZRP performance. IEEE Transactions on Industrial Informatics 3(1), 63–72 (2007)
5. Akkaya, K., Younis, M.: Survey on Routing Protocols in Wireless Sensor Networks. Adhoc Networks (2005)
6. Maltz, J.B., Johunson, D.: Lessons from a full-Scale multi-hop wireless ad hoc network test bed. IEEE Personal communications magazine (2005)
7. Cardei, Wu, J., Lu, M., Pervaiz, M.O.: Maximum network lifetime in wireless sensor networks with adjustable sensing ranges. In: Proceedings of IEEE International Conference on Wireless and Mobile Computing, Networking and Communications (WiMOB), vol. 3, pp. 438–445 (August 2005)
8. Cardei, M., Thai, M.T., Li, Y., Wu, W.: Energy-efficient target coverage in wireless sensor networks. In: Proceedings of the 24th Annual Joint Conference of the IEEE Computer and Communications Societies (INFOCOM), vol. 3, pp. 1976–1984 (March 2005)
9. Belding-Royer, E.M.: Routing approaches in mobile adhoc networks. In: Basagni, S., Conti, M., Giordano, S., Stojmenovic, I. (eds.) Mobile Ad HocNetworking. ch. 10, pp. 275–300. Wiley-Interscience, Hoboken (2004)
10. Maltz, D., Hu, Y.: The Dynamic Source Routing Protocol for Mobile Ad Hoc Networks, Internet Draft (July 2004), `http://www.ietf.org/internetdrafts/draft-ietf-manet-dsr-10.txt`
11. Perkings, C.E., Belding-Royer, E.M., Das, S.R.: Ad Hoc On- Demand Distance Vector (AODV) Routing IETF Internet draft (February 2003), `http://www.ietf.org/internetdrafts/draft-ietf-manet-aodv-13.txt`

A New Approach for Securing Mobile Adhoc Network with an Improved Trust Calculation Method

Amit Chauhan[1] and Nidhi Shah[2]

[1] Institute of Engineering & Science, IPS, Indore, India
amitcs3786@gmail.com
[2] U & P. U. Patel Department of Computer Engineering, CSPIT, CHARUSAT, Changa, Gujarat, India
nbshah999@yahoo.com

Abstract. A Mobile Adhoc Network is a group of wireless mobile computers in which nodes cooperate by forwarding packets for each other to allow them to communicate beyond direct wireless transmission range. Due to wide-ranging characteristics of the Ad Hoc Networks, it is always at a risk to internal as well as external attacks. Many solutions have been proposed and currently being improved in this area. Most of these solutions involve encryption, secure routing, quality of service etc. Each of them is designed to operate in a particular situation, which may fail to work successfully in other scenarios.

This paper offers an alternate approach to improve the trustworthiness of the neighbourhood nodes and secure the routing procedure. It helps in computing the trust in neighbours and selecting the most secured route from the available ones for communication. It also helps detecting the compromised node and virtually removing from the network.

Keywords: MANET, SID, Trust.

1 Introduction

Mobile adhoc network MANET is a new concept in wireless communication world, where the networks are formed and destroyed on the fly without any centralized controlled. MANET is a collection of independent mobile nodes that can communicate to each other via radio waves. Mobile Ad-Hoc network is a system of wireless mobile nodes that dynamically self-organizes itself in arbitrary and temporary network topologies [2]. Due to the lack of centralize management; security is a major concern in this dynamic, error prone, multi-hop wireless communication network. [1]. The network is very dynamic, here a node may enter and leave the network on frequent basis. Nodes may also be mobile, that they move within the network itself or from one ad hoc network to the other[5].

"Trust, is a particular level of the subjective probability with which an agent will perform a particular action, both before we can monitor such action (or independently of his capacity of ever to be able to monitor it) and in a context in which it affects our own action" [7]. Trust is a belief that the principal, when asked to perform an action,

D.C. Wyld et al. (Eds.): CNSA 2011, CCIS 196, pp. 587–597, 2011.

will act according to a predefined description, this implies that the principal will not attempt to harm the requester, regardless of how it carries out the request.

We can make three points of the definition above.

- Trust is subjective.
- Trust is affected by actions that cannot be monitored.
- The level of trust depends on our own actions.

Existing security trends provide the criteria to build certain level of trust in the network. For example, cryptographic algorithms for privacy and digital signatures, authentication protocols for providing authenticity and access control methods for managing authorization. However, these methods do not manage the general concept of "trustworthiness". For instance, a cryptographic algorithm is unable to say that, competent programmers have authored a piece of digitally signed code or a signed public-key certificate does not guarantee the owner's authenticity.

Trust has the following properties. [6]

Transitivity: Trust is not necessarily transitive, that is, if A trusts B and B trusts C, and A does not necessarily trust C.

Symmetry: Trust need not be symmetric, that is, A trusts B does not imply that B trusts A.

Reflexivity: Trust is assumed to be reflexive, that is, a node trusts itself completely.

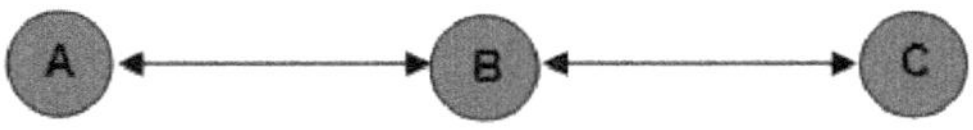

Fig. 1. Trust between Network Nodes

A trust level is requested by a "Requester" to the "Recommender", in reply a recommender send its own trust level in the requested node. Based on experience gained via hearing the channel and trust level received from the neighbor, a node calculates its own trust in a particular node for a specific entity. Ad hoc networks are based on "trust your neighbor" relationships. This relationship originates, develop and expire on the fly [4]. A trust model can secure an ad hoc network from the attacks to some extent and identify the routes with certain measure of safe and confidence.

2 Trust Relationships

Ontological Trust relationship exists between one-hop neighbors. When one neighbor holds a belief about other, the same belief in the reverse direction need not exist at the same time. Mutual trust does exist between entities, but we represent them as two separate trust relationships, which can be manipulated independently.

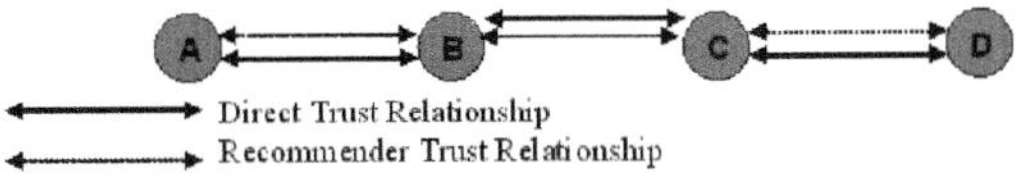

Fig. 2. Trust Relationship in the Network

Trust can be seen in two ways, viz. 1. Direct Trust Relationship and 2. Recommender Trust Relationship. Each node maintains a database for its own use. Based on experience and recommendations, these values are changed in the database at any time. Depending on the behaviour of the direct (one-hop) neighbors, a node will calculate the trust value and will recommend the same in case of requested by any other node. For calculating the trust value of the remote node, a requester can demand recommendations from its neighbors.

3 Existing Solution for Trust Calculation

A wide range of proposals are recommended to estimate the amount of trust between two communicating nodes in ad hoc network. Almost every method is based on situational trust for particular category of activity.

As suggested by Alfarez Abdul-Rahman and Stephen Halles in [3], a requester issues recommendation request message (RRQ) and receives recommendation message. These recommendations are time bound and refreshed on periodic basis. The recommended solution works as follows.

RRQ : : = Requestor_ID, Request_ID, Target_ID, Categories, RequestorPKC, GetPKC, Expiry

Categories : : = SET OF (Category_Name)

Recommendation Request (RRQ)

Recommendation : : = Requestor_ID, Request_ID, Rec_Path, [SEQUENCE OF {Recommendation_Set, TargetPKC} | NULL]

Rec_Path : : = SEQUENCE OF {Recommender_ID}

Recommendation_Set : : = SET OF Recommendation Slip

Recommendation_Slip : : = SET OF SEQUENCE {Target_ID, Category_Name, Trust_Value, Expiry}

Trust Recommendation

Where,

Requestor_ID - represents identity of the requester

Request_ID - is a unique identity of the request

Target_ID - represents identity of the target (about whom trust recommendation request is broadcasted)

Categories - set of category names that requestor is interested in inquiring about.

RequestorPKC – is a public key certificate, which can be used to encrypt the Recommendation_set (Optional)

GetPKC – requestor interested in target's public key for further communication (optional)

Rec_Path – contains the ordered sequence of recommender IDs.

Recommendatin_Set – includes multiple instances of Recommendation_Slip

Category_Name – Name of the category for which trust level is requested.

Expiry – Contains expiry period for RRQ

4 Shortcomings of the Existing Solution

There are several problems in the existing solution. Some of them are,

1. The existing solution [3], computes the trust for a node in particular category. On the contrary, the proposed solution calculates the global trust.
2. Expiry timers are maintained for the recommendations. If the timer expires and the path is still active, again the original requester has to request for the trust value of the target. Thus, the process is duplicated even in case of unchanged trust value. This incurs more delays and waste of processing time and bandwidth.
3. The recommender is simply passing on its trust value of target node to the requester and the original requestor computes the value on its own. There are chances of malicious recommendation from one of the recommender, lies in between the original requester and the target node.

5 Proposed Method for Trust Calculation

Many solutions have been proposed to compute the trust level in ad hoc networks. Every solution has its own pros and cons and also designed and developed by keeping particular situation in mind. Thus, it may or may not work in the other condition. Ad hoc networks are based on *"trust your neighbor"* relationships. Since there is no centralize control, each node is responsible for a secure data communication and as a process of providing secure communication path; each node monitors its neighbors. However, each node has to assure that, it is communicating with a trustworthy neighbor. This proposal offers a unique way of computing the trust level in the network and reduces the communication overhead by limiting the size of packet containing trust level information.

There are two different strategies in calculating target nodes trust value [3].

1. **Direct Trust Value:** This is relevant to the direct trust relationships, where a mobile node in a range can scrutinize the activities of its neighbors and calculate the trust value on its own.
2. **Recommender Trust Value:** This is relevant to recommender trust relationship. In this case, trust value of out of range node is requested using RRQ (Recommendation Request).

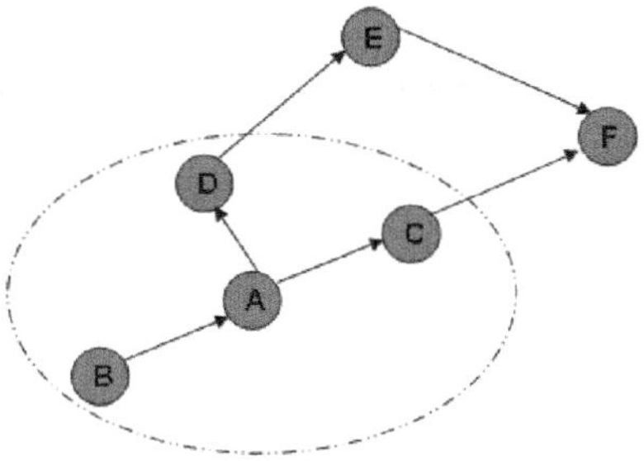

Fig. 3. Communication Range

In figure 3, node A can directly communicate with the node B, C and D, as all of them are in A's communication range. Node E and F are out of range of node A, but it can still reach these out of range nodes via D and C respectively. Thus, node C and D will relay the message for A, in case A wishes to communicate with node E and F.

5.1 Neighbor Monitoring

In wireless manner, the nodes in a direct communication range, can transfer the data packet and updates routing paths directly. But before this, a node has to assure that it is communicating with a legitimate node. At this point, the concept of trust in the network appears. Each node has a different trust level in its neighbors and as stated earlier.

A node in a radio range of its neighbors can passively overhear the channel and ongoing activity at the other end. This is possible even if a node is not actively involved in a communication. Because of this unique characteristic of wireless networks, it is viable in ad hoc networks to monitor the neighborhood activities and record any offences conducted. Each node constantly monitors the activity of its neighbors in terms of amount of successful data packets and routing updates forwarded correctly. In case of any malicious activity, a node will broadcast SID (Single Intrusion Detection) against the malicious node. The affecting nodes (which are in a radio range of a malicious and SID originator node) will recompute the trust level of malicious nodes and raise their trust level database.

5.2 Validating Single Intrusion Detection (SID)

A malicious activity by any node can be detected and other nodes are informed using Single Intrusion Detection (SID). It is quite likely that a malicious node may broadcast a false SID against a legitimate node or due to the unavoidable circumstances like poor radio connectivity, error in received packets, etc. a node may get detected as a compromised node by its neighbors and an SID may broadcasted against it. Thus, instead of blindly accepting the SID, following parameters are considered by a node receiving SID broadcast:

5.2.1 Algorithm to Validate SID

1. Trust level of a node, which is broadcasting SID against a compromised node.
2. If a compromised node is in a radio range, it will observe a compromised node for a certain period.
3. It will request other neighbors for their recommendations about the compromised node.
4. Depending on its conclusion, a node may recompute the trust level for either the compromised node or SID broadcasting node.

5.3 Trust Recommendation

Structure of the recommendation request (RRQ) message is almost same as the one used in [3].

RRQ : : = Requestor_ID, Request_ID, Target_ID

Recommendation Request

In the above message, the RRQ does not contain Category and Expiry. We have not included these two parameters because we are not judging the trust of any node for a particular category. We are calculating the global trust, based on SID, hello beacons and acknowledgements.

Recommendation::= Requestor_ID, Request_ID, Recommender_ID, Target_ID, Trust_Value

Request_ID : represents identity of the request

Target_ID: represents identity of the target .

5.4 Trust Computation

As discussed earlier, each node computes its own trust based on its observation or recommendations from its neighbors. Unlike the scheme proposed in [3], where an original requester node computes the trust level recommended by intermediate as well as final recommender, here every node computes the trust level based on its own trust in its neighbors and forwards the computed trust towards the original requester.

A node constantly observes the activities of the other nodes in its radio range and computes the trust level for each node. In case of SID broadcast, the compromised node is not evicted out of the network immediately, rather trust level is computed and if it falls below certain threshold then only the node is expelled from the network.

A node will compute the trust level of its neighbors based on SID (either broadcasted by itself or other nodes), beacons and acknowledgements. Trust level computation also depends on received / missing beacons and acknowledgements. Each parameter viz. SID, Beacon and Acknowledgement is rated on the scale of 0 to 5.

Table 1. Trust Value Semantics

Value	Meaning	Description
0	Distrust	Completely Untrustworthy.
1	Ignorance	Cannot make trust-related judgment about entity.
2	Minimal	Lowest possible trust.
3	Average	Mean trustworthiness. Most entities have this trust level
4	Good	More trustworthy than most entities
5	Complete	Completely trustworthy

It computes the trust level as follows. Consider that node A is computing the trust level of node B. A node computing trust level, rates each of these events from 0 (zero) to 5 (five) based on its experience. This scheme proposed percentage based computation. It takes 60 % of SID, 20% Hello Beacons and 20% of Acknowledgements. In case of no data transfer there will not be any communication between two nodes and hence no acknowledgements, in this case it takes 60% of SID and 40% of Acknowledgements.

$$tv = 0.6 * sid + 0.2 * bcn + 0.2 * ack \ldots \qquad \ldots\ldots\ldots (1)$$

Here, tv = Trust Value

sid = Single Intrusion Detection

bcn = Beacon

ack = Acknowledgement

Lets assume that node A has gathered following details about node B after observing it for a particular period of time.

sid = 4, bcn = 3, ack = 2

$tv = 0.6 * 4 + 0.2 * 3 + 0.2 * 2$

= **3.4**

Each node will use the above-described formula to compute its trust level in the neighboring node. Even if it is recommending the trust level of its neighbors to the requestor, it will first calculate the trust level in above described manner and forward it to the recommendation requester node. In case of recommending the trust value of the target node, the recommender will calculate the trust using the equation (1) and forward it to the requester node.

Computing Trust Proportion of the Neighbor

$$Sr = \sum_{i=1}^{n} Ni \tag{2}$$

where, S_r = Sum of trust of neighbors (recommenders) of a requester

i = Neighbors of a requester
N = Trust value of i

Computing Trust Proportion Between a Requester and a Recommender

$$T_{Rr(i)} = [100 * T_{r(i)}] / S_r \ldots\ldots\ldots \tag{3}$$

where, $T_{Rr(i)}$ = Calculated trust proportion between a requester and a recommender

$T_{r(i)}$ = Trust recommended by a recommender
S_r = Sum of trust of neighbors (recommenders) of a requester

Computing the Final Trust Value of a Target

$$T_t = \sum_{i=1}^{n} T_{Rr(i)} \ldots \tag{4}$$

Where, T_t = Sum of trust proportion of neighbor nodes.

$T_{Rr(i)}$ = Calculated trust proportion between a requester and a recommender

The original RRQ requester node will calculate the trust level of a target node in above described manner. Firstly, it will calculate the total trust value of its neighbor and compute the individual trust proportion of each neighboring node based on it. At last, it will calculate the trust value for target node by adding the recommended trust values based on the proportional trust in the recommender.

5.4.1 Algorithm to Compute the Trust in Ad Hoc Network

1. Check whether the target node is in the communication range or not. If it is not in a communication range then, broadcast RRQ in the vicinity.
2. Compute the trust percentage of each node against the sum of the trust of all the neighbors.
3. Consider the percentage of recommended trust value based previously computed trust level proportion of the neighbors.

Add the calculated recommendations from the neighbors and compute the final trust value of the target node.

Example

In this scenario as shown in figure 4, node A wishes to communicate with node E. As a prerequisite for a secure communication, node A requests for a trust level for node E. Since E is not in a communication range of the node A, it will broadcast the RRQ message to its neighbors.

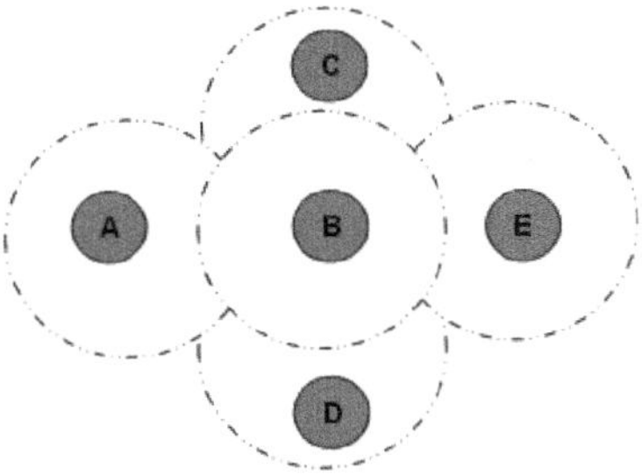

Fig. 4. Requesting Trust Level of Out of Range Node

Node B, C and D can directly communicate with node A; Node A, C, D and E can directly communicate with node B; Node A, B and E can directly communicate with node C; Node A, B and E can directly communicate with node D; Node B, C and D can directly communicate with node E.

As stated above, as a part of secure communication with node E, node A broadcasts RRQ to request. Here, node A and E is not in a direct communication link of each other. Neighbors of node A viz. node B, C and D, will receive the RRQ packets and fortunately, all of these nodes are in a direct radio communication rage of node E. All of these nodes have calculated the trust level of node E previously, using the equation (1).

A⟶B : A,rrqA01,E
A⟶C : A,rrqA01,E
A⟶D : A,rrqA01,E

As a recommendation reply each node will send its own recommendation to node A – the requestor.

B⟶A : A,rrqA01,B,E,2
C⟶A : A,rrqA01,C,E,3
D⟶A : A,rrqA01,D,E,2

Node A will calculate the trust level as follows. Initially,

- Node A trust node B value 1
- Node A trust node C value 3.5
- Node A trust node D value 5

Recommendations about node E from the neighbors of node A.

- Node B trust node E value 2
- Node C trust node E value 3
- Node D trust node E value 2

As per Equation (2)

Sr = 9.5
As per Equation (3)
$\mathbf{T_{Rr(B)} = 0.21}$
$\mathbf{T_{Rr(C)} = 1.11}$
$\mathbf{T_{Rr(D)} = 1.05}$

Finally, Trust of Node A in a Target Node E according to the equation (4)

$\mathbf{T_t = 2.37}$

6 Benefits of the Proposed Scheme

The proposed scheme has significant variations and their benefits as follows.

1. The RRQ and recommendation reply messages are simple and do not contain unnecessary parameters and hence it reduces the overhead generated in the network.
2. Each node itself computes the proportional trust level of its neighbors and forwards it to the requester. Thus, there is no need of sending the list of intermediate recommenders in form of rec_path or rec_slip.
3. We do not calculate the trust for any specific category. We are calculating the global trust, based on SID, hello beacons and acknowledgements.
4. As stated earlier, in case of any change in the trust value of any active node, the recommender will re-recommend the changed trust value to the requestor, with the help of the forward path established previously. Hence, we do not maintain any Expiry Timer.
5. The original requester node calculates the trust level of target node in proportion with the trust level of his neighborhood territory.

7 Conclusion

Security is vital in Ad Hoc Networks. Securing the Ad Hoc Networks starts from the neighbor verification in the local community also termed as a cluster – collection of wireless nodes in a particular group. As a proposed solution trust is not calculated for any particular situation instead, it is computed based on a summary of behavior of the node for a specific amount of period, instead of a target node, calculation is made on overall trust, a neighbor itself will calculate the percentage based trust and recommend it to the requester. In case of any malicious behavior, a Single Intrusion Detection (SID) packet is broadcasted against compromised node and all the participating neighbors are informed about the malevolent activity performed.

References

1. Yang, H., Meng, X., Lu, S.: Self-organized network-layer security in mobile ad hoc networks. In: Proc. 3rd ACM workshop on Wireless Security
2. Kourten, G., Schneider, J., Preuitt, D., Thompson, T.G.C., F'ickas, S., Segall, Z.: Whwn Peer-to-Peer comes Face-toFace: Collaborative Peer-to-Peer Computing in Mobile Adhoc Networks. In: 1st International Copnference on Peer-to-Peer Computing, Linkoping, Swedan, pp. 75–91 (August 2001)
3. Abdul-Rahman, A., Halles, S.: A Distributed Trust Model. In: New Security Paradigms Workshop, Proceedings of the 1997 workshop on New security paradigms, pp. 48–60 (1997)
4. Pirzada, A.A., McDonald, C.: Establishing Trust in Pure Ad-hoc Networks. In: Proceedings of the 27th conference on Australasian Computer Science. ACM International Conference Proceeding Series, vol. 56, 26, pp. 47–54
5. Perkins, C., Royer, E.: Ad hoc on-demand distance vector routing. In: Proc. IEEE Workshop on Mobile Computing Systems and Applications (1999)
6. Candolin, C., Kari, H.H.: Distributing Incomplete Trust in Wireless Ad Hoc Networks. In: Proceedings of the New Security Paradigms Workshop. ACM, New York (1997)
7. Diego, G.: Can We Trust? In: Gambetta, D. (ed.) Trust Making and Breaking Cooperative Relations, Department of Sociology, University of Oxford, electronic edition. ch. 13, pp. 213–237 (2000)

A Routing Protocol for Facilitating Multimedia Transmission over 802.11e Based Mobile Ad Hoc Networks

Sujatha P.Terdal[1], V.D. Mytri[2], A. Damodaram[3], and Uday S.B.[4]

[1] Department of Computer Science and Engineering,
PDA College of Engineering, Gulbarga, Karnataka
suja_pst@rediffmail.com
[2] Principal, GND College of Engineering, Bidar, Karnataka
vdmytri2006@rediffmail.com
[3] Professor, Department of Computer Science and Engineering, JNTU, Hyderabad
[4] Department of Information Science and Engineering,
PDA College of Engineering, Gulbarga , Karnataka
udaysb@rediffmail.com

Abstract. With a view to support delay sensitive multimedia traffic, IEEE 802.11e standard(EDCA) has been proposed as an improvement over IEEE 802. 11 based DCF mechanism. But studies show that EDCA is unable to cope with high traffic load conditions thus failing to offer QoS guarantees for multimedia traffic. This work proposes a routing mechanism that can take advantage of the service differentiation offered by the MAC and at the same time overcome its limitation under heavy load conditions thus facilitating transport of real time data. Our work measures the existing work load of the high priority queues and the level of contention caused due to neighboring nodes to assess the available bandwith and accordingly route the audio -video stream along less congested paths, to ensure better end to end delay and throughput. Simulation studies show that our protocol is able to protect delay constrained traffic under heavy traffic conditions.

Keywords: MANET, Multipath AODV, Load Balancing, Energy Aware Routing.

1 Introduction

With the recent advances in wireless technology , use of Mobile ad hoc networks (MANE T) for providing content -rich services is gaining popularity. So it has become very essential for MANET's to have a reliable, efficient Quality of Service mechanisms(QoS) to support diverse real-time multimedia applications. Ad hoc networks are wireless mobile networks without any infrastructure, where mobile nodes cooperate with each other to find routes and relay packets. Such networks can be deployed instantly in situations where infrastructure is unavailable or difficult to install, and are evolving rapidly to provide ubiquitous untethered communication. The ease with which MANET's can be formed has catalyzed its widespread

D.C. Wyld et al. (Eds.): CNSA 2011, CCIS 196, pp. 598–607, 2011.

deployment. Ensuring QoS guarantees for audio and video transport over these networks introduces new challenges due to the frequent link failures introduced arising out of mobility of nodes and time varying channel conditions. This necessitates optimizations at MAC , routing, transport layer and application layer. To reduce distortion at the receiver, mechanisms like multiple Description Coding and Layered Coding schemes are devised at the application layer. These schemes decompose multimedia data in to base and enhancement information resulting in large number of packets offered to the network which calls for efficient routing mechanisms that can handle increased amount of traffic .Additional MAC layer mechanisms are also necessary that can reserve resources like bandwith, for delay sensitive traffic. One such optimization done at the MAC layer is the enhanced distributed co-ordination function (EDCF) of IEEE 802.11e ,which is an enhancement of IEEE 802.11 DCF medium access protocol. Based on the QoS requirements , different levels of proirity can be assigned to different types of traffic. In EDCF, traffic of different priorities is assigned to one of four transmit queues[8] ,which respectively correspond to four Access Categories(AC).Each AC transmits packets with an independent channel access function ,which implements the prioritized channel contention algorithm. Priority in gaining channel access to realtime data is given by assigning smaller contention window, which would mean lesser waiting time for them. The 802.11e was initially proposed for wireless LANs in the presence of Access Points (AP). As MANET's are multi-hop networks and do not use AP's , supporting 802.11e MAC for ad hoc networks need additional modifications. Even though ,service differentiation is done at the MAC layer by IEEE 802.11e to ensure QoS ,its performance degrades when additional real-time traffic flows in to the network. This happens because of increase in the level of contention among the flows that belong to the same traffic class. At this juncture, MAC layer will have no option but to drop such frames resulting in the performance degradation. Adopting a routing layer solution can be used that detects such overloaded nodes that are busy forwarding high priority packets. The solution we propose here, estimates the load based on the medium utilization and level of channel activity around a node and selects paths that are lightly loaded and can possibly offer routing paths that can sustain delay sensitive traffic.

In the recent past suitability of multipath routing protocols have been discussed in [1][2] for transporting real-time applications over MANET. In wireless ad hoc networks for continous real-time data transfer , routing protocols have to ensure lesser frequency of route failures for which multipath routing technique is a viable alternative. From a fault tolerant perspective ,multipath routing can be achieved by using multiple paths simultaneously, for data transmission .But simultaneous transmission introduces interference among multiple paths resulting in lesser throughput and introduction of jitter which is unacceptable. Hence we use precomputed primary path for transmission and switch to alternate path, when primary path fails.

The rest of the paper is organized as follows: Section 2 discuses the literature and related works .Section 3 introduces our proposed protocol. Performance evaluation of the proposed protocol is taken up in section 4.Conclusion is presented in section 5.

2 Review of Literature

IEEE 802.11 Distributed Coordination Function (DCF) lacked built -in mechanisms for supporting real -time services which demand strict QOS guarantees. With this aim, IEEE 802.11e[3] was initially proposed for supporting multimedia applications over wireless LANs.

Though IEEE 802.11 e EDCA can improve the throughput efficiency of delay sensitive traffic , simulation studies[4][5] show declined throughput compared to that of DCF under heavy traffic loads because of the increase in retransmissions and the way contention window is reset statically without considering changing network load conditions. Aiming at reducing collisions at high load conditions, a MAC layer solution PEDCA[6] is proposed by dynamically varying the transmission probability of each Access Category depending on the network load. This measure can protect high priority AC at heavy loads. [7] conducted performance study on the suitability IEEE 802.11e protocol on multi-hop ad hoc networks. Results show that voice and video traffic is able to maintain a steady throughput, independently of lower priority traffic up to a certain limit. [8] points out that IEEE 802.11e cannot guarentee strict QoS requirements needed by real-time services without proper network control mechanisms.They propose a call admission control and rate control scheme for real-time data along with letting best effort traffic use residual bandwidth.[9] proposes a routing mechanism with distributed Call admission control algorithms which calculates available bandwidth according to local channel state and the information of the neighbor nodes.

TSLA[10] is a routing layer solution based on EDCA proposed for alleviating congestion and diverting incoming traffic over less congested paths. It uses MAC layer buffer size of the Access Categories ,to indicate congestion. Although using queue size of the Access Categories may reflect the amount of internal collision ,this is insufficient as this does not consider traffic activity of neighboring nodes. So TSLA cannot assure throughput guarantees. Energy of the nodes while routing is also ignored here , which is one of the factors that determine the lifetime of a routing path.

In the recent past , load balancing solutions suggested involved finding paths with minimum traffic and routing data over such minimum traffic paths. Minimum traffic path comprised of nodes with least queue size. CSLAR[11] makes route selection based on channel contention information ,number of packets in its queue and number of hops along the route. Busy and idle portion of the channel around a mobile node is estimated using NAV obtained from MAC layer. LBAR[12] defines a new metric for load balanced routing known as the degree of nodal activity to represent the load on a mobile node.

[13] discusses MRP-LB which spreads traffic at packet level granularity equally in to multiple paths. It distributes the load such that total number of congested packets on each route is equal. [14] defines a cost criterion that combines load information at a node with the energy expended in transmitting the RREQ packet from the previous node to the current node.

None of the above load balancing solutions distribute load without differentiating the type of data forwarded by the relaying nodes for alleviating congestion. Further in the above literature QoS and load balancing solutions are either offered independently as MAC enhancements or as routing extensions without using 802.11e. So our objective is to devise a routing mechanism that establishes less congested multiple routing paths that are long lived to facilitate multimedia transmissions.

3 Proposed Congestion Aware Multipath Routing Protocol

Load balancing is very crucial in distributing network load uniformly over all parts of the network and extend the lifetime of the network .So routing protocols need to take routing decisions by taking into account experienced channel load, in addition to shortest hop metric. Even though preferential treatment to real-time data is given by EDCA at MAC layer ,network performance degrades when additional real-time flows are injected into the network, resulting in the loss of delay sensitive audio and video packets. This is because with increasing real time traffic ,high priority queues build up. Increasing traffic in the network leads to increasing level of contention among nodes while performing channel access resulting in more number of collisions and deterioration of end to end delay. IEEE 802.11e ,nodes here experience two types of collisions namely internal and external collisions. External collision occurs when neighboring nodes simultaneously perform channel access. When more than one Access Category count their back-off counters to zero at the same time within a node, an internal or virtual collision is said to happen leading to packet drops. So with the increasing network load it is necessary to protect the delay constraints of real -time data. Our approach proposes Congestion Aware Multipath Routing mechanism, (CAMR) for improving the throughput of realtime data. Our solution , adopts a measurement based approach to assess the available bandwith between two nodes. Once bandwith is measured ,existing load status of Access Categories that carry audio and video traffic is measured. Remaining energy of the nodes is also measured. Route Discovery process is accordingly modified to consider current network load conditions.

3.1 Bandwidth Calculation

Accurate Bandwidth estimation is difficult in wireless networks as the channel is shared among the neighboring nodes. Therefore computing effective available bandwidth must not only take in to account transmission rate of a node , but also the transmissions of all neighboring nodes. We adopt bandwidth measurement technique based on the channel usage as in [15]. Every node counts the number of consecutive idle slots observed by the node over a period of time interval T_{meas}. Channel usage refers to time taken by the MAC layer in transmitting data and control frames. This reflects the available bandwidth. From a set of sample values ,a probability density function *idle(x)* of number of consecutive idle slots *x* could be derived. Later average number of idle slots *Av-idle-slots* in the measurement interval can be computed as

$$\text{Av-Idle-slots} = \sum_{x=0}^{\infty} x \cdot idle(x) \qquad (1)$$

Then the available bandwidth can be computed as

$$\text{Available-Bw} = \frac{Av - idle - slots}{Tmeas} \quad (2)$$

In multi-hop wireless ad hoc networks ,buffer capacity of the nodes increase signifying the occurrence of congestion. Once available bandwidth is measured , another measure that is taken into account, is the kind of traffic that is being processed by the node. If the node is already relaying voice or video packets, then including such a node in a routing path may effect the quality of service. Hence we take into account the existing number of packets queued up at the AC for audio and video.

3.2 Algorithm

If (intermediate node has enough energy) and
(queue-utilization of AC[audio] < thresh)
and (queue-utilization of AC[video] < thresh)
if (*Available-BW* < *BW* in RREQ packet)
BW=Available-BW
else ignore RREQ packet

3.3 Route Discovery and Path Selection

CAMR is implemented over AOMDV [16] that computes link disjoint paths. Here at the intermediate nodes , duplicate copies of RREQ are not immediately discarded. Source node initiates Route discovery when routes are not available in the cache. Route discovery begins with the flooding of RREQ packets to all neighboring nodes. RREQ packets are modified to record the available bandwidth ie, *Available-BW*. RREQ is propagated only if the intermediate node has enough energy (thresh-energy) to sustain the transmission duration. Next a RREQ packet is ignored by the intermediate node , if queue size of voice and video AC is beyond a threshold. Source node initializes bandwidth to BW which is the maximum value of the bandwidth in the RREQ packet. While RREQ is propagated ,each intermediate node checks its available bandwidth with the value stored in RREQ packet. If the *Available-BW* of the intermediate node is found to be lower than the value in RREQ header ,then it is updated with the lower one. Thus the destination will come to know about a congested node. Destination after waiting for certain time interval gathers multiple routes ,which is restricted to three paths and selects two routing paths with highest *Available-BW* value in RREQ packet. Data transmission is initiated along the primary path by the source node. Transmission over secondary path is initiated by the source when a RERR is received over the primary path.

4 Performance Evaluation

In this section, benefits of CAMR is shown by comparing the simulation results with AOMDV.

4.1 Simulation Scenario

This protocol is simulated using OMNET++ [17] patch[18] in INET framework which supports complete physical, data link and MAC layer models for simulating wireless ad hoc networks over 802.11e. We simulated a network of mobile nodes placed randomly in an area of 1500 x 600 square meters, with 50 mobile nodes. A source and a destination is selected randomly. Free space propagation model is assumed as the channel model. Each node is assumed to have a constant transmission range of 250 meters. Medium access control protocol used is IEEE 802.11e Enhanced Distributed Coordination Function (EDCF). CBR traffic is generated with an audio traffic at the rate of 120 kbps and video traffic rate of 82 kbps. Packet size is 512 bytes. Packet inter arrival time is kept at 1second for both audio and video. Source destination pairs are spread randomly over the network. Mobility pattern of the mobile nodes is generated using Random Waypoint model. A mobile node selects another node as destination in the network and constantly moves towards it at a given velocity. Once it reaches there, it waits for some pause time and selects another node and again starts moving. Speed of a mobile node is assigned a value between 0 to 20meters/sec.

4.2 Results

Working of CAMR protocol is compared with the multipath AODV. Performance metrics analysed are packet delivery ratio, end to end delay and average energy consumption. Packet delivery ratio is the ratio of total number of packets that have successfully reached the destination to the total number of packets generated by CBR sources. Figure 1 shows how CAMR reacts to increasing audio traffic. As can be seen in the figure, packet delivery ratio is better than AOMDV. Increasing audio sources results in building up of queue size of Access Category for voice. CAMR avoids such nodes ,whose queue size is beyond a threshold. Hence , there is an improvement in the packet delivery ratio.

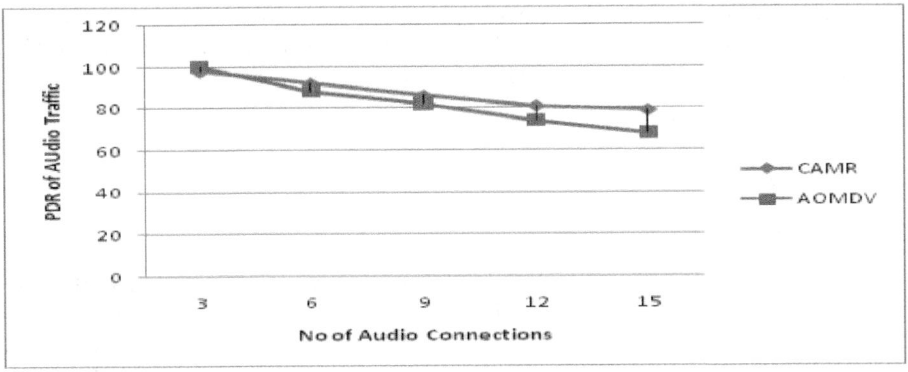

Fig. 1. Packet Delivery Ratio for increasing audio traffic

Packet delivery ratio of video packets observed in Figure 2 , is comparatively lesser than that of audio packets due to the service differentiation offered by IEEE 802.11e. Number of video generating sources is constantly increased. Packet delivery ratio of audio and video packets is improved even under increased generation of delay sensitive traffic. Packet Delivery Ratio for AOMDV is lesser as it selects shortest routing paths without considering the queue size of the Access Categories at the nodes. Performance of both AOMDV and CAMR worsens when number of traffic generating sources increase.

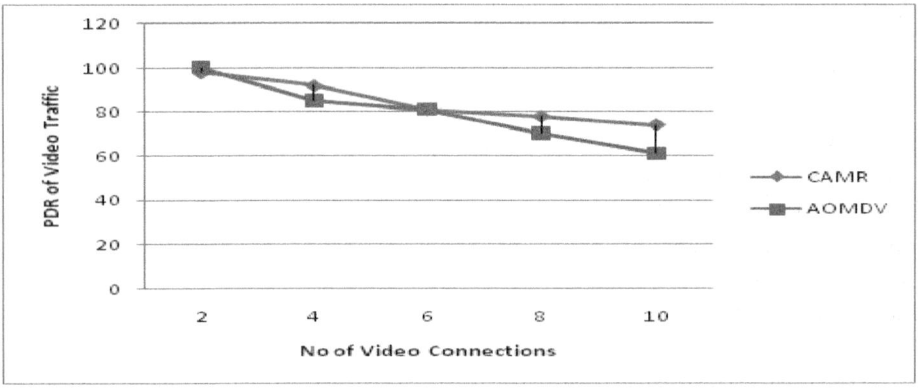

Fig. 2. Packet Delivery Ratio for increasing video traffic

Avoiding congested routes become necessary to provide QOS for multimedia data. CAMR shows betterment in end to end delay even under increased number of audio packets whereas AOMDV protocol exhibits deterioration of end to end delay as it does not adopt any mechanism to avoid congested routes. Using congested routes causes more number of packet drops and retransmissions which contribute to increase in end to end delay. Figure 3 shows the improvement achieved.

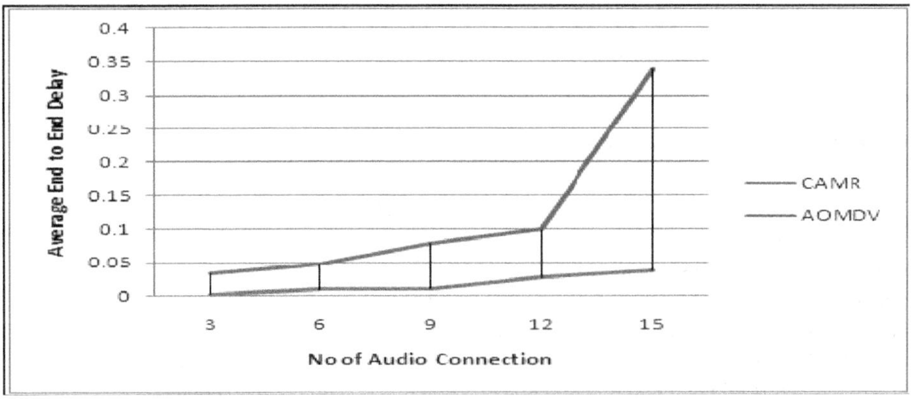

Fig. 3. End to End Delay for increasing audio traffic

Video traffic is again independently increased with respect to a constant audio and background traffic. As can be seen in the Figure 4 end to end delay of CAMR does not degrade as in AOMDV. End to end delay of AOMDV sharply increases when the number of video sources increases to 10.

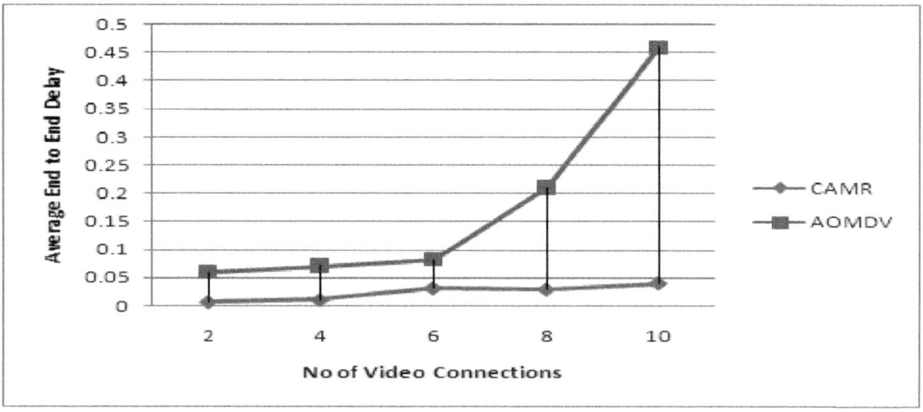

Fig. 4. End to End Delay achieved for increasing video traffic

Average energy consumption is defined as the ratio of the sum of energy spent by all nodes to the number of nodes at the end of simulation .This metric is useful as it reflects on the energy usage of the nodes .When the traffic in the network increases queue size starts building up. This increases the level of contention among nodes resulting in collisions and packet drops. Packet drops further, cause retransmissions. All these attribute to increased energy consumption by the nodes resulting in network partitions. Average energy consumed by the nodes for CAMR is lesser than that of AOMDV asserting the fact that ,AOMDV does not adapt to increasing load .CAMR is successful in detouring paths with congested nodes thereby reducing the energy consumed.

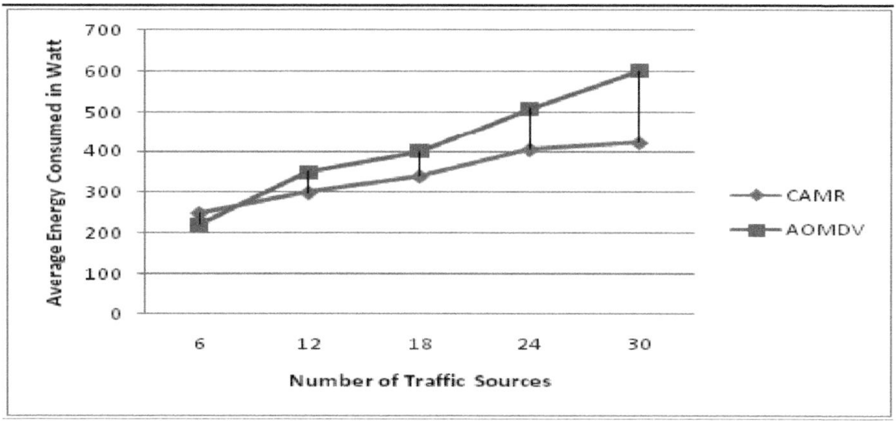

Fig. 5. Average Energy Consumed

5 Conclusion

Providing QoS assurances to multimedia applications is of vital concern in Mobile Ad hoc networks. We have proposed a simple and effective multipath routing enhancement for ensuring QoS of high-priority flows over a IEEE 802.11e EDCA based MAC. We considered the effect of internal collisions that reflects channel contentions among flows belonging to equal priority and external collisions that reflects channel contention among the neighboring nodes while establishing routing paths to achieve load balancing. Results show that CAMR can overcome the network performance degradation under increasing inflow of real -time traffic.

References

1. Li, Y., Mao, S., Panwar, S.S.: The Case for Multi path Multimedia Transport over Wireless Ad Hoc Networks. In: Proceedings of the First International Conference on Broadband Networks (BROADNETS 2004). IEEE, Los Alamitos (2004)
2. Gogate, N., et al.: Supporting Image/Video Applications in a Multihop Radio Environment using Route Diversity and Multiple Description coding. IEEE Trans. Circuits and Sys.for Video Tech. 12(9), 777–792 (2002)
3. IEEE Std 802.11e/D8.0, Draft Supplement to Standard for Telecommunications and Information Exchange Between Systems Systems – AN/MAN Specific Requirements - Pan 11: Wireless Medium Access Control (MAC) and physical layer (PHY) specifications: Medium Access Control (MAC) Enhancements for Quality of Service, QoS (2004)
4. Xi, W.H., et al.: Effectiveness of QoS provided by IEEE 802.11e for different traffic types. IEEE, Los Alamitos (2005)
5. Naoum-Sawaya, J., et al.: Adaptive Approach fo QoS Support in IEEE 802.11e wireless LAN. IEEE, Los Alamitos (2005)
6. Cheng, Y., Li, Z., Li, B.: Adaptive transmission Probability for IEEE 802.11e for MAC Enhancements. IEEE, Los Alamitos (2007)
7. Calafate, C.T., Manzoni, P., Malumbres, M.P.: Assessing the effectiveness of IEEE 802.11e in multi -hop mobile Networks environments. In: 12th IEEE International Symposium on Modelling, analysis and Simulation of Computer and Telecommunication Systems, (MASCOTS 2004) (October 2004)
8. Chen, X., Zhai, H., Fang, Y.: Enhancing the IEEE 802.11e in QoS Support:Analysis and Mechanisms. In: Proceedings of 2 nd International Conf. on Quality of Service in Heterogenous Wired/Wireless Networks(Qshine 2005). IEEE, Los Alamitos (2005)
9. Yan, Z., et al.: A Novel Call Admission Control Routing Mechanism for 802.11e based Multi-hop MANET. IEEE, Los Alamitos (2008)
10. Mbarushimana, C., Shahrabi, A.: Congestion Avoidance Routing Protocol for QoS-Aware MANETs. IEEE, Los Alamitos (2008)
11. Li, Y., Man, H.: Three Load Metrics for Routing in Ad Hoc Networks. In: Proc of Vehicular Technology Conference, IEEE, Los Alamitos (September 2004)
12. Hassanein, H., Zhou, A.: Routing with Load Balancing in Wireless Ad Hoc networks. In: Proceedings ACM MSWIM, Rome, Italy (July 2001)
13. Pham, P., Perreau, S.: Multi -Path Routing Protocol with Load Balancing policy in Mobile Ad Hoc Routing, pp. 48–52. IEEE, Los Alamitos (2002)
14. Dahlberg, L.C.T.: Path Cost Metrics for Multi –Hop Network Routing, pp. 15–21. IEEE, Los Alamitos (2006)

15. Sarr, C., Chelius, C.C.G., Lassous, I.G.: A node based available bandwidth evaluation in IEEE 802.11 ad hoc networks. Iinternational Journal of Parallel Emergent and Distributed Systems (July 2005)
16. Marina, M.K., Das, S.R.: On -demand Multipath Distance Vector Routing in Ad Hoc Networks. In: Proceedings of the International Conference for Network Protocols (2001)
17. http://www.omnetpp.org
18. http://www.hluze.cz/2008/11/omnet-80211e-patch-for-inetmanet-20080920-ver-10/

A Survey on Dataspace

Mrityunjay Singh and S.K. Jain

Computer Engineering Department,
National Institute of Technology, Kurukshetra-136119, India
mrityunjay.cse045@gmail.com, skj_nith@yahoo.com

Abstract. In many large/small organization or enterprises, managing the heterogeneity among data at various level has made a challenging task for its management community. In an organization, data may vary from fully structured to completely unstructured. The existing data management systems fail to manage such data in efficient manner. Now, Dataspace technology addresses the problem of heterogeneity present in data and solving various shortcomings of the existing systems. This paper presents a survey on dataspace and discusses issues related to the dataspace like system architecture, data modelling, querying and answering techniques, and indexing.

Keywords: Dataspace, data integration system, pay-as-you-go data integration, PIM, mediated schema, semantic mappings, inverted list.

1 Introduction

Management of heterogeneous, complex, and large volume of data is a challenging task. In many small/large organizations and enterprizes, data may be scattered in many formats; it may be structured (e.g. relational database (RDB)), semi-structured (e.g. XML, LaTeX, web data), and unstructured (e.g. text documents) and managed by several management softwares[1,2,5]. A relational database management system (RDBMS) manages only structured data; semi-structured and unstructured data required different management softwares. Consider, a university has several departments, and each department maintains its database individually using database management software. Different departments might be using different database management software. The computer engineering department may maintain its data in xml database, while accounts department manages its data using an RDBMS. At the end of month, accounts department may require information about number of days worked by the employees of the computer engineering department for the purpose of computing their monthly salary. Here, the issue of heterogeneity comes in picture that restricts the account department for retrieving data from database of the computer engineering department. The possible solutions of this problem can be: *first,* the desired data from the database of computer engineering department may be manually entered in the database of accounts department. *Second* solution may

D.C. Wyld et al. (Eds.): CNSA 2011, CCIS 196, pp. 608–621, 2011.

be data integration [8], which suggest the integration of databases of both the departments using a software tool. *Third,* solution may use of dataspace technology. Franklin et al. [1] propose the concept of dataspace for managing collection of heterogeneous data. A dataspace integrates its data in an incremental fashion and improves its performance with time [2,5,6,8]. The dataspace technology is in its development phase. The work on modeling dataspaces [11,12,13,14], querying and answering techniques [5,20,21], and indexing techniques [22] has been cited in literature. The dataspace systems e.g. iMeMex [17,26], Semex [27,28], and Haystack [29] have been implemented and cited in literature.

The rest part of this paper is organized as follows: Section 2 defines dataspace concept with examples. In section 3, we discuss a possible architecture for dataspace management system (DSMS). Section 4 has a discussion on data models for dataspace. Section 5 describes querying and answering techniques for dataspace. Section 6 describes indexing techniques for dataspace. The open research issues on this area are discussed in section 7, and finally, we concluded our discussion in section 8.

2 Dataspace

Dataspace is defined as a set of participants and a set of relationships among them. The participants of a dataspace may be data sources like XML repository, RDB, code collection, LaTeX documents, text documents, web data, a software package, and an email repository. Dataspace brings a new architecture for information integration [4]. Dataspace is merely a data integration approach. The example of dataspace may include Personal Information Management (PIM), scientific data management, google desktop search, ocean circulation forecasting system, structured query and content of WWW, ecological data analysis, environmental observation and forecasting, and social networks [1,3,9,7,17]. Here, we have discussed two of them.

Personal Information Management (PIM) : The personal information contain highly heterogeneous data (e.g. emails, word documents, XML, music files, image files, address book entries etc.) available on the personal desktop with possible extension to mobile devices, personal information on web, or even all information access during a person lifetime. Managing the personal information in efficient manner is a challenging task. PIM [9,17] offers the services for easy access and manipulation of personal information. PIM supports the query like "Find the list of student who took the dataspace topic for the presentation in current semester", "find the list of paper published in year 2010 in DASFAA conferences". The desktop search tools are the first step for developing a PIM. The implemented systems for PIM are iMeMex[17][**?**], Semex[24] , Haystak[29].

Scientific Data Management: Consider a scientific research group working on a large project, let weather forecasting system for simulating past, present, and near future events. This group is graphically distributed, use internet to coordinate scientific research, and share data from the research library.

The computation may requires importing data, and model outputs from other groups, e.g. surface weather observations requires data from cloud forecasting. The observation results of surface whether observation are the inputs to the program of cloud forecasting system. It may be possible that data manage by one group will different from the other groups in term of managing softwares, schema etc. Suppose one uses RDB and another uses XML, then the transforming of data and schema from one to another is difficult. The solution of this problem is to create a scientific dataspace for managing data and every group will retrieve required data from scientific dataspace [1,7]. Dessi et al. [7] propose a Collaborative Scientific Environment (CSE) for the scientific dataspace management.

3 Architecture for Dataspace Management System

This section presents description on system architecture of a DSMS, which is shown in Fig 1. A DSMS manages data in dataspace, provides services to dataspace participants and users, and it also supports a model management environment that allows creating new relationship and manipulating existing relationship among the participants. The required components of a DSMS should be Catalog & Browse, Search & Query, Local store & Index, Discovery component, Source extension component, and Administration [1,3].

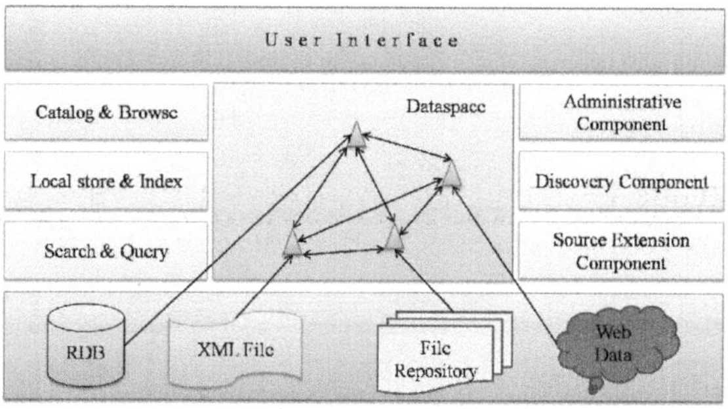

Fig. 1. Dataspace Management System

Catalog & Browse component, stores detail description about the participants of dataspace. The user can get description about the data source by browsing the catalog. *Search & Query component,* provides searching and querying facility to the users of a dataspace. A DSMS supports the keyword queries, structured queries, meta data queries, monitoring queries etc. It also supports lineage and uncertainty queries. *Local Store & Index Component,* is responsible for enabling fast query answering to the user. This component locally stores the frequently access data in its cache and answers certain queries without accessing of original data sources. Indexing is an important issue in heterogeneous environment for fast searching of data. It takes a token as a input and return the locations of token appearing in dataspace. *Discovery Component,* is responsible for locating the new participants in dataspace, discovering the new relationship with existing participants, creating semi-automatic relationship and manipulating existing relationship among the existing participants of dataspace. *Source Extension Component,* is responsible for enhancing the low level participant of dataspace by supporting backup, replication and recovery operation. *Administration component,* is a central component of a DSMS that manages interaction among all components of a DSMS. This component is also responsible for interaction of users with DSMS.

4 Models for Dataspace

This section describes data models for dataspace. Dataspace is a collection of heterogeneous data present in various data sources; each data source uses different data model for representing its data. For example, RDB uses relational model, XML uses XPath model etc. Thus, a new model is a prerequisite for representing all heterogeneous data presents in dataspace into single model. In the literature, we have identified few data models for which can be useful for dataspace, these models are iMeMex data model (iDM) [11], Unified data model(UDM) [12], Triple model [13], and Probabilistic semantic model [14]. In the next subsections, we describe iDM, UDM, triple model and probabilistic semantic data model in detail.

4.1 iMeMex Data Model(iDM)

The iDM is a unified and versatile data model [11], which is specially designed for a iMeMex PDMS. It expresses all personal information in the form of resource view and resource view graph. A *resource view* is a sequence of components that express structured, semi-structured, and unstructured pieces of the underlying data. For example, files, folders, elements of XML document etc. represents distinct resource view in iDM. The set of resource views, which have common property, forms a *resource view class.* For example, {file, folder}, {relational tuple, relation, RDB}, {XML text node, XML element, XML document, XML file} etc represent a resource view class. Resource view is linked to each other forms an arbitrary directed graph structure, called *resources view graph,* as shown in figure 2(b).

The advantages of iDM model are:

- It is the first model which able to represents all heterogeneous personal information into single model.
- It represents heterogeneous data in the form of resource view.
- This model uses database approach so easy to understand.

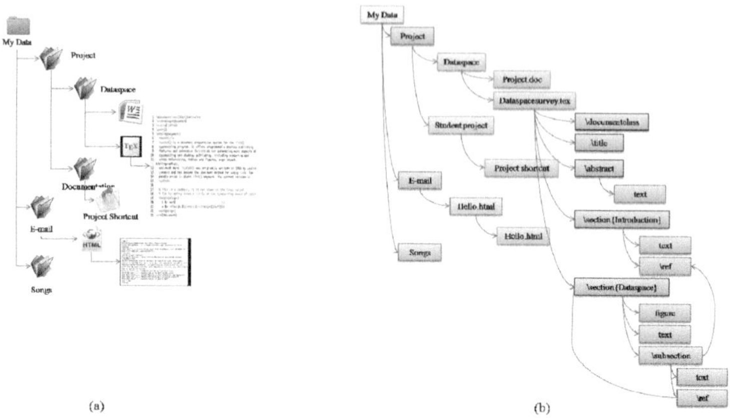

Fig. 2. Example of iDM data model

The disadvantage of iDM model, it based on graph structure and uses a new query language iQL. The iQL is based on XPath and SQL like query language so it may be very complex. Learning a new query is little difficult for normal users.

4.2 Unified Data Model

The UDM is especially design for the desktop search system [12]. This model forms a unified rooted ordered tree for data like file, folder, and content of files store in desktop dataspace. Two basic terms used for defining UDM model are *Desktop dataspace* and *Dataspace fragment* [12]. *Desktop dataspace,* represents all the personal information available on desktop in form of rooted order tree $DS{=}(V{,}E)$, where V is set of nodes and E, subset of V X V, represents a set of edges of tree. There exists a distinct root node from which all nodes of tree can be reached by traveling the edges in E. Each data item in dataspace is uniquely represented by a node in dataspace tree, and have a set of attributes and value pairs. For example, a node representing a word file may have a set of attribute $< name = report >$,$< type = doc >$,$< creationdate = 12 - 09 - 2010 >$,......$< size = 210kb >$. The node may be a file, folder, or contents of file. The nodes, in the dataspace tree, are arranged in depth-first pre-order traversal of tree.

The UDM model for the hierarchy shown in Fig. 2(a) is illustrate in Fig. 3. Each files, folders, and content of files represents a distinct node in tree. The top folder in hierarchy represent the root node, contents of a file or empty folders represent the leaf nodes, and file or folders represent internal nodes of tree. The advantage of UDM model:

- This Model uses the integrated IR-DB approach.
- This model also able to represents the partial section of a file. UDM model have advantage over the current desktop search tools.

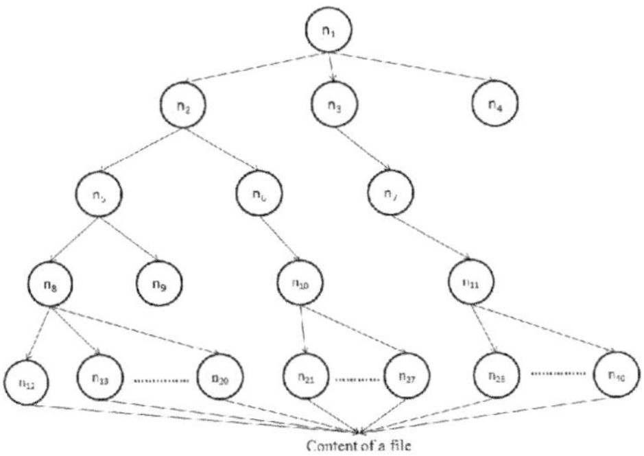

Fig. 3. Unified Data Model

- The conventional IR query language is not much powerful so the new query language is introduces, which is based on SQL query language with some extended core operations. These operations are called TALZBRA operation.

The UDM data model mainly focus on the problem of current desktop search tools. Like current desktop search tools, this model is also not able to support relational data query. For retrieving the relation data user must know about the new TALZBRA operation. This model also not able to support for representing the shortcuts of any files and folders.

4.3 Triple Model

The triple model represents heterogeneous data in triple form [13]. It decomposes the heterogeneous data into set of small chunk of information, called *information unit*, and encapsulates these information units into triples. For decomposing an item into triple, there are certain *Decomposition Rule Sets (DRS)* exist. By using DRS, an information item decomposes into triples. Initially, triple model was used by Resource Description Framework (RDF) for representing the resources on web. Now, M. Zhong et al. modify and extended this model for representing the heterogeneous data presents in dataspace. A triple is defined as 3-tuple (S,P,O), where S is subject component refer to an item, has an unique integer id, P is a predicate component, records the property of information item like name and data type i.e meta data about object component, and O is an object component, which directly stores the data as a byte array. In triple model, an information item is represented as collection of triples.

Consider, Fig. 4 exhibits the triple graph for the hierarchy of files and folders shown in Fig. 2(a). Every folder, file, or contents of file represent a unique information items. Let us consider, the contents of file Dataspacesurvey.tex are documentclass, title, abstract, sectionintroduction, sectiondataspace, subsectionpim, ref, cite etc. By applying the DRSs on folders, sub-folders, files, and content of the files, the folders will decompose into sub-folders and files, files will decompose into contents of the files. The file Dataspacesurvey.tex file will be decompose

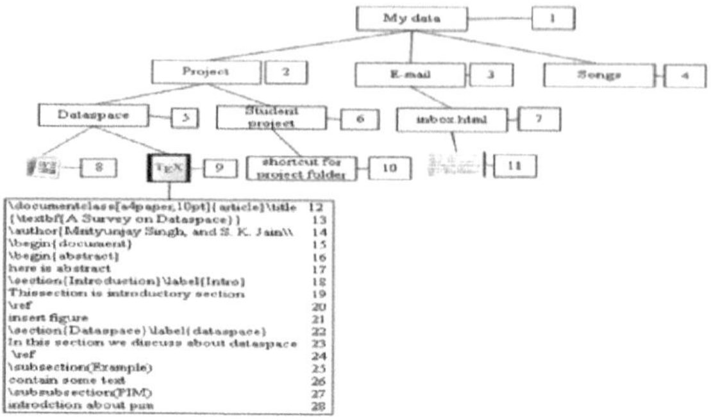

Fig. 4. Example of triple model

into documentclass, title, abstract, section introduction, section dataspace, subsection pim, ref, cite etc. As show in figure 4, all information item in shown in figure 4 have assigned an unique id from 1 to 28. Let us consider a folder "project" with id 2 as shown in figure 4. Now we decompose this folder into triple model. The attributes of any folder may name, type, creationdate, size and so on. For folder project, attribute name can be represented into triple as (2, (name,string),"project"), where subject component is 2, object component is "project", and predicate component is tuple of two values, attribute of folder is name and type of attribute name is string; For attribute creationdate the triple will be (2,(creationdate,date), 12.06.2101). The triple model also able to represents other data model like relational data model,DB, iDM model, XML model etc. Thus, the triple model is more suitable for dataspace system. The advantages of triple model:

- It is a simple and flexible solution for representing heterogeneous data.
- It supports Subject Predicate Object(SPO) query language that can be enhanced by RDF based query language.

The disadvantage of TDM model is that it does not support the path expressions queries, uncertainty and lineage lineage queries. The non-advance users are not familiar with SPO query.

4.4 Probabilistic Semantic Model

The probabilistic semantic model is purely based on probability [14]. This model uses the probabilistic mediate schema and probabilistic semantic mappings for representing the data in heterogeneous data sources, and supporting top-k query answering. The main challenge in building a data integration system is incorporating uncertainty. Previously, this model is used for solving the problem of uncertainty in data integration. Now, it is extended for modeling the data in dataspace support platform. The main objective of dataspace system is to integrate the heterogeneous data sources in "pay-as-you-go fashion". This model

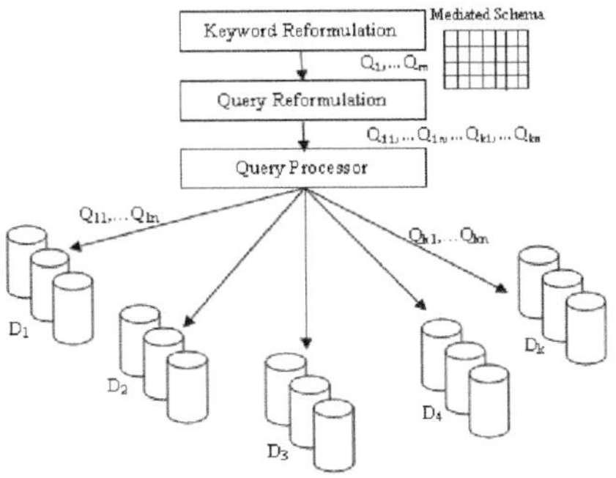

Fig. 5. System architecture of Probablistic semantic model

uses data integration approach, populates the data in dataspace system in incremental fashion, and improves its performance with time. The probabilistic data model uses probabilistic mediated schema and probabilistic schema mapping for integrating various data sources and populating them in dataspace. Firstly, the set of probabilistic mediated schemas have been automatically created from the set of source schemas by using bootstrapping algorithms [16]; then data sources schema have mapped into mediated schema by using probabilistic schema mapping, after that queries poses over mediated schema. The user queries posed over system are first reformulated into set of candidate structured query. This process is called keyword reformulation. If desired data are found in mediated schema then answer is returned from here. Otherwise, the set of structured queries are reformulated into respective data sources. This process is called query reformulation. The data is populated over mediated schema in incremental fashion that's the main characteristics of dataspace. Fig. 5 exhibits a system model of PDM [14]. This system returns top-k answers of a query posed over system.

The probabilistic semantic model handles the uncertainty present at various level. The sources of uncertainty in dataspace system are semantic schema mapping, semantic mediated schema, data and query. The mapping represents a relationship between the various heterogeneous data source and mediated schema. The probabilistic schema mapping is used for describing the relationship between the source and mediated schema without uncertainty in mapping. There are mostly two type of semantic schema mappings [10]: *by-table* semantic depends on the correct mapping between the source and target schema and *by-tuple* semantic depends on the correct mapping between the particular tuple of the schema. The advantages of PDM are returns top-k answers to the users query, handles the uncertainty at various level. The main disadvantages of PDM model are obtaining the reliable probability and less scalable due to integration approach. The comparison among the various data models are shown in table 1.

Table 1. Comparison between various data models for dataspace

	iDM	UDM	TDM	PDM
Type of data handled	Centralized heterogeneous data	Centralized heterogeneous data	Distributed and centralized heterogeneous data	Distributed and centralized heterogeneous data
Underlying model	Unified graph based	Rooted order tree based	RDF based	Probabilistic schema based
Query Processing	iQL, based on Xpath Query	TALZBRA extension of SQL	SPO query language, can be enhanced by using RDF based query language	SPJ based query language
Approach	Pure database	Integrated DB/IR approach	RDF based approach	Data integration approach
Implementation	PIM	PIM	Dataspace	Dataspace
Uncertainty handle	No	No	No	Yes
Merit	Precise Query semantic	Easy query interface	Powerful query language	Top-k answer
Demerit	Complex Query Syntax	No provision for representing the shortcut and reference	No support for query like path expression uncertainty and lineage	Obtaining reliable probability function

5 Querying and Answering Techniques

This section explains querying and answering techniques for dataspaces. Dataspace system provides an uniform access query interface to the user over several heterogeneous data sources. The users can posed query in various language over dataspace systems. Several challenges have been identified by the researchers during the designing of querying and answering techniques for the dataspace system [5]. These challenges cover queries and answers. *Queries,* keywords as well as structured queries are posed by the user over the set of heterogeneous data sources. Thus, handling such complex queries is a challenging issues because every source may have different model and query language. *Answers,* since the answers of a query can be obtained from more than one data sources. So, it can be differ in term of rank, heterogeneity, iterative, sources as answer, reflection, and in-suit. There are several quering and answering techniques are proposed in literature which are *Context-Based Query (C-Query)* [20], is a context based techniques which opt the context based reference relationship between information units, and *Integrated framework for querying collection of heterogeneous data* [21], it is a hypothetical query model which borrows the ideas from XML and linear video presentation model and basically design for querying over heterogeneous data collection.

C-Query, model has been proposed by Yukun Li et al. for personal dataspace [20]. This model is based on context-based reference relationship which is generated by user activities performing on the system. As shown in Figure 6,C-Query framework is divided into *Query Interface,* handles user query and provide refined result to the user. Query posed by the user to the system has been submitted to *C-Query Engine* and result is produced based on user input query and CDB. *CDB,* is a data structure for describing the personal data item and relationship among data items. CRR are stored in database based on the user activity. *CRR identifier,* monitors the behavior of users, and updates the CRR in CDB.

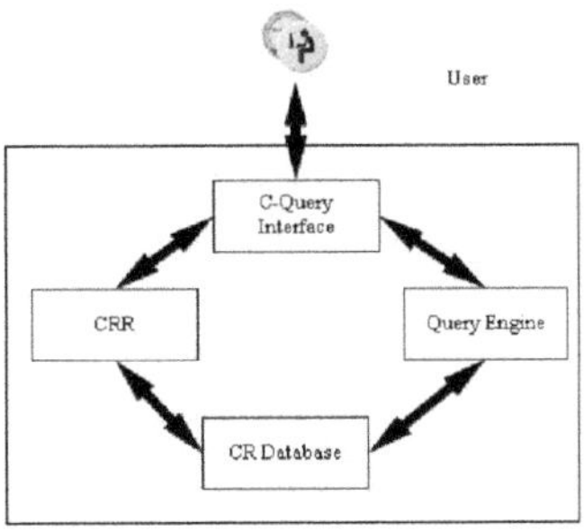

Fig. 6. Framework for C-Query Model [20]

According to Yukun Li et al., the answer of any query poses into dataspace is produces by using C-Query model in two steps: *Identifying the CRR between the participants* and *query processing.* CRR is the relationship between two personal data item access by same user. The personal data item is the basic element of personal data and is the smallest unit of personal data operation such as read, modify, delete. CRR is identified on the basis on user activity perform over the data sources. After identifying the CRR relationship, the answer of query can be obtained in *query processing* step.

6 Indexing

This section presents various indexing techniques for dataspace. Indexing is an important issue for building a dataspace for fast query answering to the user. Xin Dong et al.[22] describe the two types of query: *Predictive Query* and *Neighborhood Queries.* A *predictive query* contains a set of predicates. Each predicate is of the form (v, K_1.......K_i), where v can be either attribute name or association name, and K_1......K_i are keywords. A *neighborhood keyword query* contains set of keywords. The predicate and keyword queries are different from traditional keyword search query because it not only contains keyword or set of keywords but also contains association and instances. Xin Dong et al.[22], proposed several indexing techniques which support the predicate query and neighborhood keyword queries. In previous research, inverted list technique has been adapted for

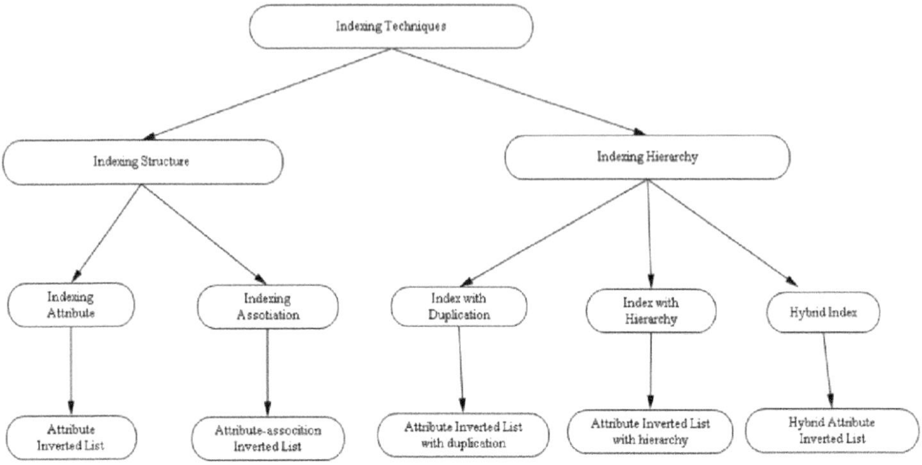

Fig. 7. Classification of indexing technique with corresponding inverted list

indexing the heterogeneous data collections. The inverted list supports keyword search on unstructured data. Xin Dong et al. have proposed various flavor of inverted list which supports collection of heterogeneous data in dataspace [22]. We can classified the indexing techniques for dataspace into Indexing structure and Indexing hierarchy. The classification of various indexing techniques with corresponding inverted list is shown in Figure 7.

Indexing Structure: Indexing structure tells how attributes and associations can be indexed to support predicate queries w.r.t keywords. Mainly, two schemes have been proposed for indexing structure for supporting predicate query: indexing attribute and indexing association. *Indexing attribute,* captures attribute type semantic for indexing. The attribute type can be captured in several ways [22]: *First*, build an index for each attribute but it increase the indexing overhead. *Second,* specify attribute name in cell of inverted list, this solution is complicated. Indexing attribute technique save the index space and lookup time. The inverted list used for this techniques is Attribute inverted list(ATIL) [22]. *Indexing Association technique* is based on associated instances. The associated instance *w.r.t.* set of keywords can be traced by finding the set of instance that contains these keywords. This indexing technique is expensive due to large number of instances and a return instance can be associated with one or more instances. The inverted list used in this technique in *Attribute-association inverted lists (AAIL)*. The drawbacks of this technique are integrating the association information in inverted list increase the size of index which slow down answering attribute predicate but speedup the association predicate.

Indexing Hierarchy: Indexing hierarchy tells how indexing can be done in presence of hierarchies for answering predicates queries. Mainly, three schemes have been proposed for indexing hierarchy: Index with duplication, Index with hierarchy path, and Hybrid index. *Index with Duplication* duplicates a row of the attribute name for each ancestor. The inverted list used for this technique is Attribute inverted list with duplication (DUP-ATIL)[22]. In DUP-ATIL, if a keyword K appear in the value of attribute and the attribute has any ancestor in hierarchy then duplicate the row with same attribute for ancestor. *Index with Hierarchy Path,* The keywords in every row include the entire Instead of duplicating the row in Invited list. The invited list is used for this purpose is attributed invited list with hierarchy (Hier-ALIT). In this method, Instead of duplicating the row for each ancestor of any attribute we include all ancestor into the hierarchy path for each attribute. *Hybrid Index,* DUP-ATIL is more suitable for the case where a keyword occurs in many attributes with common ancestor and Hier-ATIL is more suitable for the cases where a keyword occurs only in few attributes with common ancestor. *Hybrid Index scheme* combines the strength of both techniques. The inverted list used for this purpose is hybrid attribute inverted list (Hybrid-ATIL).

7 Current Research Challenges on Dataspace

This section presents the various research issues for developing the dataspace management system. We are presenting this survey during our phd research work and facing some short of problems during designing of dataspace system. Franklin et. al. listed various research challenges in dataspace [1,5]. Dataspace is a latest concept which provides a uniform view to the users for accessing the information from the various distributed and heterogeneous data sources. Dataspace system overcomes the drawback of existing information management systems like DBMS, data integration systems, current desktop search systems, search engines etc. Therefore, the development of dataspace system has several open research issues like data modeling & querying, local store & indexing, dataspace discovery, reusing human attention, correctness guarantees etc.

Data modeling & querying, modeling the heterogeneity in dataspace and providing the efficient searching and querying techniques for the users become an open research problem for the researchers. In this paper, we present several data models for the dataspace but each of them fall some short of problems. The main problem in modeling is handling uncertainty presents in the various levels and populating data in dataspace in "pay-as-you-go" fashion. Dataspace system should also have an efficient query processor for supporting all types of queries such as keywords queries, structured queries, meta data queries.

Local store & Indexing, component supports fast answering of user query without accessing the original data sources. Indexing is also important in heterogeneous environment for providing the fast searching and querying of data. So, building an efficient local store & indexing component should be also an open research issue.

Dataspace discovery is responsible for locating the new participants in the dataspace and maintaining the relationship with existing participants. Since, the data sources in various organizations are scattered everywhere. Therefore, locating these data sources and creating the relationship with existing data sources become a research challenge.

Reusing human attention, The key property of dataspace system are semantic integration and provide approximately accurate results of the user query. The most appropriate semantics can be achieve by using human attention. On the basis of these semantics, we can archives most accurate semantic mappings and system should able to return the accurate results to the user. These semantics are also helpful for creating the relationships among the various participants in the dataspace.

8 Conclusion

Dataspace technology addresses the issue of heterogeneity among data and data sources. Dataspace retrieves information from heterogeneous data sources scattered over various places. Dataspace is an enhancement over data integration systems which populate its data in incremental fashion. A dataspace management system favors least co-ordination among data sources and supports coexistence of heterogeneous data sources. Formally, a dataspace is defined as a collection of several data sources, also known as participants, and relationships among them. The participants may vary from structured to unstructured data types. The first piece of work on dataspace appeared in 2005, and since then researchers are continuously contributing in this area. The area is still open for research. This paper presents current work in area of dataspace, and to the best of our knowledge, it is the first survey paper on dataspace.

References

1. Franklin, M., Halevy, A., Maier, D.: From databases to dataspaces: a new abstraction for information management. ACM Sigmod Record (2005)
2. Podolecheva, M., Prof, T., Scholl, M., Holupirek, E.: Principles of Dataspaces. Seminar From Databases to Dataspaces Summer Term 2007. Citeseer (2008)
3. Podolecheva, M.: Principles of Dataspaces, Seminar From Database to Dataspaces. Summer term (2007)
4. Halevy, A., Maier, D., Franklin, M.: Dataspaces: The tutorial. In: PVLDB 2008 (August 23-28, 2008)
5. Halevy, A., Franklin, M., Maier, D.: Principles of dataspace systems. In: Proceedings of the Twenty-Fifth ACMSIGMOD-SIGACT-SIGART Symposium on Principles of Database Systems (2006)
6. Hedeler, C., Belhajjame, K., Paton, N., Campi, A., Fernandes, A., Embury, S.: Dataspaces, ch. 7, pp. 114–134. Springer, Heidelberg (2010)
7. Dessi, N., Pes, B.: Towards Scientific Dataspaces. In: Proceedings of the 2009 IEEE/WIC/ACM International Joint Conference on Web Intelligence and Intelligent Agent Technology, vol. 03 (2009)
8. Franklin, M.: Dataspaces: Progress and Prospects. Dataspace: The Final Frontier, 1–3 (2009)
9. Dittrich, J., Blunschi, L., Färber, M., Girard, O., Karakashian, S., Salles, M.: From Personal Desktops to Personal Dataspaces: A Report on Building the iMeMex Personal Dataspace Management System. In: SIGIR PIM Workshop (2006)

10. Dong, X.L., Halevy, A., Yu, C.: Data integration with uncertainty. The VLDB Journal 18(-2), 469–500 (2009)
11. Dittrich, J., Salles, M.: iDM: A unified and versatile data model for personal dataspace management. In: Proceedings of the 32nd International Conference on Very Large Data Bases, pp. 367–378 (2006)
12. Pradhan, S.: Towards a novel desktop search technique. In: Wagner, R., Revell, N., Pernul, G. (eds.) DEXA 2007. LNCS, vol. 4653, pp. 192–201. Springer, Heidelberg (2007)
13. Zhong, M., Liu, M., Chen, Q.: Modeling heterogeneous data in dataspace. In: IEEE International Conference on Information Reuse and Integration IRI 2008, pp. 404–409 (2008)
14. Sarma, A., Dong, X., Halevy, A.: Data modeling in dataspace support platforms. In: Borgida, A.T., Chaudhri, V.K., Giorgini, P., Yu, E.S. (eds.) Conceptual Modeling: Foundations and Applications. LNCS, vol. 5600, pp. 122–138. Springer, Heidelberg (2009)
15. Vaz Salles, M., Dittrich, J., Karakashian, S., Girard, O., Blunschi, L.: iTrails: pay-as-you-go information integration in dataspaces. In: Proceedings of the 33rd International Conference on Very Large Data Bases, pp. 663–674 (2007)
16. Das Sarma, A., Dong, X., Halevy, A.: Bootstrapping pay-as-you-go data integration systems. In: Proceedings of the 2008 ACM SIGMOD International Conference on Management of Data, pp. 861–874 (2008)
17. Dittrich, J.P.: iMeMex: A platform for personal dataspace management. In: SIGIR PIM Workshop (2006)
18. Dessi, N., Pes, B.: Towards Scientific Dataspaces. In: Proceedings of the 2009 IEEE/WIC/ACM International Joint Conference on Web Intelligence and Intelligent Agent Technology, vol. 03, pp. 575–578 (2009)
19. Levy, A., Rajaraman, A., Ordille, J., et al.: Querying heterogeneous information sources using source descriptions. In: Proceedings of the International Conference on Very Large Data Bases (1996)
20. Li, Y., Meng, X.: Supporting context-based query in personal DataSpace. In: Proceeding of the 18th ACM Conference on Information and Knowledge Management, pp. 1437–1440 (2009)
21. Pradhan, S.: Towards an integrated framework for querying collection of heterogeneous data. In: Proceedings of the 3rd International Conference on Ubiquitous Information Management and Communication, pp. 51–57 (2009)
22. Dong, X., Halevy, A.: Indexing dataspaces. In: Proceedings of the 2007 ACM SIGMOD International Conference on Management of Data (2007)
23. Dittrich, J.: iMeMex: A platform for personal dataspace management. In: SIGIR PIM Workshop (2006)
24. Cai, Y., Dong, X., Halevy, A., Liu, J., Madhavan, J.: Personal information management with SEMEX. In: Proceedings of the 2005 ACM SIGMOD International Conference on Management of Data, pp. 921–923 (2005)
25. Bush, V.: As we may think Reading digital culture. Wiley-Blackwell (2001)
26. OSGi Allience, http://www.osgi.org/Main/HomePage
27. Personal Information Management—SEMEX (SEMantic EXplorer), http://db.cs.washington.edu/semex/semex.html
28. Dong, X.L., Halevy, A.: A platform for personal information management and integration. In: Proceedings of VLDB 2005, PhD Workshop (2005)
29. Haystack group, http://groups.csail.mit.edu/haystack/

A Novel Social Network Model for Business Collaboration

Sreedhar Bhukya

Department of Computer and Information Sciences
University of Hyderabad, Hyderabad- 500046
sr2naik@gmail.com

Abstract. Recent studies on social networks are based on a characteristic which includes assortative mixing, high clustering, short average path lengths, broad degree distributions and the existence of community structure. Here, a application has been developed in the domain of 'Business collaboration' which satisfies all the above characteristics, based on some existing social network models. In addition, this model facilitates interaction between various communities (Academic/Research/Business groups). This application gives very high clustering coefficient by retaining the asymptotically scale-free degree distribution. Here the business network community is raised from a mixture of random attachment and implicit preferential attachment. In addition to earlier works which only considered Neighbor of Initial Contact (NIC) as implicit preferential contact, we have considered Neighbor of Neighbor of Initial Contact (NNIC) also. This application supports the occurrence of a contact between two Initial contacts if the new vertex chooses more than one initial contacts. This ultimately will develop a complex social network rather than the one that was taken as basic reference.

Keywords: Social networks, Neighbor of neighbor initial contact, Tertiary contact, Business collaboration.

1 Introduction

Recent days Business collaborations becoming domain independent. For example stock market analyst is taking the help of computer simulator for future predictions. Thus there is a necessity of collaboration between people in different domains (different communities, in the language of social networking.) Here we develop a novel business application for collaborations in business communities which gives a possibility of interacting with a person in a different community, yet retaining the community structure of Business network. Social networks are made of nodes that are tied by one or more specific types of relationships. The vertex represents individuals or organizations. Social networks have been intensively studied by Social scientists [3-5], for several decades in order to understand local phenomena such as local formation and their dynamics, as well as network wide process, like transmission of information, spreading disease, spreading rumor, sharing ideas etc. Various types of social

D.C. Wyld et al. (Eds.): CNSA 2011, CCIS 196, pp. 622–630, 2011.

networks, such as those related to professional collaboration [6-8], Internet dating [9], and opinion formation among people have been studied. Social networks involve Financial, Cultural, Educational, Families, Relations and so on. Social networks create relationship between vertices; Social networks include Sociology, basic Mathematics and graph theory. The basic mathematics structure for a social network is a graph. The main social network properties includes hierarchical community structure [10], small world property [11], power law distribution of nodes degree [19] and the most basic is Barabasi Albert model of scale free networks [12]. The more online social network gains popularity, the more scientific community is attracted by the research opportunities that these new fields give. Most popular online social networks is Facebook, where user can add friends, send them messages, and update their personal profiles to notify friends about themselves. Essential characteristics for social networks are believed to include assortative mixing [13,14], high clustering, short average path lengths, broad degree distributions[15,16], and the existence of community structure. Growing community can be roughly speaking set of vertices with dense internal connection, such that the inter community connection are relatively sparse. Here we have considered an existing model [2] of social networks and developed it in way which is suitable for collaborations in academic communities.

The model is as follows:

The algorithm consists of two growth processes: (1) random attachment (2) implicit preferential attachment resulting from following edges from the randomly chosen initial contacts.

The existing model lacks in the following two aspects:

1. There is no connection between initial to initial contacts, if more than one initial contact is chosen.
2. There is no connection between initial contact and its neighbor of neighbor vertices.

These two aspects we have considered in earlier model [1] and apply earlier model into this Business application. The advantage of our application can understand from the fallowing example and our application can be applicable to the real-world applications. Let us consider a business person contacting a business person in a business group for his own business purpose and suppose that he/she didn't get adequate support from that business person or from his neighbors, but he may get required support from some friend of friend for his/her initial contact. Then the only way a new business person could get help is that his primary contact has to be updated or create a contact with his friend of friend for supporting his new contact and introduce his new contact to his friend of friend. The same thing will happen in our day to day life also. If a business person contacts us for some business purpose and we are unable to help him, we will try to help him by some contacts of our business friends. The extreme case of this nature is that we may try to contact our friend of friend for this business purpose. We have implemented the same thing in our new application. In the old model [2], information about friends only used to be updated, where as in earlier model information about friend of friend also has been updated. Of course this application creates a complex social network but, sharing of business information or data will be very fast. This fulfills the actual purpose of business social networking in an efficient way with a faster growth rate by keeping the business community structure as it is. This process is going continuously in real world business activity and makes business community growing faster in internally and externally.

2 Network Growth algorithm

The algorithm includes three processes: (1) Random attachment (2) Implicit preferential contact with the neighbors of initial contact (3) In addition to the above we are proposing a contact between the initial contact to its Neighbor of Neighbor contact (tertiary). The algorithm of the business model is as follows [1], in this model we consider each vertex is as a business person.

1) Start with a seed network of N vertices
2) Pick on average $m_r \geq 1$ random vertex as initial contacts
3) Pick on average $m_s \geq 0$ neighbors of each initial contact as secondary contact
4) Pick on average $m_t \geq 1$ neighbors of each secondary contact as tertiary contact
5) Connect the new vertex to the initial, secondary and tertiary contacts
6) Repeat the steps 2-5 until the network has grown to desired size.

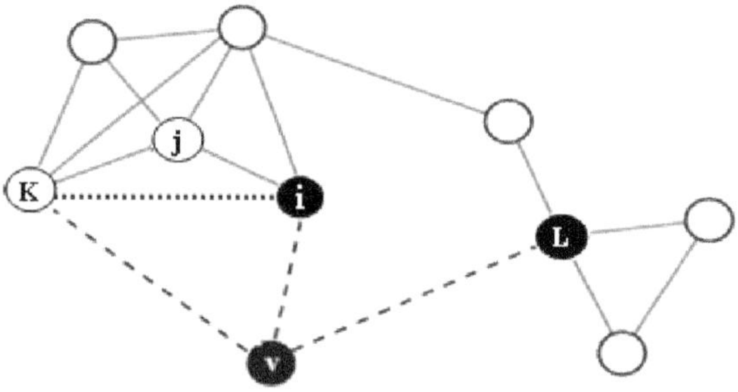

Fig. 1. Growing process of business community network

The new vertex 'V' initially connects through some one as initial contact (*say i and L*). Now *i*, updates its neighbour of neighbour contact list and hence connects to k. V' connects to m_s number of neighbours (say k) and m_t number of neighbour of neighbours of i (say k).

Below in Fig.2.Visualization of a business network graph with N=50. Number of each secondary contact from each initial contact n_{2nd}~U[0,3) (uniformly distributed between 0 and 3), and initial contact is connecting its neighbor of neighbor vertices U[1-2]. In this business model we tried 50 sample vertices and prepared a strong growing business network.

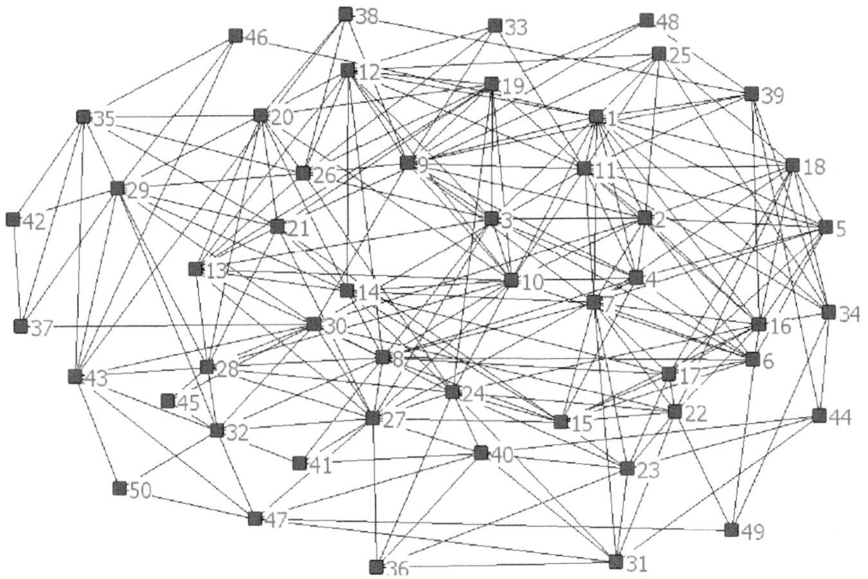

Fig. 2. Showing business social network graph with 50 Business persons

3 Vertex Degree Distribution

We derive approximate value for the vertex degree distribution for growing network model mixing random initial contact, neighbor of neighbor initial contact and neighbor of initial contacts. Power law degree distribution with p (k) ~ k^{γ} with exponent $2<\gamma<\infty$ have derived [17, 19]. In this model also the lower bound to the degree exponent γ is found to be 3, which is same as in the earlier model.

The rate equation which describes how the degree of a vertex changes on average during one time step of the network growth is constructed. The degree of vertex v_i grows in 3 processes:

1) When a new vertex directly links to v_i at any time t, there will be on average ~ t vertices. Here we are selecting m_r out of them with a probability m_r/t.
2) When a vertex links to v_i as secondary contact, the selection will give rise to preferential attachment. These will be m_r. m_s in number.
3) When a vertex links to v_i as tertiary contact, this will also be a random preferential attachment. These will be $2m_r\, m_s\, m_t$ in number.

These three processes lead to following rate equation for the degree of vertex v_i [1]

$$\frac{k_i}{t} = \frac{1}{t}\left(m_r + \frac{m_r m_s + 2 m_r m_s m_t}{2(m_r + m_r m_s + 2 m_r m_s m_t)} k_i \right) \tag{1}$$

Based on the average initial degree of a vertex is

$$k_{init} = m_r + m_r m_s + 2 m_r m_s m_t$$

Separating and integrating from t_i to t, and from k_{init} to k_i , we will get the following time evaluation for the vertex degrees

$$k_i(t) = B\left(\frac{1}{t_i}\right)^{1/A} - C \tag{2}$$

Where

$$A = 2\left(\frac{m_r + m_r m_s + 2m_r m_s m_t}{m_r m_s + 2m_r m_s m_t}\right), B = A\left(m_r + \frac{1}{2} m_r m_s + m_r m_s m_t\right), C = A m_r$$

From time evolution of vertex k_i (t), we can calculate the degrees of distribution p(k) by forming cumulative distribution F(k) and differentiating with respect to k. Since the mean field approximation[1,2] the degree $k_i(t)$ of a vertex v_i increases monotonously from the time t_i the vertex initially added to the network, the fraction of vertices whose degree is less than $k_i(t)$ at t is equivalent to the fraction of vertices that introduced after time t_i. Since t is evenly distributed, this fraction is $(t-t_i)/2$. These facts lead to the cumulative distribution [1]

$$F(k_i) = P(\tilde{k} \le k_i) = P(\tilde{t} \ge t_i) = \frac{1}{t}(t - t_i) \tag{3}$$

Solving for $t_i = t_i(k_i, t) = B^A (k_i + C)^{-A} t$ from (2) and inserting it into (3), differentiating $F(k_i)$ with respect to k_i, and replacing the notation k_i by k in the equation, we get the probability density distribution for the degree k as

$$P(k) = AB^A (k + C)^{-2/m_s + 2m_s m_t - 3} \tag{4}$$

Here A, B and C are as above. In the limit of large k, the distribution becomes a power law p (k) ~ $k^{-\gamma}$ with $\gamma = 3 + 2/m_s$, $m_s > 0$, leading to $3 < \gamma < \infty$. Hence the lower bound to the degree exponent is 3. Although the lower bound for degree exponent is same as earlier model. The probability density distribution is larger compared to earlier model, where the denominator of the first term of degree exponent is larger compared to the earlier model.

4 Clustering

The clustering coefficient on vertex degree can also be found by the rate equation method [18]. Let us examine how the number of triangles E_i changes with time. The triangle around v_i are mainly generated by three processes

1. Vertex v_i is chosen as one of the initial contact with probability m_r/t and new vertex links to some of its neighbors as secondary contact, giving raise to a triangle.
2. The vertex v_i is chosen as secondary contact and the new vertex links to it as its primary or tertiary contact giving raise to a triangles.
3. The vertex v_i is chosen as tertiary contact and the new vertex links to it as its primary or secondary contact, giving raise to a triangles.

These three process are described by the rate equation [1]

$$\frac{E_i}{t}=\frac{k_i}{t}-\frac{1}{t}\left(m_r\text{-}m_rm_s\text{-}3m_rm_sm_t-\frac{5m_rm_sm_t}{2(m_r+m_rm_s+2m_rm_sm_t)t}k_i\right) \quad (5)$$

where second right-hand side obtained by applying Eq. (1) integrating both sides with respect to t, and using initial condition $E_i(k_{init}, t_i) = m_r\, m_s(1+3m_t)$, we get the time evaluation of triangle around a vertex v_i as

$$E_i(t)=\left(a+bk_i\right)\ln\left(\frac{t}{t_i}\right)+\left(\frac{a+bk_i}{b}\right)\ln\left(\frac{a+bk_i}{a+bk_{init}}\right)+E_{init} \quad (6)$$

Now making use of the previously found dependent of k_i on t_i for finding $c_i(k)$. solving for $\ln(t/t_i)$in terms of k_i from (2), inserting into it into (6) to get $E_i(k_i)$, and dividing $E_i(k_i)$ by the maximum possible number of triangles, $k_i(k_i-1)/2$, we arrive the clustering the coefficient

$$c_i\left(k_i\right)=\frac{2E_i\left(k_i\right)}{k_i\left(k_i-1\right)} \quad (7)$$

For this equation detail explanation on refer ref [1]

For large values of degree k, the clustering coefficient thus depend on k as $c(k)\sim\ln k/k$.

This has very large clustering coefficient compared to the earlier work where it was $c(k)\sim 1/k$.

5 Results

Here a comparison has been made between the earlier model and current business application by calculating the edge to vertex ratio and triangle to vertex ratio for 50 vertices. The results are given in Table: 1.here one can see an enormous increase in secondary contacts. In addition tertiary contacts also have been added in our business model, which leads to a faster and complex growth of business network.

Table 1.

Data on our proposed model	Initial Contact (IC)	Secondary Contacts (SC)	Neighbor of Neighbor IC (NNIC)
Vertices	2.8	5.56	2.78
Triangles	0.8	6.0	6.44

5.1 Simulation Results

The below results have been represented graphically by calculating the degree (number of contacts) of a node. This also is shows an enormous growth in degree of nodes.

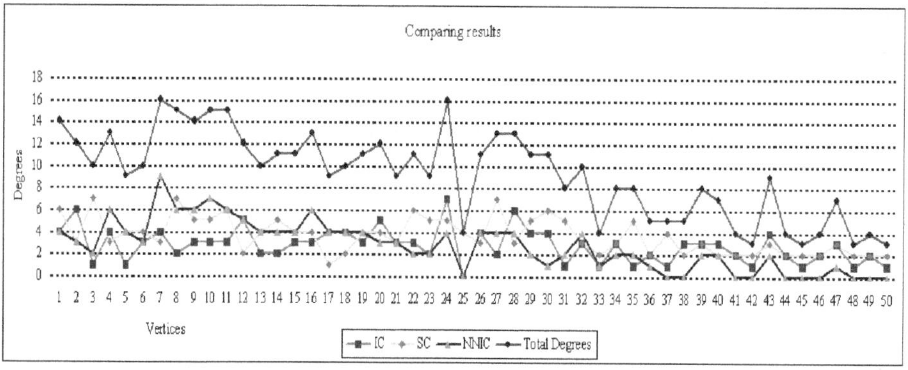

Fig. 3. Comparison results of business growing network community: initial contacts are growing very slow rate compared to secondary contact i.e. ■ indicates initial contact, ♦ indicates secondary contacts, and ▲ indicates neighbor of neighbor of initial contact connects to the vertex v_i, Finally ● indicates degree of each vertices, when initial, secondary and tertiary contact connect to a vertex v_i. Our Business network community is growing very fast and complex when compared to existing model, vertices simulation results based on Table: 1.

6 Conclusion

In this paper, an application which reproduces very efficient networks compared to real business social networks has been developed. And also here, the lower bound to the degree exponent is the same. The probability distribution for the degree k is in agreement with the earlier result for m_t =0. The clustering coefficient got an enormous raise in growth rate of $\ln(k_i)/k_i$ compared to the earlier result $1/k_i$ for large values of the degree k. This is very useful in the case of business groups, which helps in faster business information flow and an enormous growth in business. Thus here an efficient but complex application of business social network has been developed which gives an enormous growth in probability distribution and clustering coefficient and edge to vertex ratio by retaining the community structure. This application can be used to develop a new kind of business social networking among various business groups.

Tool

We have used C language, UciNet, NetDraw and Excel for creating graph and simulation.

Notations

Notation	Description
m_r	Initial Contact
m_s	Secondary Contact
k_i	Degree of vertex i
E_i	Number of triangles at vertex i
P(k)	Probability density distribution of degree k

References

1. Bhukya, S.: A novel model for social networks. BCFIC IEEE, 21–24 (February 16-18, 2011)
2. Toivonen, R., Onnela, J.-P., Saramäki, J., Hyvönen, J., Kaski, K.: A model for social networks. Physica A 371, 851–860 (2006)
3. Milgram, S.: Psychology Today 2, 60–67 (1967)
4. Granovetter, M.: The Strength of Weak Ties. Am. J. Soc. 78, 1360–1380 (1973)
5. Wasserman, S., Faust, K.: Social Network Analysis. Cambridge University Press, Cambridge (1994)
6. Watts, D.J., Strogatz, S.H.: Collective dynamics of 'small -world' networks. Nature 393, 440 (1998)
7. Newman, M.: The structure of scientific collaboration networks. PNAS 98, 404–409 (2001)
8. Newman, M.: Coauthorship networks and patterns of scientific collaboration. PNAS 101, 5200–5205 (2004)
9. Holme, P., Edling, C.R., Liljeros, F.: Structure and Time-Evolution of an Internet Dating Community. Soc. Networks 26, 155–174 (2004)
10. Girvan, M., Newman, M.E.J.: Community structure in social and biological networks. Proc. Natl. Acad. Sci. 99, 7821–7826 (2002)
11. Newman, M.E.J.: The structure and function of complex networks. SIAM Review 45, 167–256 (2003)
12. Barabási, A.-L., Albert, R.: Emergence of scaling in random networks. Science 286, 509–512 (1999)
13. Newman, M.E.J.: Assortative Mixing in Networks. Phys. Rev. Lett. 89, 208701 (2002)
14. Newman, M.E.J., Park, J.: Why social networks are different from other types of networks. Phys. Rev. E 68, 036122 (2003)
15. Amaral, L.A.N., Scala, A., Barth, M., Stanley, H.E.: Classes of small-world networks. PNAS 97, 11149–11152 (2000)

16. Boguna, M., Pastor-Satorras, R., Díaz-Guilera, A., Arenas, A.: Models of social networks based on social distance attachment. Phys. Rev. E 70, 056122 (2004)
17. Evans, T., Saramäki, J.: Scale-free networks from self-organization. Phys. Rev. E 72, 026138 (2005)
18. Szabo, G., Alava, M., Kertesz, J.: Phys. Structural transitions in scale-free networks. Phys. Rev. E 67, 056102 (2003)
19. Krapivsky, P.L., Redner, S.: Organization of growing random networks. phys. Rev. E 63, 066123 (2001)

A Novel Way of Providing Dynamic Adaptability in P2P JXTA Sockets Using Aspect Oriented Programming

Vishnuvardhan Mannava[1] and T. Ramesh[2]

[1] Department of Computer Science and Engineering,
KL University, Vaddeswaram 522502, A.P., India
vishnu@klce.ac.in
[2] Department of Computer Science and Engineering,
National Institute of Technology, Warangal, 506004, A.P., India
rmesht@nitw.ac.in

Abstract. The need for adaptability in software is growing, driven in part by the emergence of autonomic computing. In many cases, it is desirable to enhance existing programs with adaptive behavior, enabling them to execute effectively in dynamic environments. The peer-to-peer (p2p) paradigm is attracting increasing attention from both the research community and software engineers, due to potential performance, reliability and scalability improvements. P2P model has opened many new avenues for research and applications within the field of distributed computation, so performance evaluation is unavoidable. In this paper we are using Aspect oriented programming (AOP) to enable dynamic adaptation in existing p2p JXTA Sockets. We propose an approach to implement dynamic adaptability especially in existing p2p JXTA socket programs and Aspect weaving in p2p JXTA using AOP. We have used AspectJ; Java based language to create aspects in Eclipse supported framework.

Keywords: Dynamic adaptation, Aspect Oriented Programming, AspectJ, p2p JXTA Sockets and Reusability.

1 Introduction

A software application is adaptable if it can change its behavior dynamically (at run time) in response to transient changes in its execution environment or to permanent changes in its requirements. Recent interest in designing adaptable software is driven in part by the demand for autonomic computing. Autonomic computing [1] refers to self-managed, and potentially self-healing, systems that require only high-level human guidance. Autonomic computing is critical to managing the myriad of sensors and other small devices at the wireless edge, but also in managing large-scale computing centers and protecting critical infrastructure (e.g., financial networks, transportation systems, power grids) from hardware component failures, network outages, and security attacks. Developing and maintaining adaptable software are nontrivial tasks. An adaptable application comprises functional code that implements the business logic of the application and supports its imperative behavior, and adaptive code that implements the adaptation logic of the application and supports its adaptive behavior.

D.C. Wyld et al. (Eds.): CNSA 2011, CCIS 196, pp. 631–639, 2011.

The pioneering work resulting from the development of Peer-to-Peer (P2P) systems, such as Gnutella, has highlighted many interesting properties of P2P, such as dynamic adaptability, high scalability and high availability of service despite highly dynamic changes in the underlying physical infrastructure. Thanks to these desirable features, the P2P interaction model has been very successful and has recently been an influential player in many research communities. Therefore, a shift to the P2P model has become attractive for many classes of applications originally based on the traditional client-server model (e.g. collaborative applications, instant messaging, etc.). Furthermore, a growing number of projects have been quick to embrace the P2P model directly from their initial design phase. Recently, a number of P2P libraries (e.g. Free Pastry, JXTA [10], etc.) providing basic support for P2P interaction (for example discovery mechanisms) have been made available to the research community. Such libraries are intended to serve as generic building blocks for higher level P2P services and applications. In order to evaluate the cost of JXTA communications, we perform a number of bidirectional bandwidth tests (also known as ping-pong tests) between JXTA peers. We perform these tests over a Fast Ethernet local-area network for both JXTA-J2SE and JXTA-C, using each of the available JXTA communication layers (varying certain experimental parameters such as message size, buffer size and JVM options).

Our paper is organized as follows. We review related work in section 2. Section 3, we describe Aspect Oriented Programming. In section 4, we describe p2p JXTA Sockets using AOP. Try to show the Efficiency of AOP by CPU Profiling in section 5. Section 6, Try to show the affect of 'Aspects' on application through Eclipse's Aspect Visualizer. We conclude the paper and future work in section 7.

2 Related Work

Previous work has been done by Yang [13] to implement a system which performs dynamic adaptation using AOP. This approach uses join points to specify where the adaptation should take place, and a set of rules to specify the conditions when an adaptation should occur. Another solution to achieve adaptation in applications using AspectJ is proposed by Dantas et al [14]. An adaptation framework developed by Pierre-Charles David et al [15] is implemented using the Fractal component model. Peers in peer-to-peer networks are usually considered uniform in resources. So, to deal with heterogeneous peers, a "super peer" based approach was introduced [4]. Each super peer acts as a central server to a group of peers. These peers send their search requests to the responsible super peer that at first uses the super peer overlay network to process the request. Only if a key cannot be located, the regular peer-to-peer network will be used. The "super peer approach" reduces the required bandwidth and completes requests faster.

A peer-to-peer event-notification architecture called Scribe, following the publish-subscribe approach, was introduced in [3]. A peer can create topics which any peer can subscribe to. To efficiently disseminate events to the subscribers over the network a multicast tree for every topic is created. As far as we know there are very few projects which involve JXTA and "pure" DHTs. One is the JXTA subproject jxta-meteor [5, 6] which intends to provide a platform to develop DHTs (as for now the project includes Chord and CAN) over JXTA protocols (as services). Another project about DHT in JXTA is GISP [7] (Global Information Sharing Protocol): this is a proposal for a new DHT protocol, which is intended as a service to be put over JXTA.

We adopted the performance model introduced in [4, 6], where the authors study the JXTA rendezvous protocol performances, by comparing it with the policy of older versions of JXTA, and by using a JXTA subproject benchmark suite [10]. To our knowledge, there is no related work of providing dynamic adaptability to p2p JXTA Sockets using Aspect Oriented Programming.

3 Aspect Oriented Programming (AOP)

Aspect Oriented Programming (AOP) is a program development methodology proposed by Gregor Kiczales in "Aspect-Oriented Programming"[2], published in 1997. In AOP, the requirements (requests) of the program are termed ‘concerns’. Concerns are divided into core concerns and crosscutting concerns. An example that is used most frequently to explain core and cross-cutting concerns is the Distributed Auction system. In a system, core concerns are the main functions of the Auction System, which are to set the product for auction, set minimum bid, set current bid etc.

However, other features required by a distributed system, such as logging, distribution, profiling and tracing are cross-cutting concerns. Although object oriented programming is currently the most widely used methodology for dealing with core concerns, it comes up short in processing crosscutting concerns. This becomes more so for complex applications. AOP is a new methodology that enables separation of crosscutting concerns and their implementation through a new module termed the ‘aspect’. Figure 1 displays the weaving process of application code with aspect.

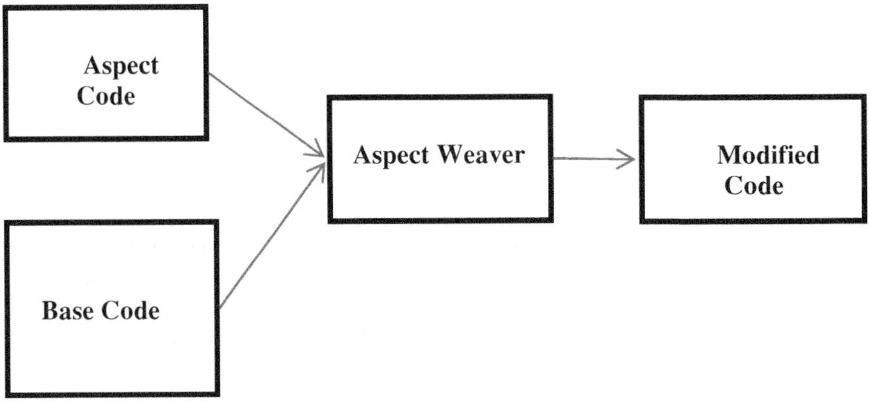

Fig. 1. Weaving of Aspect on Source Code

In the below figure 2, peers are communicating using TCP and HTTP protocols. JXTA socket are necessary to discover peer service and to advertise about peer group services. By using end point service peers can easily communicate with each other.

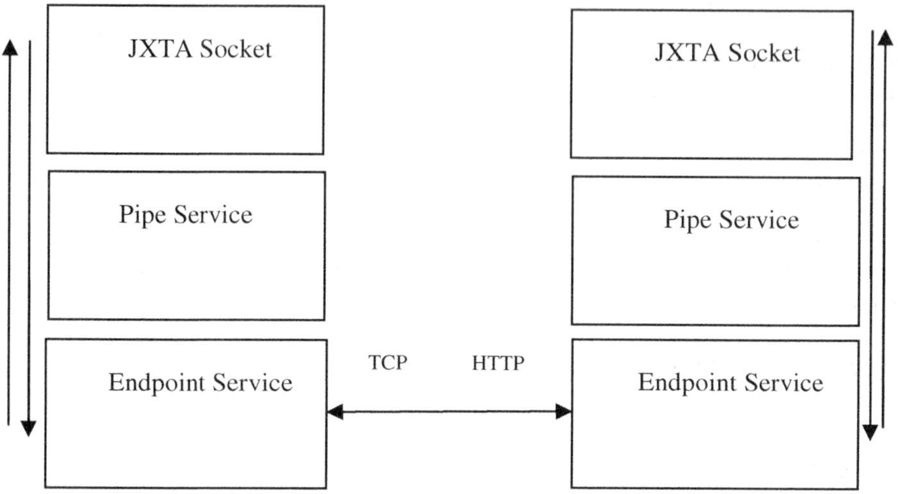

Fig. 2. Stack of JXTA communication protocol

In the following examples, we are using the traditional JXTA code of sun JXTA 2.5 tutorial. We are converting that code into dynamic adaptable using AOP.

4 P2P JXTA Sockets Using AOP

JxtaSocket is a bidirectional Pipe, which implements the java.net.Socket interface. JxtaSockets behave as closely as possible as a regular java socket, with the following differences: JxtaSockets does not implement Nagle's algorithm and therefore applications must flush data at the end of data transmission, or as the application necessitates. JxtaSockets does not implement keep alive which, for most applications it is not required, however is good to note this difference. The JxtaSocket uses the core JXTA unidirectional pipes (Input Pipe and Output Pipe) to simulate a socket connection in the platform J2SE binding.

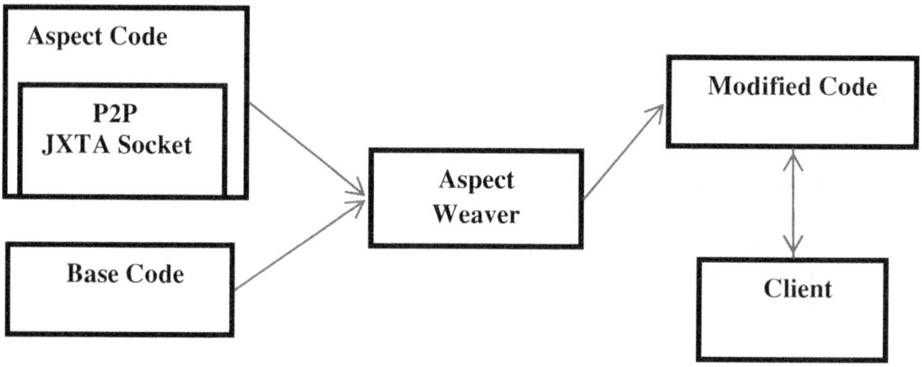

Fig. 3. Dynamic Adaptability in JXTA Sockets using AOP

The following code shows p2p JXTA ServerSocket using AspectJ which can reusable and supports dynamic adaptable. It creates a JxtaServerSocket and awaits bi-directional connections. Everyone can crosscut their method using pointcut and can change functionalities of server dynamically.

4.1 Serverside P2P JXTA Socket Using AOP

In the below code, p2p JXTA ServerSocket using AspectJ which can reusable and supports dynamic adaptable. It creates a JxtaServerSocket and awaits bi-directional connections. Everyone can crosscut their method using pointcut and can change functionalities of server dynamically. AOP main aim is to providing adaptability in existing programs, here run method of SocketServer class is cross cut by run() point cut. Here, Server will wait for Client Connections when we start the P2P network.

```
public aspect JxtaServerAspect {
pointcut run():call(public void SocketS*.run());
after():run(){
  System.out.println("Starting ServerSocket");
  JxtaServerSocket serverSocket = null;
serverSocket = new JxtaServerSocket(netPeerGroup, create-
SocketAdvertisement(), 10);
  while (true) {
  System.out.println("Waiting for connections");
  Socket socket = serverSocket.accept();
if (socket != null) { System.out.println("New socket con-
nection accepted");
Thread thread = new Thread(new ConnectionHandler(socket),
"Connection Handler Thread");thread.start();}}
  private transient PeerGroup netPeerGroup = null;
public JxtaServerAspect() throws IOException, PeerGrou-
pException {
NetworkManager manager=new NetworkManager( NetworkMan-
ager.ConfigMode.ADHOC, "SocketServer",
  new File(new File(".cache"), "SocketServer").toURI());
  manager.startNetwork();
  netPeerGroup = manager.getNetPeerGroup();} }
```

4.2 Client Side P2P JXTA Socket Using AOP

In the below code, Client will send the data to another peer through JXTASOCKET. It will also reusable and dynamic adaptable by cross cut class methods in pointcut. Hence we strongly say that AOP always provide dynamic adaptability to existing programs. If we run the following code it will connect to server peer and can send/receive the data from and to server through JXTA Sockets.

```
public aspect JxtaClientAspect {
pointcut run(boolean waitForRendezvous,PeerGroup netPeer-
Group):call(public void SocketClientSide.run(..))
  && args(waitForRendezvous,netPeerGroup) ;
```

```
after(boolean    waitForRendezvous,PeerGroup    netPeer-
Group):run(waitForRendezvous,netPeerGroup){
  netPeerGroup = manager.getNetPeerGroup();
  pipeAdv = JxtaServerAspect.createSocketAdvertisement();
if(waitForRendezvous){                                   man-
ager.waitForRendezvousConnection(0);}
  if (waitForRendezvous){
  manager.waitForRendezvousConnection(0);}
  System.out.println("Connecting to the server");
  JxtaSocket socket = new JxtaSocket(netPeerGroup,
  null,pipeAdv,
  // connection timeout: 5 seconds
  50000,   // reliable connection true);
  // get the socket output stream
  OutputStream out = socket.getOutputStream();
  DataOutput dos = new DataOutputStream(out);
  // get the socket input stream
InputStream in = socket.getInputStream();
DataInput dis = new DataInputStream(in);
long total = ITERATIONS * (long) PAYLOADSIZE * 2;
System.out.println("Sending/Receiving   "   +   total   +   "
bytes.");dos.writeLong(ITERATIONS);
dos.writeInt(PAYLOADSIZE);
  long current = 0;
   while (current < ITERATIONS) {
  byte[] out_buf = new byte[PAYLOADSIZE];
  byte[] in_buf = new byte[PAYLOADSIZE];
  Arrays.fill(out_buf, (byte) current);
  out.write(out_buf);
  out.flush();
  dis.readFully(in_buf);
  assert Arrays.equals(in_buf, out_buf);
  current++;     } out.close();  in.close();
  socket.close();
  }}
```

AOP main aim is to providing adaptability in existing programs, here run method of SocketServer class is cross cut by run() point cut and when start the network server will wait for Client Connections. Any Program can reuse this Aspect code without editing single line by cross cut their method using pointcut.

5 Efficiency of AOP by CPU Profiling

In some cases, flexibility and reusability of the design comes with the price of decreased efficiency. At the same time, performance is often a key quality attribute of distributed applications. It is therefore beneficial to investigate whether AOP may influence performance of applications. The comparison of the differences between AOP and OOP shows results that indicates influence of application quality, especially performance. To demonstrate this P2P JXTA Socket Communication is applied and the CPU profiling data is collected. It took 8 ms to execute the program without AOP and 5.01 ms to execute when AOP is applied.

5.1 Profiling Statistics before Applying AOP

The main method execution took 8 ms with one time P2P JXTA Socket Communication. The below figure 4 shows that the complete details of the p2p socket Communication connection and time spent by the processor in each time.

5.2 Profiling Statistics after Applying AOP

The main method execution took 5.01 ms with one time P2P JXTA Socket Communication of each method defined. The below figure 4 shows that the complete details of the P2P JXTA Socket Communication and the time spent by the processor in each method. By comparing these two call tree graphs we can say that the code having the AOP cross cutting is more efficient in terms of computation power usage. These both resulted has the same for memory usage.

Here, we have observed practically that execution time analysis comparison of JXTA Socket Communication without AOP and With AOP by run the above code seven times shows in Fig 4. These both resulted has the same for memory usage.

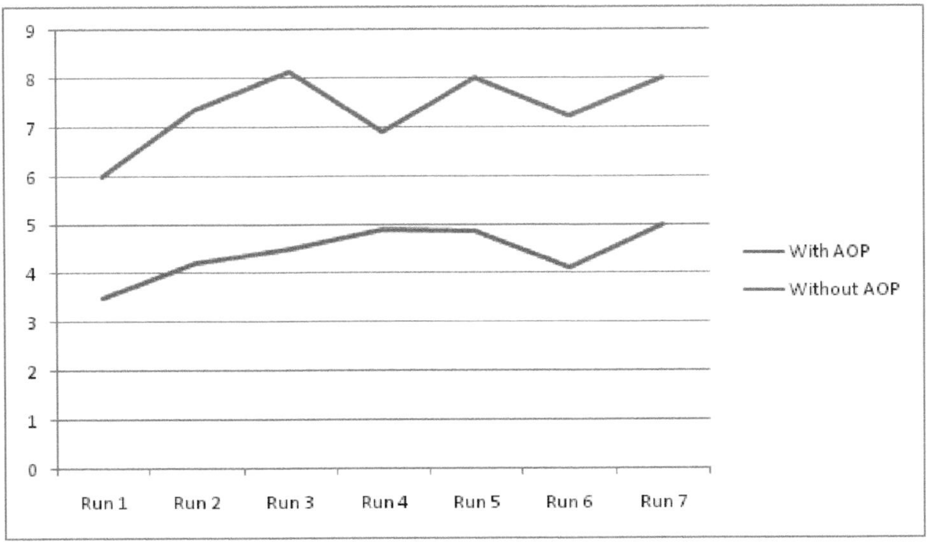

Fig. 4. Execution Time Analysis for P2P JXTA Socket Communication without AOP and AOP

6 Eclipse's Aspect Visualiser

Aspect Visualiser is an extensible plugin that can be used to visualize anything that can be represented by bars and stripes. It began as the Aspect Visualiser, which was a part of the popular AspectJ Development Tools (AJDT) plug-in. It was originally created to visualize how aspects were affecting classes in a project. As in Figure 5 we have shown the member view of distribution, tracing, and profiling aspects with class, and p2p JXTA Sockets. Here bars represent classes and aspects in AOP code and black colored stripes represent advised join points in the execution flow of AOP code, which were matched with defined pointcuts in various aspects.

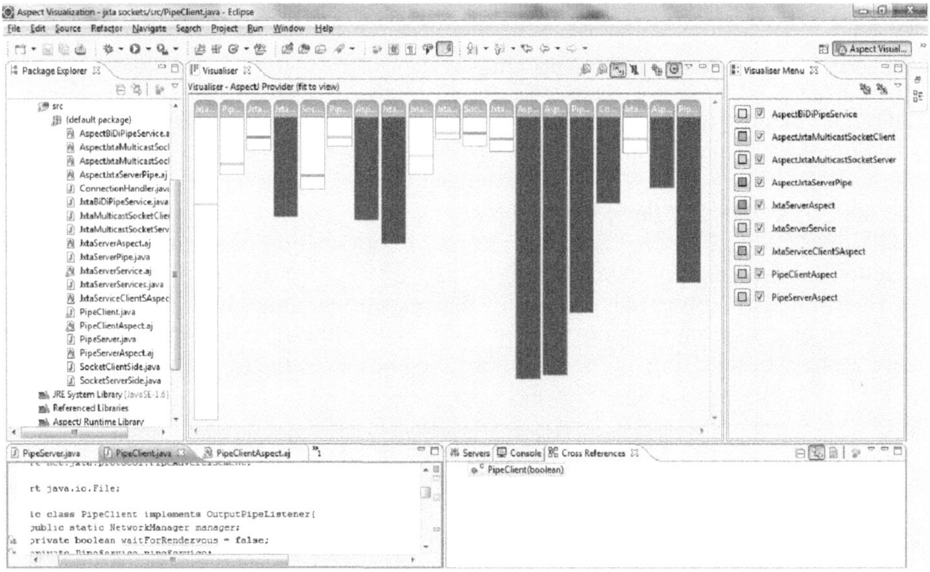

Fig. 5. Aspect Visualizer member view

7 Conclusion

In this paper, we demonstrates dynamic adaptability and reusability in p2p JXTA Sockets using Aspect Oriented Programming that supports reuse of existing programs in new, dynamic environments even though the specific characteristics of such new environments were not necessarily anticipated during the original design of the programs. In particular, many existing programs, not designed to be adaptable, are being ported to dynamic wireless environments, or hardened in other ways to support autonomic computing. In future we will address how Agent based java program communicates with p2p JXTA Service, and also we will address dynamic composition of web services between peers using AOP.

References

1. Kephart, J.O., Chess, D.M.: The vision of autonomic computing. IEEE Computer 36(1), 41–50 (2003)
2. Kiczales, G., Lamping, J., Mendhekar, A.: Aspect-oriented programming. In: Aksit, M., Auletta, V. (eds.) ECOOP 1997. LNCS, vol. 1241, pp. 220–242. Springer, Heidelberg (1997)
3. Rowstron, A., Kermarrec, A.-M., Castro, M., Druschel, P.: SCRIBE: The design of a large-scale event notification infrastructure. In: Crowcroft, J., Hofmann, M. (eds.) NGC 2001. LNCS, vol. 2233, p. 30. Springer, Heidelberg (2001)
4. Zhu, Y., Wang, H., Hu, Y.: A Super-Peer Based Lookup in Structured Peer-to-Peer Systems. In: ISCA PDCS, pp. 465–470 (2003)
5. Jiang, N., Schmidt, C., Matossian, V., Parashar, M.: Enabling Applications in Sensor-based Pervasive Environments. In: Proceedings of the 1stWorkshop on Broadband Advanced Sensor Networks, (BaseNets 2004) (2004)
6. jxta-meteor official web site: `https://jxta-meteor.dev.java.net/`
7. Kato, D.: GISP: Global Information Sharing Protocol A Distributed Index for Peer-to-Peer Systems. In: Proceedings of the 2nd International Conference on Peer-to-Peer Computing (P2P 2002), p. 65 (2002.d)
8. Ratnasamy, S., Francis, P., Handley, M., Karp, R., Schenker, S.: A scalable content-addressable network. In: Proceedings of the 2001 conference on Applications, Technologies, Architectures, and Protocols for Computer Communications, pp. 161–172 (2001)
9. Halepovic, E., Deters, R.: The Costs of Using JXTA. In: Third International Conference on Peer-to-Peer Computing (P2P 2003), p. 160 (2003)
10. jxta-benchmarking official web site: `https://jxtabenchmarking.dev.java.net/`
11. Clement, A., Harley, G., Webster, M., Colyer, A.: Eclipse AspectJ: aspect oriented programming with AspectJ and the Eclipse AspectJ development tools. Addison Wesley Prof., Reading (2005)
12. Avgustinov, P., Christensen, A.S., Hendren, L., Kuzins, S., Lhoták, J., Lhoták, O., deMoor, O.: An Extensible AspectJ Compiler. In: Proceedings of the 4th International Conference on Aspect-Oriented Software Development, pp. 87–98. ACM Digital Library, New York (2005)
13. Yang, Z.: An Aspect-Oriented Approach to Dynamic Adaptation. In: WOSS 2002 (2002)
14. Dantas, A., Borba, P.: Adaptability Aspects: An Architectural Pattern for Structuring Adaptive Applications with Aspects. In: Proceedings of SugarloafPLoP 2003 Conference (2003)
15. David, P., Ledoux, T.: Towards a Framework for Self-Adaptive Component-Based Applications. In: Proceedings of FMOODS/DAIS (2003)

A Novel Way of Providing Dynamic Adaptability in P2P JXTA Services Using Aspect Oriented Programming

Vishnuvardhan Mannava[1] and T. Ramesh[2]

[1] Department of Computer Science and Engineering,
KL University, Vaddeswaram 522502, A.P., India
vishnu@klce.ac.in
[2] Department of Computer Science and Engineering,
National Institute of Technology, Warangal, 506004, A.P., India
rmesht@nitw.ac.in

Abstract. The need for adaptability in software is growing, driven in part by the emergence of autonomic computing. In many cases, it is desirable to enhance existing programs with adaptive behavior, enabling them to execute effectively in dynamic environments. The peer-to-peer (p2p) paradigm is attracting increasing attention from both the research community and software engineers, due to potential performance, reliability and scalability improvements. P2P model has opened many new avenues for research and applications within the field of distributed computation, so performance evaluation is unavoidable. In this paper we are using Aspect oriented programming (AOP) to enable dynamic adaptation in existing p2p JXTA Services. We propose an approach to implement dynamic adaptability especially in existing p2p JXTA Service programs and Aspect weaving in p2p JXTA using AOP. We have used AspectJ; Java based language to create aspects in Eclipse supported framework.

Keywords: Dynamic adaptation, Aspect Oriented Programming, AspectJ, p2p JXTA Services and Reusability.

1 Introduction

A software application is adaptable if it can change its behavior dynamically (at run time) in response to transient changes in its execution environment or to permanent changes in its requirements. Recent interest in designing adaptable software is driven in part by the demand for autonomic computing. Autonomic computing [1] refers to self-managed, and potentially self-healing, systems that require only high-level human guidance. Autonomic computing is critical to managing the myriad of sensors and other small devices at the wireless edge, but also in managing large-scale computing centers and protecting critical infrastructure (e.g., financial networks, transportation systems, power grids) from hardware component failures, network outages, and security attacks. Developing and maintaining adaptable software are nontrivial tasks. An adaptable application comprises functional code that implements the business logic of the application and supports its imperative behavior, and adaptive code that implements the adaptation logic of the application and supports its adaptive behavior.

D.C. Wyld et al. (Eds.): CNSA 2011, CCIS 196, pp. 640–648, 2011.

JXTA encapsulates each of these mechanisms in a specific protocol. Therefore it is possible to focus on one aspect of the p2p paradigm, e.g. service discovery of peer. Different implementations are available, but the Java implementation is the most complete and thus the most convenient implementation to be used for teaching. This standard p2p platform, where the separation of concerns is respected and the active open source community continues to provide reusable software, should save time since there is no need to build core p2p software for teaching. JXTA defines six core protocols: the peer discovery protocol, the peer resolver protocol, the peer information protocol, the peer membership protocol, the endpoint routing protocol and the pipe binding protocol (PBP). One of the main abstractions in JXTA is the concept of pipe, which describes a connection between a sending endpoint - encapsulation of the native network interfaces provided by a peer - and one or more receiving endpoints. As it is familiar for users of UNIX to use a pipe to connect the output from one command to the input of another command, pipes may be used intensively by JXTA developers. A pipe - a kind of virtual communication channel is used to conveniently connect peers and to send messages between them because a network transport can be accessed without interacting directly with the endpoint abstraction. Any transport capable of unidirectional asynchronous unreliable communication can be used; indeed JXTA specifications specify that the default service pipe provides unidirectional asynchronous unreliable communication. Different endpoint transport implementations are available, e.g. TCP or HTTP.

Our paper is organized as follows. We review related work in section 2. In section 3, we describes p2p JXTA Services. Try to show the Efficiency of AOP by CPU Profiling in section 4. Section 5, Try to show the affect of 'Aspects' on application through Eclipse's Aspect Visualizer. We conclude the paper and future work in section 6.

2 Related Work

Previous work has been done by Yang [2] to implement a system which performs dynamic adaptation using AOP. This approach uses join points to specify where the adaptation should take place, and a set of rules to specify the conditions when an adaptation should occur. Another solution to achieve adaptation in applications using AspectJ is proposed by Dantas et al [11]. An adaptation framework developed by Pierre-Charles David et al [12] is implemented using the Fractal component model. Peers in peer-to-peer networks are usually considered uniform in resources. So, to deal with heterogeneous peers, a "super peer" based approach was introduced [4]. The "super peer approach" reduces the required bandwidth and completes requests faster.

A peer-to-peer event-notification architecture called Scribe, following publish subscribe approach, was introduced in [3]. A peer can create topics which any peer can subscribe to. To efficiently disseminate events to the subscribers over the network a multicast tree for every topic is created. As far as we know there are very few projects which involve JXTA and "pure" DHTs. One is the JXTA subproject JXTA-meteor [6] which intends to provide a platform to develop DHTs (as for now the project includes Chord and CAN) over JXTA protocols (as services). Another project about DHT in JXTA is GISP [7] (Global Information Sharing Protocol): this is a proposal for a new DHT protocol, which is intended as a service to be put over JXTA.

Yet, to our best knowledge, there is no related work of providing dynamic adaptability to p2p JXTA Services using Aspect Oriented Programming.

3 P2P JXTA Services Using AOP

JXTA-enabled services are services that are published by a ModuleSpecAdvertisement. A module spec advertisement may include a pipe advertisement that can be used by a peer to create output pipes to invoke the service. Each Jxta-enabled service is uniquely identified by its ModuleSpecID.

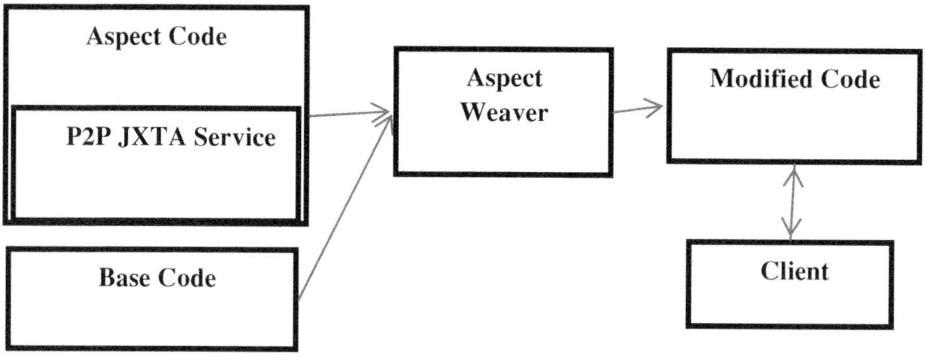

Fig. 3. Dynamic Changes in JXTA service using AOP

In the above figure 3, P2P JXTA Service is created and advertised in AOP. Aspect weaver will weave the Base code and Aspect code then generate a class file which is referred as modified code as shown in figure 3.Client can access peer service by running modified code only. If we change JXTA service details in AOP code, it will adapt that change dynamically without restart the application or communication between peers.

In our example JXTA-enabled service, we create a ModuleClassID and publish it in a ModuleClassAdvertisement. We then create a ModuleSpecID (based on our ModuleClassID) and add it to a ModuleSpecAdvertisement. We then add a pipe advertisement to this ModuleSpecAdvertisement and publish it. Other peers can now discover this ModuleSpecAdvertisement, extract the pipe advertisement, and communicate with our service.

4.1 Creating a JXTA Service Using AOP

This example illustrates how to create a new JXTA service and its service advertisement, publish and search for advertisements via the Discovery service, create a pipe via the Pipe service, and send messages through the pipe. It consists of two separate applications:

4.1.1 Server

The Server application creates the service advertisements (ModuleClassAdvertisement and ModuleSpecAdvertisement) and publishes them in the NetPeerGroup. The ModuleSpecAdvertisement contains a PipeAdvertisement required to connect to the service. The Server application then starts the service by creating an input pipe to receive messages from clients. The service loops forever, waiting for messages to arrive.

4.1.2 Client

The Client application discovers the ModuleSpecAdvertisement, extracts the PipeAdvertisement and creates an output pipe to connect to the service, and sends a message to the service.

In the following examples, we are using the traditional JXTA code of sun JXTA 2.5 tutorial. We are converting that code into dynamic adaptable using AOP.

4.2 P2P JXTA Service Server Using AOP

The following code shows p2p JXTA Service using AspectJ which can reusable and supports dynamic adaptability. It creates a JXTA Service and awaits bi-directional connections. Everyone can crosscut their method using pointcut and can change functionalities of server dynamically without restart the application to adapt changes. AOP main aim is to providing adaptability in existing programs, here start method of JxtaServer* class is cross cut by start () point cut and start the network server; server will wait for Client Connections. Here * indicates that class/method names should match to starting letters JxtaServer/star and remaining can be anything.

```
public aspect JxtaServerService
{
pointcut start():call(public * JxtaServerS*.star*(..));
before():start(){
manager=new   NetworkManager   (NetworkManager.ConfigMode.
ADHOC,"JxtaServerServices",  new  File(new  File(".cache"),
"JxtaServerServices").toURI());
manager.startNetwork();
netPeerGroup = manager.getNetPeerGroup();
groupAdvertisement=
netPeerGroup.getPeerGroupAdvertisement();
// get the discovery, and pipe service
discovery = netPeerGroup.getDiscoveryService();
System.out.println("Getting PipeService");
pipeService = netPeerGroup.getPipeService();
startServer();     }}
  public void startServer() {
System.out.println("Start the ServiceServer");
ModuleClassAdvertisement                          mcadv=
(ModuleClassAdvertisement)
```

```
AdvertisementFac-
tory.newAdvertisement(ModuleClassAdvertisement.getAdverti
sementType());
mcadv.setName("JXTAMOD:JXTA-EX1");
ModuleClassID mcID = IDFactory.newModuleClassID();
mcadv.setModuleClassID(mcID);
discovery.publish(mcadv);
discovery.remotePublish(mcadv);
ModuleSpecAdvertisement mdadv = (ModuleSpecAdvertisement)
AdvertisementFac-
tory.newAdvertisement(ModuleSpecAdvertisement.getAdvertis
ementType());
mdadv.setName("JXTASPEC:JXTA-EX1");
mdadv.setVersion("Version 1.0");
mdadv.setCreator("babu");
mdadv.setModuleSpecID(IDFactory.newModuleSpecID(mcID));
mdadv.setSpecURI("http://www.jxta.org/Ex1");
PipeAdvertisement pipeadv = createPipeAdvertisement();
mdadv.setPipeAdvertisement(pipeadv);
StructuredTextDocument    doc    =(StructuredTextDocument)
mdadv.getDocument(MimeMediaType.XMLUTF8);
StringWriter out = new StringWriter();
doc.sendToWriter(out);
System.out.println(out.toString());
out.close();
discovery.publish(mdadv);
discovery.remotePublish(mdadv);
serviceInputPipe = pipeService.createInputPipe(pipeadv);
while (true) {
System.out.println("Waiting  for  client  messages  to  ar-
rive");Message msg;
  // Listen on the pipe for a client message
   msg = serviceInputPipe.waitForMessage();
  // Read the message as a String
  String ip = null;
  // get all the message elements
  Message.ElementIterator en = msg.getMessageElements();
  if (!en.hasNext()) {  return;   }
  MessageElement msgElement = msg.getMessageElement(null,
  "DataTag");
  if (msgElement.toString() != null) {
  ip = msgElement.toString();
  }if (ip != null) {
  System.out.println("ServiceServer: receive message: " +
  ip);}}}}
```

4.3 P2P JXTA Client Service Using AOP

In the below code, AOP will cross cut the startJxta method of JxtaServiceClient class. First it will create one group and then advertise their group to outside world. It will search for JXTA-EX1 Service advertisement. If service is found, it will send the messages to related peer.

```
public aspect JxtaServiceClientSAspect {
pointcut start():call(public void
JxtaServiceClient.startJxta(..));
before():start(){
  // create, and Start the default jxta NetPeerGroup
  netPeerGroup = PeerGroupFactory.newNetPeerGroup();
groupAdvertisement=
netPeerGroup.getPeerGroupAdvertisement();
// get the discovery, and pipe service
  discovery = netPeerGroup.getDiscoveryService();
  System.out.println("Getting PipeService");
  pipeService = netPeerGroup.getPipeService();
  startClient();
  }   private void startClient() {
  // Let's try to locate the service advertisement
  Enumeration en = null;
  while (true) {  try {
  en=discovery.getLocalAdvertisements(
DiscoveryService.ADV,"Name","JXTASPEC:JXTA-EX1");
if ((en != null) && en.hasMoreElements()){break;}
discovery.getRemoteAdvertisements(null,DiscoveryService.ADV,
      "Name","JXTASPEC:JXTA-EX1",   1, null);
Thread.sleep(2000);}
ModuleSpecAdvertisement mdsadv= (ModuleSpecAdvertisement)
en.nextElement();
StructuredTextDocument  doc  =  (StructuredTextDocument)
mdsadv.getDocument(MimeMediaType.TEXT_DEFAULTENCODING);
  StringWriter out = new StringWriter();
  doc.sendToWriter(out);
  System.out.println(out.toString());
  out.close();
// we can find the pipe to connect to the service
  // in the advertisement.
PipeAdvertisement pipeadv = dsadv.getPipeAdvertisement();
  // create the output pipe endpoint to connect
OutputPipe    outputPipe=    pipeService.createOutputPipe(
pipeadv, 10000);
// create the data string to send to the server
  Scanner s=new Scanner(System.in);
  String data=null;
  System.out.println("how many masgs u want to send");
  int n=s.nextInt();
```

```
  for(int i=0;i<=n;i++)          {
System.out.println("Please  enter  Message  to  Send  to
Server");
  data =s.nextLine();
StringMessageElement   sme   =   new   StringMessageEle-
ment("DataTag", data, null);
  Message msg = new Message();
  msg.addMessageElement(null, sme);
  // send the message to the service pipe
  outputPipe.send(msg);         }
// create the pipe message
System.out.println("message \"" + data + "\" sent to the
ServiceServer");}}
```

In the above code, client will search for available services. If any service is found, client peer will send message to sever peer. AOP will prompt for messages to enter at run time. Messages count is client choice. We can change the message details and message formats at run time. Here AOP is reusable and dynamic adaptable.

5 Efficiency of AOP by CPU Profiling

In some cases, flexibility and reusability of the design comes with the price of decreased efficiency. At the same time, performance is often a key quality attribute of distributed applications. It is therefore beneficial to investigate whether AOP may influence performance of applications. The comparison of the differences between AOP and OOP shows results that indicates influence of application quality, especially performance. To demonstrate this P2P JXTA Services is applied and the CPU profiling data is collected. It took 9.63 ms to execute the program without AOP and 5.65 ms to execute when AOP is applied.

5.1 Profiling Statistics before Applying AOP

The main method execution took 9.63 ms with one time P2P JXTA Services calling. The below figure 4 shows that the complete details of the P2P JXTA Services and time spent by the processor in each time.

5.2 Profiling Statistics after Applying AOP

The main method execution took 5.65 ms with one time P2P JXTA Services of each method defined. The below figure 4 shows that the complete details of the P2P JXTA Services calling and the time spent by the processor in each method. By comparing these two call tree graphs we can say that the code having the AOP cross cutting is more efficient in terms of computation power usage. These both resulted has the same for memory usage.

Here, we have observed practically that execution time analysis comparison of JXTA Service invocation without AOP and With AOP by run the above code seven times shows in Fig 4. These both resulted has the same for memory usage.

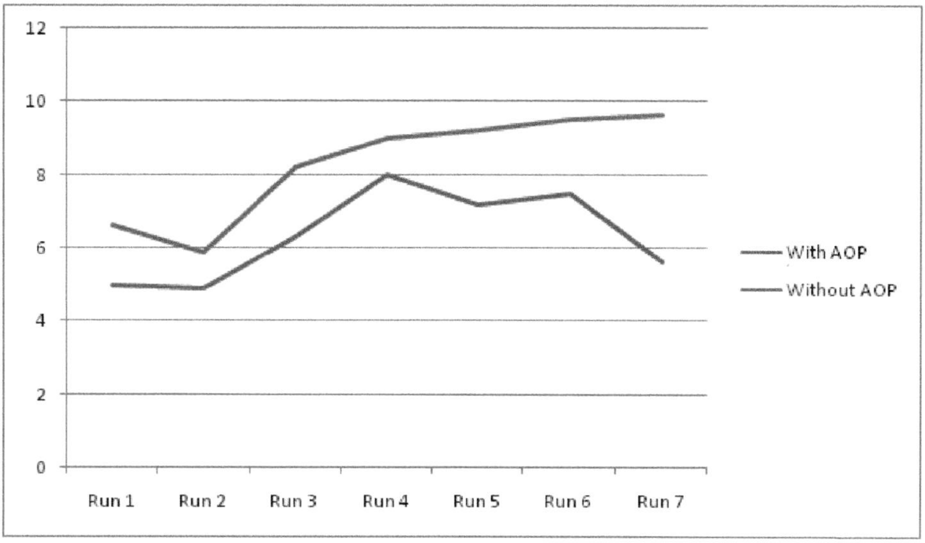

Fig. 4. Execution Time Analysis for P2P JXTA Services Connection without AOP and with AOP

6 Eclipse's Aspect Visualiser

Aspect Visualiser is an extensible plugin that can be used to visualize anything that can be represented by bars and stripes. It began as the Aspect Visualiser, which was a

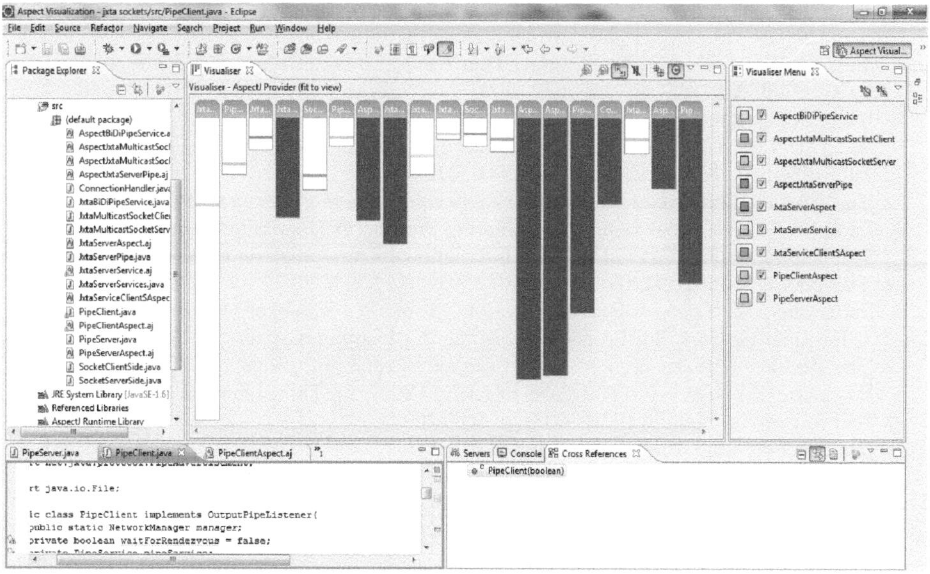

Fig. 5. Aspect Visualizer member view

part of the popular AspectJ Development Tools (AJDT) plug-in. It was originally created to visualize how aspects were affecting classes in a project. As in Figure 5 we have shown the member view of distribution, tracing, and profiling aspects with class, and p2p JXTA Service. Here bars represent classes and aspects in AOP code and black colored stripes represent advised join points in the execution flow of AOP code, which were matched with defined pointcuts in various aspects.

7 Conclusion

In this paper, we demonstrates dynamic adaptability and reusability in p2p JXTA Services using Aspect Oriented Programming that supports reuse of existing programs in new, dynamic environments even though the specific characteristics of such new environments were not necessarily anticipated during the original design of the programs. In particular, many existing programs, not designed to be adaptable, are being ported to dynamic wireless environments, or hardened in other ways to support autonomic computing. In future we will address how Agent based java program communicates with p2p JXTA Service, and also we will address dynamic composition of web services between peers using AOP.

References

1. Kephart, J.O., Chess, D.M.: The vision of autonomic computing. IEEE Computer 36(1), 41–50 (2003)
2. Yang, Z.: An Aspect-Oriented Approach to Dynamic Adaptation. In: WOSS 2002 (2002)
3. Rowstron, A., Kermarrec, A.-M., Castro, M., Druschel, P.: SCRIBE: The design of a large-scale event notification infrastructure. In: Crowcroft, J., Hofmann, M. (eds.) NGC 2001. LNCS, vol. 2233, p. 30. Springer, Heidelberg (2001)
4. Zhu, Y., Wang, H., Hu, Y.: A Super-Peer Based Lookup in Structured Peer-to-Peer Systems. In: ISCA PDCS, pp. 465–470 (2003)
5. Jiang, N., Schmidt, C., Matossian, V., Parashar, M.: Enabling Applications in Sensor-based Pervasive Environments. In: Proceedings of the 1stWorkshop on Broadband Advanced Sensor Networks, (BaseNets 2004) (2004)
6. jxta-meteor official web site: `https://jxta-meteor.dev.java.net/`
7. Kato, D.: GISP: Global Information Sharing Protocol A Distributed Index for Peer-to-Peer Systems. In: Proceedings of the 2nd International Conference on Peer-to-Peer Computing (P2P 2002), p. 65 (2002.d)
8. Ratnasamy, S., Francis, P., Handley, M., Karp, R., Schenker, S.: A scalable content-addressable network. In: Proceedings of the 2001 conference on Applications, Technologies, Architectures, and Protocols for Computer Communications, pp. 161–172 (2001)
9. Halepovic, E., Deters, R.: The Costs of Using JXTA. In: Third International Conference on Peer-to-Peer Computing (P2P 2003), p. 160 (2003)
10. jxta-benchmarking official web site: `https://jxtabenchmarking.dev.java.net/`
11. Dantas, A., Borba, P.: Adaptability Aspects: An Architectural Pattern for Structuring Adaptive Applications with Aspects. In: Proceedings of SugarloafPLoP 2003 Conference (2003)
12. David, P., Ledoux, T.: Towards a Framework for Self-Adaptive Component-Based Applications. In: Proceedings of FMOODS/DAIS (2003)

Trust Management for Grid Environment Using Rule Based Fuzzy Logic

Mohd Noman Siddiqui, Vinit Saini, and Ravinder Ahuja

Electronics and Computer Engineering Department,
Indian Institute of Technology, Roorkee, Uttrakhand
{mohdnoaman.mns,vinit.saini.ynr,ahujaravinder022}@gmail.com

Abstract. Grid computing system is an open, dynamic and service-oriented environment. There are multiple service providers, which offer services in Grid to users. In order to make the entity use the resources and deploy services with safety and reliability, the "trust" notion is addressed. Trust mechanism has been focus of much research in recent years providing a safety and reliable Grid computing environment. In this paper we have proposed a technique for calculating the trust based on the rule based fuzzy logic. Three parameters reliability, capability, and user satisfaction are taken as an input and output is trust factor. We have implemented and evaluated the performance using GridSim simulator.

Keywords: Trust management, Grid Computing, Fuzzy Trust, Fuzzy Inference.

1 Introduction

The service providers in Grid computing system offer services to users. The notion of "trust" is addressed to ensure that an entity uses the resources with safety and reliably. Trust is classified into two categories: Identity trust and Behavior trust. Identity trust is static. Once the identity is authenticated in the Grid system, its trust remains static and will not change thereafter. This trust value depends on the credentials made at the time when that entity joins the system. Behavior trust is dynamic in nature and is based on transactions between entities in the past time. If the entity do something wrong or harmful, its behavior trust value will then be dropped down, other entities may decide to give up choosing it as a service provider based on its behavior trust value. Many trust models based on entity behaviors have been proposed. In the trust model proposed by Wei Wang and GuoSun Zeng, trust is divided into Direct Trust and Recommend Trust [1], and is based on a Bayesian probabilistic framework which uses the beta distribution. Chunling Zhu and Xiaoyong Tang [2] proposed a behavior based trust model to implement the dynamic trust level, and establishes the reliable trust mechanism based on trust function which expresses the dynamic trust. But trust is a subjective and inaccurate value when decided by the Grid entity, it is difficult to describe with accurate probability distribution. It is also difficult to ensure the independency of events in Bayesian probabilistic framework. Few behavior trust models

D.C. Wyld et al. (Eds.): CNSA 2011, CCIS 196, pp. 649–657, 2011.

based on fuzzy logic in Grid are proposed [3] [4]. The weighted fuzzy comprehensive evaluation is given in [3] and is proposed for peer-to-peer network. A new behavior trust model based on fuzzy logic in Grid is proposed in [4], which evaluates the direct trust by weighted fuzzy comprehensive evaluation and a rule base is used to set and simplify fuzzy rules while used in computing of reputation. In this context trust is an entity's belief in another entity's capabilities, honesty and reliability based on its own direct experiences within a specific context at a given time. Reputation is obtained by fuzzy derivation and combination of recommendation trust from other entities.

2 Related Work

There are various trust models which have been proposed which takes different factors in to account for calculating the trust. Bayesian Model [2] was proposed for peer-to-peer network but significant in most of the networks. Eigen Trust Model [3] provides Eigen vector calculation for trust mechanism in distributed system which enables an entity to distinguish from malicious entities. In this environment entities rate each other, and every time when an entity i executes a task from entity j , it may rate the transaction as successful ($tr(i,j)=1$) or unsuccessful ($tr(i,j)=-1$). Behavior based model, this model is based on dynamic nature of trust which is dependent on several factors. It implements the management of dynamical trust level [9][10], and establishes the feasible and reliable trust mechanism, based on trust function, which dynamically expresses trust changing.

Few behavior trust models based on fuzzy logic in Grid are proposed [5] [6] [7]. But the fixed weighted fuzzy comprehensive evaluation in [5] is not suited due to its static nature. Shanshan Song and Kai Hwang suggest enhancing the trust index of a resource site by upgrading its intrusion defense capabilities and checking the success rate of jobs running on the platforms, but the computing of directed trust is not mentioned in [7].

3 Trust and Reputation

The trust helps the entities to find the trustworthy entity for the execution of job. Before looking up the role let us get into the definition of Trust and Reputation as defined in [1]:

Trust is the firm belief in the competence of an entity to act as expected such that this firm belief is not a fixed value associated with the entity but rather it is subject to the entity's behavior and applies only within specific context at a given time.

The main character to notice is that trust is subjective and dynamic in nature. It is subjective due to dependence on various factors and is dynamic, as it changes its value from time to time depending on the performance. Every entity has its own trust value and this measure changes with respect to the time.

A reputation is an expectation about an agent's behaviors based on information or about observations of its past behavior.

In order to incorporate the past behavior reputation is defined, the present value of trust is calculated on the basis of reputation earned by an entity over the past interval of time. In the later section Trust model is discussed, there both the trust and reputation is taken into account.

4 Fuzzy Logic

The subjective nature of trust results in its uncertainty and fuzziness characters. Fuzzy logic offers the ability to handle uncertainty and imprecision effectively, and is therefore ideally suited to describe trust, hence it is well suited to model trust using fuzzy logic. Fuzzy logic uses qualitative terms and linguistic labels to represent trust as a fuzzy concept, where membership functions describe to what degree a peer can be labeled as trustworthy or untrustworthy. Fuzzy logic provides rules for reasoning with fuzzy measures of this type. In modeling trust, concepts such as trustworthy, honesty, and accuracy are defined and quantified. Since these linguistic labels are fuzzy, we can apply fuzzy logic to handle the uncertainty and the imprecision in any trust model.

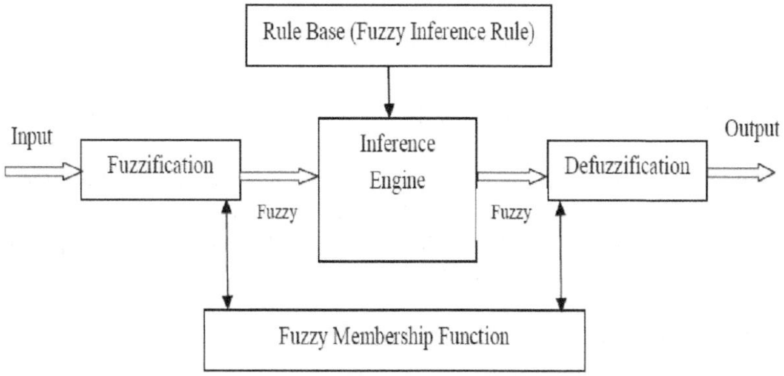

Fig. 1. Fuzzy Inference Model

Fuzzy inference is the process of formulating the mapping from a given input to an output using fuzzy logic. The mapping then provides a basis from which decisions can be made, or patterns discerned. The concrete five parts of the fuzzy inference process are described as follows:

(1) Fuzzification: The first step is to take the inputs and determine the degree to which they belong to each of the appropriate fuzzy sets via membership functions.

(2) Fuzzy membership function: A membership function is a curve that defines how each point in the input space is mapped to a membership value (or degree of membership) between 0 and 1. There are many membership functions such as Guass, Bell, Z, PI, Trapez, S-Polynome, Dreieck and so on.

(3) Fuzzy Inference Rule Base: Fuzzy Inference Rule Base comprises many fuzzy rules. In fuzzy approximate reasoning; there are two important inference rules: Generalized Modus Ponens (GMP) and Generalized Modus Tollens (GMT). Generalized Modus Pones (GMP) is defined as follows:

Implication: If X is A Then Y is B

Premise: X is A

Conclusion: Y is B.

(4) Fuzzy Inference Engine: Mamdani-type fuzzy inference method is the most commonly seen fuzzy methodology. Mamdani's method was among the first control systems built using fuzzy set theory. Mamdani-type inference, expects the output membership functions to be fuzzy sets. After the aggregation process, there is a fuzzy set for each output variable that needs defuzzification. Mamdani is a Min-Min-Max fuzzy inference method.

(5) Defuzzification: The input for the defuzzification process is a fuzzy set (the aggregate output fuzzy set) and the output is a single number. As much as fuzziness helps the rule evaluation during the intermediate steps, the final desired output for each variable is generally a single number. Perhaps the most popular defuzzification method is the centroid calculation, which returns the center of area under the curve.

5 Proposed Model

The proposed model starts by having the values of Capability(C), Reliability(R), and User satisfaction(U). We can choose any desired value between 0 and 1. This value may depend on initial credentials produced by participating entity. These values are taken as an input to the fuzzy system described in previous section. It calculates the trust value of every present entity on Grid. When any entity wants to advertise its resource, this trust value is also advertised together with computing capabilities. When any entity wants to avail service from others, it receives trust value of every other entity. Then it chooses particular entity for the transaction. On every successful transaction, a feedback in terms of C, R, and U, is received from entity which uses the service. Hence trust value of entity, which provides the service, is updated.

The trust evaluation module is updated from time to time having feedback from other entities. So we can state that direct trust is included when a feedback from availing entity is taken and Recommendation is included when feedback from every other entity is taken after specific interval of time. In this manner we reduced the complexity of accounting Recommendation Trust on every successful transaction; only direct trust is accounted every time.

6 Simulation and Results

6.1 Simulation Parameters

The behavior of fuzzy system is studied through the rule viewer and surface viewer simulated in Matlab. Figure 2 shows the trust model, having three input parameters and one output. The fuzzy inference used is mamdani as depicted is Figure1. Figure 3 shows the rule viewer of various rules taken into the consideration. The rule viewer gives the graphical representation of rule base designed. The rule are of the form IF X is A, Y is B, Z is C, THEN T is D. Figure 4 shows the surface viewer of the rules. The surface viewer is helpful in depicting the dependency of two inputs to output values. As there are three inputs to the system, hence three surface viewers are drawn to study the behavior of the system.

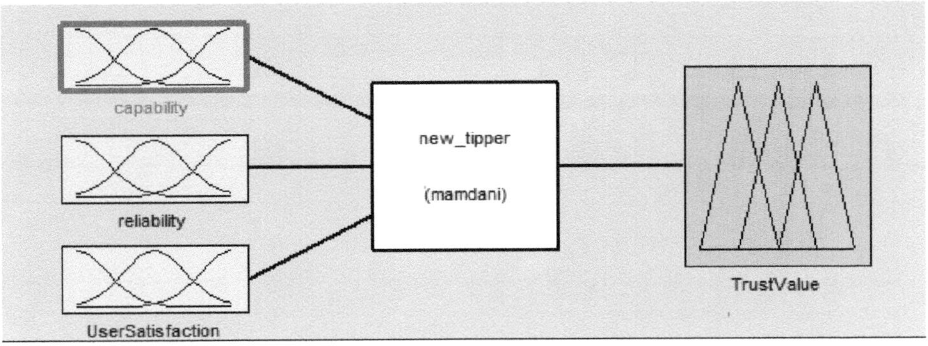

Fig. 2. Trust Model based on Mamdani-type Fuzzy Inference

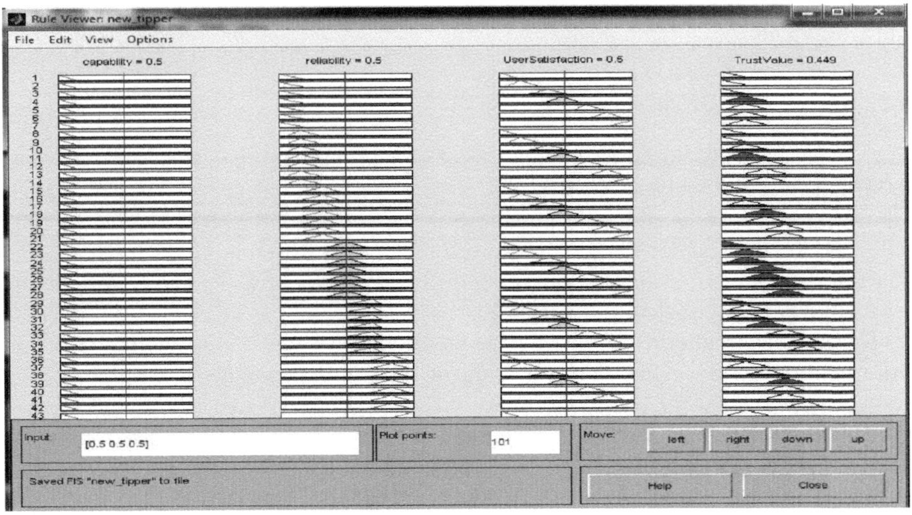

Fig. 3. A sketch map of Mamdani-type Fuzzy Inference

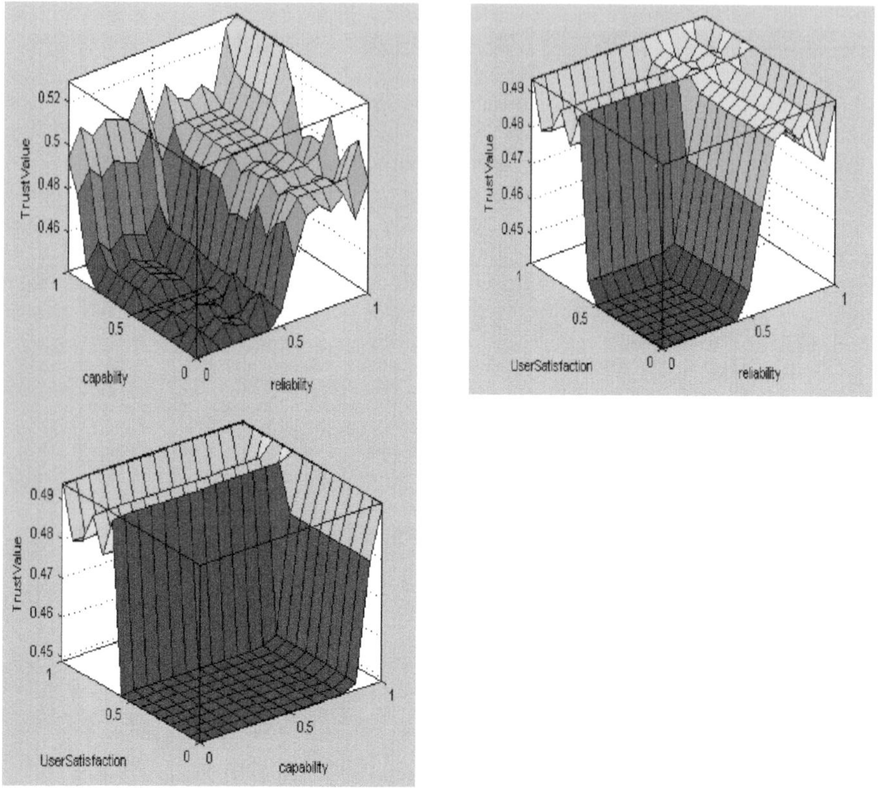

Fig. 4. A three dimensional simulative sketch map of capability, reliability, user satisfaction and Trust Value

6.2 Results and Discussion

The proposed grid system architecture is designed and simulated in gridsim version 5.0 [8]. The initial value of C, R, and U are chosen as 0.4, 0.4, and 0.4. This value is arbitrarily taken so as not give higher value to any resource. It will give a similar value to every resource. There are five resources with different characteristics. Their characteristic are simulated by assigning different values of C, R, and U, which models them from high trusted to low trusted.

The model initializes the trust degree of an entity when it contacts the GIS (Grid Information Server). After that, updating of trust is dependent on user ratings. The resource is modeled for behaving in five different situations and user updates in subsequent transaction. In Figure 5 the graph is shown between the total numbers of transactions performed on the system and mean error between the actual trust value and updated trust value. Near about after two hundred transactions the mean error stabilizes and after that becomes constant. This number of transaction is optimally achieved; as if this number is low then more weight age is given to user and it can falsely decrease the trust degree of resource. And if this number if very high, then very low weight age is given user.

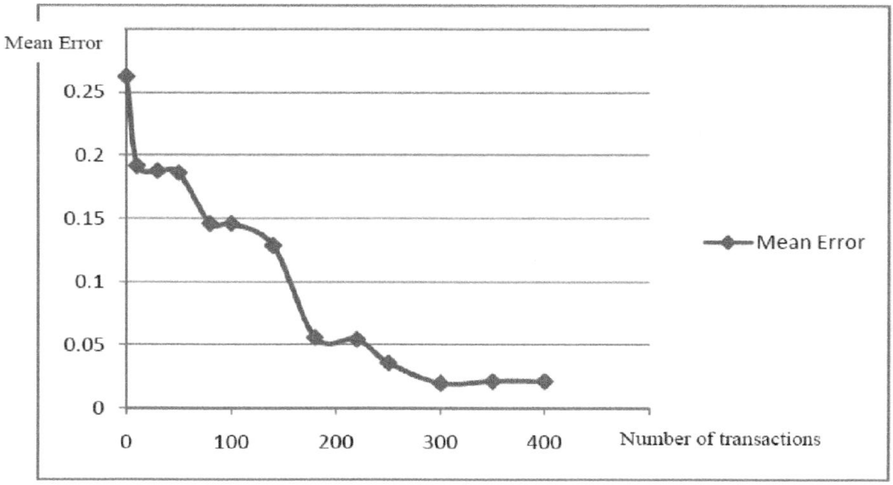

Fig. 5. Relation between number of transactions and mean error between actual and updated trust value

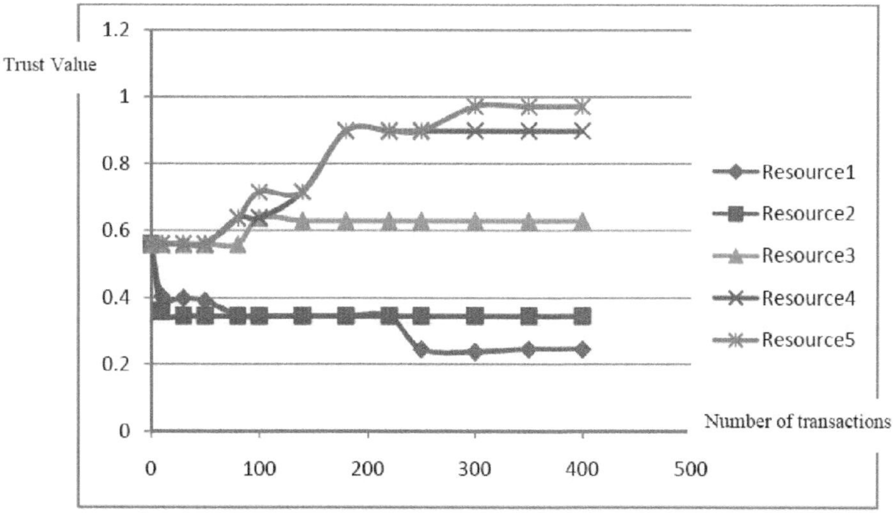

Fig. 6. Change in trust value of different resource

This curve is maintained unless the behavior of resource does not change. When the behavior changes the model adjusts the value in optimal number of transactions. The Figure 6 shows the relation between number of transaction and changing trust values of different resources. Every resource is assumed to work at particular trust factor. Then all the resources are given initial value of 0.6. Near about hundred fifty and two hundred transactions, the final values are reached, assuming the resources works as defined by its trust value.

For evaluating the proposed model, makespan is addressed. Makespan is the time interval during which specific numbers of transactions are completed. In this scenario the total execution time of transaction is the major part of makespan. In addition to it, there will be minor contribution of processing and calculating trust value. Figure 7 shows the makespan of three different models, namely with no trust, version 1, and version 2. In first model there is no accountability of rust and tasks are randomly allocated to any entity present over there. Version 1 is our proposed model. Version 2 is minor modified form of version 1, in the feedback from other entities, only two parameters are taken and third parameter, C, is the derived from the resources computing capability. For example, when entity updates that it has increased its memory from 1 Gb to 2 Gb, the value of C is also increased. Version 2 shows lowest makespan but in this case, user is given lesser importance by having only two feedbacks.

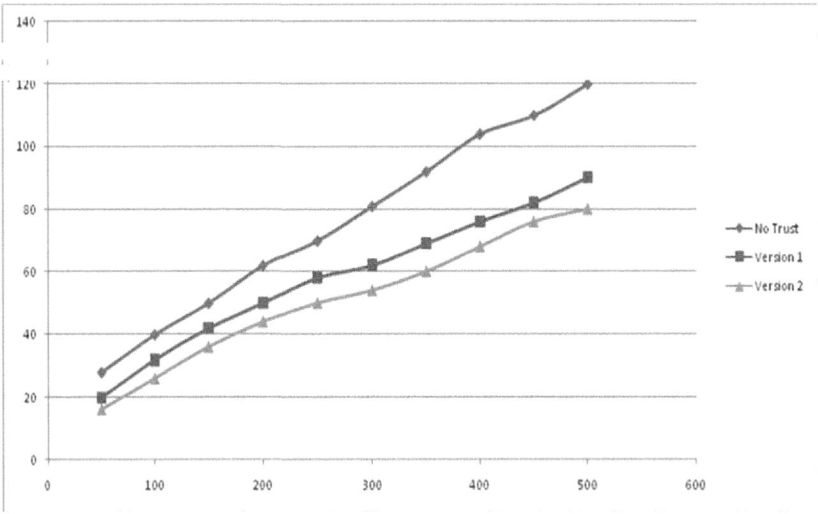

Fig. 7. Makespan of three models

6 Conclusion

A grid is definitely a valuable platform for resource virtualization which aggregates a vast amount of resource. The fuzzy rules used in the system are analyzed with the help of rule viewer of Matlab. The surface viewer shows the relation between input and output. Model initializes the trust degree of resources with arbitrary chosen value then this value is modified using rule base of fuzzy set. A model for trust evaluation is simulated for grid network using gridsim. This model is validated and proved to be useful as it requires an optimal number of transactions to stabilize.

References

1. Sun, M., Zeng, G., Wang, W.: A Trust-Oriented Heuristic Scheduling Algorithm for Grid Computing. In: Malyshkin, V.E. (ed.) PaCT 2007. LNCS, vol. 4671, pp. 608–614. Springer, Heidelberg (2007)
2. Wang, W., Zeng, G.: Trusted dynamic level scheduling based on Bayes trust model. In: Science in China Series F: Information Science. LNCS, vol. 50(3), pp. 456–469 (June 2007)
3. Chen, H., Ye, Z., Liu, W., Wang, C.: Fuzzy Inference Trust in P2P Network Environment. In: Proc. 2rd IEEE Conf. International Workshop on Intelligent Systems and Application, (ISA 2010) (2010)
4. Hongmei, L., Qianping, W., Guoxin, L.: A Fuzzy Logic-Based Trust Model in Grid. In: International Conference on Networks Security, Wireless Communications and Trusted Computing, NSWCT 2009, pp. 608–614 (August 2009)
5. Tang, W., Chen, Z.: Research of subjective trust management model based on the fuzzy set theory. Journal of software 14(8), 1401–1408 (2003)
6. Tang, W., Hu, J.B., Chen, Z.: Research on a Fuzzy Logic-Based Subjective Trust Management Model. Journal of Computer Research and Development 42(10), 1654–1659 (2005)
7. Song, S., Hwang, K., Macwan, M.: Fuzzy Trust Integration for Security Enforcement in Grid Computing. In: Jin, H., Gao, G.R., Xu, Z., Chen, H. (eds.) NPC 2004. LNCS, vol. 3222, pp. 9–21. Springer, Heidelberg (2004)
8. GridSim toolkit, `http://www.gridbus.org/gridsim/`
9. Zhu, C., Tang, X., Li, K., Han, X., Zhu, X., Qi, X.: Integrating Trust into Grid Economic Model Scheduling Algorithm. In: Meersman, R., Tari, Z. (eds.) OTM 2006. LNCS, vol. 4276, pp. 1263–1272. Springer, Heidelberg (2006)
10. Foster, C.K.: The Grid 2 Blueprint for a New Computing Infrastructure. The Elsevier series in grid computing.

Author Index

Aathira, K.S. 23
Abou-El Kalam, Anas 402
Ahuja, Ravinder 649
Anand, Sheila 483
Ananthapadmanabha, T. 393
Anitha, R. 441
Anjana Devi, V. 427
Arun, R. 113
Ashoor, Asmaa Shaker 497
Ayodele, Anthony 513
Azath, M. 356

Bag, Samiran 302, 344
Banerjee, Joydeep 526
Bansal, G. 258
Barbhuiya, F.A. 131, 258
Bhattasali, Tapolina 268
Bhukya, Sreedhar 622
Bhuvaneswaran, R.S. 427
Biswas, S. 131, 258
Boult, T.E. 513

Chaki, Rituparna 268
Chakraborty, Soubhik 178
Chandavarkar, B.R. 331
Chauhan, Amit 587

Damodaram, A. 598
Das, Ayan Kumar 577
Dash, S.S. 537
Dasmohapatra, Manas Ku. 157
Datta, Kamalika 157
Deepak, D.J. 331
Durga Bhavani, S. 43
Dutta, Sandip 178
Dutta, Tanima 281

Engineer, Pinal 184
Eswari, P.R.L. 53, 65
Ezra Prince Jebahar, I. 113

Firake, Shamal M. 78
Fraboul, Christian 402

Gangashetty, Suryakanth V. 374
Geetha, G. 472
Ghosh, Debaditya 577
Ghosh, Pradipta 526
Gopalakrishnan, K. 11
Gore, Sharad 497
Gosul, Manohar 489
Gupta, Neelima 453
Gupta, Sainath 374
Gupta, Sunil Kumar 167

Henrydoss, James 513
Himanshu, Pareek 53, 65
Hubballi, N. 131

Jain, S.K. 608
Jayakumar, C. 472
Jha, Govind Kumar 89
Jhansi Rani, P. 43
Johari, Rahul 453
John, Sapna E. 225
Joshi, R.C. 292
Jyostna, Grandhi 53

Kala, Rahul 463
Kannan, A. 113
Kavya, A.P. 393
Khilar, Pabitra Mohan 364
Kola Sujatha, P. 113
Krishna Prasad, A.V. 140
Kumar, G. Dileep 489
Kumar, Neeraj 89
Kumar, N. 258
Kumar, Parveen 167
Kumar, Shiv 292
Kuravadi, Bangaru Babu 564
Kutty, Thulasi N. 23

Lydia Elizabeth, B. 249

Mahanti, N.C. 178
Majumder, Pritam 577
Malempati, Sreelatha 239
Mannava, Vishnuvardhan 545, 552, 564, 631, 640

Mehul, Ekata 184
Meshram, B.B. 78
Mirta, Swarup Kumar 526
Mitra, Souvik Kumar 526
Modi, Dhaval 184
Mogalla, Shashi 239
Mohandas, Radhesh 383
Moses Jr., William K. 414
Mytri, V.D. 598

Nandi, Sukumar 131, 258, 281
Naskar, Mrinal Kanti 526
Nasr, Khalid 402
Nath, Hiran V. 1
Neela Madheswari, A. 356
Nesa Sudha, M. 225

Padmaja Rani, B. 140
Pais, Alwyn Roshan 331, 383
Pandu Rangan, C. 414, 502
Patel, Vipul 383
Phadnis, Swapnil 65
Piramuthu, Selwyn 150
Prakash, A. John 249
Prasad, S.D.V. 214
Prasad Vasireddy, V.S. 545, 552
Prema, K. 537
Puttamadappa, C. 393

Radhakishan, V. 502
Rahimunnisa, K. 194
Raj, Ashji S. 35
Rajaram, S. 320
Rajeswari, S. 204
Ramesh, T. 545, 552, 564, 631, 640
Rao, B. Srinivasa 214
Rao, M. Sambasiva 43
Rhymend Uthariaraj, V. 11, 249
Romana, Sandeep 65

Sabbu, Pruthvi 374
Sachan, Preeti 364
Saha, Amrita 344
Saini, Vinit 649
Sardana, Anjali 100
Sarkar, Pinaki 344
Satish Kumar, Vengala 281
Schrier, Walter 513
Sengupta, Indranil 157
Senthil Kumar, N. 537
Shah, Nidhi 587
Shah, Rahul 184
Shanthoosh, P.V. 113
Sharma, Himanshu 89
Sharma, K.G. 89
Sharmila Deva Selvi, S. 502
Shravani, D. 140
Shukla, Anupam 463
Siddiqui, Mohd Noman 649
Singh, Abhay Nath 292
Singh, Mrityunjay 608
Sitapara, Harsh 184
Soni, Pravin 78
Srinivasan, Chungath 35
Subbiah Bharathi, V. 123
Subramanian, Mohanavalli Seetha 483
Sudha, S. 249
Sunitha, K.A. 537
Sur, Arijit 281
Surekha, T.P. 393
Surendar, M. 320
Suresh, Manjula 441
Suresh Varma, P. 140
Sureshkumar, S. 194
S.B., Uday 598

Tarsauliya, Anupam 463
Terdal, Sujatha.P. 598
Tiwari, Ritu 463

Upendra Kumar, M. 140

Valarmathi, M.L. 225
Varkey, Rincy Merrin 194
Varma, Siddhartha 374
Venkataramani, Y. 204
Venkatasubramani, V.R. 320
Vijayalakshmi, B. 123
Vivek, S. Sree 502

Wahida Banu, R.S.D. 356

Yadav, Dinesh 100

Zhou, Wei 150

Batch number: 10838023

Printed by Printforce, the Netherlands